The American Campaigns of Rochambeau's Army

Jointly Published, 1972, by

PRINCETON UNIVERSITY PRESS · PRINCETON · NEW JERSEY

BROWN UNIVERSITY PRESS · PROVIDENCE · RHODE ISLAND

The American Campaigns of

ROCHAMBEAU'S ARMY

1780, 1781, 1782, 1783

Translated and Edited by Howard C. Rice, Jr., and Anne S. K. Brown

Volume I THE JOURNALS

of Clermont-Crèvecoeur, Verger, and Berthier

Copyright © 1972 by Princeton University Press
All rights reserved
LCC 71-166388
ISBN 0-691-04610-7

The printing of the color reproductions of the
Berthier maps has been made possible by a gift
from Mr. Paul Mellon, who owns a set of the
originals. Mr. Mellon has also provided access
to the rich collection on the Revolution in his
library, from which many illustrations and
references in this book have been taken. The
publishers also gratefully acknowledge gifts
in support of this publication from William D.
Wright and from Herbert S. Bailey, Jr.

This book has been composed in Janson types

Designed by James Wageman
Illustration layout designed by Howard C. Rice, Jr.

Printed in the United States of America by
Princeton University Press, Princeton, New Jersey
Illustrations printed by
the Meriden Gravure Co., Meriden, Connecticut

There is little doubt that our not being able
to crush this reinforcement immediately upon its arrival
gave additional animation to the spirit of rebellion,
whose almost expiring embers began
to blaze up afresh upon its appearance.

—SIR HENRY CLINTON

Preface

This book is essentially a collection of documents, selected and edited in such a way as to present a comprehensive story of the campaigns of the French army under Rochambeau during the American Revolution. We think of it as a contribution to both the history of the American War of Independence and the military history of the last years of the Old Regime in France. The documents, texts as well as maps and other illustrations, are (with a few exceptions) by French participants in the campaigns and thus provide an account of the war in America as they experienced it.

Volume 1 consists of three journals translated from the original French manuscripts. Although presented here as a triptych, the authors were neither The Three Musketeers nor Soldiers Three. They may have known each other's names, but otherwise they were not closely associated personally during the campaigns. The first, Jean-François-Louis, comte de Clermont-Crèvecœur (1752–ca. 1824) was a first lieutenant in the Auxonne Regiment, Royal Corps of Artillery. The second (and youngest), Jean-Baptiste-Antoine de Verger (1762–1851), was a sublieutenant in the Royal Deux-Ponts Regiment of infantry. The third, Louis-Alexandre Berthier (1753–1815), attached to the Soissonnais Regiment with the rank of captain, served on the staff as an assistant quartermaster-general.

Although the journals inevitably refer to many of the same persons, places, and events, they do not merely repeat one another but bring complementary strands to the history of the campaigns. The three men, for example, left Brest in 1780 on different ships. Berthier joined the expedition only at the last moment and was obliged to make a circuitous voyage via Martinique and Saint-Domingue before reaching Newport some three months after the other two. Berthier was also among those who took part in the Destouches expedition to the Chesapeake in March 1781, while Clermont-Crèvecœur and Verger stayed in Newport and learned of it only at secondhand. In the summer of 1781 Verger remained with a detachment in Newport, participated in a raid on Long Island, and went to Yorktown with Barras's fleet, whereas the others marched overland to the Hudson, took part in the reconnaissances of British-held Manhattan Island, and then proceeded to the head of Chesapeake Bay. At that point Clermont-Crèvecœur sailed down the Bay to the Yorktown peninsula. Berthier conducted the baggage train there by forced marches overland. During the winter quarters of 1781–1782 Clermont-Crèvecœur was stationed with his artillery unit at West Point in Virginia, while the other two were billeted in the vicinity of Williamsburg. When the army left Boston in December 1782, bound for Venezuela, each of the trio was embarked on a different ship and touched at different islands. Their parallel accounts complement each other and serve, incidentally, to call attention to this often overlooked phase of the American campaigns of Rochambeau's army. The War of the American Revolution, for the participants, did not end in 1781 with the victorious Siege of Yorktown, nor was the theatre of operations confined to continental North America. During the campaign of 1783 in the Caribbean, Berthier made an overland journey to Caracas, while Clermont-Crèvecœur and Verger remained in port at Puerto Cabello. It was also during this campaign that Berthier's younger brother Charles-Louis, his inseparable companion until then, lost his life in a duel. Unexpectedly, Verger's journal provides the clue to the identity of the antagonist. Finally, it may be noted that, whereas Berthier's journal stops short in Saint-Domingue and Clermont-Crèvecœur's account ends with the arrival at Brest in June 1783, Verger's narrative continues to the end of that year, thus giving us the impressions of a soldier returning home from the wars.

The three journals are here published completely for the first time. As explained more fully in our "Checklist of Journals," translated extracts from Clermont-Crèvecœur's journal (under another name), brief passages (in French) from Verger's journal, the first part only of Berthier's journal (in French), and selected passages from Berthier's journal (in English) have previously appeared in periodicals. The Editors' initial task has been to decipher and transcribe the variform eighteenth-century handwritings and establish a correct reading of the French manuscripts. In presenting the final English versions no attempt has been made to simulate "printed facsimiles" of the manuscripts. The writers' own corrections, marginal additions, and addenda have been incorporated into the text. Punctuation, paragraph breaks, and sentence structure have been modified for purposes of clarity. Uniform date headings have been inserted, and proper names have been standardized to conform to current usage. None of the journals was originally written with publication in mind. We have therefore felt justified in revising them in matters of form, just as the authors themselves or their publishers would have done had they been preparing the copy for printing. In respect to substance, fidelity to both the exact meaning and the spirit of the original has been our aim. In order to convey this meaning and spirit to present-day readers, recondite archaisms have been avoided where possible. We are nevertheless aware that, in casting the three journals into the common mold of normal twentieth-century American English, something of the eighteenth-century flavor of the originals has been lost, as well as the personal style and idiosyncrasies of the individual writers. Of the three, Clermont-Crèvecœur's style is the most traditionally and formally correct. Verger is less mature; his language and spelling occasionally betray his bilingual background. Berthier's writing is spontaneous and personal, but his style, especially the sentence structure, is careless if judged by a schoolmaster's standards. The original manuscripts are available in their respective repositories to specialists (paleographers, graphologists, linguists) and doubting Thomases who may wish to verify our translations.

The Editors' annotations to the journals identify the less obvious persons, places, and events and elucidate obscure terms when appropriate. We have attempted to enhance the significance of the journals further by relating them to each other through cross-reference and, by drawing upon other primary sources, both published and unpublished, placing them in the larger context of the war. Among the more important of these sources are the journals written by other French officers, a checklist of which appears at the end of Volume I. The notes are thus to some degree not merely the Editors' but also those of the authors' contemporaries. It is almost as if they were looking over our shoulders, scanning the journals of Clermont-Crèvecœur, Verger, and Berthier, interpolating their own comments: "But this is how *I* remember it . . . ," or "He forgot to say that. . . ." None of our three journal writers, being from the lower ranks, was a party to the councils of war that determined the happenings they describe. We have therefore included references to the decisions made at the higher levels, especially to the papers of General Rochambeau and of *his* commander in chief, General Washington. Here again we have cited or paraphrased the primary documents, with occasional reference to secondary works when they supply a convenient summary. The hindsight provided by the subsequent publication of contemporary source materials has also enabled us now and then to indicate how the British enemy envisaged some event or what the Americans thought of their French allies. Although such references could be extended still further, we have left this game to other historians and restricted ourselves primarily to the French point of view.

Each of the three journals is preceded by a biographical sketch of the author. Reconstructing the lives of Clermont-Crèvecœur and Verger, of whom no ready-made biographies exist, has meant ferreting out a few discernible episodes from obscure and elusive sources. In contrast, to tell the story of Berthier, who reached the summit of fame as Napoleon's marshal and chief of staff, has involved winnowing the pertinent essentials from a huge accumulation of materials. We have taken some pains to follow the threads of these parallel lives, not merely because we wanted to find answers to the natural questions—Where did this man come from? What became of him afterwards?—but also because we believe they have some significance as case histories of professional soldiers of the Old Regime who continued their careers through the wars of the French Revolution and Empire. The three journal writers were of the generation that came of age in the peaceful interlude following the close of the Seven Years' War. Their elders and superiors—General Rochambeau, for example—had fought in this and previous wars, but they had not. The campaigns in America marked their first participation in active warfare. The French Revolution, a decade later, brought the decisive turning-point in their lives. Clermont-Crèvecœur, by then a captain of artillery, became an émigré, continued his military career under foreign flags, returned home to France with the Restoration of the Bourbons, and finally attained the rank of colonel only upon his retirement. Verger, a foreigner from the Bishopric of Bâle serving in the army of the Old Regime, left French service and hitched his wagon to the House of

Deux-Ponts, which became the ruling family of the Kingdom of Bavaria. He eventually rose to the rank of lieutenant general in the Bavarian army and lived until 1851. Berthier at first embraced the cause of the Revolution with eagerness but soon found himself at odds with the new regime and relegated to inactive status. In 1796, under the Directory, he began his momentous partnership with General Bonaparte, which was to include all the great Imperial victories as well as the ill-fated Russian Campaign of 1812. Two years later Berthier rallied to the Bourbons and then, during the Hundred Days and only a few days before Waterloo, brought an end to his brilliant career by taking his own life. The lives of these three officers who made their military debut in the American Revolution embrace the multiple and contradictory aspects of the French Revolution and the Empire. Observing the dilemmas they faced, following them through these turbulent years, gives some idea of a soldier's lot during this period and helps us appreciate the full connotation of the words Alfred de Vigny used as a title for a collection of his stories: *Servitude et Grandeur militaires*. Nor are these "later lives" irrelevant in a book about the American Revolution. They enable us to view the campaigns of Rochambeau's army as an episode in European history and thus place the American War of Independence in a broader perspective.

The illustrations, which form an essential part of this book, are not merely added as an afterthought. These pictorial documents, including the maps, have been a major preoccupation since the start of our investigation. As much attention has been given to their selection and annotation as to the written texts. In Volume I, for example, are the sketches that Verger drew to illustrate his own journal, among which are unique documents on American uniforms of the Revolution. Also included in Volume I are facsimiles of manuscript and printed documents, comprising specimen pages from the three journals, several historic letters of Rochambeau, Washington, and other actors in the drama, and examples of printing done on the press of the French Fleet. The maps and views reproduced in Volume II, an indispensable accompaniment to the journals printed in Volume I, form a comprehensive atlas of the American campaigns of Rochambeau's army, as well as a fine sampling of eighteenth-century French military cartography. As explained in the special introduction in Volume II, a substantial proportion of the maps are the work of Louis-Alexandre Berthier, the third of our journal writers. The others were also surveyed and drawn by French officers who served in America. Again the fact that several of these cartographers later served in the wars of the French Revolution and Empire lends further significance to these examples of their work.

Also to be found in Volume II is a series of written documents called "Itineraries," here translated and published for the first time from the original manuscripts preserved among the Berthier papers. These are detailed, mile-by-mile descriptions of the route taken by Rochambeau's army when marching from Rhode Island across Connecticut to the Hudson and thence through New Jersey, Pennsylvania, Delaware, and Maryland to Williamsburg in Virginia. Thus for many of our maps—notably the road maps—we have contemporary annotations in the form of a commentary by French participants in the war.

Although this book may properly be considered a compilation of documents from French sources, the term "French" here needs some qualification. The greater part of our materials are not from national archives or libraries in France but from public or private collections in the United States. We have consulted the official records in France, especially for the editorial annotations, and have indeed taken a number of our maps from this source. Nevertheless, our major documents derive ultimately from the personal papers of French participants in the American Revolution that are now in the United States. The manuscript of Clermont-Crèvecœur's journal is in the library of the Rhode Island Historical Society, Verger's journal in the Anne S.K. Brown Military Collection at Brown University, and Berthier's journal and maps in the Princeton University Library. The papers of Rochambeau (frequently referred to in our notes) are preserved partly in the library of Paul Mellon at Upperville, Virginia, and partly in the Library of Congress, which has also supplied several important maps. The Mellon Library has contributed maps by Crublier d'Opterre, a French engineer. Still other American libraries are represented in our roster of sources. The transatlantic migration of manuscripts can in this instance be explained in part by their subject matter and by the fact that the American Revolution is a major event in the brief history of the United States while it is a relatively minor episode in the long span of the history of France. The chronological and ideological segmentation of French historical research and writing by the French Revolution has tended to obscure still further the last campaigns of the Old Regime. We trust that this publication under the imprint of two American university presses will reassure those who feel that manuscripts that migrate to the United States are thereby lost to the historians of their native land. Material considerations have made it impossible to publish the documents in both the original and in translation, as might ideally be desirable, but in spite of their appearance in a foreign tongue, we hope that they will find readers in France as well as in the United States and other parts of the English-speaking world.

❧

Plans for this book were laid in 1965 with the assistance of Mr. Grant Dugdale, Director of the Brown University Press, Mr. William S. Dix, Librarian of Princeton University, and Mr. Herbert S. Bailey, Jr., Director of the Princeton University Press. The assurance of eventual publication given by them at that time as well as their continuing support have enabled us to bring the project to completion. From the beginning the Meriden Gravure Company has been closely associated with the planning of the book. Mr. Parker Allen, Mr. Harold Hugo, and Mr. John F. Peckham have taken both a personal and professional interest in it, for which we are deeply grateful. Mr. Sanford G. Thatcher of the Princeton University Press has patiently and effectively edited the copy and carried the responsibility of seeing the book through the press.

During the past seven years we have inevitably incurred many obligations, and since both of us have drawn upon our earlier experience with kindred subjects, many of our obligations have accumulated over a still longer period. In many respects this whole book is a tribute to the collectors, the booksellers, the archivists, the museum curators, and the librarians who, over the years, have salvaged and preserved the documents we are privileged to publish. Their share is evident in the sources for the illustrations in Volume I and the maps and views in Volume II, as well as in our editorial introductions and annotations citing documents from still other repositories. As mentioned above, our translations of the three French officers' journals have been made from manuscripts in the Rhode Island Historical Society, the Anne S.K. Brown Military Collection at Brown University, and the Princeton University Library. The maps and other illustrations have been reproduced from originals in these three collections and from numerous others in both France and the United States.

For permission to reproduce material from their collections, and for other courtesies, we are indebted to the Comte and Comtesse Michel de Rochambeau, to the Prince and Princesse de La Tour d'Auvergne Lauraguais, and to the Société d'Encouragement à l'Elevage du Cheval Français (present owner of the Château de Grosbois) through its president, Monsieur René Ballière, and secretary general, Monsieur Pierre Van Troyen. We are also grateful to the following institutions in France for similar favors: Service Historique de l'Armée, Bibliothèque du Ministère des Armées "Terre," Archives du Génie, Service Historique de la Marine, Bibliothèque Nationale (Section des Cartes et Plans), Musée du Louvre (Cabinet des Dessins), Musée de Versailles, Bibliothèque Municipale de Versailles, Musée de la Coopération Franco-Américaine (at Blérancourt), and Musée Départemental des Vosges (at Epinal). Monsieur André Jammes, of the Librairie Paul Jammes, kindly served as our representative in Paris for obtaining photographs (executed by Raymond Lalance) of materials in French collections. The late Capitaine de Frégate le Vicomte Fleuriot de Langle, of the French Navy, read descriptions of naval battles and assisted in the translation of eighteenth-century nautical terms. Numerous individuals in France have facilitated our researches and responded generously to our appeals for assistance: among them, Baron Louis de Beaufort, Monsieur Yvon Bizardel, Monsieur Pierre Breillat, Monsieur Jean Brunon, Monsieur J.P. Busson, Monsieur François Chamonal, Général Comte Charles de Cossé-Brissac, Madame Pierre Ducourtial, Messieurs Fabius Frères, Monsieur Pierre Gérard, the late Vicomtesse Robert Grouvel, Monsieur et Madame André Jacquemin, Mademoiselle Adrienne Joly, Monsieur D. Labarre de Raillicourt, Mademoiselle Y. Lacrocq, Mademoiselle Madeleine Lenoir, Monsieur Georges Poisson, Monsieur Pierre Quarré, Monsieur Max Terrier, and the late Monsieur Gérard Vernes. Madame Ulane Bonnel, Library of Congress representative in Paris, was most helpful.

Invaluable guidance for research in Germany was initially provided by Major General Robert G. Fergusson, U.S.A. (Ret.), formerly Chief of Staff at Central Army Group Headquarters in Heidelberg, and by Mr. Charles E. Dornbusch, military historian of Cornwallville, New York. In Munich we benefited greatly from the assistance of Dr. Harald Jaeger and Dr. Tausenpfund of the Bayerische Hauptstaatarchiv, Freiherr von Reitzenstein and Fraulein Rotrand Wrede of the Bayerische Armeemuseum, Dr. Olof Wendt of the Wehrbereichsbibliothek, and Hauptmann Joachim Burth. Dr. William Schleicher of the Staatsbibliothek in Bamberg has kindly provided photographs and other useful information. In Switzerland Dr. André Rais, of Delémont and Porrentruy, has generously shared with us his knowledge of the history of the former Bishopric of Bâle.

Turning to the American side of the Atlantic, we express our appreciation to the following collections which have permitted reproduction of materials in their possession: the Library of Paul Mellon (at Upperville, Virginia), Library of Congress, Boston Athenæum, John Carter Brown Library, Historical Society of Pennsylvania, Library Company of Philadelphia, Maryland Historical Society, New-York Historical Society, the Henry Francis du Pont Winterthur Museum, and the Smithsonian Institution. From a perusal of our editorial notes it will be evident that these institutions have also contributed in various other ways to our work. Librarians and curators have been most helpful. We must mention in particular Mr. Willis Van Devanter, librarian of the Mellon collection, Mr. Walter W. Ristow of the Map Division, Library of Congress, Mrs. Dorothy S. Eaton and Mr. Paul G. Sifton of the Library of Congress Manuscript Division, Mr. Walter Muir Whitehill of the Boston Athenæum, Mr. Nicholas B. Wainwright of the Historical Society of Pennsylvania, and Mr. Edwin Wolf 2nd of the Library Company of Philadelphia. Still other American institutions have aided us by replying to our queries and, among other things, helping us to establish our "Checklist of Journals." These include the American Antiquarian Society, American Philosophical Society, Connecticut Historical Society, William L. Clements Library, Delaware Historical Society, Henry E. Huntington Library, Newberry Library, New Jersey Historical Society, University of Virginia Library, and the Library of the College of William and Mary. The research and curatorial staff of Colonial Williamsburg, through the good offices of Mr. Carl H. Humelsine, Mr. Edward P. Alexander, and Mr. Edward M. Riley, has rendered us valuable assistance. Mrs. Carl Dolmetsch, associate curator, and Miss Patricia A. Gibbs, research assistant, were particularly helpful. Mr. Charles E. Hatch, Jr., historian of the Colonial National Historical Park, has supplied information from the Park Service records. Professor Frederick Doveton Nichols has shared with us his personal knowledge of the Yorktown region.

We are fortunate in having been able, when the occasion arose, to draw upon the scholarly resources of Brown University and of Princeton University. Professor Durand Echeverria and Professor Carl Bridenbaugh of Brown have been helpful counselors, as have Mr. Thomas R. Adams, Miss Jeannette D. Black, and Mr. Stephen Ferguson of the John Carter Brown Library, and Mr. Richard B. Harrington, librarian of the Anne S.K. Brown Military Collection. We regret that Professor Gilbert Chinard of Princeton did not live to see the publication of this book, for, insofar as the Berthier journals and maps are concerned, it is the realization of a project that he himself had long cherished. We are happy to think that he was able to follow it through part of its course. Others at Princeton, including Professor Julian P. Boyd and Mr. P. J. Conkwright, have likewise long been aware of the potential interest of these materials. Members of the staff of the Department of Rare Books and Special Collections of the Princeton University Library—including Mrs. Mina Bryan, Mr. Earle E. Coleman, Mr. Alexander P. Clark, Mr. Alfred L. Bush, Mrs. Wanda Randall, Miss Helen Skillman, Mr. Charles E. Greene, and Mr. Lawrence E. Spellman—have in one way or another contributed more perhaps than they realize to the gradual evolution of this book.

Friends in various parts of the country have aided and encouraged us by their interest in our work and by their ready response to our appeals for assistance. Mrs. Evelyn Acomb-Walker, the Reverend Edwin S. Ford, Dr. Peter J. Guthorn, Mr. Richard G. Lucid, Mr. Marius B. Péladeau, and Mr. John H. Stutesman, Jr., have read portions of the manuscript and offered helpful suggestions. The response

283 CHECKLIST OF JOURNALS,
MEMOIRS, AND LETTERS OF FRENCH OFFICERS
SERVING IN THE AMERICAN REVOLUTION

349 ABBREVIATIONS AND SHORT TITLES OF
WORKS FREQUENTLY CITED IN THE NOTES

Volume II

Itineraries

3 EDITORS' INTRODUCTION

7 THE ITINERARIES

Maps and Views

111 EDITORS' INTRODUCTION

121 SYNOPSIS OF MAPS AND VIEWS

123 DESCRIPTIVE NOTES ON MAPS AND VIEWS

205 THE MAPS AND VIEWS

343 GENERAL INDEX TO VOLUMES I AND II

facing page 3

French Artillerymen at the Time of the American Revolution
From a series of watercolor drawings depicting the uniforms of the French army as prescribed by the regulations of 1779. At that time the several regiments comprising the Royal Corps of Artillery were grouped under "No. 64" in the official roster of French regiments (cf. *Etat militaire*). Clermont-Crèvecœur (of whom no portrait has been found) was a first lieutenant in the Auxonne Regiment, Royal Corps of Artillery.
Anne S.K. Brown Military Collection, Brown University, Providence, Rhode Island.

between pages 12 and 13

Illustrations, Volume I

Pages from the Manuscript of the So-Called Robernier Journal, now Attributed to Clermont-Crèvecœur
Title page and pages summarizing the allied and English losses in dead, wounded, and prisoners at Yorktown. See translation of the journal, p. 61.
Rhode Island Historical Society, Providence.

Memorandum of his Services Prepared by Clermont-Crèvecœur in 1814
This is one of several such memoranda submitted to the army authorities by Clermont-Crèvecœur when requesting his retirement and pension. It is preserved in his personal dossier among the records of the French War Department.
Archives de la Guerre, Service Historique de l'Armée, Vincennes, France.

The Château de Vaudéville, Clermont-Crèvecœur's Birthplace near Épinal in Lorraine
Jean-François-Louis, comte de Clermont-Crèvecœur, was born in the Château de Vaudéville, parish of Longchamps, on 10 January 1752. This photograph shows the château as it appeared in the 1930's; it has recently been restored by its present owners. See Editors' Introduction to Clermont-Crèvecœur's journal.
Courtesy of Monsieur and Madame André Jacquemin, Musée Départemental des Vosges, Épinal (Vosges), France.

between pages 60 and 61

De Grasse's Letter to Rochambeau, from The French Cape, Saint-Domingue, 28 July 1781, Announcing His Planned Arrival at the Chesapeake Bay
De Grasse also informs Rochambeau that his fleet will bring detachments from the army regiments stationed in Saint-Domingue, as well as funds amounting to 1,200,000 *livres*. This news, which reached Rochambeau and Washington at their Philipsburg camp, north of New York, on

14 August, determined the march of the allied armies to Virginia. See Clermont-Crèvecœur's journal, n. 54.

Original letter, signed by de Grasse and received by Rochambeau, Library of Paul Mellon, Upperville, Virginia.

Washington's Letter to Rochambeau, Chatham, New Jersey, 28 August 1781, Fixing a Rendezvous at Princeton

"I shall not have the Honor of joining your Excellency till we arrive at Princeton, where I will order Dinner to be ready at three O Clock. . . ." See Clermont-Crèvecœur's journal, n. 65. The letter, signed by Washington himself, is in the handwriting of his aide, Jonathan Trumbull, Jr.

Library of Paul Mellon, Upperville, Virginia.

Congressional Greetings to Rochambeau, Philadelphia, 4 September 1781

"The brilliant appearance and exact discipline of the several Corps do the highest honor to their Officers, and afford a happy presage of the most distinguished services. . . ." The greetings of the Continental Congress were conveyed by its president, Thomas McKean, during the French army's march through Philadelphia, 4 September 1781. See Clermont-Crèvecœur's journal, n. 72.

Library of Paul Mellon, Upperville, Virginia.

Congressional Resolution, 29 October 1781, Concerning the Victory at Yorktown

"*Resolved*, . . . That the thanks of the United States in Congress assembled, be presented to his excellency the count de Rochambeau, for the cordiality, zeal, judgment and fortitude, with which he seconded and advanced the progress of the allied army against the British garrison in York. . . ." See Clermont-Crèvecœur's journal, n. 128.

Journals of Congress, and of the United States in Congress Assembled, For the Year 1781, Vol. VII (Philadelphia, printed by David C. Claypoole, 1781). Princeton University Library.

between pages 92 and 93

Letter of Colonel Desandroüins Written at Puerto Cabello, 14 February 1783, Shortly After His Escape from the Shipwreck of the Bourgogne

The 74-gun warship *Bourgogne*, carrying troops of Rochambeau's army aboard, was wrecked off Punta Uvero on the Venezuelan coast during the night of 3–4 February 1783. Colonel Desandroüins of the Royal Corps of Engineers was one of a group of survivors who made their way overland through the wilderness to Puerto Cabello. See Clermont-Crèvecœur's journal, nn. 186–188.

Archives du Génie, Vincennes, France, article 15-1-7, No. 34[10].

The Sloth, as Depicted in Buffon's Histoire Naturelle

According to Clermont-Crèvecœur, the sloth was a "very curious and ugly animal that gets its name from the life it leads." He also mentions that Cromot Dubourg unsuccessfully attempted to take live specimens back to France for further study by the naturalists of the Jardin du Roi. See Clermont-Crèvecœur's journal, p. 94 and nn. 196–197.

Georges-Louis Leclerc, comte de Buffon, *Histoire Naturelle: Quadrupèdes*, Tome v (Paris, Imprimerie Royale, 1786), Plates LXIII and LXIV, engraved by C. Baquoy and by Baron after Jacques De Sève. Princeton University Library.

JOURNAL OF VERGER

facing page 103

Jean-Baptiste-Antoine de Verger. Self-Portrait

The nineteen-year-old sublieutenant portrays himself in the uniform of the Royal Deux-Ponts Regiment—sky blue coat with lemon yellow facings. The number "104," visible in the portrait, was used to designate this infantry regiment only during the years 1777–1787. An ordinance of 1776, which split several of the older regiments to create new ones, had placed the Royal Deux-Ponts in this numerical order, and another ordinance of March 1788 eliminating two regiments from the list moved it back to number "102." In 1791 it became the Ninety-ninth Infantry, "ci-devant Royal Deux-Ponts," and with the advent of the Republic was eventually disbanded along with the other foreign proprietary regiments in French service. Cf. *Etat militaire* for the years 1776–1793.

The cockade on Verger's hat recalls the Franco-American alliance (white and black), with the red representing Spain. Behind the French and American standards, below the medallion, a portion of the blue, white, and red Dutch flag (United Provinces) can be discerned. The anchor is evidently intended to recall the sea voyages of Rochambeau's army during its American campaigns.

Verger's drawing, reproduced here actual size, serves as the frontispiece to his manuscript journal. Anne S.K. Brown Military Collection, Brown University, Providence, Rhode Island.

between pages 126 and 127

Verger's Sketch of the Comtesse de Noailles, *the Transport Ship that Brought Him to America*

Verger was embarked at Brest, with 250 other men of the Royal Deux-Ponts Regiment, in the *Comtesse de Noailles*, one of the transports escorted by Admiral de Ternay's warships. *The Fanÿ*, also shown in the sketch, has not been identified. See Verger's journal, n. 1. The page facing the sketches provides a characteristic specimen of Verger's handwriting.

Page 2 and facing leaf of manuscript journal. Anne S.K. Brown Military Collection, Brown University.

Verger's Diagrams of the Encounter of Ternay's Fleet with an English Squadron under Captain Cornwallis, off the Bermudas, 20 June 1780

See Verger's journal, p. 119 and nn. 5–6; Clermont-Crèvecœur's journal, p. 16 and n. 4.

Page 10 and facing leaf of manuscript journal. Anne S.K. Brown Military Collection, Brown University.

Verger's Drawings of Indians from the Six Nations at Newport, 29 August–1 September 1780

According to Philip Schuyler, who made arrangements for the Indians' visit to Rochambeau's army at Newport, the "embassy" included 13 Oneidas and Tuscaroras and 5 Caghnawagas, all friendly to the Americans and the French. Verger describes the sword dance he witnessed in his journal (pp. 121–123 and nn. 12–19). At some later date Von Closen copied, or had copied, Verger's drawings for his own collection. See Von Closen's journal, ed. Acomb, plate facing p. 264, and our Vol. II, "Maps and Views," descriptive note to No. 47.

The two drawings, reproduced here on a single page, face pp. 18 and 22 of Verger's manuscript journal. Anne S.K. Brown Military Collection, Brown University. The barely legible bar of music is on p. 23.

Rochambeau's Address to the Indian Deputies, Newport, 30 August 1780

The text in both French and English, signed by Rochambeau and distributed by him to the Indian envoys, is written on an official printed form adorned with the royal arms and Rochambeau's personal seal. This copy was transmitted by Rochambeau to Washington when reporting on the Indians' visit. See Verger's journal, n. 14.

Library of Congress, Washington Papers, Series IV, Vol. 148, item 111.

Admiral de Ternay's Death, as Announced in the Gazette Françoise, *the Weekly Newspaper Printed on the Press of the French Fleet at Newport*

See Verger's journal, n. 30, and, concerning the newspaper, *Gazette Françoise: A Facsimile Reprint of a Newspaper Printed at Newport on the Printing Press of the French Fleet in American Waters during the Revolutionary War*, with an introduction by Howard M. Chapin (New York, The Grolier Club, 1926).

Masthead from p. 1 and a portion of p. 4, No. 5. From a copy of this issue in the Rhode Island Historical Society, Providence.

Official "Relation" of the Destouches Expedition to the Chesapeake, March 1781, Printed on the Press of the French Fleet at Newport

Verger, who transcribed this printed account into his journal, attributes it to Granchain, the "major," or chief executive officer of the fleet, who was largely responsible for the planning of the expedition. See Verger's journal, pp. 126–129 and nn. 30–33; Berthier's journal, pp. 242–244; "Checklist of Journals," *s.v.* Granchain; and map, Vol. II, No. 12.

Page 1 of a 4-page leaflet. This copy was preserved in the papers of L.-A. Berthier and is now in the Princeton University Library.

between pages 142 and 143

Verger's Plan of the French Attack on the Tory Fort at Lloyd Neck, Long Island, 12 July 1781

See Verger's journal, pp. 130–132 and nn. 42–47. According to Verger's narrative account, the troops embarked at Newport on the *Romulus* (commanded by La Villebrune) and the *Gentille*, the two ships shown here on the right, from which landing boats are proceeding towards the shore. The third ship, farther left, is doubtless the frigate *Ariel*, which also participated in the expedition. The fourth represents a British ship that fired at one point on the *Ariel*.

The French forces commanded by Colonel d'Angély consisted of about 200 men drawn from the detachments of Rochambeau's regiments left at Newport and from the ships' garrisons there. Verger shows them in two successive positions: first, assembled on the shore after landing, and then, after they had "debouched from a wood," re-formed in line of battle facing enemy fire from two cannon in the fort. Regimental colors identify the units: blue and yellow for Verger's own regiment, the Royal Deux-Ponts; green and white for the Saintonge; crimson and white for the Soissonnais; black and white for the Bourbonnais. The white and white may indicate the Picardie Regiment (detachments from which were presumably among the garrisons of Barras's ships that supplied part of the men for this Long Island expedition); in a report sent to Rochambeau by Choisy, the latter notes that two Picardie soldiers were wounded at Lloyd Neck, while Gallatin ([1], p. 678) mentions a Picardie captain, "M. d'Aberton," who was also there.

The red square below the woods is perhaps intended to indicate the French rear guard. For another map of this engagement, drawn by a naval officer, see Vol. II, No. 42.

Verger's plan faces p. 62 of his manuscript journal. Anne S.K. Brown Military Collection, Brown University.

Verger's Drawings of American Foot Soldiers, Yorktown Campaign, 1781. Left to Right: Black Light Infantryman of the First Rhode Island Regiment, Musketeer of the Second Canadian Regiment, Rifleman, and Gunner of the Continental Artillery

Verger probably made these sketches soon after the Siege of Yorktown, before the American army departed from Virginia for its winter quarters on the Hudson. The first, or left-hand, figure can easily be identified as a black light infantryman of the First Rhode Island Regiment, Continental Line, from his light infantry cap decorated with the anchor and blue-and-white plumes of Rhode Island, the short white jacket with fringed cape or collar, white overalls, buff leather crossbelt, and long rifle with bayonet attached.

The second figure shows a typical musketeer or line infantryman wearing a felt tricorn hat, brown regimental coat with lapels and cuffs buttoned back to show the light red facing color, black stock, white crossbelt with yellow metal belt plate, from which hangs a short saber, and holding a musket with bayonet attached. The only nonregulation garment is his light red overalls. However, in all other respects the uniform fits the description of those worn after 1779 by the battalion companies of the Second Canadian Regiment (Congress's Own), as given by Charles M. Lefferts, *Uniforms of the American, British, French, and German Armies in the War of the American Revolution* (New York, 1926), p. 20, Plate 4.

The third figure is a rifleman in the characteristic garb of these ubiquitous American frontiersmen-turned-soldiers who, as Verger points out in his journal, never ceased to inspire terror in the enemy. Dressed in linen rifle frock, fringed on cape and seams, and homespun overalls, with his axe, powder horn and capacious pouch, his belt and rifle sling of untanned leather, his long rifle with bayonet carried at the trail, his floppy wide-brimmed low-crowned hat decorated with feathers—he is typical of his branch. Because of his somewhat raffish and uniquely American appearance he was never mistaken for the enemy. Some riflemen operating in cooler climates wore the small light infantry cap decorated according to their fancy with feathers, fur, or vegetation, but the hunting frock never varied except in color. A good illustration of this latter garment appears in Robert L. Klinger and Richard A. Wilder, *Sketchbook '76* (Arlington, Virginia, 1967), pp. 16–18. (The same work, pp. 11–15, describes and illustrates the musketeer's coat and overalls.) The picturesque American rifleman was the subject of many prints published in Europe at the time of the Revolution: e.g., by C. Henning (Nuremberg, n.d.), by Johann Martin Will (Augsburg, n.d.), and by D. Berger after D. Chodowiecki in *Allgemeines historisches Taschenbuch . . . für 1784* (Leipzig and Berlin, 1784).

The last figure is a gunner of the Continental Artillery, whose blue uniform, faced scarlet, with white waistcoat and breeches, and black felt hat was prescribed in orders issued by Washington on 2 October 1779. When describing the appearance of the Continental Army at the Philipsburg camp in July 1781, Clermont-Crèvecœur noted in his journal (p. 33) that "only their artillery were wearing uniforms." The gunner in Verger's drawing carries a powder horn on his brown leather shoulder belt and wears his pouch in front. In his right hand he holds a lighted match or port-fire. The white cockade on his felt tricorn is worn, by Washington's orders, in honor of the French alliance. The regulation cockade was actually a combined black (American) and white (French) insignia, though Verger has omitted the black portion here. He also shows the uniform buttons as of white rather than yellow metal, but at this date many details worn by all Continental troops were contrary to the letter of the regulations.

As explained in the Editors' note to Albrecht Adam's commemorative painting of the skirmish at Morrisania (Vol. II, No. 47), several of Verger's drawings were copied by or for Baron Von Closen *ca.* 1825. Von Closen's copy of the four foot soldiers, now lost, is reproduced from a surviving photograph of it in Evelyn Acomb's edition of Von Closen's journal, facing p. 249. There are some discrepancies between Verger's contemporary observations and the later Von Closen copy. In the latter, for example, the artilleryman's blue coat has been changed to white (the Continental Artillery never wore white coats) and the rifleman's black hat cord has also been left white. Von Closen mistakenly labels the Rhode Island light infantryman "Massachusetts" and the Second Canadian musketeer "New Jersey." On the other hand, the artilleryman's cockade is correctly represented.

Verger's drawing of the four foot soldiers faces p. 170 of his manuscript journal. Anne S.K. Brown Military Collection, Brown University.

Articles of Capitulation, Yorktown, 19 October 1781.
Contemporary Printing of the French Translation
Prepared at French Army Headquarters

See Verger's journal, n. 83, for a discussion of this rare pamphlet, which may have been printed on the press of the *Ville de Paris*, de Grasse's flagship, then in Virginia waters.

Pp. 1 and 7 of an 8-page pamphlet (last page blank). John Carter Brown Library, Providence, Rhode Island. This copy was part of the original John Carter Brown Collection, having been bound into a volume of French pamphlets assembled by Ternaux-Compans.

Formation of a Company and a Regiment, Drawing by
Pierre-Charles L'Enfant, for Regulations for the Order and Discipline of the Troops of the United States

See Verger's journal, n. 153. This drill manual was compiled by Baron von Steuben with the assistance of Captain Benjamin Walker and of Colonel Fleury, Captain L'Enfant, and Captain Duponceau, French officers serving in the Continental Army. Steuben presented to Washington a specially bound copy of the first edition, in which original drawings were substituted for the engraved plates. Timothy Pickering of the Board of War wrote from Philadelphia to Steuben on 14 August 1779: "I delivered to the book-binder the plans for the regulations drawn by Mr L'Enfant, with directions to bind them with a copy of the regulations in the most elegant manner for his Excellency Genl Washington. . . . But after searching the city over he has not been able to procure any gold leaf for gilding. . . . I have told the book-binder to get it at any price." This is the copy now in the Boston Athenæum, from which our illustration is taken. The bookbinder was Robert Aitken; see Willman and Carol Spawn, "R. Aitken, Colonial Printer of Philadelphia," *Graphic Arts Review*, January-February 1961. According to Friedrich Kapp, *Life of . . . Steuben* (New York, 1859), p. 219, Steuben had another copy of the *Regulations* bound for presentation to the French minister (Conrad-Alexandre Gérard).

Regulations. . . . (Philadelphia, 1779), L'Enfant's drawing for Plate I. Reproduced from Washington's copy of the book, courtesy of the Boston Athenæum, Boston, Massachusetts.

Verger's Drawings of Mounted Continental Light Dragoons, 1781

The first of Verger's two drawings (above) appears to be a trooper of the First Regiment (formerly the Virginia Light Horse) of the Continental Light Dragoons. He wears a blue coat faced with white, white waistcoat, buckskin breeches, black boots, and a leather dragoon cap with a black plume and black and white band or turban. His saddle cloth, or shabraque, is blue bound with white. He carries the traditional long broadsword of the English Light Dragoons. Although Washington's orders of 2 October 1779 (cf. *Writings of GW*, XVI, 387–388) specified that all Continental Light Dragoons were to wear "Blue faced with White," with white buttons and linings, the only regiment known to have worn this uniform at Yorktown was the First Regiment under the command of Lieutenant Colonel Anthony Walton White, which participated in the Gloucester sector with the remnants of Armand's Legion. According to Lefferts (*Uniforms*, p. 64), the full dress uniform of the First Regiment was in 1780 "blue faced with white, but the fighting dress was of heavy or coarse white linen." Asa Bird Gardiner, "The Uniforms of the American Army" (*Magazine of American History*, I, No. 8 [Aug. 1877]), p. 477, points out that as early as 1778 blue short coats faced with white, with white waistcoats and black breeches, were worn by Lieutenant Colonel Henry ("Light Horse Harry") Lee's cavalry of the Legion (which was detached from the First Regiment of Light Dragoons).

Verger's second drawing (below) doubtless represents a trooper of the Second Regiment of Continental Light Dragoons. As distinguished from the first drawing, this dragoon is wearing a blue coat faced with buff; the saddle cloth is also blue bound with buff. Harold L. Peterson, *The Book of the Continental Soldier* (Harrisburg, Pennsylvania, 1968), p. 236, notes that the light blue turbans on the helmets of the Second Regiment had yellow tassels, which are clearly shown here by Verger. Although the Second Continental Light Dragoons are not listed among the Continental cavalry regiments present at Yorktown, they constantly provided escorts for the commander in chief throughout the war, and it is therefore quite likely that Verger sketched one of them at headquarters during the Yorktown Campaign. When the Second Regiment was operating along the Hudson in 1780 under the command of Major

Benjamin Tallmadge, they wore blue coats faced with buff, buff breeches, black boots, and dragoon helmets with blue turbans and white plumes (see *Military Collector and Historian*, II, No. 3 [September 1950], p. 39, Plate 28). In his studio painting of the "Surrender of Burgoyne at Saratoga" John Trumbull includes the figure of Captain Thomas Youngs Seymour of the Second Continental Dragoons. Trumbull represents the helmet as all brass, while Verger's 1781 drawing shows it as being black bound with brass (see Theodore Sizer, *Works of . . . Trumbull* [New Haven, 1967], Figs. 184–186).

To the best of the Editors' knowledge, Verger's watercolors are the only extant contemporary drawings portraying the uniforms of the Continental Light Dragoons during the Yorktown Campaign. The drawings face pages 172 and 173 of Verger's manuscript journal. Anne S.K. Brown Military Collection, Brown University.

between pages 186 and 187

The Beaver and the Opossum, as Depicted in Buffon's Histoire Naturelle

See Verger's journal, pp. 153 and 158, for his description of these animals, which he observed during the army's sojourn in Virginia. To the French officers Buffon was the chief authority on American natural history.

Georges-Louis Leclerc, comte de Buffon, *Histoire naturelle: Quadrupèdes*, Tome III (Paris, Imprimerie Royale, 1784), Plate XIX, and Tome IV (1785), Plate XXVII, both engraved by C. Baquoy after Jacques De Sève. Princeton University Library.

Prince William Henry's Visit to The French Cape in April 1783, as Described in Les Affiches Américaines

See Verger's journal, n. 184. *Les Affiches Américaines* was the newspaper published at Le Cap Français, then the largest city in the French colony of Saint-Domingue.

Page 1 of 4-page supplement to *Les Affiches Américaines*, 9 April 1783. From a copy in the Library Company of Philadelphia.

Delémont, Verger's Birthplace in the Bishopric of Bâle

See Editors' Introduction to Verger's journal, n. 2. The Bishopric of Bâle, an autonomous principality in the Jura Mountains on the borders of France and Switzerland, was also called, as in the legend of this engraving, the Principality of Porrentruy. It is now a part of Switzerland. Verger, who was born in Delémont on 7 November 1762, visited the town upon his return from America in November-December 1783.

Engraving by Helman and Née after Perignon, in Laborde and Zurlauben, *Tableaux de la Suisse, ou Voyage pittoresque*, 2nd edn. (Paris, Lamy, 1784), Vol. V, Plate CCXXXI. Princeton University Library.

Jean-Baptiste-Antoine de Verger at the Age of Fifty-two,
Commander of the Bavarian Gendarmerie Korps

See Editors' Introduction to Verger's journal, n. 25. This portrait, the original of which has not been seen by the Editors, is said to be signed "P S III/15," i.e., March 1815. Verger's uniform bears the insignia of a major-general. The decorations are the sash and Grand Cross of the Bavarian Order of the Crown, and the Legion of Honor (which had been awarded him in 1809).

Artist unknown. Reproduced from H. Schröder, *Das Königlich Bayerische Gendarmerie Korps 1812–1912* (Munich, 1912), p. 6.

JOURNAL OF BERTHIER

facing page 191

xxvi
Illustrations

Louis-Alexandre Berthier at the Age of Thirty-seven.
Painted by Lefevre in 1791

This is the earliest known likeness of Berthier, of whom many later portraits are extant. It was painted in 1791, the year Berthier attained the rank of colonel. He is here wearing the uniform of a staff officer of the Old Regime. His decorations, worn together in the second left-hand buttonhole, as the royal regulations prescribed, are the Cross of the Order of Saint-Louis (received in 1788) and, recalling his campaigns in America a decade earlier, the eagle of the Society of the Cincinnati (received in 1789).

Oil on canvas, 64 x 54 cm. Signed on back of canvas-stretcher, "Le Fevre p[in]xit 1791." Collection of the Prince de La Tour d'Auvergne Lauraguais, Paris and Buenos Aires. Reproduced here through his courtesy.

between pages 240 and 241

First Page of Berthier's Journal, Mentioning His Initial Efforts to Join Rochambeau's Expedition to America

A characteristic sample of Berthier's handwriting. The notations in the right-hand margin are in another hand and were added later, as were the underscorings in the text. The manuscript remained with Berthier's papers at the Château de Grosbois until 1936.

Manuscript in Princeton University Library, Berthier Papers, No. 1.

Page from Berthier's Journal Mentioning His "Map of Rhode Island"

The journal is cast in the form of "letters to a friend." The "letter" beginning on this page, though dated July 1781, relates what happened in October and November 1780. Berthier here notes that "I have spent all my spare time working on the map of Rhode Island, since all those we had seemed to me very inadequate." See Editors' translation of the journal, pp. 235-236, and map, Vol. II, No. 7.

Page 28 of manuscript. Princeton University Library, Berthier Papers, No. 1.

Washington's Letter to Rochambeau Informing Him of Benedict Arnold's Treason

See Berthier's journal, n. 35. The letter, dated from Washington's headquarters at West Point, 26 September 1780, reached Rochambeau in Newport on 1 October. The text is in the handwriting of Alexander Hamilton, signed by Washington.

Library of Paul Mellon, Upperville, Virginia.

Grenadiers from the Soissonnais Regiment in the Naval Battle of the Chesapeake, 16 March 1781

Grenadiers from the Soissonnais Regiment are shown fighting at close range on the deck of the 74-gun *Conquérant*, one of the ships of Destouches's squadron that had sailed from Newport on 4 March. According to Berthier's journal (p. 243), "The *Conquérant* suffered considerable damage because while she was fighting the English vanguard her rudder had been badly damaged, preventing her from being able to follow her lead ship and thus exposing her to the fire of the whole enemy line. Her principal adversary was the *London* until the *Neptune* intervened and the *London* let go." The commander of the *Conquérant*, Captain Cheffontaine, lost his life, as did Ensign Kergus; there were numerous casualties among the sailors as well as the soldiers from Rochambeau's army aboard. One of the grenadiers of the Soissonnais Regiment especially distinguished himself in an incident that soon became legendary. As depicted here, he has just had one of his legs shot off and cries out, "Thank heaven, I still have two arms and a leg to serve my King!" The anecdote was circulated in several French publications, from which the artist presumably derived his somewhat fanciful rendering of the scene—a good example of "patriotic gore," Louis XVI style.

Aquatint engraving by De Machy *fils* after Aimée Duvivier, published by Lebas in *Mémorial pittoresque de la France* (1786). Musée de la Coopération Franco-Américaine, Blérancourt (Aisne), France.

between pages 264 and 265

Page from Berthier's Journal Relating the Death of His Brother

Charles-Louis Berthier, who had been his elder brother's inseparable companion during the American campaigns, died at Curaçao on 17 February 1783 as the result of wounds received in a duel. He was then twenty-four. On the page shown here Berthier transcribes a letter from his brother written from Curaçao on 11 February. See Editors' translation of Berthier's journal, pp. 260–261.

Page 9 of manuscript in Princeton University Library, Berthier Papers, No. 3.

Death Certificate of Charles-Louis Berthier

See Berthier's journal, n. 100.

Manuscript in Princeton University Library, Berthier Papers, No. 45.

between pages 264 and 265

Berthier's Drawing of an Indigo Machine

Berthier visited an indigo plantation near Maracay, Venezuela, in March 1783. See his journal, p. 276.

Page 4 of 4-page manuscript, "Dépenses et produit d'une habitation d'indigot. . . ," Princeton University Library, Berthier Papers, No. 43.

The Hôtel de la Guerre, Berthier's Childhood Home in Versailles

The Hôtel de la Guerre (left), seat of the Ministry of War, and the adjacent building housing the Navy and Foreign Affairs ministries, constructed in 1759–1760, were designed by Berthier's father, Jean-Baptiste Berthier, who also resided in them as "governor." The Hôtel de la Guerre was thus home to Louis-Alexandre Berthier from his early childhood; he retained a personal apartment there until the royal properties were nationalized by the Republic in 1792. See Editors' Introduction to Berthier's journal, n. 2, and Berthier's journal, n. 47. The buildings are still standing, though put to other uses, in what is now called the Rue de l'Indépendance Américaine. Our engraving is one of a series by Ingouf (François-Robert, or his elder brother, Pierre-Charles); another, showing a cross-section of the Navy and Foreign Affairs building, is reproduced in *Papers of TJ*, VII, facing p. 453.

Courtesy of the Bibliothèque Municipale de Versailles (which now occupies the former Foreign Affairs building).

Berthier's Death in Bamberg, 1 June 1815

See Editors' Introduction to Berthier's journal, pp. 216–217 and nn. 86–88. This contemporary print by J. Fleischmann—"drawn on the spot"—shows the Neue Residenz, the palace of Berthier's father-in-law, Duke Ludwig Wilhelm of Bavaria. It was here that Berthier spent the last two months of his life. The legend of the engraving explains that Marshal Berthier's life came to an end here, between one and two o'clock on the afternoon of 1 June 1815, "through an unfortunate fall from the ninth window of the upper storey." A tablet placed on the Residenzstrasse side of the building in 1934 reads: "Alexander Berthier der Marschall Napoleons fand hier den Tod durch Sturz aus dem obersten Stockwerke am 1. Juni 1815 Mittags 1 Uhr."

Courtesy of the Staatsbibliothek, Bamberg (which is now housed in the Neue Residenz).

page 266

Berthier's Journey from Puerto Cabello to Caracas, 25 February–17 March 1783

Outline map. See Berthier's journal, pp. 266–279.

Journal

OF JEAN-FRANÇOIS-LOUIS,

COMTE DE CLERMONT-CRÈVECŒUR

Artillerie nº 64   Compagnie D'ouvriers D'artillerie

FRENCH ARTILLERYMEN AT THE TIME OF THE AMERICAN REVOLUTION (*see p. xvii*)

Identifying the true author of the so-called Robernier journal, an anonymous manuscript in the collections of the Rhode Island Historical Society, has proved an intriguing task. The attribution of the journal to one Louis-Jean-Baptiste-Sylvestre de Robernier, an obscure subaltern in the Soissonnais Regiment of infantry, seems to be based solely on a name written three times by as many different hands on the flyleaf of the manuscript. These notations (where the name is spelled "Robertnier") do not correspond to the handwriting of the text and were apparently added at some later date.

The journal was originally brought to Providence by Colonel George L. Shepley, a distinguished collector of Americana, who purchased it around 1923. In 1938, after Colonel Shepley's death, the bulk of his library was acquired by the Historical Society from his daughter, Mrs. E. T. H. Metcalf.[1] Meanwhile, a tentative English translation of the journal had been made by Professor Edouard R. Massey of Brown University, and excerpts relating chiefly to Rhode Island were published in 1923.[2]

An investigation of Robernier's career in America in the French War Department archives (administered by the Service Historique de l'Armée and located in the Château de Vincennes) yielded nothing beyond the fact that he came over with Rochambeau's army in 1780 as a sublieutenant in the Soissonnais Regiment and returned to France in 1783 as a second lieutenant in the same infantry regiment. His personal dossier is missing from the files, indicating that he probably quit the army not long after his return. Robernier's name appears in the *Etat militaire de France* for 1788, reappears in 1790, and vanishes thereafter.[3]

Anyone reading this journal in its entirety will promptly conclude that it could not have been written by an infantryman, since the author, from the moment the French army began its march from Rhode Island, was engaged in moving its cannon to Yorktown and, once they had arrived there, in firing them at the English. It is clear, therefore, that the author was an artilleryman.

1. "The Shepley Library," Rhode Island Historical Society, *Collections*, xxxi, No. 4 (Oct. 1938), 97–100.
2. "Rhode Island in 1780, by Lieutenant L.J.B.S. Robertnier," *ibid.*, xvi, No. 3 (July 1923), 65–78.
3. The *Etat militaire de France* was the official directory or list of army officers, published annually in Paris.

Rochambeau's army sailed with but one battalion of artillery, the Second Battalion of the Auxonne Regiment, Royal Corps of Artillery, to which the author doubtless belonged. From his comment on Washington's failure to invite lieutenants to his mess, it could be assumed that he was a lieutenant.[4] From his military duties on the march from the Hudson to the James, from Williamsburg to York, and in the French batteries before York, it could be further assumed that he was a first lieutenant.[5] Since the first lieutenant was second in command of a French artillery company, this assumption was partially confirmed by his statement that he accompanied his captain "to reconnoiter the site for a battery," and fully confirmed by his assignment to command half the Maisonneuve Company of the Auxonne Regiment on the voyage of Vaudreuil's fleet to Puerto Cabello.[6]

The published records indicate that ten companies of the Auxonne Regiment of artillery embarked with Rochambeau's army.[7] The "Inspection de 1781" (the official inspection report) in the regimental dossier at Vincennes lists by name ten first lieutenants serving at that time in America. Which one of these ten wrote the journal? Of this group, Lieutenant Bregeot died in Martinique in 1782;[8] Lieutenant La Barolière, according to the "Inspection de 1781," "was wounded by an assassin"; Lieutenants de Cremilles and d'Altecan were promoted captains before the siege;[9] Lieutenant Pusignan was wounded at Yorktown.[10] Elimination of these names left five possibilities to consider. Further scrutiny of the journal provided an additional clue: the author's informed interest in the iron industry, evident in his description of a visit to an iron mine in Maryland,[11] suggested that he might well have been a native of Lorraine, the principal iron-mining region of France. Of the two lieutenants known to have been born in Lorraine, Bregeot, as just mentioned, did not survive the American campaign, but the other, the Comte de Clermont-Crèvecœur, did. Furthermore, Crèvecœur, as well as the author, was first lieutenant of the Maisonneuve Company in 1782. From this point on it seemed probable that Crèvecœur was the author of the journal, and various pieces of the puzzle began to fall into place.

Although two small discrepancies caused momentary concern,[12] these were eventually outweighed when photocopies of leaves from the manuscript journal were placed beside documents in Crèvecœur's handwriting preserved in his personal dossier at Vincennes. The latter are chiefly communications written in 1814 to the minister of war in connection with Crèvecœur's request for a retirement pension. Despite the lapse of over thirty years between the date of the journal and the pension claims, the handwriting is strikingly similar—as can be seen by comparing the specimen pages from the journal reproduced here with one of the later documents, also reproduced. The Editors have therefore concluded that the so-called Robernier journal could have been written only by Jean-François-Louis,

4. See journal, p. 48 and n. 79.

5. See journal, pp. 40, 57–59, and n. 117.

6. See journal, pp. 58, 84, and n. 176.

7. *Les Combattants*, pp. 314–320. Although other artillery units joined Rochambeau's army in June 1781, and still others came with Saint-Simon's army from the West Indies to join the Franco-American forces at Yorktown, the Auxonne battalion is the only one

which served with Rochambeau's army throughout its American campaigns, 1780–1783 (the period covered in the present journal).

8. See journal, p. 80 and n. 165.

9. *Les Combattants*, pp. 314–315.

10. See journal, p. 60.

11. See journal, pp. 74–75 and n. 153.

12. See journal, p. 59 and n. 117; p. 84 and n. 176.

comte de Clermont-Crèvecœur, first lieutenant of the Second Battalion, Auxonne Regiment, Royal Corps of Artillery.

Of the three diarists represented in this volume, Jean-François-Louis, comte de Clermont-Crèvecœur, had the most illustrious ancestry and the most frustrating life. These two aspects of his career were banefully connected in an era when the old order was being swept away by a torrent of revolution, initiated by the very people whom Crèvecœur had helped liberate from the tyranny of an English king. In his journal, which is the most comprehensive of the three, we find Louis de Clermont-Crèvecœur (as he was generally called) committed to do battle against his own destiny. The victory for which he fought so conscientiously in America presaged the doom in France of his family and his king.

Crèvecœur's family could trace its lineage back to the year 974, when Baudouin, comte de Clermont en Beauvoisis, and his wife Adèle, sister of Thibaut de Champagne, founded a house that was to survive through some of its branches for the next eight hundred years. Clermont had accompanied William the Conqueror to England and Godefroy de Bouillon and Louis VII on the first two Crusades before Hugues de Clermont, in the twelfth century, acquired the lands and title of Crèvecœur. Two generations later Hugues's grandson Guy married the heiress of Leisquevin on condition that his descendants bear her name and arms. As late as the mid-eighteenth century, at the time of the birth of our diarist, his parents still bore the name of Leisquevin in addition to that of Crèvecœur.[13]

The family tradition of military service was also passed down from one generation to the next. Louis de Crèvecœur's great-grandfather, born in 1603, was colonel of the Montdejeu Regiment of infantry during the Thirty Years' War. This redoubtable warrior at the ripe age of seventy-two married a second wife, who bore him two sons. The younger, Charles-Alexandre, became a captain of infantry, married well, and in 1715 procured a patent of nobility as Comte de Crèvecœur, to which his son Jean-François succeeded. Jean-François (our subject's father) served as a captain in the army of Maria Theresa during the War of the Austrian Succession. Returning to Lorraine in 1750, he married Augustine-Antoinette, baronne de Steincallenfeltz, and resided in the Château de Vaudéville in the parish of Saint-Rémy de Longchamp, near Epinal.

Here, at Vaudéville, on the night of 10 January 1752, Jean-François-Louis, the future author of the journal, was born. Deemed by the attending midwife unlikely to survive, the infant was christened the next morning by Father Jacquot, curé of Longchamp and Vaudéville, in the private chapel of the château. His hastily summoned godparents included Monsieur Molet standing as proxy for the Comte de Girecourt, retired chancellor and chief minister of Her Royal Highness the Dowager Duchess of Lorraine; the baby's aunt, Baronne Louise-Julienne de Steincallenfeltz, canoness of Saint-

13. La Chenaye-Desbois and Badier, *Dictionnaire de la Noblesse, contenant les généalogies, l'histoire et la chronologie des familles nobles de la France* . . . , 3rd edn. (Paris, 1863–1876), V, 920–932; VI, 502–510. Our diarist was only very remotely related to his better-known contemporary, Saint-John de Crèvecœur (1735-1813), author of *Letters from an American Farmer* (London, 1782).

Goëry at Epinal; and his father, Comte François.[14] Three years later a sister was born and christened Gabrielle-Antoinette. Under the name of "Madame de Crèvecœur" she subsequently succeeded her aunt as canoness.

After Duke Francis III of Lorraine married Maria Theresa and became Holy Roman Emperor, he was succeeded as sovereign of Lorraine by the deposed King Stanislas of Poland, father-in-law of Louis XV. Stanislas reigned in benevolent splendor at Lunéville and Nancy, where he was a lavish patron of learning and the arts. When young Louis de Leisquevin-Crèvecœur was three years old, a patent and proof of nobility, with the title of Comte de Clermont-Crèvecœur, was drawn up for him so that he might be enrolled as a future gentleman cadet in the Pages' Corps of King Stanislas. Eventually, in March 1765, he entered service at the Court. Stanislas' sudden death the following year (after which Lorraine was united to France) was a real disaster for the boy's parents, who were in serious financial difficulties. At that time commissions in the French army were reserved for the nobility. However, the provincial aristocracy, when lacking money and influence at Versailles, often had to seek openings for their sons in the army's most lowly and arduous branch, the artillery. Thus, in July 1766, when Louis de Clermont-Crèvecœur was fourteen, he was enrolled as a candidate for the Royal Artillery School at Metz.[15]

The French artillery had just fallen heir to a genius as its inspector general. Monsieur de Gribeauval, renowned throughout Europe while serving as a field marshal under Maria Theresa, had lately been recalled to France to introduce his new system of artillery into the French army, which ultimately employed it to overrun Europe during the Republic and Empire. Crèvecœur's personal file in the War Department archives contains the following document signed by Loyauté[?]:

Artillery, 4 August 1767
M. de Gribeauval calls to your attention, on behalf of Madame the Abbess of Saint-Louis de Metz, that he has among his candidates for the School of the Royal Corps of Artillery in this city a young man whom she assures me belongs to the ancient house of Clermont-Crèvecœur, whose name he bears.
He is well-behaved, very diligent in his studies, and shows the greatest possible promise; however, due to their extreme poverty, his parents are unable to contribute towards his maintenance.
M. de Gribeauval implores Monseigneur to use his good offices to help this young man prepare himself to enter the Royal Corps, and requests that he be granted a modest pension until he is admitted to the Cadet School. During this interval he proposes that Monseigneur allot him annually 400 *livres* from the Artillery Funds.

This document, evidently destined for the Duc de Choiseul, minister of war, produced the desired result. The following December Crèvecœur was admitted to the school, of which Loyauté was the commandant. In June 1769 he was commissioned second lieutenant in the Auxonne Regiment, then stationed at Metz, and continued to serve in this regiment until April 1791.

14. The record of the birth and baptism, summarized here, is in the "Registres paroissiaux de Longchamp," Archives du Département des Vosges, Epinal. The Château de Vaudéville is still in existence. See photograph reproduced as one of our illustrations.

15. Unless otherwise indicated, statements concerning Clermont-Crèvecœur's military assignments are based on the documents in his personal dossier in the Archives de la Guerre at Vincennes.

From the beginning of his military career Crèvecœur seems to have been well regarded by his superiors, who refer to him repeatedly in the inspection reports of the regiment as a "bon sujet" (good soldier). For example, in 1770 he is described as "a very good soldier, does well in his studies." In 1772: "His conduct is excellent and he is most amenable." In 1773: "Clermont-Crèvecœur . . . is well behaved and shows zeal for his profession. He is a little too conceited." (He was then twenty-one).

On 5 April 1780, just before his departure for America, Crèvecœur was promoted first lieutenant in the company of cannoneers commanded by Captain Olivier d'Hémery. The inspection report of 1781, signed by Lieutenant Colonel Curiol de Laziers, who served with the regiment in America, bears the following notation: "De Crèvecœur—An officer who performs his duties well. His morals and his conduct are irreproachable." After Yorktown Captain d'Hémery yielded the command of Crèvecœur's company to Garret de Maisonneuve, who had formerly commanded the bombardier company. For the voyage from Boston to Puerto Cabello the company was split in two, Captain de Maisonneuve taking half aboard the ship *Northumberland*, while Lieutenant de Crèvecœur commanded the other half aboard the frigate *Amazone*. Just before he reembarked for France in May 1783 Crèvecœur was brevetted captain. Two years after his return he was commissioned second captain on the staff of the Artillery School at Strasbourg; in 1787 he was transferred to the Arsenal at Metz.

The year 1789, marking the beginning of the French Revolution, was a fateful one for the Comte de Clermont-Crèvecœur and his family, whose ties were with the Nobility and the Clergy rather than with the Third Estate. Louis' father had recently died. One of his cousins was a priest, and his aunt and sister Gabrielle were canonesses depending in part for their support upon prebends from the chapter of Saint-Goëry at Epinal.[16] In the summer of 1789 Captain Crèvecœur was sent out from Metz to inspect the armament of the garrisons of Toul, Verdun, and Nancy, where he doubtless witnessed the growing unrest with increased concern for his family, his property, and his own future in the army. In September he put in a request for six months' leave "in order to see to his affairs in Epinal." This was eventually approved by General La Chappelle de Bellegarde, director of the Metz Arsenal, and by General Perrin des Almona, inspector of artillery for Lorraine, who commented: "This officer is active and zealous and merits this favor." Beginning his leave on 4 January 1790, Crèvecœur was presumably back at his post in Metz that summer. The mutiny of several regiments at Nancy (31 August 1790), put down with firmness by the Marquis de Bouillé, must have given Crèvecœur further cause for reflection. The insurrection boded ill for the nobles of Lorraine and underlined the growing gulf between officers of an older order and the "Jacobin" rank and file. Discipline, as for-

16. According to information in the Archives du Département des Vosges at Epinal (Série G, Chapitre d'Epinal), Gabrielle-Antoinette de Crèvecœur was "apprébendée," i.e., received as a canoness and granted a prebend, in 1788. See also Léon Schwab, ed., *Documents relatifs à la vente des biens nationaux, Département des Vosges, District d'Epinal*, Collection de documents inédits sur l'histoire économique de la Révolution Française (Epinal, 1911), chap. 4, "Indemnités accordées aux émigrés du Département des Vosges en exécution de la Loi du 27 avril 1825." This tabulation of indemnities paid to émigrés includes (pp. 291–292, No. 85) the settlement in 1829 of a claim made by the "comtesse du Trésor, née de Clermont-Crèvecœur" as the heir of "la comtesse de Clermont de Crèvecœur, ex-chanoinesse d'Epinal."

merly understood, was breaking down. Many career officers had resigned or left the country to join the émigré forces that were assembling abroad.

Crèvecœur nevertheless remained at his post during the year 1791 and even received gratifying marks of recognition. He finally obtained the coveted Cross of the Order of Saint-Louis, which was presented to him in the King's name by Monsieur de Bellegarde at Metz on 1 February 1791. In April he was given command of a company in the Third Regiment of artillery (the former Régiment de Besançon). Alas, just as he achieved the rewards for which he had worked so diligently for twenty-five years past, the rush of events was destroying the old familiar army hierarchy.

King Louis XVI's abortive flight to Varennes in June 1791 raised new dilemmas for officers like Crèvecœur. The following year, in April 1792, the Legislative Assembly declared war on Austria and Prussia who, reinforced and encouraged by French émigrés, were preparing to invade France and "rescue" the King. Mutiny was rife in the armies under Rochambeau, Lafayette, and Luckner sent to the frontier, and many troops fled before the enemy. Rochambeau, finding his own plans and counsel overridden by the authorities in Paris, submitted his resignation and handed his command over to Luckner on 20 May 1792. The former commander of the expeditionary forces in America, then sixty-six, did not choose to emigrate but retired to his estate near Vendôme.

It was at about this same time that Clermont-Crèvecœur, at the age of forty, made his decision to leave the country. According to his service record, he was replaced as captain of his artillery company on 18 May 1792, "ayant abandonné son emploi."[17] Whether or not he formally resigned is not known. Henceforth, for more than twenty years, the Comte de Clermont-Crèvecœur led the precarious life of an émigré officer, faithful in his fashion to king, country, and religion, even when serving under foreign flags.

We may suppose that Clermont-Crèvecœur first returned to Epinal to escort his mother and sister out of France—thereby forfeiting such property as the family possessed there—before he joined the émigré forces in the Rhineland. His service record indicates that he campaigned with the Army of the Princes in the ill-fated Austro-Prussian invasion of northern France in the late summer of 1792.[18]

---

17. See Lieutenant Colonel L. Hartmann, *Les Officiers de l'Armée Royale et la Révolution* (Paris, 1910), where the defection of artillery officers in 1792 is discussed, pp. 438, 462–464, 479–480.

18. At this time the émigré forces were distributed into three armies: the Armée des Princes (or Armée du Centre), assembled near Trier; the Armée de Bourbon, stationed in the Low Countries for cooperation with the Austrians; the Armée de Condé, assembled near Worms for moving into Alsace. The Army of the Princes took its name from King Louis XVI's brothers, the Comte de Provence (future King Louis XVIII) and the Comte d'Artois (future King Charles X); it was disbanded by an order of 24 November 1792. The authoritative work on the émigré armies is

Vicomte Grouvel, *Les Corps de troupe de l'émigration française (1789–1815)*, 3 vols. (Paris, Editions de La Sabretache, 1957–1964). A useful general survey is in Jean Vidalenc, *Les Emigrés français, 1789–1825* (Caen, 1963), Troisième Partie, "Sous divers drapeaux," pp. 137–221. Grouvel includes a succinct account of the 1792 campaign of the Army of the Princes (III, 9–21) as well as detailed descriptions of the different units comprising it. According to Grouvel (III, 159–161), the role of the reconstituted Royal Corps of Artillery (in which Clermont-Crèvecœur presumably served) was limited to demonstrations before Thionville. Bellegarde (Crèvecœur's former commander at the Metz Arsenal) was second in command of the artillery. Third in command was Quiefdeville,

Goethe, who accompanied the Duke of Weimar during the campaign, found the French émigrés assembled in late August at Grevenmacher along the Moselle, poised for the advance into France. They had with them, he noted, their wives and mistresses, their relatives and children, "as if to display the inherent inconsistency of their present situation."[19] Whether or not Crèvecœur took his mother and sister on campaign is problematical, but we do know that one of the more picturesque officers of the Army of the Princes eventually became his brother-in-law by marrying his sister Gabrielle.[20] This was Major General Louis-Jean David, comte du Trésor de Bactot, former colonel of the Lorraine Dragoons. As instructor of cavalry to the Naval Brigade he had the novel assignment of teaching the naval heroes of de Grasse's fleet to charge on horseback through the German mud.[21] After suffering crushing defeats at the hands of Dumouriez, Kellerman, and Custine, the Army of the Princes, hungry and destitute, was disbanded in November, and its remnants turned over to the Prince de Condé. Crèvecœur, however, did not join Condé's army, having been apprized "by one of his commanders" that he had been selected to join a secret expedition departing from England. Early in 1793 (following Louis XVI's execution in January) England had joined the coalition of powers ranged against the French Republic. Lieutenant Colonel de La Grée of the Auxonne artillery was asked by the English to select officer cadres for various secret operations; Lieutenant Colonel François-Charles de Quiefdeville of the Metz artillery was appointed to command them.[22] In November 1793 Quiefdeville assembled his cadres, including Captain de Crèvecœur, at Portsmouth for participation in a cross-Channel expedition led by Lord Moira the following month. The aim was to reinforce the Royalist Vendée Army, which was besieging Granville and other points along the French coast; but after learning that the Vendéens had retired to Laval, Moira's contingent returned to England where Quiefdeville garrisoned his artillery cadres on the Isle of Wight. In May 1794 Parliament authorized the raising of a corps of Royal Emigrant Artillery under Quiefdeville's command. Crèvecœur was among the officers who served with this unit on the Continent during the evacuation of Ostend and the retreat of the Duke of York's army from Holland in 1794–1795. In August 1795 he accompanied the Comte d'Artois (later Charles X) to the Ile d'Yeu during the second Quiberon expedition, another unsuccessful attempt to support the insurrection in La Vendée. According to a testimonial signed by Quiefdeville (London, 8 June 1796), Captain Crèvecœur had "conducted himself with honor and distinc-

with whom Crèvecœur was subsequently associated in various enterprises.

19. Goethe, *Campagne in Frankreich, 1792* (first published in 1822).

20. In the summary of his services accompanying his petition to King Louis XVIII, 28 June 1814, Clermont-Crèvecœur states that he has lost his papers relating to the campaign of 1792 in the Army of the Princes and can therefore submit as proofs only "the attestation of his brother-in-law, the Comte du Trésor," and those of other surviving comrades. See also n. 16, above.

21. Chateaubriand, *Mémoires d'outre-tombe*, Part 1, Book IX, Chap. 9, "L'Armée des Princes." Cf. Grouvel, *op.cit.*, III, 93–100, "Corps Royal de la Marine." The corps of émigré naval officers included many veterans of the American war whose names appear later on in the present work: the Comte d'Hector (who had been commander of the port of Brest when Rochambeau's army embarked there), Albert de Rions, Amblimont, Cillart de Villeneuve, La Grandière, Plessis-Parscau, and Vaugirauld, among others.

22. Grouvel, *op.cit.*, I, 177–178, "Cadres d'Artillerie de Quiefdeville, 1793–1796."

tion" in these various operations. In 1796 he was quartered for a time on the island of Jersey with cadres commanded by his brother-in-law, the Comte du Trésor; then, after this unit was disbanded, he was back in England again, temporarily without employment.

The year 1797 opened a new chapter in Crèvecœur's life—a period of approximately ten years in the Portuguese service. The story of the French émigré officers in Portugal is one of the more obscure ramifications in the history of the Emigration.[23] During a period when Portugal was little more than a pawn in the power struggle between England, France, and Spain the situation of the émigrés was precarious and often paradoxical. The few ascertainable facts concerning Clermont-Crèvecœur's years in Portugal give at least a hint of the experiences of these wanderers. In 1797, the year he left England, the situation in Portugal was a desperate one. Spain had made peace with France and was at war with England, Portugal's traditional ally; plans for a partition of the country between Spain and France were being discussed. Reinforcements for the Portuguese army, including several French émigré regiments, were sent out from England. At this time Quiefdeville, Crèvecœur's erstwhile commander, was appointed brigadier general and inspector of artillery in the army of Portugal. Several of his old officers, including Crèvecœur and a young brevet captain of the Toul artillery named Jacques de Montpézat, accompanied him to Lisbon.

Crèvecœur's commission in the Portuguese army, dated 20 July 1797, was issued in Queen Maria's name and signed by her uncle, the Duque de Lafões, as minister of war. It appointed "João Francisco Luis, conde de Clermont Crèvecœur," a *sargento mor* (adjutant major) in the Faro Regiment of artillery, with back pay accruing from 1 December 1796.[24] An earlier document, dated 1 April 1797, indicates that Clermont-Crèvecœur had been incorporated into the regiment as of that date.[25]

By 1799 all but a few of the reinforcements sent by England had been withdrawn, but a new crisis in 1801 brought other French émigré officers to Lisbon, including some of Crèvecœur's old acquaintances. In 1801, when Portugal refused the terms of a Spanish ultimatum (inspired by Bonaparte) requiring the abandonment of her alliance with England, the Spanish army invaded the country and met with little resistance, except from one commander in the north (the Marquis de La Rosière, a Frenchman in Portuguese service). By the terms of the peace treaty signed in September, the Portuguese were obliged to make territorial concessions and pay a heavy indemnity to Spain. In consequence of this humiliation Lafões was dismissed as head of the Portuguese army and replaced by a veteran Prussian general, Count von der Goltz, who proposed so drastic a reorganization that he in turn was obliged to resign. The post of supreme commander was then given (upon the recommenda-

23. See Vidalenc, *op.cit.*, p. 217; *Mémoires du Marquis [V.L.A.] de Toustain, 1790–1823*, ed. Marquise de Perry de Nieüil (Paris, 1933), pp. 226–275.

24. A transcript of Clermont-Crèvecœur's Portuguese commission ("Brevet de Major") is in his dossier in the Archives de la Guerre at Vincennes.

25. The same order includes the names of "Leonardo-Alexis, cavalheiro de Chalup," assigned to the Estremoz Regiment of artillery as *sargento mor*, and "Francisco Joseph Bret de Lepinay," captain in the same regiment. Copies of this document and others from the *Arquivo Historico Militar*, Lisbon, were obtained for the Editors through the courtesy of the Baron Louis de Beaufort.

tion of the English government) to the Comte de Vioménil, who reached Lisbon towards the end of 1801.[26] Vioménil, an experienced officer, had been one of the generals in Rochambeau's army in America, and was, like Clermont-Crèvecœur, a native of Lorraine.[27]

In the subsequent reorganization of the Portuguese army undertaken by Vioménil, Crèvecœur was appointed aide-de-camp to General de Quiefdeville in 1802. That same year he requested the Prince Regent's permission to marry. According to a document in the Portuguese army archives, dated 3 December 1802 and signed by "Don João de Minerva de Mello de las N.O.," the permission was granted, but unfortunately no further details are given—not even the name of the fiancée. Crèvecœur was then fifty. In the numerous memoranda that he later prepared to secure his retirement pension, he makes no mention of his marriage.[28] We can only surmise that he was either jilted or widowed before leaving Portugal.

Although Clermont-Crèvecœur's movements during the next few years cannot be traced in detail, it is known that he remained in Portugal until 1808. These must have been uncertain and troubled years for him, as they were for Portugal, which could not escape involvement in the struggle between France and her enemies.

In 1803, when hostilities between England and France were resumed after the rupture of the Peace of Amiens, Bonaparte sent Lannes as ambassador to Lisbon with instructions to disrupt the rearming of Portugal and alienate her from England. Filling the government with spies who reduced the army and blocked all defense efforts, Lannes succeeded brilliantly. In 1805 he was replaced by Junot, who continued to make it clear that Portuguese "neutrality" could be purchased only by obedience to French wishes. Finally, a crisis came in August 1807, when Napoleon ordered the invasion of Portugal. General Junot's army of 25,000, reinforced by 27,000 Spaniards, was sent to seize the country. By choosing the most unexpected route, and without striking a blow, Junot managed to reach Lisbon with 1,500 exhausted men on 29 November, just as the Prince Regent set sail for Brazil with his court, his treasure, and his fleet, leaving a Council of Regency to govern the country. Junot proceeded warily while he rested his army and waited for the stragglers and the Spaniards to catch up. Then, on 1 February 1808, he took over the government of Portugal, keeping only the most subservient bureaucrats in office. The House of Bragança, it was proclaimed, had ceased to reign, and Portugal would henceforth be governed in the name of the French Emperor. Junot's tenure as governor proved to be short-lived. The insurrection in Madrid that summer, which set off uprisings in Portugal,

26. *Mémoires du Marquis de Toustain*, pp. 226–228. Toustain, who accompanied Vioménil to Portugal, was the General's nephew.
27. See below, "Checklist of Journals," *s.v.* Vioménil. The Vioménil name derived from the small locality of Vioménil, some seventeen miles southwest of Epinal. The Comte de Vioménil was born at Ruppes, while his elder brother, the Baron, was born at Fauconcourt, which is ten or so miles from Vaudéville, Clermont-

Crèvecœur's birthplace. These places are all within the present Department of the Vosges.
28. For example, in his letter (cited below) to the Duc de Feltre, minister of war, written at Tottenham, Middlesex, 16 February 1816, he states that he and Jacques de Montpézat "had been living together in the country during the seven years that they had been in England."

deprived him of his Spanish and Portuguese allies. On 1 August 1808 English forces under Sir Arthur Wellesley (future Duke of Wellington) landed at Mondego Bay. In a series of brilliant victories Wellesley drove Junot out of the country and restored it to Portuguese rule by 18 September 1808.

The fate of such émigré officers as Clermont-Crèvecœur during Junot's brief occupation of Portugal is far from clear. Junot disbanded the Portuguese army, except for 9,000 infantry and cavalry whom he formed into a Portuguese Legion to serve with Napoleon's Grand Army and 5,000 more whom he attached to his own army in Portugal. These Portuguese soldiers, he proclaimed, would "form one single family with the soldiers of Marengo, Austerlitz, Jena, and Friedland." One might suspect Clermont-Crèvecœur of having gone over to the French invaders were it not for several documents preserved in the Lisbon archives. There is, for example, a receipt dated 4 June 1808 and signed by Crèvecœur for his pay as adjutant major of the Algarve Regiment in which he notes that his current pay is "double the amount of his former pay scale." Even more significant is a joint letter from Crèvecœur and his friend Montpézat, written from London the following year (6 June 1809) to Don Miguel Pereira Forgas, the new Portuguese secretary of war and navy.[29] The two officers, acknowledging that six months' leave with pay has already been granted them by His Excellency, request an extension, since "nothing has changed in respect to their position" and "their presence in Portugal can be of no use to the service of His Highness the Prince Regent." According to a memorandum dated 11 July 1809, a six months' extension was granted them by order of the Prince Regent and conveyed through Dom Ant. Joares de Novonha, "general of the forces of the Court." The same memorandum mentions that Montpézat, by then a lieutenant colonel, was separated from the First Regiment of artillery on 24 August 1808 "by the occupying French government." It therefore seems likely that Clermont-Crèvecœur was dismissed at about this same time and that his reinstatement in the Portuguese army, like Montpézat's, came only after the expulsion of the French. When the British in turn took over the control of Portugal, they made short shrift of the French émigrés. In contrast, it is remarkable to find that the Portuguese continued to pay these officers who had served them in their first hour of need.

Clermont-Crèvecœur's return to England in late 1808 or early 1809 marked the end of his active military life. Although he was still technically on leave from the Portuguese army, he never returned to the Peninsula.[30] For the next few years he and his friend Montpézat lived quietly in Tottenham near London while the war on the Continent pursued its course, bringing new victories and, eventually, defeat to Napoleon's armies.

29. This letter, in French, was written from "East Street, Manchester Square No. 54." In a postscript Clermont-Crèvecœur states that "although attached to the Second Regiment of artillery . . . he has always been paid by the Treasury at Lisbon, and this by special order, as adjutant of the late General de Quiefdeville."

30. Exactly how long he continued on leave (beyond the extension mentioned above) has not been determined. It may be noted, however, that in a late résumé of his services (28 June 1814) he states that he was a "major in Portugal" from 13 December 1797 to 1814, a total of seventeen years!

Journal

des guérres faites En amerique

pendans les années, 1780, 1781, 1782. 1783.

avec quelques dissertations Sur les mœurs &

Coutûmes des americains; un recit des

batailles qui ont été livrées aux anglois aux Endroits
Differents ou l'armée de mr. le comte de Rochambeau a passée
Depuis le commencement dela géurre dans la nouvelle angletea
avec une Description des choses remarquables qui ont été apa
porté Detre vües depuis boston jusqu'a willamburg capitale
dela virginie, ou l'on compte une Etendue de 300 lieus.

TITLE PAGE OF THE SO-CALLED ROBERNIER JOURNAL (see p. xvii)

notre perte pendant le siège est montée à 4 officiers

tués dont deux d'artillerie une vingtaine de blessés

dont 2 sont morts de leurs blessures. m. de choisy

148.

Eut 5 soldats tués et 21 de blessés, nous eumes 70

soldats tués et 169 de blessés. en tout. 279.

les américains perdirent 10 officiers et 260 hommes

tués ou blessés.

les anglois 30 officiers tués ou blessés. et 300 soldats.

la garnison prisonniere de guerre se monte a 6918.

hommes de troupes. en matelots - - - - 1500

plus hommes pris pendant le siege - - - 68.

nombre des prisonniers - - - - - 8486.

non compris les deserteurs qui se montoient a 100,

non compris les torés pris. ny les marchands

ces derniers n'ont pas été regardés comme prisonniers.

artillerie prise en fer - - - - - - 140 pieces

en fonte - - - - - - - 74

Total 214 pieces.

fusils. 7320, drapeaux 22. batiments pris dans

le port. 63. il y en a de coulés qu'on peut relever.

PAGES FROM THE MANUSCRIPT OF THE SO-CALLED ROBERNIER JOURNAL,
NOW ATTRIBUTED TO CLERMONT-CREVECOEUR (see p. xvii)

Mémoire Pour le Sieur, Comte de Clermont=Crevecœur Demandant Sa

Retraite Comme Maal De Camp.   23. Xbre Ret.

Nr 4768.9495   Rec travail le 21 7bre

Services.	Campagnes de guerre.	Observations.
jean françois louis Comte de clermont Crevecœur, nié le 10 janvier 1752. chevalier de St louis depuis le 1er janvier 1790. Est Entré aux cadets de S. M le roy Stanislas. roy de pologne En 1765. Entré au corps royal de L'artillerie a l'école de metz En 1766. reçu Eleve du dit Corps. En 1768. Lt. En Second au regt d'auron= ne En juin 1769. Capitaine au même regiment En 1783. Emigré En 1792 comme capitain Commandant au 6e regiment D'Artillerie passé au Service De Sa Majesté la reine de portugal En 1797. comme Major d'Artillerie, reconnu Susceptible du grade de Lt. Colonel au 31 janvier 1797. par S. A R. Monsieur. 49. ans de services	a fait toutes Les campagnes D'amerique En 1780. 81. 82. & 83. S'est trouvé au Siege d'york. au Combat naval des bermudes. dans les dites années. a fait la Campagnes Des prises En 1792. la retraite de hollande, S'est trouvé a Differentes affaires. dans les dites années et princi= palement a tiberon. a fait une campagne de la guerre Entre l'espagne & le portugal. En 1801. 4 Campagnes En amerique 3 En 1792. 93. 94. 1 En Espagne 1801. 8. Campagnes de guerre. 57 années De Service. 17 comme Lt. Colonel. & 1. Campagne —— 18.	il ose Esperer dans les bontés De S. M. ayant tout perdu, lui & Sa famille par les Suites de la revolution, il ne lui reste d'autres Esperance En rentrant dans Sa patrie que celle que Ses Services, et Son age lui permettent D'esperer. En consequence il ose se flater qu'on lui accordera le grade De Maal De Camp. avec la retraite attaché a ce grade. ayant les 18. années requises, pour obtenir cette grace. Nota. il fut reçu chevalier de St louis En 1790. par mr de la chapelle, maal De camp. Directeur de l'arsenal a metz. Dans toutes les formes. Dont il a le Certificat. Et la Suite Confirmé par les prises En 1792. il avait presenté Son memoire pour obtenir la croix de St louis En 1788. ayant le teurs requisa à cet Epoque, mais Son age lui comptant Ses Services à 13 ans ce fut admis que deux ans après.

fait a londres le 4 juillet 1814.

Examer A la analyse

Le Comte de Clermont Crevecœur.

Lt. Colonel D'Artillerie

MEMORANDUM OF HIS SERVICES PREPARED BY CLERMONT-CREVECOEUR IN 1814 (*see p. xvii*)

THE CHATEAU DE VAUDEVILLE, CLERMONT-CREVECOEUR'S BIRTHPLACE NEAR EPINAL IN LORRAINE
(*see p. xvii*)

The Emperor's abdication and the return of the Bourbons in April 1814 (the "First Restoration") was the signal for the return of the émigrés. After an exile of twenty-two years Clermont-Crève-cœur could at last return to France. He was then sixty-two. On 28 June 1814, from the Paris lodgings of the Chevalier Durepayre, officer of the Garde du Corps, at the "petit hôtel de Crussol in the Rue du Doyenné," he wrote to King Louis XVIII requesting a commission in the artillery of the Maison du Roi with the rank of major general.[31] If, however, this should not be available, he hoped that His Majesty would be so kind as to reward his zeal and long service by retiring him as a major general, "in view of his age, the loss of his fortune, and his constancy in sharing the trials of His Majesty." He signs himself "lieutenant colonel of artillery," a brevet rank granted him in 1799 by the King's brother, the Comte d'Artois. On the margin of this letter Clermont-Crèvecœur gives a brief résumé of his forty-eight years of service, including twelve campaigns. Beneath the résumé is the following testimonial signed by the Comte de Vioménil:

> This officer served under me in the American campaigns, in which he particularly distinguished himself. He was again under my command in the Portuguese army in which his talents as an artillery officer were well known. Among his campaigns, he has forgotten to mention those of 1780–81, 82, and 83 in New England.
>
> Le Cte. de Vioménil

Clermont-Crèvecœur's petition did not bring him all that he hoped for. An undated document in his file headed "Retirement Pension 4768" indicates that he was finally retired with only the rank of colonel.

Soon after submitting his petition (the first of several) Crèvecœur went back to London, where he apparently remained throughout the Hundred Days, which culminated in the final defeat of Napoleon at Waterloo in June 1815 and the Second Restoration. He was still in London the following year. On 16 February 1816 Crèvecœur and Montpézat wrote from Tottenham to the Duc de Feltre, the new minister of war, concerning their affairs. Noting that the law of 20 December 1815 ordering all retired officers to return to France had only recently come to their attention, they explained that pressing business had kept them in England and requested permission to delay their return for three months, because of the inclement season for travel and the state of their health. Attached to this letter is an "Ordre du Roi" of 2 March authorizing them to remain in England to wind up their affairs.

The last documents in Clermont-Crèvecœur's file concern his pension as a chevalier of the Order of Saint-Louis, which apparently commenced on 9 May 1817 while he was living in Paris at 9 Place Vendôme. A final note on the pension account reads: "Ajourné en 1824 pour . . . [illegible word]." In French military parlance the term *ajourné* is most commonly used for conscripts or recruits "rejected" for reasons of health. But here we may take it to mean that Crèvecœur's pension was cancelled because, at the age of seventy-two, his life had ended.

31. This letter and the other documents cited hereafter are in Clermont-Crèvecœur's dossier in the Archives de la Guerre at Vincennes.

The following translation of Clermont-Crèvecœur's American journal has been made from the manuscript belonging to the Rhode Island Historical Society in Providence. This is a small volume bound in contemporary marble boards without label, comprising 323 numbered pages in addition to a title page and several blank pages at the end. The pages measure approximately 19.5 x 13.5 cm.; some of the paper is watermarked G. Delançon and some, N. Jeslin [?]. Internal evidence shows that the author completed the journal soon after his return to France in 1783, although he may have made this fair copy at a later date. It is written throughout in a legible hand; spelling, punctuation, and style conform to correct standards of the time. The author's notes (beginning on page 309 in the manuscript) and his occasional marginal additions have been incorporated into the text of our translation at the appropriate places.

Journal

OF THE WAR IN AMERICA

DURING THE YEARS 1780, 1781, 1782, 1783,

with some remarks on the Habits and Customs of the Americans; an account of the Battles fought, from the beginning of the War in New England, against the English in those places through which the Army of the Comte de Rochambeau passed; with a description of the remarkable sights between Boston and Williamsburg, capital of Virginia, a territory extending some 300 leagues.

[by Comte Jean-François-Louis de Clermont-Crèvecœur, lieutenant of the Auxonne Regiment, Royal Artillery]

May 1780

The French fleet, escorted by the squadron commanded by the Chevalier de Ternay, set sail from Brest on 2 May 1780.[1] The fair wind with which we left the harbor lasted about ten hours. We cleared the Pointe du Raz, a very dangerous passage, without difficulty; but once in the Gulf of Gascony [Bay of Biscay] the wind changed, the sea rose, and we encountered weather to which I was not accustomed and which, without incapacitating me, nevertheless caused me some very disagreeable moments. Some ships had their masts broken and much of their rigging damaged, but thanks to the vigilance and ministrations of the crew, these were promptly repaired.

The ship in which I embarked (the King's flûte[2] *Pluvier* of 26 guns) was a good sailer, so we did not run into any great danger. We were hove to for two weeks without making any headway because of con-trary winds. Several ships suffered a great deal and were even dismasted. Finally the wind abated and the sea calmed down, whereupon we continued on course in a good breeze and were soon within sight of Cape Ortégal. Running south, we rounded Cape Finisterre.

In leaving Brest we had absolutely no idea of our destination, though it was rumored in the ship that we were bound for our islands [the Antilles]. Eventually we fell into the trades and sailed to within four degrees of the tropics when the Admiral signaled a new course a point to the north, which we held for several days.

June 1780

We sighted a small vessel, which our frigates pursued and captured; it was an English ship bound for Europe with news of the capture of Charleston from the

1. The troops constituting Rochambeau's army had embarked a month earlier (the Auxonne artillery on 11 April), but adverse winds and other incidents had delayed the final departure. See Verger's journal, pp. 117–118, for a list of the regiments embarked and of the ships compris-ing Ternay's squadron. See also map and views of Brest, Vol. II, Nos. 1–3.

2. Supply ship, carrying only half its normal complement of guns.

Americans.[3] Thereupon the signal was given to change course to due north, and we were no longer in doubt about our destination, as we had left France in hopes of delivering this city, which we knew to be besieged. Our destination was now changed by the news of its surrender. It seemed certain that we would disembark in one of the ports of North America, either in the Chesapeake, Rhode Island, or Boston.

On 20 June several ships were sighted sailing towards us. As they approached they could be seen more clearly; they were estimated to be 5, all warships. This event did not alarm us unduly because we knew our force to be superior, since M. de Ternay's squadron was composed of 7 well-armed ships: the *Duc de Bourgogne* and the *Neptune* of 80 guns; the *Conquérant* of 74; the *Jason, Provence, Eveillé,* and *Ardent* of 64; and the frigates *Surveillante* and *Amazone* of 36.

The frigates were sent ahead to reconnoiter and judged them to be hostile. As we were constantly approaching one another, the combat was soon engaged. I shall give as brief an account as possible of what I saw, without entering into detail, since I am not a sailor.

We were to leeward of the English ships. M. de Ternay placed his squadron between his convoy and the enemy. One of their ships detached herself from the others to get to our weather and then proceed into the midst of the convoy so as to disperse it and seize or sink some vessels. The French admiral sent two ships ahead under full sail to cut her off. They soon caught up with her, but the enemy ship, realizing she was risking capture, tacked about to rejoin her fleet, during which maneuver she put herself within range of our line.

The combat began with this English ship, which was obliged to run down the whole French line in order to reach her own; then it became general, but since the two squadrons were sailing on opposite tacks, the action did not last long. The enemy ship I mentioned tacked about at some distance from her squadron and was pursued by two of ours, which attacked her a second time and did her some damage; but night fell and obliged the combatants to withdraw. We sailed feint courses all night, though with lamps lighted, in order to conceal our destination from the enemy. We could, I believe, have taken better advantage of our superiority and our situation. Many people thought that we had been too slow in attacking the enemy. On the other hand, could the Admiral expose in headstrong action a convoy, an army, that it was essential to deliver to its destination? Some of the troops and all the generals were aboard the warships; in addition, the crews and troops were very tired, and most of them were sick, since it was our fifty-first day at sea. Let the critics judge, therefore, whether the Admiral could have done better![4]

3. Ternay records in his journal, 18 June, that the frigate *Surveillante,* commanded by Cillart de Villeneuve, captured an English ship called the "*batorth*" (*Botetourt,* according to journals of the Vicomte de Rochambeau, p. 197, and of the Comte de Charlus), which had left Charleston, South Carolina, 30 May, bound for the Windward Islands. There were five English officers aboard; Ternay placed an auxiliary officer from the *Surveillante* in command of the captured ship. Charleston, defended by the Americans under General Benjamin Lincoln, had surrendered to General Clinton on 12 May after a five weeks' siege. Ternay also records that on this same day, 18 June, he assembled aboard his flagship the captains from the ships of his squadron to give them their instructions concerning the landing in America.

4. See Verger's journal, pp. 119–120, for a more detailed description, with diagrams, of the encounter with the English. Other diagrams of this naval action will be found in the journals of Brisout de Barneville, pp. 233–235, and of the Vicomte de Rochambeau, pp. 200–201. Admiral de Ternay's own terse account is in his unpublished journal, pp. [19–20]; this is a bare record, with little commentary. He notes only: "Fearing to lose sight of my convoy, I signaled to proceed to the northward. . . ." The Admiral, as Clermont-Crèvecœur attests, was criticized for not taking advantage of the situation. According to Von Closen (pp. 22–23): "Many persons reproached M. de Ternay for not having taken greater advantage of the superiority of his forces, and for not having pursued the enemy; but his convoy was too precious to him, since he knew the importance of our expedition, and his *precise* orders were to land our army *as soon as possible.* He did not pay any attention to the entreaties of the young naval officers, who, I was told, complained a great deal about his policies, as did most of the army officers, who understood nothing of the consequences of sea engagements, such as the embarrassment or dangers to a scattered convoy, as ours might have been, during the night. While the combat lasted, the frigates hovered around the convoy ceaselessly in order to hold it closely together." General Rochambeau summed things up in his *Mémoires* (p. 241) by saying that "the Chevalier de Ternay continued his route

On 6 July we sounded and found bottom; we were opposite the mouth of the Chesapeake Bay. The signal to prepare to anchor was made when suddenly we sighted sails we could not identify in the twilight and the signal was canceled. A new one was given to tack immediately, and before nightfall feint courses were set. Soon we sighted two unidentified frigates that had slipped into the middle of our squadron in the dark. They made many signals we could not understand, which made us fear the enemy was in our midst, especially after what we had seen the evening before. These frigates stayed with us all night. They even fired on several of our ships. At daybreak we identified them. When they saw with whom they had to deal, they set all sail and fled. We chased them the whole day, but fruitlessly. We have learned since that the fleet we sighted consisted of transports, escorted by two frigates, bringing 2,800 troops back to New York from the Siege of Charleston. What a pity we missed such a chance![5]

We then steered straight for Rhode Island. Nothing of note occurred until we were within sight of land, where we anchored on the evening of the 12th.[6] On the morning of the 13th, despite a very thick fog, we took coast pilots aboard and entered Newport harbor at five that evening, to everyone's great delight, after a passage of 72 days. We had aboard a large number of men suffering from scurvy, including some who were seriously ill. I had a touch of it myself; with bad food and poor sleeping quarters in contaminated air, how can one remain healthy? I had never felt seasick, but I had found the voyage so tedious that it would be difficult to express how utterly prostrated I was.

M. le Comte de Rochambeau went ashore immediately, accompanied by several others, and when he reached the town was astonished to find hardly a soul. The shops were closed, and the local people, little disposed in our favor, would have preferred at that moment, I think, to see their enemies arrive rather than their allies. We inspired the greatest terror in them. The General had all the difficulty in the world finding lodgings, but finally, with the help of some good Americans, everything turned out for the best. It should be noted that the town's leading citizens, whether from fear or from the pleasure of seeing us arrive, illuminated their houses the night we arrived.[7] The effect was beautiful from the middle of the harbor. The next morning we saluted them with 13 guns.

The first concern of the Comte de Rochambeau was choosing a campsite for the army, which was in great need of going ashore; so, after reconnoitering the

---

with his convoy, preferring its preservation to the personal glory of capturing an enemy warship."

5. Clermont-Crèvecœur's date of 6 July for this incident is questionable, since other journals (including Verger's, p. 120) situate it on 4–5 July. According to the Duc de Lauzun ([2] pp. 277–279): "We . . . learned that the convoy before which the Chevalier de Ternay had sheered off on the 4th of July carried 3,000 English soldiers, going from Charleston to New York, and was escorted by only four or five frigates. . . . It is very true that any man a little less timid would have arrived in America with three or four English vessels, five or six frigates, and 3,000 prisoners of war, and that it would have been a very brilliant manner in which to present ourselves to our new allies." Von Closen (pp. 25, 36) adds that the two roving English frigates were later identified as the *Iris* and the *Guadeloupe*. The *Iris* was eventually captured by the French the following year, 10 September 1781, off the Chesapeake Capes; see Verger's journal, p. 136. The *Guadeloupe* was sunk in the York River during the Siege of Yorktown but was later refloated by the French victors and taken to Brest, according to Clermont-Crèvecœur's journal, pp. 58, 61.

6. The dates recorded here are also questionable. The consensus of other journals and related documents gives the following chronology for the arrival of the fleet and army: *9 July*, land sighted. *10 July*, pilots came aboard while the ships lay at anchor outside Narragansett Bay. *11 July*, General Rochambeau and other staff officers were taken into the Bay on the frigate *Amazone* and went ashore at Newport, where they slept that night; that same day the entire fleet and convoy sailed into the Bay (late afternoon or early evening, about seven o'clock, according to Blanchard [1], p. 35) and anchored off Newport. *12 July*, the troops remained aboard the ships; that evening there were illuminations in the town. *13–16 July*, landing of the troops. Landing of the sick and of the artillery continued for several days, until the 19th or 20th.

7. Clermont-Crèvecœur added this in the margin of his journal.

island, he placed his camp to the south and in front of the town [Newport], which is the only one on the island and is the capital of Rhode Island.[8] The troops disembarked on the 14th and 15th and camped in the following order: the regiments of Bourbonnais and Deux-Ponts, Soissonnais and Saintonge, all on one line. The artillery covered the headquarters, and the Lauzun Legion took up an advantageous position in front so as to be able to see anyone approaching the coast. Its camp was a mile from that of the army.

The army had taken barely two days' rest before it had to go to work digging trenches and fortifying those points where an enemy attack or raid might be expected. Meanwhile, as we were working to disembark the artillery, about 20 sail were sighted heading for the island; it did not take long to recognize them as enemy ships, which caused considerable alarm since we were not yet in a state of defense. We had landed only a few field pieces, which we immediately took to the points where we feared the enemy would land. Our ships moored broadside for fear the English might try to force the channel; but not daring to undertake this, after spending several days examining us, they decided to retire.[9] We proceeded tranquilly to arm the coast and throw up several redoubts. Our artillery, consisting of twelve 24-pounders, eight 16-pounders, eight 12-pounders, sixteen 4-pounders, two 8-inch

howitzers, eight 6-inch howitzers, six 12-inch mortars, and four 8-inch mortars, was all landed and emplaced at points of vantage.

⚜ August 1780 ⚜

The enemy reappeared several times in the course of the summer, but since we were then in condition to receive them, we only hoped they would substitute action for threats.

When we first arrived in Newport, we sensed the difficulty of living in a country where language is an obstacle. We lacked practically everything; there were no shops, no markets, no gardens, and the natives avoided us. The houses that seemed to be inhabited were stripped of every resource, though the countryside, if cultivated, should be very productive, since the island of Rhode Island is about 15 miles long and 5 or 6 miles wide and the land is very good. The fields under cultivation were well kept, though there were not many of them. Very few trees were to be found on the island because, when the English evacuated it, they destroyed nearly all of them. They had evacuated the island 10 months ago, at the time the Comte d'Estaing appeared in the neighborhood.[10] According

8. In describing the camp as "to the south and *in front of the town*" Clermont-Crèvecœur is situating it in military terms: the camp faced the enemy who would presumably arrive by sea from the south; the town was thus *behind* the camp. See maps, Vol. II, Nos. 4–7.

9. Verger's journal, p. 120, dates the appearance of the "20 sail" as 21 July (confirmed by other journals). Concerning the British plans for attacking the French before they could establish themselves in Rhode Island and the subsequent failure to do so, see William B. Willcox, "Rhode Island in British Strategy, 1780–1781," *Journal of Modern History*, XVII, No. 4 (Dec. 1945), 304–331; Willcox, *Portrait of a General, Sir Henry Clinton in the War of Independence* (New York, 1964), pp. 324–338; and Willcox's edition of *The American Rebellion, Sir Henry Clinton's Narrative of his Campaigns, 1775–1782, with an appendix of original documents* (New Haven, 1954), pp. 197–208, 443–458. Willcox's authoritative studies tell the story from the British vantage point in New York but make relatively little use of French sources. Clinton in his *Narrative* (pp. 207–208), an apologia written after the war, concludes his account of the Rhode Island affair with

these characteristic reflections: "On the other hand I am unwilling to ascribe the failure of this enterprise to any particular cause, though I must acknowledge it to have been my firm opinion that we should scarcely have been disappointed of success had Mr. Graves fortunately reached New York six days sooner than he did, or even had Admiral Arbuthnot contrived by his frigates to have obtained timely information of the French fleet's arrival, and his transports had been ready as promised for the immediate reception of troops. But, let what will have been the cause, this nation will ever surely have reason to lament that anything intervened to prevent either [attack], as there is little doubt that our not being able to crush this reinforcement immediately upon its arrival gave additional animation to the spirit of rebellion, whose almost expiring embers began to blaze up afresh upon its appearance."

10. The British occupation had lasted nearly three years. A force of some 6,000 men under Clinton, arriving by sea from New York, took possession of Newport on 8 December 1776. An attempt to dislodge the British by American land forces under General John Sullivan and French naval

to several credible residents, this island was an enchanting resort before the war, when everyone prospered without the slightest hardship. The land yielded abundant returns for whatever was planted by the fortunate occupants. And the air here could not be fresher. In short, it was a delightful abode. People came in droves from the South to restore their health, which the hot southern climate had undermined. We saw everywhere the pathetic remains of what nature had once produced in abundance for the use and pleasure of the inhabitants.

September 1780

Newport harbor is superb, very spacious, and affords a safe anchorage for warships. It is full of fish, and one can catch various kinds there, all excellent. Cod is abundant as well as other varieties of fish known in Europe. The harbor was defended, at the entrance to the Bay, by a fort called Brenton, which we have re-established with twelve 24-pounders to bombard vessels seeking entry. Mortars emplaced along the channel would fire on them during and after entering. A small island [Goat Island] in front of the channel was armed with forty 36-pounders from our ships. The latter were moored along the waterfront of the town between this small island and another [Rose Island], some distance from the port, on which artillery was also emplaced.

The Bay had three entrances formed by two islands and the mainland: the right-hand passage [Sakonnet River] between the island of Rhode Island and the mainland; the left-hand passage separating the island of Conanicut from the mainland; and the middle passage, which was the main channel to the harbor. The General proceeded to fortify only the main channel and the right-hand passage, placing a battery of eight 18-pounders on the island of Rhode Island at the channel narrows, where one might expect a raid, and simultaneously securing his communications to the mainland at a point from which he could receive aid without interference. The Comte de Rochambeau did not bother about fortifying the left-hand passage, which would have involved installing camps on Conanicut Island. He had too few troops to guard two islands, the second of which was almost as large as Rhode Island. Instead, he emplaced batteries to defend the approaches to the town and others at the end of the island. Moreover, the small island [Goat Island] I mentioned that was supplied with guns from the fleet fulfilled its function perfectly: since it was round, the guns could be transported to any point as occasion demanded.[11]

The Comte de Rochambeau received deputations from several savage tribes who came to offer their services.[12] These men gave us a demonstration of their games, their dances, and their manner of scalping their enemies (which is to remove a man's hair, or rather the skin around the top of his head so that the hair comes with it).

forces under d'Estaing, in August 1778, was a failure. For a detailed discussion of this first unsuccessful attempt at Franco-American military cooperation, see Louis Gottschalk, *Lafayette Joins the American Army* (Chicago, 1937), pp. 234–269, Chap. xiv, "American Soldiers and French Sailors," and Chap. xv, "Straining the Alliance." The British eventually evacuated Newport on 25 October 1779; this was not, however, the result of any military action, nor of the appearance of d'Estaing's fleet, as implied by Clermont-Crèvecœur. Information acquired by the French in 1778 about Newport, the defenses of the island, and the navigation of coastal waters was available to Ternay and Rochambeau two years later and must have been a significant factor in their planning.

11. For the location of the various fortifications mentioned here, see map, Vol. ii, No. 7. A summary of the strategic considerations dictating their location is found in a memorandum prepared *ca.* September 1780 by Colonel Desandroüins, Royal Corps of Engineers: "Mémoire sur la ville de Newport, en Rhode-Island, avec la description de ses environs, des Ouvrages de Campagne Construits pour sa défense et celle de sa Rade, et enfin de ceux qu'on pourrait y ajouter" (Archives du Génie, Vincennes, Article 15-1-7). With the memorandum, and keyed to it, is Desandroüins's signed map, "Plan de la Position de l'Armée Française autour de Newport et du Mouillage de l'Escadre dans la Rade de cette Ville . . . 1780."

12. In his manuscript (pp. 29–31) Clermont-Crèvecœur places this description of the Indian deputations under April 1781; it has been transferred here to its proper place. The Indians arrived in Newport on 29 August and left on 2 September 1780. See the more detailed description in Verger's journal, pp. 121–123 and nn. 12–19, and his drawings, which are reproduced as illustrations.

These barbarians go naked and paint their bodies different colors, though their natural color is approximately that of copper. They pierce their nostrils, from which they hang large medallions, and likewise their ears. Some slit the edge of the cartilage of their ears so that they hang down to their shoulders. To these they attach many glass baubles. In the most intense cold they wear only a thin wool blanket. They always travel in bands, well armed. They spent four days in Newport.

We staged a gun drill for them. They seemed not to like the noise of the cannon, but that of the drums amused them very much. The oil and the dye they use on their bodies makes them stink and look disgusting. They are very fond of strong liquor and are always smoking. M. de Rochambeau sent them home loaded with gifts. The one who seemed to be in command and who addressed us was a Canadian who spoke French and who likes being associated with them. These people have many good qualities and are basically much less barbarous than they appear, as witness the war we fought in Canada in which they rendered the greatest service to France.

October 1780

I might mention here that during the month of October there was a terrible storm. The whole camp was blown apart. The vessels anchored in the harbor dragged their anchors, and several went aground. A merchantman was dashed on the rocks and could not be salvaged. This storm lasted the whole night of the 19th–20th. Some people sustained heavy losses. Most of our tents were torn to pieces.[13]

The town of Newport could pass for a city, though there is nothing pretty about the town itself. Nearly all the houses are built of wood. Sometimes they build them outside the town and, when completed, put them on rollers and pull them to the lot on which they are to stand. Mostly these are very small houses, though it is not rare to see them move fairly large ones. The houses are charming, of simple architecture, and quite well planned for the convenience of each owner. The interiors are wonderfully clean, and the exteriors painted in different colors present a varied aspect that enhances one's pleasure. The Americans do not possess much furniture, barely enough for indispensable use. Everything is simple and so clean you can see your face in it.

The American manner of living is worthy of mention. Their favorite drink seems to be tea, which is ordinarily served from four to five in the afternoon. The mistress of the house does the honors. She serves it to everyone present, and it is even rude to refuse it. Generally the tea is very strong, and they put a single drop of milk in it. They also drink very weak coffee, weakening it still further with the little drop of milk. They drink chocolate in the same manner.

In the morning they breakfast on coffee, chocolate, and slices of toast with butter. They also serve cheese, jam, pickles, and sometimes fried meat. It should be remarked that those least well off always drink coffee or tea in the morning and would, I believe, sell their

13. Clermont-Crèvecœur adds this information about an October 1780 storm in a note (MS, p. 309). He apparently misrecollected the exact date when writing up his journal, for other sources, though mentioning several such storms, indicate none on 19–20 October. Admiral de Ternay's manuscript journal, for example, records only fair weather for 19–20 October. Ternay does, however, record for Sunday, 8 October: "southwest winds, cool, clear weather. I sent my boat alongside the *Cibelle* [*Cybèle*], which had gone aground on the south coast with her bow on the rocks and stove in. I immediately had them set to work unloading this ship. The vessel *Fantasque* went aground and broke her top mast when attempting to ship it. She struggled all morning to reanchor. Nearly all the tents in the camp were blown down during the night by the wind. Monday, 9 October. The winds blew all day from the southwest. Foggy weather until 3 o'clock in the afternoon. The frigates turned around to take station outside the line of warships." Von Closen, p. 43, 9 October, also speaks of a storm at this time, when "we had a terrifying hurricane again, which overturned almost all the camp tents and obliged the troops to spend 24 hours in bivouac because so many tents were torn." This was probably the tail of the hurricane that had devastated Martinique, Barbados, and other West Indian islands in October 1780. The *Gazette Françoise*, printed by the Imprimerie Royale de l'Escadre at Newport, published several reports on the disaster in its issues of 30 November 1780 (No. 3, p. 3), 15 December (No. 5, pp. 2–4), and 22 December (No. 6, p. 1).

last shirt to procure it. The use of sugar generally marks the difference between poverty and affluence.

Their dinner consists of boiled or roast meat with vegetables cooked in water. They make their own sauce on their plates, which they usually load with everything on the table, enough to frighten a man, and pour gravy over it. On the table there is melted butter, vinegar, pepper, etc., which they use according to their taste.

In general they eat a great deal of meat and little bread, which they replace with vegetables. After dinner those in comfortable circumstances have the tablecloth removed, whereupon the ladies retire. Madeira wine is brought, and the men drink and smoke for quite a while. Among the prosperous, and especially at dinner parties, after the ladies retire the customary healths are drunk; there are so many that one rarely leaves the table without being a little tipsy from the vapors of the wine and the noise the men make when the wine begins to go to their heads.

At meals a bowl containing grog, cider, or beer is passed to those who are thirsty. (Grog is a drink made of rum and water; when there is sugar in it, it is called toddy, and if lemon is added, punch.) There are no glasses, but always this inevitable bowl that is presented to you. When you go visiting, the master of the house never fails to offer you a drink. He takes one first, being careful to drink to your health. Then comes your turn.

In the evening a rather light supper is eaten about ten o'clock.

The Americans are tall and well built, but most of them look as though they had grown while convalescing from an illness. (There are some, however, who are big and fat, but not very vigorous.) The Americans do not live long; generally one notices that they live to be sixty or seventy, and the latter are rare. There are, however, men and women here of eighty, but it is exceedingly uncommon for them to reach that age. I knew one man who was ninety and still rode horseback with ease, was possessed of all his faculties, and enjoyed perfect health.

The women are also very pale and seem frail. They are quite precocious. A girl of twenty here would pass for thirty in France. It must be admitted, though, that nowhere have I seen a more beautiful strain. As I have said, the women have very little color, but nothing can compare with the whiteness and texture of their skin. They have charming figures, and in general one can say they are all pretty, even beautiful, in the regularity of their features and in what one can imagine to be a woman's loveliest attribute.

One must see them at a dance, where they acquire the color they do not have naturally; then one is really struck with admiration. But they fall short in one very noticeable respect, and that is their frigid manner. Once off the floor, they lose much of their charm and show little vivacity and gaiety in your company. If you do not wish to be bored, you must assume the burden of conversation, animating it with your French gaiety, or else you will be lost. It is very difficult to make such an effort, especially when you do not know English. However, when these beauties get to know us, and when they deign to let us look at them, we find them absolutely ravishing.

I noticed on several occasions that the young of both sexes took pleasure in playing our innocent little game of forfeits, which they had known before we arrived.

The English had made the French seem odious to the Americans by their remarks about us. According to them, we were the meanest and most abominable people on earth. They had carried their insolence to the point of saying that we were dwarfs, pale, ugly specimens who lived exclusively on frogs and snails—and a hundred other such stupidities.

Little by little the houses and shops were opened to us, and some merchandise was offered, though at outrageous prices. Finally on both sides friendship and courtesy replaced the bad impressions we had formed of each other, and we were received as brothers rather than foreigners. We took up quarters in the town to the great delight of the residents, who lodged us very well.[14] They took the trouble to teach us their lan-

14. Speaking of the good discipline of the French troops in Rhode Island, Rochambeau recalls in his *Mémoires*, I, 255: "This contributed not a little to acceptance by the State of Rhode Island of the proposal I made to repair at our expense the houses that the English had damaged, provided they could be used during the winter as barracks for our men, and that the townspeople would lodge all the officers. We spent 20,000 *écus* in repairing these houses

guage, wishing themselves to learn French. Few members of the army had cause to complain of their lodging or their hosts. Nevertheless, one may reasonably state that the character of this nation is little adapted to society. The men are very cold, rather stiff, and reticent, except for a group called Quakers, of whom I shall speak further.

The town of Newport has many Protestant churches, nearly all built of wood, without ornament and regular in shape, for the practice of the different religions that are all tolerated in this country. The predominant religion is Anglican. Much of the town, and even the Island, is inhabited by Quakers. These men are extremely grave in their dress and manner and very temperate. They speak little—even laconically—and "thee and thou" everyone. They never remove their large wide-brimmed hats on entering or leaving a room. Their religion is based on fear of God and love of their neighbor. It is against their principles to take any interest in the war. They abhor all sanguinary acts and refuse to take part in rejoicing not only in the innocent pleasures of society but even in the success of their country. They do not permit slavery in their Society, and that is why none of them is served by negro slaves. If they have any, they grant them their freedom. They are very charitable among themselves. They will never take an oath, since they have no faith in the word of man, and refuse to pay tithes, considering the demands of the clergy a usurpation; thus they themselves have neither priests nor ministers. They are, however, obliged to pay taxes levied by Congress for the support of the war. Most of them are royalists.

Their form of worshipping the Supreme Being seems rather bizarre. Their meetinghouse is open to all. They assemble there twice on Sunday, morning and evening. The sexes are separated, and one never sees men sitting in the women's pews. The utmost silence reigns, and the members of the sect seem lost in the deepest reflection. Everyone is seated. When they feel so inspired, the men, as well as the women and girls, may speak. Whoever finds himself in this condition is easy to detect by his convulsive movements: his voice, his body, and all his limbs become agitated. Then everyone awaits the gift of the Holy Spirit and prepares to listen to the discourse that follows these quakings. It often happens that they leave the meetinghouse without having uttered a word. Sometimes the speeches turn on nothing but trivialities.

This sect is very rigid, as I have said above. Quakers allow themselves no pleasures beyond conversation and meditation; they are forbidden to sing and dance. The women, who are very pretty and are more inclined to pleasure than those of other sects (and that is not surprising, considering the constraint under which they must live) cannot become accustomed to such rigorous behavior, particularly while they are young and pretty. They detest their religion and only come to like it at an age when French women begin to become devout. If the Quaker men are even more solemn than those of other sects, one finds that Quaker girls balance the score by being much gayer and more playful. They love pleasure but are always held back by the fear of displeasing their parents. Since they have no ministers, they have no ceremonies. They marry themselves in the presence of all their friends and relatives, promising mutual fidelity. They publish banns and sign a contract in order to ensure that their mutual possessions benefit their children. Their wedding feasts are terribly dreary, since nobody speaks. You may imagine how much fun that would be!

and thus left in the town [Newport] marks of France's generosity towards her allies. A camp of barracks, because of the expense of transporting the necessary wood from the mainland, would have cost us more than 100,000 *écus*; our boats (*chaloupes*) were barely sufficient to bring in firewood. . . ." A letter outlining this proposal, from Tarlé, intendant of the French army, addressed to Governor Greene, Newport, 29 August 1780, is printed in Stone, *French Allies*, p. 219. Orders concerning the move from camp into winter quarters in town are in the army's *Livre d'ordre* (see "Checklist of Journals," *s.v.* Comte de

Vioménil), under dates of 25 October et seq.; these include detailed instructions for precautions against fire, for latrines and other sanitary measures, etc. The billeting list assigning officers to residences in Newport has survived ("Etat des logements occupés dans la ville de Newport par l'armée aux ordres de M. le Cte. de Rochambeau pendant le quartier d'hiver de 1780 à 1781"); printed in Stone, *French Allies*, pp. 221–224, and in *Washington-Rochambeau Celebration*, souvenir program (Newport, 1955), p. 19.

This country is divided between two parties called Whigs and Tories. The former, known as the "good Americans," fight for the freedom of their country and disregard the unjust laws that the English wish to impose upon them. The others, known as "royalists," are those who have remained attached to the King. One may regard the latter in several different ways or, better, from several different angles. We have been in this country long enough to be able to define and analyze the character of these Tories. The vast majority of them are cowardly and cruel, judging by their treason and innumerable crimes against their compatriots. Some, undecided whether to take sides, could be seen waiting for some happy event to indicate in which direction their interest lay. Others, feigning to be on the side of the Americans, were spies paid by the English government to betray their compatriots. Finally, a great number of these miserable creatures decided to take up arms against their country, lured by money and permission from the English to pillage and sack the homes of their fellow citizens.

It is amazing that a government as fine as England's should close its eyes to the crimes and atrocities committed by this execrable party. The English have played very poor politics in allowing these traitors to behave with such cruelty in America. Did they hope to subdue the colonists by means of these atrocious crimes? On the contrary, they have only alienated them further from the mother country and strengthened their resolve to be independent.

I have met other Tories who, bound by fortune and gratitude, declared from the start their adherence to the King. Few as they were, they were honest, and one can only pity their misfortune and the hatred they have aroused. Three-fourths of the inhabitants were Tories. Throughout the war you could not travel in

safety for fear of these brigands, most of whom you could not identify. I shall report more details in the course of this journal.

What misfortunes one can foresee from the division of opinion in a country where the public good demands that everyone think alike! It is up to the Americans to follow a prudent course if this war brings them freedom in its wake. I have witnessed some rather comical scenes at our balls where Tories and Whigs were assembled. We invited all the families indiscriminately and always noticed that a Whig lady would not dance in the same room with a Tory lady, and vice versa. The men were more politic, but the women in this country do not know the meaning of diplomacy. They carried things to such a point that, when we first gave balls, the Whigs refused to come to a house to which Tories had been invited. Since the latter were numerous in Newport, especially their ladies, we did not lack for dancing partners. But all was smoothed over in the end; the women all danced regardless, and everything went beautifully.

❧ February 1781 ☙

During the month of February the ships *Eveillé* and *Ardent* of 64 guns left Rhode Island with the frigates to intercept the reinforcements sent from New York to General Arnold in Virginia.[15] The *Eveillé*, commanded by M. de Tilly, was unable to catch up with the first division of the English, but when she arrived within the Capes of the Chesapeake Bay, she met the English warship *Romulus* of 50 guns, escorting a convoy of 10 transports, all of which she captured. M. de Tilly sent the transports to Philadelphia and kept the

15. The expedition under Le Gardeur de Tilly left Newport on the evening of 9 February, returning there on the evening of 24 February. Destouches, commander of the fleet at Newport, sent his secret instructions to Tilly on 31 January 1781 (*Destouches Papers*, No. 14); Rochambeau reported the departure on 9 February to Washington and to La Luzerne in letters dated 12 February (Doniol, v, 413–414); Destouches sent word of the return on 24 February in a communication of that date to Rochambeau (Doniol, v, 421). The expedition included

the *Eveillé* of 64 guns (but not the *Ardent*, as noted here by Clermont-Crèvecœur) and the frigates *Surveillante* and *Gentille*. The cutter *Guêpe*, which also left Newport with the others, was lost off Cape Charles, though her crew and commander, the Chevalier de Maulevrier, were saved (Deux-Ponts, pp. 21, 28; Von Closen, pp. 57–59, 80). See "Checklist of Journals," *s.v.* Colbert de Maulevrier, for his account of his adventures; also *s.v.* Beauvoir. Other comments on the Tilly expedition are in Berthier's journal, p. 240.

Romulus, which he brought back to Newport. She was armed and added to the fleet, by then under the command of the Chevalier Destouches, since M. de Ternay had just died of a putrid fever after an illness of only four days.[16]

You might like to know about this General Arnold, whom I have just mentioned. He was called the right arm of General Washington, had served well in the cause of American liberty, and had won glory in several actions, such as his retreat from Canada shortly after the death of General Montgomery, when he took command of the American army. He wanted to complete the outer works before Quebec, but the enemy had received reinforcements and he was obliged to abandon the siege in the middle of winter. He made his retreat amid the greatest dangers.

A man of humble birth,[17] Arnold was not without talent. In 1780 he was seduced by the English to surrender the fort of West Point, of which I shall speak later. Major André, adjutant general of the English army, was sent to New York by Sir Henry Clinton, commander in chief of His Britannic Majesty's forces in America, to confer with Arnold on the means of carrying out his infamous treason. Although in disguise, Major André was arrested by an American patrol as he started back to New York. Having got wind of his capture, Arnold escaped to New York, while André was hung several days later [2 October 1780] in front of General Washington's camp. The English commissioned Arnold a brigadier general and employed him in this capacity in Virginia. He had ample opportunity to repent of his infamy. The English officers were unwilling to serve under his command. They despised him, and with reason. Ashamed and disappointed, he asked to be sent to England where he is today, doubtless scorned by every thinking man and hated by the whole human race.

After M. de Tilly's expedition to the Chesapeake, the generals and admirals held a council of war where they decided that the whole squadron would leave for the Chesapeake Bay with 1,500 French troops, two 12-pounders, four 4-pounders, and two howitzers, all under the command of the Baron de Vioménil. There they would take possession of the Bay, land in Virginia, and attack the traitor Arnold, who was in command of 1,200 English troops. The Marquis de La Fayette was to join Vioménil there with 1,500 American troops provided with artillery, munitions, and guns of all calibers.

On 26 March [8 March] the squadron set sail, but on reaching the Capes they met an enemy squadron that, contrary to our expectations, was somewhat stronger than ours.[18] Battle was joined [16 March] and became very hot. The *Conquérant*, one of our ships, was badly battered after a fight with two enemy ships, while one of theirs, the *Robust*, was put out of action. The enemy was master of the wind. His ships entered the Bay, and our squadron, since it could not hope for victory by renewing the combat, made its way back to Newport, where it arrived on 16 April [26 March] to our great surprise, as you may imagine, for we could not believe it was ours.

The Chevalier Destouches, who after the death of the Chevalier de Ternay commanded the French fleet, did not wish to compromise himself, since he held only a temporary command. He could not bring himself to renew the battle when prudence indicated a retreat, even though the two forces were at that time equal. He did not know then that the enemy had suffered more than we had.

Some time before this expedition set sail, we had

16. Ternay had died on 15 December 1780. See Verger's journal, n. 28, and Berthier's journal, p. 237.
17. On the contrary, General Benedict Arnold (1741–1808), born in Norwich, Connecticut, came of a distinguished and well-to-do family. He was the great-grandson—the fourth in succession to bear the name—of Benedict Arnold (1615–1678), the first governor of Rhode Island under the royal charter of 1663. Concerning the arrival in Newport of news of Arnold's conspiracy, see Berthier's journal, n. 35.
18. Detailed accounts of the Destouches expedition to the Chesapeake, 8–26 March 1781, are included in Verger's journal, pp. 126–129, and in Berthier's journal, pp. 241–244. See also map, Vol. II, No. 12.

received a visit from General Washington, to whom we rendered the same honors as to a marshal of France.[19]

General Washington is about 5 foot 10 or 11, well built, with a good figure. His face is handsome and his expression modest. Although cold, it conveys an impression of kindliness and affability. His uniform is simple and unadorned. He responded to the courtesies shown him in an altogether admirable manner. Our generals gave fêtes and balls in his honor at which he danced indiscriminately with everyone. He was honored and esteemed even by his enemies. His justice, his benevolence, and his courage in the misfortunes he experienced at the head of the army made him even more beloved and respected by his men. The people's confidence in him added further to the glory he had won on various occasions when he employed his military talents in the service of his country. He has sacrificed his whole fortune to preserve American independence. Today he tastes the fruit of his labors in peace. He has won and is still winning the admiration of all Europe by his unselfish efforts to gain freedom for his country. In this he has but satisfied the dictates of his heart whose dearest desire is to serve his country.

The town was superbly illuminated for his arrival.[20] He spent eight days in Newport, during which the plans of the coming campaign were devised and soon put into execution.

19. Washington arrived in Newport on 6 March and left on 13 March, after observing the departure of Destouches's ships on the 8th. Rochambeau's aide-de-camp, Von Closen, who had been sent to Washington's headquarters at New Windsor on the Hudson to accompany his party to Newport, describes the journey in his journal, pp. 59–64. Much local lore concerning Washington's visit to Newport has been collected by Edwin M. Stone in his *French Allies*, pp. 362–373. Clermont-Crèvecœur's description of Washington is echoed in many of the other French officers' journals; Gilbert Chinard, *George Washington as the French Knew Him, A Collection of Texts* (Princeton, 1940), is a convenient compilation of such tributes. Although many festivities marked the occasion, the principal reason for Washington's visit was to discuss plans for the year's campaign with Rochambeau. Detailed records of these conferences, if kept, have apparently not survived, but the subjects touched upon are mentioned in Rochambeau's letter to Washington, Newport, 31 March 1781 (Library of Congress, Washington Papers; printed in Doniol, IV, 580–581). In this letter, written after news of the failure of the Destouches expedition had been received and while he was still awaiting dispatches from France with plans for the coming season, Rochambeau proposed to carry out the plan discussed at Newport and march his army to join Washington on the Hudson, there to await developments. "I will leave here 1,200 men, with 3,000 militia to be called up, to protect the King's squadron as long as it is obliged to remain at anchor here." Rochambeau also mentioned that Duportail (Washington's chief engineer), who had been present at the Newport conference and was now returning to New Windsor, would be able to discuss the proposals more fully. In his reply, dated New Windsor, 7 April 1781, Washington wrote: "Upon maturely considering the offer which your Excellency has been pleased to make, of marching all your forces to this place, . . . I am of opinion that it ought, under present circumstances and appearances, to be deferred, as it would be putting you, perhaps, to an unnecessary trouble. . . . My reasons for waiving your Excellency's offer at the present time are briefly as follow: I do not look upon the French troops as *essentially necessary* at this place untill an operation against New York shall have been determined upon, or untill we shall have been obliged to make so large detachments to the Southward that we shall have occasion for them to assist in securing the post of West Point and its dependencies. . . . It does not appear to me that an enterprise so weighty as that against New York can be decided upon, untill we hear what reinforcements of Men and Ships may be expected from Europe. I therefore think, that the Troops under your Excellency's command may remain in their present position, untill the arrival of the Viscount de Rochambeau (which I hope may be soon) or some other intelligence from Europe. . . . But as it may have an effect upon the fears of the enemy in New York and hinder them from making further detachments to the Southward, I beg your Excellency to circulate a report that you are soon to join this Army, and to make some demonstrations of preparing for a march." Original letter in the Rochambeau Papers, Paul Mellon Collection; text printed in *Writings of GW*, XXI, 426–428.

20. The *Livre d'ordre*, 6 March 1781, specifies: "As the town is illuminating this evening to celebrate the arrival of His Excellency General Washington, officers will have lampions or candles placed in the windows of the houses they occupy; the same will apply to windows of enlisted men's quarters, where feasible, and expenses are to be reimbursed."

❧ June 1781 ❧

The rumor was spread that the French army would join the American army camped at White Plains near New York. We were ordered to send all our belongings to Providence, a town on the mainland, and to keep only our campaign equipment with us. Some time previously M. de Barras had arrived on a frigate [the *Concorde*] from France to take command of Ternay's squadron.[21] Not being able to sustain himself in New-

port without troops, he was assigned a detachment of 600 men commanded by M. de Choisy, brigadier general, to which were added 1,000 American militia and one and a half companies of artillery to operate the coastal batteries.[22] The magazines were transported to Providence, at the head of the Bay of Rhode Island [Narragansett Bay], where the hospitals were already established. The latter remained there.

We were very much annoyed to have to leave our heavy baggage behind and seemed to foresee the misfortune of losing it, which eventually occurred. Offi-

21. The frigate *Concorde* left Brest at the end of March and arrived at Boston on 6 May. Among the passengers, in addition to the Comte de Barras, were the Vicomte de Rochambeau and the Baron Cromot Dubourg, who was to serve as one of General Rochambeau's aides-de-camp and who describes the voyage of the *Concorde* in his diary (1), pp. 205–208. Upon his arrival in Newport the Comte de Barras assumed command of the fleet, which had been under the temporary command of Destouches since Ternay's death; the official order, dated 15 May 1781, by which Destouches resumed command of the *Neptune* and Barras took command of the flagship *Duc de Bourgogne* is in the *Destouches Papers*, No. 3. The Vicomte de Rochambeau was returning from his mission to France (he had left Newport at the end of October 1780), bringing badly needed money—"part of the six millions which Monsieur [John] Laurens had got from the government"—and all-important dispatches to his father (Vicomte de Rochambeau, pp. 215–216). The dispatches included instructions to Rochambeau from the Marquis de Ségur, minister of war, dated Versailles, 9 March 1781, and a communication from the Marquis de Castries, minister of marine, dated Brest, 21 March (both printed in Doniol, v, 466–470). Rochambeau thus learned that the "Second Division" that had remained at Brest would not be sent, but that 6,000,000 *livres tournois* were available "to supply the needs and upkeep of the American army." Still more important, he learned that de Grasse's fleet had left for the West Indies and could be expected to cooperate with Rochambeau and Barras in North American waters during the summer. Upon the receipt of this information Rochambeau lost no time in requesting a conference with Washington at Wethersfield, Connecticut, to draw up plans for the campaign. The original minutes of the Wethersfield Conference (21–23 May 1781), including Rochambeau's propositions and Washington's observations, are in the Rochambeau Papers, Paul Mellon Collection; this crucial document is not printed in Doniol, and only an abbreviated version appears in *Writings of GW*, XXII, 105–106. In reply to one of Rochambeau's pro-

posals Washington stated: "it is thought advisable to form a junction of the French and American armies upon the North River as soon as possible, and move down to the vicinity of New York to be ready to take advantage of any opportunity which the weakness of the enemy may afford. Should the West India Fleet arrive upon this coast, the force thus combined may either proceed in the operation against New York, or may be directed against the enemy in some other quarter, as circumstances shall dictate. The great waste of men (which we have found from experience) in the long marches to the Southern States—the advanced season now to commence these in—and the difficulties and expense of Land transportation thither, with other considerations too well known to His Excellency the Count de Rochambeau to need detailing, point out the preference which an operation against New York seems to have, in present circumstances, to attempt sending a force to the Southward."

22. Rochambeau's "Instructions pour M. de Choisy, Brigadier des Armées du Roi, commandant le détachement français à Newport," dated 10 June 1781, are printed in Doniol, v, 493. The possibility of an English attack upon Newport, now less strongly defended, was a continuing preoccupation. General Clinton wrote from New York to Admiral Rodney in the West Indies, 28 June 1781: "Now, sir, permit me to suggest to you an idea which forcibly strikes me. Barras is left at Rhode Island with seven ships, all the cannon taken out of the works, and these garrisoned with twelve hundred French and thirteen hundred militia. It is therefore become the same tempting object it was before the French were fortified or reinforced. I need not say how important success against that squadron and port would be while they remain in the state I describe, and there can be no material alteration which I shall not be constantly acquainted with. I ask no more of the navy than to take a station between Conanicut Island and Brenton's Neck, covering my landing either on that neck or under the protection of frigates in Sakonnet Passage." Clinton, *Narrative*, p. 533.

cers were taxed by weight for the belongings they took with them. Captains were allowed 300 pounds and lieutenants 150. The camp equipment alone weighed this amount. Each of us bought horses, which were sold us at a very high price.

Finally the army received orders on 10 June to leave the next day in two divisions. All the troops were put in small boats to ascend the Providence River. Several of them ran aground, so that most of the troops spent the night aboard these little craft, many without food. It was only the next day with the help of the tide that the boats got up the river. All the troops disembarked on the 12th and camped beyond the town of Providence, where the army spent several days.[23]

Providence is rather a pretty town. Its environs are charming because of the varied landscape. This town seems almost deserted; there is little commercial activity. All the houses here as well as in Newport are built of wood; the streets are not paved. The air is pure and healthy, though the town is surrounded by woodlands. One sees nothing interesting here except the magnificent hospital, which has a fine location.[24]

During our stay in Providence a convoy escorted by the *Sagittaire* of 50 guns arrived in Boston.[25] After

23. See maps, Vol. II, Nos. 14 and 27.

24. The French hospital was installed in the College of Rhode Island, built in 1770, now known as University Hall, still standing on the Brown University campus at the top of College Hill. Arrangements for the use of the college building by the French (it had already been used as a hospital by the Americans during the Rhode Island campaign of 1778–1779) were made before the arrival of Rochambeau's army by M. Ethis de Corny, *commissaire des guerres*, who had reached America at the end of April 1780 on the *Hermione*. De Corny reported to La Luzerne, French minister in Philadelphia, 4 July 1780: "I arrived in Providence on 24 June fully confident not only that the use of the college building for a hospital had been granted but even that it was in readiness. I was much surprised to learn that the request made by Dr. Craik [James Craik, assistant director-general of hospitals, Continental Army] and General Heath had been refused on the most frivolous pretexts. I lost no time in protesting against this ridiculous decision, and after stammering out my reasons in bad English to the Council [Council of War, Rhode Island General Assembly] with as much warmth as conviction, I presented my requisition and the very next morning obtained the building. Sunday I put workmen in it; I went to Boston to get glass, nails, and all the other things that can't be found here. The repairs are well advanced: improvements are gradually being made in this establishment, which, furthermore, unites all desirable advantages of size, location, and salubrity. We shall have a second auxiliary hospital (*hôpital de provision*) between Providence and Newport at Poppasquash. This is strictly speaking an *entrepôt*, or summer hospital built of wood. Dr. Craik had this mediocre establishment built thinking, as did General Heath, that it could take the place of the one that had been refused him at Providence, but aside from the nature of these barracks, they will accommodate scarcely 250 or 300 sick. . . ." Letter in the Archives du Ministère des Affaires Etrangères, Correspondance poli-

tique, Etats-Unis, supplément, Vol. 17; printed in Bouvet, *Service de santé*, p. 56. Complementing the French sources used by Bouvet, the story of the negotiations for the hospital, based on records of the Rhode Island Council of War and the Providence Town Meeting, is told by Howard W. Preston in his *Rochambeau and the French Troops in Providence in 1780-81-82* (Providence, 1924). "And this same Sunday, while President Manning was preaching in the First Baptist Meeting House at the foot of the hill, the Frenchman took possession of his college at the top of the hill. . . . The French used the building from June 26, 1780, to May 27, 1782, one year and eleven months, as stated in the bill rendered for its use." Preston, p. 5.

25. This convoy of 8 transports escorted by the *Sagittaire* (commanded by the Chevalier de Montluc de la Bourdonnaye) had left Brest on 22 March with de Grasse's fleet bound for the West Indies; after passing the Azores, it was detached to pursue its own course to New England, reaching Boston on 11 June (Cromot Dubourg [1], pp. 212–213). The "eagerly awaited convoy" (Von Closen, p. 82) had been expected since early May when the Vicomte de Rochambeau had brought news of its departure (cf. Berthier's journal, 6 May, 7 June, pp. 245, 246). "My recruits were landed today in Boston, about 400 able-bodied men and 260 afflicted with scurvy: these 400 men will arrive here on Saturday, will be incorporated on Sunday, and I shall leave on Monday the 18th with the Bourbonnais Regiment" (Rochambeau to Washington, Providence, 15 June 1781, printed in Doniol, v, 494). Rochambeau ([2], pp. 279–280) says that most of the recruits were assigned to the detachment remaining at Newport under Choisy. The *Livre d'ordre*, 13 June 1781, states: "M. de Choisy is informed that the recruits (*remplacements*) just arrived from France will be distributed among the regiments according to the annexed list. After this incorporation is completed at Providence, each regiment will send to Newport 50 men drawn from these recruits, who will serve to complete the four detachments [at

anchoring in the harbor all the ships were forced by a gale to put to sea. At the end of several days they returned, all except the *Stanislas*, a 600-ton *flûte*, which was captured and taken to Halifax.

The convoy brought us two companies of artillery, some recruits, and ammunition and equipment of every kind. A detachment was sent from Providence to bring back the recruits and escort the military chest. When all were assembled, our departure was fixed for 18 June.

We marched in four divisions, each regiment forming one, which left on successive days. The Lauzun Legion formed the vanguard. The artillery was also divided into four sections, each assigned to a division. Each division was followed by a number of vehicles. Since I was assigned to the First Division, I shall follow its march in this journal.[26] Distances are here reckoned in miles, as in England, 3 miles being slightly longer than a French league.

18 June (15 miles) The army marched from Providence to Waterman's Tavern [Pottersville, Coventry, Rhode Island]. The roads were very poor, and the artillery did not arrive until eleven o'clock at night. The troops did not march well, as frequently happens on the first day's march.

19 June (15 miles) From Waterman's Tavern to Plainfield [in Connecticut] on very bad roads. The artillery and the supply wagons arrived very late. There would be a superb position for a camp of 1,200–1,500 men a mile and a half from this village on the Providence side.

20 June (15 miles) From Plainfield to Windham. The roads were better, and the situation of the little town most agreeable. A mile away is a beautiful river

with a fine wooden bridge. We camped on its banks very comfortably, though hardly militarily.

21 June (18 miles) From Windham to Bolton [Center], a very small town, which is quite pretty. The roads were frightful, with mountains and very steep grades. The artillery arrived very late, and we slept in bivouacs, since the supply wagons were still in the rear. It should be remarked that this country is heavily wooded and that often we have great difficulty finding a level spot on which to pitch a camp. The roads are badly laid out and very difficult, especially for large vehicles.

We had entered the province of Connecticut, one of the most productive in cattle, wheat, and every kind of commodity. It is unquestionably the most fertile province in America, for its soil yields everything necessary to life. The pasturage is so good here that the cattle are of truly excellent quality. The beef is exceptionally good. The poultry and game are exquisite. Among the former the turkeys, geese, and ducks are renowned, especially the wild ones. There is among the game birds a certain partridge the size of a grouse whose flesh is even whiter than that of our chickens. It perches, as do our red partridges, and lives in meadows along small streams. It is very easy to shoot. The water birds, particularly a species of snipe, are excellent here. It is surprising to find in this country so many wild walnut trees. The tree and leaves are somewhat similar to the European variety, but the nuts and the quality of the wood are different. The nuts taste quite good, but you lose patience trying to eat them. As for the wood, it is superior to all others for carriages. It is used to make wheels and shafts of incredible lightness. It is inconceivable how wheels so delicate

Newport], from which an equal number will be sent back to their regiments [in Providence]. As soon as the sick who had to be left in Boston are able to march, they will proceed to Newport to complete their recovery and will subsequently be incorporated into the detachments from their regiments. The Comte de Rochambeau has sent an officer to Boston to look after the sick and to send them on to Newport by different conveyances as they progressively recover. . . ." According to the "Etat du remplacement arrivé de France pour l'Armée de M. le Cte. de Rochambeau" (Library of Congress, Rochambeau Papers, Vol. 9, pp. 129ff.), the recruits consisted of 592 men (including 134 sick or convalescent), in addition to two com-

panies of artillery. These new arrivals assigned to the regiments already in America had been drawn from still other regiments: Auvergne, Neustrie (assigned to Bourbonnais); Languedoc (assigned to Bourbonnais, Soissonnais, or Saintonge); Boulonnais (to Saintonge); Anhalt, La Marck (to Royal Deux-Ponts); and Barrois (to the Lauzun Legion).

26. The route of the army's march from Providence to Philipsburg, near Dobbs Ferry on the Hudson, is described in detail in Vol. II, Itineraries 1 and 2, and maps of the roads and the campsites, Nos. 13–39. Information on the localities mentioned is included in the notes to these documents.

can last as long as the most massive ones. I wish our cabriolets and pleasure carriages were built of such wood; being lighter, they would not spoil our roads by their weight, and it would require fewer horses to draw them, making traveling much easier. Since there are no such walnut trees in Europe, this is but an idle dream that can never be realized in view of the difficulty of procuring the wood in France.

There are also trees here that are very useful for other purposes. There are possibly more than 12 species of oak; although it is of fairly good quality, ours is still to be preferred for a variety of uses. I have never seen any elms; this is perhaps the only European tree that cannot be found in America[!].

22 June (12 miles) From Bolton to Hartford, the capital of Connecticut. Through it runs a magnificent river, which is navigable for fairly large ships. The roads were better. We stayed there on the 23rd and 24th to rest the troops and to make necessary repairs to the artillery. Hartford is a large town, divided in two by the river that is named after the province. It is quite well built, with some pretty houses, but the streets are not paved. Three miles from town is a village called Wethersfield, whose few houses are all very pretty. This place is also notable for its fine location; climbing to the top of the church steeple, you can see the countryside for nearly 50 miles around.

Connecticut is one of America's best provinces. It has excellent pasturage, and that is why its cattle are famous for their beauty and quality. The countryside yields almost all the products of Europe except wine. Grapes grow in the woods and everywhere, but they taste entirely different from ours and only resemble ours in shape. They taste like our black currants that we call *cassis*. They claim that, if this grape were cultivated, it would flourish, but the Americans' laziness doubtless prevents them from making the effort. I hope they will one day know the pleasure of growing their own wine and substituting it for the cider they make here in great quantity, which is truly good. You would think yourself in Europe when you cast your eyes over the orchards, the apple trees, and the fields. The landscape is the same. This country has a very healthy and salubrious climate. We have seen old people here of both sexes who enjoy perfect health at a very advanced age. Their old age is gay and amiable, and not at all burdened with the infirmities that are our lot in our declining years. The people of this province are very hard-working, but they do not labor to excess, as our peasants do. They cultivate only for their physical needs. The sweat of their brow is not expended on satisfying the extravagant desires of the rich and luxury-loving; they limit themselves to enjoying what is truly necessary. Foreigners are cordially received by these good people. You find a whole family bustling about to make you happy. Such are the general characteristics of the people of Connecticut.

You often encounter Tories here. This country is unfortunately swarming with them, and the harm they have done to the inhabitants is incredible.

25 June (13 miles) From Hartford we marched to Farmington. The roads were better, and the village, tucked into the bottom of a pleasant valley, very pretty. The position of the camp was truly military. It should be remarked that on our arrival in each camp crowds of natives from the vicinity came running up to watch us pass but especially to listen to the music of our regimental bands. Enchanted to find charming young ladies in our midst, our generals and colonels had the musicians play each evening and invited the girls to dance.[27] Thus we relaxed from the fatigues of the day. As for us [in the artillery], we profited little from these pleasures, since we always arrived so late!

We lived very well during our passage through this province. The poultry here is excellent and quite cheap. The Americans crowded round, not only to hear the bands, but also loaded with every sort of produce, so that the camp was a continual market, offering the most delicious wares. This country is swarming with a species of partridge, much larger than ours, which roosts in trees. Its flesh is as white as our chicken's, though more delicate. It likes the marshes, and

27. Lieutenant Gallatin of the Deux-Ponts Regiment relates that at Bolton "the band played outside the camp and we danced on the green. General Baron de Vioménil, who was marching with our regiment, had a dispute with our Colonel [Christian de Deux-Ponts] about our band, which the latter had ordered to play without asking the General. A heated argument ensued, and the Colonel withdrew the band. M. de Vioménil gave a *louis* to the musicians but did not deign to use his authority to call the band back again." Gallatin (1), p. 675.

the meadows bordering streams, and is quite tame. When a dog flushes one in the reeds, it will fly immediately to a neighboring tree, then to another if one is near. They are at their best in the autumn; the Americans are very fond of them.

26 June (13 miles) From Farmington to Barnes's Tavern [in Marion, town of Southington]. The roads were quite good, and the day not very tiring. There was only one house in this place.

27 June (13 miles) From Barnes's Tavern to Break Neck [in Middlebury] or, in French, "casse-cou," a most appropriate name indeed. Numerous mountains and rocky roads delayed the arrival of the artillery until after three in the morning. Our horses could do no more, so we had to commandeer all the oxen we passed and go far afield to find others in order to reach camp with our guns. Many of our wagons broke down. We never had a worse day, considering the fatigues and misfortunes we endured. The village contains few houses. These are widely scattered and very ugly. There are some sawmills here where several planks can be sawn at once.

28 June (15 miles) From Break Neck to Newtown. The first 4 miles of road were very bad, and the rest quite good. We saw several unfamiliar trees along the road, such as the tulip and the choke-cherry. The tulip tree blooms during May. I have seen two different colors, one white, the other russet; its flower rather resembles those in our gardens, and that is how it gets its name. It grows very tall. I have seen such trees with a spread of 5 or 6 fathoms, or around 30 feet. Its wood is soft and of poor quality; boards for ceilings and wainscoting are made out of it. Its leaves are very beautiful.

The choke-cherry resembles our wild cherry,

though its leaves are much darker. It bears cherries in bunches like our currants. From it a kind of liqueur is made with rum, which is called "cherry rum."

One finds here another curious shrub [bayberry] that the English call "wax bush," or *arbre de cire*. The wax gathered from it is green. Pharmacists use it because of some special property it has. Candles are made from it, but its wax must be mixed with ordinary wax or spermaceti. The bush has little berries covered with wax, which one recovers by dropping them into boiling water, whereupon the wax melts and rises to the top.

The town of Newtown is in the province of New York [Connecticut]. We saw much poverty there among the inhabitants, as well as ruined fields and houses. This is the capital of the Tory country, and as you may well imagine, we took great precautions to protect ourselves from their acts of cruelty.[28] They usually strike by night, when they go out in bands, attack a post, then retire to the woods where they bury their arms. But we were too much on our guard to fear these brigands. These people are very difficult to identify, since an honest man and a scoundrel can look alike. Thus we hardly dared arrest them. The Americans, more experienced, picked up a few but were forced to turn them over to the English, who claimed they were royal troops. In this way they sometimes escaped the noose.

An aide arrived from General Washington informing us that the Americans had started the campaign on the 26th and were waiting for us to join them. I forgot to say that, according to the Comte de Rochambeau's orders, we were to serve in America as auxiliary troops under the supreme command of the American generalissimo.[29] On the 29th and 30th we remained at Newtown. We would have rested there until the 2nd

28. Ever since the British occupation of New York following the American withdrawal from Manhattan Island in the autumn of 1776, the surrounding territory had been the scene of intermittent guerrilla warfare. This so-called Neutral Ground extended over much of Westchester County, New York, adjacent parts of Connecticut, as well as parts of northern New Jersey. The raiders included regulars enlisted in British Loyalist units such as Colonel Delancey's corps, as well as numerous freebooters. Tory sympathizers were called "Cowboys" or "Refugees" (in consequence of their having taken "refuge" under the protection of the Crown); the rebel sympathizers, "Skinners." James Fenimore Cooper's novel *The Spy* (1821) has the

Neutral Ground as its setting. Cooper reminds his readers (Chap. xxxiv): "The French forces drew near to the royal lines, passing through the Neutral Ground, and threatened an attack in the direction of Kingsbridge, while large bodies of Americans were acting in concert. By hovering around the British posts, and drawing nigh in the Jerseys, they seemed to threaten the royal forces from that quarter also. The preparations partook of the nature of both a siege and a storm."

29. Rochambeau's orders, signed by the Prince de Montbarey, minister of war, Versailles, 1 March 1780, are printed in Doniol, v, 324–326. Article 1 specified that the King's intention was that "the general to whom His Maj-

of July had not the Comte de Rochambeau received orders from Washington to make every effort to accelerate his march.

ᴐᵍ⧼ July 1781 ⧽ᵍᴐ

1 July 1781 (15 miles) From Newtown to Ridgebury.[30] Instead of marching by regiments, we marched by brigades. The roads were very mountainous, and the journey difficult. This little town is not very pretty. The natives appear to be poor. There is much devastation by the English. In the evening news came from General Washington that caused a change in our route. We were to have proceeded from here to Crompond.[31]

2 July (19 miles) From Ridgebury to Bedford. The roads were execrable, the day was very long, and the wagons and artillery had a great deal of trouble in reaching their destination. The Lauzun Legion, which up to now had marched on our left, joined us. We occupied an excellent position; our camp was pitched on this side of Bedford, with the grenadiers and chasseurs and the Legion in front.[32] We had, besides, 160 American dragoons [Sheldon's dragoons, Colonel Cobb commanding], who are incontestably the best troops on the continent. They are permanently attached to General Washington and form his body-

esty is entrusting the command of his troops is always and in all cases to be under the orders of General Washington." Article 1 of the confidential "secret instruction" of the same date (Doniol, v, 327) adds: "His Majesty wishes and orders the Comte de Rochambeau, as far as circumstances allow him to do so, to keep together in a corps the French troops which His Majesty has placed under his command and, as occasion arises, to inform General Washington, generalissimo of the troops of Congress and under whose orders the French troops are to serve, that the intentions of the King are that there be no dispersal of French troops and that they are always to serve in an army corps under French generals, except in cases of temporary detachments that are expected to rejoin the main corps within a few days."

30. Ridgebury is a hamlet near the New York state line in the northern part of the "town," or township, of Ridgefield, Connecticut—not to be confused with the town's main agglomeration, Ridgefield proper, which is some 5 miles south of Ridgebury. See map of the Ridgebury camp, Vol. II, No. 37.

31. As outlined in the "Plan for marching the army from Providence to King's Ferry on the east bank of the Hudson River . . ." (Vol. II, Itinerary 1), it was expected that the army would proceed west from Ridgebury, Connecticut, to Crompond (in present Yorktown, Westchester County, New York) and thence to Peekskill on the Hudson to join the American forces there. As a result of Washington's decision to threaten the enemy in New York, the route of march deviated southwest from Ridgebury to Bedford, west to North Castle (Mount Kisco), and eventually south to the allied encampment at Philipsburg on the heights between White Plains and Dobbs Ferry. Washington to Rochambeau, Headquarters near Peekskill, 30 June 1781: "I must entreat your Excellency to put your first Brigade under march tomorrow Morning, the remaining Troops to follow as quick as possible,

and endeavour to reach Bedford by the evening of the 2d. of July, and from thence to proceed immediately towards Kingsbridge should circumstances render it necessary. Your Magazines having been established on the Route by Crompond it may perhaps be out of your power to make any deviation; but could you make it convenient you would considerably shorten the distance by marching from Ridgebury to Salem and from thence to Bedford leaving Crompond on your right." *Writings of GW*, XXII, 293; Doniol, v, 505–506; original letter in the Paul Mellon Collection. Washington to Rochambeau, Headquarters near Peekskill, 2 July 1781: "I have this Morng received your Excellency's Favr of last Evening [from Ridgebury, 1 July, 8 p.m.; Doniol, v, 508]. I think it will be very well for your Excellency to proceed Tomorrow to North Castle [Mount Kisco] where you will continue until you assemble your whole Force, unless you should hear from me within that Time. Being at North Castle will put you in a direct Rout to receive your Provisions from Crompond, and will be in a direct Way for your Troops to advance to White Plains, or any other Point below, as Circumstances shall appear to Demand." *Writings of GW*, XXII, 324; Doniol, v, 508–509; original letter in the Paul Mellon Collection. See also Berthier's journal, p. 248.

32. The route of the First Brigade (with which Clermont-Crèvecœur marched) from Ridgebury via Bedford to North Castle (Mount Kisco) is not described in the "Itineraries," nor is it shown on Berthier's road map (Vol. II, No. 24), both of which describe the slightly different route (via present Bedford Center) of the Second Brigade. Routes of both brigades are, however, schematically indicated on the general map of camps of marches, Vol. II, No. 162. The Bedford camp, or bivouac, of the First Brigade was on the outskirts of present Bedford Village, near the intersection of Seminary and Court Roads.

guard. He is always attended by an escort of these brave men. The American army came to camp several miles to our right. We can consider that this moment marked the opening of our campaign.

We learned on arrival in Bedford that the previous evening an English patrol had burned several houses just outside the village, which had already suffered much damage and, in fact, hardly had any houses left standing. This settlement is very small and denuded of every resource—not surprisingly considering that this region has been a battlefield for three years.

That evening the Lauzun Legion left for Morrisania to surprise the English dragoons of Colonel Delancey.

3 July (5 miles) From Bedford to North Castle [Mount Kisco] by a very pretty road [Guard Hill Road]. The Second Division joined us that day, having marched 24 miles. It had had only one day's rest since Providence. We remained at North Castle on the 4th and 5th. Everything here has been either destroyed or burned by the English.

We learned that Delancey's corps, which the Legion had hoped to surprise, was at Williamsbridge and had doubtless got wind of the Legion's march because, the

moment the French appeared, nearly 3,000 English debouched in several columns. This maneuver forced the French to cross a small stream and form in line of battle behind it. The American general Lincoln, leading another expedition, joined up with our troops. A few shots were fired, the Americans had 4 men killed and 15 wounded; the Legion lost none. Each retreated in good order.[33]

On the 5th General Washington came to see the Comte de Rochambeau and spent five hours with him.

6 July (17 miles) From North Castle we marched to Philipsburg at White Plains. The route was quite good to within several miles of the camp. Early in the day we suffered much from the heat. The roads were so bad that the last division of artillery, to which I was attached, did not arrive in camp until an hour after midnight. The troops had been on the road since three o'clock the morning before without anything to eat. They found nothing to drink on the way. Casting your eyes over the countryside, you felt very sad, for it revealed all the horrors and cruelty of the English in burned woodlands, destroyed houses, and fallow fields deserted by the owners. It is impossible to be more

33. Lauzun's advance from his camp (No. 7) at Bedford during the night of 2–3 July was one part of a two-part combined attack, conceived by Washington as the first of his threatening moves against the English in New York. According to Washington's plan (*Diaries*, II, 231–233), a detachment of Americans under General Lincoln was to reconnoiter the enemy posts on the northern end of Manhattan Island—Forts Knyphausen (Washington), Tryon, and George (Laurel Hill), the latter being the "preliminary object"—but if from appearances, an attempt against them was judged inadvisable, Lincoln would remain on the mainland above Spuyten Duyvil Creek and cover Lauzun's operation. Meanwhile, Lauzun would advance to Morrisania (on the east bank of the Harlem River) and cut off Delancey's and other enemy corps believed to be quartered in that vicinity. The success of these simultaneous movements depended in both cases on surprise. Lincoln decided not to attack the Manhattan Island forts; the enemy became aware of his movements, thus eliminating the factor of surprise; Delancey's corps had shifted from Morrisania farther inland towards Williamsbridge on the Bronx River, where Lauzun met up with it. The joint action thus failed to accomplish the objectives set by Washington. The localities involved are shown on maps in Vol. II, Nos. 43–46. According to Deux-Ponts, p. 35, Lauzun assured him soon after this "journée peu mémorable et peu glorieuse" that he himself did not know

exactly what had happened or why the attempt had failed; several years later, however, Lauzun confidently recounted the affair in his memoirs ([2], pp. 290–291). Freeman (*Washington*, V, 297–299) characterizes Lauzun's account—rather too harshly—as "so grossly inaccurate and self-laudatory that it scarcely deserves citation." An excellent recapitulation of "The Attempt upon the British Posts at Kingsbridge," with complete text of many of the pertinent contemporary documents, is given by John Austin Stevens in his "The Operations of the Allied Armies before New York, 1781," *Magazine of American History*, IV, No. 1 (Jan. 1880), 4–9, 34–41. Cf. Berthier's journal, p. 248. How it all looked to an American private who was in the thick of things is related by Joseph Plumb Martin in his *Narrative of Some of the Adventures of a Revolutionary Soldier* (Hallowell, Maine, 1830; reprinted as *Private Yankee Doodle*, ed. George F. Scheer, Boston, 1962), pp. 214–218. See also Maria Campbell, *Revolutionary Services . . . of General William Hull, prepared from his manuscripts, by his daughter . . .* (New York and Philadelphia, 1848), pp. 199–204. William Hull (1753–1825), then a colonel, was sent by Washington to "attend" the Duc de Lauzun during the attack on Manhattan; unfortunately his latter-day recollections as paraphrased and edited by his daughter give only a tenuous glimpse of the affair.

uncomfortable than we were that day; more than 400 soldiers dropped from fatigue, and it was only by frequent halts and much care that we brought everyone into camp.[34]

That night I saw something that surprised me very much. Spending the night in a meadow, I noticed that the top of the grass was covered with sparks. At first I attributed this to the heat, but I did not long persist in this error, for I saw that the sparks were generated by a fly that imitates our glowworms, having like them the ability to give off light at one end. The body of these flies was very long, making them look like a glowworm equipped with wings. The English call it a "fairfly" or "firefly," which means *belle mouche* or *mouche de feu*.

We camped in front, our right wing resting on the left wing of the Americans. The two armies were camped on a single line in a very agreeable and advantageous position.[35]

On 8 July General Washington reviewed the two armies. I went to the American camp, which contained approximately 4,000 men. In beholding this army I was struck, not by its smart appearance, but by its destitution: the men were without uniforms and covered with rags; most of them were barefoot. They were of all sizes, down to children who could not have been over fourteen. There were many negroes, mulattoes, etc. Only their artillerymen were wearing uniforms. These are the élite of the country and are actually very good troops, well schooled in their profession.[36] We had nothing but praise for them later; their officers, who seemed to have good practical train-

34. Washington's General Orders, Headquarters, near Dobbs Ferry, 6 July 1781: "The Commander in Chief with pleasure embraces the earliest public opportunity of expressing his thanks to his Excellency the Count de Rochambeau for the unremitting zeal with which he has prosecuted his March in order to form the long wished for junction between the French and American Forces. An Event which must afford the highest degree of pleasure to every friend of his Country and from which the Happiest Consequences are to be expected. The General entreats his Excellency the Count to Convey to the Officers and Soldiers under his immediate command the grateful sense he entertains of the Chearfulness with which they have performed so Long and Laborious a march at this extreme hot Season. The Regiment of Saintonge is entitled to peculiar acknowledgements for the Spirit with which they continued and Supported their March without one days Respite. . . ." *Writings of GW*, XXII, 332–333. The "parole" for 6 July was "Lewis the sixteenth," the "countersigns," "Luzerne" and "Rochambeau." The Chevalier de La Luzerne, French minister, had arrived from Philadelphia that day. Washington's "compliment" was transcribed into the French army's order of the day, 7 July (*Livre d'ordre*, p. [286]). Announcing his safe arrival to Admiral Barras in Newport, Rochambeau wrote on 8 July: "We have made the most rapid march to arrive here at General Washington's request, without a single complaint and without leaving a single man behind, except for ten love-stricken Soissonnais who returned to see their mistresses in Newport and whom I beg you to apprehend." Doniol, v, 510. Replying to Rochambeau from Newport, 13 July, Barras stated that M. de Choisy had found in Newport "only one of the Soissonnais deserters, whom he had placed under arrest." "Another of these soldiers," Barras continued, "has been apprehended in

Portsmouth and is to be held in irons on the ship *Marie Françoise*. Will you kindly take the necessary steps for having him brought back to your army." Original letter in the Rochambeau Papers, Paul Mellon Collection. To the Marquis de Ségur, minister of war in Versailles, Rochambeau reported on 8 July: "We have covered 220 miles in eleven days of marching. There are not four provinces in France where we could have traveled with more order and economy and without lacking anything. There have necessarily been heavy expenses, but nothing wasted, and, what is perhaps the first example of it, there was not a single regimental officer, more than half of whom marched on foot, who wasn't fed by the general or superior officers, with rough food, without their being obliged to procure their own mess. You do not complain, Sir, of money spent usefully for the good of the state, and I believe that this expense has been essential to our American allies. For heaven's sake, Sir, do not forget our money and real funds for the month of October; our neighbors lack everything, and the subsidy which they can draw on in letters of exchange will soon discredit this currency. . . ." Doniol, v, 511–512.

35. For maps of the allied camp at Philipsburg, on the heights between the Bronx and Sawmill rivers, within the boundaries of the present town of Greenburgh, Westchester County, see Vol. II, Nos. 39–41 and 46.

36. "The whole effect was rather good. Their arms were in good condition; some regiments had white cotton uniforms. Their clothing consisted of a coat, jacket, vest, and trousers of white cloth, buttoned from the bottom to the calves, like gaiters. Several battalions wore little black caps, with white plumes. Only General Washington's mounted guard and Sheldon's legion wore large caps with bearskin fastenings as crests. Three-quarters of the Rhode Island regiment consists of negroes, and that regiment is

ing, were the only ones with whom we occasionally lived. I returned, following the generals of the French army, who looked quite different and much more glamorous.

On 10 July we learned that the *Romulus* and 3 frigates under the command of Captain de La Villebrune had left Newport and entered the Sound (between Long Island and the mainland) bound for Huntington Bay. The English ship of 44 guns stationed there retired at their approach, and some small vessels fled into the Bay. The pilots aboard the French ships did not dare enter by night, preventing M. d'Angély, a colonel attached to the army who was in command of the 250 troops aboard, from landing that night on the point [Lloyd Neck] at Oyster Bay where Fort Lloyd, which he wished to capture, was located. He was therefore obliged to postpone his operation until the next morning. Landing with his small force, he found the fort more strongly held than he had expected and the enemy defenses entirely different from what he had been told. After a lively cannonade and sustained musketry fire he was obliged to retreat. He lost 4 men killed.[37]

On 11 July the Lauzun Legion passed in review, a sight that gave no small pleasure to the Americans. It was camped at Chatterton Hill, 2 miles from our left wing.[38]

On the 12th our generals were at Dobbs Ferry, 3 miles from our camp on the famous river known as the Hudson, or North River, which at this spot is about 2 miles wide. Warships of 64 guns can ascend this river to a point 30 miles beyond Albany, 250 miles from its mouth. Its bank on the Dobbs Ferry side is fairly low, but the opposite bank is rocky and is very high and very steep. The Americans have built a redoubt here and erected two batteries to prevent enemy ships from going up the river, thus ensuring the passage of the army stores, which are more conveniently transported by water.[39]

On 14 July at nine in the evening we heard rather a heavy cannonade and fusillade. They beat the Call to

the most neatly dressed, the best under arms, and the most precise in its maneuvers. The American army is always drawn up in *two lines*, a custom which we have also adopted." Von Closen, pp. 91–92. Writing at about this same time, one of Washington's aides, Jonathan Trumbull, Jr., commented on the appearance of the French army in a letter to Col. Varick (then in Poughkeepsie): "The Junction of the two Armies is formed at this Place, & has commenced with high seeming Cordiality & Affection, demonstrated by constant Acts of Conviviality & social Harmony. A very fine Body of Troops compose the French Army, which seems anxious to give some Marks of Heroism, to distinguish their Attachment & Military Pride." Jonathan Trumbull, Jr., to Col. Varick, Headquarters near Dobbs Ferry, 13 July 1781, letter in Princeton University Library, Andre deCoppet Collection.

37. See Verger's journal, pp. 130-132, for his more detailed account and map of this expedition, in which he took part. See also map in Vol. II, No. 42. The expedition left Newport on 10 July, returning there on the 14th. This unsuccessful attempt to capture the Lloyd Neck fort (Fort Franklin) near Huntington, Long Island, and burn the British stores at Huntington was the second in the series of threatening moves against New York, following the Lincoln-Lauzun attempt of 2–3 July and preceding the reconnaissance in force of 21–23 July.

38. Chatterton Hill, a commanding elevation on the west bank of the Bronx River in White Plains, was the scene of the Battle of White Plains, 28 October 1776, during Washington's retreat from New York. According to Cler-

mont-Crèvecœur (p. 35), Lauzun's Legion moved on 17 July to another camp at "Red House," about 2 miles to the northeast; at the same time the grenadiers and chasseurs of the Second Brigade took over the Legion's Chatterton Hill camp. See maps, Vol. II, Nos. 40–41, which show the Lauzun Legion in its later position, as does No. 25.

39. The supply depots for both Americans and French were up the Hudson, near Peekskill, or even higher up the river. When it was still expected that the French army would march, according to the original plan, directly west from Ridgebury, Connecticut, to Peekskill, Commissary-general Blanchard was sent ahead to make arrangements for hospitals and supply depots. He relates, for example, in his journal ([1], pp. 78–79) that arrangements were made for bakeries at Fishkill Landing (Beacon), which is north of West Point at the upper entrance to The Highlands. Although Blanchard (or his editor) consistently confuses "Peekskill" and "Fishkill," it is clear from the context that these bakeries were first set up at Fishkill Landing. The change in the army's route required quick readaptation, which in turn produced some unpleasantness between Blanchard and Rochambeau. "On 15 July I went back to the camp [at Philipsburg]. That evening M. de Rochambeau criticized me because there had been a shortage of bread. I tried in vain to justify myself by telling him that I was not specifically responsible for this service, but he would not listen to me. I had nevertheless warned him that bread would be lacking in view of the distance from the ovens." Blanchard (1), p. 83.

Arms, and we did not doubt for an instant that the camp was being attacked, or at least the Lauzun Legion at the outpost. The firing continued but an hour, after which they beat Retreat. We had hardly returned to our tents before an order came to send 200 men with six 12-pounders and two howitzers to Tarrytown, 4 miles from camp on the river above Dobbs Ferry, to which two English frigates had sailed under cover of night. When all was ready, the order was countermanded. Only the American general [Robert] Howe marched out with a detachment of his own troops.

On 16 July at five in the morning we heard the frigates firing, and once again our camp was alerted. We sent two 12-pounders with two howitzers to Tarrytown.[40] That afternoon I went to watch the cannonade; but since the frigates were some distance out in the stream, we could do them little harm. The previous night the English frigates had captured a vessel loaded with flour, bread, and uniforms for Sheldon's American dragoons. When they put their crews in boats to attempt a landing at Tarrytown, where the army bake-ovens were located, a sergeant of the Sois-sonnais Regiment with his guard of 12 men kept up such a lively and effective fire that he prevented the landing. (This sergeant and all his men were invited next day to dine with the Comte de Vioménil. The sergeant was made an officer.)[41] The Americans arrived a moment later: two 18-pounders were emplaced to fire on the frigates, which were obliged to retire out of range. In the English attack the Americans lost one sergeant and had one officer seriously wounded. The latter was taken prisoner.

On 17 July the Lauzun Legion moved its camp to Red House, while the grenadiers and chasseurs of the Second Brigade took over the Legion's camp.[42]

During the night of 17–18 July M. Hartman, an officer of the Legion, was killed by Delancey's dragoons while on patrol with a detachment of hussars. The infantry went to the rescue of the hussars, but the enemy fled to the woods and vanished in the darkness.[43]

On 18 July the French and American generals advanced quite near New York to examine the enemy works through their field glasses.[44] They saw 5 or 6

40. The cannonade was commanded by Captain Bernard de Neurisse and Second Lieutenant Jean-Philippe de Verton, both of the Auxonne artillery, Clermont-Crèvecœur's regiment. Recalling the incident some forty-five years later, Verton claimed: "My action, among others, on the North River, against two English frigates when I was fortunate enough to set fire to the larger with one of my shells, so completely deceived the English general who was in command at New York that he straightaway sent orders to Lord Cornwallis (who himself gave me these details in a private conversation) to send him 1,200 to 1,500 men from his army, because there seemed no further doubt that the combined armies intended to attack him in New York, since they had their siege artillery. (He had mistaken the shells I had fired on the frigates for bombs.)" Verton, p. 22. Writing at the time, Washington recorded in his *Diaries*, II, 236, 16 July 1781: "two french twelve pounders, and one of our 18 prs. were brought to bear upon the Ships which lay off Tarrytown, distant about a Mile, and obliged them to remove lower down and move over to the West shore." See also Berthier's account of the incident, p. 251.

41. "Our commanding officers outdid themselves in bestowing praise upon these brave soldiers: '*Mon Général*,' the sergeant replied to the Baron de Vioménil who was praising him for his conduct, 'I am indebted to the advice and the bravery of my corporal, who perfectly seconded my endeavors.' Courage is not such a rare virtue in France; modesty is somewhat more so; and yet this was a pattern of the most perfect modesty in a circumstance very delicate for a soldier. I have, I must admit, heard with pain a superior officer criticize the praise bestowed upon these men and blame the Baron de Vioménil for having invited them to dine with him. Can virtue ever be too much honored or too well rewarded?" Abbé Robin (1), pp. 59–60, "letter" dated from Camp at Philipsburg, 4 August 1781. Abbé Robin was a chaplain marching with the Soissonnais Regiment.

42. See maps of the Philipsburg encampment, Vol. II, Nos. 40–41, which show Lauzun's Legion in its "Red House" camp and the grenadiers and chasseurs of the Second Brigade on Chatterton Hill. Cf. n. 38.

43. "That is not the whole story. The dead officer's horse, which none of the hussars had been able to catch, galloped back to his picket, but since he could not reply to the sentinel, who cried out twice, *Qui vive?* and once, *Wer da?* he was killed 15 paces from the guard, some minutes after his master." Von Closen, p. 96.

44. This reconnaissance was made from the Palisades on the New Jersey shore, opposite Manhattan Island. Washington, *Diaries*, II, 237–239, 18 July: "I passed the North River with Count de Rochambeau—Genl. de Beville his Qr:Mr. Genl. and Genl. Duportail in order to Reconnoitre the Enemy Posts and Encampments at the North end of York Island—took an Escort of 150 Men from the Jersey Troops on the other side. From different views

small encampments established in support of the redoubts. (The camp at Philipsburg was only 10 miles from New York [i.e., Manhattan Island]).

On 19 July the English frigates that I mentioned above came down the river again in a good breeze on their way back to New York. They were heavily shelled while passing the batteries at Dobbs Ferry, which were now in very good condition. The howitzers started a fire aboard one of the ships. One of our soldiers whom they had captured during the night of the 15th–16th took this opportunity to escape. He jumped overboard and swam to the bank on our side. He told us that the English had had several men killed and wounded during our various cannonades.

It was also on the 19th that we arrested two spies in camp, both French.

On 21 July we received orders to prepare to march.[45] The Retreat served as the signal for getting under arms, whereupon the First Brigade of the army, the grenadiers and chasseurs of the four regiments with

two 12-pounders, two 4-pounders, and two howitzers, an American division, and the Legion were ordered out. This army formed up and marched in three columns throughout the night. We arrived at five in the morning of 22 July at the height that dominates King's Bridge (a bridge leading from the mainland to New York Island), except for the two 12-pounders, which were delayed by the bad roads and by an accident that occurred during the night when a caisson fell down a precipice 40 feet deep. We had to light a fire and work very hard to extricate the lot. The horses, 6 drivers, and the vehicle all fell in, but none of them was hurt. The artillery did not arrive until eleven that morning. The English seemed amazed, not having had the slightest suspicion of our march.[46]

On arrival at King's Bridge we formed in line of battle, above, and on our side of the bridge. A battalion of grenadiers and chasseurs was posted on a small eminence in front, to the left of our position. Several English dragoons came to reconnoiter, and a few musket

the following discoveries were made. . . ." A detailed description follows. Von Closen (p. 96) adds the name of Colonel Desandroüins, chief engineer of the French army, to those accompanying the generals on this reconnaissance. General Duportail, a French officer in the American service, was Washington's chief engineer.

45. Orders concerning the reconnaissance in force of 21–23 July (originally scheduled for 13 July but postponed because of bad weather) are in the French army *Livre d'ordre*, 13, 14, 21 July (pp. [288, 290–291]); Washington's "Instructions for Reconnoitering the Enemy's Posts at the North End of York Island" are in *Writings of GW*, XXII, 370–372, and his narrative account in his *Diaries*, II, 241–245; Rochambeau's brief report is printed in Doniol, V, 518–519 (also MS in the Paul Mellon Collection). The French troops were commanded by Major General Chastellux, the Americans by General Benjamin Lincoln. Under the subheading "The Reconnaissance in Force of the New York Defenses" John Austin Stevens includes a convenient recapitulation of the event in his "The Operations of the Allied Armies before New York, 1781," *Magazine of American History*, IV, No. 1 (Jan. 1880), 23–25, 41–43; although additional documents have become available since its publication, this is still the most satisfactory study. Maps incorporating the information gathered during the reconnaissance and showing the localities mentioned in Clermont-Crèvecœur's journal are reproduced in Vol. II, Nos. 43–45, and 46. Other accounts are by Von Closen, pp. 97–102; Cromot Dubourg (1), pp. 302–303; Deux-Ponts, pp. 37–38; Dumas (1), I, 70–72; Gallatin (1),

pp. 680–681; Charlus, who commanded the Second Battalion of grenadiers and chasseurs, in letter to his father (the Marquis de Castries) dated Philipsburg, 29 July 1781, Archives de la Guerre, A¹3732, pièce 81.

46. Recalling these events in his apologia, General Clinton wrote: "Nothing, certainly, could have been more alarming as well as mortifying than my situation at the present crisis—the most important advantages presenting themselves hourly, of which I could not avail myself for want of force; the enemy's parading on the heights on my front for two days, and no possibility of my stirring against it was I in ever so great force, as I had not an armed vessel to cover either of my flanks and Mr. Washington had, by an unexpected move, masked the only *débouché* (over King's Bridge) I then had to the continent. And, should the Count de Grasse happen to arrive on the coast in the Admiral's absence, everything was to be apprehended, not only for all the distant points of my army, but even for those at New York. . . ." Clinton, *Narrative*, p. 321. Lieutenant von Krafft, serving with one of the German regiments on Manhattan, observed "the Rebels and French" from the vantage point of Fort Washington (or Fort Knyphausen, as he called it). Describing their movements, he noted in his diary, 22 July: "Altogether one could see by their camps which were on the plain above Independence, that they must be very strong. Tonight, though we had certainly expected an attack, they were very quiet." Thomas H. Edsall, ed., *The Journal of Lt. Charles Philip von Krafft*, New-York Historical Society Collections for 1882 (New York, 1883), pp. 142–143.

shots were exchanged. The various forts, that known as No. 8 in particular, which was below the bridge on our side,[47] saluted our army with a few cannon-shots that did us no harm. An American regiment sent to capture a small work gave a very good account of itself. The troops reached the position under fire from the enemy guns, which took off the leg of one of their officers.

After thoroughly inspecting the points in front of the army, the generals crossed the Harlem River to examine the opposite bank. There they were shelled without result, whereupon they came back across the river and continued along their original route in order to reconnoiter the island as far down as the city of New York.[48] The frigates anchored in the North River kept up a continuous fire on the generals without consequence. Then the group fell back on Morrisania, where the cannonade and musketry were rather more lively. M. de Damas, aide-de-camp of M. de Rochambeau, had his horse shot from under him, and the French took four prisoners.[49]

We received an order to emplace batteries in front

of Redoubt No. 8 in preparation for an attack on it, but the order was countermanded almost immediately. We could doubtless have captured this redoubt, though not without loss. It held about 150 men and 3 or 4 guns and was dominated by the three famous forts called Washington, Tryon, and Laurel.[50] The first is the largest. They form a sort of triangle and are connected by strong entrenchments mounted with cannon. Those in the forts are very large, including calibers up to 48-pounders. The English fired several shots that reached our army.

I believe it would be impossible to find a position more ideal for defense than this. The three forts are built on top of three high hills. Fort Washington, on the highest and most inaccessible of these, dominates the others, which could not hold out if it fell. This central fort is joined to the two others by lines of circumvallation running from one side of the island to the other. The English camp is located behind these lines, and there are several advance posts in front.

On 23 July the generals made further reconnaissances,[51] and a dragoon of General Washington's

47. See map, Vol. II, No. 43. Redoubt No. 8 ("L" on the map) was situated on the east bank of the Harlem on present University Heights, campus of New York University in the Bronx. The exterior defenses of the northern end of Manhattan Island, located on commanding eminences on the mainland across Spuyten Duyvil Creek and the Harlem River, were begun by the Americans in 1776 and later reoccupied in part by the British when they in turn held Manhattan Island. These defenses consisted of a series of numbered redoubts, beginning on the west with "No. 1" on Spuyten Duyvill Hill and extending in a semicircle to "No. 8" on what is now known as University Heights. No. 8 was the only one of these redoubts occupied by the British in July 1781 at the time of the French-American reconnaissance. See Reginald P. Bolton, "The Exterior Forts and Encampments," in his *Relics of the Revolution* (New York, 1916), pp. 200–214; John Christopher Schwab, *The Revolutionary History of Fort Number Eight on Morris Heights, New York City* (New Haven, 1897).

48. The route of the generals (which can be traced on map 46 in Vol. II) might be described in the language of 1970, very approximately, as south along the Grand Concourse of the Bronx (State Route 22) down to the Triboro Bridge. Although no pictorial sketches done by French draftsmen at the time of the July 1781 reconnaissance have been found, a watercolor drawing made four years and four months earlier by an English officer, Cap-

tain Thomas Davies of the Royal Regiment of artillery, gives a good idea of the appearance of the northern end of Manhattan Island and the route down the Harlem Valley. Davies's "A View of the Attack against Fort Washington and Rebel Redoubts near New York on the 16 November 1776 by the British and Hessian Brigades" is reproduced in I.N. Phelps Stokes, *The Iconography of Manhattan Island*, Vol. VI (New York, 1928), frontispiece II (description, p. 38); other reproductions are in, e.g., John A. Kouwenhoven, *The Columbia Historical Portrait of New York* (New York, 1953), p. 74, and Richard M. Ketchum, ed., *The American Heritage Book of the Revolution* (New York, 1958), p. 201.

49. Berthier, who was with Damas, Vauban, Lauberdière, Von Closen, and other skirmishers, gives a full account of this incident in his journal (pp. 252–253), as does Von Closen (pp. 99–100). Many of the other journals also mention the *escarmouches*, which seem to have gained considerably in the retelling. Gallatin ([1], p. 681) remarks that "the aides-de-camp couldn't let this opportunity pass without trying to distinguish themselves." See Albrecht Adam's commemorative painting, reproduced in Vol. II, No. 47.

50. See maps, Vol. II, Nos. 43 and 46. Forts Washington (or Knyphausen), Tryon, and Laurel Hill (Fort George) were all on Manhattan Island, that is, across the Harlem from No. 8.

51. "Went upon Frogs [Throgs] Neck, to see what com-

bodyguard was killed. The grenadiers and chasseurs who had been detached to the left flank returned to the army, as did the Legion in the afternoon. We departed at five that evening, undisturbed by the English. The light troops beat the woods, where they found many weapons that the Tories had cached there, as was their custom. We searched every house, since all in this neighborhood were suspect.

We arrived in camp at Philipsburg in the best possible order between eleven and twelve o'clock that night. On the next day, 24 July, two men deserted from the Legion. That day we finished the redoubts at Dobbs Ferry, which were never used. During our stay at Philipsburg we sent out in view of the enemy several foraging expeditions, which were not disturbed.[52] Each day it was announced that Lord Cornwallis was embarking his troops in Virginia to bring them to New York to reinforce the position the English expected us to besiege. We shall see that none of this was true.

English deserters appeared in camp almost daily, and sometimes our men deserted, too. An English soldier who arrived on the 8th assured us that the troops who had just arrived in New York belonged to the garrison of Pensacola that had recently been captured by the Spaniards[53] and were not from Cornwallis's army as we had thought.

On 11 August a woman was arrested who had come from New York on the pretext of seeking her father who, she claimed, was a soldier in the American army; but doubtless her intentions were not so pure. She was put in a safe place to rest from her journey, which she had made on foot.

This anecdote leads me to make a brief observation on the subject of American women, or girls. In a country so new where vice should not be deeply rooted,

---

munications could be had with Long Isld. the Engineers attending with Instrumts. to measure the distance across it. Washington, *Diaries*, II, 245, 23 July. See map, Vol. II, No. 45. Rochambeau ([2], pp. 283–285) relates: "While our engineers were making this survey (*faisoient cette opération géométrique*), we fell asleep, overcome with fatigue, at the foot of a hedge, under fire from guns on enemy vessels that tried to disturb this work. Awaking first, I called General Washington and pointed out to him that we had forgotten the hour of the tide. We quickly returned to the mill dam on which we had crossed over the little inlet (*bras de mer*) that separated us from the mainland: we found it covered with water. Two small boats were brought up, in which we embarked with the saddles and harnesses of our horses. Then two American dragoons went back and pulled by the bridle two horses that were good swimmers; these were followed by the others, urged on by the whips of some dragoons left on the other side, to whom we sent back the boats. This maneuver was accomplished in less than an hour; fortunately the enemy was not aware of our predicament." Von Closen, who accompanied Rochambeau to Throg's Neck, also describes this incident (p. 101).

52. "At first we had been given no other forage (*fourrage long*) than the pastures around the camp. Later on orders were given for armed foraging expeditions as far as the enemy's advanced posts. On one of them we went to a little town or village called New Rochelle, which is inhabited by a colony of French who took refuge here and built it at the time of the Wars of Religion; they have kept the use of the French language." Gallatin (1), p. 679.

Orders for such expeditions appear in the army's *Livre d'ordre*, for example, under dates of 3, 6, 8, and 13 August. A typical order (8 August) specifies: "The army will forage tomorrow for grass and hay; scythes must be taken. Rendezvous at 4 A.M. on the road near the Intendant's quarters. Each regiment will supply 3 wagons for the artillery; the others will be used for the officers' food. Wagons must be completely loaded. The police of each regiment will see to this. Oxen will be brought into camp this evening, so that the wagons can reach the rendezvous at the appointed time. The escort will be composed of a company of grenadiers and chasseurs from the battalion of the Soissonnais Brigade, of one second captain, one lieutenant and 50 men per brigade, and of a picket of 30 of Lauzun's hussars. The rendezvous for this escort will be at the camp of the Saintonge grenadiers and chasseurs. Police guard as usual. M. de Gambs [Bourbonnais] will command this foraging expedition."

53. Pensacola, West Florida, on the Gulf of Mexico, surrendered on 8 May 1781, after a two months' siege. Although the expedition was nominally a Spanish one, under Bernardo de Gálvez, it included French naval vessels (*Palmier, Destin, Intrépide, Triton, Andromaque*) "garrisoned" with troops from the West Indies. For accounts by French participants, see "Checklist of Journals," *s.v.* Cadignan, Saint-Exupéry, Soret de Boisbrunet. See also the recent work by N. Orwin Rush, *The Battle of Pensacola. . . . Spain's Final Triumph over Great Britain in the Gulf of Mexico* (Tallahassee, 1966), which, though drawing heavily on Spanish and British archives, makes no use of French sources. Cf. map, Vol. II, No. 163.

why should there be such a large number of prostitutes? Only one reason seems to me to be the cause. Although the fathers and mothers keep an eye on their daughters during their childhood, once they reach the age when human nature demands that they know everything, they become their own mistresses and are free to keep company with anyone they wish. Among the country people (for today in the towns education has corrected the abuses of which I shall speak) the girls enjoy so much freedom that a Frenchman or an Englishman, unaccustomed to such a situation, straightaway seeks the final favors. It is actually the custom, when a young man declares himself to be in love with a young girl, without even mentioning marriage, to permit him to bundle with her. This permission is granted by the parents. He then shuts himself up in a room with the young lady to lavish the most tender caresses upon her, stopping short of those reserved for marriage alone; otherwise he would transgress the established laws of bundling. If the young lady should take offense at his intrepidity, her parents will give him a hard time. The truly virtuous girls, who are not governed by temperament, easily resist and conform to the letter of the law of bundling, but it is to be feared that those more amply endowed by nature in this respect succumb to this tender sport. Bundling, it would seem, is made for Americans only. The coldness and gravity of their faces proclaim that this sport suits them perfectly. The bundling period is not defined; you can play this game for five or six years before deciding to marry, and even afterwards if you wish, without committing yourself finally to marry the girl after receiving these initial favors.

The women are generally very faithful to their husbands. You find few libertines among them. Yet some girls lead a most licentious life before they marry, though once married they, too, become good. The men are not fussy in this respect; they believe a girl should be free and do not despise her unless she is unfaithful after marriage. Thus a girl who has proved her worth, if she is pretty or rich, is quite sure of finding a husband; if she has had the misfortune to be seduced and the seduction bears its unfortunate fruit, it is not she who is disgraced, but the man. Respectable houses are henceforth closed to him, and he cannot marry into a respectable family.

It is rare to find a woman committing adultery here, though it does happen. In this situation the husband announces the delinquency of his wife and publishes it in the papers. No dishonor falls upon the husbands for the misconduct of their wives, and no one points the finger of scorn at a cuckold. Instead, they pity him. If the wife absconds with her lover, the husband announces in the gazette that his wife has quit his bed and declares that he will not pay her bills or be liable for any debts she may have contracted. The husband always assumes responsibility for his wife's obligations, but in this circumstance his conscience is clear, since a wife who abandons her husband becomes a criminal. This is no excuse, however, for dissolving the marriage, which rarely occurs, since their laws do not permit it. The husbands are quite patient about waiting for their wives to repent. If they do, their husbands take them back, forget the past, and live with them in perfect harmony. I leave it to the European husbands to ask themselves whether they are capable of doing as much.

On 14 August we received letters from Newport reporting that the frigate *Concorde*, which had gone to meet M. de Grasse's fleet, had left the fleet on 26 [28] July and that de Grasse was departing on 3 August to join M. de Barras, so we expected him to arrive any day.[54] (M. de Barras had recently arrived in Newport to take command of the squadron the Chevalier

54. Washington, *Diaries*, ii, 253–254, 14 August 1781: "Received dispatches from the Count de Barras announcing the intended departure of the Count de Grasse from Cape François, with between 25 and 29 Sail of the line and 3200 land troops on the 3d. Instant for Chesapeake bay, and the anxiety of the latter to have every thing in the most perfect readiness to commence our operations in the moment of his arrival as he should be under a necessity from particular engagements with the Spaniards to be in the West Indies by the Middle of October, at the same time

intimating his [Barras's] Intentions of enterprizing something against Newfoundland, and against which both Genl. Rochambeau and myself Remonstrated as impolitic and dangerous under the probability of Rodney's coming up this Coast. Matters having now come to a crisis and a decisive plan to be determined on, I was obliged, from the shortness of Count de Grasse's promised stay on this Coast, the apparent disinclination in their Naval Officers to force the harbour of New York and the feeble compliance of the States to my requisitions of Men, hitherto,

Destouches had temporarily commanded at the death of the Chevalier de Ternay.) The whole army was convinced that the siege of New York was certain. We shall soon see that our generals' plans were quite different.

On 15 August a flag of truce from New York was arrested at the main guardhouse. This was the fourth to be sent with ordinary letters. The Comte de Rochambeau was greatly annoyed and expressed his opinion very pointedly in a letter to the English general, Sir Henry Clinton, as these flags of truce appeared to be spies.

On 17 August two deserters were caught, one from the Bourbonnais and one from the Deux-Ponts regiments. The first was hung, and the second got off with a flogging out of consideration for his family, thanks to the good offices of the Comte de Deux-Ponts.

❧ Departure of the Army from Philipsburg ❧

On 19 August the Call to Arms was beaten and the order issued for our immediate departure. When the army was under arms, the General noticed that there were not enough supply wagons and that 5,000–6,000 rations of bread still remained in camp. This postponed our departure from six in the morning, as ordered, to midday. The artillery park had left the evening of the 18th by a different road than the one the infantry was to take.

I left on 18 August with the artillery park's wagon train, but that day we were only able to go 4 miles, and we slept in bivouac.[55] The American army left on

the 19th, but by another route, so that we marched in three columns, the artillery forming the center column. One cannot imagine how many afflictions we had to endure during the six days it took us to march from Philipsburg to King's Ferry on the Hudson River, a distance of 40 miles. It took us six days because of the terrible weather and incredible roads. We slept every night in bivouac. There was a terrific storm on 20 August. I floundered in the mud and in a horrible marsh with all the wagons and the artillery train, not knowing where I was or how I could get out of it. Not until daybreak was I able, with great difficulty, to extricate myself. During the march from Philipsburg I was in command of the rear guard of the artillery. I have no doubt that, had the enemy been able to predict our march, he would have caused us much anxiety.

Philipsburg to King's Ferry (40 miles) As I have said, it took us six days to cover this distance. Halfway we crossed the Croton, quite a pretty river with a fine wooden bridge [Pines Bridge], which was, however, in ruins. We passed through Peekskill, a village of 20 houses on the Hudson River. We camped on the high ground at the edge of the river and remained there on 23 and 24 August;[56] the two armies had joined one another here. Meanwhile, we took the artillery and the army wagons across the river on flatboats. This was a long and tedious procedure, since there were very few boats. At this point the river is about 2 miles wide.

It is most surprising that the English, who controlled the river from New York to King's Ferry, did not send one or two frigates to undermine our feeling of security; for as we had been marching for seven days, they must have heard about it, especially since they probably thought we were going to attack New York by

and the little prospect of greater exertion in the future, to give up all idea of attacking New York; and instead thereof to remove the French Troops and a detachment from the American Army to the Head of Elk to be transported to Virginia for the purpose of cooperating with the force from the West Indies against the [enemy] Troops in that State." De Grasse's letter outlining his plans, dated from The French Cape, 28 July 1781, reached Newport by the frigate *Concorde* on 11 August; it was immediately forwarded by Barras, whose courier arrived at the Philipsburg headquarters on 14 August. See Doniol, v, 520–522. The original of de Grasse's historic letter, which is in the Paul Mellon Collection, is reproduced

here as one of our illustrations. De Grasse set sail from The French Cape early in the morning of 6 August; he anchored off Cape Henry on 31 August.
55. Berthier, assistant quartermaster-general, conducted the column in which Clermont-Crèvecœur marched. It was the left column of the French army, the center column of the allied armies as a whole. See Berthier's journal, pp. 253–255, and Vol. II, Itinerary 3. The maps, reproduced in Vol. II, Nos. 48, 61, and 62, do not show the route of this column from Philipsburg to Pines Bridge, but only the subsequent portion, when the two French columns were following the same route.
56. See maps, Vol. II, Nos. 48 and 62.

way of Staten Island, which was on the other side of the river nearer the mainland. Doubtless they had their reasons, and we ours, and it is certain that they could not have suspected the latter because, except for Generals Washington and Rochambeau, no one knew our plans. If the English had wished to oppose our passage at this point, they could have forced us to go up the river as far as West Point. This would have really delayed our march, though it would not have changed our plans, as you shall see.

DESCRIPTION OF THE STRONGHOLD OF WEST POINT[57]

West Point, the fort that General Arnold had been on the point of delivering to the English, is a very respectable fortress that belongs to the Americans. It is situated so as to cut the communications of the Hudson River with Canada and, in the present circumstances, is a very important post. This fort has become the key to America, for New York is in the center of the American territory, which extends from Charleston to Halifax. The English occupy these three important positions. The Hudson River flows through New York, where its mouth is situated, and cuts the united provinces in two. One can therefore imagine how important it is for the Americans to control the navigation on this great river, which, if the English controlled it, could separate absolutely their northern from their southern provinces.

The fortress of West Point is 40 miles from New York. It deprives the English of all communication, not only with Canada but also with the interior of America, where they would expose themselves to the fate of General Burgoyne, who was caught there with his whole army on his way from Canada. The local militia forced him to surrender when he could no longer procure food for his troops.

The fortress of West Point is in a very formidable position, being perched on high rocks with very steep sides above a plateau on which 1,200–1,500 men can deploy in line of battle. Six forts, raised one above the other, defend the approach and protect the troops below. Several fine batteries overlook the river, which at that point makes a wide elbow turn. At the point where the river bends back on itself a chain is placed across the bend to prevent any ship from passing through. A small island called Constitution Island is mounted with batteries whose fire crosses that from the forts.

All the forts are built of wood except one, which is of stone. Along the parapet have been erected stockades, which remain lowered while the cannon are firing and can be raised again the moment an escalade is threatened.[58] This parapet is very low. Some people criticize this form of fortification. It seems to me that a parapet 4½ feet high is more effective than one 2 feet high fitted with stockades; however, the latter has its advantage. There is no embrasure, so the cannon have a much larger field of fire. The battery is quite high above the water, and the stockades may be instantly raised in case of danger. These fortifications were built to fulfill the same function as our high coastal gun carriages. The American carriages are all very low. They therefore had to invent some method of adapting them to their purpose at a time when they could not build others.

One of the principal works is Fort Clinton, built on a rock that seems to grow out of the river; it is large enough to provide a very strong *place d'armes*, so it is used for the artillery park.

———

The crossing of the North River at King's Ferry is defended by two forts. The first, on the east bank, is called Verplanck, or Fort La Fayette. It is built of wood and is very small. There are a few miserable iron guns there, badly mounted and poorly maintained. The second, opposite the first on the west bank, is called Stony Point. It is also very small and is built of earth

57. Clermont-Crèvecœur presumably did not himself turn aside to visit West Point at this time; the description inserted here is a paraphrase or summary of other accounts. See, e.g., Cromot Dubourg (1), pp. 307–308: "23 August—M. de Rochambeau was not willing to pass so near West Point as nine miles, without seeing it. He left by boat at eight o'clock in the morning to visit it with General Washington and several officers. I mounted a horse and went by land, in order to arrive as soon as he. . . ." Other descriptions are given by Von Closen (pp. 60–61, 108), who had visited West Point in March 1781, and by Chastellux ([4], 1, 88–95), who was there in November 1780. See map, Vol. 11, No. 48.

58. See the drawings on Berthier's map, Vol. 11, No. 48.

with a double row of abatis. It, too, is fitted with 4 or 5 pieces of artillery, 12- and 18-pounders that are as poor as those in the first.

The artillery and most of the army's wagon train crossed the river on 23 August and camped 3 miles beyond the crossing, in the Jerseys.[59] On the 24th the First Brigade crossed the river and marched to a camp a little above the place where the park was stationed. That same day we received news that M. de Barras had sailed from Newport with M. de Choisy, who had been left there in command of an army detachment and 1,000 Americans.[60] The latter were militia who had already been discharged. He had embarked in his ships all the heavy artillery with all types of ammunition and equipment. M. de Choisy had left only 100 men in Providence to guard the army stores and hospitals, under the command of M. de Prez, major of the Deux-Ponts Regiment.

25 August (15 miles) The First Division left for Suffern while the Second crossed the river and marched to the camp we had occupied the night before, a procedure that was followed all along the route.[61] The roads were quite good, and the country pleasant and well cultivated.

26 August (15 miles) From Suffern to Pompton [Pompton Plains]. We crossed the river of that name three times. It had many wooden bridges, also two fords. The road is excellent and very smooth. This country, known as the Jerseys, is populated by Dutchmen who seem very prosperous. The land is well cultivated and yields abundant harvests. Ten miles from Pompton, near a village called Totowa, is a waterfall [Passaic Falls] that is regarded in these parts as a great curiosity.[62] The river flows very tranquilly down to a rock ledge imbedded in its course, which contains a crevice about 15 feet wide into which the river rushes precipitately and falls in a cascade from 70 to 80 feet. The crevice gradually diminishes until it practically disappears at the foot of the ledge, from which the river emerges and resumes its course as quietly as before.

27 August (16 miles) From Pompton to Whippany. Four miles from Whippany we passed a very large estate in one of the most pleasant spots in the whole countryside.[63] Whippany is a small village on the banks of a river of that name. We halted there on the 28th, and the Second Division joined us. Until then we had been marching down river and believed we were bound for Staten Island. What confirmed us in this belief was the fact that the American army and the Lauzun Legion had made a reconnaissance in the vicinity. A dummy camp had been pitched facing

59. They were not yet in the Jerseys, but still in the state of New York, at the locality known today as the village of Stony Point. It was then within the limits of the township of Haverstraw and is so designated on the map in Vol. II, No. 63.

60. Clermont-Crèvecœur's statement under this date (which he subsequently repeats, more plausibly, under 7 September, Elkton, Maryland; below, p. 51) is questionable, since Barras's squadron sailed from Newport only on 23 August, as recorded in Verger's journal (p. 135). It was not until 21 August that Fersen, Rochambeau's aide-de-camp, arrived back at headquarters from Newport bringing Barras's letter of 17 August announcing his intention of sailing for the Chesapeake "at the first favorable wind." Fersen (2), pp. 118–119; Von Closen, p. 107; Barras to Rochambeau, Newport, 17 August 1781, printed in Doniol, v, 524–526, original in the Paul Mellon Collection. Barras, who was preparing to go off on an expedition of his own to Newfoundland, acquiesced in this course only after the most urgent representations from Washington and Rochambeau (cf. their letters of 15 August 1781 in Doniol, v, 523–524, and *Writings of GW*, xxii, 499–500). It is thus possible that rumors of Barras's *intention* to sail

could have been circulating among the lower ranks by 24 August; if so, Clermont-Crèvecœur retrospectively expanded such rumors into a *fait accompli* when writing up his journal.

61. The route from Suffern, New York, through New Jersey, Pennsylvania, and Delaware to Elkton, Maryland, is described in Vol. II, Itineraries 3, 4, and 5, and maps, Nos. 50–60 and 64–76.

62. Several officers made an excursion from the Pompton camp on 26 August to see this famous "natural wonder," which is now in the city of Paterson, New Jersey. See, e.g., Cromot Dubourg (1), p. 376; Von Closen, p. 112; Deux-Ponts, p. 420. An elaborate description was penned by Chastellux, who visited the Falls in November 1780. Chastellux (4), 1, 104–105, and Plate facing p. 73.

63. The "large estate" was "Beverwyck," the property of Lucas von Beverhoudt, who was at this time sharing it with Abraham Lott, a patriot refugee from New York. See Vol. II, Itinerary 3, and map, No. 51. Several of the officers dined at Beverwyck (Von Closen, p. 113). Verger was entertained here when the army was marching northward in September 1782; see his journal, p. 164.

Staten Island, where fires were kept going for several nights in order to screen our march and keep the English thinking that we planned to besiege New York.[64] We were much surprised when General Rochambeau left for Philadelphia, thus upsetting our forecasts.[65]

From Whippany to Bullion's Tavern [Liberty Corner] the road was very good. Five miles beyond Whippany we passed a pretty little town called Morristown containing between 60 and 80 houses. It is situated on a small hill in pleasant surroundings. The American army camped here in 1778. Their camp was behind the woods to the left of Whippany. The American general Sullivan was then at Chatham, 7 miles to the left of the town. General [Charles] Lee, who commanded an American force, was ordered to march from Morristown to Newtown [in Pennsylvania] on the other side of the Delaware, but while marching with his army the General and his staff took a different fork in the road from the rest of his troops. Learning of his blunder, the English sent out a body of light troops who captured the General and his staff while they were at lunch.[66]

In the meantime, his troops were marching along 9 miles from there.

In 1779 the Americans camped again between Morristown and the river to great advantage, since they held the key to all roads in the countryside that led to this much frequented spot.[67]

30 August (12 miles) From Bullion's Tavern to Somerset Courthouse [Millstone] the roads were superb and traveling was easy. We finally realized that we were leaving New York behind and marching to the Delaware, the river that flows past Philadelphia. We learned that M. de Rochambeau had just received a letter from the Marquis de La Fayette, commanding 1,500 troops in Virginia, saying that Lord Cornwallis had retired to York on the river of that name where he had entrenched himself. The plan of the campaign was at last unveiled, for it was now clear that we were marching against this general, though many happy events had yet to occur before this splendid operation was concluded.

31 August (12 miles) From Somerset [Millstone] to

64. "In order better to conceal our movements from General Clinton . . . I immediately sent M. de Villemanzy, *commissaire des guerres*, to set up a bakery at Chatham, which is only three leagues from Staten Island; his work was covered by a small corps of Americans until the arrival of our vanguard. I confided the secret to him and told him that my real intention was to feed the army from this bakery on its march to Philadelphia, but that the enemy must be persuaded by all sorts of demonstrations that the object was to attack the Hook at Staten Island." Rochambeau, *Journal des opérations*.

65. Washington to Rochambeau, Chatham, 28 August 1781: "I do not find that the force upon Staten Island is large, or thrown over for any other purpose than that of defence, for which reason it is submitted to Your Excellency's judgment to march your Troops in one or two divisions, as shall be most easy and convenient to them; their moving in two divisions, & on succeeding days, will occasion no delay, as the Second will be up by the time the first will have embarked. As I propose to go the lower Road I shall not have the honor of joining your Excellency till we arrive at Princeton, where I will order dinner to be ready at three OClock, that we may lodge at Trenton (12 Miles further). As this will be a journey of 54 Miles from Whippany I would suggest to you the expediency of making part of it this Afternoon. Colo. [William Stephens] Smith, one of my Aides, who is well acquainted with the Roads, will have the honor of attending you to the rendezvous at Princeton." *Writings of*

GW, XXIII, 58–59; the original letter, reproduced as one of our illustrations, is in the Paul Mellon Collection. "28 August — MM. de Rochambeau, Chastellux, Fersen, Vauban, and I left Whippany at 4 o'clock in the afternoon. . . ." Von Closen, pp. 113–114.

66. General Charles Lee was captured at Widow White's Tavern in Basking Ridge on 13 December 1776 by an English scouting party led by Lieutenant Colonel William Harcourt of the Sixteenth Light Dragoons. Many legends concerning the circumstances of Lee's capture soon flourished (see, e.g., Von Closen, p. 114). A strictly contemporary account by one of the captors, Colonel Banastre Tarleton (who was to be the Duc de Lauzun's opponent at Gloucester during the Siege of Yorktown in 1781), is in his letter to his family, dated Princeton, 17 December 1776. Richard M. Ketchum, ed., "New War Letters of Banastre Tarleton," *New-York Historical Society Quarterly*, LI, No. 1 (Jan. 1967), 61–81. Lee was subsequently exchanged, 21 April 1778, for General Richard Prescott, who had been captured by the Americans at Newport; Lee played a controversial role in the Battle of Monmouth, was court-martialed, and lived under a cloud until his death in Philadelphia, 2 October 1782.

67. For the role of Morristown, strategically situated in the New Jersey mountains, see Melvin J. Weig and Vera B. Craig, *Morristown National Historical Park, A Military Capital of the American Revolution*, National Park Service, Historical Handbook No. 7 (Washington, 1950, and later editions).

Princeton the road was very good. This town is well built and pleasantly situated. There is a very handsome college here, which possesses some most interesting physics apparatus, including a clock that marks the passage of time in months and years, as well as the revolutions of the moon, of the earth around the sun, of this orb from tropic to tropic, and the course of the seven planets. This instrument, which is more like a terrestrial and celestial globe than a clock, seems most ingenious.[68] The English have done much damage to the college. This place is notable for the victory the Americans won here in 1777.

BATTLE OF PRINCETON[69]

On 2 January 1777 General Washington, by a very bold and well-planned march, left Trenton (a town 4 miles from Princeton) at dusk with his whole army, leaving his fires lighted facing General Cornwallis, who had come to attack his camp. Taking a road the enemy could not have anticipated, he was joined en route by a body of militia and arrived at daybreak [3 January] at a point 1 mile from Princeton. On his left he noticed some English troops retreating in disorder down the main road. At his approach they turned and fled towards the camp of the Seventh [Seventeenth] Regiment 2 miles from the town, on the left. The American general ordered his troops to double their pace and had the good fortune to fall upon the Seventh [Seventeenth] Regiment before it could join forces with the rest of the English troops. This regiment beat a retreat but, on being hard-pressed by the Americans, surrendered in the vicinity of the Col-

lege, leaving 280 men as prisoners. The rest escaped into the woods and fell back towards Lord Cornwallis at Trenton.

Meanwhile, General Sullivan had been sent to take up a position at Kingston across the Millstone River, where he destroyed the bridge after his troops had crossed. General Washington had sent him there to prevent the enemy from being reinforced by their troops stationed at Brunswick, which he succeeded in doing.

After a desultory fire several fugitives formed up at the bridge. General Washington pursued them, dispersed them, and continued along the road to Rocky Hill from where he marched to Somerset [Millstone] and finally halted at Pompton Plains where he took up a position. Crossing the Millstone River by another bridge 3 miles below, which he also destroyed, General Sullivan joined him there. When his Lordship was informed of this affair, he marched rapidly to the support of his troops but arrived too late. He had the first bridge repaired and retired to Brunswick. (See map of the Jerseys.)

What is remarkable about this operation of General Washington's is that, being encamped in a very poor position facing the English at Princeton [Trenton], he must have expected Lord Cornwallis to attack him at daybreak. His poor position and the inferiority of his force facing the English prompted him to slip away during the night and fight the English on the road to Princeton. Had his army not been exhausted by several forced marches, he was planning to continue on to Brunswick to capture the rest of the British before Lord Cornwallis arrived.

68. The ingenious instrument was an orrery, completed in 1771 by David Rittenhouse for the College of New Jersey. See H. C. Rice, Jr., *The Rittenhouse Orrery, Princeton's Eighteenth-Century Planetarium, 1767-1954, A Commentary on an Exhibition Held in the Princeton University Library* (Princeton, 1954); and "A Check-list of Items shown in the Exhibition. . . ," *Princeton University Library Chronicle*, xv, No. 4 (Summer 1954), 194–206. What is left of the orrery is now (1970) on display in William Charles Peyton Hall, Princeton's new astrophysics building.

69. Clermont-Crèvecœur's recapitulation of the Battle of Princeton—like those of Trenton, Germantown, and Brandywine, included below—is a good example of the historical accounts that many of the officers inserted as a

matter of course in their journals (often copying or paraphrasing one another). Although lacking the authority of eyewitness accounts by participants, they are nevertheless interesting evidence of how the recent military operations of their allies were understood by the French in 1781. Such theoretical exercises in military history and topography formed part of the education of young officers during their campaigns. Berthier's journal (pp. 250–251) gives a glimpse of them at work on such "studies." General Chastellux, among others, set an example with the elaborate descriptions of American battles and battlefields included in his *Travels*. Cf. Samuel Stelle Smith, *The Battle of Princeton* (Monmouth Beach, N.J., 1967), a convenient recapitulation, with maps.

1 September (12 miles) From Princeton to Trenton the roads were excellent. This town is larger than Princeton but less well built and not as pretty. On its outskirts there is a large creek that is a branch of the Delaware and that is spanned by a bridge. The Delaware, where there is both ford and ferry, is half a mile beyond. This town is also notable because of two battles won here by the Americans. The first was fought on 24 [26] December 1776.

BATTLES OF TRENTON[70]

The enemy had established their winter quarters along the Delaware at Trenton, Bordentown, and farther north at Princeton, Brunswick, etc. At the same time the American army was occupying barracks at Newtown and Wrightstown across the Delaware above Trenton. On the night of 24 [25] December 1776 General Washington took his army across the river on boats at McKonkey's Ferry, 9 miles above Trenton. Forming it into two columns, he led the right-hand column and put General Sullivan in command of the left, which was followed by the reserves. At daybreak the troops reached the various pickets the Hessians had posted along the roads leading into town. At the first alarm the latter rushed into the church, almost in the center of the town, where they defended themselves for some time against the right-hand column as it debouched along the road bordering the river. The enemy suffered heavy losses until Colonel Rall, their commander, decided to form them up on a small eminence nearby; thereupon General Washington deployed his column before the town on their left flank, while General Sullivan formed in front and the reserves filed through the small ravines to turn their right. Seeing himself surrounded, Colonel Rall surrendered with 1,000 men, while about 400 succeeded in crossing the bridge over the creek below Trenton and reaching the cantonments at Bordentown.

The second battle took place six days later. The General again crossed the river and took up a position behind the creek flowing south of Trenton along which are 3 miles of impracticable marshes reaching to the edge of the woods. Cornwallis came up immediately with his whole force to attack him, leaving only one reserve corps of two regiments at Princeton to maintain communications with Brunswick, etc., and to halt, or at least retard, the march of the Americans. General Washington sent work parties into the woods to destroy the bridge over the aforementioned creek, obliging the English to seek other crossings, which the Americans defended foot by foot. In addition, two American battalions proceeded with a cannon to a height across the creek in front of Trenton. Pushing back the work parties after a spirited resistance, his Lordship sent the troops of his right flank to turn the two battalions, who discharged a lively fire upon them, recrossed the bridge, and joined their own army. Then the English general deployed his troops on a small eminence facing the creek where he had several batteries set up to knock out the American guns emplaced above the ravines across the creek. Near a mill at the left of the bridge General Washington had a redoubt thrown up to protect his left flank where the creek was fordable. His Lordship sent a column forward to turn his flank on this side, but it was obliged to retire before a brisk cannonade that lasted until night. The troops remained facing one another. From this position, as soon as it was dark, General Washington marched that same evening to Princeton for the operation I have already described in my journal under 31 August. I should mention here that the American army numbered 4,000 men and the English 10,000.

────────

2 September (18 miles) From Trenton to Red Lion Tavern. The Pennsylvania country is very flat. We crossed the Delaware by ford and ferry.[71] It is not deep here. In summer the average depth is only 2 to 3 feet; however, in winter it is very deep. We followed the river to Bristol where we saw, on the low bank opposite, the pretty little town of Burlington, which has a charming situation. At Bristol the army and the artillery separated, the former crossing the Neshaminy River by ferry, and the latter by ford 6 miles upstream. We arrived very late in camp, having covered 24 miles with our wagons.

---

70. Cf. Samuel Stelle Smith, *The Battle of Trenton* (Monmouth Beach, N.J., 1965).

71. See map of the ford, Vol. II, No. 71.

3 September (11 miles) From Red Lion Tavern to Philadelphia the roads were still good. We passed through some pretty villages that were thickly settled. This country shows signs of being near a large city because of the density of its population and the manner in which it is cultivated. When we came within sight of the city, the army halted and the troops spruced up. With drums beating and flags unfurled, we entered it at a walk in the following order: The cavalry of the Legion led the march, followed by its infantry. Next came the artillery of the Bourbonnais Regiment followed by the regiment, then the artillery of the Royal Deux-Ponts followed by the regiment. The artillery of the park, escorted by pickets of cavalry and infantry, brought up the rear. (The Second Division entered the following day in the same order.) The streets and the line of march were crowded with people who were absolutely amazed to see such a fine army. The prejudices the English had aroused in them against our country were soon dispelled, for they saw superb men. They could not conceive how, after a long and tiring march over such frightful roads, we could be in such good condition, or how we could possibly have brought so much artillery in our train; for we had with us sixteen 4-pounders, six 6-inch howitzers, eight 12-pounders, and 200 rounds of ammunition per piece in the caissons.

It took us an hour and a half to cross this large and beautiful city. We passed the State House [Independence Hall] where the members of Congress were assembled on the front steps.[72] We saluted them, then passed the house of the Chevalier de La Luzerne, the ambassador of France to Congress, where the quality of the town were assembled.[73] We then went to camp on the Schuylkill River a mile from town.[74] This river flows into the Delaware below Philadelphia within sight of the city. If the Philadelphians continue to build, the city walls will be bathed by both rivers; I am told this is their plan. This will certainly be the largest city in the world. It is built on a plain 10 to 12 miles in diameter on the right bank of the Delaware. Fairly big ships can come up to the city, which is extremely large and well built.

The houses are of brick, and the streets are wide and perfectly straight, with sidewalks for pedestrians on both sides. There is a large number of richly stocked shops. The city has a population of 40,000. In Market Street there are two immense brick markets, one of which is the meat market. I can find no fault with them except that they stand in the middle of a superb street, which they completely spoil. The port along the Delaware is about 2 miles long and consists simply of a quay, which is remarkable only for its length.

The State House where the Congress meets is quite a large building without ornament. There is nothing

72. "On Monday and Tuesday last the French army, under the command of his Excellency Count de Rochambeau, passed in review before his Excellency the President and the Honorable the Congress of the United States, at the State House in this city . . . The President was covered, his Excellency General Washington, Commander-in-Chief, the Count de Rochambeau, etc., stood on his left hand, uncovered. The President took off his hat and bowed in return to every salute of the officers and standards. The troops made a most martial and grand appearance. The orders of his most Christian Majesty are to pay the same honours to the President of Congress as to the Field Marshal of France and a Prince of the Blood, and to Congress the same as to himself. The spectators were impressed with the most lively gratitude to the brave, noble, and virtuous prince, who so happily governs the French nation; whose shining reign and magnanimous acts are rather to be conceived than recorded. Angels envy him his acquired glory." *The Pennsylvania Packet*, 8 September 1781. Thomas McKean, president of the Continental Congress, wrote to General Rochambeau, Philadelphia, 4 September 1781: "I have the honor to express to your Excellency the satisfaction of Congress in the compliment which has been paid to them by the Troops of his most Christian Majesty under your command. The brilliant appearance and exact discipline of the several Corps do the highest honor to their Officers, and afford a happy presage of the most distinguished services in a cause which they have so zealously espoused." The original letter is in the Paul Mellon Collection. See illustration.

73. The French minister occupied a house rented from John Dickinson (also known as "Carpenter's Mansion" or the "Old Graeme Place") at the northeast corner of Chestnut and Seventh Streets, diagonally opposite the Pennsylvania State House (Independence Hall). The house has long since disappeared.

74. See maps, Vol. II, Nos. 57 and 73. The site is now well within the town, corresponding roughly to the vicinity of present 23rd and Market Streets, opposite the 30th Street Station, and extending southward to Locust or Spruce.

magnificent about the chamber where the members sit, which has no decoration. A long table covered with a green cloth and some chairs are the only furniture. There are several very pretty Protestant churches, as well as two beautiful Catholic churches, a large college that bears the title of university, and a well-placed hospital that is vast and comfortable; but all these buildings are of simple architecture and are not especially handsome.

The arts and sciences are little in vogue in this country; however, there are a few individuals engaged in such pursuits. Among these are M. Du Simitière,[75] born in Geneva, and Dr. Chovet. The former has a museum of natural history that is still unfinished. Among other interesting exhibits he showed us, we noticed a pair of heavy boots in the corner. We asked him why he had introduced objects that seemed so definitely out of place here. He burst out laughing and replied that the Americans had admired them so much that he had convinced them that they were the boots of King Charles XII [of Sweden]. We were immensely amused by this joke, as well as many others he told about this country, which he rather ridiculed. We conversed with him for an hour. He appears to be very learned, yet he works only for himself. He is between sixty and seventy and speaks very good French. He showed us many of his

drawings and engravings. It was he who sent to Paris the portraits of the members of Congress.[76]

We went from there to see Dr. Chovet, who is no less interesting, but of an entirely different type. He is of English origin, has traveled extensively, and is endowed with an infinite variety of knowledge. Anatomy is the subject in which he is most distinguished. He has in his collection two life-size wax figures of a man and a woman. The figure of the man is open on one side, revealing the insides of half his body that are made in such a way that they can be removed and then returned to their original positions. The woman's figure has the belly cut away to reveal a child in its natural position in the eighth month of pregnancy. These figures are so well made and so lifelike that one cannot behold them for the first time without shuddering. From them he has given lessons in anatomy.[77] He has assembled in his house everything relating to this study to an amazing degree of perfection. He is quite old and speaks French in an intelligible manner. The only thing that surprised me was to find so few pupils at his house; there were not more than fifteen.

Most of the inhabitants of Philadelphia are Quakers. We know that the founder of this great city was a Quaker named Penn (see the Abbé Raynal's chapter on Pennsylvania).[78] Little by little this superb city has

75. Du Simitière's museum is also described in other French journals: Chastellux (4), I, 144–145; Cromot Dubourg (1), p. 380; Von Closen, p. 118.

76. Du Simitière's portraits, drawn from life *ca.* 1779, were sent to Paris through Conrad-Alexander Gérard (La Luzerne's predecessor as French minister in Philadelphia), were engraved by Benoît-Louis Prévost and published there in 1781. An announcement in the *Mercure de France*, 24 February 1781, describes them as "Portraits des Généraux, Ministres et Magistrats qui se sont rendus célèbres dans la Révolution des Treize Etats-Unis de l'Amérique Septentrionale." After the signing of the preliminary peace treaty the set was several times pirated in London, where it appeared, for example, under the title *Thirteen Portraits of American Legislators, Patriots, Soldiers* (engraved by B. Reading, published by Richardson, 1783). See Edna Donnell, "Portraits of Eminent Americans after Drawings by Du Simitière," *Antiques*, XXIV (1933), 17–21, illus.

77. Dr. Abraham Chovet's collection of anatomical models in wax (also described in the journals cited in n. 75) was acquired after his death by the Pennsylvania Hospital, then by the Wistar Museum, University of Pennsylvania,

where it remained until the 1880's, when it was destroyed by fire. However, at least one item presumed to be from Chovet's collection has survived: see "Wax Model of a Heart, by Abraham Chovet," in Philadelphia Museum of Art, *The Art of Philadelphia Medicine*, exhibition catalogue (Philadelphia, 1965), p. 90, Fig. 82. Duponceau's *Autobiography* includes some delightful recollections of Dr. Chovet. Duponceau (1), LXIII, 323–329.

78. Abbé Guillaume-Thomas Raynal, *Histoire philosophique et politique des Etablissemens et du Commerce des Européens dans les Deux Indes* (Amsterdam, 1770 and many later editions), Vol. VI, Book 18, "Colonies angloises fondées dans la Pensilvanie. . . ." Clermont-Crèvecœur's reference to this widely read work is a further bit of evidence confirming its influential role in forming the European "image" of America. "All that I knew in fact, on my arrival in this country respecting the United States, and other parts of this continent, is what is contained in the Abbé Raynal's history of the European Colonies, which I read with Baron Steuben on board of the ship which brought us from Marseilles [in 1777]." Duponceau (1), LXIII, 449.

been settled by people from every country in Europe and has become quite a commercial center. Since the war this seems to be the only city in America whose trade has not declined; in fact, the war seems to have made it even more prosperous.

Philadelphia probably contains every religious sect in the world. Freedom of conscience is tolerated here. The Catholic churches are served by ex-Jesuits. The Philadelphians seem to take very little interest in the war. They are almost all merchants. I saw several who assured me that peace would only hurt their trade; thus, for business reasons, they did not want it.

I was not there long enough to be able to dwell more extensively on the habits and customs of the residents, who they tell me are quite different from the northerners. The young people here receive as fine an education as they could in Europe. Their schools offer every kind of instruction. There is neither rank nor distinction among the citizens. The rich alone take precedence over the common people. As for the civil and military posts, they are obtained on merit alone; a locksmith, a cobbler, or a merchant may become a member of Congress. They all believe themselves equal. The sensible people respect merit and admit their inferiority to those who are so gifted. But among men are there many who admit they are inferior to others?

There is a scramble for the lucrative posts. They are generally bestowed upon the rich, who always obtain the nation's vote by making their alleged talents shine in the light of their gold, which they know how to pour forth in order to satisfy their vanity. However, here as everywhere else one often sees merit prevail over envy; I should say that this happens more frequently in a republic than elsewhere. We saw ordinary individuals, simple artisans, attain high civil and military rank. A shoemaker or a butcher will enter the army as a captain, colonel, or even a general, if he has the knowledge required for his rank. Having served his country, he will then return to his class and begin making shoes again or slaughtering animals for the public.

The military profession is not as highly regarded here as it should be. Colonels and higher-ranking officers are hardly slighted, of course; and even majors and captains receive some consideration. However, lieutenants are virtually scorned. Only the higher ranks are held in esteem, to the extent that the American generals never invite a lieutenant from the French army to dinner. Our generals were surprised at this discrimination and somewhat offended. General Washington excused himself by saying that, since it was not the custom to invite his own lieutenants, he could not for political reasons invite those of the French army, though he knew that ours were selected differently than his. Since the two armies were now joined, the same rules and customs had to apply to both. For a long time we were unhappy about this situation, but after a while no longer thought about it.[79]

Although Americans consider themselves equal, they show a certain deference towards the rich, who associate only with one another. In general all societies are formed exclusively on equality of fortune. Vanity and pride are not unknown. In America, especially in the cities, I have known very poor families whose daughters could not be better dressed. They would rather dress well and look rich than eat better food. The wardrobe of these girls is not very large; it usually consists of two garments of each kind. One sees no girls here in town or country whose hair is not dressed in the French fashion. Those who cannot afford jewelry make up for it by substituting ordinary ribbons and feathers, and in summer their gardens furnish them with nature's richest ornaments—flowers.

Americans are so much attached to their own habits and customs that nothing can make them change. They have an unrivaled casualness. Whoever tries to instill in the Americans a taste for the social life we enjoy in France is simply wasting his time and trouble. If one wishes to be welcome in society, one must conform to its customs, not laugh at them, take it all seriously and do what the others do. Sometimes they do extraordinary things here that a polite and well-bred Frenchman could never bring himself to do. They give no parties. They sometimes pay visits, but they are short and ceremonious. The women are accustomed

79. The writer speaks as a lieutenant. Every commissioned officer in the French army at this date, with few exceptions, had to produce a patent of nobility—hence the un- usually free social intercourse between officers of high and low ranks.

to visit one another at greater length. A neighbor who lives next door will go to visit her friend and sleep with her for five or six days and be treated in her house as a stranger who has come from afar. The young girls are generally the ones who make such visits. It will doubtless come as a surprise to learn of such a custom. What can one make of it? Certainly nothing favorable to these belles. Do they not bundle with one another? This is what many people think. One dare not state it as a fact, but their attitude towards men, their conduct when in their company, the disappearance of the lilies and roses of their youth at the age of twenty to twenty-eight, and their distaste for bundling with men are all good reasons for believing that one is not mistaken.

Six miles from Philadelphia is a small town called Germantown, consisting of a single street about three-fourths of a league long. It is notable for the battle fought there on 4 October 1777; this did not turn out as well for the Americans as those I mentioned above, however. The road leading to this village is very wide and quite beautiful.

BATTLE OF GERMANTOWN[80]

The English were encamped there, occupying both sides of the town so as virtually to cut it down the middle. General Washington was then at Skippack Creek. Having learned that the enemy had sent detachments to Philadelphia, to Chester, and to Wilmington to protect their incoming transports, he left his camp on the evening of 3 October and marched all night to attack the English in Germantown. He at first proceeded in a single column but, 5 miles short of the town, formed two columns, taking command of the right-hand column, seconded by General [John] Sullivan, and giving command of the other one to General [Nathanael] Greene, who was accompanied by General [Adam] Stephen.

The right-hand column marched along the main road leading into the town. Washington detached Brigadier General [John] Armstrong with the militia to turn the enemy's left. At three in the morning the advance guard fell upon the English pickets posted by the Fortieth Regiment and the Light Infantry at various points along the road into town. When these two units were alerted, they immediately shouldered arms, put up some resistance, fell back, and were pursued into the town. Lieutenant Colonel [Thomas] Musgrave, who commanded the Fortieth Regiment, estimating the importance of maintaining communication between the flanks of the army, rushed with six companies into a large brick house in the middle of the camp lines.[81] Meanwhile, General Sullivan deployed part of his column to attack the left flank. This maneuver, made jointly with that of the militia, completely upset the left flank, which fell back on the right, leaving 150 prisoners behind.

The six companies in the brick house kept up a very lively fire. They held the key to the position, completely dominating the English right. It was for this reason that General Washington decided to attack it. To this end he sent forward two 6-pounders, whose balls barely pierced the walls and did no damage. Monsieur de Mauduit,[82] a French officer serving with the Americans, volunteered to go set the house on fire, but he did not succeed, so the project had to be abandoned.

The fighting on the American left flank was taking a less favorable turn than on the right. The field was shrouded in a thick mist. General Stephen, who by many reports was not quite sober, contributed to the confusion. His column deployed but could never form a battle line. When it arrived in great disorder, the English it hoped to surprise were in formation. General Washington came up, rallied his troops, then retired by the same road he had taken that morning. He

80. Freeman (*Washington*, IV, 501–519) gives a good account of the Battle of Germantown and its significance.
81. "Cliveden," the Chew family mansion, still standing in Germantown.
82. Chevalier Thomas-Antoine de Mauduit du Plessis served with the Americans from 1777 to 1779, distinguishing himself at Brandywine, Germantown, Red Bank, and Monmouth; he came back to America in 1780 with Rochambeau's army, as *premier aide-major de l'équipage*

d'artillerie (senior adjutant of the artillery park). Mauduit appears again in Clermont-Crèvecœur's journal (p. 59) at Yorktown and in Berthier's journal (pp. 261–263) as the compassionate friend who informed Louis-Alexandre Berthier of the circumstances of his brother Charles's death in February 1783. See also Vol. II, Itinerary 5, p. 77, and "Checklist of Journals." Mauduit's exploit at Germantown is described at length by Chastellux (4), I, 138–140.

took up a position 6 miles nearer the enemy than the one he had occupied the night before. The English owed their victory that day to Colonel Musgrave and the brick house.

═════════

Below Philadelphia are three forts: Mud Island [Fort Mifflin], Red Bank [Fort Mercer], and Billingsport.[83] These three forts were built to defend the chevaux-de-frise the Americans had installed in the river to prevent ships from coming up to the city. The English lost several men during an attack on Red Bank in 1777 and were obliged to retreat. Colonel von Donop, their commander, was killed. Of the three forts only Billingsport remains in good condition. Red Bank has been destroyed, and Mud Island is unfinished. The banks of the Delaware are rather marshy, but the land is well cultivated. The scenery is pleasant.

5 September (15 miles) After staying two days in Philadelphia, we left on the 5th for Chester. We crossed the Schuylkill on a fine pontoon bridge that rises and falls with the tides. It was on this bridge that M. du Coudray, a French artillery officer in the service of the United States, met his death. He was on horseback when the horse took sudden fright and precipitated them both into the river. Du Coudray was a very

ambitious man and wanted to be promoted major general in command of the artillery. He had already got into difficulty by wanting the sole command. General Knox, whom he wished to replace, was known throughout the American army for his talents, and since the Americans were anxious to keep Knox at the head of their artillery, they spoiled the ambitious plans of M. du Coudray. When he died, the French officers he had brought over with him experienced many difficulties. Without employment many returned to France, while others remained in this country to seek some other means of livelihood.[84]

Chester is a small town, well built and pleasantly situated on the banks of the Delaware. The roads are very good. We learned that M. de Grasse had anchored in the Chesapeake Bay with 28 ships of the line, which had put 3,000 troops ashore under the command of the Marquis de Saint-Simon. These had already joined forces with the Marquis de La Fayette, who was occupying a position designed to prevent Lord Cornwallis from retreating by land, while the French squadron blockaded him by sea. There was great joy throughout the camp. Even the generals expressed it in a satisfying way, and the siege of York was openly declared to be the object of the campaign.[85]

83. The river forts are described in more detail by Von Closen (pp. 121–122) and by Cromot Dubourg ([1], pp. 383–384), who visited them at this time with General Rochambeau, and by Chastellux ([4], I, 154–160), who had inspected them in December 1780. See Vol. II, Itinerary 5, pp. 76–77, and map, No. 57.

84. Philippe Tronson du Coudray, whose accidental death on 16 September 1777 seems to have been regretted neither by the French nor the Americans, had achieved some distinction in French military circles for his technical writings on gunpowder, metallurgy, and artillery—for example, *L'Artillerie nouvelle, ou examen des changements faits dans l'artillerie française depuis 1765* (Amsterdam and Paris, 1772), and *L'Ordre profond et l'ordre mince considérés par rapport aux effets de l'artillerie* (Paris, 1776). Du Coudray was one of those early French volunteers who had been recruited in Paris by Silas Deane with promises of commissions from the Continental Congress but whose inadaptability tried the patience of both Congress and General Washington. Fortunately men like Lafayette, Fleury, Mauduit, La Rouërie, and Duportail redeemed the reputation of French arms in American eyes—as did, later, General Rochambeau and his army.

85. Rochambeau had come down the Delaware by boat

from Philadelphia to Chester in order to see the river forts. His aide-de-camp, Von Closen, describes their arrival at Chester on 5 September: "We discerned in the distance General Washington, standing on the shore and waving his hat and a white handkerchief joyfully. There was good reason for this; for he informed us as we disembarked that M. de Grasse had arrived in the Chesapeake Bay with 28 ships of the line and 3000 troops, whom he had already landed so that they might join M. de Lafayette, in order to prevent Cornwallis from escaping by land, while he would block his egress by sea. One must experience such circumstances to appreciate the effect that such gratifying news can have, particularly upon young people who are burning with the desire to try their strength against the enemy and avid for glory, as we all were. MM. de Rochambeau and Washington embraced *warmly* on the shore. . . . The soldiers from then on spoke of Cornwallis as if they had already captured him. . . ." Von Closen, p. 123. The good news had been relayed from Baltimore by General Mordecai Gist; a French translation of his letter of 4 September to Washington is preserved among Rochambeau's papers in the Paul Mellon Collection. The original of a similar letter sent by Gist to Governor Thomas Sim Lee (at Annapolis) is in the

6 September (11 miles) From Chester to Wilmington by a beautiful route. The town is charming and in a good location for commerce on the Delaware. We crossed the creek and village of Brandywine, which is notable for the battle of that name.

BATTLE OF BRANDYWINE: AMERICAN DEFEAT[86]

Advised that a large part of the English army had embarked at New York and, soon after, that it was coming up the Chesapeake Bay, General Washington suspected that it would make a stand at Head of Elk at the upper end of the Chesapeake Bay. He left his position at Middlebrook in the Jerseys, crossed the Delaware at Bordentown, and proceeded by forced marches towards the Chesapeake. He took up a position at Clay Creek, between Head of Elk and Chester, but when the enemy marched in force against him, he fell back about 10 miles and took up another position behind the village of Brandywine on the high ground in front of the ford at Chadds Ford on 11 September 1777. There General Howe attacked him at the head of the English troops. The enemy army advanced in two columns. Its right, commanded by General Knyphausen, marched to Chadds Ford and attacked with vigor as if it intended to force the ford. Meanwhile, Lord Cornwallis at the head of the left column filed behind the mountain, crossed both branches of the creek without obstacle four miles farther up, and took the road along the river in order to surprise and fall upon the left flank of the Americans. General Washington learned of the English general's march only at noon. He immediately detached General Sullivan to oppose him, with orders to take up a position from which he could halt him. Sullivan chose in advance a very good one on a height dominating the road from which Lord Cornwallis would debouch, with his right flank resting on a road to ensure his retreat and part of his artillery placed in the center to command the road by which Cornwallis was approaching. His left, however, bordered a crest at whose foot was a very marshy terrain, which prevented him from resting it on the artillery he had counted on placing there.

On arrival at this point Sullivan was attacked. The English column pierced his left flank and seized there the artillery that had not yet been emplaced. Cornwallis advanced on his center with his troops formed in line of battle, throwing into great disorder the Americans, who fell back into the woods. Only the right wing held fast until night, under cover of which it retired beyond the woods to rejoin the rest of Sullivan's troops, who took up a new position there. Informed of his retreat, General Washington made his own in good order and marched to Chester and on to Philadelphia. It seems that the unhappy end of this battle resulted from Sullivan's insufficient knowledge of the country; losing his way on the march, he arrived at the same time as the enemy and had no time to reconnoiter the terrain. For it seems to me that, had he been able to set up his artillery on his left flank, he would certainly have stopped the enemy and taken every advantage of his position, since the marsh was not, as he thought, everywhere impracticable.

―――――

7 September (20 miles) From Wilmington to Elkton. The roads were very good at this season, but one could tell that in winter they could be very bad. Two miles from Elkton we crossed the Christina River,[87] the troops in boats and the artillery at a ford 3 miles upstream. Elkton is a small hamlet and not at all pretty. At Elkton we learned that M. de Barras had left Newport with his entire squadron, after embarking all the French troops remaining there, as well as the heavy artillery and munitions. Only the magazines and hospitals were left in Providence with 100 men to guard them.

Princeton University Library, Andre deCoppet Collection: "the French Fleet consisting of 28 sail of the line arrived in our Bay the 26 ult. with 3000 Land forces which are landed to form a junction with the Marquis De La Fayette. Part of the Fleet have Blocked up the British Vessels in York River. . . ."

86. There is an excellent discussion of the Battle of Brandywine in Freeman, *Washington*, IV, 469–78, 485–92.

87. There seems to be some confusion in Clermont-Crève-cœur's recollections here. According to the road map (Vol. II, No. 60) and Itinerary 5, the only point at which the route crossed the Christina River was at Cooch's Bridge, which is some 6 or 7 miles from Elkton and on the eastern side of Iron Mountain, the height separating the Delaware and Chesapeake Bay watersheds.

On 8 September we made a halt and the Second Brigade joined us. Generals Washington and Rochambeau left to join the troops that the Comte de Grasse had landed on the James River in Virginia, now under the command of M. de La Fayette.[88] They wanted to embark at Head of Elk the whole First Division and, in fact, as many troops as possible to join the Marquis de La Fayette by sea, but there were not enough boats. Only the grenadiers and chasseurs with eight 12-pounders, six mortars, and two 4-pounders were embarked, and it was decided that the rest of the army would push on to Baltimore where enough boats could be found to transport them.[89]

I did not embark at Head of Elk. Very much annoyed, I followed the army; but later I was consoled to have avoided all the misfortunes that befell the troops who had embarked there. They had to sail 300 miles in small boats virtually stripped of provisions.[90] The weather was so terrible and the winds so adverse that the journey took them 18 days. We arrived almost the same time they did, without having suffered any inconvenience. The hardships the other detachment had endured were incredible. Several vessels, battered by winds and storms and on the point of shipwreck, had lowered their boats and sent their men to take refuge in the warships anchored at the entrance to the York River to blockade Cornwallis. They were expecting to rest there and spend a pleasant night after the bad experiences and the dangers of the preceding days when Cornwallis sent fire-ships to attack them. These rained firebrands down on the crews all night and spread terror among them. By the greatest good fortune they escaped injury, though they were attacked by no less than 7 fire-ships.[91]

88. "Judging it highly expedient to be with the Army in Virginia as soon as possible . . . I determined to set out for the Camp of the Marqs. de la Fayette without loss of time and accordingly with the Count de Rochambeau who requested to attend me, and the Chevr. de Chastellux set out [from Elkton] on the *8th*. and reached Baltimore where I recd. and answered an address of the Citizen's. *9th*. I reached my own Seat at Mount Vernon [his first visit there since May 1775] . . . where I staid till the 12th. and in three days afterwards that is on the 15th. reached Williamsburg." Washington, *Diaries*, II, 259–260. Washington's statement notwithstanding, other sources indicate that the generals reached Williamsburg on the afternoon of 14 September; see, e.g., Rochambeau's letter to de Grasse, dated from Williamsburg on the morning of 15 September, mentioning that "We arrived here yesterday evening, General Washington and I . . ." (Doniol, v, 540). Others who accompanied the generals on their overland ride were Rochambeau's aides, Fersen and Damas, as mentioned by Cromot Dubourg ([1], p. 385) and Von Closen (p. 125). The latter writes: "Our general expressed to his other aides-de-camp his great regret at not being able to take us all, but he gave us the choice between embarking or following him by land. Du Bourg and I decided on this last course. . . . As for the army, it was decided that it would continue its route overland as far as Baltimore or Annapolis, where it would find, without fail, the ships necessary to carry it to the meeting-place on the James River."

The troops landed by de Grasse were under the command of the Marquis de Saint-Simon. Pending the arrival of Washington and Rochambeau, Lafayette, then the ranking American general in Virginia, was temporarily in command of Saint-Simon's regiments. In a letter to his wife, 22 October 1781, Lafayette remarked that the time he had commanded Saint-Simon was among his "most beautiful moments." Lafayette (1), I, 471–472.

89. According to Rochambeau's "Instruction pour M. de Custine," Head of Elk, 8 September 1781 (printed in Doniol, v, 538), the detachment which embarked at Elkton under command of the Comte de Custine (colonel, Saintonge Regiment) included a battalion of grenadiers from the Bourbonnais Regiment under the Vicomte de Rochambeau, a battalion of grenadiers from the Soissonnais under the Vicomte de Noailles, and the infantry of the Lauzun Legion under the Duc de Lauzun. On the same day Rochambeau issued instructions to Baron de Vioménil and his brother, who were to command the main part of the army on its way south (printed in Doniol, v, 537). Vioménil's instructions to the Vicomte d'Arrot, commanding Lauzun's cavalry, dated Head of Elk, 9 September, are among other papers of d'Arrot in the Manuscript Collections of Colonial Williamsburg.

90. Blanchard, chief commissary, who accompanied the Comte de Custine on this trip down the Chesapeake Bay—"a little Mediterranean," as he describes it—notes in his journal that their ship, carrying 50 grenadiers and several officers, was too small to permit any cooking; the men had only cheese and biscuit, the officers some cold meat. Blanchard (1), p. 94. Lieutenant Gaspard de Gallatin, of the Deux-Pont grenadiers, also made the voyage down the Bay on a small schooner carrying 36 of his men; he left Plumb Point, near Elkton, on 12 September, and eventually disembarked at College Landing near Williamsburg on 23 September. Gallatin (1), pp. 683–686.

91. Saint-Exupéry, a second lieutenant of the garrison of

9 September (21 miles) From Elkton to Octoraro Creek. We found the roads frightful and arrived in camp extremely late. The country is abominable, cut up by deep ravines and many small rivers, which the soldiers were obliged to ford after removing their shoes and stockings.[92]

10 September (24 miles) From Octoraro to Bushton [Bush]. The roads were virtually impassable. We crossed the Susquehanna River, the troops in boats [at Lower Ferry] and the artillery and wagons 10 miles upstream by a ford 2¼ miles wide.[93] This was the only one practicable, but barely so, since the bottom was so rocky that the horses risked breaking their legs. All

the way across we were in water up to our waists, and the horses up to their knees. The wagons crossed with the greatest difficulty. We lost several horses. The crossing took an hour and a quarter. That day the artillery marched 29 miles; still, when we reached camp, we had no time to rest as we had to leave at once.

The landscape is very picturesque here. Approaching this wide river, we came down a very steep mountain that descended abruptly to its bank, leaving no room to walk at the bottom. We saw only one house on the whole route.

11 September (12 miles) From Bushton [Bush] to

the *Triton*, one of de Grasse's ships stationed at the entrance to the York River, records in his journal ([1], pp. 371–373) the progressive arrival of the troops from up the Bay and vividly describes the fire-ship attack during the night of 22–23 September: "Six ships in flames and proceeding abreast offered a horrible spectacle, when a seventh ship, which had until then remained hidden behind the others, bore down upon the *Triton* and burst into flames at a distance of a pistol-shot. This sudden explosion made the sailors on the *Triton* lose their heads. Two hundred of them either jumped overboard or into the various boats alongside. . . . Fortunately for the rest of the crew our vessel at that moment swung about and made sail; the fire-ships, whose sails were already consumed, could not follow her. . . . The *Triton*, during this night, lost 17 men, her bowsprit, and her stem."

92. No detailed road maps or itineraries for the army's march beyond Elkton have been found; Berthier's series stops at this point. However, the route is shown on the comprehensive map of the camps and marches of Rochambeau's army, Vol. II, No. 162. The infantry proceeded from Elkton to Lower Ferry near the mouth of the Susquehanna (the present Perryville-Havre de Grace crossing); the map of its camp there is reproduced in Vol. II, No. 77. The artillery and wagons (whose route Clermont-Crèvecœur is describing), with the cavalry of Lauzun's Legion under Colonel Vicomte d'Arrot, made a detour via Bald Friar Ford, some 7 miles north of Lower Ferry. The general map of the camps and marches shows camps or bivouacs for the Legion at "Cuming-Taverne," southeast of Octoraro Creek, and at "Dear Church" on the other side of the Susquehanna. Cummings Tavern, an eighteenth-century stone house, is still standing at the locality known as Battle Swamp, some 3 or 4 miles northeast of Port Deposit near the corner of Craigstown Road and the Jacob Tome Memorial Highway (State Route 276). "Dear Church," on the western side of the Susquehanna,

is the Deer Creek Friends Meeting, on the northern outskirts of Darlington near the junction of State Routes 161 and 623, south of U.S. Route 1. The detachments making this detour via Bald Friar Ford rejoined at Bush the route taken by the rest of the army. Further instructions from Vioménil to Colonel d'Arrot, commanding Lauzun's cavalry, dated "Au camp de Bush," 10 September 1781, are in the Manuscript Collections of Colonial Williamsburg.
93. Bald Friar Ford crossed the Susquehanna from the mouth of Conowingo Creek on the eastern bank to Peddler Run (Glen Cove) on the west. The ford, now flooded, is about 1½ to 2 miles north of present Conowingo Dam (over which U.S. Route 1 passes). See the description, with aerial photograph (1921), in J. Alexis Shriver, *Lafayette in Harford County, 1781* (Bel Air, Md., 1931), pp. 25–27. Clermont-Crèvecœur understandably extends the actual width of the ford by a mile or so. Rochambeau had instructed Baron de Vioménil (8 September) to cross the Susquehanna "by ferry as well as by ford, according to the reconnaissances already made, which are to be corrected and confirmed by the reconnaissance that M. Dumas has had made . . ." (Doniol, v, 537). Dumas ([1], pp. 77–78), who was in charge of the crossing, states that the boats available at Lower Ferry were sufficient only to transport the infantry, very slowly; accompanied by local guides, he reconnoitered the Bald Friar Ford upstream, below the falls, finding the depth of the water from 3 to 4 feet, the bed covered with loose stones (*galets mobiles*) but with no underwashing (*sans affouillement*). He thereupon directed "the artillery, the horses, and all our *impedimenta*" over this route. Rochambeau's aides-de-camp, Cromot Dubourg and Von Closen, also took the route via Bald Friar Ford, which the latter describes as "diabolic"; they lodged on the night of 9 September at Porter's Mill (Porter Bridge?) on Octoraro Creek, some 4 miles this side of the ford. See Cromot Dubourg (1), p. 441, and Von Closen, p. 125.

... Tavern.[94] The roads were the same as on the previous day. We had to cross several creeks and rivers in excessive heat and dust, which caused us extreme discomfort.

12 September (10 miles) From ... Tavern to Baltimore. The roads were better. On the way we crossed three small shallow rivers, one of which had a very fine wooden bridge. We could not see the city until we were practically there. It looks quite pleasant, being large and well built and perfectly situated for commerce at one of the upper reaches of the Chesapeake Bay.[95] Frigates can come up to the wharves. The streets are perfectly straight and have sidewalks, as in Philadelphia, but are not yet paved. It is one of the prettiest cities in America and is still only at the beginning of its growth. Many Dutch and Germans live here. There is a French quarter where some Canadians live, but they have not prospered and look quite poor. They associate very little with the English. These are good folk who deeply regret not being under French rule any longer and who are so much attached to our nation that they would give their lives to come back. The country we passed through contains many of these people who come from Acadia or Canada. After conquering these countries, the English sent most of the inhabitants away and parceled them out among various English colonies. Wherever we went, these good people came to see us, bringing their wives and children. Their faces lighted up with joy at seeing Frenchmen again. When we stopped at their houses, they wanted to give us everything they possessed.[96]

In Maryland there are many Roman Catholic parishes, served by ex-Jesuits. Baltimore is the capital city.[97] Later I shall describe this country in more detail, as it deserves. We did not find enough boats here in which to embark, but were promised more within two days.

The grenadiers and chasseurs who were embarked at Head of Elk were obliged to put in at Annapolis because of bad weather and the shortage of provisions. We learned also that M. de Grasse had left his anchorage in the Chesapeake to attack the British, who had appeared at the mouth of the Bay. You will recall that M. de Barras had sailed from Newport, and M. de Grasse was rather anxious about him. To ensure the safe arrival of the Newport squadron, so essential to our generals' plans since it carried our siege artillery, the Admiral gave battle to the English squadron on 11 [5] September and beat them. After forcing them to retire, he returned to his anchorage to find to his great satisfaction that M. de Barras was anchored there with his whole squadron.

Meanwhile, M. de Barras had captured two English frigates, the *Richmond* and the *Iris*, which the English admiral had sent into the Bay to cut the cables of our ships. Had the English had the good fortune to meet up with Barras's squadron, he would doubtless have been beaten, for he had only 7 warships to the English squadron's 24. It was really lucky that M. de Barras had arrived so opportunely and without meeting any disaster, for on him depended the success of the siege of York.

When he saw that there were no boats arriving to embark the army, the Baron de Vioménil, who commanded the army in M. de Rochambeau's absence, got tired of waiting and decided to continue his march by

94. Clermont-Crèvecœur leaves the name of the tavern blank in his manuscript. It was presumably some distance beyond the village of Whitemarsh, along the "Old Philadelphia road." See maps, Vol. II, Nos. 78 and 79, and notes thereto.

95. See maps, Vol. II, Nos. 80 and 81, which show the position of the army. It will be noted that part of the troops camped on the western outskirts of what was then the city, while other units were in Old Town, east of the mouth of Jones's Falls, adjoining the Basin, and thus in readiness for the expected embarkation, which did not finally take place.

96. The Acadians, who had lived under English rule since the Treaty of Utrecht (1713), were deported in 1755 for refusing to take the oath of allegiance. For a measured discussion of this tragic episode, which has endlessly stirred the emotions of later generations (thanks in part to Longfellow's "Evangeline"), see George M. Wrong, *The Rise and Fall of New France* (New York, 1928), II, 761–783. A letter describing the arrival of the exiles in Maryland (Colonel Edward Lloyd to James Hollyday, 9 December 1755) is printed in William D. Hoyt, Jr., "Contemporary View of the Acadian Arrival in Maryland, 1755," *William and Mary Quarterly*, 3rd ser., v (1948), 571–575. The Acadians lived in the vicinity of present lower Charles Street in a section of Baltimore long known as "Frenchtown."

97. Annapolis, not Baltimore, was then as now the capital of Maryland.

land.[98] Orders were issued, and we left on the 17th.

17 September (18 miles) From Baltimore to Bryon's Tavern.[99] It was excessively hot. We could find no spring along the route, and the troops suffered extreme discomfort. After Retreat that evening M. de Vioménil received an express from Annapolis informing him that Captain de La Villebrune, commanding the *Romulus*, had just arrived there with some vessels to embark the army.[100] We were quite far away, but the next day we headed for Annapolis.

18 September (17 miles) [From Bryon's Tavern to the outskirts of Annapolis.] The journey was very long, and we were unable to reach Annapolis that night, so we camped 7 miles short of the town[101] and arrived there at seven the next morning.

19 September (7 miles) Annapolis is a small town that is quite well built.[102] It is situated on the Chesapeake Bay. The streets are not paved, nor so wide as in Baltimore. There are several fine houses here. The State House[103] of the province is the most beautiful of any in America. This building is built of brick and has a square shape. One enters by climbing five or six steps to a beautiful colonnaded peristyle elevated above the ground. Though of wood, the columns are very well constructed. The great entrance hall is lit by a dome in rather poor taste, since its contour is pierced by only six windows that are too small for the space they must light. At either side of the hall, which one might call the lobby, are two other rooms of vast proportions that are lit by very large windows. A cornice made of wood, which one would think to be plaster, runs all round the interior; it is beautifully carved. In an alcove is the tribune, which is very handsomely finished. The double staircase leading from the first room at either side of the hall to the rooms above is quite steep but very well built. Everything is delightfully clean. There is nothing else here worth mentioning except a fine hospital, which the English have destroyed.

20–25 September (250 miles, by sea) From Annapolis to Jamestown, Virginia. On the afternoon of the 20th we embarked the artillery, and on the morning of the 21st all the troops came aboard. All the army baggage, the horses, and vehicles proceeded by land.[104] Four hours after our arrival on board we set sail. With

98. Colonel Deux-Ponts (p. 45) explains that upon arrival in Baltimore on 12 September the Baron de Vioménil, thinking that the transports assembled there would be sufficient to accommodate the Bourbonnais Brigade, ordered him and the Marquis de Laval to make an exact estimate of the number of men each boat would hold. "We have done so as carefully as possible, but in spite of our earnest desire to effect a successful embarkation here, we see that it is impossible. The General has ordered for tomorrow a trial embarkation, which will decide whether we march by land or sail down the Chesapeake Bay. On 13 September, in the morning, the trial was made. The Baron de Vioménil has judged it impossible to expose the troops to the torture of such discomfort and restraint for several days and to the great risks we would run in these little boats, shamefully equipped in every respect. He has decided to march us overland. . . ." Vioménil's instructions to Colonel d'Arrot, commanding Lauzun's cavalry, dated Baltimore, 13 September, are in the Manuscript Collections of Colonial Williamsburg. According to these instructions and the schedule of march enclosed, the cavalry was to leave in advance of the main army corps, on the morning of the 14th, proceeding from Baltimore to Snowden's Iron Works, Georgetown, Pohick, Fredericksburg, Todd's Bridge, and thence via King and Queen Courthouse to Gloucester Courthouse. Lauzun's cavalry did take this overland route, but the main army corps eventually embarked at Annapolis, as explained hereafter.

99. "Bryon's Tavern" (so spelled in the manuscript), where Clermont-Crèvecœur camped with the artillery, must have been in the same vicinity as the infantry's camp at Spurrier's Tavern, which was near present Waterloo, Howard County, on U.S. Route 1. See the general map of camps and marches, Vol. II, No. 162, which shows the Spurrier's Tavern camp (No. 35), and No. 128, which shows in detail the vicinity of Spurrier's Tavern, where the army camped again in July 1782. Colles, *Survey*, Plate 60, indicates a "Boyan's" Tavern on this road, about 18 miles from Baltimore. See also map of ford over the Elkridge River, Vol. II, No. 82, which was on this day's route.

100. According to Deux-Ponts (p. 47), La Villebrune's little squadron included the *Romulus*, the frigates *Gentille*, *Diligente*, *Aigrette*, the two recently captured English frigates *Iris* and *Richmond*, and 9 transports, making a total of 15 sail.

101. According to the general map of camps and marches, Vol. II, No. 162, the 36th camp of the infantry was at "Scot's House." See also Itinerary 6.

102. See map, Vol. II, No. 83, and descriptive note thereto.

103. Clermont-Crèvecœur in his manuscript calls it "le palais des Etats de la province" by analogy to such Old Regime terms as "Les Etats de Bourgogne," "Les Etats de Bretagne," etc.

104. For a description of this overland route, see Vol. II, Itinerary 6.

a splendid breeze it took us only five days to reach the mouth of the James River. It was while passing through the middle of the French fleet that we learned that on the night of 23–24 [22–23] September Lord Cornwallis had sent the fire-ships I spoke of previously to attack the three ships blockading the York River.

26 September (6 miles) To Williamsburg. The grenadiers and chasseurs had disembarked on the 23rd on the James River in Virginia and gone to join the troops commanded by M. de La Fayette at Williamsburg. On arrival before Jamestown our troops went ashore, but we had hardly set foot on land before we were sent back aboard to load the artillery into boats.[105] We were ordered up a creek half a mile from Williamsburg to unload it. Meanwhile, the troops at Jamestown left to join the army encamped at the gates of Williamsburg.[106]

Williamsburg is situated on a charming plain between two creeks that flow into the James and York rivers. The town itself is not particularly pretty and consists of a single very long street at either end of which are very handsome buildings. One is called the Capitol and the other the Exchange.[107] There is also the Governor's Palace, whose large size indicates a fine building. (It was used as a hospital by the Americans during the siege. The following winter it accidentally caught fire and burned down.) The streets are not paved and are very rough in both summer and winter. There are several Protestant churches. The residents are all Anglican. In peacetime Williamsburg was an important commercial center, but the war has ruined most of its inhabitants.

I was immediately detached to the artillery of the Bourbonnais Regiment. On the 27th we remained in Williamsburg and were kept busy landing the stores, which could not join the army until five days later owing to the lack of vehicles.[108] We did not even have our tents, as had happened to us more than once on the journey, so we spent these nights in bivouac with the rest and thought nothing of it.

We learned that the English had captured from us several small vessels loaded with flour that were carrying about 2,500 rations for the army. M. de Choisy left that day to take command of the troops ordered to besiege the village of Gloucester, a post opposite the town of York held by the English, in which they had 1,100 men in addition to their hospitals and stores. The troops under M. de Choisy included the Lauzun Legion, 800 men from the garrisons of our ships,[109] and 1,500 militia.

28 September (12 miles) From Williamsburg we went to camp in front of York.[110] The combined ar-

105. The landing place was at Archer's Hope, about 3 miles downstream from Jamestown, as shown on the map of the army's 38th camp (counting from Providence, Rhode Island), Vol. II, No. 85. The present Colonial Parkway passes along this shore.

106. See map, Vol. II, No. 86, showing the armies "encamped at the gates of Williamsburg."

107. "La bourse" in Clermont-Crèvecœur's manuscript.

108. According to the dates given in Itinerary 6, pp. 106–107 and n. 65, the wagon train, which had come overland from Annapolis, reached Williamsburg only on 7 (or 6) October.

109. The ships of de Grasse's fleet were all "garrisoned" by detachments from army regiments for use as landing troops during the campaign in the West Indies. They served the same purpose as what was later known as the *infanterie de marine* (or *infanterie coloniale*), corresponding to the U.S. Marine Corps. These ships' garrisons are not to be confused with the army regiments (Agenois, Gâtinais, Touraine) under command of the Marquis de Saint-Simon, which were transported by de Grasse's ships to Yorktown. Saint-Simon's division had disembarked at Jamestown, 2 September, and was already in camp near Williamsburg when Rochambeau's army arrived; concerning their landing, see journals of the Chevalier d'Ancteville and the Marquis de Saint-Simon ([1], p. 387). The assignment of detachments from the ships' garrisons to Choisy's command at Gloucester is discussed in Choisy's letter to Rochambeau, 29 September 1781 (Doniol, v, 551) and de Grasse's letter to Rochambeau, same date (Doniol v, 550). The original recipient's copies of these two letters are in the Paul Mellon Collection. Joachim du Perron, a sublieutenant in the Régiment d'Infanterie de Monsieur, of the garrison of the *Languedoc*, was among those assigned to Choisy's command; his journal, one of the few firsthand accounts of the operations at Gloucester, gives detailed tabulations of the officers and units comprising the forces there (pp. 137–140). The ships' garrisons account for the large number of French regiments nominally represented at the siege in addition to those under Rochambeau and Saint-Simon. Du Perron mentions the following: Angoumois, Bourbon, Bresse, Brie, Colonel-général, Maine, Monsieur, Picardie, Rohan-Soubise, La Sarre.

110. See maps of the siege, Vol. II, Nos. 87–89. Most of the extant French "journals" of the Siege of Yorktown follow closely, or transcribe verbatim, one of the two

mies of France and America left at four in the morning in a single column. They marched thus to within 5 miles of the town, at which point they formed into three columns. The Americans formed the right-hand column, and the French the other two. I was in the center column. The heat that day was incomparably worse than anything we had previously endured. We had to march very slowly and make frequent halts. I was on foot, since my horses had not yet arrived, a plight I shared with all the other officers in the army. Even the generals were not all mounted. I can testify to having suffered every affliction imaginable. We left nearly 800 soldiers in the rear. Two fell at my feet and died on the spot. The roads that the enemy should have defended foot by foot were clear. We were never molested in any way, though we had expected to be.

We arrived about six o'clock that evening before the town of York and immediately began its investment. We spied an enemy column composed of infantry and cavalry coming to reconnoiter us and sent forward an infantry picket with 6 guns (2 of which I commanded). We fired on the English, killing several of their horses, so they decided to retire. Thus the American column that emerged from ambush was able to capture the enemy outpost.

29 September We spent the 29th reconnoitering the English works. We had 3 men killed and 3 wounded.

30 September On the 30th we discovered to our great surprise that during the previous night the enemy had evacuated two redoubts in front of their works.[111] General Washington, commander in chief of the combined armies, immediately sent the grenadiers and chasseurs to take possession of them. We converted a redan they had also abandoned into a redoubt and built a fourth to tie them all together. This work was entrusted to the Baron de Turpin, captain of engineers. We lost only 4 or 5 men during the course of its construction. Several cannon shots were fired by the English on our left. M. Drouilhet, an officer of the Agenois Regiment, had his leg shattered. One hussar was killed and another wounded.

❧ October 1781 ❧

1 October The whole army began making fascines; and the artillery, gabions and *saucissons* (long fascines).[112] During this time I went with my company to help with the landing of the siege guns on the James River 9 miles from camp. The Americans built redoubts, which the English kept under continuous fire, killing many men.

2 October An American patrol was wiped out by a single cannon-shot that killed 4 out of 5 men and wounded the other. Nothing much happened on the 3rd.

4 October When the troops under M. de Choisy went to seize an outpost at Gloucester, they found it occupied by the enemy. He attacked it and forced the English to retire. The Duc de Lauzun at the head of his Legion charged them several times in succession with the greatest success. He pushed them back to the town, then retired under orders from M. de Choisy. What is infinitely to his credit and only enhances his

official accounts: the General Staff (*Etat-Major*) journal (e.g., Verger, Menonville, Cromot Dubourg, Gallatin), or the Engineers' journal (e.g., Crublier d'Opterre, Cromot Dubourg, Querenet de La Combe). Clermont-Crèvecœur's journal for 28 September–19 October, relating his participation in the siege as an artillery lieutenant, is noteworthy as one of the few extant personal journals; another is that of Comte Guillaume de Deux-Ponts.

111. See map, Vol. II, No. 87, where the two redoubts are designated as "Redoutes de Pigeon's Hill abandonnées le 30 [septembre]."

112. See foreground of Van Blarenberghe's gouache of the siege, Vol. II, No. 92. "We made fascines and gabions, the former, bundles of brush, and the latter are made in this manner, viz.—after setting sticks in the ground in a circle, about two feet or more in diameter, they are interwoven with small brush in form of a basket; they are then laid by for use, which is in entrenching. Three or more rows of them are sent down together (breaking joints), the trench is then dug behind and the dirt thrown into them, which, when full, together with the trench, forms a complete breastwork. The word is pronounced *gabbeens*. The fascines (pronounced *fa-sheens*), are, as I said, bundles of brush bound snugly together, cut off straight at each end; they are of different lengths, from five to twelve feet. Their use is in building batteries and other temporary works." Joseph Plumb Martin, *Narrative of Some of the Adventures . . . of a Revolutionary Soldier*, ed. George F. Scheer (Boston, 1962), pp. 218–219.

noble conduct and the good example his bravery set the army is that, during his retreat when he saw one of his hussars assailed by three of Tarleton's cavalrymen, the Duc himself rushed to his defense and, fighting alongside his hussar, managed to rescue him. The man was badly wounded and, according to several of my comrades who have spoken with him, cannot sufficiently express his gratitude to his generous benefactor. The Duc has never mentioned this episode; it was the hussar who revealed it.[113]

In reporting the skirmish, M. de Choisy requested that the General assign him several pieces of artillery, but since we were short of men for the siege, the General took a long time to make up his mind. Upon his second request the General detached two of my comrades with two squads and four 4-pounders.[114]

In the combat described above the enemy lost 50 men and left an officer on the field. We had only 3 men killed and 11 wounded. MM. Billy de Dillon and Dutertre, officers of the Legion, were slightly wounded.

5 October Several patrols from both sides met and exchanged shots.

6 October We opened the trench, and the next day we built batteries. The one on the left was heavily shelled. The Chevalier de La Loge, who had his leg shot off there, died three days later. He was a lieuten-

ant in our battalion. Charming and witty, he was very erudite, not only in his profession, but in poetry as well. We often saw his poems in the *Almanach des Muses*. He was barely twenty-five and had already shown great aptitude for learning. We very much regretted his loss.[115]

I returned on the 6th from landing the artillery and went that evening with the captain of my company [Garret de Maisonneuve] to reconnoiter the site for a battery. Later that evening we returned there with the work troops and a squad from the company to lay out and build the battery. During the night the enemy gave us a pounding but did us little harm. We lost 1 man killed and 1 wounded. At daybreak we were not yet entirely under cover because the earth was very difficult to move, being full of tree trunks; besides, the workmen were very tired and much bothered by the enemy fire. The English resumed their fire at daybreak but again did not do us much damage.

8 October Several batteries were completed, though they had orders not to fire. The enemy kept up a heavy cannonade on the night of the 8th–9th.

9 October Because of the threatening moves made by the 26-gun enemy frigate *Guadeloupe*, the General sent an order to the left-hand battery, composed of four 12-pounders, two 24-pounders, six 6-inch howitzers, and a mortar, to shell the frigate and also the 50-

113. The Duc de Lauzun ([2], pp. 298–299) relates with evident relish his own joust with Colonel Tarleton but says nothing of his rescue of the hussar. Tarleton's account, in his *History of the Campaigns of 1780 and 1781, in the Southern Provinces of North America* (London, 1787), pp. 376–378, lacks anecdotal detail. The scene of the skirmish of 3 October is depicted on Du Perron's map of the environs of Gloucester, Vol. II, No. 90. Guillaume-Henry Billy de Dillon (d. 1788)—mentioned hereafter by Clermont-Crèvecœur—was at this time a captain (hussar) in Lauzun's Legion. "Billy" is part of his family name, not a nickname. He is not to be confused with such other Dillons as Robert-Guillaume Dillon (1754–1837), second colonel in the Legion.
114. "On the 5th there arrived for us 4 field pieces with 2 artillery officers and 32 gunners sent by M. de Rochambeau." Du Perron (1), p. 148.
115. La Loge's poems, appearing in the *Almanach des Muses* for 1779, 1780, and 1781, include light verse reminiscent of La Fontaine's fables and *contes* under such titles as "Le Bon Père," "Le Conseil de Momus, conte imité du grec," "Les Trois Novices, vieux conte," "Les Cygnes,

fable," "Tout est pour le mieux, fable," and "Vers attachés au cou d'un Perroquet." The apostrophe "To Neptune" (*Almanach*, 1780), with its topical theme, must have particularly appealed to La Loge's comrades. The poet calls upon Neptune to bring peace to the world and subjugate the "despot of the seas," not with the usual storms and thunderbolts, but by a more effective ruse. Transform his ships into sea nymphs, led by Love. Then entrust the fate of England to these beauteous maidens, and "if in a twinkling you would end the war—leave the field free to the French!"

Confie à ces beautés le sort de l'Angleterre,
& si dans un clin d'œil, tu veux finir la guerre,
laisse le champ libre aux Français.

A book published at the time of the 150th anniversary of the siege by a collateral descendant of the Auxonne lieutenant is dedicated to the memory of the writer's ancestor, Pierre-Louis de La Loge, who was posthumously decorated by the King with the Cross of Saint-Louis. Comte de La Loge d'Ausson, *Yorktown, ou comment la France royale libéra l'Amérique* (Paris, 1931), p. [v].

gun ship *Charon.* The frigate retired in time, but the *Charon* was set afire by hot shot and burnt.

The American batteries commenced firing and kept it up all night. We were delayed by the lack of vehicles and horses to pull our guns and ammunition caissons. The Americans had all they needed and, when they were finished with them, lent us their horses and wagons. They had made every effort to be ready before we were; however, since their resources were greater, this was not difficult. At ten o'clock on the 9th the French batteries opened fire and kept up so lively and well-directed a cannonade that within an hour the enemy batteries were silenced, having all been put out of action.

10 October My battery, not being quite finished by the 9th, did not open fire until the 10th.[116] That day it was my turn to go on twenty-four-hour duty, and I maintained a barrage that never let up for an instant.[117] I quickly put out of action the enemy batteries on which mine was trained. That night the enemy tried to cross the river on flatboats, but M. de Choisy had been forewarned and was on his guard. The fire of the batteries was very well sustained that day, and especially during the night, despite a very bad storm.

11 October The enemy fire slackened to such a degree that it really was not dangerous. It was not until night that they began to fire in earnest, but their shots were not too well aimed; nevertheless, they managed to kill several men in the trench. During the night we opened the second parallel and 7 men were wounded. It was completed the next day.

12 October On the night of the 12th–13th three redoubts were built in support and batteries emplaced.[118] There were 3 in all, composed of 6 guns each. They were mounted in a semicircle so as to cover a wider field and were placed 160 yards from the *place d'armes.* A mortar battery containing 10 mortars and two 8-inch howitzers was placed in the center to deliver shells and bombs to all the enemy works. That day 6 men were killed and 11 wounded. MM. de Miollis[119] and Dursuë, second lieutenants of the Soissonnais Regiment, were seriously wounded.

13 October The day was spent in cannonading and firing bombs at each other in such profusion that we did one another much damage. The enemy seemed to have been saving up their ammunition for the second parallel. It was of very small caliber and very effective, being fired at short range. That night we had 6 men killed and 28 wounded.

M. de Mauduit, who had formerly served in the American army, having joined it at the same time as M. du Coudray, was now captain and adjutant of the artillery park. He requested permission to go that night with several grenadiers to set fire to the enemy abatis in front of the works of their *place d'armes.* He went out three times on this mission, without any success. He burned nothing, but he and his men returned safe and sound.

15 [14] October We directed most of our fire towards the two redoubts that we intended to attack.[120] That night at eight o'clock 400 Americans, commanded by the Marquis de La Fayette, marched on

116. Clermont-Crèvecœur's battery (manned by Auxonne artillery) was one of those shown along the first parallel on the map, Vol. II, No. 88. Cf. Verger's journal, p. 141, where he notes under the date 10–11 October: "Our Nos. 3 and 4 batteries have been firing continuously since daybreak."

117. Von Closen (p. 146) notes under the date 10–11 October: "We continued to carry on a very active fire from all our batteries on the 2 assault lines. M. de *Chauteclerc*, commanding a battery of mortars, directed many 12 inch bombs on the enemy magazines, behind the escarpment of the mountain and near the river. . . ." "M. de Chauteclerc" may possibly refer to Clermont-Crèvecœur. The original manuscript of Von Closen's journal is no longer extant; the text survives only in the form of a handwritten transcript (Library of Congress) on which Evelyn Acomb's edition is based. The name, which Von Closen himself may have garbled, appears in the transcript as

"Chauteclerc," as printed by Miss Acomb. Balch (II, 11) and *Etat militaire* (1782, p. 250) mention a second captain attached to the Strasbourg Regiment (Royal Artillery), named "Chanteclair," who was on detached service in Saint-Domingue. Although he was thus "in America," we have found no evidence that he was at Yorktown.

118. The redoubts built by the French as part of the second parallel are shown on Berthier's map of the siege, Vol. II, No. 89.

119. See "Checklist of Journals," *s.v.* Miollis.

120. British Redoubts "No. 9" and "No. 10" on the allied right. The redoubts are shown, but not so identified, on Berthier's map of the siege, Vol. II, No. 87. Reconstructed versions of the two redoubts may be seen today on the Yorktown Battlefield, Colonial National Historical Park; see Charles E. Hatch, Jr., *Yorktown and the Siege of 1781,* National Park Service, Historical Handbook No. 14 (Washington, 1954 and later issues).

the redoubt [British No. 10] nearest the river and captured it. At the same moment 400 grenadiers and chasseurs of the Deux-Ponts and Gâtinais[121] regiments, under the command of the Baron de Vioménil, whose second in command was Comte Guillaume de Deux-Ponts, attacked the left-hand redoubt [British No. 9] and captured it at bayonet point. I was detached that day with two 4-pounders to take up a post between the two redoubts to support the battalion of grenadiers and chasseurs in case of resistance. One of my horses was wounded by a bomb that burst in the midst of my artillery. Because of the cries of "Vive le Roy!" that reverberated through the trench, the English believed that this was the signal for a general assault and consequently fired furiously from their ramparts. The place where I was seemed to be the target of the balls and cannister shot, but I had the good fortune to have not a man scratched. Comte Guillaume was among the first to jump into the redoubt.[122] He was wounded, though not seriously, by a ball that struck his feet. The attack lasted several minutes. We had 46 men killed and 62 wounded, including 6 officers. Among the wounded were Comte Guillaume, whom I have mentioned; the Chevalier [Charles] de Lameth, aide-de-camp of the Comte de Rochambeau, who was wounded in both knees; de Sireuil, captain in the Gâtinais, whose leg was shot off and who died the following winter; de Berthelot, de Siraque [captains in the Gâtinais Regiment], and de Lutzow [lieutenant in the Deux-Ponts Regiment]. We took 47 men and 3 officers prisoner, and the Americans captured 19 men in their redoubt and 3 officers.

The majority of the English had either escaped or been killed. During the real attack on the redoubts feint attacks had been made on the left by M. de Saint-Simon and the Comte de Custine, who lost 4 men killed and 12 wounded.

15 October The firing was heavier than ever. The enemy made a sortie with 1,200 men. They entered a deserted battery whose gunners had gone to fetch the last two guns that had been accidentally overturned in the trench. The enemy had first entered its protecting redoubt and captured the French captain in command, then the undefended battery where they spiked its four guns. The alarm spread throughout the trench. The Soissonnais Regiment, led by its commander, the Vicomte de Noailles, advanced and pushed the enemy back. The spikers were massacred as they were finishing their work, and several men were captured. There were 11 men killed and 37 wounded on our side, including 5 officers: MM. de Marin, captain of the Soissonnais; de Bargues [first lieutenant] of the Bourbonnais; d'Houdetot Colomby and de Laumont [lieutenants of the Agenois]; and de Pusignan [second lieutenant] of the artillery. M. Bourguisson [captain of the Agenois] was taken prisoner.

This sortie did not reflect great credit on the English. It was of no significance, since they could have done better. They were nearly all drunk, judging by the gun-spikers; and by the way they maneuvered they would have had great difficulty surprising a trench where the men were on the alert. Nevertheless, much damage can certainly be done by a sortie if it is well led, and especially if the enemy cannot predict at what moment he will be attacked. We must confess that we hardly dreamed of being attacked that night. The time was propitious, for the night was very dark.

16 October The batteries of the second parallel were entirely completed and began to fire. M. d'Aboville[123]

121. Clermont-Crèvecœur's note: "This was one of the three regiments that came from the islands under M. de Saint-Simon, the others being the Agenois and the Touraine. We were assigned soldiers from the Gâtinais to serve the artillery and were extremely satisfied with them. This regiment won the name 'Royal Auvergne,' which they had lost when the regiments were expanded [in 1776] to four battalions. They proved that they well deserved not to lose a name made so famous by their various military exploits." See Verger's journal, n. 75.

122. Comte Guillaume gives his own vivid and detailed account of the attack in his journal (pp. 56–61) and appends (pp. 66–71) Baron de Vioménil's report to Rocham-

beau. In December 1781 Comte Guillaume was made a chevalier of the Order of Saint-Louis for his valor on the night of 14–15 October; the honor came through special dispensation of the King, since he did not have the years of service normally required for admission to the Order. The storming of the redoubt was depicted, it would seem, in a later portrait of Guillaume de Deux-Ponts; see reproduction in Contenson, *Cincinnati*, Fig. 56, where a map (presumably of Yorktown) and a secondary figure pointing to a painting-within-the-painting can be discerned.

123. Clermont-Crèvecœur's note: "Colonel commandant of the artillery in the army of the Comte de Rochambeau. His actions during the siege and his talents have won for

J'ai reçu, Monsieur le Comte, à mon arrivée au Cap, le 16. juillet, les dépêches que vous avez eu la bonté de m'adresser dans cette partie et qui m'ont été remises par M. de Raynaud. J'ai vu avec bien du chagrin la détresse où se trouve le continent et la nécessité du prompt secours que vous sollicitez. J'en ai conféré avec M. de Lillancourt qui a pris le commandement de ce Gouvernement le jour même de mon arrivée et je l'ai engagé à me donner sur la garnison de St. Domingue en général, les détachements des Régiments de Gatinois, D'Agenois et de Touraine, faisant ensemble 3000 hommes, 100 hommes d'Artillerie, 100 dragons ~~et la compagnie des Grenadiers et des chasseurs du Régiment du Cap~~, 10 canons de campagne, quelques canons de siège et .. mortiers. Le tout sera embarqué sur 25 à 29 Vaisseaux de guerre qui partiront de cette Colonie le 3. août, pour se rendre en toute diligence dans la Baye de Chesapeak, lieu qui m'paroit indiqué par vous Monsieur le Comte, et par M. M. Virginton, de la Luzerne et de Baras, comme le plus sûr à opérer le bien que vous vous proposez. J'ai fait aussi mon possible pour vous apporter les 1,200,000 que vous dites être de la dernière nécessité. La Colonie n'a pas été en état de vous faire cet envoy, mais j'en prends à la Havane par une frégate et vous pouvez compter sur cette somme. Comme je ne puis rester sur le Continent, moy et mes troupes qui sont commandées par M. de St. Simon Maréchal de Camp, que jusqu'au 15. 8bre je vous serai obligé, Monsieur le Comte, de m'employer promptement et utilement, afin que ce tems soit efficacement mis à profit, soit contre les forces maritimes de vos Ennemis, soit contre leurs forces terrestres: mais il me seroit de toute impossibilité de vous laisser ces troupes plus longtemps, et ce pour bien des raisons. D'abord parce qu'une partie est aux ordres des Généraux Espagnols et ce n'est que sur la promesse qu'elles seront renvoyées dans ce temps, où ils comptent opérer, que j'ai obtenu la permission de m'en

continued

DE GRASSE'S LETTER TO ROCHAMBEAU, FROM THE FRENCH CAPE, SAINT-DOMINGUE, 28 JULY 1781, ANNOUNCING HIS PLANNED ARRIVAL AT THE CHESAPEAKE BAY (*see p. xvii*)

servir, ensuitte parceque l'autre partie servant de garnison à St. domingue, M. de Villement ne peut s'en passer, dans le moment où les forces maritimes sont occupées ailleurs. Toute cette Expédition, n'ayant été concertée que sur votre demande et sans que les Ministres de France et d'Espagne, en fussent prévenus, je me suis crû authorisé à prendre quelque chose sur moy pour la cause commune, mais je croirois changer tout le plan de leurs projets par une transplantation d'un corps de troupes aussi considerable. Vous sentez donc, Monsieur le Comte, la necessité de bien employer un tems précieux. j'espere que la Frégatte me devancera assés pour que je trouve tout prêt et que dès le lendemain de notre arrivée, nous puissions remplir les vües que vous vous proposés et dont je desire aussi ardemment que vous la réussitte.

Par les efforts que j'ai fait pour exécuter et satisfaire à toutes vos demandes et aux besoins tant de l'armée que vous commandés qu'au soulagement de vos alliés, vous devez concevoir le desir que j'ai d'apporter du changement à votre position et à la face des affaires. je marque à M. de Barras et à M. de la Luzerne, mon arrivée: au premier, afin qu'étant instruit, il puisse agir séparement ou de concert pour la cause commune; au second, pour qu'il nous fasse préparer nos besoins dans le voisinage de nos opérations, afin que je puisse donner tout le tems possible au soulagement des Provinces unies de L'Amérique.

J'ai l'honneur d'être avec un bien sincere attachement, Monsieur le Comte, Votre très humble et très obéissant serviteur.

le Comte de grasse

Au Cap le 28. juillet 1781.

P. J'ay des gillets à l'entrée de la riviere de Chesapeak outre ceux de notre part je me reporterai sur vos filets servant ou entre l'or des le plus favorable, mais nous n'emmenons nos troupes et nos forces navales ne pouvant quitter partageons leur tems de la garde de St. domingue et toute la saison des isles du vent.

22 8.
3. 6 Chatham 28th August 1781

Sir

I do not find that the force upon Staten
Island is large — or thrown over for any other
Purpose than that of Defence; for which Reason
it is submitted to your Excellency's Judgment
to march your Troops, in one or two Divisions,
as shall be most easy & convenient to them —
their moving in two Divisions, & on succeeding Days
will occasion no Delay — as the second will be up
by the Time the first will have embarked —

As I propose to go the lower Road, I
shall not have the Honor of joining your Excellency
till we arrive at Princeton, where I will order Dinner to be ready at three OClock, that we may
lodge at Trenton (12 miles further). — As this
will be a Journey of 54 miles from Whippany, I
would suggest to you the Expediency of making
Part of it this Afternoon — Cole Smith one of
my Aids, who is well acquainted with the Roads, will

have

WASHINGTON'S LETTER TO ROCHAMBEAU, CHATHAM, NEW JERSEY, 28 AUGUST 1781,
FIXING A RENDEZVOUS AT PRINCETON (see p. xviii)

the Honor of attending you to the Rendez:
vous at Princetown.. —

With great Esteem & Regard — and much
personal Attachment. —

I have the Honor to be

Your Excellency's

Most Obed'd Servant

G: Washington

His Excellency

Count D Rochambeau —

Sir,

  I have the honor to express to your Excellency
the satisfaction of Congress in the compliment which
has been paid to them by the Troops of his
most Christian Majesty under your Command.
  The brilliant appearance and exact
discipline of the several Corps do the
highest honor to their Officers, and afford
a happy presage of the most distingui=
shed services in a cause which they
have so zealously espoused.
  I have the honor to be,
with sentiments of the highest respect,
  Your Excellency's,
  Most obedient & most humble Servant

Philadelphia
September 4. 1781.

His Excellency
The Count de Rochambeau

Tho M. Kean President

CONGRESSIONAL GREETINGS TO ROCHAMBEAU, PHILADELPHIA, 4 SEPTEMBER 1781 (*see p. xviii*)

bled, be prefented to his excellency count de Graffe, for his difplay of fkill and bravery in attacking and defeating the Britifh fleet off the Bay of Chefapeake, and for his zeal and alacrity in rendering, with the fleet under his command, the moft effectual and diftinguifhed aid and fupport to the operations of the allied army in Virginia:

That the thanks of the United States in Congrefs affembled, be prefented to the commanding and other officers of the corps of artillery and engineers of the allied army, who fuftained extraordinary fatigue and danger in their animated and gallant approaches to the lines of the enemy:

That general Wafhington be directed to communicate to the other officers and the foldiers under his command, the thanks of the United States in Congrefs affembled for their conduct and valour on this occafion:

Refolved, That the United States in Congrefs affembled, will caufe to be erected at York in Virginia, a marble column, adorned with emblems of the alliance between the United States, and His Moft Chriftian Majefty; and infcribed with a fuccinct narrative of the furrender of earl Cornwallis, to his excellency general Wafhington, commander in chief of the combined forces of America and France; to his excellency the count de Rochambeau, commanding the auxiliary troops of His Moft Chriftian Majefty in America, and his excellency the count de Graffe, commanding in chief the naval army of France in Chefapeake.

Refolved, That two ftands of colours taken from the Britifh army under the capitulation of York, be prefented to his excellency general Wafhington, in the name of the United States in Congrefs affembled.

Refolved, That two pieces of the field ordnance, taken from the Britifh army under the capitulation of York, be prefented by the commander in chief of the American army, to count de Rochambeau; and that there be engraved thereon a fhort memorandum, that Congrefs were induced to prefent them from confiderations of the illuftrious part which he bore in effectuating the furrender.

Refolved, That the fecretary of foreign affairs be directed to requeft the minifter plenipotentiary of His Moft Chriftian Majefty, to inform his majefty, that it is the wifh of Congrefs, that count de Graffe may be permitted to accept a teftimony of their approbation, fimilar to that to be prefented to count de Rochambeau.

Refolved,

Rhode-Ifland,	Mr. Mowry	no] *
Connecticut,	Mr. Sherman	no } no
	Mr. Law	no }
New-Jerfey,	Mr. Witherfpoon	no }
	Mr. Clarke	no } no
	Mr. Boudinot	no }
	Mr. Elmer	no }
Pennfylvania,	Mr. Montgomery	no }
	Mr. Clymer	no } no
Maryland,	Mr. Hanfon	no }
	Mr. Carroll	no } no
Virginia,	Mr. Madifon	ay }
	Mr. Randolph	ay } ay
North-Carolina,	Mr. Hawkins	ay] *
South-Carolina,	Mr. Middleton	ay }
	Mr. Motte	ay } ay
	Mr. Eveleigh	ay }
Georgia,	Mr. Telfair	ay }
	Mr. N. W. Jones	ay } ay

So it paffed in the negative.

M O N D A Y, OCTOBER 29, 1781.

On motion of Mr. Clymer, feconded by Mr. Ofgood:

Ordered, That the committee of commerce deliver the books and papers of their department to the comptroller of accounts; and that thereupon, they be difcharged.

On a report of the committee, confifting of Mr. Randolph, Mr. Boudinot, Mr. Varnum, Mr. Carroll, to whom were referred the letters of the 16th and 19th from general Wafhington:

Refolved, That the thanks of the United States in Congrefs affembled, be prefented to his excellency general Wafhington, for the eminent fervices which he has rendered to the United States, and particularly for the well concerted plan againft the Britifh garrifons in York and Gloacefter; for the vigor, attention and military fkill with which that plan was executed; and for the wifdom and prudence manifefted in the capitulation:

That the thanks of the United States in Congrefs affembled, be prefented to his excellency the count de Rochambeau, for the cordiality, zeal, judgment and fortitude, with which he feconded and advanced the progrefs of the allied army againft the Britifh garrifon in York:

That the thanks of the United States in Congrefs affembled,

CONGRESSIONAL RESOLUTION, 29 OCTOBER 1781, CONCERNING THE VICTORY AT YORKTOWN (*see p. xviii*)

had ordered the guns to be unspiked immediately, so they were in firing condition. He now ordered the guns to ricochet their fire, and we could watch the progress this fire was making against the enemy, who could not stand it for long.

17 October The firing continued until three in the afternoon when General Cornwallis proposed capitulation. That day there were 2 men killed and 1 wounded. M. Bellanger, third lieutenant of the artillery, was killed in the battery he commanded. The Chevalier de Capriol, major of the artillery, was slightly wounded by the same shell.

18–19 October 1781 The Articles of Capitulation were discussed and formulated. They were signed on the 19th, whereupon at one in the afternoon we took possession of the enemy's works. At two o'clock the English garrison marched out and laid down its arms at the end of our line.[124] The garrison at Gloucester did the same before M. de Choisy's army. The English general Cornwallis excused himself for reasons of health from appearing at the head of his army. His second in command, General O'Hara, represented him. The British army marched between the allied armies; the Americans were on the right and we on the left. The generals and admirals with their numerous staff assembled at the head of our army. We could see on their faces the satisfaction they felt in garnering so gloriously the fruits of a campaign that will do eternal honor to France and in having reached the decisive stage in the struggle for American liberty that the Commander in Chief had conducted so well. How much glory he personally has won, as well as his nation!

The Comte de Rochambeau and the other French generals have gained no less glory—the former for his vigilant concern to maintain strict discipline in his army, for his care to avoid any incidents, and for winning the friendship of the Americans, who were not naturally drawn towards our nation. General Washington did not hesitate to consult him and follow his advice. He often had need of the Comte de Rochambeau's firmness; and although the American general was endowed with every talent necessary to a general, he found in his second in command an abundance of resources that would not otherwise have been available to him.

Our losses during the siege amounted to 4 officers killed, including 2 from the artillery, and 20 wounded of whom 3 died of their wounds. M. de Choisy had 15 men killed and 21 wounded; and we, 70 killed and 169 wounded, making a total of 299.

The Americans lost 10 officers and 260 men in killed and wounded.

The English lost 30 officers and 600 men in killed and wounded. The garrison taken prisoners of war numbered 6,918 soldiers and 1,500 sailors. There were 68 captured during the siege, making a grand total of 8,486, not counting 100 deserters, or the Tories and sutlers who were not reckoned as prisoners of war. The guns captured included 140 iron and 74 bronze pieces, totaling 214; in addition, there were 7,320 muskets and 22 flags. Vessels captured in the port numbered 63. Some that were sunk can easily be raised, such as the frigate *Guadeloupe* of 26 guns (which is now in Brest).

The 22 flags captured from the enemy have been sent to the Court of France as a gift from Congress, delivered by the Marquis de La Fayette. This gentleman departed for France immediately after the siege, taking with him the flags that Congress had presented to the King.[125]

---

him in the army as a whole the esteem and regard he has long held in the corps." He was later Bonaparte's First Inspector-General of Artillery in 1800.

124. See Van Blarenberghe's rendering of this scene, Vol. II, Nos. 95–97.

125. Despite Clermont-Crèvecœur's statement, Lafayette did not leave for France until 25 December 1781, when he sailed from Boston on the American frigate *Alliance*, commanded by Commodore John Barry. He had been granted leave from the American army by the Continental Congress and carried their dispatches to both Franklin and Vergennes. See Louis Gottschalk, *Lafayette and the Close of the American Revolution* (Chicago, 1942), pp. 341–347. Lafayette returned to America for several months in 1784. The Editors have not been able to confirm Clermont-Crèvecœur's further statement that Lafayette took with him flags for the King of France. Colonel Tench Tilghman, who was sent to Philadelphia with the Articles of Capitulation, mentioned in a verbal report to Congress "22 stands of colors" received "under the capitulation." *Journals of the Continental Congress*, ed. Gaillard Hunt, XXI, 1083. Washington's letter to the President of Con-

I shall not speak here of the Articles of Capitulation or of General Washington's letter of thanks to the army; since all these have been published in the newspapers, it seems useless to repeat them.[126]

24 October The Duc de Lauzun left on the frigate *Surveillante* to announce the news of the capture of York to the Court.[127] The surrender of Cornwallis produced a tremendous effect in Philadelphia. Several persons expressed their joy by illuminating their houses. This event furnished material to the journalists with which to attract attention, something the Americans never neglect, any more than do the British. They are only too happy when their newspapers are not full of malicious statements and lies.

26 October The frigate *Andromaque* left for France. Comte Guillaume de Deux-Ponts carried the duplicate dispatches. Many noblemen also left, including the Marquis de Laval, the Vicomte de Noailles, the Comte de Charlus, the Comte de Damas, etc.

29 October The Congress met and passed the following resolution, which it sent to the Comte de Rochambeau:[128]

By the United States,
in Congress Assembled,
29 October 1781.

Resolved, . . . That the thanks of the United States, in Congress assembled, be presented to his

gress, 27–29 October 1781, states that "24 Standards . . . are ready to be laid before Congress." *Writings of GW*, XXIII, 294. Resolutions of Congress, 29 October 1781, specify "that two stands of colours taken from the British army under the capitulation of York, be presented to his excellency General Washington, in the name of the United States in Congress assembled" (*Journals*, XXI, 1081), but we have not found a similar Resolution concerning a present to the King of France.

126. The Articles of Capitulation and General Washington's Order of the Day (20 October) are included in Verger's journal, pp. 144–147, 150–151.

127. Rochambeau's dispatch to Ségur, minister of war (printed in Doniol, V, 567): "Camp before Yorktown, 20 October 1781. Sir, I have the honor to send to you the Duc de Lauzun who is bringing to the King the news of the capture of Lord Cornwallis and his corps of troops. Comte Guillaume de Deux-Ponts will bring the duplicate and the recommendation for *grâces*. These are the two superior officers who have performed the two most distinguished feats, as you will see in the journal that will inform you of all the details [Rochambeau's official report on the campaign, his *Journal des opérations*]. . . ." Ségur acknowledged receipt of the news in a letter to Rochambeau dated Versailles, 22 November (original in the Paul Mellon Collection). The frigate *Surveillante*, commanded by Cillart de Villeneuve, made the crossing in twenty-two days, arriving at Brest on the evening of 19 November. Lauzun lost no time in reaching Versailles where, according to his *Mémoires* ([2], p. 300), "My news caused great joy to the King; I found him in the Queen's apartments; he asked me many questions and had many kind words for me. He asked me if I intended to return to America; I replied that I did; he added that I might assure his army that it would be well rewarded, better than any other ever had been. M. de Ségur was present. . . ." The *Surveillante* also brought the navy's courier, *Capitaine de vaisseau*

Duplessis-Parscau (who had distinguished himself aboard the *Languedoc* in the Battle of the Chesapeake Capes) bearing the Comte de Grasse's dispatches to the Marquis de Castries, minister of marine. Cf. letter from Paris, 23 November, printed in the *Gazette de Leide*, 30 November 1781, supplement. The frigate *Amazone*, with Comte Guillaume de Deux-Ponts aboard, though she arrived after the *Surveillante*, made a still more rapid crossing; after her false start on 24 October she finally left on 1 November and reached Brest on 20 November. "After a passage of nineteen days we saw the coasts of France, and on 24 November I experienced at Versailles the inexpressible happiness of embracing those who are dearest to me." Deux-Ponts, pp. 63–65.

128. Clermont-Crèvecœur copied into his journal a somewhat abbreviated version of the Resolutions, omitting the portions addressed to General Washington, to "the commanding and other officers of the corps of artillery and engineers of the allied army," and to the "other officers and soldiers" under Washington's command. An extract from the minutes of Congress was sent by the secretary, Charles Thomson, to General Rochambeau; Rochambeau sent his acknowledgment to President Thomas McKean, Williamsburg, 25 November 1781, and that same day forwarded a copy of the Resolutions to the Marquis de Ségur. Doniol, V, 587–589. The English version given here follows the text as printed in *Journals of Congress, and of the United States in Congress assembled, For the Year 1781*, III (Philiadelphia, Claypoole, 1781), 213–216. See illustration. An annotated text based on the original manuscripts is in Gaillard Hunt, ed., *Journals of the Continental Congress*, XXI (Washington, 1912), 1080–1082. The Resolutions were drafted by a committee consisting of Messrs. Edmund Randolph (Virginia), Elias Boudinot (New Jersey), James Mitchell Varnum (Rhode Island), and Daniel Carroll (Maryland).

excellency the count de Rochambeau, for the cordiality, zeal, judgment, and fortitude, with which he seconded and advanced the progress of the allied army against the British garrison in York [and Gloucester]: That the thanks of the United States in Congress assembled, be presented to his excellency count de Grasse, for his display of skill and bravery in attacking and defeating the British fleet off the Bay of Chesapeake, and for his zeal and alacrity in rendering, with the fleet under his command, the most effectual and distinguished aid and support to the operations of the allied army in Virginia: . . .

Resolved, That the United States in Congress assembled, will cause to be erected at York in Virginia, a marble column, adorned with emblems of the alliance between the United States, and His Most Christian Majesty; and inscribed with a succinct narrative of the surrender of earl Cornwallis, to his excellency general Washington, commander in chief of the combined forces of America and France; to his excellency the count de Rochambeau, commanding the auxiliary troops of His Most Christian Majesty in America, and his excellency the count de Grasse, commanding in chief the naval army of France in Chesapeake. . . .[129]

Resolved, That two pieces of field ordnance, taken from the British army under the capitulation of York, be presented by the commander in chief of the American army, to count de Rochambeau; and that there be engraved thereon a short memorandum, that Congress were induced to present them from consideration of the illustrious part which he bore in effectuating the surrender.[130]

Resolved, That the secretary of foreign affairs be directed to request the minister plenipotentiary of His Most Christian Majesty, to inform his majesty, that it is the wish of Congress, that count de Grasse may be permitted to accept a testimony of

129. The monument thus authorized by Congress was not erected for another hundred years. The "Victory Monument," seen today in Yorktown, was begun at the time of the Yorktown centennial celebration in 1881 and completed three years later. Descendants of Rochambeau and other French officers were present at the laying of the cornerstone. See "Centennial Commemoration of the Surrender of Yorktown," in Stone, *French Allies*, pp. 535–595.

130. "I may tell you in confidence," Rochambeau had written to La Luzerne, the French minister in Philadelphia, when sending him the news of Cornwallis's surrender, "that it would mean a great deal to me were Congress pleased to grant me as a token of appreciation four little pieces of field cannon engraved with the date of this event and the gift made me by the United States, to be placed in my Château de Rochambeau in order to preserve for my grandchildren the memory of this event and the appreciation shown to their grandfather by Congress." Rochambeau to La Luzerne, Camp before York, 19 October 1781, Archives du Ministère des Affaires Etrangères, Etats-Unis, Correspondance politique, Supplément, Vol. 15. La Luzerne evidently lost no time in dropping the hint in the appropriate Congressional ears, as the Resolutions of 29 October testify. When sending to the Marquis de Ségur, minister of war, a copy of these Resolutions, Rochambeau commented: "I have avoided replying definitely about the two pieces of cannon that Congress is so kind as to offer me, because I cannot accept them without His Majesty's approval, which I beg you to request. . . ." Rochambeau to Ségur, Williamsburg, 25 November 1781, printed in Doniol, v, 589. His Majesty's approval was presumably received, for in December 1782 Washington forwarded the trophies, duly inscribed, to Philadelphia, where they arrived only after Rochambeau's departure for France. The story can be traced in the following letters: Washington to Rochambeau (mentioning difficulty in getting the cannon engraved), 9 February 1782, *Writings of GW*, XXIII, 394; Rochambeau to Washington (suggesting that the cannon could be sent to Nantes and thence up the Loire to Tours), Williamsburg, 27 February 1782, Library of Congress, Washington Papers; Washington to Rochambeau, Newburgh, 29 December 1782, *Writings of GW*, XXV, 492; Rochambeau to Washington, Annapolis, 11 January 1783, Library of Congress, Washington Papers. The cannon were eventually forwarded to France and remained at Rochambeau's estate near Vendôme until the Comtesse de Rochambeau, during the French Revolution, entrusted them *ca.* 1790 to the local authorities. After figuring prominently in various patriotic parades and fêtes, the cannon became a bone of contention between the municipality (Vendôme) and the department (Loir-et-Cher), which eventually gained possession of them. The trophies were subsequently lost sight of, but during the Restoration Rochambeau's widow received from Louis XVIII, by way of replacement, another pair of smaller cannon. A photograph of these substitute trophies is in Forbes and Cadman, I, 127. These "Congressional cannon," as they are sometimes called, are still preserved in the Château de Rochambeau; letter to the Editors from Comte Michel de Rochambeau, 24 August 1967.

their approbation, similar to that to be presented to count de Rochambeau . . .[131]

I have not given a very extensive account of the siege itself. There are minute details that have not seemed to me worth writing down here. These relate only to my profession and will be the subject of a separate memoir.

After the siege the excessive fatigues the army had been subjected to, as well as the bad food, caused a great deal of illness among the troops. We were short of nearly everything. Many officers also paid their toll in the form of serious illnesses. We lost many from bloody flux.

The English suffered no less than we. The large number of negroes they had requisitioned as laborers spread the plague in town. These miserable creatures could be found in every corner, either dead or dying. No one took the trouble to bury them, so you can imagine the infection this must have engendered. Still, a large number of them survived. Most were reclaimed by the inhabitants. Negroes without masters found new ones among the French, and we garnered a veritable harvest of domestics. Those among us who had no servant were happy to find one so cheap.

The magazines at York were filled with every kind of dry stores. Most of the French officers were in great need of the basic necessities. Entrance to the town was forbidden to the French for four or five days, at the end of which time the Americans granted us freedom to enter and buy what we pleased; but by then they had plundered everything and there was nothing left.

The English and French got on famously with one another. When the Americans expressed their displeasure on this subject, we replied that good upbringing and courtesy bind men together and that, since we had reason to believe that the Americans did not like us, they should not be surprised at our preference [for the English]. Actually you never saw a French officer with an American. Although we were on good enough terms, we did not live together. This was, I believe, most fortunate for us. Their character being so different from ours, we should inevitably have quarreled.

Lord Cornwallis needed 100,000 *écus* to pay his troops. The French generals and colonels lent him this sum. When he arrived in New York, the General returned the money together with 100 bottles of porter to express his appreciation to those who had rendered him this service.[132]

131. Through a comedy of errors involving several American officials de Grasse eventually received, not two, but four cannon. After a pair had been engraved in Philadelphia with an appropriate inscription, Elias Boudinot, then president of the Continental Congress, discovered that "the pieces pitched upon were not of those taken at Yorktown and therefore were improper to be sent." Thereupon General Knox had a proper duplicate pair engraved at Poughkeepsie, but when these reached Philadelphia, Samuel Hodgdon, commissary of military stores there, was mortified to find that the earlier "improper" pair had already been sent to France. Overriding Hodgdon's hesitations, Washington nevertheless ordered him to entrust the second pair to the French minister for forwarding to de Grasse. Letters concerning the cannon from Boudinot to Washington, Philadelphia, 14 June 1783, Knox to Washington, West Point, 3 November 1783, and Samuel Hodgdon to Washington, Philadelphia, 11 December 1783, are in the Library of Congress, Washington Papers, printed in de Grasse (1), pp. 164–166; Washington's reply to Hodgdon, Philadelphia, 13 December 1783, is printed in *Writings of GW*, XXVII, 270. A royal order of 21 July 1786, countersigned by Castries, minister of marine, permitted de Grasse to "accept from the United States of America four pieces of 6-caliber cannon" and authorized him to place them at the Château de Tilly, his residence situated between Mantes and Dreux west of Paris. This must have been some small consolation to the Admiral, who was then living in virtual disgrace (cf. Verger's journal, n. 192). The cannon were engraved with the following inscription in French: "Pris à l'armée anglaise par les forces combinées de la France et de l'Amérique à Yorktown en Virginie, le 19 octobre 1781. Offert par le Congrès à S.E. le comte de Grasse, comme témoignage des services inappréciables qu'il a reçus de lui dans cette mémorable journée." A few days after the Admiral's death his son, Auguste de Grasse, wrote on 19 January 1788 to Jefferson, then United States minister in Paris, that the four cannon presented to his late father now figured in his own coat of arms and that his gratitude had dictated the device uniting them: "Libertas Americana." Auguste de Grasse's letter is printed in *Papers of TJ*, XII, 521. According to a recent biographer of de Grasse, the four "Yorktown" cannon were removed from Tilly during the French Revolution and melted down at Dreux to make bronze money; the same writer was unable to confirm a tradition according to which one of them had escaped the melting pot and was preserved at the Musée des Invalides in Paris. Jean-Jacques Antier, *L'Amiral de Grasse, Héros de l'Indépendance américaine* (Paris, 1965), pp. 381–382, 451.

132. "When Lord Cornwallis and his army left York, he

The frigate *Andromaque*, which had left on 26 October, was obliged to return after being pursued by the English squadron. It left again on 1 November. This squadron was sighted off the Capes, proceeding south. Several of our politicians maintained that the English were taking reinforcements to Charleston, in the belief that a victorious army would continue its conquests by recapturing this city, so important to the Americans. They claimed that this was the plan of M. de Rochambeau and General Washington, a project, however one looked at it, that seemed entirely feasible. But the Comte de Grasse would not consent, on the pretext that his ships were needed in the Windward Islands.[133]

4 November. The French squadron set sail for the Antilles, leaving at York the *Romulus* and 3 frigates under the command of Captain de La Villebrune to protect the shipping in the York and James rivers.

The English troops left by stages, and once the Articles of Capitulation were fulfilled, the Americans left also, some to join General Greene in the south, others for the north in the vicinity of West Point (not to be confused with the hamlet in Virginia of that name).

While Arnold was commanding English troops in Virginia, he had had trenches built around Portsmouth. These we now destroyed.[134] All the outer works around York were also razed. After completing this task, the French army took up winter quarters on 15–18 November. The headquarters was at Williamsburg, and the other quarters were at York, Gloucester, Hampton,[135] and West Point [in Virginia], to which I was sent.

The town of York is rather small and ugly.[136] It was very prosperous before the war. We destroyed it almost entirely during the siege. There was only one pretty house, and that was not spared by the bombs and shells and is now beyond repair. It belonged to Governor Nelson, one of the American generals who had most distinguished himself at the siege. As he knew the gunners had been told to spare his house, he came himself into the French batteries and said: "True, it is my house; but, my friends, it is full of English. Do not spare it." He did not have to tell us twice, and the house received a hail of shots.[137]

---

informed me of his need of money, and I shared with the greatest pleasure the few funds that we then had in our military chest. I placed but a single condition on the reimbursement, which was that it be made to us by the [English] chest in New York. . . ." Rochambeau to Sir Henry Clinton, Williamsburg, 9 December 1781, printed in Doniol, v, 589–590. A letter from Clinton to Rochambeau, New York, 31 December 1781, concerning the loan, is in the Library of Congress, Rochambeau Papers, Vol. III, p. 301.

133. Washington had indeed considered a move on Charleston, contingent upon "water conveyance" provided by de Grasse's ships. The question was raised even before the Siege of Yorktown during the conference with de Grasse aboard the *Ville de Paris* (cf. "Questions proposed by General Washington to Comte de Grasse," 17 September 1781, *Writings of GW*, XXIII, 122–125), and again after the capitulation (cf. Washington to de Grasse, 20 October 1781, and de Grasse's reply, 23 October, *Writings of GW*, XXIII, 248–250). In both cases de Grasse's replies were negative, "the orders of his court, ulterior projects, and his engagements with the Spaniards" rendering it "impossible to remain here the necessary time for this operation." Thus, as Washington reported to Congress (letter to President of Congress, 27[–29] October 1781, *Writings of GW*, XXIII, 294–299): "The prosecution there-fore of the Southern War, upon that Broad Scale which I had wished, being, as I judged, to be relinquished, nothing remained in my Opinion more eligible, than to reinforce Genl. Greene's Army to such a State of Respectability, as that he may be able to command the Country of So. Carolina . . . and to march myself with the Remainder of the Army to the North River; where they would be ready, at the ensuing Campaign, to commence such Operations against N. York as may be hereafter concerted. . . ." For the same reasons Washington abandoned a plan for an expedition against Wilmington, North Carolina, which was to have been commanded by Lafayette.

134. See maps of Portsmouth, Vol. II, Nos. 102 and 103, and descriptive notes thereto.

135. See map of Hampton, where the Lauzun Legion was quartered, Vol. II, No. 106.

136. See map and views of Yorktown after the siege, Vol. II, Nos. 98, 99, and 101.

137. The story seems to have become confused in the retelling, no doubt because of the numerous Nelsons and several Nelson houses. The house belonging to Governor and General Thomas Nelson (who commanded the Virginia militia at the siege) was not destroyed and still stands (sometimes referred to as "York Hall"). However, the house of Governor Nelson's uncle, the elderly "Secretary" Thomas Nelson, on the eastern edge of the town,

I did not arrive in West Point until the end of November 1781. First I had been sent to York to see to the embarkation of the heavy siege pieces, as well as the large artillery park, for their trip to West Point. We had only three companies from the artillery corps with us there, plus the miners' company, the whole under the command of M. de Chazelles [Chazelles de Bargues, lieutenant of the Bourbonnais Regiment].

West Point, otherwise known as Delaware, is a little hamlet of 7 or 8 houses at the confluence of the Mattaponi and Pamunkey rivers.[138] We had great trouble finding lodgings. The soldiers occupied the abandoned houses, and eventually the officers were fairly comfortable. We built batteries on the two rivers and set up a bomb battery in between.

This point was fortified and put into a state of defense only to protect the army's retreat in case of attack by a superior force. Thus communications were maintained with the rear. The army could retire to this place and, with the aid of several redoubts that could be located at points of vantage, defend it against superior forces. Furthermore, this position, being between two wide rivers navigable for 50 miles inland, was provided with natural defenses.

During the winter of 1781–1782 we had very little to do. Our batteries were soon completed, and we rested quietly from the fatigues of the last campaign. I made several acquaintances in the neighborhood, where there were some charming plantations along the two rivers I have mentioned. These people are very hospitable and receive you in a most cordial manner, but they are exceptionally lazy. The gentlemen, as well as those who claim to be but are not, live like lords. Like all Americans they are generally cold, but the women are warmer. They have the advantage of being much gayer by nature than the northern women, though not so pretty. They love pleasure and are passionately fond of dancing, in which they indulge in both summer and winter. When a gentleman goes out

of his house—something he does rarely—he is always followed by a negro groom who rides behind him.

The Virginians live almost exclusively on salt meat, of which they keep an ample store. The summer heat here restricts them to this diet, for fresh-killed meat must be consumed within twenty-four hours or else it will spoil. The beef is very poor in Virginia. The lamb and poultry are excellent, but in summer they have to be eaten immediately. Salt meat is therefore their staple diet; consequently the men and women all have poor teeth. A girl of twenty here, even more than in the north, has lost her freshness. She would pass for thirty-five in France. The men, as I have said, are not very active. While they drink a lot and chew tobacco, they leave the responsibility of the household to their wives. The latter manage things admirably but are very wary and lock up everything, a necessary precaution against the negroes, who are great thieves. Wherever else you travel in this country you find nothing locked; Americans sleep peacefully with their doors unlocked, whether in Pennsylvania, the Jerseys, or Connecticut.

Bundling is unknown in Virginia, but in its stead are other practices that rather tend, in my opinion, to go out of bounds. To begin with, when a girl has chosen her "beau,"[139] she is free to shut herself up with him for hours on end without ever tiring of his company. Since we were little used to these new-fangled ways, we expressed our surprise to these young ladies, only to be told: "What harm do you see in that, he's my best beau!" After that retort there was nothing to be said. What amazed us was that all these "beaux" do not urge them to go too far. This happens occasionally, but what of it?

Virginia is a beautiful and fertile province. Sometimes the winters are very cold, according to the Marquis de Vaudreuil who spent the winter of 1778–1779 [1779–1780] here with the *Fendant*. At that time the York River froze, obliging him to remain longer

which served as Cornwallis's headquarters, was in fact destroyed. See "Old Houses and Other Places of Interest in the 'Town of York,'" map in Hatch, *op. cit.*, p. 46. Chastellux ([4], II, 384–385) gives still another version of the story.

138. See maps of West Point, Vol. II, Nos. 104 and 105.
139. Clermont-Crèvecœur uses the word *amant* meaning "lover," but since this has rather different connotations in English, the American "beau" has been substituted.

than he wished.[140] But this is exceptional. The winter we spent here was quite mild except for three very cold days in January. On several occasions I even had to wear summer clothes. We noticed that the cold weather arrived only with west or northwest winds. During four months of the year the heat is unbearable, and when there is no breeze one suffocates. It is even hotter here than in the Antilles, because in the islands you are at least sure of a cooling breeze morning and evening, whereas in Virginia you may go four or five days without a breath of air. What is even more surprising is that when a west wind begins to blow in the middle of summer you feel the cold keenly. Several residents have assured me that they have seen ice here in June. What an odd climate, where the sky is so beautiful and the earth so fertile! For in addition to its native products, of which I shall speak directly, the country produces an abundance of those we grow in Europe.

The fruits here are excellent, especially the peaches, but the inhabitants are too indolent to grow what is useful and beautiful and do not devote themselves to raising what would satisfy the taste and eye of a real cultivator. Their gardens are limited to a few vegetables, and they have no inclination to embellish them. Since the dry season is often long, this would require watering, which they neglect; thus they lose interest in their gardens.

Among the natural products of Virginia, tobacco forms the basis of their economy, and Virginia tobacco is much esteemed in Europe. Indigo, too, does well here, but less well than in Carolina. Cotton also grows successfully and serves to clothe the inhabitants, who make all sorts of garments out of it. The negresses card and spin it, and it then goes to the weaver. They grow excellent yams, which the English call sweet potatoes. This is a most tasty vegetable, and Europeans generally like it.

No white man works in the fields unless driven by poverty to this extremity. An individual's wealth is gauged by the number of negroes he owns. The English took many away from the proprietors, thus ruining most of them in spite of their vast domains. The blacks are naturally lazy and can only be made to work through punishment. In this respect the Virginians are quite cruel to their slaves and do not spare them.

Virginia is covered with forests and intersected by immense rivers navigable for 250 miles inland. They all flow into the Chesapeake Bay. As I have said, the plantations are all situated on the river banks to facilitate navigation and increase the wealth of the proprietors. Ships come to pick up their tobacco, bringing in exchange everything they need.

Two or three hundred miles inland are the Blue Ridge Mountains. The Baron de Turpin, a captain in the Royal Corps of Engineers, was sent on a trip there and brought back a very good memorandum, which I have not yet had time to read. It is said to be a charming country where the heat is not nearly so intense and where there are new settlements being established whose inhabitants live happily and can satisfy every need of a pleasant, though restricted, life. I should have liked to go there to see for myself its much

140. After the unsuccessful Siege of Savannah (September–October 1779) by American land forces and d'Estaing's French fleet, the 74-gun *Fendant*, commanded by the Marquis de Vaudreuil, came north to Virginia and remained off Yorktown from 20 November until 25 January 1780; the ship carried a large number of sick and wounded, who were lodged in makeshift hospitals on shore. The Marquis de Vaudreuil, the Comte de Pontdevaux, the Chevalier de Tarragon, and other officers were received at Williamsburg by Governor Jefferson, who discussed with them the "throwing up proper works at York" as defenses against the threatened British invasion. *Papers of TJ*, III, 210–211, 246–253. In his account of his visit to Virginia, Aristide Du Petit-Thouars, a *garde-marine* on the *Fendant*, writes romantically of the Virginian maidens he met (*la tendre Patsy, la chère Pauly, la grosse Betsy, la petite Nancy, . . .*) and speaks movingly of the sufferings of the sick and wounded, which were aggravated by the extreme cold weather, "10° below zero" during most of their stay. "We got out of the bay only after struggling for eight days against the impenetrable ice floe. . . ." Du Petit-Thouars (2), pp. 29–47. According to Jefferson, the thermometer (Fahrenheit) at Williamsburg in January 1780 "was at 6.° corresponding with 11½ below zero of Reaumur . . . at that time, York River, at York town, was frozen over, so that people walked across it. . . . Chesapeake bay was solid, from its head to the mouth of Patowmac." Jefferson, *Notes on the State of Virginia*, ed. Peden (Chapel Hill, 1955), p. 78.

vaunted wonders. I heard a few details from the Baron de Turpin. He spoke to me particularly of a very beautiful natural bridge formed by the mountain streams. The arch that has been cut through the rock is very high, though I do not know its exact dimensions.[141] There are also many natural hot springs where baths have been established like those in England.

I have already mentioned that the cattle here are very poor and small. There is, however, one species of goat that is much valued because it replaces cows in supplying milk during the winter. The cows usually calve only in spring. They are puny and thin, owing to the lack of pasturage during eight months of the year, including four months of winter and four of drought.

The horses are highly esteemed. I have seen some fine specimens. They are handsome, fleet-footed, and extremely gentle. The English have almost destroyed the breed, and it will take years to bring it back. One does not see meadows like those in the north. There are marshes that become good pastures in the spring but dry up completely in the summer. Thus the horses are fed corn and cornstalks during the winter. This is a poor food for cattle but seems to be excellent for horses, which do not appear to lose either their vigor or their flesh during the winter.

As for the hogs, which are consumed in quantity (since, as I have said already, they provide the principal food), the people here have a special way of curing them that consists of salting and smoking them almost as we do in France; however, ours cannot touch theirs for flavor and quality. Little structures called smokehouses are used for this purpose. The roof where the meat is hung has openings all round. A small fire is lit and banked with care to prevent it from flaming and is kept going for up to six weeks, at which point the meat is properly smoked and reaches perfection.

141. Baron de Turpin's account of his visit to the Natural Bridge (in May 1782) and views of it engraved after his drawings were published by Chastellux in his *Voyages . . . dans l'Amérique Septentrionale* (Paris, 1786). See Chastellux (4), II, 445–456. The engravings were the first published pictures of Virginia's famed natural wonder.
142. The opossum, as a curious and exotic American animal, was a subject of great interest to the French. During the winter quarters at Williamsburg, Colonel d'Aboville (commander of the French artillery at the siege) pursued

Various species of wild animals are found in Virginia—for instance, deer much smaller than ours that are nevertheless very good to eat. They are generally seen in the mountains, where one also finds small bears that are very vicious. Beavers are to be found, too, but since they live in colonies and are very shy when hunted or when the virgin land where they live is cleared, they are rarely seen except in wild and uninhabited country. There is a very common species of hare that some people call a rabbit because its meat is white like the rabbit's. These are hunted the same way as our hares; they never burrow and have the same instincts as ours. Foxes are very common, but they are smaller than ours. Their pelt, which is better, is a lucrative article of trade, especially in the northern provinces. The opossum, an animal with a fox's head and a rat's tail, is the size of a cat. The female carries her young in a small pouch under her belly to which they are attached before birth. People claim that four or five days after the mating of male and female the young appear in the pouch. When the female drops her young, they detach themselves naturally. When chased she puts her young in the little pouch and carries them to a place of safety.[142]

The squirrels here are grey and somewhat larger than ours; however, they have the same habits as ours and make charming pets. Their meat is very appetizing. The flying squirrel deserves mention also; the size of a large rat, it has, like a bat, two membranes on either side that it uses as wings, but it does not fly any distance. This animal is very pretty. There is still another species [chipmunk] that is smaller and lives in hedges. It is brown with white stripes on its back from head to tail. The regularity of these stripes makes it look very pretty.

One also finds from the north to Virginia a certain

observations that enabled him to determine, with a gunner's eye for precision, the span of pregnancy of the opossum (13 days) and the period of incubation of the young in the mother's pouch (2 months). D'Aboville's authoritative "scientific paper" was published in Chastellux's *Voyages* ([4], II, 462–468). Chastellux also sent back to France in February 1782, via the frigate *Hermione*, a live possum destined for Monsieur Buffon, the great naturalist who presided over the Jardin du Roi. See our illustration.

animal called a skunk (*puant*), which is very well named because of the stink it leaves behind. This, its only means of defense, comes from a liquid it releases the moment it believes itself in danger. Its walk is slow and sedate, and it seems to say: "Approach if you dare!" The skunk is the size of a small cat and is black and white.

The raccoon is a water animal somewhat like a fox, but with very short paws, a large head, and a small neck. It is grey. Its paws are like a monkey's, and it uses them the same way as a squirrel. Its flesh is good eating and its pelt much esteemed for making hats. One also sees water rats, otters, and muskrats. The latter belong to the beaver family and build dams and underground lodges along the banks of streams and ponds. They smell very strongly of musk, a liquid they secrete in little sacs in the genital region.

THE BIRDS OF VIRGINIA

There are in Virginia many kinds of birds whose shapes and colors are striking. Some are much like European birds, so I shall confine myself to those I have found especially curious. The Carolina bird [waxwing], which is the size of a finch, is ashy brown on top, shading to dark brown, with a small brown crest and a pale yellow belly. The tip of its tail is also yellow. Its neck and wing tips are quite dark. On its wings are small spots of the most vivid red that seem made of neither feathers nor hair, and in fact nobody knows what they are. Nothing strikes me as prettier, but at the same time very singular. Only the males have these red spots.

The male redbird or cardinal is the most beautiful color red with a crest of the same color. The color of the female is less vivid. There is a smaller species whose wings and head are tipped with green; I do not know what the Americans call it. The bluebird, which is said to belong to the same family as our robin, is a most brilliant blue with a reddish breast. It is a pleasure to see one fly in the sunlight, for no sight is more dazzling. It is the size of a sparrow. You see bluebirds also in the north. The small yellow bird called a "bobins" is greyish in winter and in summer becomes a beautiful yellow. It, too, is found in the northern provinces.[143]

The quail or yellow bird has a back somewhat like our species, though the colors are darker. Its breast is yellow with black spots. The males have brighter coloring and very dark necks. The mockingbird is the size of a thrush and does not have particularly pretty plumage except for its throat. The people here claim it can imitate anything it hears. The jay is much smaller than ours and has the same markings on its wings. The blackbird is most extraordinary, though quite common. It is black like ours, but with a black beak, and on its wings are patches of brilliant scarlet (we have dubbed it the "colonel"). This colored patch is generally covered by the large feathers, but when near its mate it spreads its wings and shows off this charming color. The females also have colored patches, though less brilliant.

There are several species of woodpecker, all pretty because of their varied colors. The largest is black with a red crest and is called the cock of the woods. It is as large as a crow and looks a little like one except for the crest. The partridge here is very small; its flesh is as white as a chicken's and very delicate. I have already mentioned the large partridge that one finds up north, but not here. The small partridges are plentiful. The negroes catch them with corn kernels soaked in rum. Although markedly different from ours, having black curved beaks, they look somewhat the same.

One also sees eagles in Virginia, but of the small species. However, I saw one that must have weighed 25 or 30 pounds. It was not more than eight months old then and seemed not yet full grown. Eagles turn white as they grow older.

The turkey buzzard has a neck like a turkey's and marbled brown feathers on its back. The wild turkeys one sees here are delicious eating, but they rarely leave the mountains. There are a large number of geese, duck, and waterfowl that are like ours and are very

143. Clermont-Crèvecœur's word "bobins" is presumably his phonetic transcription of "bobolinks," or "boblinks." "In Pennsylvania they are called *Reed-birds*, in Carolina *Rice Buntings*, and in the State of New York *Boblinks*"; J. J. Audubon, *The Birds of America* (New York, 1840– 1844; Dover Publications reprint, New York, 1967), IV, 11. Although the male bobolink has a yellow patch on his neck, what Clermont-Crèvecœur describes here sounds more like a goldfinch.

good to eat. It is amazing to see the rivers in winter covered with them; one must see this sight to believe it. However, they are difficult to approach.

One finds hummingbirds (*oiseaux-mouches*) in Virginia that swoop down upon flowers like a fly and suck their honey. They move through the air as a fly does and make the same noise, but they have feathers like other birds. Some varieties are prettier than others. The hummingbird builds a nest the size of a small *écu* and lays three or four eggs in it the size of peas.

There are still other birds whose colors are not very striking and that rather resemble our European birds; however, there is a species they call "the tyrant" [kingbird, *Tyrannus tyrannus*] that is the size of a starling. It makes war on all the others, large or small, attacking them under their wings. With its beak, as sharp as a needle, it pierces their breasts and kills them. When attacked by a larger bird the kingbird slips under the attacker's wing and lets itself be picked up in the other's claws, then kills it in flight. At "the tyrant's" approach all birds, large and small, take flight.

SNAKES

Although there are in America snakes of all colors and sizes, none except the rattlesnake is dangerous. It is said that after being bitten by this creature, if you do not receive help within five or six minutes, you die. There are many in America, particularly in Virginia; fortunately Nature has provided and scattered in plain view a plant called serpentaria, or snake-root, that cures snakebite if applied immediately. We know that ammonia is also a good remedy. Negroes are often exposed to these bites. One is readily warned of a rattlesnake's approach by the noise it makes. It has on the end of its tail a series of hollow rings filled with hard objects that constantly strike the edge of the rings, making a noise only a little less loud than a cricket, but much less shrill. The age of this animal can be determined by the number of rings on its tail. The people here maintain that some grow as big around as a man's leg and are 15 to 16 feet long. The more thickly settled a country is, the fewer rattlesnakes there are, because the negroes kill them. It is very dangerous to sit down in the woods and fall asleep lest one surprise you.

There are snakes of different colors and some are striped and very pretty, but black snakes are the most common. In some places we found several of these creatures in our tents. I was not very much bothered by their presence, though I confess in all good faith that I could do without these nocturnal visitors. The soldiers found many snakes in straw they had to sleep on, none of them dangerous. They feasted on them the next day.

❧ May 1782 ❧

During May a frigate arrived from France bringing us the King's bounties (*grâces*) for the capture of York.[144] M. de Rochambeau was awarded a governorship with a salary of 30,000 *livres*. (On his arrival in France in 1783 he was also made a chevalier of the Saint-Esprit.) The Baron de Vioménil was appointed governor of La Rochelle, and his brother was granted a pension of 5,000 *livres*. M. de Béville, quartermaster-general of the army, received a pension of 1,200 *livres*. The Duc de Lauzun was allowed to keep his Legion,

144. According to Von Closen (pp. 193–194), news was received at Williamsburg on 9 April (via a small schooner from Providence) of the arrival in Newport (26 March) of the frigate *Emeraude*, which had left France on 16 February, bringing the impatiently awaited lists of the King's *grâces*. The ministerial dispatches were sent overland from Newport by an express, finally reaching Williamsburg on 25 April, but only after Rochambeau had sent Collot, then Fersen, to meet the slow-moving courier. The complete lists (signed at Versailles, 5 December 1781), summarized here by Clermont-Crèvecœur, are in the Paul Mellon Collection (Rochambeau Papers, letters from Ségur, Nos. 30–37); also in the Archives de la Guerre (Vincennes), A¹ 3734–3735, from which latter source they are summarized in Noailles, *Marins et Soldats*, pp. 297–299. Not everyone was pleased with the bounties granted. Commissary-general Blanchard, in a rather sour and disgruntled letter written from Williamsburg, 30 April 1782, to M. de Veymerange, intendant of the King's armies, complained: "the *grâces* were impatiently expected but have been received with dissatisfaction. They are certainly unfairly distributed and men who merited much have been wholly forgotten . . . ," etc. Blanchard's letter is published by André Girodie in " 'Soissonnais' et l'Amérique, Lettres inédites," *Franco-American Review*, I, No. 3 (Winter 1937), 237–239.

and the Marquis de Laval was promoted brigadier. M. de Tarlé, intendant of the army, was awarded the Cross of Saint-Louis. M. d'Aboville, commander in chief of the artillery, was promoted brigadier. The Chevalier de Lameth, who was wounded at the Siege of York, received the Cross of Saint-Louis, the command of a regiment, and a pension of 2,000 *livres*. Comte Guillaume de Deux-Ponts was given command of a regiment of dragoons, as was also the Vicomte de Noailles. Several officers were named chevaliers of the Order of Saint-Louis. M. de Buzelet, major of artillery, was granted a pension of 400 *livres*, and M. de Boisloger, first captain, one of 300. M. de Pusignan, wounded at the siege, was awarded the Cross of Saint-Louis and a bonus of 500 *livres*; M. d'Heméry, the Cross of Saint-Louis; M. de Mauduit, adjutant of the park, a pension of 600 *livres*.

All the regimental officers, and those of the artillery who had not drawn a forage allowance during the campaign, were granted bonuses as follows: first captains, 400 *livres*; second captains, 300; first lieutenants, 240; second lieutenants, 180; sublieutenants, 120. The engineers were also rewarded. M. de Querenet [de La Combe], lieutenant colonel in command of the trench works during the siege, was promoted colonel with a pension of 1,200 *livres*. M. de Plancher, a lieutenant wounded during the siege, was awarded a pension of 300. All the other engineer officers received bonuses.

ᴥᔤ June 1782 ᔥᴥ

On 12 June we received the sad news of the naval battle fought by the Comte de Grasse in the Antilles [Battle of the Saints] on 12 April.[145] What anxiety this news caused us! Even the Americans were petrified; at this moment they thought the war would never end. What an even more disagreeable position we were in! Having believed after the surrender of Lord Cornwallis that we should soon see our native land once more, our expectations were again postponed by the confirmation of this unhappy event.

We suffered greatly from the heat. The nights seemed even hotter than the days. We did not know where to turn. Added to this discomfort was an invasion by gnats, whose bite is far more venomous than those of Europe. You could guard against them only by smoking and burning tobacco in your room. Its odor drives them away. It is dangerous to go bathing in this country. One sees few Americans indulge in this pastime. They maintain that the water loosens their bowels and causes fevers, and that one can bathe only before dawn or after sundown and stay in the water but a very short time. Nevertheless, I went bathing at all hours and never felt the slightest ill effect. Since the country is very hot and one perspires a great deal, I followed the American custom of drinking grog (rum and water), which fortifies and invigorates you without stopping perspiration.

During the summer it is impossible to go out of the house in the daytime. The houses are designed to stay cool, being built round a large hall or vestibule with a cross draft running through it. This serves as a sitting-room during the day. In the evening you go out, but you do not stay long outdoors since the dampness of the night air is dangerous. The Americans stand the heat better than we do, or at least they are less sensitive to it.

I have already said they are so lazy that they provide nothing pleasant or convenient out-of-doors such

145. The Battle of the Saints, in which Admiral Rodney defeated the French fleet under de Grasse and in which the latter was taken prisoner, took place in two successive engagements, 9 and 12 April 1782, off Guadeloupe near the small islands known as "Les Saintes." In contemporary eyes de Grasse's defeat, which seemed to alter the balance of naval power in England's favor, somewhat unjustly dimmed his decisive role at Yorktown—as his vindicators have been pointing out periodically ever since. Numerous French accounts of the Battle of the Saints have survived; see "Checklist of Journals," *s.v.* de Grasse, Bougainville, Cadignan, Du Perron, Du Petit-Thouars, Goussencourt, Saint-Simon, Tornquist, Comte de Vaudreuil, Villebresme. Mahan, *Operations of the Navies*, pp. 207–226, provides a good analysis, as does Charles Lee Lewis, *Admiral de Grasse and American Independence* (Annapolis, 1945), Chap. xix, "The Engagement off Saints Passage," pp. 225–254. Concerning the post-mortem controversy, see Verger's journal, n. 192. From the French ships that survived the battle was formed the squadron commanded by the Marquis de Vaudreuil, which came to Boston in August 1782 and which eventually transported Rochambeau's army back to France via the Caribbean, as related by Clermont-Crèvecœur hereafter.

as groves of trees or pools. Their wells and springs are not usually covered, so that the water is mostly warm and unpleasant to drink. Elsewhere in this country it is brackish and tastes bad. But in this, as in other respects, they have a lack of concern that is difficult to explain.

I gauged their taste by a small talent I have for playing the violin. I played several pretty airs with variations composed by our best masters, which impressed them no more than would the singing of our peasant girls. But when I played several of their own tunes, their expression changed to one of pleasure. It is fair to say that most of their tunes are fit only to bury the devil. They have neither taste nor sentiment; there is something pitifully uncultivated about them. I confess, however, that I made a young lady cry by playing her a sentimental air that she had taken a fancy to; but I beg my reader not to believe that I wish by this statement to claim any special talent for this instrument, which I took up only to amuse myself.

To convince you of the truth of what I have said, this young lady had a "beau" whom she loved very dearly, so she had a tender heart; in every country a

sentimental air always recalls the best moments of one's past. The women of this country who fall in love with someone really love him and are faithful. One must give them their due. Although difficult to arouse, once in love they succumb to the most tender and sincere feelings. Here as elsewhere the women are natural coquettes. They wish to please, but when you want to persuade one that you love her and find her to your taste, she replies ingenuously that she already has a "beau" and can love no one else, but that she will let you be her friend. Then she will ask you for a lock of your hair, which she will make into a bracelet, while she wears her lover's around her neck. This is the custom, and it is not equivocal, since the moment you see a girl you know whether she already has a "beau" or a friend.[146]

⤙ July 1782 ⤚

In the midst of our peaceful life at West Point we received orders to be in Williamsburg on 25 June. On

146. Clermont-Crèvecœur's comments on the young ladies of Virginia find an echo in other journals. The Chevalier de Coriolis, a twenty-eight-year-old lieutenant in the Bourbonnais Regiment, was so charmed with American ways that he seriously proposed marriage to Miss Blair, daughter of John Blair of Williamsburg, who maintained open house for the French officers during their winter quarters there. As Coriolis explained in a letter to his parents written from Baltimore, 29 July 1782 (printed in Coriolis [1]), he had obtained a fortnight's leave (with the cordial encouragement of General Chastellux but grudging approval of his brother-in-law, Commissary-general Blanchard) to visit Miss Blair, who was then staying with cousins in the country, only thirty or forty miles distant from the army's northbound route. This was at "Scotchtown," then the estate of Miles Cary in Hanover County, about eight miles northwest of present Ashland; Von Closen, Mauduit, and Billy de Dillon also made this jaunt to bid farewell to the ladies (Von Closen, pp. 209–210). Coriolis played with the idea that he might remain in America as a sort of military attaché but regretfully reported to his brother from Providence, 12 November 1782, that the imminent departure of the army for the West Indies made it difficult to reconcile his plans for marriage with his military career: "I thought I was reaching the moment that would make me the happiest of men, and now I am farther than ever from it. However,

I am reasonable enough to accept my lot and bow to what cannot be prevented. . . ." Miss Blair was one of the American ladies whose silhouette portraits were preserved by Von Closen among his keepsakes of his American campaign; see Von Closen, pp. 163–164 and Plate facing p. 137. Another Franco-Virginian romance can be read between the lines of two letters addressed to Mrs. William (Mary Willing) Byrd III of Westover by the Chevalier de Mauduit, who writes from Boston, 21 December 1782, on the eve of his departure: "Now is the time of War, all the scenes are to be at the West-Indies. If I fall, a tear from each of my family, I say my family, for really your family and mine are together in my heart. . . . Adieu my Dear Mama my worthy mother, the example of the best mother, love your son for till death, he will love you all very heartily. Adieu, perhaps forever, if it is so, I shall look to you and your family an instant before my Last Moments. . . ." "Letters from M. Mauduit to Mrs. Byrd," *Virginia Magazine of History and Biography*, 2nd ser., XXXVIII, No. 1 (Jan. 1930), 56–59; the two letters are in English. A less innocent episode involving a titled French officer resulted in the birth on 3 November 1782 of a son to Miss Rachel Warrington, niece and ward of Mrs. Susanna Riddell, then a resident of Williamsburg. Lewis Warrington (1782–1851), who had a distinguished career in the U.S. Navy, was never recognized by his father.

1 July we departed in four divisions, as last year, leaving at York a company of artillery with 400 men under the command of M. de La Valette, brigadier of the royal army. The little squadron commanded by M. de La Villebrune remained also. The siege guns were left at West Point with two companies of artillery.

I was attached to the Third Division, which left on the 3rd, the First and Second having departed on 1 and 2 July. This time the artillery had perfectly good teams, and we suffered only from the terrific heat. We marched from Williamsburg to Baltimore, 200 miles overland, in twenty-three days. I shall mention only the principal places through which we passed.[147]

14 July At Fredericksburg. Fredericksburg is a small town on the Rappahannock, which would be very pretty had it not suffered much during the war. Its commerce has been dormant for some time. Since our arrival in Virginia it seems to have revived somewhat. The Rappahannock is navigable for 200 miles inland. We forded it a short way above the town. The ford was as bad as can be.[148] We camped across the river a mile beyond the town of Falmouth where we made a halt.

Fredericksburg is where General Washington's mother lives. We went to call on her but were amazed to be told that this lady, who must be over seventy, is one of the most rabid Tories. Relations must be very strained between her and her son, who will always be the right arm of American freedom.[149] I should call attention to the fact that in many families you find two brothers, or sometimes a father and mother, holding opposite opinions. One is a defender of liberty, while the other is a confirmed Loyalist. What evils result from this division of opinion, which disturbs the union and sows discord in the midst of families who should be happy together!

20 July To Alexandria. Alexandria is also a small town, but on the Potomac, one of the largest rivers in America after the Hudson. However, this town appears to be still in its infancy. Twenty years ago there was not a single house here. It will be very pretty, for every day very nice houses are being built here. It is very well situated for commerce. Vessels can go 250 miles up the Potomac. This river marks the boundary between Maryland and Virginia. We crossed it in boats 8 miles beyond Alexandria where it was quite narrow, not over 1,000 to 1,200 yards wide, and went to camp across the river a mile above the village of Georgetown. This village is ugly, badly built, and poorly situated.

21 July To Bladensburg. We halted in Bladensburg, quite a pretty town on a fairly large creek [Anacostia] that can accommodate boats up to 100 tons. We stayed there two days and arrived in Baltimore on the 26th.

26 July To Baltimore. We found the city still handsomer than the year before, for 150 new houses had been built. Its commerce seems to have revived. Soon it will unquestionably be one of the most prosperous cities in America, not only because of its strategic location for commerce but because of the numbers of foreigners who settle here each day.

⚜ August 1782 ⚜

On 28 July we received news that the squadron of the Marquis de Vaudreuil had just appeared off the Capes of the Chesapeake Bay. It was composed of 13 warships and 3 frigates. One of the latter arrived at Hampton, bringing dispatches for the Comte de Rochambeau. The General immediately ordered M. de Choisy to go to Boston, where the squadron was bound, and take with him three artillery officers and two engineers, who were named in the orders. It was rumored that M. de Choisy was going to take com-

147. See Verger's journal, pp. 159–160, for a day-by-day itinerary of the army's march northward through Virginia and across Maryland to Baltimore. Verger, sublieutenant in the Deux-Ponts Regiment, was with the Second Division and thus marched a day ahead of Clermont-Crèvecœur. The route is shown on the general map of camps and marches, Vol. II, No. 162; the successive campsites are represented by Berthier's maps, Vol. II, Nos. 108–129.
148. See map of "Gué de Falmouth," Vol. II, No. 120.

149. Although he does not mention Mrs. Washington's Tory sympathies, Douglas S. Freeman in his biography of *Washington* (V, 491) refers to the "lack of affection for his mother" as "the strangest mystery of Washington's life." Mrs. Augustine (Mary Ball) Washington's house at the corner of Lewis and Charles Streets in Fredericksburg, where she lived from 1772 until her death in 1789, has been restored and is maintained as a historic site by the Association for the Preservation of Virginia Antiquities.

mand of the 2,000 troops aboard M. de Vaudreuil's squadron.[150]

The arrival of the squadron and the departure of M. de Choisy intrigued us not a little and gave the politicians a lot to figure out; however, the fact is that no one except General Rochambeau knew anything. We learned only some time after the arrival of the squadron in Boston that nearly all the ships had run aground there on arrival. The *Magnifique* of 74 guns struck so hard that she could not be freed and was a total loss.[151]

M. de Vaudreuil's squadron had suffered greatly in the battle of 12 April, so it went to Boston for repairs. We shall subsequently see that this squadron came to this country for several reasons.

The Baltimoreans seemed to us the most courteous of all the people we have met, except the people of Newport. Their social assemblies are well managed, and the ladies are elegantly turned out. Since trade is their principal occupation, it is not surprising to find almost all the inhabitants well off. Their manners are very pleasing, and the women, without being so pretty as elsewhere, are charming and amiable. They love entertaining and good food. Although everything is very dear, you can find here something to satisfy every need and taste. Private carriages are numerous; you see few well-to-do people who do not have their own cabriolet. The women here are excellent equestriennes and enjoy riding horseback and driving their own carriages.

Our camp was erected on a charming site in the midst of a woodland near the city, from which we enjoyed a most agreeable view.[152] In front of each brigade the soldiers had erected arches of foliage that added to the pleasant effect. Each evening after Retreat the regimental bands played and crowds of people on foot, on horseback, or in carriages swarmed around the musicians. The music seemed to please them. The bands were careful to play many of their favorite tunes, and often there was dancing as well.

DESCRIPTION OF MARYLAND

The province of Maryland is abundantly endowed with everything. One can find here every necessity of life. Many inhabitants are Roman Catholics. The colony was founded by Queen Mary of England after whom it was named the "Land of Mary." This province, which is still very young, requires only strong arms and cultivation to make it a delightful locality.

There are mines here of every variety—silver, copper, iron, lead, etc., and even, so it is said, gold—as well as many deposits of lesser metals. Students of chemistry and natural history would find much to write about. Few of the many mines, except the iron mines, are being worked. The inhabitants content themselves with asserting that their land holds hidden

150. Vaudreuil had in mind an expedition against the British-held fort in Penobscot Bay (a recurring magnet to the French navy), but both Rochambeau and Washington dissuaded him; see Washington to Vaudreuil, 10 August 1782, *Writings of GW*, xxiv, 497–500. The role of Choisy and the officers who accompanied him was therefore limited to investigating the coastal defenses of Boston and vicinity; see hereafter, p. 80.

An expedition from Boston to Penobscot Bay had already been envisaged, but abandoned, in the spring of 1781. It was to have been led by La Pérouse, then commanding the frigate *Astrée*; see La Pérouse's correspondence with Destouches in *Destouches Papers*, Nos. 70–86. In the summer of 1782, at the time Rochambeau's army was marching northward, La Pérouse (later famous as the ill-fated explorer of the Pacific) led an expedition to Hudson Bay, where he destroyed the British posts there—Fort Prince of Wales (Churchill, Manitoba) on 11 August and Fort York (York Factory, Manitoba) on 22 August. A summary of this brilliant but little-known exploit is in

Noailles, *Marins et Soldats*, pp. 284–288. For an account by a participant, see "Checklist of Journals," *s.v.* Lannoy.

151. The *Magnifique* was wrecked on "Man-of-War Bar" off the northwest point of Lovell's Island at the entrance to Boston Harbor on 9 August 1782. To replace her the Continental Congress, by a resolution of 3 September 1782, presented to His Most Christian Majesty a comparable ship, the *America*, then being built for the Continental Navy in Portsmouth, New Hampshire. The story of the unfortunate *America* is told by Samuel Eliot Morison in his *John Paul Jones* (Boston, 1959), pp. 318–330. Morison relates that the local American pilot responsible for the wreck of the *Magnifique*, who was obliged to give up his job for that of sexton in a Boston church, was long thereafter taunted by small boys with the couplet:

> Don't you run *this* ship ashore,
> Like you done the Seventy-four!

152. See maps of the 1782 Baltimore encampment, Vol. II, Nos. 129 and 130.

treasures. Up to now they have been permitted to open only the iron mines. I have seen some of their forges and furnaces as I passed through the country. At the moment, however, everything suffers from the evils of war, everything languishes; only a long peace could enable the inhabitants to take possession of their underground treasure.

The iron mines I had an opportunity to see are rich and produce ore of comparable quality to that of France, but much inferior to that of England. They extract 100 pounds of iron from 300 of ore. If they used exactly the same process as we do, they would extract even more. They do not wash their ore sufficiently. This operation is performed by their negroes, who, being by nature soft and lazy, take little trouble, and thereby reduce the yield.[153]

The prevalence of iron mines in Maryland makes the water here more or less healthy. There are plenty of mineral springs, though many of these flow also through the copper mines, making their water most unhealthy. Doubtless much of the soldiers' illness came from drinking from springs along the route. It is very dangerous to let soldiers drink along the route; on the other hand, it seems cruel to prevent a poor wretch, overcome by the heat, from seeking relief from his sufferings. In camp it is the responsibility of the army doctors—in fact, their first responsibility—to analyze the local water. I am amazed that they do not take these precautions more often, which would surely prevent much illness. It is known that the water from springs is not as healthy as that from rivers or brooks. A soldier ought to confine himself to the latter; but he likes to drink cold water, and running waters are rarely cold, especially in the summer. This subject should be discussed in more detail, but I shall leave it to others more eloquent than I to employ their pens on behalf of the soldiers' health.[154]

There are not in the whole world so many peach trees as there are in Maryland. They abound along the roads and on all the plantations. It is, in fact, the fruit tree that does best in America. The Americans make peach brandy that is very strong without being disagreeable to the taste; this is yet another article of trade for the province. In general the Americans are very fond of hard liquor. Their grog is always very strong, as is their punch, with which we are familiar in Europe. But they rarely drink it since the rum or the rye with which they make it is very scarce. Here it is also made with brandy, which many people prefer because it is not so strong.

5 August The General reviewed his army. The troops were in their most brilliant full dress. The General passed along the lines of the camp, followed by a large crowd of Americans, the ladies and their cavaliers on horseback and others in carriages. The Comte de Rochambeau was accompanied by His Excellency General [Thomas Sim] Lee, governor of the province. He watched the troops march past. Never, I believe, had the Baltimoreans enjoyed so fine a spectacle as these regiments all dressed in new uniforms, the soldiers' faces ruddy with health. It was hard to believe that these were the same troops who last year had suffered so many fatigues and hardships.

Rumors of a general peace reached us about the middle of August. We learned that peace negotiations were under way in France and hoped that they would be successful. This news was sent to the Comte de Rochambeau by Congress. He received another letter from General Carleton, the former governor of Canada who had relieved Sir Henry Clinton in command of the British troops in New York, which also gave him great hope because of the latter's news from the English court. M. de Rochambeau sent an express to General Washington to ask if his plans of campaign would proceed despite these rumors. All this, as you will see later (in spite of the actual peace rumors spread abroad), was no more than a device employed by our general to cover up his plans. It was therefore

---

153. Clermont-Crèvecœur's interest in iron mines and his special attention to smelting processes doubtless sprang from his observations in Lorraine, his native province, where the chief iron mines of France were (and are) located. Among the forges that he might have seen near the route of march through Maryland were the Snowden iron works on the Patuxent River and the Nottingham Company forges at Whitemarsh.

154. Problems of army hygiene are touched upon in Bouvet, *Service de santé*. See also "Checklist of Journals," *s.v.* Coste.

decided that we should leave Baltimore.[155] The Legion's departure was fixed for 23 August, and that of the other divisions on successive days.

The artillery from West Point (in Virginia) under M. de Chazelles, as well as the troops remaining at York under Brigadier General de La Valette, lieutenant colonel of the Saintonge Regiment, arrived in Baltimore on the 19th, escorted by the *Romulus*. The artillery, consisting of three companies, together with an infantry detachment of 400 men, were left in Baltimore, still under the command of M. de La Valette and M. de Chazelles.[156]

The order was issued on 22 August for the army to depart on the 23rd in four divisions. The route was designated as far as King's Ferry on the Hudson River. It is useless to repeat the description of precisely the same route as last year's.[157] Up to now the objective seemed to be to join the American army encamped on the Hudson at Peekskill.

People said that the English were about to evacuate Charleston, and even New York, and take their troops to the Antilles to make the most of their naval victory of 12 April by recapturing the islands we had taken from them. Having a superior fleet and being masters of the sea, all this seemed possible and well conceived on their part. Our reunion with the Americans before New York could upset their plans. Our thinking was correct, but as you will see later, we had not yet guessed the secret.

After our departure from Baltimore we thought no more of the current rumors of peace and regarded them as chimerical, especially in the face of English supremacy on the sea, which would hardly lead them to submit to the French demands communicated to the British ambassador, namely, that despite her losses in the Antilles France would not retreat from her position in favor of free trade and American independence. Thus we believed the peace to be far from concluded and desired nothing more than to distinguish ourselves against another Cornwallis and, after this double blow,

155. Rochambeau had not himself accompanied the army on its march from Williamsburg to Baltimore (General Chastellux was in command) but had gone ahead to confer with Washington. A memorandum entitled "Substance of a Conference between Comte de Rochambeau and General Washington," dated Philadelphia, 19 July 1782, is printed from the manuscript in the Library of Congress, Washington Papers, in *Writings of GW*, xxiv, 433–435; Rochambeau's copy, a two-column document in his and in Washington's hand, is in the Paul Mellon Collection. In Washington's opinion, "New York . . . has ever been, and ought to be the primary object of our Arms." A possible second object, Charleston, was "morally impossible" unless siege artillery and heavy stores could be transported by water. The alternatives remaining, therefore, were to threaten New York or to undertake an offensive "into the Bowels of Canada." For either of these purposes a junction of the two armies on the Hudson was necessary. "For these reasons it is, as the French Corps has already left their Cantonments, and proceeded to Maryland; and because Baltimore is not within supporting distance of York Town, and West Point in Virginia, and too far from the Enemy's principal post of New York . . . that I have advised Count de Rochambeau to continue (by slow and easy movements) his March to the North River. . . . It is for these reasons also, I readily assented to the propriety of removing the artillery and Stores from York Town, and West Point, and to the evacuation of those Posts." Rochambeau could not assent to the Canadian proposal without further authorization from the French Court.

Washington confirmed the plan for a junction of the allied forces on the Hudson in a communication to Rochambeau dated 16 August 1782.

156. Concerning the quartering of these detachments, see La Valette's correspondence with the local authorities in *Journal and Correspondence of the State Council of Maryland, 8 (1781–1784)*, ed. J. Hall Pleasants, Archives of Maryland, xlviii (Baltimore, 1931), pp. 252ff. Officers were lodged in town, the troops in temporary barracks or huts on Whetstone Point. The detachments under La Valette and Chazelles remained in Baltimore until the following spring, when they returned directly to France in May 1783. When the main part of Rochambeau's army left Boston for the Caribbean in December 1782, these detachments and such others as were left in America (chiefly the sick), as well as Lauzun's Legion, were placed under the command of the Duc de Lauzun, who was himself under Washington's direct orders. See "Instructions pour M. le duc de Lauzun," 21 October 1782, summarized by Gontaut-Biron in his *Le Duc de Lauzun* (Paris, 1937), p. 165. Details concerning the gradual departure of the sick and wounded are given by Bouvet, *Service de santé*, pp. 104–106. Millet, a surgeon, returned to France with the last of them only in February 1784.

157. Verger, who had not taken this route the previous year (having gone by sea from Newport to Virginia), gives a day-by-day description of it in his journal, pp. 161ff. See Vol. ii, Nos. 131–143, for maps of the successive camps.

to return to our country. All our thoughts therefore turned on New York, and we firmly believed at that moment that the army was marching there with this aim in view.

September 1782

Once again we crossed the Susquehanna, but this time in boats, which enabled us to avoid the bad roads and made the journey much shorter.[158]

We arrived in Philadelphia on 3 September and remained there one day. The troops paraded before Congress as they had done the year before. The Chevalier de La Luzerne, the French envoy to the United States, had us to dine both days in the pavilion he had had built for the fête he gave to celebrate the birth of the Dauphin.[159] This room was beautifully decorated and the various emblems on its walls very well conceived. Of these I shall cite only two that seemed to me to do honor to the designer. At the east end of the room was a rising sun surmounted by 13 stars (the arms of America) with an Indian watching the sunrise and apparently dazzled by its rays. Beside the Indian in the same picture was a woman, representing England, emptying a sack of gold into the

hands of another Indian, who throws the gold at her feet with obvious contempt. At the opposite end of the room were the arms of France with a sun at its zenith lighting the world. And there were also several other emblems appropriate to the event that had occasioned the fête. The pavilion was 100 feet long; its walls were supported by a colonnade 30 to 40 feet high.

We learned in Philadelphia that the unfortunate case of Captain Asgill had not yet been resolved. Each day he awaited execution in reprisal for the cruelty of a Loyalist captain [Richard Lippincott] who had captured a captain of the American militia [Joshua Huddy] and, after subjecting him to unspeakable torture, had hung him from a tree, attaching a placard to his back (while exposing his body on a public highway) reading: "Thus we shall treat all who rebel against their king and country." When General Washington heard of this atrocity, he wrote the English general asking him to turn over the Loyalist captain to him. If he refused, Washington said he would have lots drawn among the officers captured with Cornwallis and would hang whichever officer fate decreed. This turned out to be Captain Asgill, who came of a very good family in England, was an only son, and would be heir to a very large fortune. The English general was much embarrassed because, although he

158. The crossing was made at Lower Ferry (Havre de Grace); the previous year Clermont-Crèvecœur had crossed upstream at Bald Friar Ford (above, p. 53).

159. The designer of the pavilion ("a large frame building erected for a dancing room") on the grounds of the French Legation at the corner of Chestnut and Seventh Streets was Pierre-Charles L'Enfant (future planner of the city of Washington), a French engineer in American service whom Washington had lent to La Luzerne at the latter's request; La Luzerne to Washington, 22 April 1782, in Library of Congress, Washington Papers, and Washington's reply, 27 April 1782, in *Writings of GW*, XXIV, 174. Several contemporary descriptions of the great fête of 15 July have survived. The most elaborate is the one written by Dr. Benjamin Rush, first published in the *Columbian Magazine*, February 1787, reprinted in L. H. Butterfield, ed., *Letters of Benjamin Rush* (Princeton, 1951), I, 278–284; see also J. T. Scharf and T. Westcott, *History of Philadelphia* (Philadelphia, 1884), I, 420–421, and Stone, *French Allies*, pp. 505–508 (with facsimile of one of the printed invitations). According to Dr. Rush, "the Minister had borrowed thirty cooks from the French army to

assist in providing for an entertainment suited to the size and dignity of the company." Although they did not go to Philadelphia specifically for this purpose, the fortuitous presence of both Rochambeau and Washington lent added *éclat* to the occasion. Annis Boudinot Stockton, in her sylvan retreat in Princeton, was inspired to compose "An Ode on the Birth of the Dauphin of France"; see L. H. Butterfield, "Morven: A Colonial Outpost of Sensibility, with some hitherto unpublished Poems by Annis Boudinot Stockton," *Princeton University Library Chronicle*, VI, No. 1 (Nov. 1944), 1–15. Speaking through the Princeton muse, the "Genius of America" bade

> Tritons, convey to Gallia's royal ear
> The pleasing transport on our heart engraved:
> To none more dear is France's blooming heir
> Than to the people whom his father sav'd.

"France's blooming heir," born at Versailles on 22 October 1781, died in 1789; his younger brother (b. 25 March 1785) then became Dauphin and, after his father's execution, the hapless Louis XVII—the "lost Dauphin" of American frontier mythology.

wished to deliver the guilty man to the Americans, the Loyalists declared that if he did they would lay down their arms. There were long conferences between the English and American generals from which the Americans derived no satisfaction, and Asgill's execution was declared necessary. The mother of this unfortunate man wrote the Comte de Vergennes, begging him to intercede for her son. This great minister deigned to take an interest in the fate of the distressed family and spoke to the King, who ordered him to write on his behalf to Congress. The touching letter this minister wrote on behalf of his sovereign had the desired effect, since it obtained Asgill's pardon. All Europe had been concerned with his misfortune.[160]

We heard no other news in Philadelphia. We left on 5 September and stayed in Trenton until the 8th. From there we departed in two divisions and arrived on the 16th at the Hudson River.[161] On the 17th we crossed the river and camped on the other side at Peekskill,[162] where we found 8,000 men of the American army. They were far different troops from those of the previous year. Now they were all uniformed and well groomed. We were struck with the transformation of this army into one that was in no way inferior to ours in appearance. Their officers, too, were well turned out.

On 21 September General Washington reviewed our army. The troops filed past him and, despite the long journey they had just made, still appeared magnificent. On the 22nd we went to watch the maneuvers of the American army and were truly impressed.[163] This proves what money and good officers can do to make good soldiers.

In general the American troops are quite good. They stand fast under fire and give a good account of themselves. The Americans have always had a certain number of fine soldiers, albeit very few. From these the Continental regiments were formed at the beginning of the war. The Americans put all told about 20,000 troops into the field, but the majority were militia, raised for a particular expedition, who went home the moment after their victory or defeat.

How can one expect such men to be good soldiers? They cannot, nor could they ever be, equal to our militia in France. Living with their families in peace and quiet for a hundred years, the Americans became accustomed to a soft life in the midst of plenty, their fertile soil supplying their every need. How could these people be soldiers, especially now that the war seems to have no end and they have grown thoroughly tired of it, most of them from disillusionment and others from sheer inconstancy?

It is true that at the beginning of the Revolution they struck the enemy some mighty blows, but then they were dealing with small English forces and the spirit of liberty had filled them with fanaticism. After their initial successes this spirit was carried to a degree of inconceivable fervor. Later on, before the arrival of Rochambeau's army, General Washington had the greatest difficulty collecting enough troops to defend the indispensable posts. True, Washington ran out of money, and half of Congress had sold out to the English and supplied him with very little. It is to this general's further credit that he managed to hold on to important positions with his feeble resources, despite the powerful opposition of England who seemed during this time to be occupying the whole American empire.

The arrival of the French army raised the Americans' spirits to some degree. They had been almost ready to submit to the yoke and abandon the project of becoming free and independent when their hopes

---

160. The French intervention in the Asgill affair was based on the fact that Captain Charles Asgill was among the Yorktown prisoners who were protected against reprisals by Article 14 of the Articles of Capitulation; see Rochambeau (2), I, 304–305. Washington's letter to Asgill, dated from his headquarters, 13 November 1782, and enclosing the Act of Congress of 7 November "by which you are released from the disagreeable circumstances in which you have so long been," is in *Writings of GW*, xxv, 336–337. Katherine Mayo, *General Washington's Dilemma* (New York, 1938), provides a good account of the Asgill affair and its international repercussions. A sentimental novel entitled *Asgill, ou les désordres des guerres civiles*, by M. de Mayer, was published in Amsterdam and Paris, 1784.

161. A note dated Haverstraw, 16 September 1782, from M. de Villemanzy, commissary, to M. de Menonville, acting chief of staff, requests the latter to specify in the day's orders that officers must take provisions for two days and the men for four, preparatory to their crossing the Hudson. D. B. Updike Autograph Collection, Providence Public Library.

162. See map of the French camp at Peekskill, Vol. II, No. 143.

163. Cf. the description in Verger's journal, p. 166.

were revived by the protection guaranteed America by the King of France. From that time on Washington's army grew from day to day.

Now, after the defeat and capture of the army of Cornwallis, General Washington has under his command 10,000–12,000 regular troops with which to oppose the English, who have a like number in New York. He has prevented his enemies from making, or even attempting, any incursion into the country he controls. The English are thus prevented from securing meat for their army on this continent and are obliged to remain in New York to await supplies from England. At the same time General [Nathanael] Greene commands part of the southern territory, where he has managed to contain the English in Charleston. They are bottled up in that place as they are in New York.

The English have already lost two armies in this country. The expense of holding New York and Charleston is incredible. Although ostensibly in possession of these two places, can they ever hope to conquer a country that can defend itself and that has so extensive a coast? It seems impossible, and one cannot conceive how the English government can pretend to prosecute a plan so utterly chimerical. People maintained, furthermore, that everything had changed after the battle of 12 April [Battle of the Saints] and that the English were determined to evacuate in America all posts that belonged to the thirteen colonies. The moves made by the English clearly indicated their intention. They had already evacuated Savannah [11 July 1782]. Troops were being embarked in New York and Charleston. Everything pointed to an evacuation. Our march until then was to oppose this plan, for fear that their troops might descend upon our colonies [in the West Indies] where their ships were blockading most of our ports. But we had yet to discover how the English would dare evacuate New York within sight of an American army of 10,000 men plus 5,000 French, not counting 20,000 militia whom General Washington could call up within three or four days in case of need. I believe that the English really wanted to evacuate New York but that they were much embarrassed to find some means of executing such a plan. The interests of France were clearly to try and prevent this for the sake of the future security

of our islands. The English would not have been able to evacuate New York without heavy losses while the French fleet was in Boston and the Americans faced them in force.

Subsequent events justified the opinions I have just expressed. The English could not send their forces to the Antilles, since they would have had to abandon New York and its immense stores, leaving a weak garrison to be besieged by 10,000 good American troops who could watch their every move. Moreover, this would have meant abandoning the Loyalists, who had no other protection than the King's troops. We can see today the miserable fate of these Loyalists, abandoned by the Americans whom they had forsaken, who are now wards of the English government, which does not know how to get rid of them.

24 September We learned that the frigates *Aigle* and *Gloire*, bringing back to America the Baron de Vioménil (who had returned to France two months after the surrender of Cornwallis) as well as the Duc de Lauzun, the Marquis de Laval, the Comte de Ségur, the Prince de Broglie, and other passengers, had been pursued in Delaware Bay by 6 enemy frigates. M. de La Touche, who commanded the *Aigle* (in which the Baron de Vioménil was embarked), seeing himself pursued, decided to run up the Delaware River, though he had no pilot aboard. The *Gloire*, preceding the *Aigle* up the river, ran aground but luckily succeeded in freeing herself from the sandbank that no one knew was there. However, the *Aigle*, which drew more water, went hard aground on the same bank.

Realizing that it was now impossible to escape the enemy, M. de La Touche decided to unload his passengers into the ships' boats with all the King's money he had aboard and send them ashore. Seeing the boats lowered, the English sent their own boats in pursuit. When the Baron de Vioménil saw that the English boats were gaining on ours, he ordered part of the money thrown overboard to lighten the boats, being careful to mark the spot so that it could be retrieved at an opportune moment. This maneuver was successful. He reached the opposite shore, and the enemy returned to their ships. The Chevalier de Fontenay and MM. de Verton and de Silleul, officers of the artillery who were returning to America from France, displayed great energy in this affair and guarded the treasure day and night. Meanwhile, the enemy returned to the King's frigate and shelled her for a short time until she surrendered, since she could not hold out against the combination of forces against her. Before surrendering M. de La Touche ordered a hole punched in his ship to scuttle her, but this did not prevent the enemy from raising her and towing her into New York.

On the next day the French went back for the money they had thrown overboard and retrieved all but 150,000 *livres*. The *Gloire* had the luck to escape to Philadelphia. The passengers on the *Aigle* lost all their possessions. The Baron de Vioménil's loss was about 20,000 *écus*, and those of the others were in proportion. This event was even more unfortunate for M. de La Touche, who lost heavily. Two or three days earlier his ship and the *Gloire* had had a fight with an English warship that they presumed to be the *Hector* of 74 guns (a French vessel captured by the English in the battle of 12 April), and he was on the point of capturing her when superior enemy forces appeared and forced him to flee, abandoning his prey. These were the same ships that later chased him into the dangerous waters in which he ran aground.[164]

M. de Choisy and the other officers who had left Baltimore for an expedition returned from Boston. They informed us that there had been a question of besieging the fort held by the English at Penobscot Bay, a few leagues beyond Boston Bay, but that Washington, for very good reasons, had not wished them to undertake this venture. They also told us that, to compensate for the loss of the 74-gun ship *Magnifique* in Boston Harbor, Congress had begged M. de Vau-

dreuil to accept on behalf of His Majesty the 74-gun ship *America*. The Marquis de Vaudreuil had taken possession of this ship, which he accepted in the King's name. The ship was not completed and was as yet only a hull; however, the rigging of the *Magnifique* could be used aboard her. We learned also that M. de Bregeot, captain of the artillery, had died in the Antilles. He was a very learned man whose loss we much regretted because of his fine qualities.[165]

25 September On the 25th the whole army left the camp at Peekskill to encamp at Crompond, 9 miles beyond, where we acted as the vanguard of the American army.[166] Our new position was very military but very disagreeable, since it had no water. We had to drink from a neighboring pond where the water was not good. Autumn was beginning and we already felt the cold. The troops built barracks, for we expected to remain there two more months before taking up our winter quarters. We did not yet know where these would be, but each man expressed his feelings on the subject. However, we were far from believing those whose guess came nearest to the truth. They said that Rochambeau's army would soon leave for Boston to embark for the Islands. How could anyone reasonably devise such a plan? Nevertheless, you shall soon see that this was the one that the Comte de Rochambeau had been ordered to execute.

Nothing remarkable happened at Crompond. The English did not disturb us, and we did not seek to disturb them. The order to depart was issued on 23 October, together with our route to Hartford. We arrived there the 30th, passing through the same places as last year.[167] We found that the roads had not im-

164. Several of the passengers on the *Gloire* and *Aigle* wrote vivid accounts of their adventures. See Broglie (1), pp. 28–35; Ségur (1), pp. 163–166 (letter to his wife from Philadelphia, 16 September 1782), and (2), I, 364–383; Montesquieu (3), pp. 258–260 (letter to Saint-Chamans from Philadelphia, 18 September 1782); Lauzun (2), pp. 310–311. A brief report written by the Baron de Vioménil to the Marquis de Ségur, minister of war, dated 17 September 1782, was printed in newspapers of the day (e.g., *Courier de l'Europe*, 22 November 1782); translation in *Magazine of American History*, VII (1881), 34–35, and in Vioménil (1), pp. 46–48.

165. Louis-Georges Mollet de Bregeot, born in Epinal on 5 September 1749, arrived in America with Rochambeau's army as one of the senior first lieutenants of the Auxonne artillery, of which Clermont-Crèvecœur was the junior.

By 1781 Bregeot had been promoted captain and was waiting for a company command to fall vacant at the time of his death at Fort Royal, Martinique, in 1782. Having been born but a few miles from Crèvecœur's own birthplace, and being only two years older, his death must have been keenly felt by the author. See *Les Combattants*, p. 314; *État militaire*, 1780, 1781, 1782.

166. See map of the "Hunt's Tavern" camp, Vol. II, No. 145, and, for its relationship to the surrounding region, the large map of the "Position of the American and French Armies at King's Ferry, Peekskill, Crompond and Hunt's Tavern, from 17 September to 20 October 1782," No. 146.

167. Maps of the 1782 campsites along the route from Crompond to Hartford are in Vol. II, Nos. 147–151.

proved one whit; however, the artillery had better teams. We supposed when leaving Crompond that Hartford was the town in which we would take up our winter quarters, but no sooner had we arrived there than these hopes were dashed.

❧ November 1782 ❧

The Comte de Rochambeau no longer concealed from us that the army was bound for Boston to embark in the squadron of the Marquis de Vaudreuil. Our fate was no longer in doubt. It was really very disagreeable, after such a hard campaign, to be deprived of the rest that we believed we had earned. This news made the whole army sad. Still, we had to make the best of it.

We stayed four days in Hartford. The artillery marched in a single column and arrived in Providence on 9 November.[168] I cannot express how uncomfortable we were while camping in a country where the cold was already very intense. We were frozen in our tents. And the tents were frozen so stiff that, after the pegs and poles were removed to take them down, they stood alone. So you can judge how cold it was.[169]

While in Providence I had nothing better to do than go and see my old friends in Newport. I found that city quite deserted, but in compensation all faces lighted up when they saw the French returning. I stayed three days in this town with much satisfaction. It is perhaps the town in all America where the French received the greatest tokens of friendship from the Americans. I confess that I left Newport with regret. It was in Newport that I learned English during the ten months the army spent there.[170] I believe that the regrets I express here are only natural, considering that I was leaving a charming country and warm friends to go to a wild and torrid land, as will presently be seen. Such is the soldier's lot.

Since we were about to depart for Boston, I returned to Providence, which we quit on 16 November, leaving the infantry in barracks 3 miles from town.[171] As M. de Vaudreuil's squadron was not yet ready to sail, we had had to put the troops in barracks. The artillery left first because of the large amount of matériel to be embarked.

We arrived in Boston on the 19th. The troops were lodged in vacant houses, the officers also. We had fairly comfortable lodgings, but those of the troops were most inadequate. The distance from Providence to Boston is 45 miles. The roads are charming. The cities and towns [Wrentham, Dedham], as well as the country we passed through, intimated what Boston would be like. It is one of the finest cities not only in America but in the whole world.

The city is very large and well built, but not as beautiful as Philadelphia. It is situated on a peninsula that makes it a fortress in itself, since it is surrounded by water, except for a single causeway that connects the city with the mainland. This causeway is on the town side and is defended by two redoubts. On two high hills in the middle of town, which dominate the harbor, forts have been built to protect the anchorage. They are equipped with very good guns. Farther back

168. From Hartford to Providence the army took the same route as the previous year; see maps, Vol. II, Nos. 152–156.

169. Lieutenant de Coriolis, of the Bourbonnais Regiment, wrote to his brother from Providence, 12 November 1782: "You may imagine what it is to be under canvas in very heavy frosts, which will soon be accompanied by two feet of snow, usual in this region at the beginning of December. As for myself, I am fortunate in experiencing none of these inconveniences and I am campaigning in the most agreeable way possible. The Marquis de Laval [colonel of his regiment] . . . has been good enough to take me into his household on the same footing [as his newly arrived aide-de-camp, the Comte de Langeron], so that I am always lodged and, what is still more agreeable, have no inn to pay for at the end of the month, either for myself or my servant. True, my new situation has necessitated a bit more expense for horses: I have three, which cost me a lot of money, and I shall have to sell them for almost nothing when we leave." Coriolis (3), p. 814.

170. The French were still a subject of conversation in Newport when Francisco de Miranda visited the city in September 1784. "I had tea with Miss Champlin and her mother; their company was so gracious and so instructive in matters relating to the character, procedures, and way of living of the French during their stay here in the army of Monsieur de Rochambeau that I remained there until nine o'clock." *The New Democracy in America, Travels of Francisco de Miranda in the United States, 1783–84,* tr. Judson P. Wood, ed. John S. Ezell (Norman, Okla., 1963), p. 135.

171. See map of the camp in North Providence, Vol. II, No. 156.

in the city is another hill on which is located the famous beacon that is lighted to alert the whole coast and call out the militia.

From this hill one can enjoy the most beautiful view imaginable. The whole city is spread out before you, as well as the harbor with its islands in the middle and the various forts built to prevent the approach of enemy ships. You can see across the harbor the town of Charlestown, which the English burned after the battle the Americans won at the beginning of the Revolution. You can also see the position that General Washington occupied during the battle. The Americans were blockaded in the city by the English fleet and on the land side, where the city joins the mainland, by their army. Washington succeeded in posting part of his troops on a hill that dominated the harbor.[172] There he emplaced his batteries. This position was so advantageous to the Americans that the English retired, not wishing to expose their ships to the fire from the batteries; thus the much inferior force was victorious.

The amount of commerce carried on in Boston makes it one of the richest cities in the world. All the inhabitants are merchants. The large number of foreigners who have been attracted here by trade add no little to the city's prosperity. Its commerce consists principally of hides, leather, wood for construction, flour, etc. The townspeople are so engrossed in their business affairs that they seem to have time for little else. They are casual and inscrutable. All I can say is that, of all the people in America, we have found them the coldest; however, those of us who have gotten to know some Bostonians declare that they were received with coldness at first but later with frankness and graciousness or, if you will, with more courtesy. Actually one cannot expect too much of this from Americans. For the rest, they have one individual characteristic in that, when you get to know them, you find them at least sincere and satisfactory to deal with.

As a rule their "assemblies" could not be drearier.

When you arrive, you find tea on the table and you drink some. This ceremony accomplished, the ladies retire to their own apartments (into which you are never admitted, by the way, until you are well known to the family, and even then only with great ceremony). The men linger to smoke or chew tobacco and talk politics. This is what is generally known here as "good company," which is found only among the rich.

The governor's mansion is one of the prettiest houses in town; it is situated on the side of a hill and enjoys a most pleasant view.[173] His Excellency General [John] Hancock is the governor. He is the man in America who has contributed most to the Revolution. His great spirit and intellect furnished him with infinite resources with which to parry the crushing blows of the English. He was president of the Continental Congress at its inception. Afterwards he was appointed governor of Boston for life, though this was contrary to American law, which generally limits the term of a governor to three years. Today he is an old man of eighty, and although he takes little part in American affairs, he is beloved and esteemed by his fellow citizens.[174]

Besides the governor's mansion there are a number of Protestant churches and public buildings that are quite handsome. I have rarely in my life seen such pretty private houses, in both the exterior architecture and the symmetry, comfort, and cleanliness that reign within. They are almost all built of wood and painted different colors, which lend a pleasing variety to the view.

The dominant religion here is Presbyterian [Congregationalist], which is at war with all the others, especially the Quakers. The latter are in constant fear lest the former, being the stronger, will persecute them, and not only them but all the other sects. This could in time start a revolution perhaps more frightful than that which has taken place.

I note with sorrow the unhappy results for mankind of that religious tolerance which is said to ensure the

172. Clermont-Crèvecœur seems to be referring to the siege of British-occupied Boston, in 1776, when Washington occupied Dorchester Heights.

173. Hancock's mansion, no longer standing, was on a site close to the west wing of the present State House. See Walter Kendall Watkins, "The Hancock House and Its Builder," *Old-Time New England*, XVII (July 1926), 3–19.

174. Actually John "Encôque" (as Clermont-Crèvecœur writes his name) was only forty-five at this time, though his recurrent attacks of the gout no doubt made him seem much older; he died in 1793 at the age of fifty-six. James Bowdoin succeeded Hancock as governor of Massachusetts in 1785.

well-being of a state but which, in my opinion, becomes on the contrary a source of evil when a sect as intolerant and fanatic as the Presbyterian dominates through sheer numbers those living peaceably within their respective faiths. The Roman and Presbyterian religions are made to live alone and, furthermore, far apart. How many revolutions England has had, all started by the Presbyterians! Literary men have come out in favor of religious tolerance, but in expressing these sentiments they believed men were what they hoped they were, not what they are.

Happy Americans—I speak now of the country people—who live with your families in peace and plenty, whose anxieties are confined to rearing your children in the sound principles you yourselves profess! Far from the cities with their corrupt morals, your virtue derives solely from your innocence. You know nothing of the vices, nor even suspect that you may be corrupted by the very simplicity that you profess. Such are the rural Americans. But how different are those living in cities like Boston! Commerce brings in wealth, but all peoples leave their vices there. Suspicion, fraud, and insincerity characterize most American merchants. There are some honest ones, but they are very rare.

The women leave their houses very seldom. In general they are very pretty. They possess little wealth in their own right, since the law of the land allows them nothing. Their brothers inherit all their fathers' property, leaving little for their sisters. However, in this country the women enjoy many other advantages. When they are pretty and well brought up, they are sure of finding husbands. Men here do not look for fortunes but for a companion of their choice; when they are sure of her virtue and morals, they marry her. A father cannot dispose of his children against their will. However, before living their own lives, they are obliged by law to submit for a fixed term to the will of their parents. The term ends at twenty for a girl and twenty-five for a boy.

Life in Boston is very expensive yet one finds here an abundance of every sort of goods. One thing I noticed was that in the evening an oyster vendor passes through the streets crying his wares. The residents invite him into their houses to open the oysters and then have a feast. Sometimes they even stop him in the streets and eat them on the spot. These remind me of our sweetmeat vendors—but what a difference![175]

In general the habits, customs, and manners of the Bostonians are pretty much like those of the Americans I have come to know personally. You meet the same type from the Hudson River to the part of Acadia occupied by the English. I shall not stay in Boston long enough to get to know the people personally; however, I stand on what I have said, that we found the Bostonians less to our liking than any other people we met. Were a foreigner to judge the whole nation by the inhabitants of this city, he would certainly not have a very favorable impression of it.

Americans tend to express the same opinions of the French as the English do, a national prejudice that is not very favorable to either of us. We have opened many people's eyes, but I believe the Bostonians are less reasonable in this respect than others.

American cities are as much inclined towards luxury and all its trappings as ours. There is little difference between them. But go into the back country and you will find the candor, the innocence, the hospitality that characterizes the heart of a virtuous man. Simplicity still reigns there. Nature alone guides these good Americans. These are the people who suffer the calamities of war, which is ruinous for them; having very little money, they pay their taxes in produce, in cattle whose milk is their principal food. It was in the course of our travels here that we perceived the truth of what I have just said. A Frenchman can hardly be expected to like their customs because they are too simple, but a reasonable man cannot help admiring them and wishing he could live such a life as they enjoy.

During the whole course of our stay in Boston we were kept busy embarking all the artillery with the ammunition and equipment, which was hard work in

175. Clermont-Crèvecœur's term, translated here as "sweetmeat vendors," is *vendeurs d'oublies*. In eighteenth-century France *oublies* (*oublayes*) were thin waffles or wafers made of sugar, eggs, and honey; the *oublieurs* (*oublieux*), known to later generations as *marchands de plaisir*, hawked their wares through the streets in a char-

acteristic basket strapped to their backs, generally at night, as the police regulations for their guild required. See Marguerite Pitsch, *La Vie populaire à Paris au XVIIIᵉ siècle, d'après les textes contemporains et les estampes* (Paris, 1949), pp. 65–67 and Figs. 92–94.

the cold weather we were having. The officers mounted guard at the park and we spent the nights in bivouac, which was not very amusing; but the service of the king demanded it.

December 1782

Finally everything was loaded, and on 1 December we received orders to go aboard ourselves. I was assigned to the *Amazone* together with half of the Maisonneuve Company, which I commanded. The rest of the army arrived, regiment by regiment, for the same purpose. I embarked on 1 December.[176] The Comte de Rochambeau, who had led us as far as Providence, went from there to Philadelphia to embark for France.[177] He quit his army at a very critical moment, leaving his command to the Baron de Vioménil. We were grieved that the Comte de Rochambeau should leave us when we were involved in an expedition such as this. We were bound for the Islands, and this idea, together with the loss of our general, only deepened our despondency, though this was somewhat diminished by the presence of the Baron de Vioménil, who replaced him.[178] We ought to have been satisfied, since

176. A list of the vessels comprising the Marquis de Vaudreuil's fleet is included in Berthier's journal, p. 257. Detailed embarkation lists indicating the assignment of army officers and units to the different ships are given in the "Etat Général d'Embarquement fait à Boston en Décembre 1782," Cromot Dubourg (2), pp. 19–31. A somewhat similar but less complete list is printed in Noailles, *Marins et Soldats*, Appendix XI, pp. 406–409. Under the heading "Second Bataillon du Régiment d'Auxonne, Individus attachés au Parc, & Autres" the Cromot Dubourg embarkation list (p. 27) places in the *Northumberland*: Crèvecœur, Lieutenant en 1er, Thiballier, Lieutenant en 2me, Haen, Lieutenant en 3me d'ouvriers, with one-half of Maisonneuve Company, 23 men. The same list places in the *Amazone*: Maisonneuve, Capitaine, Siccard, Lieutenant en 3me, with one-half of Maisonneuve Company, 23 men. There is therefore a discrepancy between this list and the author's statement in the journal that he was embarked in the *Amazone*. This contradiction was taken into account by the Editors when attributing the journal to Clermont-Crèvecœur (see Introduction to journal, p. 4) but was outweighed by other evidence. We have concluded, despite the Cromot Dubourg list, that First Lieutenant Crèvecœur was in the *Amazone* with half the Maisonneuve Company of the Auxonne Regiment, while the other half of the company, with Captain Maisonneuve, was in the *Northumberland*.

177. Rochambeau embarked on the frigate *Emeraude* at Annapolis on 8 January 1783. Among the other passengers (seventeen officers in all) were: the Vicomte de Rochambeau (the General's son), Chastellux, Choisy, Béville, Béville's two sons, Vauban, Lauberdière, Montesquieu, the Vicomte de Vaudreuil (a young cousin of the Marquis and Comte de Vaudreuil who had served as Chastellux's aide-de-camp), Dr. Coste. The *Emeraude*, commanded by M. de Quémy, cleared the Chesapeake Capes on 14 January, was pursued for thirty hours by an English 64, ran into a violent storm on the 16th, sighted the Azores on the 30th, lost a man in a thunderstorm off Cape Finisterre,

and finally anchored off Saint-Nazaire at the mouth of the Loire on 10 February 1783. Rochambeau's narrative report, "Journal de notre Navigation," is in the Archives de la Guerre (Vincennes), A 3734; a rewritten version of this is in his *Mémoires*, I, 318–319. Chastellux's account of the crossing is in a letter written to Jeremiah Wadsworth from Paris, 31 May 1783; original in Wadsworth Papers, Connecticut Historical Society; excerpt printed in Chastellux (4), II, 660.

178. On his departure from Boston with the French army Vioménil wrote the following letter to Washington, in reply to one from the Commander in Chief expressing his regret at not being able, owing to the requirements of military secrecy, to bid the French farewell in person:

"Boston, December 18, 1782. Sir: The veneration with which this army has been imbued for you since the first instant it was presented to you by Count Rochambeau, its confidence in your talents, the wisdom of your orders, the ineffaceable memories of your kindnesses, of your attentions, and of the examples you have given us when danger was near, and the approval, regrets, and wishes with which you have so generously now honored our departure, are reasons enough to make us bound in duty to say that there is not a single general or officer in the army which has just been entrusted to me who is not more deeply moved rather than flattered by your praise. There is not one among us who does not regret infinitely that the secrecy attending our departure has prevented us from keeping our agreement to be presented again to you by Count Rochambeau, that we might pay you our respects, thank you, and let you see our faces, beaming with appreciation. Having thus conveyed the general sentiments of all of us towards you, I beg you to permit me to take this occasion to assure you again that every sentiment I have expressed for my comrades will be as lasting as the very deep respect with which I am, Your Excellency's very humble and obedient servant, Vioménil. P.S. At this very moment the Marquis de Vaudreuil is giving order that his fleet be ready to sail on Sunday, and from

the latter was beloved and esteemed throughout the army. However, we had not been at all prepared for this event and it filled us with alarm. Such is the soldier's lot. Since he owes his livelihood to the state, he therefore owes it any sacrifice.

A moment of pleasure and repose makes us forget all the hardships we have had to endure. Perhaps one day I shall enjoy this long-awaited moment; then I shall savor all the pleasure I have found in supporting my country and furthering its interests. But how could men exhausted in mind and body by the fatigues of a long campaign feel this?

I shall not try to explain here the political reasons for the voyage we were about to make. That is a mystery it is not up to me to unravel at the moment. We were told only that the squadron of the Marquis de Vaudreuil was going to the Antilles. Several officers of the staff had already returned to France, among them the Chevalier de Chastellux, major general and chief of staff of the army. Many infantry officers had resigned, despite the Comte de Rochambeau's positive assurances that within six months the army would be in France. At that moment this was too much to hope for. Subsequent events, however, justified our general's prediction.

I faithfully stayed aboard ship as long as we remained in Boston harbor.[179] It was very cold and, besides, the ships were anchored 6 miles from the city. The journey back and forth had to be made by water, and I did not enjoy it. Thus, after being embarked for 22 days, we waited each day for orders to set sail.

22 December The *Amazone* finally left for Portsmouth, a city 45 miles north of Boston. We arrived on the 23rd at the entrance to the harbor, but bad weather prevented our entering. We sent the Comte de Vaudreuil the dispatches that had been entrusted to the captain of our frigate by the Marquis, his brother.

The Comte de Vaudreuil had gone to Portsmouth to have his ship, the *Auguste*, repaired and had been joined there by the *Pluton* for the same purpose.

25 December Thanks to a favorable wind we were able to enter, and we anchored alongside the *Auguste* and *Pluton*. The Comte de Vaudreuil was ready to sail. He awaited only a favorable wind to leave the harbor. The two vessels he commanded were needed by the Marquis's squadron, which had left Boston on the 24th. But it was impossible for us to leave the harbor until the evening of the 29th because of head winds.

Portsmouth is quite large.[180] There are pretty houses here, but the town, like others in America, seems nearly ruined as a result of the war. Its commerce has been reduced to a minimum; it exports nothing but cod, which it sends to the Antilles. Actually this trade is quite profitable. It also exports cattle and other produce in which the country abounds. The men here are more inured to hard work than anywhere I have been. The women have stronger characters, are more active, and are generally pretty. It is very cold here in the winter. We felt the cold keenly, but the air is healthy and salubrious.

We left in Portsmouth the staff officers of the *Magnifique* who were to take over the *America*. We saw this ship, which is very handsome and very well built but which has no stern gallery. There is still six months' work to be done on her before she will be ready for sea.[181]

29 December We finally set sail together with the two warships *Auguste* and *Pluton*, the transport *Reine de France*, and several American vessels.[182] On the night of 30–31 December we ran into a storm which scattered the fleet. On the morning of the 31st we sighted no other ship except the *Reine de France*. It is useless to relate all that we suffered during the bad weather. The severe cold only added to our difficul-

all signs, when this letter is relayed to you, we shall have lost sight of this continent. . . ." Library of Congress, Washington Papers; translation in Vioménil (1), pp. 58–59.

179. See map of Boston harbor, Vol. II, No. 159.

180. See Crublier d'Opterre's map, Vol. II, No. 160, "Plan de la Ville et du Port de Portsmouth, dans la New-Hampshire" (Paul Mellon Collection). Crublier d'Opterre, captain in the Royal Corps of Engineers, embarked at Portsmouth on the *Auguste*.

181. Concerning the *America* (which did not live up to its promises), see n. 151.

182. Aristide Du Petit-Thouars was second in command, under M. de Gaston, of Clermont-Crèvecœur's ship, the frigate *Amazone*; see Du Petit-Thouars (2), pp. 92ff., which complements this part of Clermont-Crèvecœur's journal. The voyage of the *Auguste*, from which Clermont-Crèvecœur's ship the *Amazone* became separated, is recorded in the journal of the Comte de Vaudreuil (*Neptunia*, No. 50, pp. 31ff.).

ties. I felt the most disagreeable sensations, since for the first time in my life I was seasick; but the weather was so bad that it would have been difficult not to have succumbed. The gale, which lasted two or three days but which did not hold us back, was followed by delightful weather. We regretted only having been separated from the two warships; being responsible for the *Reine de France* was not exactly a pleasure.

ᚎ *January 1783* ᚎ

For the next three or four days the weather was so pleasant that we hardly expected to encounter a new storm a hundred times worse than what we had just been through. We were not far from the Bermuda islands off the American coast at 32° north latitude when, during the night of 6–7 January, the wind rose and the sea increased until our frigate was laboring painfully, particularly on the crests of the waves. She was shipping a lot of water, and at each moment the deck was lashed by waves of such monstrous size that they seemed about to engulf her. You could not stand up in any part of the ship, her motion was so violent and so unpleasant. At one moment she was knocked down on her port side with such violence that the shock knocked my hammock, where I was at the time, off its hooks and the hammock and I went careening into space and landed in the corner of the cabin. Tired and sleepy as I was, I awoke with a start and found myself afloat as I heard the sound of a wave rushing into the ship and through it from stem to stern. Just imagine what a waterfall sounds like when pouring from the top of a cliff to the bottom of a valley and you will have a very faint idea of the noise water makes when it pours into the hollows of a ship. Added to this were the lamentations of the crew, who believed that we were sinking and were invoking the aid of every saint in paradise.

I sincerely believed that we were about to die. All my troubles were annihilated in grief. I was no longer capable of making sad reflections on the danger ahead and the horrors I was witnessing, since I had already made up my mind that this was the end. However, when I no longer heard water rushing into the ship, I extricated myself from my corner as best I could and went on deck. Everyone told me in hushed tones of the danger we had been in. The frigate had been knocked down and held under for two or three minutes by a wave she had been unable to avoid. Axes had been passed out to chop down the masts, which is the only recourse in such an emergency. But the vessel righted herself, and we got off with a good soaking.

During this storm the frigate suffered considerable damage. Our masts were broken, our sails torn, and one of our quarterhouses (a locker protruding from the stern) was carried away. We were obliged to jettison one of our boats. Our cattle, sheep, several chickens, and a large part of our provisions were lost. Since the ship was badly damaged on the port side, the captain was obliged to run off before the wind, in the opposite direction to our course for the Antilles.

The storm lasted three days and three nights. On the morning of the fourth day the weather was once more serene, and we resumed our course and repaired as best we could the damage we had suffered. We had become separated from the *Reine de France*, which we met again five days later. The previous day she had been engaged in combat by a 14-gun privateer. Having only 2 guns herself, she fought this vessel for five hours and would have captured it had not darkness intervened. The *Reine de France* was carrying 300 men of The Cape and Champagne regiments,[183] but she had very little ammunition.

11 January We ran into bad weather again, but it was nothing in comparison to the last two storms. We were approaching the trade winds, which you pick up at 28° north latitude. The cold had departed and the temperature was delightful. We crossed the Tropic of Cancer on the 18th and on the 21st sighted the island of Puerto Rico. We spoke the fort at San Juan, where we were informed that the Marquis de Vaudreuil's squadron had spent six days cruising up and down before the island, that English forces were to windward and leeward of us, that Admiral Pigott's squadron of 19 warships was waiting off Saint-Domingue to

183. These detachments were ships' garrisons, brought to New England from the West Indies in Vaudreuil's squadron only in the late summer of 1782; they were not, strictly speaking, a part of Rochambeau's (now Vioménil's) army. See n. 117 on ships' garrisons.

prevent us from joining up with the Spaniards there, and that M. de Vaudreuil had picked up at Puerto Rico 16 transports of a fleet that had been escorted out from France by M. de La Bretonnière, commander of the frigate *Cérès*. These vessels were loaded with ammunition and provisions of all sorts.[184]

23 January Once we had all the news, we set our course for the entrance to the Puerto Rico Channel, which we entered on the 23rd. Meanwhile, we ordered the *Reine de France* to proceed into Puerto Rico harbor. Whether through disobedience or through inability to reach the harbor, she allowed herself to fall down to leeward where she ran into an enemy squadron south of Santo Domingo that captured her and took her into Jamaica.

24 January In the morning we sighted several sail heading south that, according to the information we had been given at Puerto Rico, we took to be our own squadron. We were not mistaken, and we made a reunion with the squadron at noon.[185] Up to this time we had not known where we were to rendezvous. Having cleared the Puerto Rico Channel and evaded the enemy, we learned that the squadron was bound for Puerto Cabello on the coast of Caracas [Venezuela] in South America. Thus we still had 140 leagues [490 miles] to go.

28 January We sighted Curaçao, but unfortunately we mistook it for Bonaire, a small island containing several houses inhabited by Dutchmen; we were far down to leeward at that time and Bonaire was well to windward. We passed Curaçao to leeward. Night had fallen by then. The next day we sighted the mainland at Cape San Román, indicating that we were well to leeward of Puerto Cabello. As the transports were lagging far behind, we were ordered to go back, with the *Cérès*, to round them up and consequently became separated from the rest of the fleet. Almost all our efforts were in vain, since we only succeeded in rallying 6 or 7. We thought it would be very easy to return to windward, but were much mistaken. We could not manage to round the point to windward of us, so after fighting headwinds and adverse currents for eight days, M. de La Bretonnière gave special instructions to the convoy and we concentrated on our own efforts

to come up to windward. The *Cérès*, which was faster than the *Amazone*, was soon out of sight, so that next day we found ourselves alone.

For two or three days we saw nothing more. Finally we spied a little schooner. We tacked up and took off a Spanish pilot, who gave us the great pleasure of telling us where we were, since we did not have the least idea. Our charts were poor, and no one in our crew had ever sailed in these waters before. The pilot, whose presence on board reassured us, told us the dreadful news that one of our warships had been lost on the coast and that he himself had picked up 13 men from the wreckage. He could not remember the name of the ship but assured us that the captain and 400 men had been landed safely. He also told us that we ourselves had been in great danger and that, had we not tacked when we did, we should have been wrecked on a reef two or three minutes later. It was a stroke of luck that we met the pilot when we did.

❧ *February 1783* ❧

5 February We sighted the port and town of Curaçao. We recognized three of our ships anchored in the harbor: the *Couronne*, the *Neptune*, and the *Hercule*. By then we were very anxious about the rest of our ships, though we had every reason to believe they had reached Puerto Cabello. We also sighted two ships we believed to be the *Souverain* and the *Northumberland*. By next day we had gained a good distance on them to windward when the *Souverain* signaled us to come within hail. This was a cruel blow to us, for in one moment we saw the work of several days undone; but we had to obey. We bore away and came back to the *Souverain*, which informed us that it was the *Bourgogne* that had sunk, but that no further details were known. The commander also told us that he had been cruising here for several days and that he was very much worried about the Admiral, whose ship [*Triomphant*] he had seen falling way down to leeward; that, furthermore, he had heard several merchant vessels sending distress signals and begged us to

184. See Verger's journal, under date of 16 January, p. 171, and Berthier's journal, p. 258.

185. Verger's journal (p. 172) notes the arrival of the *Amazone* on this date.

go and see if we could give them any assistance, and also tell them that the convoy was to rendezvous at Curaçao.

We immediately sailed back before the wind and soon reached one of them. We asked for news of the Admiral and of the vessels that had fired distress signals. They replied that they had no information; however, several declared that they had run out of provisions. We gave them as much as we could spare and told them they should go and anchor in Curaçao, which was not more than 25 or 30 miles away. They received this news with joy. We were also pleased to have been able to make ourselves useful to them, which consoled us for having lost so much time. It was really depressing to see the pitiful state these vessels were in. They had had only two weeks' supply of food and water aboard, yet it had been three since we had left Puerto Rico together.

We went back to the *Souverain* to report on the results of our mission. We told her we had a pilot,

and she replied that she would follow us and that we should go on ahead and signal our courses. For three days we tried to make headway without result; then, since we had run out of water, we asked permission to put into Curaçao, which was granted.

13 February The *Hercule* had just left the harbor, so the *Souverain* followed her. As for us, we entered the port and dropped anchor on 13 February.

There we learned all details of the loss of the *Bourgogne*.[186] There were 9 officers drowned, 2 from the navy and 7 from the army, including 4 from the Bourbonnais Regiment and 1 from the artillery. They had been put on a raft which, being too heavily laden, capsized; few of its occupants were saved. The disorder that reigned on board the ship immediately after it ran aground had been appalling. This was said to have been the fault of the captain [M. de Champmartin], who had neither the common sense nor the presence of mind to bring order out of the chaos that resulted from the lack of discipline on board. There

186. The Chevalier de Coriolis, a lieutenant in the Bourbonnais Regiment, who was on the *Bourgogne*, gives a detailed account of the wreck and timetable of events in his "Relation du naufrage de la *Bourgogne*," later published in the *Revue Militaire Française*, II (1870), 262–289. Coriolis places the time when the ship went aground during the night of 3–4 February 1783 at a quarter past midnight. The spot was a league and a half off Point "Lubero" (Punta Uvero) on the northern coast of Venezuela (map, Vol. II, No. 168). The first survivors to bring news to Puerto Cabello were Ensign Pinsun and Colonel Desandroüins, who arrived there on the evening of 6 February. The frigate *Néréide*, dispatched that same evening, reached the scene of the wreck at seven in the morning of 7 February. Coriolis himself, with a detachment of 30 soldiers and 30 sailors, left Punta Uvero on 7 February, proceeding overland via Capadare, Rio di Tocuyo, Sanare and Yaracuy, to Puerto Cabello, which they reached on 13 February; other detachments arrived on the days following. Like the journals of Clermont-Crèvecœur, Verger (pp. 172, 173), and Berthier (p. 260), virtually all the extant journals for this campaign give hearsay comments on the wreck of the *Bourgogne* and severely criticize the commander of the ship, M. de Champmartin. Coriolis's vivid but restrained eyewitness account also blames the commander: "The conduct of M. de Champmartin has been sharply blamed by his entire corps and by everybody in general. The King's ordinance is positive: the captain of a ship, in all cases whatsoever, will be the last to leave his ship and will save himself last. Never-

theless, when the frigate *Néréide* came alongside the *Bourgogne*, she found 250 men without officers. The danger was not so very pressing (and M. de Champmartin should have realized this), since a month later a part of the wrecked vessel could still be seen above the water. The public even placed a part of the blame on the officers commanding the different detachments on board; but the order to embark, which had been definitely given them, was their justification, M. de Champmartin having assured them that he would be the last to leave the ship. They would certainly have done better to refuse, but it seems to me that they cannot be blamed for having obeyed their chief." Coriolis estimated the total casualties as 120 drowned. His figure included 9 officers and a chaplain, as well as 27 men from the three companies of the Bourbonnais Regiment that were aboard. Other estimates of the casualties vary greatly. According to Von Closen (pp. 295–296), the Marquis de Vaudreuil immediately sent Champmartin home via Curaçao on a neutral ship. After his return to France Champmartin was court-martialed. His conduct was judged reprehensible, and he was suspended from his functions for three months; the sentence was not, however, carried out, and he was permitted to request retirement, which was granted "for reasons of health." Proceedings of the investigation are in the Archives Nationales, Marine B⁴, Vol. 266. A secondary account of the wreck of the *Bourgogne* is given in Noailles, *Marins et Soldats*, pp. 330–335 (but does not cite Coriolis's "Relation"). See also Maurice Lachesnais's notes to the printed version of Coriolis's "Relation."

were almost 300 men lost who might have been saved if order had been maintained. I shall say no more about this unhappy event, which, according to reports, did little honor to the ship's commander.

M. Desandroüins, colonel of engineers, was aboard. It was thanks to him and to Ensign Pinsun that the lives of the 300 men left on board were saved. Without food they marched overland through a dreadful wilderness to Puerto Cabello to seek aid.[187] The *Néréide* was sent to rescue the 300 survivors abandoned by their captain. They had not wanted to follow the example of their comrades, some of whom had drowned before their eyes when the rafts were launched. When the *Néréide* arrived, they had had nothing to eat or drink for three days except the few chickens that remained on deck, mixed with salt water.[188]

I have already said that the dangers you incur on this coast are incredible. I cannot understand how anyone could venture coming to these virtually unknown parts, where uncharted currents expose you to the risk of a shipwreck with all hands just when everything appears to be safe. M. de Vaudreuil's fleet and the remnant of M. de Rochambeau's army could not have counted for much! The former was in the worst possible condition from the storms it had been through, and the latter from sickness and the loss of men on transports scattered by the various storms and captured by the English. We heard only of misfortunes and disasters. One can truly say that, had M. de Vaudreuil's fleet been defeated in battle, it would not have suffered more damage than it sustained from being buffeted by wind and wave for 60 days, the time it took to reach this famous rendezvous with Admiral Solano, commander of the Spanish squadron at Havana, and his fleet. In the meantime, this admiral had remained peacefully at Havana, while we endured the most painful privations and frustrations.[189]

The rumors of peace that had been going the rounds every day revived our jaded spirits somewhat, for to

187. A letter written by Colonel Desandroüins to his chief in France is preserved in the Archives du Génie, Vincennes, Article 15-1-7, No. 34[10]: "At Porto-Cabello on the Coast of Caracas, 14 February 1783. Sir, The event to which I have just been exposed is so cruel and so interesting that I cannot refrain from informing you of it in a few words, the vessel that is to take this letter being about to sail. During the night of the 3rd to the 4th of this month the vessel *Bourgogne* that I was on was lost on the Coro coast a league and a half from land off Pointe D'Ubero 40 leagues from here. There were drowned 4 officers of the Bourbonnais, Messrs. de Caupenne, Trogoff, Mérindol, and de la Faige, one officer of the Regiment of the Cape, M. de Brossard, one officer of the Royal Corps of Artillery, M. de la Faguette, the first lieutenant of the vessel, M. de Pénandreff, two auxiliary officers, and the chaplain of the ship [Father Onésime]. We underwent unbelievable hardships and sufferings to reach this place across uncultivated and almost totally uninhabited country. I have lost everything even to my last slipper (*jusqu'au dernier chausson*). My comrades d'Opterre, de Turpin, and Plancher, who had previously arrived here on the *Pluton* and the *Auguste*, have lavished on me all the help and care that my sorry situation and my state of exhaustion required. M. d'Albert [de Rions], captain of the *Pluton*, immediately offered to take me on his ship, and I shall henceforth remain there. Since my arrival I have regained my strength and my health does not seem to be affected by this cruel crisis. Once again, Sir, I bespeak your kindnesses, I hope that your health is perfect and I am with respect, Your very humble and very obedient servant, Desandroüins." The original letter is reproduced as one of our illustrations.

188. Cromot Dubourg, then serving as assistant quartermaster-general under Baron de Vioménil, noted in his journal ([2], pp. 55–57): "The 7th [February] we saw arrive by land M. Desandroüins, Colonel of Engineers, who told us that he had escaped from the *Bourgogne*, which had run aground on the Coro coast, at Icaque Point. He came to ask help for this vessel. . . . M. de Vioménil requested me to arrange with the administrator to send help to the victims. The frigate *Néréide* left in the evening to go to the rescue of those who might still be on the ship. A Spanish brig (*goëlette*) was sent along the coast to go into all the different inlets (*anses*) and take food to such unfortunates as might be along the shore. Another convoy of food was sent overland to meet them. These different convoys left at 9 o'clock in the evening, and we had heard of the disaster only at 5 o'clock. . . . The *Néréide* returned here the 12th [February]. She had reached the ship at 8 o'clock on the morning of the 7th and had found there 250 men, whom she rescued. The captain, as well as all the officers, had abandoned them." The Comte de Vaudreuil's journal (*Neptunia*, No. 50, p. 35), under the date 6 February, also mentions the arrival of "two officers" and the measures taken for the relief of the *Bourgogne* survivors.

189. See Berthier's journal, p. 258, for his comment on the rendezvous with Don Solano.

look at the situation philosophically, peace could not have been concluded at a more opportune moment. From another quarter came the announcement that the Comte d'Estaing was leaving Cadiz with 50 warships, both French and Spanish, and 18,000 troops to land in case the English did not wish to submit to the French conditions, which actually retracted none of the proposals France had made to England prior to the unfortunate battle of 12 April 1782. This large force, plus the abandonment of the Siege of Gibraltar by the Spaniards,[190] posed a threat to the English, since it would release a formidable reinforcement for the conquest of Jamaica, which was the objective of this year's campaign. The English were too interested in keeping this large, rich island, which, once it fell to the Spaniards, would be lost to them forever. Thus we awaited the peace and watched each day for the arrival of a vessel announcing it.

We learned at Curaçao that 9 warships had arrived at Puerto Cabello, including the *Auguste* and the *Pluton*, and that the latter had had a combat by night off Puerto Rico with an English ship of 50 guns that, seeing with what she had to deal (the *Pluton* carried 74 guns), vanished in the darkness. Meanwhile, the second captain of the *Pluton* had been killed.

190. "Until near the close of the war, it may be said that the chief ambitions of France were in the West Indies; those of Spain, in Europe—to regain Minorca and Gibraltar. In this way Gibraltar became a leading factor in the contest, and affected, directly or indirectly, the major operations throughout the world, by the amount of force absorbed in attacking and preserving it." Mahan, *Operations of the Navies*, pp. 120–121. Cf. Von Closen, pp. 297–298. By the terms of the secret Franco-Spanish convention of Aranjuez (12 April 1779), agreed upon prior to Spain's formal declaration of war on Great Britain on 21 June 1779, there would be no peace until Gibraltar was restored to Spain. Although Gibraltar was blockaded, this did not prevent its successful "relief" by British fleets in January 1780 and again in 1781. In 1782 a combined Franco-Spanish expedition under the Duc de Crillon (a Frenchman in Spanish service) was undertaken, using floating batteries invented by d'Arçon, a French engineer. The grand assault of 13 September 1782 (represented in John Singleton Copley's famous painting of "The Siege of Gibraltar") resulted in failure. In spite of the earlier agreement with the French, Spain accepted preliminary peace terms (20 January 1783), by which Gibraltar re-

DESCRIPTION OF THE ISLAND AND TOWN OF CURAÇAO[191]

The town of Curaçao [Willemstad] is not at all pretty. The houses are of quite different architecture from those of Europe. The island, which is about 35 miles long and 12 to 15 wide, belongs to the Dutch, who had two 50-gun warships there and five or six frigates of 26 to 36 guns. The harbor is safe and charming. The entrance is rather narrow, and all ships touch bottom there on entering, without serious consequences. They moor to the quay and along the shore, for the water is never rough but is always as smooth as oil in spite of the stiff breeze outside. What makes a stay here agreeable are these breezes that cool the air and diminish the excessive heat. When there is no breeze one feels it, for Curaçao is situated 12° above the equator.

The majority of the white inhabitants are very rich Jews who do a big business. The town is inhabited by a large number of free negroes who earn their living as small merchants by buying produce from the mainland and reselling it; for the island, which is nothing but a large rock, produces little except a few coconuts. Whatever grows is soon dried up by the prevailing shortage of water. It hardly ever rains here. It had

mained in possession of the British. As compensation Spain received the island of Minorca in the Mediterranean and both East and West Florida in America. The adventures of a young Virginian, Lewis Littlepage, who served as a volunteer aide-de-camp on the Duc de Crillon's staff at Gibraltar, are related by Curtis Carroll Davis, in *The King's Chevalier, A Biography of Lewis Littlepage* (Indianapolis, 1961), pp. 57–77.

191. See map of Curaçao, Vol. II, No. 167. Further glimpses of Curaçao and somewhat similar comments on the Dutch are found in Du Petit-Thouars (2), p. 95; Ensign Du Petit-Thouars was second in command of the frigate *Amazone*, Clermont-Crèvecœur's ship. See also the contemporary Dutch description of the island: J. H. Hering, *Beschryving van het Eiland Curaçao, en daar onder hoorende Eilanden, Bon-Aire, Oroba en Klein Curaçao* (Amsterdam, 1779; facsimile reprint, Aruba, De Wit N. V., 1969). Another interesting description is in Justin Girod-Chantrans, *Voyage d'un Suisse dans différentes colonies d'Amérique pendant la dernière guerre* (Neuchâtel, 1785), pp. 89–110. The Swiss traveler, who was aboard one of the French warships that escaped from the Battle of the Saints, visited Curaçao in April 1782.

not rained for thirty-five months when we arrived, though it rained a little during our short stay.

The town is surrounded by a strong wall containing several bastions fitted with artillery, which is kept in good condition. Across the harbor is another town called "Spanish Town," which has no wall. All the streets but one are very narrow in order to keep them cool and shaded, so that the sun never shines into the houses. Since the latter are inhabited by Jews and negroes, you can imagine that the smell is not very agreeable. All the houses have fairly large arcades in front that are rather convenient, but they have neither chimneys, kitchens, nor windowpanes. There is no need of chimneys or kitchens, for the cooking is done out-of-doors. Windowpanes are replaced by canvas awnings that permit a constant flow of air in the rooms.

The governor of the town has a rather nice house. He seemed to us a very worthy man, but he is not a professional soldier and has never been one.[192] Nevertheless, there are troops here who seem to be very well equipped, in addition to a militia that is quite sizable because of the large number of negroes and mulattoes who are required to bear arms in an emergency.

The Dutch do not have a high regard for the military profession. In a nation that thinks only of commerce and that has not for a long time experienced the calamity of war, this is not at all surprising; however, they should also feel now (after the conduct of the British towards them) how essential it is, if one wishes to maintain the glory of an empire, not to give oneself up blindly to the sole object of acquiring wealth. This nation resembles a miser who ends by

neglecting to guard his treasure; when he leaves his door unlocked, thieves enter and steal everything he holds most dear. The English have profited handsomely from the avarice of the Dutch. The capture of the island of St. Eustatius is certainly proof of what I have just said.[193]

This nation was for a long time admired by all Europe. But today what is there to admire about her? What did she do during the war? Nothing but supply England with money to make it easier to continue the war against France. I believe that she will not be able to rise again unless she gives some consideration to her army, which she scorns. For what can she expect from mercenary officers who have no object but personal gain and to whom the glory and honor of serving their country are completely alien?

Many languages are spoken in Curaçao; with French and English you are sure to make yourself understood. After taking on water and as many provisions for the army as we could load aboard the transports, we set sail on 19 February. We had stayed six days on this island, which we left without regret. It is notable only as a center of trade betwen the Dutch Company and the Antilles. There is a great deal of commerce here, especially since the capture of St. Eustatius by the English.

19 February We left Curaçao and sailed in a good breeze to Puerto Cabello in four days. We arrived there the morning of the 23rd. I confess that I was horrified the moment I beheld the coast surrounding the bay of Puerto Cabello. We had been told of the tigers, lions, bears, and ox-eating snakes there. When I looked at the shore I was not at all surprised, since

---

192. Johannes de Veer (successor to Jean Rodier) had been governor of Curaçao since August 1782; he had previously held various administrative posts on the island and was to serve as governor until 1796. Joh. Hartog (*Curaçao van Kolonie tot Autonomie,* 2 vols. [Aruba, De Wit, 1961], I, 318–319 and 620, n. 193) gives a brief account of the visit of the French ships, with references to Dutch and French archival sources. In the one-volume English abridgment of Hartog's history, *Curaçao from Colonial Dependence to Autonomy* (Aruba, De Wit, 1968), the visit of the French in 1783 is entirely omitted, as are all footnotes.

193. From the beginning of the war the Dutch West Indian island of St. Eustatius had served as a neutral entre-

pôt for contraband trade among the belligerent islands and with the North American continent. Soon after Great Britain declared war on the United Provinces (20 December 1780) Admiral Rodney captured the island on 3 February 1781, and with it a rich booty, including over 150 merchant ships and merchandise valued at more than £3,000,000. St. Eustatius was recaptured from the English on 26 November 1781 by a French expedition led by the Marquis de Bouillé, governor-general of the French Windward Islands. The important role of this small Dutch island during the war is well summarized by J. Franklin Jameson in his article, "St. Eustatius in the American Revolution," *American Historical Review,* VIII, No. 4 (July 1903), 683–708.

it clearly indicated the abode of everything frightful and ugly that nature can produce. The houses were badly constructed, and most of the inhabitants seemed poverty-stricken. However, there were several families of consequence, those of the few Spanish officers whose wives had settled here.

The harbor is defended by a rather handsome fort that, though small, is in good condition.[194] There are other small forts, which did not strike me as worth much, perched on several very high hills. The guns mounted in them could not do much harm to an enemy below, since they are of low caliber and in poor condition. For the rest, the fort at the harbor entrance is quite formidable, but being built of stone it could not long resist against 36-pounders, with which ships moored in the harbor half a cannon-shot away would certainly be equipped.

As soon as I arrived, I made inquiries about lodgings ashore. My health was not of the best, and I was extremely tired from the sea voyage. I was greatly in need of refreshment after such a long crossing. I had the good fortune to find as comfortable a room as the country afforded, which I occupied at once, seeking to recuperate in peace. Had I been able to speak Spanish, I could have satisfied my curiosity about many objects of which I remained in ignorance; in view of our short stay, however, I did not even consider studying a language to which I had perhaps taken an unreasonable dislike.

The country, the plants, the animals were all new to my eyes, for nothing looked in the least like its European counterpart. Everything is different here on account of the climate and the wide variety of specimens it affords. The heat is both excessive and continuous. Your only defenses are light clothing and the breeze that springs up daily at certain hours. Without these you could not stand it, since Puerto Cabello is only 10° 30″ [10° 15″] north of the equator.

Very little of the country is cultivated. There are a few *casas* scattered here and there, occupied by Indians who are all Catholics and subjects of the King of Spain. A little over 100 miles away you meet savage bands who are cannibals and are said to be very cruel, especially to the Spaniards. There are several towns

in the country that are reputed to be very beautiful. The principal ones are Caracas, which is the capital, Valencia, etc. The former is 50 miles from Puerto Cabello and is the residence of the governor and also of a bishop. The roads leading to it are very bad, and the heat, fatigue, and quantity of provisions required discouraged us from making the journey. However, several officers conquered all these difficulties and reported themselves very pleased with both the people and the sights they saw.[195]

There are three racial types in this country besides the white man: (1) Indians who are almost white, with a pale or livid complexion and long black hair, and are tall and well built, (2) negroes, and (3) Caribs. You can imagine how many shades the mixture of all these races produces. The resultant combinations are very singular, so that you cannot tell which is which. In addition, all these motley peoples are subjects of the King of Spain. Some have the right to the title "Don" and are consequently admitted to officer's rank, to the magistrature, and to the Church. It is not unusual to see a mulatto, and sometimes a negro, saying Mass, and others who are captains, colonels, and above. A mulatto is more highly regarded if he is born of a white Spanish father; then he inherits his father's rank as well as his noble lineage, which the Spaniards usually claim to be very ancient. Even if the mulatto should be a bastard, he inherits the title "Don" and may keep it for life.

After investigation one is no longer surprised to see so much of the land untilled, for the subjects of the Court of Spain are not permitted to engage in any form of commerce. There is in Spain a West India Company that alone has the right to sell and buy the produce of the Caracas coast. It alone fixes the prices as it sees fit and exacts enormous duties on everything that enters and leaves the countries of New Spain. Thus natives are kept in the depths of poverty, since the Company discourages industry by the low prices it sets on the valuable products it buys from them. The natives therefore stand to gain nothing from the fertile soil, which under present conditions barely furnishes them with the means of subsistence. The Company alone has the right to buy and sell the gold or

194. See map, Vol. II, No. 169.
195. See Berthier's account of his journey to Caracas, pp. 266ff. Other accounts are in the journals of Broglie, Coriolis, Dumas, Ségur.

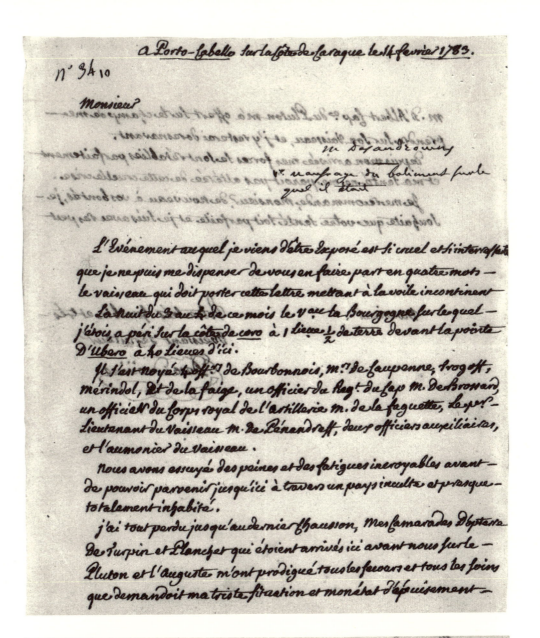

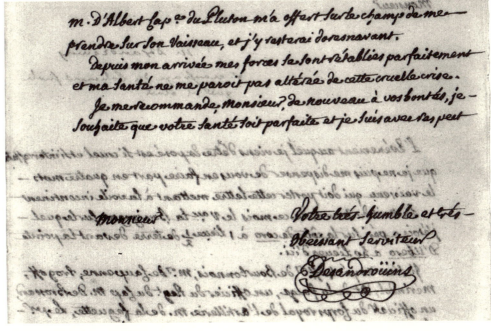

LETTER OF COLONEL DESANDROUINS WRITTEN AT PUERTO CABELLO, 14 FEBRUARY 1783,
SHORTLY AFTER HIS ESCAPE FROM THE SHIPWRECK OF THE *BOURGOGNE* (*see p. xviii*)

de Seve delin.   *Baron Sculp*   *De Seve delin.*   *C. Baquoy Sculp.*

L'AI ADULTE.   JEUNES AIS.

THE SLOTH, AS DEPICTED IN BUFFON'S *HISTOIRE NATURELLE* (*see p. xix*)

silver mined in Mexico and Peru. A certain percentage of every quintal of gold or silver is owed to the king. Thus, when a Mexican has an immense fortune, he is not master of its disposition and can neither leave the country nor move to another and take his fortune with him. If he leaves his own country, he must leave his treasure behind. The coast is lined with well-manned forts to prevent smuggling. The punishments the government metes out to those found guilty are very severe. It is surprising (incredible to those who have not seen it) to find how many troops and guards the Court of Spain and the Company maintain here to enforce their orders and prerogatives. One can judge by the foregoing the immense revenues of the Court of Spain, its resources, and its grandeur. It is really lucky that this nation has not more nerve, for then she would make the whole universe tremble with her immense territory, her armies, and her wealth.

I have been told more than once incredible tales about the religious fanaticism and practices of the Spaniards. They must be seen to be believed, for they are carried to the ultimate extremes. Their priests are veritable gods. It is amazing how they have gained the people's respect. They are all-powerful. The large number of confraternities they have founded has gained them very large salaries, or rather perquisites. This is almost all the revenue, incidentally, that their cures or benefices bring in, since so little of the land is cultivated that the tithes yield very little. Every Spaniard—man, woman, or child—carries a rosary, large or small, or a relic of almost every saint in paradise. Their priests, who are among the most ignorant of men, make them believe whatever they wish, so long as it is not contrary to the fabrications they themselves invent to earn fat incomes. The houses are rather reminiscent of Capuchin cloisters. Their furnishings consist mostly of a cross and those images or relics one finds in our convents. When you knock at a door, it is the custom to say *Ave Maria!* The person opening the door counters with a *Gratia plena!* Finally, these people who seem so religious and who should be simple and kind are anything but that, according to my information, and willingly commit the most heinous crimes under cover of their religion, since they believe that by confessing them all will be forgiven. Their priests, who actually dishonor their calling, are

not loath to give them absolution so long as they pay for it. When the Inquisition is mentioned, all nature trembles at the word, but once it is pronounced they fall on their knees and adore the person who pronounces it. How could the priests fail to be adored when this terrible and unnatural word is constantly on their lips? How thankful we French should be to have none of this Inquisition!

Nevertheless, in the short time we were in Puerto Cabello we had no reason to complain of its inhabitants. The Spanish Americans are naturally sweet-tempered and are very different from what I am told of the European Spaniards, whom I do not know. The women go out rarely, except to church; however, we were invited to parties at their houses where the women gathered on one side of the room and the cavaliers on the other. There we made conversation—or rather those who knew Spanish did—and talked a great deal about rosaries and saints. Sometimes they sang hymns and sometimes love songs, and they all ended up dancing sarabands, *passe-pieds*, and the fandango. The latter dance would make the most licentious woman blush. I saw it danced several times, and I could not help being amazed to see it danced by two young ladies. At the most formal balls they always dance this particular dance. The young lady has as her partner a cavalier whose movements exactly coincide with hers. I have said enough to give you an idea of the fandango and the way it is danced.

I have already mentioned that this country is full of very high mountains and that generally the soil does not produce anything like as much as it could. I noticed that, if nature had a little help from the farmer, the land would reproduce in abundance whatever is planted. However, I have already explained why the natives do not clear their land. The vineyards cultivated to some extent in Caracas yield three harvests a year; grapes are gathered in January, May, and September. This should give you some idea of the nature of the soil, which yields continuously.

This country, fallow as it lies, is full of wild animals unknown in Europe. [Buffon's] *Natural History* gives fairly detailed accounts of the species of animals found on the South American continent, but the descriptions of certain animals do not seem entirely accurate. I shall leave to those who have been busy writing on this subject the responsibility of transmitting their notes to the naturalists, so the latter can revise the history of those species for which they had not been able to obtain accurate descriptions.[196] M. Dubourg, brigade-major of the army, has amused himself preparing several articles. No doubt the work he has compiled in his spare time will be welcomed, since truth has guided his pen. The sloth, a very curious and very ugly animal that gets its name from the life it leads, is one that especially deserves study. M. Dubourg attempted to bring live specimens back to France, but they all died during the passage.[197]

All quadrupeds here are different from those in Europe, and even from those of North America, except the bears, the only ones that are the same. This is also true of the birds, which in this country are surprisingly beautiful and wonderfully varied. A naturalist, chemist, or botanist would find each individual specimen here worth examining, while the ensemble could not be more interesting. One sees no single tree like any European tree and very few like any in North America. There are several fruits of which the people here are very fond, including pineapples, apricots, sapodillas, coconuts, custard apples, pink apples, avocados, etc. One should not forget the cacao, which is excellent and which is the sole article of export on the coast of Caracas. Here again the Company holds the exclusive rights to it. The cocoa tree requires little cultivation. It grows in the woods where there is a great deal of humidity and shade. There are whole valleys full of coconut palms (quite different from cocoa trees), which grow to a great height and bear coconuts weighing 5 to 6 pounds. One cannot enter these valleys for fear of being bombarded by coconuts falling from great heights.

Since the plants here are always green, it is not un-

usual to see flowers grow on trees together with ripe fruit and others in the process of ripening. However, there are some seasonal fruits, in addition to those available all year round. Oranges and lemons grow in the woods. Few people cultivate them, except in Caracas. Furthermore, the oranges are very poor; you cannot eat them because they are too bitter. The people here make a drink from them, not as good as punch, which they call orangeade. It is refreshing and healthful. Wild lemons and limes are delicious in punch or lemonade. These two drinks are essential here, since the heat and the high rate of perspiration make you terribly thirsty and in constant need of refreshment.

The water we drank in Puerto Cabello came from a little river a mile below the town. It was not first-rate; however, it was hard enough to procure, even when you paid for it. (A barrel of water containing 20 bottles costs 1 *real*, that is 14 *sous* and 6 *deniers*.) We had not yet had much sickness, but we were assured that the following month would be very unhealthy because of the rains. This is what happens in these climates; the moment the breeze is cut off you are suffocated by the heat. We had already felt the results during the small showers we had.

Of all the wild animals the most deadly is the tiger, and next comes the lion. The former is very quick and cunning when it is after its prey. In this country there are many wild cattle, which the natives hunt. The tiger waits in a tree near a stream for these animals to come and quench their thirst. The moment the animal starts to drink, the tiger springs on it; however, the latter, seeing the tiger's image reflected in the water, pulls back its head and, the moment the tiger is ready to fall upon it, gores it in the belly with its horns. It is also said that these tigers often sit in the water almost up to their necks with their tails between

196. The publication of Buffon's *Histoire naturelle, générale et particulière*, compiled with the assistance of Daubenton and others, was begun in 1749, continued throughout Buffon's life, and completed by his disciples after the master's death in 1788. As new specimens and new information were received at the Jardin du Roi various supplements and revisions were issued. Buffon's great work did much to stimulate interest in natural history and to popularize the study of it among amateur scientists, as evidenced by the journals of the French officers in Rochambeau's army.

197. An unpublished fragment of Cromot Dubourg's journal ([2], pp. 51ff.) includes his notes on natural history, with references to Buffon. On the last page of this manuscript (p. 57), which has dated entries for February 1783, he notes in the margin: "I have bought a Sloth, which I am keeping carefully: this is an '*Ai*,' according to the description given by M. de Buffon, Tome 11, p. 72. I shall try to take it back to France alive. If I am unsuccessful, I shall at least have it stuffed and will be able to prepare some notes on this animal, which is really most extraordinary." See our illustration taken from Buffon's *Quadrupèdes*.

their legs. With one of their paws they will move their tails back and forth in the water, thereby attracting fish. Then, with the free paw, they seize the fish and toss it out of the water. They continue this little exercise until they have caught enough fish, then they eat them. I heard both of these facts from a Spaniard.

I have already said that there are snakes here that can eat an ox. I thought this was a myth until credible persons confirmed it, so how could I not believe it? A tiger will attack a man provided he is off his guard, for it is instinctively wary of anyone who is armed. A lion takes flight at a man's approach, provided the man says nothing to it, but becomes furious if provoked. The Marquis de Vaudreuil brought two tigers back to France with him, as well as several other animals including a bird known as the "king of vultures." See [Buffon's] *Natural History*.

March 1783

On 15 March we learned that a small vessel had arrived at La Guaira (a port 20 leagues from Puerto Cabello) from Martinique, announcing the arrival from France of the frigate *Andromaque* with news that the peace had just been signed in Paris. This frigate had anchored at Fort Royal but was bound for the fleet of M. de Vaudreuil to bring him the official dispatches from the French Court. A week elapsed before we received any positive news, and the delay somewhat dampened our joy; however, the *Andromaque* arrived on the 24th with the confirmation of this welcome intelligence. The peace had been signed on 3 February [20 January], though hostilities would not cease in America until 3 April.[198]

We sincerely desired peace, especially after our departure from New England, for when all is said and done, that is a charming country whose climate is much like the European climate. It lies within the same latitudes, so that nature is almost the same there and presents the same landscape, as well as other amenities that add immeasurably to the pleasure of life. How different from life under the burning and unpleasant skies of Puerto Cabello!

Nevertheless, some parts of this country have a delightful climate. The city of Caracas is one, according to our generals who went there because they could not resist visiting a city of which so many marvelous things had been reported. They could not say enough about the affability of the inhabitants. The women are charming, though even they receive you with pious ceremonies, as in our convents. Otherwise they converse well and enjoy a joke. Many of our young Frenchmen could not resist their charms, and most of them left their hearts in Caracas—for several days, at least. Those who could play the guitar did not fail to employ their talent to express their tender martyrdom in the Spanish fashion.

Caracas has a very temperate climate and is a land of perpetual spring. The landscape shows off the beauty of nature all year round. There are flowers and trees and fruits at all seasons. The city is built on the side of a very high mountain at whose base is a small valley with a river flowing through it, making it as fertile as can be. This valley belongs to the nobility and clergy and is cultivated for them by slaves. The natives who live in the *casas* scattered throughout the valley do not dare to clear the land for the reasons stated above. But an even more cogent reason is that, if they did, the nobles and clergy would extort the fruit of their labors from these wretched people the moment it became valuable.

One travels on muleback here as in Spain; however, there are horses as well, though I have never seen a fine one here. A brisk business is done in mules, which are exported to the Islands. The merchants buy them for practically nothing and sell them in the Islands, Saint-Domingue in particular, for a fortune. I have seen horses go for 3 or 4 *gourdes*, that is, 5 *livres* and 10 *sols* apiece. The mules cost very little more.

The number of wild cattle I spoke of earlier is simply incredible. These animals, which have become

198. Preliminary and conditional articles of peace between Great Britain and the United States were signed in Paris, 30 November 1782; preliminaries between Great Britain and France and between Great Britain and Spain on 20 January 1783. The definitive treaties were not signed until

3 September 1783. Meanwhile, as indicated here, the end of hostilities had been proclaimed. The treaty of peace between Great Britain and the Dutch was not finally signed until 1784.

wild, are as mean as can be and are dangerous to meet on the road. They travel in herds, and the natives are more afraid of them than they are of lions and tigers. They go out and hunt them. The Indians, who are very adroit, take many alive. Before we arrived, they sold for about 1 *gourde* a head, but the price has now risen to 7 or 8. Although small and lean, they are quite tasty. There is also an extensive trade in their hides, which are sold raw, without being tanned. The manner in which the Indians kill them is quite skillful. They use a very sharp stiletto. They approach the animal, who is in a fury, having been deliberately tormented until it reaches that point, and attach it to a post on a long tether. Each time it is prodded in the rear with the stiletto it bellows and jumps into the air, meanwhile unconsciously going round and round the post and winding up its tether until it is suddenly brought up short. The Indian takes this opportunity to sever its spinal cord with one stroke of the stiletto, and it falls dead. The Indian rarely misses, and the animal rarely escapes, in which case it would be very dangerous.

I have only one peculiarity to report about the climate. Since the mountains here are extremely high, when you travel you often reach the top of one by a narrow path, since there are no roads, and you are astonished to find yourself in an almost ice-cold temperature, so that in place of your light clothing you would be better off in winter furs. Several army officers have assured me that when they spent the night in a *casa* on one of these mountains they suffered intensely from the cold and were obliged to keep a fire

going all night. I asked the inhabitants about this, and they told me that it was not uncommon to find ice up there. What a surprising quirk of nature! One can hardly imagine ice forming practically on the equator, but it is true.

On 28 March we learned that the Comte [Christian] de Deux-Ponts and several other French officers returning with him from Caracas in a small bark had met an English frigate called the *Attelante* [*Albemarle*], which had captured them. These gentlemen were nevertheless sent back to Puerto Cabello. But since hostilities had not ceased at that time, the *Couronne* and the *Amazone* were sent to meet the *Néréide*, which was escorting our generals back.[199] We cruised about for two days outside the bay of Puerto Cabello looking for the English frigate; then the *Néréide* appeared, and all three of us entered the port.

᪥ *April 1783* ᪥

Since the Admiral did not wish to depart until hostilities had ended, he issued orders to prepare to leave on 3 April. We left the harbor at four that afternoon, but since the flagship did not come out, we tacked up and down all night waiting for her. The Admiral got under way the next morning and ordered us [the *Amazone*] to take on board the Comte de Ségur, whom we were to land on the southern coast of Saint-Domingue at Jacmel where he had a large plantation, and then join the fleet at The French Cape as soon as possible.[200]

199. The French officers returning along the coast from La Guaira to Puerto Cabello in an armed Spanish coastal patrol boat were intercepted by the *Albemarle*, an English frigate commanded by Captain Horatio Nelson, who was later to be known as the victor of Trafalgar (1805). In addition to Comte Christian de Deux-Ponts, the party included Schmidt (one of the Colonel's aides?) and Isidore Lynch, then serving as *aide-major-général* (brigade-major). The Comte de Ségur, who was a passenger on another boat immediately ahead of the one carrying Deux-Ponts and Lynch, relates in his *Mémoires* (I, 507-511) that Lynch (an Irishman in French service) narrowly missed detention when his London birth was almost revealed to his captor. Verger (p. 175) and Berthier (p. 279) both mention Deux-Ponts's adventure. See also Von Closen, pp. 312-313; Karl Theodor v. Heigel, "Die Beteilung des

Hauses Zweibrücken am nordamerikanischen Befreiungskrieg," in *Sitzungsberichte der Königlich Bayerischen Akademie der Wissenschaften, Philosophisch-philologische und historische Klasse* (Munich, 1912), Abhandlung 6. Cf. map, Vol. II, No. 168. Detailed maps of La Guaira, the nearest port to Caracas, will be found in Bellin, *Petit Atlas Maritime* (Paris, 1764), II, Plate 25, and in De Pons, *Voyage à la partie orientale de la Terre-Ferme dans l'Amérique Méridionale* (Paris, 1806), III, between pp. 124 and 125.

200. The Comte de Ségur was accompanied by Blanchard and by Berthier. See Ségur (1), I, 515-523; Blanchard (1), pp. 127-129; and Berthier's journal, pp. 28off. Aristide Du Petit-Thouars, second in command of the *Amazone*, also mentions the voyage via Jacmel; Du Petit-Thouars (2), p. 99.

During the short time he was with us the Comte de Ségur appeared to us a most courteous and amiable nobleman; his conversation was very animated and witty. He has a vast amount of knowledge, but it is not superficial like that of many other noblemen. He reasons with the convincing air of one who really knows. He has devoted much of his time to literary pursuits. He restricts his military duties to those required of a man of honor in the service of his country. This explains his coming to America. Literature is his recreation, I daresay, as well as his avocation.[201]

We left the rest of the fleet, which was also bound for The Cape, but by a much shorter route than ours, since we had to sail completely round the French part of the island of Santo Domingo.[202] It took us 9 days to reach Jacmel, where we left the Comte de Ségur as well as M. Blanchard, the chief commissary of the army. We wasted no time there, and the moment the ship's boat returned we resumed our voyage to The Cape. We had great difficulty rounding Cape Tiburon, for lack of wind. It took us even longer to clear Môle Saint-Nicolas because of strong headwinds. For several days we remained within sight of Cape Maisí on the island of Cuba, as well as of Môle Saint-Nicolas, without being able to round it. Finally we succeeded, only to run into a little storm. It was evidently decreed by fate that I should never go to sea again without running into a storm.

We broke two topmasts and were obliged to enter La Tortue Channel in an effort to anchor in Port-de-Paix to make repairs, but we met with every possible obstacle. The wind had risen and was blowing from directly ahead. We made signals of distress to summon aid. Our frigate, which had lost her upper masts, showed clearly enough the sorry condition she was in; still, no pilot appeared, and we were obliged to spend the night hove to in the middle of La Tortue Channel at the mercy of a most violent wind, though the sea was fairly smooth. Next day we found ourselves at the channel entrance and made further efforts to reach Port-de-Paix. We were almost there despite the wind, which was steadily increasing, when suddenly the current took charge and dragged us down towards a fort at the right of the entrance to the bay. I believed at that moment that there was nothing to be done and that the ship would perish (by this time the harbormaster was aboard). Fortunately the vessel bore away in the nick of time and brought us off the wind, putting us out of danger.

When our captain saw that it would be dangerous to anchor in such a harbor in a strong breeze, he resolved to spend the night in the channel (for the second time) to wait for the wind to moderate so he might come up next day and round La Tortue Island. Actually we found ourselves clear of the channel the next morning with a much lighter breeze. We thought no more of reentering the channel. Since the harbormaster was still aboard, the captain of the frigate forced him to pilot us to The Cape as a punishment for having left us to perdition in the channel for a whole day and night without sending aid. You may imagine that he had a very cool reception on board. He tried to make some feeble excuses, but we did not even listen to them.

The winds now became more manageable, and on 26 April we entered the harbor of The French Cape where we found the Spanish squadron on the point of departure[203] and M. de Vaudreuil ready to sail for France. Since leaving Puerto Cabello we had been at sea 23 days, though the squadron had made the journey in 11. I had no time to lose. I had to work very hard to finish my errands, for the squadron was getting under way for Brest on 30 April with the whole of Rochambeau's army aboard.

I shall not go into a detailed description of the city of The French Cape, since it is quite well known in

---

201. The varied and voluminous literary productions of Louis-Philippe, comte de Ségur (1753–1830), were eventually gathered into the thirty-four volumes of his complete works. In addition to his *Mémoires, ou Souvenirs et Anecdotes* (3 vols., 1824–1826)—often cited in the present work—Ségur's writings included ancient and modern history, political speeches, light verse, short stories, fables, songs, and plays. Several of the plays were written for

Catherine the Great's Hermitage Theatre, when Ségur was French ambassador to Russia in 1784–1789. See *Catalogue . . . de la Bibliothèque Nationale, Auteurs*, CLXIX, 995–1013.

202. See maps and views, Vol. II, Nos. 171, 172, and 173.

203. Verger's journal (p. 176) lists the ships comprising the Spanish squadron.

France.[204] Besides, my stay was so short that whatever I might say about it would be very little in comparison to what there is to say. I have seen only one other large city as well built as this. The streets are perfectly straight, but the houses are mostly of one storey. The immense wealth of the citizens is well known, since they trade with all the world. Gold circulates here by the fistful, and life is incredibly expensive. The inhabitants are reckless gamblers and accept only gold. Silver is proscribed. They give themselves up entirely to voluptuousness and take delight in the most sensual pleasures. The white women here are charming, dress with taste and elegance, and seem incredibly pleasure-loving. Dancing is a passion with them. It is true that they dance in a ravishing manner; their lightness, grace, and gaiety figure largely in this innocent pastime. One cannot imagine how they enjoy this exercise so much in such a hot climate.

The men do not limit their folly to paying court and homage to these charming creatures but indulge their special taste for the colored ladies. The mulatto women are their goddesses, and the men lavish immense sums on them. True, they are also very elegant and often have very good figures. But when you look at their skin—horrors! These girls nevertheless acquire some polish. They educate themselves by reading many novels. Their style and their manners are much above those of their counterparts in France. If you go to their houses, they will receive you with a certain dignity, but you cannot help smiling to see those brown faces putting on little airs of nonchalance, complaining of headaches and stomach aches, staging appropriate migraines in order to be left alone with a favorite lover; for whoever ruins himself for them is obliged to allow them a caprice or two. All this is truly comic to a reasonable foreigner who is genuinely amused by the singularity of these women, without being tempted to fall in love with them or ruin himself to gain their favors. If you wish to pay them court, it will cost you dearly, for they will consider nothing less than 20 Portuguese dollars (one Portuguese dollar being worth about 44 *livres*); however, this holds only for the "high-toned" girls. What fools men are! Will they never realize their gross stupidity? For, after all, what adds to your pleasure in loving a woman? It is her beauty, her face, the whiteness of her skin. Shave a monkey, a she-monkey, and you will come near having the face of the enchantresses I have just described. You could sooner grow accustomed to looking at a negress than at a mulattress; at least the former has a

204. See map and view, Vol. II, Nos. 174 and 176. Other descriptions of The French Cape (Le Cap Français, known today as Cap Haïtien) will be found below in Verger's journal (pp. 176–177) and in Berthier's journal, describing his brief stop there in September 1780 (p. 233). For an exhaustive account of the French colony of "Saint-Domingue," see Médéric-Louis-Elie Moreau de Saint-Méry, *Description topographique, physique, civile, politique et historique de la Partie Française de l'Isle Saint-Domingue . . . accompagnée des détails les plus propres à faire connaître l'état de cette Colonie à l'époque du 18 Octobre 1789; et d'une nouvelle Carte de la totalité de l'Isle*, 2 vols. (Philadelphia, Chez l'auteur, 1797–1798). Although published when the author was living in the United States as an émigré, this remarkable work treats of the colony as it was before the French Revolution, presenting, as the author says, "a tableau of its past splendor." Moreau de Saint-Méry had been gathering material for many years; he had already published six volumes of the Laws and Constitutions of the French colonies (Paris, 1784–1789) and in 1791 issued a large volume of engraved plates entitled *Recueil de vues des lieux principaux de la Colonie Françoise de Saint-Domingue, gravées par les soins de M. Ponce . . . accompagnées de cartes et plans de la même*

colonie, gravés par les soins de M. Phelipeau, Ingénieur-Géographe (Paris, 1791). A new edition of Moreau de Saint-Méry's *Description*, edited by Blanche Maurel and Etienne Taillemitte, has recently been published in 3 vols. (Paris, Société de l'Histoire des Colonies Françaises, Librairie Larose, 1958); with the exception of the maps of Le Cap François and of Port-au-Prince (greatly reduced), this edition does not reproduce the plates of the *Recueil*.

The French colony of "Saint-Domingue" was limited to the western part of the island of Santo Domingo or Hispaniola; this is now the French-speaking, "black" Republic of Haiti. The eastern part of the island, formerly a Spanish colony, is now the Dominican Republic. Moreau de Saint-Méry also compiled and published a *Description topographique et politique de la Partie Espagnole de l'Isle Saint-Domingue* (Philadelphia, 1796), with an English translation by William Cobbett. There is, however, no English translation of his *Description* of the French colony. An extensive account of French Saint-Domingue by a traveler who visited it in 1782 is in Justin Girod-Chantrans, *Voyage d'un Suisse dans différentes colonies d'Amérique pendant la dernière guerre* (Neuchâtel, 1785), pp. 115–373.

definite color, whereas if a white woman were to daub herself with soot, this would approximate the color of the other.

There is every delight imaginable to be found in this colony, but also the diseases that are the lot of indiscreet people who do not exercise moderation in their pleasures. Every European who lands here pays what is called the "tribute" within four or five days of his transgression. It is a stroke of luck if he recovers, for the period of convalescence is long and requires much care. I was so afraid of this "tribute" that I did not dare sleep ashore but returned on board each evening. Even though they say you have only to land to catch this disease, I nevertheless believe that many Europeans have escaped and that, so long as you exercise restraint, you can manage to stay well in all countries, or at least resist these diseases better than those who do not.

I saw almost everything I possibly could at The Cape during the four days I spent there. I went to the theatre, which is not very good, but my long fast from plays, which I like very much, enabled me to enjoy it.[205] Fêtes and dances were given during the stay of the squadron, but I could attend very few. Prince William Henry of England had been here and was received with the distinction due his rank. He stayed only twenty-four hours.[206]

The Spanish squadron had left for Havana. It had taken along all the Spanish troops stationed in Saint-Domingue, under the command of General Gál-vez, who is beloved and esteemed by the whole nation for his candor, his courtesy and his military accomplishments.[207] His wife accompanied him. She was much admired for her talents and amiability.

On 28 April I received orders to disembark my half-company [Maisonneuve] from the *Amazone* (which was to transport the Enghien and Touraine regiments later on) and embark with it on the *Néréide*. The army's departure was fixed for 30 April. Several ships departed that day, but a dying wind kept the rest in harbor until the next morning, when we got under way. I left the island of Saint-Domingue without having had the pleasure of seeing in the back country the plantations whose soil yields so much wealth to France.[208] I was really sorry about this; on the other hand, I was comforted by the thought of returning to my country for which I had long yearned, especially after leaving New England.

⌁ May–June 1783 ⌁

We finally departed on 1 May, promising ourselves a short and happy voyage, which one might reasonably expect at this season. We were much mistaken, however, for the weather alternated between storms and calms, increasing our anxiety in no small measure. Nevertheless, nothing really bad happened to us until we were within sight of the French coast, where we were disturbed to find ourselves in a thick fog. We

205. For another comment on the theatre in the French colonies, see Berthier's journal, p. 230, describing a performance of *Le Barbier de Séville*, which he witnessed at Saint-Pierre, Martinique, in August 1780. Moreau de Saint-Méry (*Description . . . de la Partie Française de l'Isle Saint-Domingue*, ed. Maurel and Taillemite, I, 356–367) gives a detailed history of the theatre at The Cape, with many anecdotes. The theatre was located in the Place Montarcher.

206. The Prince's visit had taken place on 5 April, two days after the official cessation of hostilities. He later became King William IV. See Verger's journal, n. 184.

207. The Spanish troops assembled in Saint-Domingue were to have participated in the French-Spanish expedition against the English island of Jamaica along with Vioménil's army. Verger's journal, pp. 177, 178, makes similarly favorable comments about both Gálvez and his wife, as do several of the other French officers' journals; see,

e.g., Von Closen, pp. 326–327. Bernardo de Gálvez (1726–1786), governor of Spanish Louisiana since 1776, had played a considerable role in the war by capturing the British posts of Baton Rouge (1779), Natchez (1779), Mobile (1780), and Pensacola (1781). He was subsequently appointed captain-general of Louisiana and the Floridas, captain-general of Cuba, and viceroy of New Spain (1785). Soon after acceding to this latter post he died in Mexico in 1786. Gálvez's wife was Félicie de Saint-Maxent, of a Louisiana Creole family. John W. Caughey, *Bernardo de Gálvez in Louisiana, 1776–1783* (Berkeley, 1934). An English translation of the text of Carlos III's royal proclamation (12 November 1781), honoring and rewarding Gálvez for his conquests in the Gulf of Mexico, is included in N. Orwin Rush, *The Battle of Pensacola* (Tallahassee, 1966), pp. 10–15.

208. Verger's journal, p. 178, describes the Chevalier de Walsh's sugar plantation.

were within a league of the island of Ushant before we knew it, in heavy seas and a high wind. We had to sail very close to the wind to clear the island and had to crowd on sail to make headway against the current, which is very strong in these parts. Despite the danger, we arrived in the harbor of Brest at three in the afternoon on 17 June 1783.

I was in a great hurry to land, having firmly resolved never to set foot again on the frigate. I had taken such a great dislike to the sea that now, as I finish my journal, I cannot think of it without a shudder. All the dangers I had faced, all the afflictions I had suffered, were buried in complete oblivion when I finally found myself safe ashore on the land I had been longing to see once more. I had suffered every affliction one can suffer at sea except shipwreck, which I had escaped; I had come near it, though, and had been threatened with starvation as well when the provisions ran out. But when I saw my country again all was forgotten.

The men of my company disembarked on 19 June and left for Morlaix to await orders. The infantry regiments went into rest quarters in the outskirts of Brest.

One can truly say that, in order to enjoy the pleasures of life to the full, you must first suffer many ills and misfortunes, both physical and moral. To have reached the goal of my heart's desire is the pleasure I am now savoring. I am writing the account of all events I have witnessed, recalling all my emotions, all my thoughts. Today I am delighted to have been able to investigate places, manners, customs hitherto unknown to me; I have gained in experience and profited much. If the picture I have painted pleases and amuses my friends, how glad I shall be to have attempted it!

Journal

OF JEAN-BAPTISTE-ANTOINE DE VERGER

JEAN–BAPTISTE–ANTOINE DE VERGER
SELF-PORTRAIT (*see p. xix*)

Editors' Introduction

Jean-Baptiste-Antoine de Verger (1762–1851), a sublieutenant in the Royal Deux-Ponts Regiment, was the youngest of our trio of journalists and was, like most of the other men in his regiment, of foreign birth. He was born on 7 November 1762 in the town of Delémont (Delsberg), the fourth son of the eleven children of Henri-Joseph-Antoine de Verger and his wife Jeanne-Baptiste-Joachine-Henriette de Hennet.[1] Although Delémont is today in the Canton of Berne, Switzerland, it was not a part of the Swiss Confederation at the time of Verger's birth. Like its neighbor Porrentruy, Delémont was then in the Bishopric of Bâle, a predominantly Catholic and French-speaking episcopal principality lying to the southwest of the city of Bâle along the French frontier. Since the time of the Reformation the city of Bâle and the bishopric of that name had been distinct territorial entities. The ruler of this small buffer state in the Jura Mountains was the Prince-Bishop of Bâle, who was both a prelate of the Church and, with respect to his temporal possessions, a prince of the Holy Roman Empire. The Prince-Bishop generally held court in his fine palace at Porrentruy, making occasional sojourns at Delémont, where another château (built in 1716–1719 by the architect Racine de Renan and still standing, though now put to other uses) served as his summer residence. Verger's native land was thus one of those innumerable small states that, through an intricate web of feudal relationships, still made up the Holy Roman Empire.[2]

The Verger family, which descended from Perin de Verger, burgomaster of Porrentruy (Pruntrut, Brundrut) in the fifteenth century, was closely identified with the ruling class clustered around the Prince-Bishop of Bâle.[3] Being strongly Catholic and attached to the Holy Roman Empire, the family was ennobled in 1717 by the Emperor Charles VI. Our diarist's paternal grandfather, Jean-François-Joseph de Verger (1678–1728), was a doctor of laws, aulic councillor, and diplomat who had been sent by the Emperor on various missions to the Federal Diets of the Swiss cantons. His great-uncle, Jean-Conrad, who served as intendant of finance to the Elector of Bavaria, had established a Bavarian

1. There is no complete biography of Verger; the present sketch has been compiled from widely scattered sources. Statements concerning Verger's military services are based on his personal dossiers in the French Archives de la Guerre at Vincennes and in the Bavarian Kriegsarchiv in Munich.

branch of the Verger family. His father, Henri-Joseph (1718–1783), as "lieutenant of the chatelleny of Delémont" and aulic councillor, represented the authority of the Prince-Bishop in Delémont. When Jean-Baptiste-Antoine de Verger was born there in 1762, he was baptized by the Prince-Bishop; Jean-Baptiste d'Andlau, knight of the Teutonic Order, and Baroness Maria-Regina von und zu Bodmann, wife of the bailiff of Delémont, served as godparents.

Families such as the Vergers traditionally looked to the Church and the army to provide honorable careers for their sons. Two of Jean-Baptiste-Antoine's brothers, François-Xavier and Conrad, thus became canons of the abbey of Moutier-Grandval, while he himself turned to the army. To those who were subjects of small states like the Bishopric of Bâle, a military career generally meant service in the army of one of the greater powers such as France. Under the Old Régime the French army included a number of foreign proprietary regiments, Irish, Swiss, or German.[4] One such regiment,

Further information has been gleaned from the following volumes of the *Geschichte des Bayerischen Heeres* (8 vols. in 12, Munich, 1901–1935): Vol. IV, Part 1, Oskar Bezzel, *Geschichte des kurpfälzischen Heeres . . . bis zur Vereinigung von Kurpfalz und Kurbayern 1777, nebst Geschichte des Heerwesens in Pfalz-Zweibrücken*; Vol. V, Oskar Bezzel, *Geschichte des kurpfalz-bayerischen Heeres von 1778 bis 1803*; Vol. VI, Part 1, Oskar Bezzel, *Geschichte des königlich bayerischen Heeres unter König Max I. Joseph von 1806 (1804) bis 1825.* Also consulted were Ernest H. Kneschke, *Neues Allgemeines Deutsches Adels-Lexicon*, 9 vols. (Leipzig, 1859–1870), IX, 373–374, and *Göthaisches Genealogisches Taschenbuch der Freiherrlichen Haüser* (1856). Comprehensive notes on Verger are found in Marcel Dunan, *Napoléon et l'Allemagne, Le Système Continental et les débuts du Royaume de Bavière, 1806–1810* (Paris, 1943), p. 663, n. 144, and in Otto Rieder's biography of "Karl August Graf von Reisach," *Oberbayerisches Archiv für vaterländische Geschichte* (Munich), LX (1916), 347–348, n. 1. At some time in the 1820's Verger evidently prepared a brief recapitulation of his career through 1822, which was added as a preface to later transcripts of his journal (see our "Checklist of Journals," *s.v.* Verger). This résumé is the chief source of the "Notes biographiques" in Mgr. Eugène Folletête's article, "Un officier jurassien à la Guerre de l'Indépendance des Etats-Unis d'après le journal du lieutenant Jean-Baptiste-Antoine de Verger de Delémont," *Actes de la Société Jurassienne d'Emulation, Année 1943* (La Chaux-de-Fonds, 1944), XLVII, 231–250. Folletête's article also includes a "Table Généalogique de la Famille de Verger" and a "Généalogie de la Famille du Général Nouvion"; these tables are based on notes compiled by André Rais. We are greatly indebted to Dr. Rais, Conservateur des Archives de l'ancien Evêché de Bâle à Porrentruy and Conservateur du Musée jurassien à Delémont, for further information about the Verger family, which will be included in a forthcoming volume of his *Livre d'Or des Familles du Jura* (Porrentruy, Editions du Jura, 1967–). Other sources used by the Editors are mentioned in subsequent notes.

2. A good general survey of the history of the Bishopric of Bâle, with map and bibliography, is in Marcel Godet et al., *Dictionnaire historique et biographique de la Suisse*, 7 vols. and suppl. (Neuchâtel, 1921–1934), I, 558–565, "Bâle, Evêché de." See also Gustave Amweg, *Bibliographie du Jura bernois, ancien Evêché de Bâle* (Porrentruy, 1928); Virgile Rossel, *Histoire du Jura Bernois* (Geneva, 1914); Abbé A. Daucourt, *Histoire de la Ville de Delémont* (Porrentruy, 1900). Daucourt's history is heavily weighted with church affairs; writing in 1900, the author, an unreconstructed Jurassien, still resents the annexation of the old Bishopric of Bâle to the Canton of Berne. Engraved views of the town and château of Delémont are in Laborde and Zurlauben, *Tableaux de la Suisse, ou Voyage pittoresque*, 2nd edn. (Paris, Lamy, 1784), V, 410, Plates 230–231; see our illustration.

3. *Dictionnaire historique . . . de la Suisse*, VII, 100, "Verger"; H. J. Leu, *Schweitzerisches Lexicon*, 20 vols. (Zurich 1747–1765), XVIII, 491–492, "Verger oder Vergier."

4. A convenient tabulation of the "Régiments étrangers" is in Louis Susane, *Histoire de l'ancienne infanterie française*, 7 vols. and plates (Paris, 1849–1853), I, 315–316.

informally known as the Prince-Bishop of Bâle's regiment but generally designated by the names of its successive commanding colonels (Eptingen, Schonau, Rheinach), was, by an agreement made with France in 1758, recruited in the bishopric.[5] Contrary to what might be expected, young Verger was not enrolled in this regiment, but rather in another of France's foreign regiments, the Royal Deux-Ponts. The regiment took its name from the Duchy of Deux-Ponts (Zweibrücken), a small Rhine valley state that, through family inheritance, had become linked to the Electorate of Bavaria.[6]

The Royal Deux-Ponts Regiment, then commanded by Colonel Christian de Deux-Ponts, was one of the four infantry regiments assigned to Rochambeau's army for the expedition to America. Verger, fresh from school and only seventeen,[7] entered the regiment as a gentleman cadet in February 1780 and was promoted sublieutenant in April, a month or so before departure for America. As a reward for his conduct during the Siege of Yorktown he was transferred to the élite company of chasseurs in June 1782. He served throughout the American campaigns, returning to France with the rest of the army in June 1783, as he tells us in his journal, which he continued for several months after his landing at Brest. During July and August 1783, the Deux-Ponts Regiment proceeded across France to its quarters at Landau, the garrison town on the eastern frontier, which it reached on 5 September. Along the way Verger had several days' leave in Paris, saw the sights in Rheims, Toul, and Nancy, and visited two of his sisters at Saverne in Alsace. Later that autumn he had a few weeks' leave to visit his home in Delémont and then returned to his regiment at Landau in mid-December. Shortly thereafter he received news of his father's death at Delémont on 18 December 1783, at the age of sixty-five.

The next few years were relatively peaceful ones for the Deux-Ponts Regiment. In May 1786 Verger was promoted second lieutenant in Rühle's company, which Lieutenant General de Falkenhayn characterized in his inspection report of 1 October 1788 as follows: "This company is more uniform than the others, and its rear rank better trained; it is smartly turned out and well commanded." In August 1789 Verger was promoted first lieutenant in the company of Hainault, and in September 1791, after the regiment had been rechristened the Ninety-ninth Infantry, he was adjutant major.[8] Verger's

5. *Ibid.*, VII, 355–358, "Régiment de Rheinach"; Daucourt, *op.cit.*, pp. 425–427, "Le Régiment de l'Evêché." Daucourt mentions that Ferdinand-Joseph de Verger (b. 1770) of Delémont entered the regiment in 1786 as a sublieutenant; he was a younger brother of our subject.

6. Susane, VII, "Régiment Royal de Deux-Ponts." Journals or letters of other officers of the Deux-Ponts Regiment are listed below in our "Checklist of Journals," *s.v.* Closen, Deux-Ponts (Guillaume), Fersen, Gallatin, Schwerin. Evelyn Acomb's introduction to Von Closen's journal includes valuable material on the Deux-Ponts family and the regiment. See also Johann Georg Lehmann, *Vollständige Geschichte des Herzogthums Zweibrücken und seiner Fürsten, der Stamm- und*

Vorältern des k. bayer. Hauses (Munich, 1867), which includes a "Genealogische Tabelle der noch blühenden pfalz-birkenfeld-bischweiler Linie."

7. Verger's dossier at Vincennes says that he had attended the "gymnase de Delémont." It has been suggested that he may also have attended the Abbé de Luce's boarding school at Bellelay. This was considered a model establishment where young noblemen from the bishopric (as well as from Alsace or the Swiss cantons) were given the rudiments of military training, since most of the pupils were destined for a military career. Rossel, *op.cit.*, pp. 204–205.

8. See Susane, *op.cit.*, I, 324. An army reorganization law voted by the National Assembly, 1 January 1791, prescribed the suppression of the names traditionally

service record in the French army archives ends with the statement that he had left his regiment on 6 May 1792. From this point on his trail must be picked up elsewhere and will eventually lead to Bavaria.

The year 1792 marked a decisive turning-point in Verger's life. War broke out in April, with France ranged against Austria, Prussia, and the émigré armies; in August came the downfall of the monarchy and the establishment of the French Republic. Our previous diarist, Clermont-Crèvecœur, decided to leave his country and join the émigrés; Berthier, the author of the next journal, chose to remain in France, though he was temporarily relieved of his military duties. Verger, like other foreign-born officers in French service, could view the question of allegiance in somewhat different terms. Although he might have cast his lot with the Revolution, heredity prevailed over heresy and he chose to follow his chief to Germany to take up arms in behalf of the Catholic Empire. The commanding colonel of his regiment, Christian de Deux-Ponts (then known in France as the Marquis de Deux-Ponts), had already (in 1791) returned to Zweibrücken, where a number of his old officers eventually joined him. On 26 June 1792 Verger was enrolled as captain in the Zweibrücken Lifeguards (which bore the resounding title of Herzog Pfalz Zweibrückische Leibgarde zu Fuss).[9] From then on he styled himself Johann Baptist Anton von Verger, occasionally using his perfectly legitimate but long-discarded family title of Freiherr (baron). By the autumn of 1792 Verger was serving on the staff of the Duke of Brunswick-Oels and campaigning with the Prussians in Champagne. After the Prussians were halted at Valmy—the first victory of the French Republic—Custine's Army of the Vosges took the offensive and advanced towards the Rhine. Bavarian lands in the Palatinate, including the Duchy of Zweibrücken, were occupied and subsequently, after changing hands several times, annexed to France. The former duchy eventually found itself absorbed into the Department of Mont-Tonnerre.[10]

Meanwhile, a revolution in miniature was taking place in Verger's homeland, the Bishopric of Bâle.[11] Encouraged by the example of their French brothers, the inhabitants were presenting their grievances to their sovereign and demanding reforms similar to those instituted by the National Assembly in France. Deeming his authority threatened by the unrest of his subjects, Prince-Bishop Joseph de Roggenbach appealed to the Austrians, who in March 1791 sent a garrison of some four to five hun-

used to designate the regiments and substituted numbers, assigned according to regimental seniority. This was in line with the general elimination of all titles. The distinction between French and "foreign" regiments was wiped out by a decree of 21 July 1791.

9. Bezzel, *op.cit.*, IV, Part 1, 554–555.
10. Philippe Sagnac, *Le Rhin français pendant la Révolution et l'Empire* (Paris, 1917), with a useful map, "Carte du Pays Rhénan divisé en Départements (An VII)."
11. For a detailed history, see Gustave Gautherot, *La Révolution française dans l'ancien Evêché de Bâle: (1) La République rauracienne, (2) Le Département du*

Mont-Terrible, 1793–1800, 2 vols. (Paris, 1907); and the more recent work by Jean-René Suratteau, *Le Département du Mont-Terrible sous le régime du Directoire (1795–1800), Etude des contacts humains, économiques et sociaux dans un pays annexé et frontalier*, Annales littéraires de l'Université de Besançon, Vol. LXXI (Paris, 1964). Suratteau includes an exhaustive bibliography. Earlier accounts: Charles F. Morel, *Abrégé de l'Histoire et de la Statistique du ci-devant Evêché de Bâle, réuni à la France en 1793 . . . avec une carte du pays* (Strasbourg, 1813); A. Quiquerez, *Histoire de la Révolution dans l'Evêché de Bâle, 1791* (Porrentruy, 1881).

dred men to restore order. A year later, when war broke out between Austria and France, the Austrian troops were withdrawn from the bishopric. Thereupon the French, in turn, invoking a treaty of 1780, occupied the principality. In November 1792 a popular assembly declared the *ci-devant* bishopric independent and proclaimed the "Rauracian Republic." A few months later, in March 1793, the tiny republic voted its "reunion" to France and became the Department of Mont-Terrible, the eighty-fourth and smallest department of the French Republic.[12] Upon the arrival of the French the Prince-Bishop took flight from his capital at Porrentruy and eventually emigrated to Constance, where his courtiers and counselors followed him.

The archives of the former Bishopric of Bâle indicate that Verger was in touch with the small court at Constance and that he was involved in various schemes for restoring the émigré Prince-Bishop to power.[13] For example, in a communication dated 12 April 1793 Captain Verger, "formerly adjutant major of the Deux-Ponts Regiment," submitted a plan for driving the French from the bishopric. The Prince rewarded Verger with a gratification of 12 *louis d'or* but merely handed the plan along to the Austrian minister at Bâle—and nothing came of it. During the summer of 1793 an insurrection against French Republican rule took shape in the mountains near Delémont. This incipient peasant revolt, which resembled the *chouannerie* in La Vendée, raised great hopes among the Prince-Bishop's supporters. Verger was one of the envoys (with Lieutenant Fischer and a lawyer named Babey) sent by Baron d'Andlau to plead with the Imperial minister (Buol) at Berne for Austrian subsidies and armed support of the insurrection. These efforts proved fruitless, as did similar attempts (in which Verger was also involved) to obtain financial assistance from the Swiss authorities in Berne and Bâle. For lack of outside support the insurrection came to a pathetic end. One of its leaders, Georges Roll, was beheaded on 17 November 1793, on which day the guillotine appeared for the first time in the town square at Delémont. Joseph de Roggenbach, the Prince-Bishop, died in exile at Constance in 1794; his successor, François-Xavier de Neveu, was destined never to reign. The former Bishopric of Bâle remained under French rule until 1814; the following year the Congress of Vienna annexed it to the Canton of Berne.

Verger's participation in the futile attempts to restore the old regime in the Bishopric of Bâle must have marked a particularly discouraging period in his life. For the time being he was an exile, a man without a country. After 1793 his fortunes were linked to the House of Deux-Ponts and thus to Bavaria, which eventually became his adopted land. The meager records concerning his life during the next few years indicate that on 1 September 1794 he was formally commissioned a staff captain in the Kurpfalzbayerische Zweibrückische Garderegiment.[14] In 1797, when the French under General Joubert were striking at the Austrians in the Tyrol, we find Captain von Verger serving as an intelli-

12. In 1800 the Département du Mont-Terrible was incorporated into the Département du Haut-Rhin.
13. Gautherot, *op.cit.*, II, 48–51, "Intrigues des émigrés." The archives of the former Evêché de Bâle, cited by Gautherot, were transferred from Berne to Porrentruy in 1963.

14. Bezzel, *op.cit.*, IV, Part 1, Anlage 34, pp. 100*–101*, "National-Liste deren sämmentlichen Staabs- und Oberofficiers des Kurpfalzbayerischen Zweibrückischen Garderegiments, Amberg, den 13. April 1799."

gence officer on the staff of Quartermaster-General Baron Hohenhausen, assisting in the organization of frontier defenses.[15]

The Elector of Bavaria, Karl Theodor, died in 1799 and was succeeded by his nephew, Maximilien Joseph de Deux-Ponts (1756–1825).[16] "Prince Max" was a cousin of Christian de Deux-Ponts, Verger's former commander, and an old friend of the disbanded Deux-Ponts Regiment. He had been the "proprietor," and for a time the acting commander, of another French regiment, the Régiment d'Alsace and had owned a fine mansion in Strasbourg (the Hôtel de Deux-Ponts), which had been confiscated with his other properties in France early in the Revolution. Indeed, as he himself once said: "I was raised in France, and beg you to look upon me as a Frenchman." Maximilian (to use the German form of his name) proved a capable and patriotic ruler who, with the assistance of his all-powerful minister of state, the Comte de Montgelas, charted a devious course through the rocky channel of the Napoleonic era and managed to come through unscathed. His accession released Bavaria from bondage to Austria and brought about a rapprochement with France. In 1806, by the grace of Napoleon, he became the first King of Bavaria—Maximilan I Josef.

Verger's fidelity to the House of Deux-Ponts was to be well rewarded. His career now began to advance at a brisk pace. In 1799, soon after Maximilian came to power, he was assigned to the Elector's Foot Guard (Leib-Regiment) stationed in Nymphenburg and Munich. Meanwhile, Christian de Deux-Ponts had been promoted lieutenant general and, in January 1800, was put in command of the Bavarian Auxiliary Forces, with Verger as his aide.[17] In April 1800 Verger was promoted to the rank of major; a few months later he was appointed assistant quartermaster on the Bavarian General Staff.

His new duties soon brought him into contact with the French. The Treaty of Lunéville (March 1801) provided for the evacuation of French troops from Bavaria (where they had defeated the Austrians at Hohenlinden in December 1800). Major von Verger, in collaboration with a French representative, General Lahorie, worked out the details of the withdrawal of Moreau's army.[18] The departure of the French armed forces from Munich marked the beginning of the new era of friendship between Maximilian Josef's Bavaria and Bonaparte's France.

The nature of Verger's tasks as a staff officer eventually led him into the field of diplomacy. The first of several such assignments was his appointment in October 1803 to the post of Bavaria's minister resident in Berne, the Swiss capital. Verger thus found himself very close to his native land and could renew old acquaintances there. The former Bishopric of Bâle was still under French rule (as part of the Department of Haut-Rhin), but the political climate was not what it had been ten years earlier. Indeed, the French occupation of Delémont had had certain unexpected consequences for Verger. In 1796 his sister, Marie-Louise de Verger, had married a French Republican general, Jean-Baptiste-

15. Bezzel, *op.cit.*, v, 500.
16. Dunan, *op.cit.*, p. 438, n. 2, provides a good summary of Maximilian Josef's early career. See also Susane, *op.cit.*, v, 373–396, "Régiment d'Alsace"; Hans Haug, *Le Château des Rohan et les grands hôtels du*

XVIIIe siècle à Strasbourg (Strasbourg, Editions des Musées de la Ville, 1953), pp. 17–19, "L'Hôtel de Deux-Ponts."
17. Bezzel, *op.cit.*, v, 42.
18. Bezzel, v, 651–652.

Théodore Nouvion (1753–1825), who was military commander in the region.[19] The Nouvions and their two young sons were still living in Delémont at the time Verger was appointed minister in Berne. A third son, Ferdinand Nouvion, was born on 23 January 1806. The baby's godparents were Maximilian Josef, King of Bavaria, and Princess Maria Anna of Sigmaringen. This royal sponsorship was obviously arranged by the boy's uncle. Later that same year, on 16 July 1806, Verger, then forty-three, was married at Porrentruy (capital of the former bishopric) to Anne-Antoinette-Suzanne de Noël, daughter of an infantry major who had seen service in France. Since the marriage was childless, Verger maintained a deep interest in his sister's children and eventually, when his nephew Ferdinand Nouvion reached the age of eighteen, adopted him as his son and legal heir.[20]

In September 1806, soon after his marriage, Verger was promoted colonel on the General Staff. The following year he was given a new diplomatic assignment, the post of Bavarian minister in Stuttgart, the capital of Württemberg. Like Bavaria, Württemberg had just been raised to the status of a kingdom, as part of Napoleon's scheme for building a league of strong German states (the Confederation of the Rhine) to counterbalance the power of Austria and Prussia. Napoleon's protégés and allies were, among other things, expected to supply contingents to the Grand Army. Under these circumstances it was no doubt deemed appropriate and useful to have Bavaria represented in Stuttgart by a military man. Verger must have performed his duties to his sovereign's satisfaction, for the King's first honors list, announced in May 1808, named Colonel von Verger commander of the Civil Order of the Bavarian Crown, granting him the title of Freiherr (Baron) in the Bavarian nobility. The following June he was promoted major general.

Napoleon was now at the zenith of his power. When he embarked on his Essling-Wagram campaign in Austria, General von Verger was sent as a special Bavarian envoy to Napoleon's court and attached to his field staff during the campaign. Years later, when recalling this episode in his career, Verger wrote: "I had several long audiences with the Emperor, who always received me well. He honored me, on 16 October 1809, with the title of member of the Legion of Honor, decorated me with its gold eagle, and then, by a brevet dated 20 October, named me officer of the Legion of Honor."[21]

19. "Genéalogie de la Famille du Général Nouvion," *Actes de la Société Jurassienne d'Emulation . . . 1943*, p. 237; also, pp. 373–374, note by André Rais on "Henriette Nouvion," a granddaughter of General Nouvion, who died in 1938, aged eighty-nine, at Delémont. With her death the Nouvion family disappeared from the region. The original manuscript journal of J.-B.-A. de Verger (her great-uncle) is believed to have been at one time in Henriette Nouvion's possession; see "Checklist of Journals." Concerning General Nouvion, see Gautherot, *op.cit.*, II, 185; Quiquerez, *op.cit.*, pp. 216–217, 239; G. Six, *Dictionnaire biographique des Généraux et Amiraux de la Révolution et de l'Empire* (Paris, 1934), II, 261–262; Suratteau, *op.cit.*, index. Suratteau points out (pp. 131–132) the political implications of Nouvion's marriage to one of the local aristocrats. He also mentions (p. 435) that in 1801 another of Verger's sisters, Henriette, married a French officer (Jean-Antoine Garobuau) and concludes that "On aimait bien l'uniforme dans la famille . . ."

20. Ferdinand Nouvion (1806–1867), who inherited his uncle's title of Freiherr von Verger, served creditably in the diplomatic corps of Bavaria from 1834, when he was first secretary in Vienna, until his death in 1867 while ambassador to the Vatican. He was at one time the Bavarian minister in Berne. Nouvion had three daughters by his marriage to Anne de Provenchères.

21. Folletête, *op.cit.*, p. 233.

In spite of such honors, not all the audiences with Napoleon were as serene as Verger implies. On at least one occasion, which we know about from other sources, he was obliged to calm the Emperor's wrath. The incident took place in the interim between the Armistice of Znaim (12 July 1809, following the victory at Wagram) and the conclusion of peace at Vienna (22 October).[22] During this period hostilities were still continuing in the Voralberg and Tyrol, where Marshal Lefebvre commanded the French and Bavarian forces. Thwarted in his attempts to subdue the insurrection that had broken out in this region, Lefebvre angrily blamed his Bavarian allies and subordinates, including the young Crown Prince, the future Ludwig I of Bavaria, who was in nominal command of one of the Bavarian divisions. The withdrawal from Hallstein by Baron von Stengel, one of the Crown Prince's subordinates, particularly incensed the French marshal.[23] Tension mounted, and ugly scenes took place at Salzburg. As news of this interallied dissension reached Napoleon's headquarters in Vienna, the Emperor finally replaced Marshal Lefebvre, but at the same time conveyed his displeasure in no uncertain terms to Prince Ludwig. The Bavarian foreign minister, Montgelas, relates in his memoirs:

> The Emperor was much aroused by these occurrences. He summoned General Verger and complained vehemently about the Crown Prince. Verger was made to understand that the Prince was for the moment only a subordinate general liable to punishment like any other, that his noble birth had nothing to do with his military service, that a man might rule as he saw fit in a peaceful capital but must prove himself on the battlefield or not appear there at all. At the same time the Emperor demanded that General Verger proceed immediately to the Prince's headquarters to communicate what he had just said. He also sent a letter in the same vein through the Prince's brother-in-law, the Viceroy of Italy [Eugène de Beauharnais]. General Verger had no choice but to do as he was bid. He therefore set out via Munich, where he was given further instructions, and managed to accomplish his awkward mission with great adroitness. Thereupon the whole affair seemed to be forgotten and was never mentioned again. These are the real facts of the case which came officially to the attention of the Ministry, and the truth of which can be vouched for. . . .[24]

While engaged in these special missions Verger was still, nominally at least, the Bavarian minister to Württemberg. He retained the Stuttgart legation until 1812, when he was appointed commander in

22. The course of Franco-Bavarian relations during this period is treated in elaborate detail by Marcel Dunan, *op.cit.*, pp. 254–272, "De l'Armistice à la Paix [1809]."

23. Dunan, p. 661, n. 140. E. Schnackenburg, "Der Feldzug von 1809 in Tirol, im Salzburgischen und an der bayrischen Südgrenze," in *Jahrbücher für die deutsche Armee und Marine*, LXXXVIII (July–Sept. 1893), 270, where it is stated that an Imperial order of the day for 9 October set up a court of inquiry composed of: General Andreossy, then the French military governor of Vienna; Major General Verger, the Bavarian envoy in Vienna; General Montmarie; and General Mathieu Dumas, chief of staff to the Prince of Neuchâtel (Marshal Berthier). Stengel appeared before the court in Vienna on 27 October and

was exonerated after a hearing lasting only three-quarters of an hour; however, he was never reinstated by the Bavarians. From evidence such as this we can assume that Verger's path crossed that of Berthier, our third journal-writer, here at Vienna in October 1809. Cf. Editors' Introduction to Berthier's journal, p. 207.

24. Maximilian, Graf von Montgelas, *Denkwürdigkeiten des Bayerischen Staatsministers . . . 1799–1817*, translated from the French original by Max von Freyberg-Eisenberg, edited by Ludwig von Montgelas (Stuttgart, 1887), pp. 199–200. Cf. Dunan, *op.cit.*, pp. 257–259. Napoleon also upbraided the Prince in a letter to General Wrede, 8 October 1809 (printed by Dunan, p. 257). For a bibliographical note on Montgelas's memoirs, originally written in French, see Dunan, pp. 446–447, n. 13.

chief of the newly created Royal Bavarian Gendarmerie Corps, his duties to begin with the new year 1813. This military gendarmerie, patterned after Napoleon's famous *gendarmerie d'élite*, was responsible for the internal security of the kingdom.[25] The transfer from the Stuttgart legation to the command of the Gendarmerie Corps presented difficulties for Verger. Despite rank and honors, Verger, at fifty, was evidently worrying about his finances and his future. Without personal fortune, married to a lady who likewise lacked a substantial inheritance, how was a man living on army pay to maintain the state to which he had risen? Verger's concerns are reflected in a letter that he wrote to the Comte de Montgelas in December 1812, soon after learning of his new appointment.[26] While assuring His Excellency of his willingness to obey His Majesty's orders, Verger nevertheless expressed his regrets at leaving a post he "had become accustomed to consider the fruit of thirty-two years of service." He had, he reminded the King's minister, spent his personal savings on the furnishing of his house in order to represent His Majesty worthily and had cherished the hope that his seniority and zeal might be rewarded by appointment to "one of the big legations." His income had hitherto consisted of his military pay of 3,604 *f*. 48 plus his salary as minister at Stuttgart, 12,000 florins, making a yearly total of 15,604 *f*. 48. But now, he pointed out, his annual salary as commander of the Gendarmerie Corps was to be only 7,500 *f*.—and this sum included the allowance of 150 *f*. for office expenses, travel, entertainment, and a new household establishment! Was it not in the interest of the service and of the nation, Verger concluded, to grant the commander a salary commensurate with his rank and responsibilities? Meanwhile, Verger had been awarded the Grand Cross of the Order of the Crown, the first such award to be granted outside the royal family and the Knights of Saint Hubert. Thus his title of Freiherr in the Bavarian nobility became hereditary.

In 1813 Napoleon's star began to set. After the disastrous campaign in Russia (in which Bavarian combat forces, but few of the staff, had participated), King Maximilian Josef put his ear to the ground and heard the growing discontent among his subjects. "My position," he wrote Marshal Berthier in May 1813, "is becoming more critical by the minute. . . . Public opinion is no longer what it was in 1809 and people are out of all patience with the war."[27] On 8 October 1813 Bavaria signed, with Austria, the Treaty of Ried, by which she withdrew from the French-sponsored Confederation of the Rhine and agreed to join the great coalition against Napoleon. Consequently, when the remnants of the French army began their homeward march after the debacle at Leipzig (the "Battle of the Nations," 16–19 October 1813), a Bavarian division under General Wrede, instead of bringing aid, placed itself squarely across their path at Hanau (30 October).

25. Bezzel, *op.cit.*, VI, Part 1, 96–97. H. Schröder, *Das Königlich Bayerische Gendarmerie Korps 1812–1912* (Munich, 1912). This centennial publication includes (p. 6) a portrait of Verger that is reproduced in the present volume. See also Heinrich Junker's sesquicentennial article, "Die Entwicklung der Bayerischen Landpolizei, von der Gründung als Königlich Bayerische Gendarmerie 1812 bis zur Grossstation 1962," in *Bayerische Landpolizei*, V (1961–1962), 7–11.

26. Verger to "Monsieur le Comte" [Montgelas], Munich, 2 December 1812. Munich, Kriegsarchiv, Offizierspersonal Akt 83365. The letter is in French.
27. Max Joseph to Berthier, Munich, 14 May 1813. Marcel Dunan, ed., "Nouveaux Documents sur l'Allemagne Napoléonienne, Lettres du Roi de Bavière au Maréchal Berthier (1806–1813)," *Revue Historique*, CLXXXVI (1939), 112–143.

Verger was deeply involved in the events of 1813 and 1814. As commander of the Royal Bavarian Gendarmerie Corps he had a hand in organizing a field gendarmerie to escort General Wrede during the campaigns and provide military and civil intelligence.[28] Still more important, he was accredited as Bavaria's special envoy to the Allied Powers. Verger's performance in this role is described with considerable acerbity by Montgelas, the Bavarian prime minister:

> The relations entered into with the Allied governments and the obligations assumed towards them required the sending of a plenipotentiary to headquarters, where he would represent the interests of the state and serve as a general observer. The Allied courts suggested the appointment of General Verger, then chief of the Gendarmerie Corps, formerly envoy to Switzerland and Stuttgart. This choice, stemming from the recommendation of Baron von Binder, an old acquaintance of the General, brought no advantages to Bavaria. Verger, though basically a worthy man, was . . . better at dealing with subordinates than at approaching the higher ranks. . . . Furthermore, he was inordinately concerned with the state of affairs in his original homeland and harbored a good many personal prejudices that were equally inconsonant with Bavarian interests. The situation of the former Bishopric of Bâle and the terms of its incorporation into the Canton of Berne, as well as the restoration of the Bourbons, were of more urgent concern to him than the problems touching the interests of his sovereign. Indeed, these shortcomings were exploited in order to divert his attention from the real purpose of his mission and to let him know only as much as was desirable. It was only at the beginning, before people knew him, that he was received with special distinction and assured of complete confidence. Count von Wrede, too, had at the time of Verger's arrival, lost a good deal of prestige: the serious wound he had received at Hanau forced him to remain there for some time. . . .[29]

Verger's credentials as special envoy to Allied headquarters, signed by King Maximilian Josef and Montgelas, were dated 24 October 1813. Reports sent by him to Munich indicate that he was in Frankfurt in early December, in Freiburg-im-Breisgau from mid-December until early in the new year, and in Bâle by mid-January 1814.[30] The actual invasion of France by the Allies began in January; representatives of the "Big Four" (Austria, Prussia, Russia, and England) gathered in February at Châtillon, where the agreement known as the Treaty of Chaumont (9 March) was drawn up. Although Bavaria was not an official participant in the Châtillon conferences, Metternich regularly communicated the proceedings to the Bavarian envoy and observer. Nevertheless, Montgelas complained, "General Verger was unable, or did not feel entitled, to send to his government excerpts or even clear summaries of these proceedings," and it was necessary to obtain information from other sources.[31] Before Bavaria had an opportunity to adhere to the treaty, as she was invited to do, the rush of events had already rendered it superfluous. Allied troops entered Paris on 31 March; Napoleon abdicated on 11 April; King Louis XVIII, restored to his throne, returned to Paris on 2 May. As a consequence of these events Verger found himself in Paris at a memorable moment in its history. The Bourbons, as he had long hoped, were again the rulers of France as they had been three decades earlier when he returned from the campaigns in America wearing the Royal Deux-Ponts uniform of the King's army.

28. Bezzel, *op.cit.*, VI, Part 1, 98; Schröder, *op.cit.*, pp. 8–9.
29. Montgelas, *op.cit.*, p. 312.
30. Rieder, *op.cit.*, p. 348, with references to the Bavarian archives.
31. Montgelas, *op.cit.*, p. 351.

At the end of May 1814 peace was concluded between France and the Allies, and a general congress scheduled to meet in Vienna that autumn for the purpose of reorganizing Europe. At this juncture it was essential for such lesser powers as Bavaria to watch out for their special interests lest they be lost sight of in the impending general settlement. General Verger's role as special envoy soon came to an end. Henceforth General Wrede was entrusted with defending Bavaria's claims and reaching a preliminary understanding with Austria. Again Montgelas takes us behind the scenes:

> General Verger was at first entrusted with opening negotiations with Prince Metternich, but he was by nature shy and exceedingly cautious, liked the seclusion of his home, seldom saw the Prince, and preferred to deal with him through intermediaries. Furthermore, he was more preoccupied with the affairs of Switzerland, his homeland, than with our own, and worked on a plan for partitioning the district of Porrentruy when he should have been endeavoring to obtain compensations for Bavaria. Since he obviously lacked the zeal and activity necessary to carry out the task committed to him, it was handed over to General Wrede, whose prestige, accruing to him from the glory gained at the outset of the campaign, was such that he could exert some personal influence. . . .[32]

Montgelas's reiterated reference to Verger's preoccupation with affairs in his homeland raises the question: what was happening there to give him so much concern? Until the end of the year 1813 the former Bishopric of Bâle was still an integral part of France, as it had been for the past twenty years. However, when the Allies launched their offensive against France, one of the invasion routes led through this border department. Towards the end of December 1813 and at the beginning of 1814 Austrian troops (with some Bavarians) occupied Delémont, Porrentruy, and neighboring localities. In their wake came a temporary ruler in the person of Baron d'Andlau of Birseck, a former resident of the old bishopric,[33] and a protégé of Metternich. What would be the ultimate fate of this small state in the general European peace settlement? Would it be restored to the Prince-Bishop? Would it remain French? Or, again, would it become a new Swiss canton or be annexed to one of the existing cantons? Such were the questions that troubled and preoccupied General Verger during the year 1814. The answer eventually came from the Congress of Vienna, which by an act dated 20 March 1815 decided that the territory of the former Bishopric of Bâle (with a few very minor exceptions) would be incorporated into the Canton of Berne.[34] The action of the Congress was duly approved by

32. Montgelas, p. 378.

33. A summary history of this complicated period will be found in Rossel, *op.cit.*, pp. 243ff.; a detailed treatment in Arthur Beuchat, *L'Evêché de Bâle sous le gouvernement général du baron d'Andlau, janvier 1814–août 1815*, doctoral diss., Faculty of Philosophy, University of Berne (Delémont, 1912). See also *Dictionnaire historique . . . de la Suisse*, articles on "Bâle, Evêché de," "Berne (23., 'Réunion de l'Evêché de Bâle')," "Vienne, Congrès de," and "Andlau." Baron d'Andlau was associated with Verger in 1793, as mentioned above. Like Verger, he had been in French service before the Revolution. See *Etat militaire*, 1782–

1792, under Eptingen, Schonau, or Reinach Regiments; also Daucourt, *op.cit.*, p. 588.

34. Text in Rossel, *op.cit.*, pp. 248–249; Johann Ludwig Klüber, ed., *Acten des Wiener Congresses in den Jahren 1814 und 1815*, 9 vols. (Erlangen, 1815–1816, 1835), v, 310–318, "Déclaration des puissances . . . rassemblées en congrès à Vienne, sur les affaires de la Suisse, en date de Vienne le 20 mars 1815"; Articles 3 and 4 of the Declaration concern the Bishopric of Bâle. This solution of the problem, one of many such territorial adjustments discussed in committees at Vienna, was reached only after much bargaining and several compromises (which can be traced through the index to Klüber's compilation).

the Swiss Federal Diet, a formal "Act of Reunion"[35] was drawn up, and then, in a ceremony at Delémont on 21 December 1815, a federal commissioner transferred the territory to the Canton of Berne. One more of the small vassal states of the Holy Roman Empire thus disappeared from Europe.

In January 1816, scarcely a month after the old principality was joined to its Bernese neighbor, Verger was named a member of the Sovereign Council of the Republic of Berne.[36] Since he continued to reside in Bavaria and never went back to live in Delémont, this was probably little more than an honorary membership and mark of recognition accorded one of the old patrician families of the region as well as a reward for his share in the negotiations that had led to the Act of Reunion. Verger's participation in the Campaign of France—the Befreiungskrieg, as the Germans call it—also brought him new decorations: the Order of the Red Eagle, first class, from the King of Prussia and the Order of Saint Anne, first class, from the Emperor of Russia. In 1816, when the Bourbons were back on the French throne again (after the interval of the Hundred Days), he was at last awarded the Cross of the Order of Saint-Louis in recognition of his early services with the French in America.[37] To complete this array of medals, Verger received in 1817 his first military decoration from his adopted country, the Denkzeichen Armee of Bavaria, instituted by Maximilian Josef on 27 May.

Meanwhile, General Verger had resumed his routine military duties in Munich. He continued to hold the post of commander of the Royal Gendarmerie Corps until his retirement. In June 1822 he was promoted lieutenant general and chief of the Fifth Section of the Bavarian General Staff. It was during these years, in 1824, that Verger and his wife formally adopted their nephew Ferdinand Nouvion. In 1831 the General was disabled by an eye ailment that threatened him with blindness, but by 1833 he had completely recovered. A more pleasurable interruption came the following year, when he was sent to represent the King of Bavaria at the unveiling of the Alexander I column in St. Petersburg. As a participant in the ceremony he received a gold commemorative medal, a souvenir that no doubt sent his thoughts back to the 1814 Campaign of France when he had seen the glamorous Tsar in the field.

Verger remained on the active list of the Bavarian army until 1840, when he retired at the ripe old age of seventy-eight, being granted a fine pension and "the right to wear the uniform." By then he had worn the light blue of the Palatine-Bavarian armies for over sixty years, and in any other garb he would doubtless have felt improperly dressed. He died on 10 March 1851 in Munich, aged eighty-eight, and was given a grand funeral at St. Boniface Pfarrkirche by his wife and adopted son.

❦

35. Full text in Rossel, *op.cit.*, pp. 257–263. This "annexation" of the former bishopric to the Canton of Berne is at the root of today's "Jurassian" autonomist movement.

36. Folletête, *op.cit.*, p. 233.

37. *Staatshandbuch des Königreiches Bayern*, 1835, 1839.

The translation of Verger's journal has been made from the manuscript in the Anne S.K. Brown Military Collection, Brown University, Providence, Rhode Island. The journal is written on paper in two small octavo volumes bound in contemporary boards with leather backs, measuring approximately 16 x 9.5 cm. each. The two volumes are separately paginated: "Tome I," pp. 1–183 (last page blank); "Tome II," pp. 1–186 (last ten pages blank). The watercolor drawings bound into the first volume are reproduced here and also provide specimens of the author's youthful handwriting, which is not always easy to decipher. This is the original manuscript begun by Verger at Williamsburg in December 1781 and terminated, rather summarily, in January 1784. Two nineteenth-century transcripts of Verger's journal are described below in our "Checklist of Journals," *s.v.* Verger.

Journal

OF THE MOST IMPORTANT EVENTS

that occurred to the French Troops under the command of M. le Comte de Rochambeau, after their departure from Brest; with various particulars concerning the Squadron commanded by the late Chevalier de Ternay.

Begun at Williamsburg in Virginia this [1st] day of December 1781 by de Verger, officer of the Royal Deux-Ponts Regiment.

HONI SOIT QUI MAL Y PENSE

Volume I

The Embarkation at Brest, 4 April 1780

The regiments selected to go to America embarked successively on 3, 4, and 5 April. The grenadier companies were divided among the warships assigned to escort us, which were 7 in number:

Duc de Bourgogne, 80 guns, flagship——
Flag Captain, M. [le Comte] de Médine
Neptune, 74 guns——Capt. M. Destouches
Conquérant, 74 guns——Capt. M. de La Grandière
Eveillé, 64 guns——Capt. M. Le Gardeur de Tilly
Provence, 64 guns——Capt. M. de Lombard
Jason, 64 guns——Capt. M. de La Clocheterie
Ardent, 64 guns——Capt. M. [le Chevalier]
de Marigny

FRIGATES

Surveillante, 32 guns——Capt. M. [le Chevalier]
de Cillart [de Villeneuve]
Amazone, 32 guns——Capt. M. [le Comte]
de La Pérouse

REGIMENTS EMBARKED

First Brigade
Bourbonnais——Col. Marquis de Laval
Royal Deux-Ponts——Col. Comte [Christian]
de Deux-Ponts
Second Brigade
Soissonnais——Col. Comte de Saint-Maîme
Saintonge——Col. Comte de Custine

ARTILLERY

First Battalion, Auxonne Regiment——
Col. M. d'Aboville

Legion of Lauzun——Col. Duc de Lauzun

ARMY STAFF

Comte de Rochambeau,
Grand Cross of the Royal and Military Order of Saint-Louis, lieutenant general of the King's armies and commander in chief
Baron de Vioménil,
commander of the Order of Saint-Louis, major general
Chevalier de Chastellux,
major general and chief of staff

Comte de Vioménil,
major general
M. de Béville,
brigadier and quartermaster-general
M. de Tarlé,
intendant

15 April The fleet weighed anchor and moved to an anchorage at Bertheaume in the narrows at Brest. On this day the *Comtesse de Noailles*, a vessel of 550 tons in which I was embarked with 250 men of the Royal Deux-Ponts Regiment,[1] ran before the wind into the *Conquérant*, because of the clumsiness of our captain, Jouisse. Fortunately the second captain dropped anchor in time to prevent greater damage. Nevertheless, our bowsprit was broken, and we had to be towed back to port. Having disembarked the troops onto a reserve frigate, M. Hector, commander of the port of Brest, ordered the damage repaired with all dispatch, so that by nine o'clock the next morning we were able to return to the roadstead on the rising tide.

May 1780

2 May Meanwhile, headwinds had obliged the fleet to return to port, and it was not until the night of 1–2 May that the wind turned fair; at three in the morning the signal was given to up anchor and, shortly after, to make sail. By approximately ten o'clock that morning 39 transports had cleared the narrows, and very soon the coast of Brittany was out of sight. Off Ushant

we saw the wreck of the *San José*, a Spanish ship sunk there recently.

10 May We entered the Bay of Gascony, or Biscay, where a southwest wind, which blows very fresh in these parts, set us in towards the coast, bringing with it a heavy fog and frequent squalls that forced us to tack in very close to shore. Six leagues[2] off we sighted the Spanish coast, and had the wind not shifted, we should have had to anchor in La Corunna or face the peril of shipwreck. Several of our vessels had lost their fore-topmasts. Among others the *Provence* signaled that she had sustained irreparable damage from the sea and requested permission to put into the nearest port. This was refused by signal from M. de Ternay, and the damage was repaired in one hour.

That day the *Amazone* chased a ship that turned out to be Swedish. Next day the *Surveillante* chased a large English privateer and had already fired a cannon-shot at her when, contrary to everyone's expectation, she received a signal to tack just as she was about to catch up with her prey.

The heavy weather left us after we rounded the Cape of Ferrol. It was in these latitudes that we saw a species of flying fish. They average about 8 inches in length. They have two large hollow fins shaped like wings which, when inflated, permit them to rise into the air and fly about 50 feet, so long as their wings are wet. This is the only defense nature has provided them against the dorados, some of which are 3 feet long. The latter are a lovely shade of sky-blue with yellow-tipped heads and yellow tails. They are always pursuing flying fish, which, thanks to their wings, can es-

---

1. Von Closen, second captain in the Deux-Ponts Regiment, who was also embarked on the *Comtesse de Noailles* (depicted in Verger's sketch, reproduced here), characterizes it as an "old tub." Von Closen's journal (see "Checklist of Journals") provides a parallel and complementary account of the Atlantic crossing. He states (p. 6) that Ternay's entire fleet, including the transports, consisted of 47 sail. Verger lists only the escorting navy ships. Brisout de Barneville ("Composition de l'Escadre commandée par M. le Chevalier de Ternay," pp. 222–223) adds the following names:

Cutter, 16 guns: *Guêpe*
Armed "flûtes" (supply ships): *Fantasque, Isle de France*
"Gabares" (armed transports): *Pluvier, Saumon, Barbue, Ecureuil, Spritly* (cutter), *Henry* (privateer)

Transports: *Aimable Marie, Amazone, Aventure, Baron d'Arros, Casa Major, Cibelle, Comtesse de Noailles, Doyard, Drack* [Drake?], *Félicité, Harmonie, Jeune Mercure, Loire, Lion, Marquise de Lévi, Mars, Patrocle, Père de Famille, Petit Cousin, Pressigny, Saint Esprit, Vigilant, Rover*

A similar list, included in the Vicomte de Rochambeau's journal (pp. 195–196), gives these additional names: *Duc de Chartres, Française, Jument, Turgot, Vénus.* He also states that the frigate *Bellone* and the cutters *Levrette* and *Prudence* accompanied the fleet only to the end of the channel at Cape Finisterre. None of these lists identifies the *Fanÿ* shown in Verger's sketch.

2. A nautical league is 5½ kilometers, or approximately 3½ miles.

cape. Both make very delicate eating. During the bad weather we also saw a kind of fish as big as a horse that the sailors call a devilfish. We caught many tuna, which travel in schools and like to follow ships. Their flesh is appetizing and a great boon to the crews.

For several days we were treated to the spectacle of dolphins, which spout water through two small tubes, like a fountain, to a height in proportion to their length, which extends to 20 feet in some. They usually travel in schools and swim a meandering course. We also saw several whales. Whenever we were threatened with bad weather, a dusky bird called a halcyon appeared. These birds are very common and are certain harbingers of storm.

After passing the Azores in an excellent breeze we fell into the Trades, which we held for a month, being driven from 40 to 50 leagues a day in most beautiful weather and a very smooth sea.

Towards the end of May we saw a prodigious quantity of floating weed called "sea grapes" in bunches averaging 2 feet in diameter. At times it was so thick that the sea looked like a marsh. We met it, though in diminishing quantity, to within a short distance of the land.

One sees in the colonies a kind of fish that looks like a shell.[3] Of a clear violet color, it is sticky and looks quite lifeless; however, when you touch it, it burns like hot water. As we approached the torrid zone it became insufferably hot.

June 1780

20 June About three o'clock, while in the latitude of the Bermuda Islands and 80 leagues from shore, we sighted some ships astern.[4] After the *Surveillante* signaled that they were superior in number to their pursuers, the *Neptune* and the *Eveillé* were sent on reconnaissance, while our squadron sailed to windward of the convoy and the signal for general quarters was given. They discovered 5 ships of the line, led by a frigate that had covered half the distance between them and our reconnaissance vessels. When the *Eveillé* and the *Neptune* were almost within range of the *Robust*, which was at least 2 miles from the rest of the fleet, they were preparing to put her in their crossfire when M. de Ternay signaled them to heave to, an order that astonished and even angered many of the sailors.

The time it took the rest of our squadron to join these two vessels enabled the English fleet to come to the support of its leading vessel and form its battle line. After we had made recognition signals, to which they failed to reply, the Admiral gave the signal to begin combat, each side being then within normal range of the other's guns. Although the English were to windward, they had to sail very close-hauled. The vessel at the tail end of their line, unable to hold course and in danger, if she tacked, of falling down upon our line, performed a very handsome maneuver that was also very bold and that would have been impracticable had she not been a smart sailer. She bore away, passed directly in front of our whole line, and received the broadside of every ship; then she sailed, firing briskly, to the head and to windward of her own line, thus preventing her own ships from being cut off from her.[5]

After the two battle lines had passed one another, we and the English made simultaneous signals to tack about and resume combat. This time we shelled one another at closer range without, however, doing one another much harm. It was then six o'clock in the evening, and after we had passed them, M. de Ternay changed course. The English went their way, unpursued by M. de Ternay. As we were stronger by two vessels, one cannot blame him enough for his mediocre performance; for had our Admiral maneuvered according to the normal rules observed by mariners, it is certain that he would have captured a vessel or would at least have inflicted much damage on the enemy, whereas Arbuthnot can now boast of having suffered none.[6]

3. Doubtless a Portuguese man-of-war.
4. See Clermont-Crèvecœur's journal, p. 16 and n. 4.
5. Diagrammatic sketches of the engagement of 20 June off the Bermudas, similar to those reproduced here from Verger's journal, are in the journals of Brisout de Barneville (pp. 233–235) and of the Vicomte de Rochambeau

(pp. 200–201). See also the diagram (based on British sources) in Mahan, *Operations of the Navies*, between pp. 156 and 157.
6. The British fleet engaged by Ternay was not Arbuthnot's but a squadron returning from escorting a large convoy to Bermuda under Captain Cornwallis (the brother

Nevertheless, we held our fire during the night, and by morning no enemy was in sight.

We captured a privateer of 12 guns that was carrying [dispatches announcing] the surrender of Charleston.[7]

July 1780

4 July We were entering the Chesapeake Bay when towards eight o'clock that evening, after land had been signaled, we sighted several sail in the beautiful twilight. Without waiting to ascertain whether the vessels were large, or sending a frigate to find out, M. de Ternay tacked us about precipitately and ran feint courses through the night. The ships we had sighted consisted of a large convoy, two warships of 64 guns, and one of 50.

Next morning we spied two unidentified frigates in the midst of our squadron. When they were called to the Admiral's attention, he did not even give the order to chase them. When the frigates perceived that they were in the midst of a French fleet, they fired two cannon-shots at the *Duc de Bourgogne*. This insult aroused the good M. de Ternay from his lethargy, and he signaled the *Surveillante* and the *Amazone*, as well as the *Eveillé*, to pursue them. Our vessels were gaining visibly on the English frigates, especially the *Surveillante*, which was making such speed that she forced the two frigates to jettison their boats and several cannon. The *Surveillante* would shortly have caught them had our admiral not signaled her to tack about—from jealousy, it was said, at the *Surveillante*'s having passed the *Amazone*.[8]

When we had turned north, half the men in our crews fell sick from the almost continuous fog. On my ship alone four or five were added to the number each day. In the evenings we enjoyed watching the *aurora borealis* and the firmament, which is much more beautiful than anywhere in Europe.

10 July We anchored off Newport, and on the 11th

we entered this long-desired harbor. On the evening of our arrival the city was all illuminated, and our ships set off quantities of rockets.[9]

On the 13th we disembarked all our troops, half of whom were suffering from scurvy. We camped that evening above the city on a good site. The number of our sick prevented us from immediately taking measures for our security.

21 July On the 21st, 22 sail were sighted; they were all large ships, and we learned that Clinton was embarked in them with 6,000 men. Our situation was such that we had great cause to fear that we should be taken by storm. With no fort, with not a gun unloaded, after the grenadiers and chasseurs of our brigade had been detached to march to the Neck [Brenton's Point], we had left only 400 men in condition to face the enemy. The rest were absolutely tent-bound, or else unable to stand up for an hour. The brigade of the Soissonnais Regiment had fared better and still had 1,000 men fit for service; but the artillery and Lauzun's Legion were very weak. Our sailors as well had suffered terribly from scurvy. The *Conquérant* alone had 400 sick.

Had Clinton been more resolved to attack us, it is certain he would have met with but feeble resistance; with three landing-points to guard, we owed our safety to his irresolution alone.[10]

The day after he appeared I was embarked with a captain and 50 men on the *Conquérant* to reinforce her garrison, since she would have been the first vessel under fire because M. de Ternay had neglected to moor his squadron broadside. At the same time the Second Battalion of the Soissonnais Regiment was sent to camp on the island of Conanicut.

25 July By the 25th we no longer feared the enemy's arrival, as by then all our artillery was in firing condition and we had set up a fine battery for firing hot shot. The enemy frigates sometimes sailed so far inshore that we could make out the dress of their crews. That day some [American] militia arrived to join us.

---

of the General); it consisted of two 74's, two 64's, a 50-gun ship, and the frigate *Triton* (not the *Robust*). Mahan, p. 155.

7. The capture of the privateer took place on 18 June. See Clermont-Crèvecœur's journal, n. 3.

8. See Clermont-Crèvecœur's journal, n. 5.

9. For chronology of the arrival and landing at Newport, see Clermont-Crèvecœur's journal, n. 6.

10. See Clermont-Crèvecœur's journal, n. 9.

❦ August 1780 ❧

10 August The enemy disappeared and returned to Sandy Hook.

16 August During the night the wind was so strong that most of our tents were blown down. The *Fan-tasque* went aground, and the *Cybèle*, a pretty privateer, went on the rocks. This was the same storm that did so much damage in Barbados.[11]

19 August The English fleet returned and block-aded us.

29 August On the 29th about 20 savages [Indians] arrived.[12] These were deputies of the Four Nations

11. Admiral de Ternay's manuscript journal mentions "beaucoup d'orages" during the night of 15–16 August; Gallatin's journal (MS, p. 16), 16 August, also speaks of heavy winds that blew down many of the tents. There is, however, no mention of mishaps to the *Cybèle* and *Fantasque*. On the other hand, Ternay, recording a storm during the night of 8–9 October, mentions that the *Cybèle* was then on the rocks and the *Fantasque* aground; see Clermont-Crèvecœur's journal, n. 13. Verger, when writing up his journal, probably confused these two storms.

12. The circumstances of the Indians' visit to Newport are explained in a letter from Philip Schuyler to Lafayette, Albany, 18 August 1780; although the letter was addressed to Lafayette, it was delivered in his absence to Rochambeau, who in turn enclosed it in a letter to Washington (Newport, 31 August 1780) when reporting on the visit. Library of Congress, Washington Papers, Vol. 146, item 134A; Vol. 148, item 139. Schuyler wrote: "Immediately after it had been determined at head quarters to offer some of the Indians an Opportunity of seeing Count De Rochambeau, Chevalier de Ternay and the Army and fleet under their respective commands, as happy consequences would probably result from the interview, I directed Mr. Deane, the agent for Indian affairs, to conduct eight or ten of them to Rhode Island. Unhappily at the time my letter arrived, the hostile part of the Six Nations were collecting in force and threatened destruction to the Oneidas, then too weak to make effectual resistance. . . . This event has hitherto prevented Mr. Deane from prosecuting the intended Journey. He will however leave this to-morrow, not with eight or ten, as I at first proposed, but with eighteen, the increase of number was in consequence of the anxiety that the whole expressed to see the troops of the King, their Father, for this is the appellation they invariably bestow on His Most Christian Majesty. Thirteen of them are Oneidas and Tuscaroras, and I have expressly selected a few, whose wives and children are carried off by the Enemy, and who will probably go in quest of them as soon as they return from Rhode Island. This is what I wish, as they will communicate the arrival of His Majesty's fleet and troops to the hostile Savages, whom the Enemy with great Industry have taught to believe that France was not in alliance with us, and never intended to afford us any assistance, and that whatever I had said on the subject was mere forgery and only calculated to prevent them from attacking her.

The remaining five are Caghnawagas from the Sault of St. Louis near Montreal in Canada, four of them, men of influence and consideration in their nation, and whose attachment to us has induced them to leave their country and follow our fortunes. — I do not know how far His Excellency Count de Rochambeau and Chevalier de Ternay will conceive themselves authorized to address the Nations of which these people are a part, in His Majesty's name, but if they could do it with propriety, I should not hesitate to recommend it, persuaded that a variety of salutary consequences would flow from it, for both the Iroquois and the Indians of Canada still retain a strong and lively attachment to the French Nation. Indeed I have very little doubt but that their disposition with respect to these States will take a material turn the moment they are convinced of the generous interposition of the King in our favor. Under this conviction I most earnestly wish, if the French Commanders should see cause to address them, that His Majesty's determination effectually to support the American cause in the present contest should be forcibly impressed on them, nor would it be improper to observe that the King has heard with chagrin that the Indians who considered him as their Father have, not only insulted the Americans whom he regards as his brethren, that a continuation of Hostilities on the part of the Indians cannot fail of drawing his resentment on them, and that he will certainly chastise them unless they desist. — When however De Vaudreuil surrendered Canada, he gave before his departure thence a token of recognition to the Indians. It consisted of a Golden Crucifix and a watch; perhaps it would be proper on this occasion to remind the Caghnawagas of it, and to send those tokens by them with a message to all the Canadian Indians, requesting them to send deputies to the Count, and giving assurances for their return whenever they choose. Whatever Communications the Count may choose to make, either to the Indians of Canada or the Inhabitants, will be faithfully conveyed by the Caghnawagas. — If any goods are [arrived?] which were by the King intended as a present to the Savages I wish it would be mentioned to those now going to Rhode Island, and the goods delivered to Mr. Deane for distribution when he returns to Schenectady. . . . Mr. Deane, who accompanies these people, is a person of Abilities, well versed in the Manners and Customs of the Indians, and perfect master of their language; full confidence may be placed in him in any matters rela-

who had come to make sure of our arrival and to offer us their alliance.[13] They were taken to see the General, to whom they made the following address through a Canadian interpreter who spoke their language and repeated each phrase in French in these terms:

O my Father, whom we have chosen of our own free will to lead us in war, we promise you every assistance. We should have been pleased if some of our neighboring tribes had not gone over to the enemy, but the English have such good *tafia*, such good rum! Besides, they give us gunpowder to go

hunting. They are very bad when you resist them, but it is by all these things that we are often seduced and brought over to their side.

M. de Rochambeau replied that the King thanked them and would not let them lack for spirits.[14] Then he gave them a medal struck with the arms of France, together with swords, shirts, blankets, and rouge.[15] They seemed well satisfied and hastened to try on their new garments. As soon as they got to their quarters, they combed the rouge into their hair and daubed it all over their shirts and blankets, since it is their cus-

tive to these people."

The "Mr. Deane" who accompanied the Indians to Newport was James Dean (1748–1823), a native of Groton, Connecticut, who had lived as a boy among the Oneidas and mastered the Iroquois languages; a protégé of Eleazar Wheelock, employed during the Revolution as an agent of Congress, Dean had graduated from Dartmouth College in 1773.

13. See Verger's drawing of the standing Indian chief (reproduced here) that appears at this point in his manuscript. This figure and the one following (Indian dancing with sword) were copied from Verger's journal by, or for, Baron von Closen, probably in the 1820's when both men were residing in Bavaria. In Von Closen's copy the two figures, which have been slightly prettified, are combined into a drawing on a single sheet. Only a photograph of the Von Closen drawing has survived; this is reproduced in Evelyn Acomb's edition of Von Closen's journal, facing p. 264. For the later relationship between the two former officers of the Deux-Ponts Regiment, see our descriptive note to Albrecht Adam's painting of the Morrisania Skirmish, Vol. II, No. 47.

14. The official version of Rochambeau's reply (with no mention of "spirits") is printed in Doniol, v, 370–371. Rochambeau distributed to the chiefs copies of his address in French and in English, written on official stationery engraved with the royal arms and his own. One such copy is preserved in the Library of Congress, Washington Papers, Vol. 148, item 111 (see illustration). Informing Washington of the Indians' visit, Rochambeau reported from Newport, 31 August 1780: "Before Yesterday, I received a Deputation composed of 19. Indians of Different Nations. . . . I received them most heartily, I shewed them yesterday the French Troops mixed with the American. I put some regiments a manoeuvring before them, with field pieces and firing. They were overjoyed at what they saw and heard. The huzzars of Lauzun have surprized them, in camp, as did likewise great Lobsters of which they laughed very heartily at Table. They Drank the King of France, The United States, and the Indian

nations, who are allied to us. I have given them my answer, of which I send your Excellency a copy, and I desired them to send several Copys to those nations who have taken up the Hatchet. I made them several Gifts and gave to the chiefs, some pieces representing the coronation of his Majesty. They will go to Day, on board the fleet and I believe they will set off to morrow." LC, Washington Papers, Vol. 148, item 139, in English, signed by Rochambeau.

Admiral de Ternay noted in his journal (MS, p. [27]), 31 August, that he received 19 "sauvages oneidas" on board his flagship the *Duc de Bourgogne*: "I offered them dinner and sent them ashore after giving them some presents and exhorting them to join our allies in fighting against the English, the enemies of the French."

15. Presents for the Indians had not been overlooked by the planners of Rochambeau's expedition. For example, a memorandum entitled "Observations sur quelques articles relatifs à la Marine pour une expédition dans l'Amérique septentrionale," prepared by Lafayette and dated Versailles, 21 February 1780, specified: "Presents for the Savages . . . raw vermilion, striped woolen blankets, silver bracelets, medals with the portrait of the King and the arms of France. The presents will serve to revive the savages' love for the French. . . . To these articles should be added tomahawks, scalping knives, munitions and long rifles." Archives Nationales, Marine B⁴, Vol. 172, foll. 105–106; cited in *La Fayette*, exhibition catalogue (Archives Nationales, Paris 1957), p. 44, No. 88. An "Etat des effets de campement et habillement jugés nécessaires à la suite du corps de troupes qui doit incessamment s'embarquer," dated 10 March 1780, included: "presents for the Savages—1000 blankets, red and blue stripes; 200 silver medals with the King's arms; 50 long rifles; 200 ear pendants." Archives de la Guerre, A⁴ 48, pièce 50; cited in *La Fayette*, exhibition catalogue, p. 47, No. 98. Blanchard, commissary general, noted in his journal ([1], p. 49) that among the presents given by Rochambeau to the Indians were "red blankets that had been strongly recommended to us when we were leaving Brest."

tom to rouge their faces as well as their hair and the rest of their bodies.

I went to the room where they were assembled. They were listening intently to one of their comrades who was amusing himself by beating a small drum in a very monotonous fashion and who seemed utterly entranced by the sounds he was making. They abandoned their music in order to examine my epaulet and asked for my sword-knot, explaining by signs that they would hang it from their nose as an ornament. But a watch-chain worn by one of my comrades struck their fancy just then, so they left me to go and ask him for it.

They habitually oil their bodies and paint certain parts with rouge. Red is their favorite color. They slit the lobes around the edges of their ears until they hang down to their chins, weighed down by various small ornaments. They also pierce the cartilage of their noses and attach several baubles. They pull out the hair at the nape of their necks and attach small locks of hair to the top of their heads. When young they cut various designs in their faces. They have an olive complexion. They prefer rum above all things, and when drunk they are very dangerous.

The following day M. de Rochambeau paraded his army before these savages, but nothing pleased them so much as our pioneers with their axes. We drilled, then fired our muskets to the accompaniment of cannon fire, which alarmed them no end. That evening they all gathered in a large room to dance, and we were admitted.[16] They marched in, two by two, their chief at their head, singing a war song. Each held two small pieces of wood which he struck together by way of accompaniment. When they got ready to dance, half remained standing and the rest, having removed their animals skins and displaying very well-proportioned bodies that were oiled and rouged, began to

dance with swords in their hands while their comrades intoned a very monotonous chant, accompanying themselves with the little sticks and jumping in strict rhythm.[17]

They danced with great strength and agility, assuming various postures symbolizing a man in combat and breaking out from time to time into war-cries or dirges so piercing and violent that they filled one with terror. With them was a German from near Mannheim, who lived in their country.[18] We asked him if he had no desire to return to his native land. He replied that he would be very loath to leave a country where he was his own master and to part from these good people to return to a place where he would be a slave.

The Indians returned home well satisfied with the French.[19]

❧ October 1780 ❧

26 October Three frigates left port: the *Amazone* for France and the *Surveillante* and *Hermione* on a cruise.

31 October Our navy had a sharp alert. It happened that snow had fallen in the narrows during the night, covering the ships by morning, and their sails were enveloped in a thick mist. There was great activity as they hoisted their anchors to proceed to moor broadside.

On the 30th and 31st M. de Rochambeau's army entered winter quarters in Newport. This town is situated on a small island about 12 leagues long by 6 wide.[20] Like the province to which it gave its name, it is called Rhode Island. It is the capital of the province and contains between 800 and 1,000 houses, mostly built of wood, occupied by 6,000–7,000 inhabitants.[21]

16. Verger's drawing of an Indian dancing with sword is inserted at this point in his manuscript. See illustration.
17. The bar of music, introduced here in Verger's manuscript, is evidently intended to indicate the monotonous chant and rhythm of the Indians' dance.
18. Von Closen, in his account of the Indians' visit (p. 39), identifies the man as "a person named Frey, a German (native of Schwetzingen) and a tailor by trade, who had lived among them since the year 1758, and who, since he had served with the English, had learned their language, which he spoke rather well."

19. Verger's account of the Indians' visit to Newport is one of the most detailed of those extant and the only one to include a pictorial and musical commentary. Other interesting accounts are found, for example, in the journals of Blanchard (1), pp. 48–49; Charlus (1), pp. 76–80; Gallatin (1), pp. 330–332; Von Closen, pp. 37–39.
20. A land league equals 4 kilometers, or approximately 2½ miles. The island of Rhode Island is actually 15 miles long by 5 miles wide.
21. Newport and Providence both served as meeting places for the General Assembly of the "State of Rhode Island

The town has few notable buildings.[22] The town hall, which we used as our large hospital, is quite handsome, however, and is built of brick. There is also quite a good public library where the General Assembly meets in the summer. It is built in the Greek style of architecture, with a pretty portico adorned with four Doric columns at the entrance. There is also a lodge for the Freemasons. The meat market is built of brick and is rather pretty. All the buildings consecrated to religious worship, except the Jewish synagogue, are built of wood and are not especially notable. These include one church, two Presbyterian meetinghouses, one for Quakers that is fairly spacious, three for the Baptists, another for the Moravian brethren, and the aforementioned synagogue. Most of them were used for our hospitals.

The harbor, though rather difficult to enter, is one of the best in the world.[23] Easily a hundred vessels can winter there. It extends all the way to Providence, which is accessible to frigates. On a small island masking the entrance is an excellent emplacement for a fort containing a double-star battery, but since it was not

yet finished, we fitted it with 60 cannon from our ships. Fort Brenton contained twenty 24-pounders and six mortars. At the harbor entrance there is a lighthouse.

Three miles from town one may see the house where Dean Berkeley lived.[24]

The province of Rhode Island lies between 41° and 42° north latitude and 72° and 73° west longitude in the healthiest climate of North America. The winter is quite cold, and the summer very pleasant, especially on this island where the excessive heat common in America is cooled by the sea breezes. The land is generally quite fertile, though stony; its normal crop is corn. Before the occupation by General Prescott and his army there were many trees, every one of which they cut down, as well as those along the public promenades.[25] The higher land contained principally white pine whose needles, while still tender, are used to make beer. In addition, this province has several advantages, including two large rivers on the mainland and an excellent post road on the island. The surrounding sea, and even the harbor, abound in delicious fish—

and Providence Plantations" and continued to serve as joint capitals until 1900. The population of Newport in 1783 was 5,531, according to the statistics compiled by Evarts B. Greene and Virginia D. Harrington, *American Population before the Federal Census of 1790* (New York, 1932), pp. 68–69.

22. Most of the notable buildings mentioned by Verger have survived in some form and are described, with illustrations, in Antoinette F. Downing and Vincent Scully, Jr., *The Architectural Heritage of Newport, Rhode Island, 1640–1915* (Cambridge, Mass., 1952; 2nd rev. edn., New York, 1967). The *Town Hall* is the Colony House, built by Richard Munday, 1739–1740. The *good public library* is the Redwood Library, built by Peter Harrison in 1748. The *meat market* is the Brick Market, designed by Peter Harrison, 1760–1772. The *Jewish Synagogue*, also by Peter Harrison, 1759–1763, is the Touro Synagogue. The *one church* mentioned by Verger is Trinity Episcopal Church, Spring and Church Streets, designed by Richard Munday in 1726. The *two Presbyterian meetinghouses* refer to the First Congregational Church in Mill Street and the Second Congregational Church in Clarke Street; the original buildings, designed by Cotton Palmer of Taunton in 1729 and 1735, have survived only in mutilated form and now serve other purposes. *The meetinghouse for Quakers*, the earliest part of which dates to 1700, is at the corner of present Marlborough Street and

West Broadway. Of the *three Baptist meetinghouses* one survives: the Sabbatarian (Seventh Day Baptist), meetinghouse, designed by Richard Munday in 1729, now on the grounds of the Newport Historical Society in Touro Street. The *Moravians* met in a building that occupied the site of the present Kay Chapel on the corner of Church and High Streets. The *Freemasons* apparently had no building of their own at this time but met around in various places, including the Colony House. Several French officers with Masonic affiliations established relations with their brother Masons in Rhode Island; cf. Blanchard (1), pp. 61, 63–64. See map, Vol. II, No. 6, and the view of Newport, No. 11.

23. See Clermont-Crèvecœur's journal, n. 11; maps, Vol. II, Nos. 4, 5, 6, and 7. The *small island* mentioned by Verger is Rose Island. *Fort Brenton* was on the site of the present Fort Adams. The *lighthouse* (designated as "fanal" on the Berthier brothers map of Rhode Island, No. 7) was at Beaver Tail, the southern tip of Conanicut Island.

24. "Whitehall," restored in recent years, still stands in the town of Middletown. The philosopher George Berkeley (1685–1753), Dean of Londonderry and later Bishop of Cloyne, built the original house in 1729 and resided there until his return to Ireland in 1731.

25. See Clermont-Crèvecœur's journal, n. 10, on the British occupation of Newport.

blackfish, lobster, eel, skate, mackerel, bluefish, succulent cod, and plenty of excellent oysters. The garden produce does not amount to much because the land is chiefly laid out in meadows and pastures. The horses are strong-hocked and vigorous, and the cattle are much larger than those in the rest of America. The butter and cheese here are excellent, as are all kinds of poultry.

There are partridges here that are smaller than ours and rather resemble our quail, as well as rabbits, wild duck, and an abundance of plovers and snipe, which make very delicate eating. One also finds humming-birds of astonishing minuteness, who sing very sweetly, and a kind of blackbird with brilliant red feathers at the joints of its wings. Other birds found here have no resemblance, either in song or plumage, to those of Europe.

Before the war the number of inhabitants of this province, including negroes, had reached 35,000.[26] Nevertheless, goods produced in the province itself were few and limited principally to horses, foodstuffs, a small quantity of wheat, spermaceti candles, and rum, which they traded chiefly with Connecticut and the neighboring colonies. Actually, however, Rhode Island carries on a very extensive commerce in peacetime. They normally trade with England, Holland, Africa, the Windward Islands, as well as with the neighboring colonies. From these countries they import the following articles: from England, cloth from her factories; from Holland, specie; from Africa, slaves;[27] from the Windward Islands, sugar, coffee, and syrups; and from the neighboring colonies, building materials, produce, and lumber. The goods they buy in one place they export as payment to another. They pay for the manufactures of London with silver from Holland, export to Holland the sugar they import from the Islands, send to the Islands the slaves they procure in Africa, and keep the building materials and produce for themselves. They export the rum they distill to Africa, and the cloth bought in London to the neighboring colonies. Even during the war the inhabitants live by trading continuously. They also distill rum and manufacture candles from sperm oil.

Every year they elect a governor and a committee of five to police the province and try law cases. The Presbyterians and Baptists are the dominant religious groups. The people in general are very little attached to their religion, and each child has the right to practice his religious duties or not, without being forced to by his parents.

15 December The Chevalier de Ternay died. The whole army was paraded for his funeral. He was buried in the Baptist cemetery.[28]

26. Greene and Harrington (*op.cit.*, p. 67), estimate the total population of Rhode Island as 59,678 (including 3,761 negroes) in 1774 and as 51,869 (including 2,342 negroes) in 1783.

27. In June 1774 the General Assembly of Rhode Island passed an "Act prohibiting the importation of Negroes into this Colony." The complete text is in *Records of the Colony of Rhode Island and Providence Plantations*, ed. John Russell Bartlett, VII (Providence, 1862), 251–253.

28. Charles-Louis d'Arsac, chevalier de Ternay (1723–1780), is buried in the churchyard of Trinity Episcopal Church (not the Baptist cemetery) where a monument to his memory was placed at the King's expense in 1785. Ternay died in the Hunter House (on present Washington Street), which served as the navy's headquarters ashore. The army's *Livre d'ordre*, 15 December 1780, gives instructions for the funeral services the next day: the chaplains were to meet at Ternay's house at half past nine in the morning. The Bourbonnais Regiment was ordered to be there at the same hour; its first battalion would escort the funeral procession. Other units, which would receive their orders from Colonel Comte de Saint-Maîme, would be stationed as follows: Royal Deux-Ponts in the "place d'armes" (Washington Square) with its right extending northward, Soissonnais also in the square, Saintonge in Spring Street, the Second Battalion of Auxonne artillery in Spring Street near the "grand temple" (Trinity Church). Staff officers were to meet at the Baron de Vioménil's residence (Joseph Wanton House in Thames Street) at a quarter to ten. Blank cartridges, three per man, would be issued at the artillery park. After the salute of three volleys the officers, with the exception of those escorting the colors, would join the Comte de Saint-Maîme while the petty officers marched the troops back to quarters.

A brief notice of Ternay's death, couched in properly eulogistic language, appeared in the *Gazette Françoise*, No. 5 (15 December 1780), the newspaper issued by the Imprimerie Royale de l'Escadre at Newport (see illustration), but it is evident from references in several of the officers' journals (including Berthier's, p. 237) that Ternay was not generally popular nor was his loss greatly lamented. Further details about Ternay's death and about his memorial monument (a marble tablet inscribed in

[On 21 January] the *Culloden*, an English ship of 74 guns, appeared at the entrance to the harbor and made as if to enter. We all thought she was French, but soon she fired a gun, hoisted her flag, and made off in the direction of New York. That evening there was such a storm that she was blown ashore and sunk, though the crew was saved.[29] That same evening the *Bedford* was dismasted while chasing the *Surveillante*.

25 January The *Surveillante* and the *Hermione* returned from their cruise and captured two small vessels.

March 1781

The following description was written by M. de Granchain, adjutant of the fleet:[30]

Relation of the sortie of the French squadron commanded by the Chevalier Destouches, and of the engagement that took place on 16 March 1781, between this Squadron and the English squadron commanded by Admiral Arbuthnot

The results of the storm of 21 January having been to bring the naval forces of France and England in North America into approximate equilibrium, the Chevalier Destouches took immediate advantage of this circumstance to halt the depredations and brigandage committed by the enemy along the Virginia coast during the past two months. For this purpose he promptly detached a ship of 64 guns and two frigates under the command of Captain de Tilly to the Chesapeake Bay with orders to destroy the English flotilla and its escorting frigates there. The enemy had taken the precaution to run their vessels up the little Elizabeth River, preventing M. de Tilly from completely fulfilling his mission. However, his expedition was not fruitless, since he captured or destroyed 10 enemy vessels and brought back to Newport the warship *Romulus* of 44 guns, which he had seized at the entrance to the Bay.[31] The success of this first attempt, and the ardent desire of the Chevalier Destouches to give effective help to the state of Virginia, determined him to undertake a new expedition with more ample means.

Latin, now in the vestibule of Trinity Church), with illustrations, are in Stone, *French Allies*, pp. 338–351, and Forbes and Cadman, ii, 47–55. Francisco de Miranda transcribed in his journal, 5 September 1784, an inscription in French that apparently marked Ternay's grave prior to the arrival of the marble tablet in 1785; Miranda, *Travels in the United States*, tr. J. P. Wood, ed. John S. Ezell (Norman, Oklahoma, 1963), p. 139.

Upon Ternay's death the command of the fleet at Newport passed to the Chevalier Destouches, captain of the *Neptune*, who retained his interim command until the arrival of Barras in May 1781.

29. See Berthier's journal, p. 238, and Von Closen, pp. 56–57. News of the movements of the British fleet was regularly relayed to Newport by various observers along the Connecticut coast of Long Island Sound. There are, for example, letters to Rochambeau from William Ledyard, dated New London, 28–30 January 1781, among the papers of Rochambeau in the Paul Mellon Collection. Ledyard wrote on 28 January that "a 74 was dismantled in the late gale of wind. This we saw plain with our glasses. Another is said to be on shore, but this last wants confirmation." Later that same day Ledyard wrote: "a 74 gun ship got on Shagwomanock Rief this side Montock Point and their sunk & the whole ship's crew per-ished—a 74 gun ship was intirely dismasted which was obligd. to heave all her guns over board except her lower deck guns—this ship I saw towed into the Bay." Later that same year (while Rochambeau was hastening south to Virginia) Ledyard lost his life, 6 September 1781, when defending Fort Griswold at Groton, Connecticut, against British raiders led by Benedict Arnold. Letters and maps were sent to Destouches from New London by an agent who signed himself "Pennevert," January–April 1781; *Destouches Papers*, Nos. 15–20, 23–28. Pennevert, in his letter of 2 March, expressed some suspicion of Ledyard.

30. The "Relation" Verger transcribed in his journal was printed at Newport soon after the event by the Imprimerie Royale de l'Escadre, the French Fleet Press, which had been set up ashore on the "Rue de la Pointe," near the naval headquarters along the waterfront (present Washington Street). A few copies of this 4-page leaflet have survived; see our illustration. Verger's attribution of this official report to Granchain is confirmed by the latter's own correspondence; see "Checklist of Journals," *s.v.* Granchain.

31. On Tilly's expedition, see Clermont-Crèvecœur's journal, n. 15. The *Romulus* is depicted (far left, "K") in the "Vue de la Ville, Port et Rade de Newport" drawn about this time; Vol. ii, No. 11.

etat Major de l'armée

le Comte de rocham bault. grand croix
de l'ordre royale et militaire de St. louis
lieutenant general des armées du roi
comendant en chef.

le baron de viomenil comendeur de
l'ordre de St. louis. Marechal de camp

le chevalier de chatelux Marechal
de Camp. et major general.

le comte de viomenil Marechal de Camp

Mr. de bevile marechal general des
logis. et brigadier

Mr. de tarlé intendant

le 15. le 15. d'avril, la flotte leva l'encre et
alla mouiller a bertome, dans le
goulet de brest.
ce même jour la comtesse de noille
batiment de 550 toneaux ayant 250
homes du regt royale deux-ponts avec
les quels j'étois embarqué, par malador
du capt. nomé juife, dona vent arriere
sur le Conquerant et heureusement
que le Nord mouilla a tems pour
empecher que l'avari ne soit plus

la comtesse de noailles. de 550 toneaux

la fany.

VERGER'S SKETCH OF THE *COMTESSE DE NOAILLES*, THE TRANSPORT SHIP THAT
BROUGHT HIM TO AMERICA (*see p. xix*)

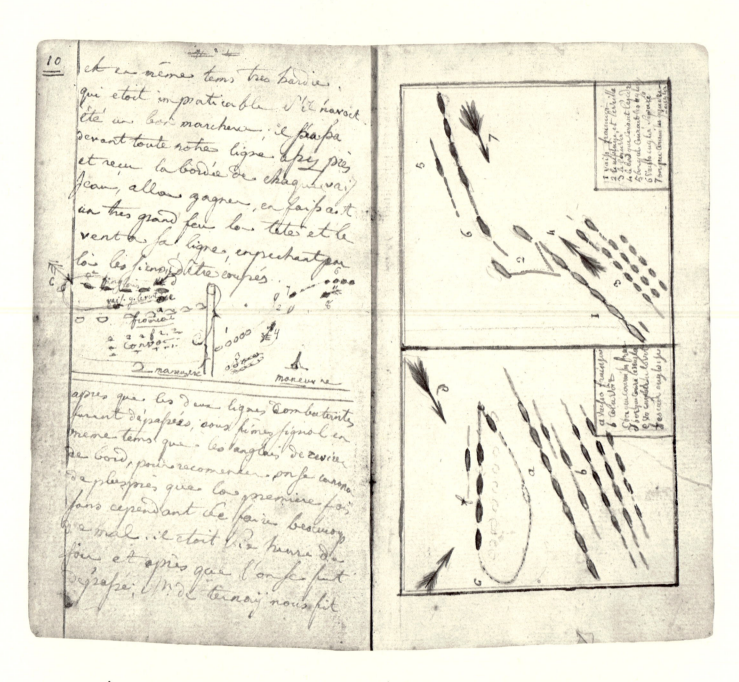

VERGER'S DIAGRAMS OF THE ENCOUNTER OF TERNAY'S FLEET WITH AN ENGLISH SQUADRON UNDER
CAPTAIN CORNWALLIS, OFF THE BERMUDAS, 20 JUNE 1780 (*see p. xx*)

VERGER'S DRAWINGS OF INDIANS FROM THE SIX NATIONS AT NEWPORT,
29 AUGUST – 1 SEPTEMBER 1780 (*see p. xx*)

NOUS, JEAN - BAPTISTE - DONATIEN DE VIMEUR, Cᵀᴱ. DE ROCHAMBEAU,

Lieutenant-général des armées du Roi, Grand'Croix de l'Ordre Royal & Militaire de St. Louis, Gouverneur de Villefranche, en Roussillon, commandant un Corps de Troupes de Sa Majesté très-chretienne.

Le roy de France votre pere, n'a point oublié ses enfants, il m'a chargé de presents pour vos deputés, comme marques de son souvenir. il a appris avec douleur que plusieurs nations trompées par les artifices des Anglais ses Ennemis avoient attaqué et levé la hache contre ses bons et fideles allies les Etats Unis de l'amerique. il me charge de vous declarer qu'il est l'ami ferme et fidele de tous les amis des americains et l'ennemi decidé de tous leurs ennemis. Il espere de ses enfants qu'il aime tendrement qu'ils ne tiendront jamais dans cette guerre contre les anglais, d'autre parti que celui de leur pere.

The King of France your father has not forgot his children. as a token of his remembrance I have offered gifts to your Deputies, from him, he learned with concern that many nations, deceived by the English, who are his ennemies, had attacked and lifted up the hatchet against his good and faithfull allyes the United States of America. he hath desired me to tell you that he is a firm and faithfull friends to all the friends of america, and sworn enemy to all its foes. he hopes that his children whom he loves sincerely, will take part with their father, in this war against the English

le Cte de Rochambeau

FAIT à Newport, le Trente Aout 1780.

Given under our hand and seal, the thirtieth of August, 1780, at Newport of Rhode island

PAR MONSEIGNEUR.

Defibulle

ROCHAMBEAU'S ADDRESS TO THE INDIAN DEPUTIES, NEWPORT, 30 AUGUST 1780 (*see p. xx*)

N° 5.

GAZETTE FRANÇOISE.

Du Vendredi 15 Décembre 1780.

tes au bord de la lame ; elle en gagna fucceſſivement d'autres affez éloignées du rivage, dont elle mina les fondemens. On en compte 10 à 12 qui ont befoins de grandes réparations. Le baſſin ayant toujours été regardé comme un afile sûr, dans lequel les bâtimens ne couroient point de rifques, ils étoient mouillés fans précaution fort près les uns des autres ; le vent d'O. & la groſſe mer y ont occafionné quelques abordages : deux navires de Bordeaux prêts à partir, fe font échoués à terre, il étoit poſſible de fauver une partie du chargement ; on efpéroit remettre à flot la plupart des autres bâtimens qui avoient eu le même fort. Il s'eſt perdu un navire à moitié chargé dans le port de la baie ; un vaiſſeau hollandois qui prenoit fon chargement au vent de la Grenade, eſt venu à la côte. Quelques maifons peu folides ont été renverfées dans les différens bourgs de cette colonie : les bâtimens de manufacture n'ont été que foiblement endommagés à la campagne ; le ravage que le coup de vent a fait fur les plantations de cannes, n'a pas été général ; il en a été de même des cafés, des cacaos, & les habi-

Les lettres d'Amſterdam confirment l'arrivée de M. John Adam à la Haye, pour entrer fans doute en négociation avec les Etats-Généraux.

De Newport, *le* 15 *Décembre*.

CHARLES-LOUIS DE TERNAI, Chevalier de St. Jean de Jérufalem, Chef-d'efcadre des Armées navales, ancien Gouverneur des Ifles de France & de Bourbon, commandant l'Efcadre Françaife fur les côtes de l'Amérique feptentrionale, eſt mort aujourd'hui en cette Ville ; fes talents, fon zèle & fes fervices diftingués lui avoit mérité la confiance & les faveurs du Gouvernement de la Patrie, & il emporte les regrets de l'Efcadre & de l'Armée. Le commandement de l'Efcadre par cet événement, paſſe entre les mains de M. Deſtouches, Capitaine de Vaiſſeau, Brigadier des Armées navales, Officier très-eſtimé de tout le Corps de la Marine Françoife, & qui s'eſt particulierement diftingué dans le combat de Oueſſant.

Il fera fait mention, à l'ordinaire prochain, des pertes que l'ouragan a caufé dans la Jamaïque & la Barbade.

A NEWPORT, *de l'Imprimerie Royale de l'Efcadre, rue de la Pointe,* N°. 641.

ADMIRAL DE TERNAY'S DEATH, AS ANNOUNCED IN THE *GAZETTE FRANÇOISE*, THE WEEKLY NEWSPAPER
PRINTED ON THE PRESS OF THE FRENCH FLEET AT NEWPORT (*see p. xx*)

RELATION

*De la sortie de l'Escadre Française, aux ordres du Cher. DESTOUCHES, &
de l'affaire qui a eue lieu le 16 Mars 1781, entre cette Escadre & celle
des Anglais, commandée par l'Amiral ARBUTHNOT.*

LES suites du coup de vent du 21 Janvier, ayant rapproché de l'égalité
les forces navales de France & d'Angleterre, dans les mers de l'Amérique
Septentrionale, le Chevalier Destouches profita sur le champ de cette cir-
constance, pour tâcher d'arrêter les déprédations & les brigandages que les
ennemis commettoient depuis deux mois sur les côtes de la Virginie. Pour
cet effet, il détacha avec la plus grande célérité, un vaisseau de 64 canons &
deux frégates, commandés par M. de Tilly, Capitaine de Vaisseau, avec
ordre de se porter dans la baye de Chesapeak, & d'y détruire la flotille Anglaise & les frégates qui lui servoient d'escorte. La précaution que prirent
les ennemis de mettre leurs bâtimens à l'abri dans la petite riviere d'Elisabeth, ne permit pas à M. de Tilly de remplir complettement cet objet.
Son expédition ne fut cependant pas infructueuse : il prit ou détruisit dix
bâtimens aux ennemis, & ramena avec lui à Newport, le bâtiment de guerre
le Romulus, de 44 canons, dont il s'étoit emparé à l'entrée de la baye.
Le succès de cette premiere tentative, & l'extrême desir qu'avoit le Chevalier Destouches de secourir efficacement l'Etat de Virginie, le déterminerent
à entreprendre de nouveau cette expédition avec de plus grands moyens. Il
fit préparer son escadre & armer la prise *le Romulus* ; & pour assurer autant
qu'il étoit possible la réussite de l'entreprise, il se concerta avec le Comte
de Rochambeau, & reçut à bord de ses vaisseaux & de la flûte le Fantasque,
un détachement de l'armée de ce Général, commandé par le Baron de Viomenil.

Le 8 Mars au soir l'Escadre mit à la voile. Les vents contraires qui re-
gnerent dans les jours suivants, la pousserent d'abord assez loin dans le sud-est.
Cependant, en profitant de la variété des vents, elle se rapprocha de la côte,
& le 14 au matin, on eut connoissance du cap Charles de la baye de Chesapeak. Les vents violents qui regnoient alors de la partie du sud, ne per-
mirent pas à l'Escadre de s'élever pour gagner le cap Henri ; elle fut au
contraire repoussée au nord, & passa deux jours à louvoyer & à lutter contre
le vent. Le 16 à la pointe du jour, les vents soufflant toujours de la même

OFFICIAL "RELATION" OF THE DESTOUCHES EXPEDITION TO THE CHESAPEAKE, MARCH 1781, PRINTED
ON THE PRESS OF THE FRENCH FLEET AT NEWPORT (*see p. xx*)

He prepared his squadron, armed the prize ship *Romulus*, and, to ensure as far as possible the success of the enterprise, joined forces with the Comte de Rochambeau and took aboard his ships and the supply ship *Fantasque* a detachment of the General's troops under the command of the Baron de Vioménil.

On the evening of 8 March the squadron set sail. The headwinds prevailing during the following days pushed it quite far to the southeast. However, by taking advantage of some variable winds, it approached the coast and, on the morning of the 14th, sighted Cape Charles at the mouth of the Chesapeake Bay. The strong winds then prevailing from the south prevented the squadron from holding up towards Cape Henry and pushed it away to the northward, where it spent two days tacking about and struggling against the wind.

At daybreak on the 16th the wind still blew from the same quarter, but more moderately, and the horizon was obscured by fog. The squadron was running on the port tack when it sighted a frigate two cannon-shots to windward. At first the Admiral gave the signal to chase her, but soon afterward several vessels loomed out of the fog. He was then convinced that this was the English squadron that, warned by some enemy of America, had been able to run down the coast before west and northwest winds and, by sailing farther off the wind than the King's squadron, had arrived off the Virginia coast almost simultaneously.[32] Consequently he recalled his launches just as the wind veered to northeast and signaled his squadron to form in line of battle on the port tack. The English squadron was then about 2 leagues to the southward and sailing on the same tack.

At nine o'clock the French squadron came about in stays in countermarch, and half an hour later the English squadron followed suit. At half past ten, noticing that the wind had freshened considerably and that they were tacking in too close to the north shore of Virginia, the Admiral ordered the squadron to wear ship in countermarch and resume the port tack.

From then on the Chevalier Destouches felt that,

as he had not expected to find the enemy fleet in the Chesapeake, his mission could no longer be accomplished. He realized the impossibility of disembarking troops under fire, even from his warships, while opposed by a superior squadron. He therefore concerned himself only with the problem of preserving the honor of the King's arms without endangering his fleet.

The enemy was taking advantage of their considerably greater speed and, encouraged by their superior strength, continued to come up to windward, crowding on sail and running on the starboard tack. At noon they tacked into the wake of the King's squadron. Before one o'clock their vanguard had approached to within half a league of the French rear guard and seemed to be planning to attack it to leeward.

Until then the Chevalier Destouches had maneuvered so as neither to seek combat nor to avoid it, because he felt that even the most fortunate result he could hope for would still leave him powerless to fulfill his mission. But the honor of the King's arms, which he had to maintain in American eyes, would not permit him to give the boastful English any opportunity for claiming that he had been chased away by a fleet of comparable strength to his own.

He himself decided to attack the enemy upon reaching the head of their line in countermarch and running down it to leeward on the opposite tack so as to make it easier for his ships to fire their lower batteries. At one o'clock the lead ship of the French line was within range of the lead ship of the enemy, and several moments later both sides began firing. The head of the English line bore away, and the vanguard of the French squadron followed suit in order to remain broadside to her, so that these units of the two squadrons fought for some time running before the wind.

Shortly before two, seeing that the English vanguard's maneuver permitted him no longer to run down their line to leeward, the Admiral had his ships tack to port in succession, whereupon they all filed past the head of the enemy fleet.

This maneuver was completely successful. The

32. General Clinton attributed Arbuthnot's speed to the fact that he was not encumbered by transports. Clinton, *Narrative*, p. 255.

moment the lead ship of the English line received the broadside of the fifth French ship, she bore away, tacked over to starboard, and retired from the combat under escort of a frigate that came to her assistance.

However, the tail end of the English squadron had kept up to windward by crowding on sail. It found itself within combat range of the French rear guard as the latter was edging down to get back into the wake of the head of the French line. This attack by the enemy rear guard caused relatively little damage to the ships at which it was directed. The *Conquérant*, however, suffered considerably, since after fighting the English vanguard she found herself again under fire from their whole battle line. Her particular adversary was a three-decker [the *London*] which, however, paid for the damage she inflicted on the *Conquérant* by the loss of her topsail yard and a large part of her rigging.

At a quarter to three, after the firing ceased on both sides, the French squadron found itself ahead and to leeward of the English. The Admiral gave the signal to close up the battle line on the port tack, without regard to the ships' regular positions. The line was formed promptly, and the squadron ran with shortened sail, waiting for the enemy to threaten a second attack before it tacked about and fell once more upon his vanguard. But the English had been so roughly handled during the first clash that they thought it imprudent to expose themselves to a second; during the rest of the day they sailed close to the wind behind the French, without taking advantage of their superior speed to renew the combat.

At nightfall the enemy squadron bore away, and the French squadron continued its course to the southeast with shortened sail and all its lamps lighted.

The next day brought no news of the enemy. The Chevalier Destouches, obliged despite his successful combat to renounce his ultimate plan to free Virginia, decided to return to Newport to repair his damaged vessels and put his squadron in condition for new operations.

One cannot praise too highly the intrepidity shown by the captains, officers, and crews, and by the troops traveling aboard the vessels. Their valor had made up for the enemy's advantage in the number and strength of their ships and would have assured success to the expedition had it depended upon superior courage. The loss sustained by the squadron that day amounted to around 80 killed or dead of wounds and 120 wounded. Among the former one must regret the loss of Captain de Cheffontaine and Ensign de Kergus.

Order of Battle of the French Squadron

Conquérant		74 guns
Jason		64 guns
Ardent		64 guns
Duc de Bourgogne		80 guns
Neptune		74 guns
Romulus, frigate		44 guns
Eveillé		64 guns
Provence		64 guns
Hermione, frigate		32 guns
Fantasque, supply ship		22 guns

[Total: 7 ships of the line, 3 frigates, 582 guns]

English Squadron, in order of rank

London		98 guns
Royal Oak		74 guns
Robust		74 guns
Bedford		74 guns
Europe		64 guns
America		64 guns
Prudent		64 guns
Adamant		50 guns
frigates:		
Roebuck		44 guns
Iris		32 guns
Medea		22 guns

[Total: 8 ships of the line, 3 frigates, 660 guns]
[End of official *Relation*][33]

33. Other accounts of the Destouches expedition by participants include those by Berthier (embarked on the *Neptune*), pp. 242–244; Blanchard (1) (*Duc de Bourgogne*), pp. 67–72; Brisout de Barneville (*Duc de Bourgogne*), pp. 256–263; Losse de Bayac (*Jason*), pp. 24–29; Villebresme (*Jason*), pp. 79–83; Charlus, letter of 20 April 1781, in Archives de la Guerre, A¹3732, pièce 65. Destouches's official letters are in the Archives Nationales, Marine B⁴ 191 ("Campagnes, 1781, Amérique du Nord"); other documents in the Destouches Papers, Huntington Library. A

The *Romulus* maneuvered courageously, holding very high on the wind opposite the *London*, which fired a broadside at her. It was fortunately short, or she would have been sunk. A soldier of our regiment was killed aboard her, as well as several sailors. She fired 360 shots in all from her 21-gun battery. The *Ardent*, commanded by M. de Marigny, fought at pistol range and prepared to board the enemy. The sailors admitted that there had been few combats between squadrons as heated as this one. Arbuthnot remained aboard a frigate throughout the combat in order to watch the maneuvers more closely. The *Robust*, which had received two broadsides in her stern from the *Neptune*, had to be towed into the Chesapeake Bay.

When the Marquis de La Fayette, who had advanced overland to support the landing of the French troops, saw the English squadron enter the Bay, he planned an immediate retreat. He had insufficient strength to make a stand, but he did not retire soon enough to prevent the capture of his baggage.

Arnold and Phillips continued to lay waste to Virginia, but the latter was killed during an attack,[34] leaving the command to Arnold, who did not keep it for long, since he was soon recalled to New York.

The English say that they lost 120 men in killed and wounded, and that the *Robust* was dismasted. They

are not too pleased with Admiral Arbuthnot, according to what I have since heard from M. Wittershausen, an Anspach officer.[35]

26 March The squadron suddenly appeared off Newport in foggy weather. We thought it was English, and there was great activity. Had it really been an enemy squadron, it would have entered without receiving a single cannon ball, since by the time the grenadiers marched out one vessel had already entered the harbor and others were arriving at a good pace.

The *Hermione* captured the *Union*, loaded with sugar and molasses.

27 March The troops disembarked. The grenadiers of the Soissonnais Regiment had suffered some losses in the action.

❧ *April–May 1781* ☙

18 April Our transports left for The [French] Cape, escorted by the *Surveillante*, and the *Hermione* departed for Philadelphia.

6 May The *Concorde* arrived in Boston.[36]

8 May The English fleet left Sandy Hook.

9 May The Vicomte de Rochambeau and M. de Barras arrived at Boston on the *Astrée*.[37]

---

series of diagrams of the engagement, entitled "Plan du Combat du vendredy 16 mars 1781. . . ," is in the Bibliothèque du Ministère des Armées "Terre," Paris, L.I.D. 43; reproduced below, Vol. II, No. 12.

Although the Destouches expedition failed to achieve its objective, its significance in the sequence of events can best be appreciated if it is seen as a "dress rehearsal" for the successful Yorktown campaign six months later. It foreshadowed, on a much smaller scale, the pattern of the later combined operation. In both instances naval supremacy was the decisive factor. In March 1781 Destouches's failure to outmaneuver Arbuthnot's squadron prevented him from landing the French troops under Vioménil that were to have joined the American forces under Lafayette sent overland to Virginia, whereas de Grasse's victory over the British off the Chesapeake Capes on 5 September 1781 made possible the decisive junction of forces in Virginia. In spite of the general disappointment, Destouches's "enterprize" was, as the soothing Congressional Resolution of 5 April 1781 expressed it, "a happy presage of decisive advantages to the United States." The copy of the Resolution sent to Destouches, with a

covering letter signed by Samuel Huntington, is in the Musée de Blérancourt.

34. General William Phillips died of a bilious fever in the house of Mrs. Robert Bolling at Petersburg, Virginia, 21 May 1781. After his treason at West Point was discovered and he had escaped to New York, Arnold was ordered to Virginia with 1,800 men to disrupt enemy communications and commerce in the Chesapeake, in conjunction with a naval force, and to destroy stores destined for Gates's army in North Carolina. Phillips was subsequently sent by Clinton with 2,000 men to reinforce Arnold and assume command of their combined forces. Clinton, *Narrative*, pp. 234–237, 254.

35. Verger mentions (p. 151) meeting Hessian and Anspach officers after the capitulation of Yorktown.

36. See Clermont-Crèvecœur's journal, n. 21, on the arrival of the *Concorde*.

37. Other sources indicate that the Vicomte de Rochambeau and M. de Barras arrived on the *Concorde*. The frigate *Astrée*, commanded by La Pérouse, was at this time operating out of Boston.

18 May This morning the English fleet was sighted —the same fleet we had fought in the Chesapeake.[38] Consequently some troops were immediately embarked aboard the ships to serve the guns, and the fleet prepared to go out; however, it did not leave. The reason given by our sailors was that, when forces are equal, a large battle would serve no purpose but to kill men without advancing the cause; therefore, they remained on the defensive.

26 May The General returned from Hartford.[39]

28 May The *Hermione* arrived, also the *Ariel*, commanded by M. de Capellis.

June 1781

The convoy having arrived at Marblehead, orders were given for the departure of the army. Each officer

was issued a portemanteau. These were transported in wagons at the King's expense.

Some artillery was left in Newport, together with a detachment of 50 men per regiment and the major [De Prez] of the Royal Deux-Ponts, under the command of M. de Choisy, brigadier general. All the troops that arrived in Boston in the convoy escorted by the *Sagittaire* were to join us.[40] I was ordered to remain at Newport on guard duty with a captain, a lieutenant, and a sublieutenant from each regiment.

18 June The First Division left Providence. . . .[41]

July 1781

10 July Contrary to our expectations, the troops remaining at Newport under the command of M. de Choisy went on a little expedition.[42] Troops from the

38. The appearance of the British squadron foiled Barras's plan to go out to meet the convoy momentarily expected from France with reinforcements for Rochambeau's army. It also prevented Barras from attending the Wethersfield Conference.

39. See Clermont-Crèvecœur's journal, n. 21, on the Wethersfield Conference.

40. Concerning the assignment of these reinforcements, see Clermont-Crèvecœur's journal, n. 25.

41. Here follows in Verger's manuscript (MS, pp. 59–60) the itinerary of the troops who marched to the Hudson. It has been omitted here since it is recorded in the journals of both Clermont-Crèvecœur and Berthier, who were present on this march.

42. Verger's narrative of the so-called Huntington Bay expedition is of particular interest as an eyewitness story. It is the only account by a participant known to the Editors, though there are several secondary reports. Among the latter, Choisy's letters to Rochambeau, Newport, 13 July, 15 July 1781, and Barras's letter to Rochambeau, 13 July, give further authoritative information; these unpublished letters are in the Paul Mellon Collection. The accounts given in the journals of Von Closen (pp. 93–94) and of Cromot Dubourg ([1], pp. 299–300), both aides-de-camp to Rochambeau, seem to be based largely on Choisy's letters to Rochambeau. The expedition is also mentioned by Gallatin ([1], pp. 677–679) and by Clermont-Crèvecœur (p. 34). Documents from American sources, including a "Narrative of the . . . affair as related to me [i.e., Onderdonk, *ca.* 1846] by Wm. Ludlam, an eye witness, aged 90," are in Henry Onderdonk, Jr., *Documents and Letters intended to illustrate the Revolutionary Incidents of Queens County* (New York, 1846), pp. 219–

224, sections 407–411. See also the supplementary note to section 410, in Onderdonk, *Revolutionary Incidents of Suffolk and Kings Counties* (New York, 1849), Appendix, p. 260.

The significance of this expedition in the general strategy of the moment can best be appreciated if it is viewed as the second in a series of Franco-American threats against the British position in New York; it had been preceded by the abortive Lincoln-Lauzun move against Manhattan Island, 2–3 July, and was followed by the reconnaissance in force of 21–23 July. See Clermont-Crèvecœur's journal, nn. 33 and 45.

An expedition by the French against the Lloyd Neck fort in Huntington Bay had already been contemplated, but postponed, in April 1781. Washington sent Major Benjamin Tallmadge to Newport to discuss the "proposed enterprise" with Rochambeau and Destouches. The proposal can be traced in Washington's letters, to Tallmadge, 8 April 1781; to Rochambeau and Destouches, 8 April; to Rochambeau and Destouches, 30 April (*Writings of GW*, XXI, 434–436, and XXII, 12–13); and in the joint letter of Rochambeau and Destouches to Washington, 25 April 1781 (Library of Congress, Washington Papers). In his letter of 30 April Washington concluded: "The absence of your light Frigates renders the plan which Major Tallmadge proposed impracticable for the present. We will, however, keep the enterprise in view, and may, perhaps, at some future time, find an opportunity of carrying it into execution with success." It was probably at this time that Tallmadge gave to the French, for planning purposes, the manuscript map still preserved in the Library of Congress, Rochambeau map No. 22, entitled in English "Map of Queens Village on Lloyd Neck

various detachments left in Newport, together with others from the ships' garrisons, were embarked on the *Romulus* and the *Gentille*.[43] Along with us also came some militia on two privateers, whose orders were to land on Block Island and seize several Refugee [Tory] posts there; however, at the sight of our ships the Tories escaped.[44] We continued down Long Island Sound with a fair wind. We anchored around one o'clock the next morning, thinking we were off Huntington, which was our landing point; when it appeared that we were mistaken, we got under way again, anchoring a league beyond, which was still half a league from Huntington.

It was five o'clock in the morning [12 July] before we landed, and the boats did not finish disembarking the troops before nine.[45] Consequently we were discovered by the enemy. The Baron d'Angély, who had been given command of these 200 men, had divided his force into three platoons. The center platoon had orders to form in line of battle when it arrived before the fort, with the other two on its right and left, then to surround it and take it by storm. On the assumption that the place was poorly guarded, each platoon officer

had been issued torches to set fire to the magazines. However, since we had planned to surprise the post in the dead of night and had now been discovered, it was against all rules to advance. Nevertheless, we debouched from a wood where we had already received several volleys from the fort. This resistance somewhat disconcerted our troops. We proceeded to form a line of battle within half a cannon-shot of the fort, then halted while the enemy kept shelling us with grapeshot from two cannon. M. d'Angély recalled the officers to the rear and asked us what should be done. All of us replied that, having advanced so far, we should risk an assault, especially since their palisade had already been breached in several places and we estimated that there were no more than 50 men guarding the fort and magazines. We returned to ranks expecting to march to the assault. We were all very much astonished to hear the command to retreat. The soldiers of the Soissonnais detachment forming the wing marched a little faster than they should have, and the center lagged behind, giving the soldiers in front the impression that they were being pursued by the enemy, so that the vanguard commanded by a sergeant and the

---

in Queens County on the north side of Long Island in the Province (now state) of New York." For the continuing interest in such an expedition, see Tallmadge's letter to Rochambeau, Wethersfield, 2 May 1781, transmitting intelligence received from one of his spies about the British and Hessian troops stationed at Lloyd Neck, Oyster Bay, and Herricks (Rochambeau Papers, Paul Mellon Collection). The post at Lloyd Neck was also known as Fort Franklin, so named by the British after William Franklin (son of Benjamin Franklin), president of the Board of Associated Loyalists. It was on the Cold Spring Harbor shore of the Neck, not on what is now called its Huntington Bay side.

43. Choisy, in his letter to Rochambeau, 13 July, says that the troops embarked for Long Island, commanded by M. d'Angély (Colonel Baron d'Angély, one of the Baron de Vioménil's aides-de-camp), consisted of 200 men, of which 140 were from the garrisons of Barras's ships and 60 from the army detachments at Newport. Also according to Choisy, the *Romulus*, the *Gentille*, the *Ariel*, and the *Prudence* took part in the expedition.

44. Both Barras and Choisy (letters cited in previous notes) speak of the Block Island and the Huntington Bay raids as two different "expeditions," though they were sent out from Newport within a short time of each other. According to their reports to Rochambeau, the Block Island expedition was prompted by information received

from Governor Greene of Rhode Island, who reported that 100 Tories were gathered there. Acting on this "certain intelligence," an American privateer carrying 50 men lent by Barras from his ships' garrisons escorted three or four schooners carrying 100 American militia. The militiamen returned to Newport on the 13th without having accomplished their mission, but the privateer apparently continued down the Sound with the Huntington Bay raiders. Choisy reported (15 July) that the American militia did in fact surprise the Tories on Block Island but allowed them to escape in their boats, to the great disgust of the militiamen, who were loud in criticism of their captain's "cowardice." Stung by this criticism, the captain came to Choisy and asked for a council of war to judge his conduct; however, since no French troops were involved and since he had no desire to "get mixed up in the business," Choisy prudently sent the American captain back to his own colonel, who was "fort embarassé."

45. Complementing Verger's map (reproduced here) is an unsigned "Plan de la baie D'Huntington," reproduced in Vol. II, No. 42. See also the "Plan of the attack on Lloyd's Neck," based on William Ludlam's recollections, in Onderdonk, *Documents*, p. 222. Although it is difficult to reconcile these three maps, it appears that the fort was in the southwestern part of present Lloyd Neck on the Cold Spring Harbor side.

rear guard, which had been sent to beat the woods on our right, began firing at one another without recognizing their comrades. Fortunately they did one another no harm. Our surgeons, who had already unpacked their instruments, retreated so precipitately that they forgot to retrieve them. We were nearly half an hour waiting for our boats, which we thought would never come. Finally we got back on board our ships in the disagreeable knowledge that we had lost 3 men killed, plus an American officer who died of wounds, all for nothing.[46] We set sail for Newport, well favored by the wind.

We had been ordered to remain only four hours on Long Island, but had stayed six, and to burn the rich stores at Huntington; we had failed on both counts. The navy had landed us too late, and once we were disembarked, M. d'Angély had failed to do the only thing left, which was to make an assault.[47]

We heard that on 3 July the American vanguard commanded by General Lincoln, advancing with assurance to surprise an enemy post, was itself surprised. His retreat would have been cut off had not the Duc de Lauzun been advantageously posted in the rear with his hussars to protect it. Lincoln's line of retreat had in fact already been cut off by Delancey's English dragoons, who, however, did not dare take on the hussars.[48]

24 July Nearly 50 ships were sighted in the Sound sailing to Rhode Island. Consequently we spent the night in bivouacs; but they never arrived.

At this time the *Hermione* and the *Astrée* were cruising off Boston to intercept a convoy bound for Canada, which indeed they met, escorted by the English frigate *Charlestown*. After a fight with the *Astrée*, the *Charlestown* captured her and was about to take her into port when the fog closed in and saved her. Meanwhile, the *Hermione* sailed into the midst of the convoy and was received far more warmly than she had anticipated. Six armed barges, crowded bowsprit to poop, shelled her lustily, doing her a fair amount of damage; nevertheless, she forced five of them to surrender. Then the same fog that had driven off the *Charlestown* separated her from two of her prizes, so that she succeeded in bringing only three, all richly laden, into Boston.

The *Surveillante* returned to Newport [from her voyage to The French Cape], shepherding her convoy without difficulty. But on her return she met a warship off the Bahamas and made recognition signals, to which the latter made no reply. The ships commenced the combat by moonlight, running before the wind on the same tack. Suddenly the French officers perceived that they had engaged a warship of 50 guns, nevertheless, they shelled one another for two and a half hours.

46. Choisy, in his letter of 15 July to Rochambeau, reported the casualties only as 3 wounded: 2 soldiers of the Picardie Regiment (presumably from the ships' garrisons) and a young American seriously wounded in the arm. Of the latter Choisy wrote: "This young man, of attractive mien and bearing, had followed the detachment as a volunteer; we are taking the best possible care of him here." Ludlam's "Narrative" (Onderdonk, *Documents*, pp. 222–223) mentions that Heathcoat Muirson of Setauket, an American patriot, served as guide to the French landing forces. While Muirson was examining the works with a spy-glass, a shot from the fort took off his arm. "He died of the wound, but described the spot so exactly, that his sister afterwards found the spy-glass in a bunch of briers where he had thrown it."

47. Choisy, in his report to Rochambeau, Newport, 15 July, summed things up in these terms: "The Huntington detachment returned yesterday at noon, without having accomplished anything. We were very badly informed about the location of the stores we intended to burn, which were protected by the fort that M. d'Angély found redoubtable and absolutely impregnable (*hors d'insulte*). He nevertheless approached close to the fort in an at-

tempt to set fire to the stores, but the guns would have wiped out his whole detachment had he not decided to withdraw. . . ." A report addressed to William Franklin by Lieutenant Colonel Upham, deputy inspector general of refugees, commanding at the Lloyd Neck fort at the time of the French raid, is printed in Onderdonk, *Documents*, p. 223; "Fort Franklin, 13 July 1781. Three large ships, five armed brigs, and other vessels appeared in Huntington Harbor, July 12, and landed at 8 o'clock 450 men, mostly French, on the back of Lloyd's Neck, two miles from the fort. At 11, they formed in front of the fort, at a distance of 400 yards, in open view. Fearing that they would get possession of a height on the right, the fort fired grape shot from two twelve pounders, when the French suddenly retreated. They left on the ground where they halted to dress the wounded, a number of surgeon's instruments, a great quantity of lint, bandages, &c., a bayonet, sword, and a very large quantity of port-fire and other materials for burning our houses; also, some few fragments of coats and shirts; and the grass besmeared with blood. . . ."

48. See Clermont-Crèvecœur's journal, n. 33.

The *Surveillante* lost 14 men killed and 22 wounded and took 6 balls in her foremast, 10 in her mainmast, and more than 70 in her freeboard. The warship, now identified as the *Jason*,[49] was rendered very uncomfortable by her adversary and retired from the combat, whereupon, as the *Surveillante* was some distance away, she fired 17 guns, apparently to summon aid.

The American frigate *Confederacy*, loaded with equipment for 12,000 men, was captured by the *Roebuck* without firing a shot, though she carried 36 guns and the *Roebuck* could not use her lower battery.[50]

The *Trumbull*, an American frigate, also of 36 guns, was captured at the entrance to the Delaware Capes by the *Chatham* of 50 guns, without firing a shot.[51] She was loaded with arms and uniforms. The *Washington*, a handsome privateer of 26 guns, was also captured by the *Charon*. . . .[52]

⚜ August–September 1781 ⚜

15 August On 15 August M. de Rochambeau received by the frigate *Concorde* M. de Grasse's reply, announcing his imminent arrival in the Chesapeake Bay with 3,000 men under the command of M. de Saint-Simon. He was consequently resolved to set the French army in motion on 19 August, together with 2,000 Americans.

The rest of Washington's army was to remain on the left bank of the North River under the command of General Heath to cover West Point, as well as to screen the army's movements from M. de Clinton and convince him that we had moved to the right bank to help M. de Grasse force a passage to Sandy Hook and capture Staten Island. M. de Villemanzy, commissary of war, was sent forthwith to establish a bakery at Chatham, only 3 leagues from Staten Island, under cover of a small American corps until the arrival of our vanguard. M. de Rochambeau had let him into the secret and disclosed to him his intention to feed the army from this bakery during its march to Philadelphia, but had emphasized that the enemy must be convinced by every possible ruse that its real objective was an attack on Sandy Hook and Staten Island. Villemanzy drew fire from Clinton's batteries when he went to collect bricks from ruined houses on the Raritan River near Sandy Hook Bay. This maneuver prevented M. de Clinton from sending any help to Lord Cornwallis.[53] In the last letter that Cornwallis received

49. According to Von Closen (p. 93), this was the *Unicorn*.

50. The *Confederacy* of 32 guns commanded by Captain Seth Harding was returning from The French Cape with military stores and produce when she was attacked by the *Roebuck*, 44 guns, and the *Orpheus*, 32 guns, on 14 April 1781, and obliged to surrender. Charles O. Paullin, *The Navy of the American Revolution* (Cleveland, 1906), pp. 207–208; James L. Howard, *Seth Harding Mariner, A Naval Picture of The Revolution* (New Haven, 1930), pp. 144–147.

51. The captor of the *Trumbull* was the *Iris*. The *Trumbull*, 28 guns, had just cleared the Delaware Capes on 8 August, bound for Havana with dispatches and a cargo of flour, when she was pursued by the *Iris*, 32 guns. When a storm came up and dismasted her, putting her at the mercy of her adversary, a majority of her crew, including some British deserters, mutinied. The rest, led by Captain James Nicholson, bravely defended the ship, losing 16 men and 2 officers wounded, before they were forced to surrender. William L. Clowes, ed., *The Royal Navy* (London, 1897–1903), IV, 72–73; Paullin, pp. 238–239. The *Iris* was captured by the French a month or so later, as mentioned by Verger hereafter, p. 136.

52. Verger's manuscript (MS, pp. 70–74) includes at this

point, under the heading, "From the Camp at Philipsburg," a brief second-hand report of the army's activities there during July and the beginning of August; it has been omitted here since these activities are more fully covered in the journals of Clermont-Crèvecœur (pp. 28ff.) and of Berthier (pp. 246ff.). There follows, as given here, an account of the army's march from the Hudson to Virginia. Verger's narrative is largely based on Rochambeau's official report, *Journal des opérations du Corps François sous le commandement du Comte de Rochambeau*. Rochambeau's "journal," compiled immediately after the Yorktown capitulation, was printed in the newspapers and issued separately late in 1781. It would thus have been readily available to Verger when he was writing up his journal at Williamsburg during the winter of 1781–1782. See "Checklist of Journals," *s.v.* Rochambeau (1).

53. Clinton did not notify Cornwallis that Washington was marching south until 2 September. In a letter of that date, from New York, he wrote: "By intelligence which I have this day received, it would seem that Mr. Washington is moving an army to the southward with an appearance of haste, and gives out that he expects the co-operation of a considerable French armament. Your Lordship, however, may be assured that, if this should be the case, I shall either endeavour to reinforce the army under

from him he asked for reinforcements for New York, when the latter was already besieged in Virginia.

The army arrived on September 3 and 4 in Philadelphia, where the French troops paraded in the best order, with flags flying and cannon at the head of each regiment with matches lighted. They rendered to the President of the Continental Congress assembled there the honors prescribed by the Court. The Congress expressed its profound gratitude for the generous help of our king and the effort he was making for his allies and for the admirable discipline and splendid appearance of the French regiments after their long and tiring march.[54] The President of the Congress, wearing a black velvet coat and dressed in a most singular fashion, asked M. de Rochambeau if it would be proper for him to salute the field officers. He replied that the King of France usually did. His Excellency concluded from this that he might do likewise without demeaning himself. . . .[55]

6 September On 6 September the army was at the head of the Elk River flowing into the Chesapeake Bay. There M. de Rochambeau found a letter from M. de Grasse announcing his arrival in the Chesapeake on 28 August and the landing of the troops of M. de Saint-Simon to join forces at Jamestown with [the Americans] under M. de La Fayette. The officer who brought this letter had arrived just an hour before, so that by the most extraordinary coincidence a combined expedition from the Leeward Islands and one from the northern part of America had succeeded in making a rendezvous within an hour.

Since few transports could be assembled in the Bay,

where the English had destroyed everything during the past five months, we could embark only the grenadiers and chasseurs and the infantry of Lauzun's Legion, under the command of M. de Custine, the Duc de Lauzun, the Comte de Deux-Ponts, the Vicomte de Noailles, and the Vicomte de Rochambeau. They could not set sail before the 11th. The Baron de Vioménil continued to march overland with the rest of the army to Annapolis.

8 September Generals Washington, Rochambeau, and Chastellux went on ahead and arrived at Williamsburg, where they found the Marquis de La Fayette already joined by M. de Saint-Simon, who had taken up a good position in which to await an attack from Cornwallis. The latter was busy entrenching himself in York and Gloucester and barricading the York River with moored vessels, as well as several sunk in the river channel. His forces, including the sailors, were estimated at between 7,000 and 8,000 men. . . .[56]

❧

I shall now return to the troops remaining at Newport. As soon as the Comte de Barras was advised that M. de Rochambeau, in consequence of M. de Grasse's dispatch, had begun his march, he prepared to leave Newport. All the troops left there with M. de Choisy were embarked, except for 100 men who were left in Providence under the command of M. de Prez to guard the army's equipment.[57]

21 August A total of 480 infantry and 130 artillery troops were embarked aboard the squadron.[58] I was on

your command *by all means within the compass of my power*, or make every possible diversion in Your Lordship's favour. . . ." Clinton, *Narrative*, Appendix, p. 563.

54. See Clermont-Crèvecœur's journal, n. 72.

55. Verger includes at this point in his manuscript (MS, p. 79) the army's itinerary from Philipsburg to Philadelphia, omitted here. Cf. Clermont-Crèvecœur's journal, pp. 40ff.; and maps, Vol. II, Nos. 48–58 and 61–73.

56. There follows at this point in Verger's manuscript (MS, pp. 82–83) the itinerary of the army from Philadelphia to Williamsburg, which has been omitted here. Cf. Clermont-Crèvecœur's journal, pp. 50ff.; and maps, Vol. II, Nos. 58–60 and 73–86.

57. "At a town meeting, held August 30, 1781, Mr. John Dermount, Overseer of the Work-house, was directed to clear that building of its inmates, and to deliver it to

Major De Prez, for the purpose of barracking the troops of His Most Christian Majesty. A large and capacious building improved as a hospital was also given up to the use of the officers. In March, 1782, most of the French troops being withdrawn, the commanding officers and the few officers occupying it with him, were requested to vacate it, unless they chose to contract with the owners to continue there at their own charges, as the finances of the town did 'not admit of rent being paid by the town for the same any longer time than till the first day of April next.'" Stone, *French Allies*, p. 604. See also H. W. Preston, *Rochambeau and the French Troops in Providence* (Providence, 1924), pp. 15–18, for fuller citations from the Providence town records.

58. Verger's journal provides one of the few surviving accounts of the passage from Newport to Virginia with

board the *Eveillé* of 64 guns, one of the smartest sailers in the French navy, commanded by M. de Tilly. All the prisoners of war that we had captured during our stay were embarked aboard the *Ecureuil*, which went to New York under a flag of truce. She took almost 400, including as many soldiers as sailors.

23 August We set sail in a fairly good breeze and soon lost sight of Newport, which all of us left with regret, each having his private reasons. One can say in praise of the fair sex there that there are few places, or indeed none in the world, where the strain is so beautiful and so amiable. *Champlin, Hunter, Brinley, Lawton, Wanton,* CROWELL, *Peckham, Easton, True, Scott, Handy, Robinson, Clarke, Townsend, Arnold.*[59]

We had headwinds for a very long time, which obliged us to sail nearly 100 leagues off the coast.

Off the Delaware Capes we struck a flat calm. Next morning we sighted 9 sail. When a breeze sprang up, favoring us first and thus giving us a head start, the *Eveillé*, the *Surveillante*, and the *Concorde* were or-

---

Barras's squadron. For other accounts by those who took the sea route to Yorktown, see "Checklist of Journals," *s.v.* Dubouchet, Villebresme.

59. Verger spells these names "Champelin, hundert, brindlé, léton, ouenton, *crowell*, bekam, isten, true, Scot, handi, relinton, clarke, tanzen, arnold." They are nevertheless easily identifiable, since all, belonging to old Newport families, appear in the Newport telephone directory today. Several of the names listed by Verger evoke particular belles who were much admired by the French. Of Margaret CHAMPLIN, daughter of the banker Christopher Champlin, who left her descendants "a valentine from Kosciusko . . . sent to her in a box of mother-of-pearl, inlaid with gold, and lined with the same," and who eventually became the mother-in-law of Oliver Hazard Perry, the Prince de Broglie (who visited Newport in November 1782) wrote: "That evening M. Vauban introduced us at the house of Mr. Champlin, well enough known for his wealth, but much better known in our army for the lovely face of his daughter. She was not in the parlor when we entered, but appeared an instant later. It is unnecessary to say that we examined her with attention, which was to treat her handsomely, for the result of our observation was to find out that she had beautiful eyes and an agreeable mouth, a lovely complexion, a fine figure, a pretty foot, and the general effect was altogether attractive. She added to all these advantages that of being dressed and coiffed with taste, that is to say, in the French fashion, besides which she spoke and understood our language." Broglie (2), pp. 65–66. The HUNTER girls were the daughters of an eminent physician, William Hunter, and first cousins of the celebrated miniaturist Malbone. The Duc de Lauzun wrote: "I was not in love with the Misses Hunter; but had they been my sisters, I could not have liked them better, especially the eldest, who is one of the most amiable persons I have ever met." Lauzun (2), p. 280. Katherine Hunter became the Comtesse de Cardigan, whose husband was guillotined in the Revolution. Nancy, who married a Neapolitan banker named Falconet, was the mother of the Comtesse de Pourtalès and of Mrs. John Middleton of Charleston, S.C. The Hunter house still stands in Newport. Miss BRINLEY, the daughter of Thomas Brinley, on whose property the Battle of Rhode Island was fought, received this passing notice from Broglie: "Miss Brinley . . . and some other ladies to whom I was introduced . . . convinced me that Newport possessed more than one rosebud." Broglie (2), p. 69. Of the Quakeress Polly LAWTON (pronounced "Leighton" in the eighteenth-century) we have so many panegyrics that it is hard to choose between them. Her favorite pastime seems to have been chiding the French officers on their immoral profession. The Comte de Ségur calls her "a nymph rather than a woman." "Her eyes," he continues, "seemed to reflect, as in a mirror, the meekness and purity of her mind and the goodness of her heart. . . . Certain it is that, if I had not been married and happy, I should, whilst coming to defend the liberty of the Americans, have lost my own at the feet of Polly Leiton." Ségur (2), I, 423–426. The Prince de Broglie writes of her: "Suddenly the door opened and in came the very goddess of grace and beauty. It was Minerva herself, who had exchanged her warlike attributes for the charms of a simple shepherdess. This was the Quaker's daughter. Her name was Polly Lawton. . . . Her costume . . . had the effect of giving to Polly the air of a Holy Virgin. I confess that this seductive Lawton appeared to me as the *chef d'œuvre* of nature. . . ." Broglie (2), pp. 67–68. Polly's father, Robert Lawton, was a wealthy Quaker who owned a farm, a town house, and a number of vessels engaged in the coastal trade. Polly married a Philadelphia Quaker named John Bringhurst but left no descendants. (It must be observed that any woman who can evoke in the minds of sophisticated Frenchmen at once a nymph, Venus, Minerva, and the Holy Virgin, deserves to be remembered!) Polly WANTON, granddaughter of two governors and godchild of Bishop Berkeley, married Daniel Lyman, General Heath's chief of staff. The ROBINSON girls were Quakers who appealed even to the enemy, since Earl Percy pronounced them "fit to grace the Court of St. James," which, however, they did not see fit to do. One of the Robinsons married John Morton, a Philadelphia Quaker. For further details about the Newport belles, see Stone's chapter on "Newport Society in 1780" in his *French Allies*, pp. 256–274.

dered in pursuit. We chased the 9 ships all day but did not come up with them until eight o'clock that evening. Darkness prevented our capturing all of them, so we had to be content with two. One we took was carrying 36 women, 32 children, 100 infantrymen, and all the baggage of the Ninetieth Foot. The other was laden with munitions.

This was a convoy from Saint Lucia, escorted by the frigate *Pegasus*. At the end of the chase the wind freshened to a point where we were making 9 knots. Two days later we ran into heavy weather and a storm that rolled up an angry sea for three days, during which we ran 4 knots under bare poles.

Eighty leagues off the entrance to the Chesapeake Bay we sighted 40 sail off our starboard bow, all large ships, plus 2 ships a couple of cannon-shot to windward of the *Glorieux*. Towards noon we made recognition signals to which they did not reply. Orders were promptly given the convoy to crowd on sail and head for the entrance to the Bay, then to run up the James River as far as possible. Our squadron also crowded on sail, and we soon lost sight of the squadron we believed to be hostile. The *Saint Marc de Rille*[?], a transport loaded with bombs, had been dismasted the previous day and could not keep up with us. Lagging behind, she was chased by two frigates. M. de Barras ordered us to go back and take her in tow, which we did. The frigates tacked about at our approach, and we rejoined our squadron at nightfall.

Next morning we sighted land and saw the same squadron approaching us in line of battle. After we had rounded Cape Charles to enter the Bay, the *Concorde* was sent back to make recognition signals. When the fleet did not respond, we prepared to shepherd our convoy, which had been halted at the entrance to the river by two warships. However, the latter replied to our recognition signals, as did two frigates coming down the Bay. We anchored on 10 September in a spot where we saw a number of buoys, leading us to believe that a squadron had recently anchored there.

As the other fleet, which had now hoisted the white [French] ensign, approached, we saw a rather lively cannonade begin. When the ships came closer, most of our mariners estimated that there were at least 9 enemy vessels in the midst of them; consequently M. de Barras gave orders to cut our cables and fire on the enemy ships. When the firing ceased, however, we saw that there were only two 32-gun frigates, the *Iris* and the *Richmond*, which had been fighting for the past hour and a half against 9 of M. de Grasse's warships and, despite the odds, had lost only 3 men killed. M. de Grasse received their captains very kindly and gave them back their swords.

On the next day [11 September] we entered M. de Grasse's anchorage. The *Cormorant*, an English corvette captured by M. de Grasse, had on board Lord Rawdon and his wife, who, though prisoners of war, were being treated with the greatest consideration and had lost none of their possessions.[60]

We remained in the roadstead eight days, during which we caught a large number of fish. The day [18 September] that MM. de Washington and de Rochambeau called on board the flagship of M. de Grasse, an English brig, thinking the squadron was English, sailed into the midst of the French vessels. On being hailed in English by the *Ville de Paris* to anchor alongside her, she complied. The captain launched his gig and, together with some other English officers and a Hessian, sailed over to call on the Admiral. The moment they arrived on deck on one side of the ship MM. de Washington and de Rochambeau arrived on the other. They were much surprised to find themselves on board

---

60. Von Closen (p. 137), relates that on 27 September, when returning from a mission to de Grasse's flagship, he stopped on board the *Diligente* to request supper but also out of curiosity to see Lord Rawdon who had been captured on the *Cormorant* together with Mr. and Mrs. Doyle: "Gossip asserts that this very pretty lady, with whom we supped, was the Lord's mistress during his campaigns in the South. It is certain that Mr. Doyle, whom Lord Rawdon made lieutenant colonel of his regiment, seemed to be *a very easy-going fellow*. After we had talked a good deal about the various events that had trans-

spired in the Carolinas [where Rawdon commanded the British forces after Cornwallis moved north to Virginia], and after Lord Rawdon had lamented the fate with which Cornwallis was threatened, we returned to our launch at 10 o'clock." The *Cormorant*, the *Queen Charlotte*, and a small coaster had been captured from the British off the coast of the Carolinas, when de Grasse was en route to the Chesapeake. Bougainville (1), pp. 15–16; Du Perron (1), p. 117; Tornquist (3), pp. 54–55; Comte de Vaudreuil (*Neptunia*, No. 46), p. 40.

the flagship of M. de Grasse, having believed it to be that of Admiral Graves.

18 September We received orders to land, which we executed that afternoon in a heavy sea. I was embarked on board the *Andromaque*, and the rest on the *Experiment*, to sail up the [James] River. Headwinds delayed us two days in reaching the farthest point navigable by frigates. The troops were reembarked in sloops and brigs with two days' provisions. I was on board the *Worteley*, an English prize. The wind being still against us, we were five days reaching our landing point.[61] It would be hard to describe what we officers and our men suffered from hunger and thirst. Our provisions had run out, and our warships were already far away and out of sight. I was rowed over with 25 men to the vessel in which I had embarked to get some peas, which luckily I found there, though in a very small quantity. These the men cooked in the grease they use to clean their muskets.

At two cannon-shots from shore we were put into boats from which we had to land in water up to our waists. We were immediately formed up to march to Williamsburg, 8 miles beyond. I fell ill on arrival from the heat, from hunger, and from the bad water. I had to pay 36 *sols* for half a pound of bread, which I was happy to obtain at this price. After landing we had nothing more pressing to do than find a well to quench our thirst. After we found one, it was not until after most of us had drunk that we learned that the wells had been poisoned by the English, who had thrown corpses into them. As a result there were many cases of dysentery, of which several men have died.

On arrival in this part of Virginia at Jamestown I was nearly an eyewitness to the atrocities committed by the English. Some of Tarleton's dragoons, after pillaging a house, violated a young woman who was pregnant. After fastening her to a door, one of them split open her belly with a sabre, killing the infant, then wrote over the door the following inscription, which I saw:

> *You dam rebel's Whore,*
> *you shall never bear enny more.*[62]

We camped above the town of Williamsburg, where we remained eight days before the rest of the army arrived. For three of them we were without bread, and often without meat. The countryside had been entirely devastated.

Meanwhile, on 4 September M. de Grasse [after landing the troops under Saint-Simon that his ships had brought from the West Indies] had returned to the Capes of the Chesapeake.[63] Admiral Hood had rejoined

61. The exact location of the landing place of Choisy's troops from Newport is not clear from Verger's narrative. However, according to Washington (*Diaries*, II, 261), they landed at "the upper point of College Creek," that is, at Archer's Hope, where Rochambeau's troops were to go ashore a few days later (25 September). Washington also refers to the spot as "the usual point of debarkation above the College Creek." See map, Vol. II, No. 85. On the other hand, Saint-Simon's troops from the West Indies had landed earlier (2 September) at Jamestown Island. Cf. map, No. 84; also "Plan du débarquement et de la Marche de la division Commandée par le Mis. de St. Simon, sa réunion avec le Corps du Mis. de La Fayette, et celle de l'Armée combinée de Washington et de Rochambeau, et le siège d'Yorck, 1781," manuscript map in the Bibliothèque du Ministère des Armées "Terre," Paris, L.I.D. 174.

62. In his manuscript (MS, p. 95) Verger gives the inscription in English, followed by his French translation of it. Stories of atrocities committed by the English, especially by Tarleton's dragoons, are repeated in several other French journals, for example, Du Perron (1), pp. 124–125. Lieutenant Tornquist, a Swede serving in the French navy, who arrived in Virginia with de Grasse's fleet, repeats substantially the same story as the one related here by Verger but situates it "on a beautiful estate 2 miles from Hampton," and adds: "In another room was just as horrible a sight, five cut-off heads, arranged on a cupboard in place of plaster-cast figures, which lay broken to pieces on the floor." Tornquist (3), p. 57. "Previous to the surrender, Tarleton waited upon general Choisè [Choisy] and communicated . . . his apprehension for his personal safety if put at the disposal of the American militia. This conference was sought for the purpose of inducing an arrangement, which should shield him from the vengeance of the inhabitants. . . . We . . . conclude that it must have arisen from events known to the lieutenant colonel himself, and applying to the corps under his command." Henry Lee, *Memoirs of the War in the Southern Department of the United States* (Philadelphia, 1812), II, 362–363.

63. Verger here interrupts the chronological sequence of his narrative to relate what had happened prior to his own arrival with Barras's squadron. For detailed discussions of the decisive naval battle of 5 September, see Mahan, *Operations of the Navies*, pp. 184–223; Charles Lee Lewis,

Graves's squadron before New York on 28 August. Together they had set sail for the Chesapeake the moment the allied army's march overland to Philadelphia had been revealed. The English squadron, 20 ships strong, arrived on the 5th at Cape Charles, counting on being ahead of M. de Grasse. The latter, notwithstanding the fact that 1,500 of his men were still manning the boats that were ferrying ashore M. de Saint-Simon's troops and had not yet returned, did not hesitate to cut his cables and go out to fight the enemy with 24 ships, leaving the rest in the York and James rivers to blockade Cornwallis. As Graves came up to windward, M. de Grasse's vanguard, under the command of M. de Bougainville, reached the English rear guard, which was rather badly mauled after being pursued by M. de Grasse for some time. The *Terrible*, an English ship of 74 guns, no longer able to keep afloat, was burned the day after the battle.

On 11 September M. de Grasse returned to the Bay, where he found M. de Barras's squadron, which had left Newport on 24 August with 10 transports carrying the siege artillery. M. de Barras's ten transports were immediately detached, together with M. de Grasse's prizes, to bring the troops from Annapolis; they were escorted by the *Romulus* commanded by M. de La Villebrune who, together with the Baron de Vioménil, went to work with such energy that he arrived on the 25th in Williamsburg Creek, where the troops were landed on the 26th and 27th.[64]

Lauzun's infantry disembarked on the 23rd and marched under the command of the Duc de Lauzun to join their hussars, who were stationed in the County of Gloucester.[65]

The Siege of York

28 September We began our march from the camp in Williamsburg at eight in the morning, the Americans in front, M. de Saint-Simon's three regiments in the center, and M. de Rochambeau's army in the rear. We marched 12 miles in oppressive heat. The regiments fanned out to form the blockade of York. Before our regiment [Deux-Ponts] set up its camp, a picket of 50 men with several field pieces were sent out to drive off a party of foot and horse facing us beyond the woods.[66] After several cannon-shots were fired, the latter retired in short order.

That night the enemy, fearing to be attacked in their outer works, which were too far from their supporting redoubts, abandoned them to us and retired to their main fortifications. This shortened their front and gave us the greatest possible advantage. We proceeded at once to garrison the abandoned works. During the day the transports bringing the siege artillery arrived at Trebell's landing, 7 miles from camp, where the troops proceeded at once to unload them.[67] Since the baggage

Admiral de Grasse and American Independence (Annapolis, 1945), Chap. 16, "The Engagement off the Virginia Capes," pp. 156–170; Harold A. Larrabee, *Decision at the Chesapeake* (New York, 1964), esp. pp. 184–223. An official account entitled *Précis de la Campagne de l'Armée Navale, aux ordres du Comte de Grasse* was printed as a 4-page leaflet aboard de Grasse's flagship, *Ville de Paris*, shortly after the Yorktown capitulation; see "Checklist of Journals," *s.v.* de Grasse. Accounts by participants are noted in the "Checklist," *s.v.* Bougainville, Goussencourt, Jennet, naval officer (unidentified), Tornquist, Comte de Vaudreuil.

64. See map, Vol. II, No. 85, which shows the landing place of the troops from Annapolis at Archer's Hope, which was along the shore of the James River to the west of the mouth of College Creek and east of Jamestown. The same map gives 24 September as the date of arrival of La Villebrune's squadron off Archer's Hope.

65. Lauzun's infantry had embarked at Head of Elk and thus preceded the main body of Rochambeau's troops. See

Clermont-Crèvecœur's journal, nn. 89–90. Lauzun's hussars, commanded by the Vicomte d'Arrot, took the overland route; see Vol. II, Itinerary 6, n. 38.

66. These were Tarleton's dragoons and Abercrombie's light infantry; Johnston, *Yorktown Campaign*, pp. 105–106. Lieutenant Clermont-Crèvecœur commanded two of the French guns, as noted in his journal, p. 57.

67. "Much deligence was used in debarking and transporting the Stores, Cannon, &ca. from Trebells Landing (distant 6 Miles) on James Rivr. to Camp; which for want of Teams went on heavily. . . ." Washington, *Diaries*, II, 263. The siege artillery had been brought from Newport on Barras's ships; field artillery had come down the Chesapeake Bay from Annapolis. Trebell's Landing was on the shore of the James River, southeast of Williamsburg. Cf. Desandroüins's map, "Carte des environs de Williamsburg en Virginie où les Armées Françoise et Américaine ont campés en Septembre 1781" (Archives du Génie, 15-1-7, pièce 29); *State Historical Markers of Virginia* (Richmond, 1948), p. 128; marker W-49.

train was not due to arrive overland until 5 October, only 30 wagons and 180 artillery horses could be rounded up to transport the provisions.[68] During the first days we suffered much from hunger.

The Comte de Grasse turned over 800 men from the garrisons of his ships to M. de Choisy, who marched on ahead to contain Gloucester, taking up a position 3 miles from the town. M. de Choisy's corps was composed of the Lauzun Legion, the infantry from the ships, and 1,200 American militia under the command of Brigadier General Weedon.[69]

Tarleton was stationed there with 600 men, including 400 cavalry. M. de Lauzun's maneuver deserves to be reported. He pushed his hussars forward, leaving his infantry in the rear. They marched at a brisk pace until they were within a musket-shot of the enemy. Then the hussars retired to right and left, leaving the infantry uncovered. The latter opened a heavy fire to which Tarleton's troops replied. Then M. de Lauzun, re-forming his squadron behind the infantry, charged vigorously, upsetting the enemy, wounding Tarleton, and driving the detachment back to Gloucester with a loss of 50 men. M. Billy de Dillon and Captain Dutertre were wounded. M. de Choisy's advance posts were but a mile from Gloucester.[70]

4 October In the evening several patrols were sent to fire on the redoubts so as to engage the enemy and reveal the location of their batteries. This same day we began building a redoubt on the enemy's right from which to shell a frigate that was greatly hindering the work parties.

6 October At four in the afternoon 1,000 French work troops were marched into the ravines whose left rested on the redoubt of Pigeon Hill. They were sup-

ported by the Bourbonnais and Soissonnais regiments. The trench was opened by means of a parallel whose left rested on the aforementioned redoubt and whose right joined the left of the American redoubt, which squarely blocked the highroad into York. This parallel was supported by four redoubts, two in French territory and two in American.[71]

The approach of the Americans, which actually formed one with ours, had its right flank resting on the river. Their task that night had been constructing their portion of the parallel. At the same time, on our left, a trench had been opened at the head of the river, defended by a battalion of the Touraine Regiment and its grenadiers and chasseurs, whose battery was manned to clear that part of the river of enemy ships. The enemy discovered this approach very early and paid it a good deal of attention,[72] though they did not know about our grand approach and did not fire on it, contenting themselves, as in the previous nights, with firing on their abandoned redoubts and on the two built by the Americans at either side of the Hampton road, behind our works. Their random shots had no effect beyond slightly wounding M. de Wisch, an officer [captain] of our regiment, and, more seriously, a soldier in my company, who were with the work parties.

At the approach of the Touraine Regiment an artillery officer was gravely wounded,[73] as well as 6 grenadiers (2 very slightly) and a soldier of the Agenois Regiment. By daybreak nearly all the works of the grand approach were in condition to be manned. The day was employed in perfecting the parallel with 400 workmen from the trench battalions.

7–8 October[74] Major general: the Chevalier de Chas-

68. The overland route of the baggage train, which left Annapolis on 21 September, is described in Vol. II, Itinerary 6. "5th [October]. Means of transportation increased by the arrival of ox teams, &c. Proceeds now with better dispatch. Park of Artillery begins to look respectable, & preparations for offensive measures ripen fast." Jonathan Trumbull, "Journal," Massachusetts Historical Society, *Proceedings*, XIV (1875–1876), 335.

69. Lauzun ([2], pp. 296–297) describes Weedon as "a rather good commander, but hating war that he had never wanted to wage, and above all, mortally afraid of gun shots." Concerning the infantry from the ships' garrisons, see Clermont-Crèvecœur's journal, n. 109.

70. For further details on the skirmish at Gloucester, see

Clermont-Crèvecœur's journal, n. 113, and map, Vol. II, No. 90.

71. For the position of the parallels and redoubts, see maps, Vol. II, Nos. 87–89.

72. Its location was reported to the British by "a deserter from the Huzzer," according to Washington, *Diaries*, II, 263–264.

73. The wounded officer was Lieutenant de La Loge of the Auxonne artillery, as mentioned in Clermont-Crèvecœur's journal, p. 58 and n. 115.

74. From here on Verger's account follows closely the official "Etat-Major" journal of the siege, with only occasional personal interpolations. The same official record, compiled at Headquarters on the basis of Rochambeau's

tellux. Regiments: Agenois, Saintonge. Night work party: 900 men. This night 50 workmen were employed in building the rear communications on the left of the parallel, under the direction of the engineers, and in perfecting the redoubt and digging communicating trenches to the batteries. The remaining 400 joined those of the artillery in constructing the battery, which was ready to fire at daybreak. The day crew of 400 men from the trench battalions spent the day perfecting the work of the two previous nights and continued work on the batteries. On the American approach they have also started to build two batteries.

Wounded at the grand approach: 6 men.

Condition of the batteries begun the night of 7–8 October:

140

Verger

Journal

American

On the right adjoining the river: one battery of 6 cannon and 4 howitzers. Near the first French redoubt: one battery of 5 cannon.

French

No. 1: A large battery of four 16-pounders, two 12-inch mortars, four 8-inch mortars, and two 8-inch howitzers a little to the left of the main Hampton road and behind the parallel.

No. 2: A battery of four 24-pounders, also in the rear of the parallel and to the right of the ravine on which it rests.

No. 3: A battery of three 24-pounders in the direction of and behind the parallel.

No. 4: A battery of three 24-pounders and two howitzers to the left of the ravine flanking the parallel.

8–9 October Major general: M. de Saint-Simon. Regiments: Gâtinais, Royal Deux-Ponts. Auxiliaries: grenadiers of the Soissonnais and Saintonge regiments. Night work party: 800 men.

Half the night workmen were employed under the direction of the engineers in finishing the communications begun the previous night, and the rest, with the

artillery, in constructing old batteries and beginning a new one, No. 5, of 7 mortars in front of the left parallel.

The 400 day workmen from the trench battalions worked on the same projects. The Americans continued their work of the preceding day and night. Their battery of 6 cannon and 4 mortars adjoining the river was ready to fire two hours before nightfall. At three in the afternoon the battery on the approach at the head of the river began firing on a frigate, which promptly cut her cables.

Killed: 1. Wounded: 1.

9–10 October Major general: M. le Comte de Vioménil. Regiments: Bourbonnais, Soissonnais. Auxiliaries: chasseurs of the Agenois and Gâtinais regiments. Night work party: 700 men. Four hundred workmen were employed under the engineers' direction in palisading the redoubts of the parallel and perfecting the communications; 2,000 men, with those of the artillery, worked on the batteries. We learned from the deserters' reports that the English army was convinced that we had no heavy artillery and that, having beaten M. de Grasse, Clinton was coming to their rescue; however, by morning they were undeceived, since we began to fire from the following batteries: the American battery of 6 guns; French batteries Nos. 1 and 2. At the end of two hours all enemy fire had ceased. The 200 day workmen from the trench battalions were employed in perfecting the communications and working on the unfinished batteries.

Wounded at the grand approach: 2 men.

10–11 October Major general: Baron de Vioménil. Regiments: Agenois, Saintonge. Auxiliaries: chasseurs of the Royal Deux-Ponts and Soissonnais regiments. Night work party: 300 men. The night workmen were employed in perfecting the batteries and redoubts. Our batteries continued to fire bombs throughout the night. One set fire to a powder caisson.

M. de Saint-Simon's battery fired hot shot on the warships and set fire to the *Charon*, which was burned up with several sick and wounded aboard.[75] We heard

---

Orders of the Day, is included in other journals. See "Checklist of Journals," *s.v.* Gallatin, Cromot Dubourg, Menonville.

75. Cf. Clermont-Crèvecœur's journal, p. 59, which places

the burning of the *Charon* a day earlier. A "Draught of His Majesty's Ship Charon of 44 Guns built at Harwich in the Year 1778" is reproduced in Homer L. Ferguson, "Salvaging Revolutionary Relics from the York River,"

the cries of these unfortunates. Two transports were also burned. We learned through the deserters' reports that our bombs were doing great damage. Our Nos. 3 and 4 batteries have been firing continuously since daybreak. Since three this afternoon the enemy has resumed firing from their right flank on No. 5 battery and its adjacent works.

Killed: 1. Wounded: 3.

11–12 October Major general: Chevalier de Chastellux. Regiments: Gâtinais, Royal Deux-Ponts. Auxiliaries: chasseurs of the Bourbonnais and Saintonge regiments. Night work party: 800 men.

Under the direction of the engineers 750 men of the night work party were employed in commencing a second parallel about 280 yards ahead of the first. Like the latter, its left rests on the large ravine that serves as a point of arrival. The American workmen have built their section of this parallel on the right where it extends to a point facing their 5-gun battery; they have also made an opening from the ravine on the left of our extreme right-hand redoubt and another that starts at the left of our No. 2 battery and runs a zig-zag course to the second parallel. This parallel is covered by two redoubts.

Eighty night workmen were employed in completing No. 8 battery and repairing the others. To protect the work and screen it from the enemy, all our mortar and howitzer batteries, as well as those of the Americans, kept firing throughout the night; meanwhile, our cannon kept up a moderate fire. The enemy fired bombs and a few cannon at us without interrupting our work, which, with that of the Americans, was well advanced at daybreak.

Early in the morning our No. 8 battery began to fire, and the cannon in all our batteries kept firing until nine. However, fearing to disturb the day work party of the Americans, they ceased fire. Our shells and bombs had already killed one man and wounded two others who were working out in front of our batteries. When the enemy battery resumed firing around eleven o'clock, our Nos. 3 and 4 batteries replied. Work on the parallel was continued by 300 day workmen from

the trench regiment, including myself. I had one man wounded. Wounded at the grand approach: 4; at that of the Touraine Regiment: 3.

12–13 October Major general: M. de Saint-Simon. Regiments: Bourbonnais, Soissonnais. Auxiliaries: grenadiers of the Gâtinais and Agenois regiments. Night work party: 600 men.

The night workmen perfected the work of the previous day. Three hundred day workmen put the finishing touches to the parallel and began to construct new batteries.

Killed: 6. Wounded: 11. MM. de Miollis and Dursue, officers of the Soissonnais Regiment, wounded.

13–14 October Major general: M. le Comte de Vioménil. Regiments: Agenois, Saintonge. Auxiliaries: grenadiers of the Soissonnais and Royal Deux-Ponts regiments. Night work party: 600 men.

Half the night workmen were employed in perfecting the redoubts and the other works of the trench; the other half, in continuing work on the batteries. This work was continued by 300 day workmen from the trench battalions.

Killed: 1. Wounded: 28 at the grand approach.

Condition of the batteries begun during the night of 13–14:

No. 6: Between the two communications [trenches] and slightly in advance of the second parallel——6 cannon.

No. 7: To the left of the outlet of the left communication and of the parallel——6 cannon.

No. 8: In the parallel to the right of the left redoubt ——6 cannon.

No. 9: In front of the left of the parallel——8 mortars, 2 howitzers.

14–15 October Major general: Baron de Vioménil. Brigadier: M. de Custine. Regiments: Gâtinais, Royal Deux-Ponts. Auxiliaries: grenadiers of the Saintonge Regiment; chasseurs of the Bourbonnais, Agenois, and Soissonnais regiments. Night work party: 800 men.

The attack ordered on the two advanced redoubts of the enemy, one resting on the river, the other on its left, was executed at nightfall. The American light in-

William and Mary Quarterly, 2nd ser., xix, No. 3 (July 1939), 257–271. Reconstructed sections of the *Charon's* gundeck and of the captain's cabin are on display in the Visitor Center, Colonial National Historical Park, Yorktown.

fantry, supported by two of their trench battalions, under the command of the Marquis de La Fayette, attacked the river redoubt [British No. 10] and captured it at bayonet point with the loss of 4 officers wounded and 20 men killed or wounded.

The French troops were ordered to attack the other redoubt [British No. 9]. They debouched from the right flank of the American 5-gun battery and were posted in the following order: the grenadiers and chasseur companies of the Gâtinais[76] and Royal Deux-Ponts regiments, commanded by Comte Guillaume de Deux-Ponts, second colonel of the latter, and Lieutenant Colonel de l'Estrade of the Gâtinais; the first battalion of the Gâtinais and the auxiliaries (grenadiers and chasseurs of the Soissonnais Regiment assigned to make a diversion from the left of our grand approach). The latter division, under the command of M. de Rostaing, colonel of the Gâtinais Regiment, was in support. The overall commander was the Baron de Vioménil, who debouched with the troops and led them in perfect order and absolute silence.

The enemy discovered the column early and opened a very lively musket fire upon it. We found their abatis in far better condition than we had anticipated, since much of our artillery had been battering the redoubt for several days. Ignoring the enemy fire and slashing those that resisted with their axes, our pioneers had opened passages for us through which the grenadiers and chasseurs of the Royal Deux-Ponts and Gâtinais regiments entered the fosses together with the aforementioned pioneers, who were still obliged to

cut through several palisades to open the fraises of the redoubt. These same grenadiers and chasseurs took advantage of the openings to mount the parapet, where they formed up and soon forced the surviving enemies to surrender. Several, wishing to continue the fight with bayonets, paid with their lives.

We captured 3 officers and 40 men, after counting 18 dead. Another 120, under a lieutenant colonel, escaped. During the attack our loss in officers and men was about 80 killed or wounded.[77] The enemy at once commenced a lively cannonade on the redoubt we had just captured, killing and wounding many men.

The moment the redoubt was taken, the men cried "Vive le Roi!" which was echoed along our whole line. This the English took to be the signal for a general assault and rained on us a volley of musketry accompanied by quantities of bombs and shells from all their redoubts and batteries. Once the redoubt was in our hands, 500 workmen debouched from the right of the second parallel to prolong it to the redoubt. American workmen continued this parallel between the two redoubts and opened a communication between the first parallel running from the right between their grand battery and their first redoubt to the one they had just captured.

All these works were pushed forward with the greatest zest and were well advanced by daybreak. The feint ordered at the left of our works was pressed home a little too enthusiastically by M. de Custine, who came to within 30 paces of the redoubts and lost a lot of men.[78] At nightfall the enemy's attention had

76. "The grenadiers of the regiment of Gâtinais, which had been formed out of that of Auvergne, were to lead the attack. . . . I said to them, 'Mes enfants, if I should want you this night, I hope that you have not forgotten that we have served together in that brave regiment of Auvergne Sans tache, an honorable name that it has deserved ever since its creation.' They answered that, if I would promise to have their name restored to them, they would suffer themselves to be killed—even to the last man. They kept their word, charged like lions, and lost one-third of their number. . . ." Rochambeau (2), I, 294. The General also kept his word. In the Etat militaire for 1783 is the following note: "This [Eighteenth Royal Auvergne] Regiment . . . , known by the name of Gâtinais, has resumed that of Auvergne by Ordinance of 11 July 1782." The newspaper published at Le Cap Français, Affiches Américaines, 5 March 1783, notes that the royal ordinance

was read to the regiment in a special ceremony held there on 22 February.

77. "The cause of the great loss sustained by the French troops in comparison with that of the Americans, in storming their respective redoubts, was that the American troops when they came to the abattis, removed a part of it with their hands and leaped over the remainder. The French troops, on coming up to theirs, waited until their pioneers had cut away the abattis secundum artem, which exposed them longer to the galling fire of the enemy." James Thacher, Military Journal (Boston, 1823), p. 342n. An abatis is an obstruction made of felled trees whose sharpened ends are pointed towards the invader. See "Profile of Yorktown Fortifications," Vol. II, No. 100.

78. Von Closen reports that Custine got drunk and made his feint attack, ordered for half past seven, an hour late "when all was quiet," losing 9 chasseurs of the Soissonnais

VERGER'S PLAN OF THE FRENCH ATTACK ON THE TORY FORT AT LLOYD NECK, LONG ISLAND,
12 JULY 1781 (*see p. xxi*)

VERGER'S DRAWINGS OF AMERICAN FOOT SOLDIERS, YORKTOWN CAMPAIGN, 1781. LEFT TO RIGHT:
BLACK LIGHT INFANTRYMAN OF THE FIRST RHODE ISLAND REGIMENT, MUSKETEER OF THE
SECOND CANADIAN REGIMENT, RIFLEMAN, AND GUNNER OF THE CONTINENTAL ARTILLERY
(*see p. xxi*)

4.:   5

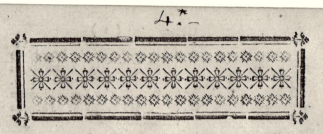

ARTICLES

DE LA

CAPITULATION

FAITE entre son Excellence le Général WASHINGTON,
commandant en chef les forces combinées de l'Amérique
& de France. Son Excellence le Comte de ROCHAMBEAU,
Lieutenant Général des Armées du Roi de France,
Grande-Croix de l'Ordre Royal & Militaire de St.
Louis, commandant les Troupes Auxiliaires de Sa
Majesté très-Chrétienne en Amérique : Et Son Excellence le Comte de GRASSE, Lieutenant Général des
Armées Navales de Sa Majesté très-Chrétienne, Com-
mandeur de l'Ordre Royal & Militaire de St. Louis,
commandant en chef l'Armée Navale de France dans
la baye de Chesapeak, d'une part :

Et le très-honorable le Comte CORNWALLIS, Lieutenant
Général des forces de Sa Majesté Britanique, com-
mandant des Garnisons de York & de Glocester ; &
Thomads Symonds, Ecuyer, commandant les forces
Navales de Sa Majesté Britanique, dans la Riviere
d'York en Virginie, de l'autre part.

ART. PREMIER.

ARTICLE PREMIER.

Les Garnisons d'York & de
Glocester, y compris les Officiers & Marelots des Vaisseaux
de Sa Majesté Britanique, ainsi
que tous autres Marins, se ren-
accordé.   dront prisonniers de guerre aux

(5)

---

(7)

XIV.

XIV.

accordé.

On ne violera aucun article de
la Capitulation, sous prétexte de
représailles ; s'il y a quelque expression douteuse, elle sera in-
terprétée selon le sens & la teneur
ordinaire des mots.

Fait à York en Virginie, le 19 Octobre 1781.

Signé, CORNWALIS.

Thomas Symons, sur l'original entre les mains du
Général WASHINGTON.

ARTICLES OF CAPITULATION, YORKTOWN, 19 OCTOBER 1781. CONTEMPORARY PRINTING OF THE
FRENCH TRANSLATION PREPARED AT FRENCH ARMY HEADQUARTERS (*see p. xxiii*)

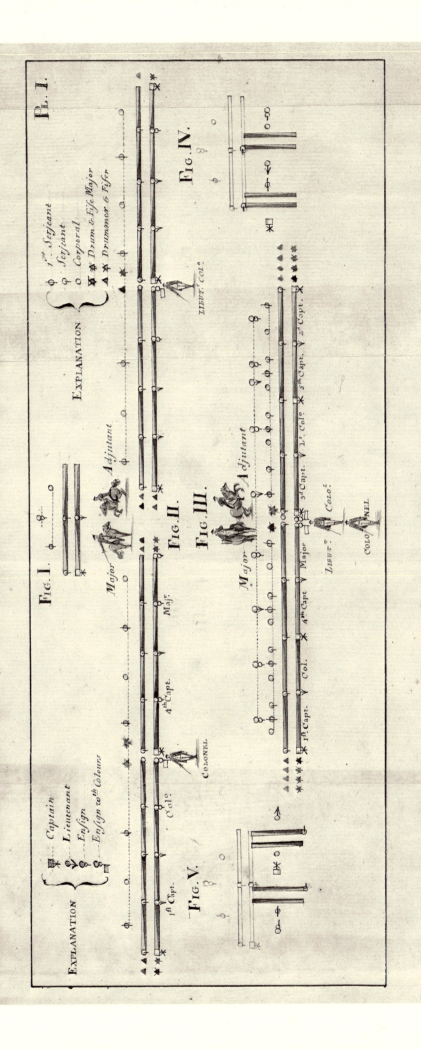

FORMATION OF A COMPANY AND A REGIMENT, DRAWING BY PIERRE-CHARLES L'ENFANT, FOR
REGULATIONS FOR THE ORDER AND DISCIPLINE OF THE TROOPS OF THE UNITED STATES
(see p. xxiii)

VERGER'S DRAWINGS OF MOUNTED CONTINENTAL LIGHT DRAGOONS, 1781 (*see p. xxiv*)

also been attracted to the head of the river by a feint executed without loss by the Touraine Regiment.

Two hundred night workmen were employed in continuing the work on the batteries, and 100 others in perfecting communications in all our works of the preceding nights.

The enemy kept up a fairly heavy fire of bombs and howitzers on our works, which interfered with our workmen. The Bourbonnais Regiment entered the trench at ten in the evening to reinforce it in case the enemy should make a sally.

Killed: 46. Wounded: 68. At the grand approach the following officers were wounded: Comte Guillaume de Deux-Ponts; Chevalier de Lameth; MM. de Sireuil and Berthelot, captains in the Gâtinais Regiment;[79] M. de Sillegue, sublieutenant in the same; M. de Lutzow, lieutenant in the Royal Deux-Ponts Regiment.

15–16 October Major general: Chevalier de Chastellux. Regiments: Bourbonnais (until the evening of the 15th), Agenois. Auxiliaries (for the night): grenadiers of the Soissonnais Regiment. Auxiliaries: the Royal Deux-Ponts Regiment. Night work party: 500 men.

One hundred night workmen were employed in perfecting the batteries, and the rest, the parallel and the redoubts. Towards five in the morning the enemy made a sally with 350 men. They fell upon a picket of the Agenois Regiment whom they massacred, took the captain prisoner, and entered the trench where the Soissonnais put up only a halfhearted resistance, abandoning the place of arms and the redoubt to the advancing enemy. This facilitated the enemy's entry into No. 6 battery and another where they spiked 6 guns

with their bayonets. However, six hours later the guns were firing again.

M. de Ch[astellux] had been warned by a deserter that the enemy was planning a sally at daybreak. He had even designated the point of attack, but the General had paid no attention to the warning and in consequence had made no dispositions. The English troops conducted themselves very well and, had they penetrated the trench earlier, would have met with little resistance. The colonel commanding the trench battalion ordered his drummers to beat the Charge to make believe the French were advancing. Our chasseurs had turned the trench to fall upon the enemy as they were returning to their lines, but lost their way when only 60 paces from the enemy redoubts.

Killed: 1. Wounded at the approach: 37. Officers wounded: MM. de Marin,[80] captain of the Soissonnais Regiment; de Bargues, lieutenant of the Bourbonnais; d'Houdetot Colomby, lieutenant of the Agenois; de Laumont, sublieutenant of the same; Lieutenant de Pusignan of the Auxonne artillery. Captain Bourguisson of the Agenois Regiment was taken prisoner.

16–17 October Major general: M. de Saint-Simon. Regiments: Gâtinais, Saintonge. Auxiliaries: grenadiers of the Agenois and Gâtinais regiments. Night work party: 800 men.

The night work party perfected the works at the trench and fortified the batteries, which began firing at daybreak. Towards ten in the morning the enemy sent a flag of truce asking for a twenty-four hour armistice to discuss surrender of the position and the fate of the troops. But M. de Washington, not finding the proposals sufficiently explicit, replied by a salvo of artillery that killed many of the enemy who were on the parapets and had not expected this.[81]

and drawing fire from the British, who supposed the attack was being renewed. "He got off with 24 hours' arrest and many jests." Von Closen, pp. 149–150.

79. Both Sireuil and Berthelot died later of their wounds. Dawson, *Français Morts aux Etats-Unis*, p. 39.

80. Marin later died of his wounds in the hospital at Williamsburg. *Ibid.*, p. 66.

81. Verger's statement, implying that Washington replied to Cornwallis's peace overtures with "a salvo of artillery," is misleading. According to Jonathan Trumbull and Ebenezer Wild, the British were exposed on the 17th to the "heaviest fire yet poured on them," which ceased only

momentarily when the British emissary appeared, was blindfolded, and taken to Washington in the rear to deliver Cornwallis's brief note. At 2 P.M. Washington replied: "I wish previously to the Meeting of Commissioners, that Your Lordship's proposals in writing, may be sent to the American Lines: for which Purpose, a Suspension of Hostilities during two Hours from the Delivery of this Letter will be granted." At 4:30 Cornwallis replied, and although his terms were unacceptable, Washington agreed to a continued suspension of hostilities, overlooking the possibility that the "enemy might wreck or burn equipment before such acts were forbidden." Ebenezer

Killed: 1. Wounded: 10 at the grand approach.

17–18 October Major general: Comte de Vioménil. Regiments: Bourbonnais, Royal Deux-Ponts.

A new flag of truce arrived around three o'clock with proposals that resulted in the cessation of hostilities on both sides until the signing of the capitulation at noon on the 19th.

Killed: 2. Wounded: 4. Lieutenant Bellanger of the artillery, killed; M. de Drouilhet, lieutenant of grenadiers in the Agenois Regiment, wounded on the evening of the 17th during a feint attack.

Bearers of flags of truce were sent from either side. They asked us to explain why we were continuing to work on the fortifications, since this was forbidden under the terms of the cease-fire. We replied that we would do what we liked but would not permit them to work on their side.

Recapitulation of killed and wounded

September [October]	SOLDIERS Killed	OFFICERS Killed	SOLDIERS Wounded	OFFICERS Wounded
1	—	—	6	1 [2]
6	—	—	8	2 [1]
7	—	—	6	—
8	1	—	1	—
9	—	—	2	—
10	1	—	3	—
11	—	—	7	—
12	6	—	11	2
13	1	—	28	—
14	46	—	62	6
15	1	—	37	5
16	1	—	10	1 (St.-Simon)
17	2	1 (Bellanger)	1	—
	59	1	182	17

The officer casualties were as follows: M. Bellanger, killed; MM. de Bée, officer of artillery, Sireuil, Berthelot, Marin, died of wounds; MM. de Drouilhet, Wisch, Miollis, Dursue, Guillaume de Deux-Ponts, [Charles de] Lameth, Sillegue, Lutzow, Bargues, Major General Saint-Simon, Houdetot Colomby, Laumont, Pusignan, wounded.[82]

Wild, "Journal," Massachusetts Historical Society, *Proceedings*, 2nd ser., VI (1890–1891), 155; Jonathan Trumbull, "Journal," Massachusetts Historical Society, *Proceedings*, XIV (1875–1876), 337; *Writings of GW*, XXIII, 236–237; Washington, *Diaries*, II, 268.
82. To this list should be added MM. Billy de Dillon and Dutertre, wounded before Gloucester on 1 October, and

Articles of Capitulation settled between his Excellency General Washington Comander in Chief of the combined Forces of America & France — His Excellency The Count de Rochambeau Lieutenant General of the Armies of the King of France — Great Cross of the Royal & Military Order of St. Louis — Commanding the Auxiliary Troops of his most Christian Majesty in America — And His Excellency the Count de Grasse Lieutenant General of the Naval Armies of his Most Christian Majesty, Commander of the Order of St. Louis, comand^g in Chief the Naval Army of France in the Chesapeak — on the One Part — And ~~His Excellency~~ The Right Honble Earl Cornwallis Lieu. General of His Britannick Majesty's Forces, Commanding the Garrisons of York & Gloucester and Thomas Symonds Esqr Commanding his Britannick Majesty's Naval forces in York River in Virginia on the other part.

Article 1st

The Garrisons of York & Gloucester including the Officers & Seamen of his Britannic Majesty's Ships as well as other Mariners, to surrender themselves Prisoners of War to the Combined Forces of America & France.— The Land Troops to remain prisoners to the United States. The Navy to the naval Army of his Most Christian Majesty.—

Article - 1st

Granted —

Article 2nd

The Artillery, Arms, Accoutrements, Military Chest and public Stores of every Denomination, shall be delivered, unimpaired, to the Heads of Departments appointed to receive them.—

Article 2^d

Granted.—

M. de La Loge of the Auxonne artillery, wounded on 6 October, who later died. Names of both enlisted men and officers who died at Yorktown are recorded in the "Liste des Français Morts en Virginie de Septembre 1781 à Août 1782," in Warrington Dawson, *Les Français Morts pour l'Indépendance américaine . . . et la Reconstruction Historique de Williamsburg* (Paris, 1931), pp. 27–49. This

Article 3ᵈ

At 12 °Clock this Day the two Redoubts on the left Flank of York to be delivered — the one to a Detachment of American Infantry — the other to a Detachment of French Grenadiers — The Garrison of York will march out to a Place to be appointed in front of the posts at 2 °Clock precisely, with Shouldered Arms — Colours cased and Drums beating a British or German March — they are then to ground their Arms, & return to their Encampment, where they will remain untill they are dispatched to the place of their Destination.— Two Works on the Gloucester Side will be delivered at One °Clock to Detachments of French & American Troops appointed to possess them.— The Garrison will march out at three °Clock in the Afternoon — The Cavalry with their Swords drawn, Trumpets sound*g* & the Infantry in the Manner prescribed for the Garrison of York — they are likewise to return to their Encampments untill they can be finally marched off.—

Article 3ᵈ

Granted.—

Article 4ᵗʰ

Officers are to retain their Side Arms — both Officers & Soldiers to keep their private property of every kind, and no part of their Baggage or papers to be at any Time subject to search or Inspection.— The Baggage & papers of officers & Soldiers taken during the Siege, to be likewise preserved for them. It is understood that any Property obviously belonging to ~~any of~~ the Inhabitants of these States, in the possession of the Garrison, shall be subject to be reclaimed.—[84]

Article 4ᵗʰ

Granted.—

Article 5ᵗʰ

The Soldiers to be kept in Virginia, Maryland, or Pennsylvania, & as much by Regiments as possible, & supplyed with the same Rations of Provisions as are Allowed to Soldiers in the Service of America: — A field officer from each Nation, viz — British, Anspach & Hessian, & other Officers on parole, in the proportion of One to fifty Men, to be allowed to reside near their respective Regi-

list of the Virginia dead is incorporated into Dawson's more extensive compilation covering the French dead in all regions of the United States, *Français Morts aux Etats-Unis*; see our list "Abbreviations and Short Titles."

83. In lieu of a retranslation of the French translation of the Articles that Verger copied into his journal, the Editors give here the original English text as preserved in Jonathan Trumbull's handwriting in the Library of Congress, Washington Papers (microfilm edition, reel 81). The manuscript retained by Washington is signed only by Cornwallis and Symonds. A second manuscript, retained by Cornwallis, bears also the signatures of Washington, Rochambeau, and Barras, the latter "en mon nom et celui du Comte de Grasse." The Cornwallis manuscript is now in the Public Record Office, London, 30/11/74, foll. 128–134; cf. George H. Reese, comp., *The Cornwallis Papers, Abstracts of Americana* (Charlottesville, University Press of Virginia, 1970), pp. 136–137. The Cornwallis copy served as the prototype for early printings of the document with all five signatures. It is so printed, for example, in Banastre Tarleton, *A History of the Campaigns of 1780 and 1781 . . .* (London, 1787), pp. 438–442; Jared Sparks, *Writings of Washington* (1837); B. F. Stevens, *Campaign in Virginia* (1888). It is of some interest, in the present context, to note that the instrument to which the French representatives put their signatures was in English; there was no parallel French text as there was, for exam-

ple, in the Franco-American treaties signed in 1778. Nevertheless, a French translation of the Articles of Capitulation was prepared at the time by the French staff for their own information and for transmission to Europe. A small 8-page pamphlet, *Articles de la Capitulation*, was printed shortly after the event—perhaps on the printing press of de Grasse's flagship *Ville de Paris*, then in Virginia waters. Copies of this rare plaquette are preserved, for example, with the papers of General Rochambeau, Library of Congress, Vol. 3, p. 28, and with papers of the Vicomte d'Arrot, Manuscript Collections of Colonial Williamsburg. There is also a copy in the John Carter Brown Library; see our illustration. This printed French text, which includes only the signatures of Cornwallis and Symonds, specifically states that it is from "l'original entre les mains du Général Washington." The French translation of the Articles transcribed by Verger follows the text of this pamphlet, which was presumably available to him when he was writing up his journal in Williamsburg. There were still other contemporary printings of this same French text of the Articles; see "Checklist of Journal," *s.v.* de Grasse (2).

84. The property included negro slaves, many of whom had taken refuge with the English; this article provided a legal basis for their eventual recovery. Clermont-Crève-cœur remarks in his journal (p. 67) that in Virginia "an individual's wealth is gauged by the number of negroes

ments, to visit them frequently and be witnesses of their Treatment — And that there Officers may receive & deliver Cloathing and other Necessaries for them, for which passports are to be granted when applied for.—

Article 5th

Granted —

Article 6th

The General, Staff & other Officers not employed as mentioned in the above Article, & who choose it, to be permitted to go on parole to ~~England~~ Europe, to N York, or to any other American maritime posts, at present in possession of the British Forces, at their own Option, & proper Vessels to be granted by the Count de Grasse to carry them under flags of Truce to New York within ten Days from this Date, if possible, & they to reside in a District to be agreed upon hereafter, untill they embark — The Officers of the civil Departments of the Army & navy to be included in this Article.— passports to go by Land, to be granted to those, to whom Vessels cannot be furnished.—

Article 6th

Granted.—

Article 7th

Officers to be allowed to keep Soldiers as Servants according to the common practice of the Service.— Servants not Soldiers are not to be considered as prisoners & are to be allowed to attend their Masters.

Article 7th

Granted

Article 8th

The Bonetta Sloop of War to be equipped & navigated by its present Captain and Crew & left entirely at the Disposal of Ld Cornwallis, from the Hour that the Capitulation is signed, to receive an Aid de Camp to carry Dispatches to Sir H^{ry} Clinton — and such Soldiers as he may think proper to send to N York[85] to be permitted to sail without Examination, when his Dispatches are ready. His Lordship engaging on his part, that the Ship shall be delivered to the Order of the Count de Grasse if she escapes the Dangers of the Seas — that she shall not carry off any public Stores — Any part of the Crew, that may be deficient on her Return, & the Soldiers passengers, to be accounted for on her Delivery.—

Article 8th

Granted —

---

he owns. The English took many away from the proprietors, thus ruining most of them in spite of their vast domains." For a recent discussion of the subject, see Benjamin Quarles, *The Negro in the American Revolution* (Chapel Hill, 1961), Chap. 9, "Evacuation with the British." The question of fugitive slaves also arose between the French and the Virginians, when the army was preparing to march northward the following year. See Governor Benjamin Harrison's letters to Rochambeau, 26 June 1782, to the Virginia Delegates to Congress, 6 July, and to Washington, 11 July, in H. R. McIlvaine, ed., *Official Letters of the Governors of the State of Virginia*, III (Richmond, 1929), 257–258, 262–263, 266. Chastellux attempted to smooth things over by assuring Governor Harrison: "I know well the intentions of the General [Rochambeau], and can assure you that I have no less attention than he has to preserve with the greatest care the property of the inhabitants of Virginia. . . . I know that all the officers have been forbid, under the most severe penalties, to take any Negro into their service, or even to receive them into camp. These precautions are not only dictated by justice, but also by reciprocal interest. Your Excellency having taken the same steps to have our deserters apprehended that we have taken to prevent the desertion of your Negroes, but I am sorry to be obliged to tell Your Excellency in confidence, that we had claimed as property of the inhabitants of Virginia several horses and Negroes, the first of which bought more than a year ago in Connecticut, and the latter purchased from prizes taken by French ships. . . ." Chastellux's letter, dated New Castle, Virginia, 6 July 1782, is printed in Stone, *French Allies*, p. 503. According to Du Perron ([1], p. 176), who mentions it reprovingly, some of de Grasse's naval officers, when leaving for the West Indies after the siege, had taken negroes with them and then sold them in the French colonies.

85. This provision gave a means of escape to certain key Loyalists in British service.

Article 9th

The Traders are to preserve their Property, & to be allowed three Months to dispose of, or remove them — And those Traders are not to be considered as prisoners of War —

Article 9th [*as revised*]

The Traders will be allowed to dispose of their Effects — the Allied Army having the right of pre-emption — The Traders to be considered as prisoners of War on parole —

Article 10th

Natives or Inhabitants of different parts of this Country at present in York or Gloucester are not to be punished on Acc° of having joined the British army —[86]

Article 10th [*as revised*]

This Article cannot be assented to — being altogether of civil Resort —

Article 11th

Proper Hospitals to be furnished for the Sick & Wounded — they are to be attended by their own Surgeons on parole, and they are to be furnished with Medicines & Stores from the American Hospitals —

Article 11th [*as revised*]

The Hospital Stores now in York & Gloucester shall be delivered for the Use of the British Sick & wounded — Passports will be granted for procuring them further Supplies from N York as Occasion may require — & proper Hospitals will be furnished for the reception of the Sick & wounded of the two Garrisons —

Article 12th

Waggons to be furnished to carry the Baggage of the Officers attending the Soldiers, and to Surgeons when travelling on Acc° of the Sick — attending the Hospitals at public Expence

Article 12th [*as revised*]

They will be furnished if possible —

Article 13th

The Shipping & Boats in the two Harbours, with all their Stores, Guns, Tackling, & Apparel shall be delivered up in their present State, to an officer of the Navy, appointed to take possession of them — previously unloading the private property, part of which had been on board for Security during the Siege.

Article 13th

Granted.

Article 14th

No Article of the Capitulation to be infringed on pretext of Reprisal, & if there be any doubtful Expressions in it, they are to be interpreted, according to the common Meaning & Acceptation of the Words.—

Article 14th

Granted.—

Done at York in Virginia
this 19th day of October 1781
　　　　　CORNWALLIS
　　　　　THO⁸ SYMONDS
[Done in the trenches before York Town in Virginia October 19 1781.
G. WASHINGTON
LE COMTE DE ROCHAMBEAU
LE COMTE DE BARRAS, en mon nom
　　　　& celui du COMTE DE GRASSE[87]]

———————

The French and American armies formed in line of battle on either side of the road by which the English

86. This provision, also relating to the Loyalists, was firmly rejected by Washington.

87. "Since M. de Grasse had a bad attack of asthma, he charged M. de Barras with the conclusion of the different articles of capitulation concerning the navy." Von Closen, p. 156. Jonathan Trumbull, Washington's military secretary, records that on 21 October the "General goes a visit to Admiral de Grasse who is unwell on board his ship, and by this means prevented embracing the General on land as was intended. Colonel Laurens attended the General." Trumbull, "Journal," Massachusetts Historical Society, *Proceedings*, XIV (1875–1876), 337.

troops were to march out, beginning at the old trenches and following the lines to the American redoubt. The English came out of the town at noon with drums beating and colors cased,[88] in the following order: a battalion of Foot Guards; the Third Foot; Seventeenth Foot; Twenty-third Foot; Thirty-third Foot; Forty-third Foot; the Highlanders: Seventy-first, Seventy-sixth, Eightieth; and the garrison of Gloucester: the Queen's Rangers (light infantry), the British (or Tarleton's) Legion; Germans: the Erbprinz and von Bose regiments of Hesse; the Anspach and von Seybothen regiments of Anspach.

Returns of the forces surrendering

General Cornwallis, General O'Hara; colonels, 2; majors, 11; captains, 52; lieutenants, 89; ensigns, 36; chaplains, 2; adjutants, 12; quartermasters, 10; surgeons, 10; aides, 22; sergeants, 295; drummers, 121; fusiliers, 3,273. Total: 3,943 [3,937]. Sick: sergeants, 90; drummers, 44; fusiliers, 1,741. Total: 1,875. At Gloucester: 1,100. Sailors: 750.

Recapitulation

Parading			Small arms	7,326
at York	3,943	[3,937]	Iron cannon	140
Sick	1,875		Brass cannon	74
At Gloucester			Flags	22
	1,100		Mortars and howitzers	22
Sailors	750		Barrels of powder	300
	7,668	[7,662]		

Ships

Charon, 44 guns, burned
Guadeloupe, frigate, 32 guns, sunk
2 sloops of war
60 transport vessels

Losses of the English from
8 September to 9 October 1781

2 captains, 4 lieutenants, 13 sergeants, 4 drummers, 133 rank and file killed. 5 lieutenants, 1 ensign, 24 sergeants, 11 drummers, 285 rank and file wounded. 1 major, 2 captains, 1 subaltern, 5 sergeants, 63 rank and file missing. Total: 552 [554].

French and American Forces engaged in the siege and their generals[89]

General Washington, commander in chief of the armies of France and America. Comte de Rochambeau, lieutenant general commanding the French army.

French generals
Baron de Vioménil
Chevalier de Chastellux
Marquis de Saint-Simon
Comte de Vioménil

American generals
Major General Lincoln
Major General the Marquis de La Fayette
Major General Baron von Steuben
Governor Nelson

At Gloucester
M. de Choisy, brigadier, commandant
Brigadier General Weedon

Navy
Comte de Grasse, commander in chief
Comte de Barras
M. de Bougainville
M. de Monteil
ships, 36
frigates, 8
corvettes, 8
transports, 20

French regiments
Bourbonnais
Royal Deux-Ponts
Soissonnais
Saintonge
Gâtinais
Agenois
Touraine

88. This provision of the Articles of Capitulation was a military insult. It was, however, copied verbatim from Clinton's terms at the capitulation of Charleston (May 1780) by which he required the American garrison to march out with its colors cased.
89. The *Journal of the Siege of York-Town* (Gallatin [3], pp. 31–32) adds the names of Brigadier Generals Duportail, Knox, and Wayne to the list of American generals and the Comte de Custine, Duc de Lauzun, and Chevalier de Béville (all brigadiers) to the French. The same source gives the figure of 9,300, including 300 Volontaires de Saint-Simon, 600 artillery, miners, etc., as the total of the French forces engaged. It lists the French ordnance as twelve 24-pounders, ten 16-pounders, ten 12-pounders, eight 12-inch mortars, and eight howitzers, or 48 pieces in all.

Royal Artillerie: 1 battalion of
the Auxonne Regiment; 2 companies
of the Metz Regiment
Light Infantry of the Lauzun Legion
400 hussars of the Lauzun Legion
200 Volontaires de Saint-Simon
800 garrison troops from the ships
Total: 8,000 men

Ordnance
14 siege guns
6 12-pounders
21 mortars and howitzers
1,500 bombs
600 shells per piece

American regiments
(some of which mustered less than 200 men)
Pennsylvania Line [Second and Third Battalions]
Congress's Own [Second Canadian Regiment]
[First] Rhode Island [Regiment, Continental Line]
La Fayette[90]
Hamilton [Colonel Alexander Hamilton's
Light Infantry Battalion]
Connecticut[91]
Lincoln
Steuben
Canada [see Congress's Own]
Stewart [First Pennsylvania Battalion]
Massachusetts [Colonel Vose's Light
Infantry Battalion][92]

Light Infantry[93]
Gimat [Lieutenant Colonel Gimat's Light
Infantry Battalion]
Riflemen [Colonel Lewis's Blue Ridge Mountain
Virginia Riflemen]
Maryland [Third and Fourth regiments,
Continental Line]
New Jersey [First and Second regiments,
Continental Line]
[Moylan's Fourth Continental] Dragoons
[Armand's Legion]
Artillery [Second Regiment, Continental Artillery;
detachments of First and Fourth regiments]
Total: approximately 5,000[94]

Militia
Virginians [3 brigades of Virginia Militia;
Dabney's Virginia State Regiment]
Maryland
Carolina[95]
New Jersey
Blue [Ridge] Mountain [Riflemen]
Total: 2,500
Grand total: approximately 15,500
[French and American]

Ordnance[96]
Siege guns: 13
Mortars and howitzers: 7
(plus several small howitzers)

90. Individual names without other designation signify division commanders who had no titular regiments.

91. Connecticut companies were attached to Gimat's, Huntington's, Hamilton's and Laurens's light infantry battalions. Johnston, *Yorktown Campaign*, pp. 113–114.

92. There were also light infantry companies from the Massachusetts Line serving in Gimat's, Huntington's and Laurens's light infantry battalions, making a total of 15. Johnston, p. 114.

93. There were in all 6 light infantry battalions recruited from New York, New Jersey, and New England, plus the Second Canadian Regiment, in Lafayette's division. Johnston, p. 114.

94. The *Journal of the Siege* (Gallatin [3], p. 32) gives the total of Continental troops as 5,550. Henry Lee (*Memoirs of the War in the Southern Department of the United States* [Philadelphia, 1812], II, 363) gives the figures of

5,500 Continental troops and 3,500 militia, or a total of 9,000.

95. The Carolina militia remained in their own state to guard the approaches to Virginia. Verger incorrectly lists the Maryland and New Jersey Line under "Militia" and the Riflemen under the Line. Troops present at Yorktown not included in his list are the First and Second New York Regiments, Continental Line; Lieutenant Colonel Gaskin's Virginia Battalion, Continental Line; Captain McKenna's Delaware Recruits; and three or four companies of the Sappers and Miners' Battalion. Johnston, *Yorktown Campaign*, pp. 109, 114. The American regiments varied in strength between 200 (Virginia State Regiment) and 550 (Third Pennsylvania, Third and Fourth Maryland) and averaged approximately 380 per regiment. *Ibid.*, p. 195.

96. The *Journal of the Siege* (Gallatin [3], p. 32) gives the number of pieces of American ordnance of all kinds as 60.

General Washington's "After Orders,"
20 October 1781[97]

The General congratulates the Army upon the glorious event of yesterday.

The generous proofs which his most Christian Majesty has given of his attachment to the Cause of America must force conviction on the minds of the most deceived among the Enemy: relatively to the decisive good consequences of the Alliance and inspire every citizen of these States with sentiments of the most unalterable Gratitude.

His Fleet the most numerous and powerful that ever appeared in these seas commanded by an Admiral whose Fortune and Talents ensure great Events.

An Army of the most admirable composition both in officers and men are the Pledges of his friendship to the United States and their co-operation has secured us the present signal success.

The General upon this occasion entreats his Excellency Count de Rochambeau to accept his most grateful acknowledgements for his Counsels and assistance at all times. He presents his warmest thanks to the Generals Baron Vioménil, Chevalier Chastellux, Marquis de St. Simon and Count Vioménil and to Brigadier General de Choisy (who had a separate command) for the illustrious manner in which they have advanced the interest of the common cause.

He requests that Count de Rochambeau will be pleased to communicate to the Army under his immediate command the high sense he entertains of the distinguished merits of the officers and soldiers of every corps and that he will present in his name to the regiments of Gâtinais and Deux-Ponts the two Pieces of Brass Ordnance captured by them; as a testimony of their Gallantry in storming the Enemy's Redoubt on the Night of the 14th instant, when officers and men so universally vied with each other in the exercise of every soldierly virtue.

The General's Thanks to each individual of Merit would comprehend the whole Army. But He thinks himself bound however by Affection Duty and Gratitude to express his obligations to Major Generals Lincoln, de La Fayette and Steuben for their dispositions in the Trenches.

To General Du Portail, and Colonel Carney [Querenet],[98] for the Vigor and Knowledge which were conspicuous in their Conduct of the Attacks, and to General Knox and Colonel D'Aberville [d'Aboville] for their great care and attention and fatigue in bringing forward the Artillery and Stores and for their judicious and spirited management of them in the Parallels.

He requests the Gentlemen above mentioned to communicate his thanks to the officers and soldiers of their respective commands.

Ingratitude which the General hopes never to be guilty of would be conspicuous in him was he to omit thanking in the warmest terms His Excellency Governor Nelson[99] for the Aid he has de-

---

97. The English version of Washington's "After Orders" given here follows the manuscript in the Library of Congress, Washington Papers. The spelling of proper names has been normalized. A printed version from this same source is in *Writings of GW*, XXIII, 245–247.

98. Verger in his manuscript writes the name "Kerneÿ." It is written "Carney" in the manuscript in the Washington Papers and is so printed in Fitzpatrick's *Writings of GW*, where a misleading footnote (XXIII, 246, n. 54) erroneously identifies him as "Col. Ethis de Corny." Ethis de Corny, a commissary in the department of supplies, had returned to France in February 1781 and thus took no part in the siege. Johnston (*Yorktown Campaign*, p. 179) correctly surmises that "Carney" is meant to be Querenet. Guillaume Querenet de La Combe (1731–1788), lieutenant colonel in the Royal Corps of Engineers, was the acting head of the French engineers at the siege, sharing with Duportail (chief of the American engineers) the command of the allied engineers at Yorktown. Illness had prevented Querenet's superior, Colonel Desandroüins, from exercising his command (as the latter pointed out in numerous petitions for preferment). Several of Querenet de La Combe's maps of the siege have survived; one of them, preserved in the Archives du Génie, is still filed with the covering letter of transmittal dated York, 24 October 1781. Querenet de La Combe was promoted to the rank of "Colonel sous-brigadier" by an order of 5 December 1781.

99. Governor Thomas Nelson, Jr. (1738–1787) had been responsible for facilitating the provisioning and movement of the troops towards Yorktown, and particularly for assembling and equipping at his own expense the militia that took part in the siege, which ruined him financially and caused his political downfall. He served as governor of Virginia only from June to November 1781, when he was

rived from him and from the Militia under his Command to whose Activity Emulation and Courage much Applause is due; the Greatness of the Acquisition will be an ample Compensation for the Hardships and Hazards which they encountered with so much patriotism and firmness. . . .

(Signed) Washington

By the greatest luck M. de Barras evaded the English Grand Fleet that had arrived in the Chesapeake Bay at almost the same time as M. de Grasse, who came from the Islands. The army of M. de Rochambeau, after a march of 360 leagues, arrived at the rendezvous only a few days later.

The English, Hessian, and Anspach troops, the elite of those who had been in Carolina, those who threatened America and were already in possession of Virginia, began the first proposals for capitulation on the anniversary of Burgoyne's surrender! The English troops are very well dressed; their highlanders, or Scots, are excellent soldiers. The Hessian regiments, and especially those of Anspach, are as handsome troops as one could see anywhere. The English soldiers have received their regular rations throughout the siege, including issues of sugar, chocolate, coffee, and rum.

The tokens of sympathy shown by the French army towards the English and Hessian officers aroused much jealousy in the American officers, who, instead of seeking their friendship, or ours, seemed to confine themselves to bringing up unpleasant subjects with us. We tried in every way to soften the lot of the defeated officers by offering to do for them whatever was in our power as individuals. We amused ourselves with the Hessians and Anspachers as far as their situation would permit.[100] They set off in batches, escorted by militia, for the different localities of their confinement; some went to New York and some to England.

The din and disorder caused by our bombs in the town defy description. Hardly a house remains that is not destroyed, either wholly or in part, by shells or bombs. One could not go ten steps without meeting the wounded or dying, destitute negroes abandoned to their fate, and corpse after corpse on every hand.[101]

22 October M. de Lauzun left on the *Surveillante* to carry the dispatches to the Court of France.[102]

25 October The *Andromaque* left with the Chevalier [Comte Guillaume] de Deux-Ponts. On the 28th she came within sight of 45 enemy sail, of which 23 were warships, including some of 50 guns.

❧ *November–December 1781* ❧

The American army left York in the first few days of November. The militia had already departed. At the same time General Wayne left with the light infantry to join General Greene. There was great rejoicing in Philadelphia, where one of the spectators saw portraits displayed of Washington and Rochambeau, illuminated and encircled with rays.[103]

---

succeeded by Benjamin Harrison. The Vicomte de Rochambeau noted in his journal (p. 249): "This brave man was harassed by his fellow citizens for having overstepped the law during that crisis in greatly contributing to the success of the campaign. It is true that he requisitioned the slaves and horses of the country for use by the army. They reproached him for his illegal acts and he resigned. It is very rarely that republics are grateful for services given them in any unusual manner." Chastellux ([4], II, 382) also expresses sympathy and respect for Governor Nelson, remarking that because of the ingratitude of his fellow citizens "those laws and customs which would have been wiped out had the state been conquered were now invoked against the defender of the state."

100. See above, p. 129, where Verger mentions an Anspach officer, M. Wittershausen.

101. "I have this day [22 October] visited the town of York. . . . It contains about sixty houses, some of them are elegant, many of them are greatly damaged and some totally ruined. . . . Rich furniture and books were scattered over the ground, and the carcasses of men and horses half covered with earth, exhibited a scene of ruin and horror beyond description." James Thacher, *Military Journal* (Boston, 1823), p. 350.

102. See Clermont-Crèvecœur's journal, n. 127.

103. Contemporary descriptions of the illuminations in Philadelphia are quoted (from the *Freeman's Journal* and other sources) in Stone, *French Allies*, pp. 488–489. On one of the windows of Alexander Quesnay's lodging in Second Street, between Chestnut and Walnut, "was drawn the picture of the illustrious American commander, with his lance in his hand, trampling under foot the crown of Britain, with the motto, *British Pride*. Over this were three fleurs de luce standing about the Count de Rochambeau's

On 16 November we [the Deux-Ponts Regiment] entered winter quarters at Williamsburg with the Bourbonnais Regiment and several companies of artillery. The Soissonnais was at York, the Saintonge and the Lauzun Legion at Hampton, and the artillery at West Point.[104]

On 28 December we lighted bonfires to celebrate the capture of St. Eustatius.[105]

The English suffered quite a lot from the American riflemen, some of whom are very expert marksmen with the carbine [long rifle.][106] They never faced the enemy as a unit, but individually, hiding from bush to bush until they brought their quarry within range; then they picked off a sentry and, having fired, fled as fast as their legs could carry them. They rarely missed their mark. I learned from an Anspach officer that the day we arrived the riflemen killed 8 sentries in this fashion. When the English catch them, they give them no quarter. One day we saw one coming back after killing a sentry on the parapet of a redoubt the previous night. He had been caught by a patrol who disarmed him and would have beaten him to death had he not been rescued by an American patrol.

The American Continental troops are very war-wise and quite well disciplined. They are thoroughly inured to hardship, which they endure with little complaint so long as their officers set them an example, but it is imperative that the officers equal their troops in firmness and resolution. They have supreme confidence in General Washington and march with courage and enthusiasm behind the Marquis de La Fayette. Of all their corps their light infantry is the most praiseworthy.

The militia seem a bit worse here than elsewhere. However, they give occasional examples of bravery when they are in superior numbers or when in possession of some defile the enemy must pass through, into which they can fire from ambush. But they must have enough room in their rear to ensure their retreat, else their high opinion of the English and, even more, their fear of capture would render them of little account in a fort or on campaign. We have seen parties of militia in this country perform feats that veteran units would have gloried in accomplishing. They only do so, however, when the persuasive eloquence of their commander has aroused in them an enthusiastic ardor of which immediate advantage must be taken.

Some American officers were heard to say in a café that, when Cornwallis saw the militia and the French arrive, he wasn't much worried, but that, when he saw the Continental troops,——!

A detachment of 100 of Cornwallis' troops who were prisoners of war embarked on the Rappahannock River and landed on a beach where they had been promised wagons and provisions. They landed in a desert where they found no means of subsistence. Eighty of them died of hunger and destitution through the negligence of the officers responsible for their maintenance.

Williamsburg is the capital of Virginia and used to be the residence of the English governor. Although built of wood, it is quite handsome. The main street is a mile long and very broad; all the other streets, which lead into it, are of little consequence. There are several fairly notable public edifices here.[107] The Col-

name, with the motto *Huzza!* which also diverged three rays of joy towards the aforementioned illustrious hero. The whole was formed by different colors . . . and attracted the universal admiration of the numerous spectators." Not to be outdone, Charles Willson Peale's home at Third and Lombard also blossomed forth with transparencies, including portraits and the motto "Shine, Valiant Chiefs!" See Charles Coleman Sellers, *Charles Willson Peale* (New York, 1969), pp. 188ff., and Sellers, *Charles Willson Peale with Patron and Populace*, in *Transactions of the American Philosophical Society*, n.s., Vol. LIX, Part 3 (Philadelphia, 1969), pp. 16–17.

104. See maps, Vol. II, Nos. 99, 104, 105, and 106.

105. St. Eustatius (Statia), which had been taken from the Dutch by the British earlier in the year, was recaptured by the French under the Marquis de Bouillé on 26 November 1781. See Clermont-Crèvecœur's journal, n. 193. Du Perron, who was in Martinique when Bouillé returned there on 5 December 1781, learned the details of the St. Eustatius raid from the participants and in turn recorded the whole story in his journal ([1], p. 181–186).

106. Verger's drawings of American soldiers, which illustrate his comments and which are reproduced here, are bound in his manuscript journal, between pp. 170 and 171, facing p. 172, and facing p. 173.

107. The public edifices mentioned by Verger—including the College [of William and Mary], the government house [Governor's Palace], the Capitol, and the insane asylum—are shown on Berthier's map, Vol. II, No. 86. Desandroüins's signed map of Williamsburg and environs (cited in

lege is built of brick and is very spacious, with two large buildings as wings where the professors are lodged. One of them, which was used for a hospital for officers, burned down shortly after our arrival.[108]

The government house, which was very handsome, was burned to the ground when it accidentally caught fire.[109] The Capitol is at the head of the town and merits a visit. There is a very beautiful white marble statue there of the celebrated Berkeley.[110] The English barracks were also consumed by flames.

The town is very sparsely populated and at present contains no more than 1,500 inhabitants. The insane asylum is very large and is one of the handsomest edifices.[111] The inhabitants are chiefly Presbyterian,[112] but all other religious groups are tolerated except the Catholics. There are many French in these parts who came here as refugees after the revocation of the Edict of Nantes.

Six miles from town are some beaver lodges. There I saw these animals cut down trees and drag them long distances to build their dams, which are constructed with astonishing neatness and solidity. We inspected one of their lodges at the foot of a tree, near a little pond; it is round, about 3 feet across, and consists of three stories built on piles. Thus, when the water rises, the beavers retire to the second floor, then to the third

---

n. 67) also shows the town in some detail. An even larger-scale map, "Plan de la Ville et Environs de Williamsburg en Virginie," known as "The Frenchman's Map," has been reproduced in facsimile by Colonial Williamsburg, Inc. This map by an unidentified French officer provided essential documentation for the twentieth-century restoration of eighteenth-century Williamsburg. It is dated by the author 11 May 1782; although the last figure of the date is difficult to interpret, other indications on the map (such as the "quartier général" in the Wythe House) confirm 1782 as the correct year.

108. The journal of Lauberdière (p. 99) describes the "université" as "composée d'un gros corps de logis et de deux gros pavillons qui n'y sont point attenants en avant," that is, a principal building and two large detached pavilions in front of it. The two pavilions, or "wings," were the Brafferton building and the President's House, the latter of which was damaged by fire on 23 November 1781. Von Closen (p. 166) mentions that the fire did not reach the main college building and that all the wounded officers in the "wing" were removed in time: "The King got off for £12,000 in damages, in a settlement that M. de Rochambeau negotiated with the President, Mr. Madison, who had lost a large part of his library and several fine physics instruments."

109. The Governor's Palace, then being used as a hospital for American wounded, burned on 22 December 1781. Writing the next day to Washington, Rochambeau reported: "We saved all the sick, most of the effects, and prevented the fire from spreading to the neighboring houses, notably my own [the Wythe House], which is the first of those occupied by Your Excellency and which was covered all night with a rain of fire. We have gathered all our sick in the Capitol and this day I have given them all the help in my power." Rochambeau to Washington, Williamsburg, 23 December 1781, in the Library of Congress, Washington Papers. Dr. James Tilton, in his *Economical Observations on Military Hospitals* (Wil-

mington, Delaware, 1813), pp. 63–64, recalls: "After the siege and capture of Yorktown in Virginia, General Washington returned to the northward and the French troops were cantoned in Williamsburg. I was left in charge of the sick and wounded Americans, who could not be moved. Being thus in a French garrison, I had some opportunity of observing the French practice and management of their sick. . . ." Washington later thanked Dr. Coste, physician general of Rochambeau's army, for "your humane attention to the American Hospitals which were established at Williamsburg after the siege of York." Washington to Coste, 7 October 1782, in *Writings of GW*, xxv, 244.

110. Norborne Berkeley, baron de Botetourt, royal governor of Virginia from October 1768 until his death in October 1770. The full-length marble statue of this well-loved governor, by the London sculptor Richard Hayward, originally stood at the Capitol; it was later moved to the College of William and Mary at the opposite end of the town. The statue was removed from the College yard in 1957 after standing there since 1801 except for a brief sojourn on the grounds of Eastern State Hospital during the Civil War. It is now located on the ground floor of the Earl Gregg Swem Library of the College of William and Mary.

111. The "lunatic hospital," later known as the Eastern State Hospital, was completed in 1773 pursuant to an act passed by the House of Burgesses "to make Provision for the support and maintenance of ideots, lunatics, and other persons of unsound minds." The designer was the Philadelphia architect Robert Smith, who had built Nassau Hall at Princeton in 1756. The original buildings were destroyed by fire in 1876 and 1885. Verger calls it the "maison des fous," the designation also used on the map of Williamsburg, Vol. II, No. 86.

112. Most of the inhabitants of this part of Virginia were actually Anglicans. Verger, like his brother officers, often uses the term "Presbyterian" to designate any or all of the Protestant sects.

if necessary, but they always keep their tails in the water. In a corner of each storey they deposit provisions for the winter. Beside the house, and sometimes inside it, they build a tunnel through which they can escape when they see hunters approach. They knock on the ground with their tails to warn their comrades of the danger. Then they remain under water until the coast is clear, which fact they also announce by tail signals.

There are several methods of hunting them. The most amusing one is as follows: Without making any noise, you come out in the evening to one of their dams and make a hole in it so that the water runs out of the pond; then you quickly go off and hide nearby. The beavers in the lodge immediately notice that the water level is falling and come out to locate the leak. Once they find it, they beat three times with their tails to summon the other beavers to work. Some bring earth, which stems the flow of water somewhat, others bring sticks, and still others apply mortar on the dam with their tails, working with incredible diligence. Meanwhile, you have time to select the animal you wish to shoot. But immediately afterwards the rest jump into the water, and you do not see them again for the rest of the day. The beaver lodges smell of amber, and the beavers communicate this odor to everything on which they lie.

A certain Mr. Egleson, one of the richest inhabitants of these parts, hearing that the British were on their way to pillage his house, retired with two negroes to an inaccessible marshland whose entrance was known only to himself.[113] With all his treasure and some provisions he moved into a beaver lodge. One of his negroes betrayed him and led in a party of British soldiers to capture him. When they came within gunshot, they had to crawl through a narrow defile, whereupon Egleson shot the negro and, reloading his musket, picked off a British soldier. This discouraged the rest, who, having lost their guide, beat a retreat. Mr. Egleson remained in his marsh six weeks; even though a price had been put on his head, no one had the courage to go out and attack him. This country is very difficult to penetrate.

113. Verger in his manuscript writes the name "Egleson"—probably Eggleston, or Eccleston, who has not been further identified.

Volume II

CONTINUATION OF THE JOURNAL,

containing a brief account of the Discovery of Virginia, its Products and Commerce, a description of its Birds and Game, and some remarks about the land; also my travels in North America, my Voyage to the Islands, our return to France, and our journey from Brest to Landau.

[Begun] at Williamsburg, this 18th day of January 1782 by de Verger, officer of the Royal Deux-Ponts Regiment.

It was on 27 April 1584, in the reign of Queen Elizabeth, that the first adventurers to go and settle in Virginia left the mouth of the Thames and, sailing past the Canary and Windward Islands, arrived on 2 July off the Florida coast.[114] On Roanoke Island at the mouth of Albemarle Sound they established themselves under Governor Ralph Lane and Admiral [Captain] Philip Amadas. From this island they made several trips to reconnoiter the mainland, coming within 130 miles of the Chesapeake Bay, whose shores were inhabited by a tribe of Indians of that name.

Most of these Indians believed in a god existing for all eternity who created the heavens after having created other gods to serve as his instruments in the creation of the universe and to help him govern it. First among these were the sun, moon, and stars; then he created the waters from which the earthly creatures were formed. Woman was formed first, and by mating with one of the gods she had four children, whence sprang the human race. They believed that all the gods were of human form; hence they represented them in their temples by images that they honored by their prayers, songs, dances, and offerings. They believed

that the soul is immortal and that the dead, depending upon their works during life, are transported to the abode of the gods or else to Popogusso (a great hole in the place where the sun sets) amid torments and eternal fire. This doctrine they had received from two persons who claimed to have risen from the dead.

They were very anxious to learn from the English, whose compasses, telescopes, magnifying glasses, bells, writing, muskets, and cannon astonished them so much that they believed they were fashioned by gods rather than men. Their high opinion of the English was greatly increased when an epidemic malady afflicted precisely those persons who had planned to do harm to the English. They went to some colonists to seek a cure from heaven.

Perceiving that the English had no women with them, the Indians believed that they had descended from the immortals of old and that some were invisible and incorporeal, would soon come to destroy them, and would kill those who displeased them with invisible projectiles that made a loud noise.

1590 After various accidents befell the colony, Captain [John] White sailed from Plymouth with three

---

114. The following digest of the early history of Virginia is based on William Stith, *The History of the First Discovery and Settlement of Virginia* (Williamsburg, William Parks, 1747, and later editions). Other French officers' journals include similar summaries; in the Berthier Papers (No. 44), Princeton University Library, there is a 9-page manuscript in Berthier's hand entitled "Découverte

de la Virginie en 1586," which also derives from Stith's *History*. Like the accounts of battles inserted in their journals, these historical summaries are another example of the way the French officers improved their time by adding to their knowledge of the country where they were campaigning.

ships. They arrived off Hatteras, where he had left the colony three years before. He sent his boat ashore, but the crew found nothing; only on their return did they spy a post on which was inscribed, in large letters, "Croatan." The colonists had agreed that, if they were obliged to retreat, they would inscribe thus the name of their destination.

The next morning the party set sail for Croatan, an Indian village in the southern part of Cape Lookout. When one of their cables parted, the vessel drifted at such a rate that they were on the verge of shipwreck. Since their provisions were nearly exhausted, they decided to go to the Windward Islands to rest. They arrived there on 23 September, leaving their comrades to their unhappy fate among the savages, and nothing more was heard of them.

The miserable failure of the first expeditions was so discouraging that, although several individuals tried in vain to organize others, no further explorations were planned during the next twelve years.

1606 Bartholomew Gosnold, who had already made a voyage to the northern part of Virginia, had boasted in such extravagant terms of the bounty and fertility of its soil that he persuaded Captain [John] Smith and two other men, who were very rich, to join him in this enterprise [the Virginia Company]. When the King took the Company under his protection, the merchants of several cities, including London, became interested and contributed towards it success. Having obtained two ships and a small bark, the colonists set sail that year.

1607 After passing the Windward Islands, they sighted land on 26 April. The first point they named Cape Henry, and the point north of it Cape Charles. Captain Newport sent ashore thirty men whom five Indians attacked, wounding two.

The colonists chose a site on a peninsula about forty miles from the mouth of the Chesapeake Bay, which they called Jamestown in honor of the reigning King, and everyone went to work. Their council ordered some to build a fort and the rest to clear land on which to pitch their tents. The natives enjoyed visiting them frequently, and although never allowed by the president to watch the colonists drill or build fortifications, they helped clear the brush within a semicircle.

Some time thereafter Captain Newport took twenty men to look for the source of the Powhatan River, henceforth called the James. After a six days' journey they arrived at a village of a dozen houses, called Powhatan, which was the residence of the local king. They were everywhere very well received, but on their return to Jamestown they found seventeen of their comrades wounded and one killed by the savages. Had the latter not been terrified when a cannonball was fired from a ship into their midst, it would have been all over for the English, who had gone to work unarmed.

After that episode the new colonists were drilled and a guard was set; nevertheless, Englishmen were constantly being killed. Their losses, after they had been ravaged by famine and disease, amounted to sixty men. The rest had nothing but crabs to eat until the end of September. In spite of all this, the president [Edward Wingfield] remained insensible to their sufferings, since he had commandeered all the grain, etc., and was living in plenty. Later, when he planned to escape to England in a small bark, he so aroused the people's indignation that they elected Ratcliffe in his stead. Meanwhile, the natives were conciliated and brought them quantities of fruit and provisions.

When Martin and Smith became the leaders, the latter, a very enterprising man, realized that their provisions would soon be exhausted. He embarked in a small boat with six companions and descended the river to Kicquotan. There the savages mocked them as poor starving creatures, derisively offering them a handful of corn in exchange for their muskets and swords. When Captain Smith saw that he could not trade with them, he was of necessity obliged to transcend his authority. Saluting them with a volley of musketry, he ran his boat ashore. The Indians fled to the woods, and the English marched to their settlement, where they found a large quantity of corn. Smith had great difficulty restraining his soldiers from pillage, suspecting that they would soon be attacked. What he had foreseen came to pass. Sixty Indians, some painted black and others red and white, came out of the woods, singing and dancing and making a frightful noise, following their Okée. This was an idol made of skins, stuffed with moss, and loaded with chains and copper plates. Armed with clubs, bows, and arrows, they charged the English, who gave them so warm a reception with a second volley that several fell, including their divinity, and the rest took to the woods. Shortly afterwards they sent one of their priests to ransom their Okée and sue for peace. Smith replied that, if they would send six unarmed men to load his boat with corn, he would not only give them back their Okée but would be their friend and would give them copper coins and axes in return. The bargain was concluded to the satisfaction of both parties, and then the Indians returned, singing and dancing, bringing them game, wild fowl, and bread.

Reascending the river, Captain Smith discovered on one of its tributaries the town of Warrasqueake, where he disembarked to go in search of provisions. All of a sudden he found himself surrounded by Indians. After killing several of his assailants in self-defense, he was obliged to surrender. To the accompaniment of singing and dancing he was conducted with great pomp to an Indian village, where he was so well fed that he feared they intended to fatten him in order to eat him. From there the Indians took him to the banks of the Pamunkey (now the York) River, where Opechancanough was king. They brought with them a barrel of gunpowder that they were saving with great care to plant the following spring as they planted their corn.

Powhatan, who was emperor of the whole country, had under him about thirty petty kings or *caciques* over whom he held the power of life and death. He had a guard of two hundred men and as many women as he wished. His subjects rendered him unlimited obedience, since they looked upon him as a demigod.

When Smith was presented to him, he was seated before a fire, dressed in a great robe of the finest furs, and flanked by two young girls of about seventeen. The lodge was lined on either side with armed warriors as well as a number of painted women. When Smith entered, everyone cried aloud, and the leader of the women was ordered to bring him water to wash his hands. Then Powhatan held a long council. At its conclusion two great stones were brought, on which Smith was placed to be beaten with clubs. Realizing that nothing could change the sentence, Pocahontas, the Emperor's favorite daughter, hid her face in her hands and threw herself across his body to save his life. At this Powhatan decided to spare him to make hatchets, etc., for the Indians.

After many misfortunes the colony achieved stability. Some pious folk sent large sums of money to found a school for the Indians. It was called St. Mary's. Later a college was founded at Williamsburg. Peace was maintained with the natives for quite a while, but once they came across the James River to ravage the environs of the college, obliging the colonists to remain on the defensive.

When the number of inhabitants became large enough, a governor was sent out from England. He established his residence at Williamsburg, the capital of the province, where a garrison was sent out to protect the new colonists from Indian raids.

❦

Virginia is very large and its western portion is not yet fully explored. It has several navigable rivers, including the James, the Pamunkey, the Occoquan, and the Rappahannock, all navigable for some distance inland. Its largest ports are Norfolk, Hampton at the mouth of the Bay, and York, and there are other smaller ports. Its principal trade is in tobacco, which is highly esteemed, particularly that raised on the banks of the James. It, as well as corn, is cultivated for the inhabitants by their negroes. The tobacco is planted and grows on all the rich land, but does best on newly cleared land. It requires great care to keep it cleared of all the weeds that flourish in the surrounding soil. When it reaches maturity, it is picked and dried in the sun until it is almost free of moisture, then packed in great barrels holding 1,000 pounds, called "hogsheads."

The corn is used to feed the negroes in the form of flour that they make into cakes and bake over the fire. The poorer inhabitants eat no other kind of bread. The corn shucks are stripped from the ears and fed to the horses during the winter, for in summer they are all let out to pasture, which makes them very strong. There are thoroughbred horses in this country, comparable to the finest in England, which are generally esteemed. They fetch high prices in the French colonies, thus providing still another branch of commerce that is very lucrative.

The people here are very fond of horse races, on which they bet considerable sums. They have another sport, which is cock-fighting. Here is how it is conducted: Certain inhabitants raise cocks that look very strong and that they bring in a covered cage to the battlefield. Those disposed to bet choose one, which is then weighed, and if he is of the same weight as his adversary, the neck feathers that might hinder him are plucked out. The cocks are next fitted with very sharp, long, curved steel spurs which are attached to their natural spurs. Then they are put into a ring enclosed by a rope, around which the circle of spectators sits. Each man launches his cock, and the fight is on. The moment one falls a man picks him up and makes him take a drink. The fight continues until one of the combatants is killed. I heard that after one of these fights Messrs. Graves and Nicholson, who had made a bet of £300 on the outcome, got into a fist-fight—the usual outcome of disputes between Americans.

The stags here are very much like the deer in our country. The hares are much smaller than the European variety, and some claim they are rabbits. The foxes are also smaller, and the fox-hunts are quite amusing. Several inhabitants keep excellent packs of hounds and hunt on horseback. We went fox-hunting several times a week with M. de Rochambeau.[115] We rarely failed to run two foxes in a day.

One finds here a quadruped the size of a cat called an oppossum[116] and observes in the female a singular trick of nature. Under her belly she has a pouch that opens and shuts, in which she keeps her young. When she is chased by hunters and her young are on the ground, she picks them up and puts them in this pouch, which immediately closes. We saw this performance.

The muskrat lives on the edge of the ponds and imparts a strong odor to whatever it touches.

The birds here are entirely different from those in Europe. The most notable are: the cardinal, which is a beautiful shade of red and has a crest (the female is the same yellow as the belly of a doe, tinged with red); the Carolina chatterer [waxwing]; the mockingbird, a yellowish-grey bird whose song imitates those of all other birds; the hummingbird; the bluebird; and the goldfinch, a small yellow bird with black-tipped wings. The partridge is smaller here than in Europe, as are the woodcock and snipe. The grouse, heath hen, etc., are found in abundance. The most remarkable of the water birds are the garganeys or "summer ducks." They are crested, and their plumage combines all the brightest colors; their crest forms a perfect helmet. There are also teal and plover here.

The land is generally marshy and sparsely cultivated. The immense woods one encounters are the prettiest imaginable in summer when the flowering laurels and other sweet-smelling trees give off a delicious scent. Parts of the countryside have been ruined by the English armies, who committed the greatest atrocities here.

❧ February 1782 ❧

[*2 February*] The *Hermione* left for France,[117] accompanied by the *Diligente*, which was bound for Boston. Not far from the Virginia coast the latter vessel was sent inshore by a violent storm and driven on the rocks a musket-shot from land by her American pilot, who was at the helm. M. de Clouard immediately sent 10 of his best swimmers ashore for help, but the seas were so steep that 8 of them perished. Meanwhile, the frigate was taking in water so fast that the men on deck were submerged to their waists. It was also bitterly cold that day. The boats were launched, but one, being overloaded, capsized. The rest of the crew was

---

115. "M. de Rochambeau, who liked hunting very much, amused himself during the whole winter riding through the woods, followed by twenty or so enthusiasts. We ran down more than 30 foxes. The dog packs belonging to the gentlemen of the neighborhood are wonderful. It is only a pity that the species of foxes is not as strong as that in Europe; ordinarily, after an hour of hunting, they are tracked down, sometimes in even less time, and rarely in more. The country around Williamsburg favors this kind of hunting. There are many clear woods and little thickets, across which one can always follow the hounds, and although there are several creeks and swamps, the fords are not dangerous and are always marked." Von Closen, p. 177.

116. Verger in his manuscript (MS, II, 22) calls it a "bossum." Chastellux ([4], II, 462–468) gives an extensive account of "The Opossum." See also our illustration.

117. Among the passengers on the *Hermione* was General Baron de Vioménil, who returned to America the following September.

saved, except for 24 men, including 2 soldiers. M. de Clouard had the two pilots shackled hand and foot and thrown into the sea.[118]

✑§ June–July 1782 §℺

28 June We received orders to get ready to march in a few days, which took everybody by surprise.[119]

1 July The Bourbonnais Regiment departed.

2 July Our regiment [the Royal Deux-Ponts] left for Drinking Spring——8 miles

3 July To Byrd's Tavern——8 miles.

4 July To Radelassen's [Ratcliffe's] House——7 miles.

5 July To New Kent Courthouse——7½ miles.

6 July To New Castle, where we made a halt——17 miles. This is a small settlement on the Pamunkey, a tributary of the York River. Here we saw a magnificent bay stallion, belonging to Colonel Syme, which had been bought for 2,000 guineas.

8 July To Hanovertown, or [Little-] Page's Bridge ——[7] miles. We encamped very near the town, which carries on a large trade in tobacco from the interior.

9 July To Hanover Courthouse——11 miles.

10 July To Burk's Bridge——12 miles.

11 July To Bowling Green, so named because of the fertility of its soil——8 miles.

12 July To Charles Thornton's, remarkable to us

because of its excellent spring water, the greatest rarity in this hot season——10 miles.

13 July Via Fredericksburg to Falmouth——10 miles. Fredericksburg is quite a large town whose surrounding country is very well cultivated. A mile from town there is a superb estate whose proprietor owns 1,000 negroes.[120] He trades extensively in tobacco. We skirted the lower end of the town on our way to Falmouth. The artillery crossed the Rappahannock, which is not navigable beyond this point, at a ford. We found the Lauzun Legion at Falmouth, where we camped on miserable ground. We stayed there two days and visited a rather fine Protestant church and a ropewalk.

15 July To Peyton's Tavern——13 miles.

16 July To Dumfries, a small settlement with nothing notable about it except a very pretty view overlooking Quantico Creek——8 miles.

17 July To Colchester, a small town on the Occoquan River inhabited before the Revolution chiefly by Scottish merchants and now almost deserted——10 miles. We went to see the forges on the Occoquan, 4 miles from town, which are very fine, and a waterfall over the rocks that is a beautiful spectacle. There is also in the middle of the river a small island that is very fertile, and in general the banks of this river are lovely.

18 July To Alexandria——17 miles. This is a fairly large town on the Occoquan [Potomac] and is a very busy port. Ships of 300 tons can easily come up to it. There are several fine buildings to be seen here. We camped on an immense plain.[121]

118. According to Von Closen (pp. 173–174), "the pilot (we are assured) was immediately thrown into the sea by the crew, who sacrificed him to their rage."

119. The various units quartered in Yorktown, Hampton, and other places on the peninsula proceeded to Williamsburg, whence the army moved northward in four divisions, marching a day apart. Verger marched with his regiment, the Royal Deux-Ponts, commanded by the Comte Christian de Deux-Ponts and led by Cromot Dubourg, which left Williamsburg on 2 July. Maps of the successive camps mentioned hereinafter by Verger are in Vol. II, Nos. 108ff.

The route followed by the army northward to Baltimore in 1782 was virtually the same as the one taken by the wagon train on its overland southward march in September 1781; see Vol. II, Itinerary 6.

120. Doubtless "Chatham," which is still standing and which in 1782 belonged to Colonel William Fitzhugh. See Vol. II, Itinerary 6, n. 28.

121. George Grieve, the English translator of Chastellux's *Travels*, who was himself in America at this time and who "attended the French army on their march, nearly the whole way from Alexandria to the North River," witnessed the following scene: "When they encamped at Alexandria, on the ground formerly occupied by Braddock [in 1755], the most elegant and handsome young ladies of the neighborhood danced with the officers on the turf, in the middle of the camp, to the sound of military music; and (a circumstance which will appear singular to European ideas) the circle was in a great measure composed of soldiers, who, from the heat of the weather, had disengaged themselves from their clothes, retaining

19 July To Georgetown, where we crossed the Potomac, a very wide, navigable river——8 miles.

20 July To Bladensburg in the province of Maryland, where we made a halt——7 miles.

23 July To Rose's Tavern[122]—— 13 miles.

24 July To two miles this side of Spurrier's Tavern——11 miles.

25 July To Baltimore——14 miles. We camped very near a street called Fredericktown Road in a rather pretty location.[123] As the army gradually assembled, we were ordered to construct an arbor along the color-line of the camp, which made a very pretty sight.[124] The Lauzun Legion was camped ahead on our left.[125]

Baltimore is one of the largest cities in North America. Even though very modern, it is thickly populated. Several public buildings are worthy of notice, such as the large church,[126] the Catholic church, and the market. Most of the dwellings are built of brick. The streets are wide and have sidewalks on both sides. The population is large, and more than two-thirds are Germans who came to America under various auspices.[127] They were each indentured to an American for a cer-

tain period at the end of which they were free. Those who behaved well had no trouble becoming established. Land was distributed to all who wished to cultivate it at a very modest sum to be paid when they were able.

The commerce here is very extensive because this city handles the trade of a large hinterland. It deals principally in flour, which it exports to the Islands, receiving sugar and coffee in exchange. During my stay here a barrel of flour could be bought for 4 piasters and sold for 35 at The French Cape. The Point [Fell's Point], actually an outlying district, is where the large vessels arrive and where frigates can come up to the wharves. However, the ships must keep quite close to the battery, which is a mile away. This battery was not then in a state of defense but is capable of being heavily fortified.[128] Three-deckers cannot approach it within less than 2 miles.

All religions are sanctioned here: the Catholics have a church here, as well as the Lutherans, Calvinists, Presbyterians, Quakers, Herrnhuter [Moravians], and Anabaptists.

not an article of dress except their shirts, which in general were neither extremely long, nor in the best condition; nor did this occasion the least embarrassment to the ladies, many of whom were of highly polished manners, and the most exquisite delicacy; or to their friends or parents; so whimsical and arbitrary are manners." Chastellux (4), II, 615.

122. See Vol. II, No. 127, map of the camp at Snowden's Iron Works, which shows "Rose's Tavern" on the road leading to Spurrier's Tavern and Baltimore. Snowden's Iron Works was on the Patuxent River in the vicinity of present Laurel, Maryland. Blanchard, who was marching with the Fourth Division, stopped here on 25 July; he notes in his journal ([1], p. 112) that he was well lodged in the house of a wealthy major [Thomas] Snowden, where he had excellent ham for dinner and again for supper, in the company of Major Snowden's attractive wife and daughter.

123. See maps of the Baltimore camp, Vol. II, Nos. 129 and 130. The Fredericktown Road was later known as the Reistertown Turnpike and is now Pennsylvania Avenue.

124. The custom of erecting ornamental bowers and arbors, known in French as *feuillées*, along the color-line of military cantonments evidently persisted into the nineteenth century. See, e.g., the various photographs in Francis Trevelyan Miller and Robert S. Lanier, *Photographic*

History of the Civil War (New York, 1911), V, 233, 257, 275, and VII, 58, 151, 241, 243, 258–259.

125. On the height now occupied by the "old" Roman Catholic Cathedral grounds, originally bounded by Charles, Mulberry, Cathedral, and Franklin Streets.

126. Old St. Paul's Protestant Episcopal Church, at Charles and Saratoga Streets; the present edifice is the fourth to occupy the site, the first having been built in 1739. See map, Vol. II, No. 129, where it appears as "Church." The "Meeting-house" on the same map is the Roman Catholic "mass house," built 1770–1775 on a hillside at the corner of present Saratoga and Little Sharp Streets. Building of the present Catholic Cathedral at Cathedral and Mulberry Streets was begun only in 1806; it was dedicated in 1821.

127. Probably an exaggeration, stemming from Verger's bilingual background, affiliation with the Deux-Ponts Regiment, and consequent awareness of German-speaking people. The German element was nevertheless important in Maryland. See Dieter Cunz, *The Maryland Germans, A History* (Princeton, 1948). From a study of the first published directory of the City of Baltimore (1796) Cunz concludes (p. 161) that about ten percent of the 3,000 names in the directory are undoubtedly German.

128. See map, Vol. II, No. 130, which shows this battery to the east of Fell's Point, in the vicinity of present Thames Street.

During our stay we held maneuvers, often with live ammunition; during a firing exercise of the Soissonnais Regiment a stray bullet broke the hip of an American doctor's wife.[129]

The Comte [Robert-Guillaume] de Dillon, second colonel of the Lauzun Legion, was riding very fast through the city streets followed by a hussar, who knocked down a child. When the father, who was present, abused the soldier, the latter wanted to knock *him* down. Meanwhile, a crowd had gathered and beat the hussar, who was left for dead in the street. Had M. de Dillon not made his escape, he would have suffered the same fate. He went to lodge a complaint with the justice of the peace, who ruled that, if the hussar died of his wounds, the inhabitant would be condemned to pay a fine of 4 shillings.

We learned in Baltimore that M. de Vaudreuil had arrived in Boston with a squadron of 13 warships.

I went often to the house of Dr. Wiesenthal, a Prussian, where a man named Zollikoffer from Zurich lived.[130] A M. ———— from Neufchâtel was married to the doctor's daughter. M. de Rochambeau and several individuals in the French army gave some very enjoyable balls.[131]

August 1782

Shortly before our departure the detachment we had left in Yorktown arrived by sea in the *Romulus* and the *Guadeloupe*. We left our large hospital in Baltimore with upwards of 400 sick, together with 30 men from each regiment and a company of artillery.[132]

We attended a ball at the house of Mr. Stuart.

25 August We left Baltimore for Great Falls[133]——— 14 miles.

26 August To Bushtown [Bush], where we saw a man over 6 feet tall mount a horse 6 feet 6 inches high.

27 August To Harford at the mouth of the Susquehanna,[134] a very large river, which the artillery crossed by a ford 2 miles from the ferry.

129. "It resulted in the arrest of the commander of the regiment (le Comte de Saint-Maime), who was in despair." Von Closen, p. 219. Blanchard ([1], p. 114) mentioning the same or a similar incident, says that the victim, an Acadian woman of about thirty, received good care and that the wound was not serious.

130. Carl Friedrich, or Charles Frederick, Wiesenthal (1726–1789), sometimes called "the father of the medical profession in Baltimore," came from Prussia in 1755. For a survey of his career and role during the Revolution, with references to other sources, see Cunz, *op.cit.*, pp. 108–110, 142–144. Zollikoffer was probably John Conrad Zollikoffer (or perhaps a brother[?], Dr. William Z.). Wiesenthal and Zollikoffer were among the founders of the German Society, established to aid German redemptioners. See Louis P. Henninghausen, *History of the German Society of Maryland* (Baltimore, 1909), p. 43, where a letter signed by Zollikoffer as secretary of the Society is printed. At the time Verger saw him J. C. Zollikoffer appears to have been engaged in trade and speculation in privateers; *Journal and Correspondence of the State Council of Maryland, 8, 1781–1784*, ed. J. H. Pleasants, Archives of Maryland, XLVIII (Baltimore, 1931), 255, under the date of 6 September 1782.

131. Von Closen (pp. 218–219) describes the ball he gave on 8 August: "I invited all my acquaintances; my hostesses asked theirs, and I persuaded my friends and some dancers from the army to come. The generals and heads of corps also did me the honor to attend, and I endeavored to make the evening pass for this charming and large company as pleasantly and merrily as I could. . . . The dance and the parties continued until 3 o'clock in the morning. . . . I called next day on all the ladies who had attended my ball, and they were good enough to assure me that they had enjoyed it very much; Madame Lee, wife of the Governor, was among them." Von Closen, because of a sudden illness, was unable to attend the ball given by the assistant quartermasters-general (including Berthier) on 14 August, but he received a detailed account of it the next day from his hostesses, as related in his journal, p. 225.

132. Concerning the detachment left at Baltimore (the last to leave the United States), see Clermont-Crèvecœur's journal, n. 156.

133. The first camp after Baltimore was near Whitemarsh Forges, according to the map, Vol. II, No. 131. The Whitemarsh Forges were on Whitemarsh Run, which is actually the head of the Bird River, which in turn flows into the "Great Falls" of the Gunpowder River.

134. See map of camp at Lower Ferry, Vol. II, No. 133. The camp was on the eastern bank of the Susquehanna between the river and Mill Creek (now Perryville). The western end of the ferry (now Havre de Grace) was in Harford County, which may explain Verger's designation. Several other officers noted in their journals for this date that plans were afoot for building a town near the ferry on the western bank of the river, to be called Havre de

29 August Via Charlestown, on the Little Elk River,[135] and Northeast to Head of Elk [Elkton], where the grenadiers and chasseurs had embarked last year——10 miles.

30 August Via Christine Bridge [Christiana] to Newport in Newcastle County [in Delaware].

31 August At Newport I asked permission to go on to Philadelphia, which was granted. I left the morning of the 31st and passed through Wilmington, whose location is the most agreeable one could possibly find. Its streets are quite regular and its houses built of brick.[136] It is on the Christiana River, whose banks are very gay. I stopped there for only a short time and went on to lunch at Chester, a rather pretty town. Eighteen miles from Philadelphia you pass quite near the battlefield of Brandywine where the Americans were beaten.

❦ September 1782 ❧

I arrived in Philadelphia in time for dinner on 31 August and took lodgings at the Black Horse.[137] Philadelphia is a large and beautiful city. All the streets are perfectly straight; the houses are tall and built of brick. You see several notable buildings here, including the mansion where the Congress meets [Pennsylvania State House, later Independence Hall], which is very large. Ascending the staircase, you see the statues of Christopher Columbus and of Penn, to whom Pennsylvania once belonged. Opposite the Congress Hall is the resi-

dence of M. de La Luzerne, the ambassador of France, and behind it is the large prison, which was still full of English prisoners from Burgoyne's army.[138] Before our arrival they had plotted to escape and had procured arms and commenced digging a tunnel, which they had nearly completed. They were resolved to kidnap General Washington and the Comte de Rochambeau, who were then in Philadelphia, and try to take them to New York. Since there were 1,500 of them, they would certainly have done a lot of harm before they were caught. Fortunately the plot was discovered by a woman in whom one of the English confided when he was drunk.

The market is very large. The town hall, the large church, the barracks, the residence of the Spanish ambassador, and the large hospital are all worth seeing. The city is on the Delaware, whose banks are charming. Frigates can come up and anchor along the quays. When I was there I saw the *Caroline*, which carries 36 guns. The suburbs of this city used to be charming and had several avenues lined with trees, all of which were cut down by the English when they were here. The commerce here is very considerable, and all the shops are very well stocked. The city conducts a flourishing trade with the Islands. It is thickly populated, and two-thirds of the inhabitants are Germans; hence the countryside is very well cultivated. Most of the houses are insured against fire.

We camped a mile above the city, where a great many people came to see us, and our regiment in particular.[139] Some were seeking a brother, others a

---

Grace. Blanchard (1), p. 114. The Vicomte de Rochambeau (p. 251) mentions that "Mr. Stock [Stokes?]," owner of the land, had already sold lots to a dozen people; Von Closen (p. 288) says that the town was to be called Frenchtown, in view of the fact that many French who wanted to settle and carry on trade there were participating in the scheme.

135. Charlestown is not on the Little Elk River. The army crossed it after passing through Northeast and just before entering Elkton.

136. Mentioning the changes that had taken place since his visit there a year earlier, Von Closen noted in his journal, p. 229 (30 August 1782), that Wilmington was greatly enlarged and embellished: "They have built 50 brick houses, very handsome and spacious, since our passage [in 1781], which makes the main street charming. The dollars that the army spends wherever it marches are beneficial to

the country, for you can perceive at a glance that they are prospering. . . ." For another comment on the economic effects of French hard money, see George Grieve's note, Chastellux (4), II, 572, n. 31.

137. The Black Horse Inn was at the corner of 2nd Street and Black Horse Alley, not far from Market Street and the waterfront.

138. La Luzerne's residence was on the corner of Chestnut and 7th Streets. The Walnut Street prison, which was completed in 1776 and which served until 1784 as a military and political prison, was in the block now known as Washington Square. The Editors have not been able to confirm from other sources Verger's story of the prisoners' plot to kidnap Washington and Rochambeau.

139. See map, Vol. II, No. 137. The 1782 camp was north of the then populated part of the city, on high ground beyond Cohocksink Creek, along the Germantown Road.

cousin; what was cruel for our soldiers was that they dared not venture outside the camp beyond the line of stacked arms, while no American dared come inside.

The whole of Pennsylvania is populated with nothing but Germans. The country around Lancaster, where Cornwallis's army is interned, is extremely well cultivated. There are many of our Moravians living in communities that share their possessions in common.[140] Until they reach the age of puberty, the girls are shut up in a sort of convent where they engage in various occupations and all dress alike.

We halted two days in Philadelphia. The march from Chester to Philadelphia was 16 miles.

3 September Via Frankford to Red Lion Tavern.

4 September Via Bristol to the Delaware, which we crossed near Trenton——18 miles. The artillery forded the river. We camped to the left of Trenton and stayed there three days.[141]

This was the site of the famous engagement that did so much honor to General Washington.[142] We saw the barracks where the Hessians had been quartered. Here is how the event occurred: The English, puffed up with success and knowing their forces to be vastly superior, divided them into two parts, consisting of a detachment of 900 Hessians under the command of M. de Rall, quartered in Trenton, and the rest of the army, commanded by Lord Howe [Brigadier General Leslie], stationed at Princeton.

The American army had been reduced to practically nothing and could muster only a few hundred militia. It was mid-winter, when the river was frozen. General Washington undertook to surprise the Germans by crossing the frozen Delaware River during the night. He had previously sent several patrols across to see what the enemy was doing. Luckily one of these was encountered by a party of Hessians who had been sent on reconnaissance after receiving several warnings of the Americans' approach. As soon as the militiamen spied the Hessian troops, they retired, leaving the latter convinced that they were only a patrol sent to gather intelligence. The Hessians then returned to their barracks, and everyone went to bed. But in the middle of the night Washington suddenly appeared and surrounded the barracks. One battalion alone managed to escape and offer some resistance, but was soon obliged to surrender. M. de Rall, whose battalion it was, was killed in the action.

When Washington learned that an enemy detachment was being sent in support from Princeton, he set out immediately in spite of his greatly inferior force from which he had been obliged to detail a strong guard for his prisoners. The Princeton troops were amazed to find themselves suddenly attacked. Although some resisted, 200 more men were captured, whereupon Washington retired with all speed to the banks of the Delaware.[143] It was bitterly cold, and his troops, without tents or bread, were tired after their forced marches.

We, on the contrary, suffered greatly from the heat in our camp, where there was no shade.

7 September To Princeton, where there is a very beautiful college[144] at which I saw several pieces of

It was not far from the village of Kensington and the road to Frankford and Red Lion Tavern, over which the army would resume its march northward. Von Closen noted in his journal (p. 120), 3 September 1781, that, when the army was proceeding south the previous year, "the soldiers of the Deux-Ponts Regiment found many relatives in Philadelphia, who came to see them in camp. This necessitated our redoubling our efforts to prevent desertion, for there are many of them who would prefer to seek their fortune in this country. . . ." He also mentions (p. 116) that he found at Frankford two former subjects of the Günderrode family (related to his own), natives of Duckroth, who had left Germany in 1763. Von Closen subsequently learned that several deserters from the Royal Deux-Ponts Regiment settled in Frankford.

140. Chastellux ([4], II, 522–525) gives an extended account of the Moravian community at Bethlehem. There were other communities at Nazareth and Lititz in Penn-sylvania and at Hope, New Jersey.

141. The camp was on the same site as the previous year. See maps, Vol. II, Nos. 70 and 138. After Trenton the main army marched northward through New Jersey in two brigades: the first included the Bourbonnais and Royal Deux-Ponts (Verger's regiment); the second, the Saintonge and Soissonnais.

142. See accounts of the affairs at Trenton and Princeton (December 1776–January 1777) in Clermont-Crèvecœur's journal, pp. 44–45; and Vol. II, Itinerary 5.

143. After the Battle of Princeton Washington retired, not to the banks of the Delaware, but north through the Millstone Valley and then via Pluckemin to his mountain fastness in Morristown (3–6 January 1777).

144. Nassau Hall, which General Chastellux, academician and connoisseur of the arts, characterized as "an immense building . . . visible from a considerable distance . . . re-markable only for its size." Chastellux (4), I, 122.

physics apparatus, including a superb pneumatic machine. From behind the college one has a superb view of the surrounding country, which is very rich and well cultivated——12 miles.

Trenton marks the beginning of the Jerseys, which used to belong to the Dutch. Most of the inhabitants speak nothing but Dutch to one another. In my opinion New Jersey is one of the most fertile and best cultivated provinces to be seen.

8 September Via the west bank of the Millstone River to Somerset [Somerset Courthouse, present Millstone], where the grenadiers and chasseurs were detached to march ahead and take up advantageous positions on the flanks of the army——14 miles.

9 September To Bullion's Tavern [Liberty Corner] ——14 miles.

10 September Via Morristown to Whippany, where we occupied an excellent position——16 miles. We were only 16 miles from Staten Island, where the nearest enemy posts are located.[145] While I was on guard duty at headquarters, I talked with an Indian who was carrying a letter from Fort Pitt to the President of Congress. He had his ears slit, like all the men of his tribe. I was invited to a party at the house of a Danish gentleman who had lived in this country for the past thirty years. His name is Biberhausen [von Beverhoudt].[146] He entertained us very well. He has a very fine estate. One of his woods was on fire, but that dis-

turbed him very little. It is the custom of the country to let forest fires burn without doing anything to halt their progress.

We lost our way going out there. With no little surprise we found ourselves near Chatham,[147] heading straight towards the enemy, when we were set back on the right road. We remained two days at Whippany.

12 September To Pompton, where we climbed a very high hill from which we could see the Hudson River——16 miles.

13 September To Suffern [in New York].

14 September To Colonel [Joshua Hett] Smith's house [at Haverstraw], 3 leagues from the Hudson. It was here [in 1780] that the conspiracy was hatched by the traitor Arnold, who wished to deliver to the English the important post of West Point. Here is how it was discovered: Major André, General Clinton's principal aide-de-camp, landed near West Point and was arrested by a militiaman who told him he would take him to his commanding officer. André begged him not to do this and offered him a bribe of 100 *louis* and his watch if he would let him go, whereupon the American, seeing the man's desire to escape, became suspicious and absolutely refused to take any money. He threatened to take him straight to General Arnold. Hearing this, André was delighted. Just then the Marquis de La Fayette passed by.[148] He noticed

145. Mathieu Dumas, serving at this time as one of Rochambeau's assistant quartermasters-general, recalls in his *Souvenirs*, I, 102: "The General, having been informed that an English fleet had been reported at the mouth of the Hudson, ordered me to go and reconnoiter it from as near as I could get without risking myself among the enemy pickets posted along the west bank of the Hudson on this side of Staten Island. A very intelligent American officer served as my guide. Taking along with us three well-mounted dragoons who knew the country perfectly, he conducted me to the very point of the Hook [Sandy Hook], where there is a sand bar that warships can cross only by unloading a part of their guns. We stopped at the highest dune, from the top of which, as we lay in the sand and out of sight, we counted, at our leisure, the 26 vessels of Admiral Pigot, at anchor outside the bar, and we observed their maneuvers as they crossed it and went up the river. Our return was no less lucky, and I owe it to my brother officer that I was able to accomplish this delicate mission to the satisfaction of General Rochambeau." See Rochambeau's letter to Washington, written from

Princeton, 7 September 1782 (Library of Congress, Washington Papers), in which he mentions: "It is however certain that M. Dumas, Deputy Quartermaster-General, has seen yesterday a great part of the fleet under sail before the Hook."

146. Concerning Lucas von Beverhoudt (who had come to New Jersey in 1778 from the Danish West Indian island of St. Thomas) and his house called "Beverwyck," see Clermont-Crèvecœur's journal, n. 63; Vol. II, Itinerary 3, n. 36, and map, No. 51.

147. "We re-discovered the ovens that M. de Villemanzy had ordered to be constructed at Chatham last year to supply the army. They are in very good condition and are being used to provision the army until it reaches the North River. (You will recall that these ovens had a rather good effect upon M. Clinton, since they fortified him in the fear that we were going to attack New York!)" Von Closen, pp. 236–237.

148. Verger's account of Lafayette's fortuitous appearance would seem to indicate that the magic of the Lafayette legend was already at work. Actually Lafayette had no

the stranger being scolded by the sentry and asked what was going on. When the soldier explained the situation, La Fayette ordered him to search the man in his presence and took possession of his papers. Imagine his astonishment at discovering that it was Arnold himself who was arranging for Clinton to send troops to make a feint attack on the forts at West Point under his command, which he was prepared to surrender immediately!

The Marquis de La Fayette went at once to warn General Washington, who also had difficulty believing his own eyes. He sent a guard to arrest Arnold, but the latter, being on *his* guard, had been warned that he had been found out. He went to his room, threw his papers into the fire, told his wife that his plot had been discovered, then mounted a horse that was kept in readiness for such an emergency and rode straight to the Hudson, where a boat kept there at his disposal took him to New York.

We have marched a total of 439 miles to the Hudson River.

17 September We crossed the Hudson at King's Ferry. En route to the crossing we marched under the fort at Stony Point that was captured by M. de Fleury.[149] On the opposite bank stands Fort La Fayette on which rests the right flank of the American army. On its left was a wood, and far in advance was a corps of 500 men commanded by Lord Stirling.[150] Between this corps and the army was a large marsh. The whole color-line of the American camp was bordered by a very beautiful arbor, decorated with various designs and coats of arms (which were very well executed) representing the different regiments.[151] The American soldiers do not stack their arms in piles like ours but simply lean them against three posts set up in the form of a scaffold before their tents, which they erect on one line.

From there we marched 4 miles to our camp at

share in André's apprehension, though he was indeed with General Washington at the Robinson House, Arnold's headquarters on the east bank of the Hudson opposite West Point, when the papers discovered on the person of "John Anderson" were delivered there by a courier from Colonel John Jameson of the Second Continental Dragoons. Jameson was in command of a detachment at North Castle. Lafayette was also one of the board of general officers who tried André and condemned him as a spy to death by the gibbet. For a detailed account of Lafayette's connection with the Arnold-André affair, see Louis Gottschalk, *Lafayette and the Close of the American Revolution* (Chicago, 1942), Chap. vi, "Benedict Arnold's Treason," pp. 121–142. See also Berthier's journal, n. 35.

149. The Vicomte de Fleury, then lieutenant colonel in the American service, was awarded a silver medal by Congress for his courage and boldness at the taking of Stony Point, 15 July 1779. This medal by Benjamin Duvivier, like those by Nicolas Gatteaux awarded at the same time to Brigadier General Anthony Wayne and to Major John Stewart, was designed and executed in France. The inscription on the medal—the only one awarded by Congress to a foreign officer—specified that Fleury was the first to mount the walls: *primus super muros*. J. F. Loubat, *The Medallic History of the United States of America* (New York, 1878), i, 22–27, and ii, Plate IV. See also Lasseray, ii, Plate VII, facing p. 430, where it is said that the medal was attached with a ribbon made from the enemy flag.

150. "Lord Stirling" was Major General William Alex-

ander of the Continental Army. According to Chastellux ([4], i, 106), "the title of 'Lord,' which was refused him in England, is not here contested: he claims to have inherited this title and went to Europe to support his pretensions, but lost his case." Lord Stirling had an extensive estate in Basking Ridge, New Jersey, near the French army's route; see Vol. ii, Itinerary 4, and map, No. 52.

151. "The American camp here presented the most beautiful and picturesque appearance: it extended along the plain, on the neck of land formed by the winding of the Hudson, and had a view of this river to the south; behind it, the lofty mountains, covered with wood, formed the most sublime background, that painting can express. In the front of the tents was a regular continued portico, formed by the boughs of trees in verdure, decorated with much taste and fancy; and each officer's tent was distinguished by superior ornaments. Opposite the camp, and on distinct eminences, stood the tents of some of the general officers, over which towered, predominant, that of General Washington. I had seen all the camps in England, from many of which, drawings and engravings have been taken; but this was truly a subject worthy of the pencil of the first artist. The French camp during their stay at Baltimore was decorated in the same style. At the camp at Verplank's, we distinctly heard the morning and evening gun of the British at Kingsbridge." George Grieve, translator of Chastellux's *Travels*, in Chastellux (4), i, 281. At least one artist *did* find this subject "worthy of his pencil." See Trumbull's painting, reproduced in Vol. ii, No. 144.

Peekskill.[152] This was on top of an arid mountain surrounded by wilderness.

20 September Our whole army turned out under arms and passed in review before General Washington.

22 September The whole American army paraded before M. de Rochambeau. At nine in the morning M. de Rochambeau, followed on horseback by most of his officers, rode down the line with M. de Washington to the beating of drums and dipping of colors in salute. The light infantry was dressed in brown coats with green revers and cuffs and white linen pantaloons tucked into black gaiters reaching to the calf; the rest of the infantry, in royal blue coats with white revers and cuffs. The soldiers' hair was powdered, their carriage was good, and they stood absolutely still. After riding down their line, we went to their parade ground to watch them march. At a shot from a cannon they formed in column, led by 50 dragoons of the American general's guard. This little troop was very well mounted. Then the infantry marched past. The regiment from the province of New York had a good band, as did another from Massachusetts.

After the parade they closed ranks in mass formation, and some of the troops deployed on the high ground while the rest formed in line of battle on the plain below. Then they executed a deployment on the river bank to repel an imaginary landing. The light infantry had to form its battle line in the marsh, where the men stood in water up to their waists. All these maneuvers were very well executed in absolute silence. The Americans drill in the Prussian style. They are indebted to General Steuben for the progress they have made.[153]

Since we were never sure how many troops they had, we amused ourselves by counting the ranks and files of each platoon, from which we estimated that 5,500 men had marched past. Counting those guarding West Point, etc., this would bring the total to 7,500 uniformed men.[154]

General Washington was on the point of taking a

152. See maps, Vol. II, Nos. 143 and 146.

153. In noting the Americans' debt to General Steuben, Verger might have added that Steuben was in turn indebted to several Frenchmen serving with him in the Continental Army. The preparation for publication of the *Regulations for the Order and Discipline of the Troops of the United States* (first printing, Philadelphia, 1779) was a truly international endeavor. When requesting from Congress "some recompense" for "the officers who assisted me in Composing the Regulations for the Troops," Steuben listed them in this order: Colonel Fleury, 1,000 dollars; Captain Walker, 600 dollars; Captain L'Enfant, 500 dollars; Captain Duponceau, 400 dollars (Steuben to the Board of War, 30 March 1779, in the National Archives). Congress accepted Steuben's recommendations, which presumably reflect his assessment of the relative contribution of each individual. Fleury had worked with Steuben in preparing the original manuscript copies of the regulations, which were circulated throughout the army even before they were available in printed form, and as one of the subinspectors he had been responsible for their distribution among the Maryland and Delaware troops. L'Enfant drew the diagrammatic plans necessary to illustrate the various maneuvers described in the text of the drill manual. (See illustration.) Duponceau, serving as Steuben's military secretary, translated Fleury's polished French into not very good English, while Captain (Benjamin) Walker, the other member of the quartet, in turn reduced Duponceau's translation into idiomatic English. Still another Frenchman, the Chevalier de Ternant, played a part in superintending the implementation of the "Regulations."

Writing to Henry Laurens, then President of the Continental Congress, 30 April 1778, Washington noted: "The Inspectors are Lt. Colonels [Francis] Barber of Jersey, [John] Brooks of Massachusetts, Davis [William Davies] of Virginia, and Mr. Ternant a french gentleman; the reason for employing him apart his intrinsic merit and abilities, was his possessing the french and english languages equally, which made him a necessary assistant to the Baron de Steuben." *Writings of GW*, XI, 328–331. (The Editors are indebted to William D. Wright for the above information.)

154. Recalling this review at Verplanck's Point, Rochambeau ([2], I, 309) wrote: "General Washington, wishing to express his respect for France and his gratitude for her benefits, had us pass between two lines of his troops, who were clothed, equipped, and armed for the first time since the beginning of the Revolution, with cloth and arms that had come partly from France and partly from the English stores captured from Cornwallis's army, which the French army had generously turned over to the American army. General Washington had his drummers beat the French march throughout this review, and the two armies met here again with the most evident marks of mutual satisfaction." The Prince de Broglie, who had just arrived from France and was seeing the Americans for the first time, wrote in his journal ([1], p. 52): "I found the American Army camped in a place called Verplanck's Point; it consisted of about six thousand men, who for the first time since the beginning of the war were decently uniformed, well armed, properly equipped and camped in tents of regular form. I passed along the camp with pleas-

house when he decided to set an example to his soldiers by living in camp. He is so much adored that even the foreigners who see this extraordinary man cannot resist according him their admiration and respect. He offered us some refreshments in his tent. When he receives any wine, a rare commodity in these parts, he announces the fact in his orders, and all those who wish to are invited to drink it as long as it lasts.[155] When his supply is exhausted, he drinks rum and water, which is called "grog." Without wishing to appear in the least critical of his generosity, I should add that all of us went to the greatest amount of trouble to feed our horses, since forage was exceedingly scarce.

It was here that we received the Comte de Fersen as second colonel of our regiment.[156]

24 September We arrived at Crompond, where we stayed for a month.[157] This place is a wilderness where we had no recreation save fishing, since hunting was forbidden because of the Refugee [Loyalist] bands in the neighborhood. We captured three who were plotting to kidnap some officers of our army.

October 1782

As the weather grew perceptibly colder our regiment built barracks for itself, and a very amusing thing

happened. Since we had been cutting wood and had burned several fences, the inhabitants of Crompond came to the General to complain of the injury his troops had done them by building barracks in their fields and asked an exorbitant sum in damages. He replied that it was only just to pay for whatever had been destroyed, and consequently a commissary of war was appointed on our side, and an American on theirs, to assess the damage. They agreed on a rather moderate sum.

The evening before our departure M. de Rochambeau was in his room when an American asked to speak with him and was admitted. It was the sheriff, or mayor, who began by saying that he was very much embarrassed by his mission but that he had come to arrest him, whereupon he clapped his hand on M. de Rochambeau's shoulder. The General was taken aback by this compliment and demanded an explanation, to which the man replied that, since the General had not seen fit to pay all the damages, according to the law of the land he would be held prisoner until the sum was paid. More surprised than angered by the sheriff's insolence, the General advised him to make himself scarce very quickly if he did not wish to become a prisoner himself, which advice the latter deemed it expedient to follow.

M. de Rochambeau wrote of the incident to General Washington, who sent a party of dragoons to

ure, astonishment, and admiration . . . so strong was the contrast with the incorrect notions I had formed that I had to keep reminding myself that I beheld in this army the same which formerly had no other uniform than a cap, on which was written *Liberty*."

155. George Grieve, suffering from the ague when he called upon Washington here, noted: "The General . . . told me he was sure I had not met with a good glass of wine for some time, an article then very rare, but that my disorder must be frightened away; he made me drink three or four of his silver cups of excellent Madeira at noon, and recommended to me to take a generous glass of claret after dinner, a prescription by no means repugnant to my feelings, and which I most religiously followed. I mounted my horse next morning, and continued my journey to Massachusetts, without ever experiencing the slightest return of my disorder." Chastellux (4), I, 280–281.

156. Axel Fersen, who had up to this time served as aide-de-camp to General Rochambeau, confessed in a letter written to his father (in Sweden) from the camp at Crompond, 3 October 1782, that he was delighted to be an aide-

de-camp no more and to have entered upon his new duties as second colonel of the Deux-Ponts Regiment: "The regiment has a fine appearance, is well disciplined, and has excellent officers. Most of them know you and all speak of you to me; the lieutenant colonel, Baron d'Esebeck, who once served in your regiment as ensign . . . , requests me to remember him to you. He had hoped for the position I now occupy and even expected to obtain it—which means that he looks askance at me, but he is a good officer and a gentleman and I hope, through my conduct, to conciliate him. If you please, my dear father, when you write to me, be so kind as to mention him, which will please him very much. The Comte de Deux-Ponts, my commanding colonel, treats me with friendship and trust, and seems delighted to have me. I shall do all I can to deserve the continuing confidence and esteem of the regiment." Fersen (2), pp. 156–161. Von Closen (p. 242) also notes Esebeck's disappointment, adding the remark: "N.B. The Comte de Fersen was too well liked at Court!!!"

157. See maps, Vol. II, Nos. 145 and 146.

apprehend the man and take him to prison in Philadelphia; however, M. de Rochambeau requested that he be pardoned.[158]

We were joined at Crompond by the Baron de Vioménil and several aides-de-camp who had come from France on the *Aigle*, commanded by M. Destouches [de La Touche], which had been captured in the Delaware after the passengers and money had been unloaded.[159]

22 October We broke camp and marched to Salem Courthouse——10 miles.[160]

23 October To Danbury [in Connecticut], where we saw several tumbledown shacks, formerly well-furnished magazines, which had been burned by the British [in 1777]——12 miles.

24 October To Newtown, where we stayed two days——10 miles. The grenadiers and chasseurs were detached to camp on a hill from which there was a charming view of the surrounding country. Here we repaired the army wagons, which were by then in very bad condition.

26 October We left very early in the morning and had scarcely begun our march when it began to rain in torrents. This was the worst thing that could have happened to us, for during our whole journey we had never found so bad a road. Our destination's name, "Break Neck," describes its miserable location. When we reached our camp, we had to do without our tents for a whole day and bivouac in the middle of a ploughed field without a single house in sight. The continual rain, added to the cold, caused us inexpressible suffering. To cap the climax, we had to go so

158. The story of "The General and the Sheriff" circulated widely at the time and was subsequently preserved for posterity by Rochambeau in his *Mémoires* (1809), I, 312–313. With Rochambeau's memories to jog his own, the Comte de Ségur, when compiling *his* memoirs of the American campaign, was reminded of the incident, which he cited both as an example of Rochambeau's tact in dealing with the Americans and of the Americans' respect for the inviolable power of the law; Ségur also recalled that the Crompond affair had been cited with telling effect during the debates in the National Assembly at the beginning of the French Revolution. Ségur, *Mémoires* (1824), I, 445–446. In addition to Verger's journal, several other near-contemporary accounts of the episode have survived: Blanchard (1), p. 117; Vicomte de Rochambeau, pp. 259–260; Coriolis, letter to his mother from Providence, 30 November 1782, in Coriolis (1), pp. 817–818; Von Closen, pp. 257–259. From these various accounts it appears that the disgruntled claimant was an American militia captain, Samuel Delevan, the owner of the house (on present Hallock's Mill Road in Yorktown) in which Rochambeau had his headquarters and on whose land the Soissonnais Brigade camped. Delevan's name is mentioned by Blanchard ([1], 117), who also notes that at Salem, the next camp after Crompond, he was lodged in the house of the sheriff (not mentioned by name), "a lively little old man," who treated Blanchard very well, offered him tea, and who had a "pretty and very friendly daughter." Von Closen, Rochambeau's aide, who served as interpreter between the General and the Sheriff, found it ironic that the claim for firewood and damaged fences should come from the same man whose millrace had been greatly improved by the labor of the French soldiers. The sums involved in the claim as cited in the different journals vary considerably, but there was evidently a substantial reduction. The compromise settlement of Delevan's claim by Villemanzy and the American arbiters seems to have closed the incident. For further identification of Delevan and the localities involved, see Cortlandt Pell Auser, "Le Comte [de Rochambeau] at Crompond: October, 1782," *The Westchester Historian*, Westchester County Historical Society, XXXVI, No. 2 (April-June, 1960), 39–40, and No. 3 (July-Sept., 1960), 64–67. In the 1950's the Yorktown Grange named its fairgrounds "Rochambeau Park."

159. Concerning the *Aigle* and *Gloire*, see Clermont-Crèvecœur's journal, pp. 79–80 and n. 164.

160. The successive camps from here to Boston, noted by Verger, are shown in maps, Vol. II, Nos. 147ff. Upon leaving the Crompond encampment the Bourbonnais and Deux-Ponts regiments marched together as the "Bourbonnais Brigade," followed at a day's interval by the Soissonnais and Saintonge regiments as the "Soissonnais Brigade." Verger's dates are thus those of the First Division's marches.

It may be noted here that the Lauzun Legion did not make this march across Connecticut as it had done the previous year. The Legion, of which Lauzun himself had resumed active command, remained at Crompond and then proceeded south to Wilmington, Delaware, where it would be near the detachments left at Baltimore. It returned from the United States directly to France in the spring of 1783. See Rochambeau's "Instructions pour M. le duc de Lauzun," 21 October 1782, summarized in Gontaut-Biron, *Le Duc de Lauzun* (Paris, 1937), p. 165. Lauzun thus became the ranking French officer in the United States and was under Washington's direct orders. See also Lauzun (2), pp. 312–316; Von Closen, pp. 259, 270.

far to find wood that we could not make our soup. We passed the whole night in this fashion.[161]——18 miles.

27 October To Barnes's Tavern [in Marion, town of Southington]——14 miles.

28 October To Farmington, a pretty town with charming surroundings. A large number of visitors came to see us, and we danced in front of the camp. The ground around our tents stank of skunk. This beast is larger than a squirrel; the upper part of its body is white and the rest black, with a white tail that it holds erect like a squirrel. It has no other defense than its urine, which it squirts from a distance at anyone who wishes to attack it. Its horrible stink obliges one to undress immediately, and despite all one's efforts to remove the spot, it never loses its very unpleasant odor. One of our officers had such a spot on his coat and had to throw it away. It is said that, when one of these animals is kept for some time in a house, its urine loses its stench entirely.

29 October We camped across the Connecticut River 2 miles beyond Hartford. Hartford is a fairly large town and the capital of the province. It has a rather handsome town hall, and the surrounding country is very pretty. The other side of the city beyond the river is called East Hartford and is not as large. The river is navigable only by small boats.

At this time there was much talk of our departure from America, but many denied it.

The inhabitants of Connecticut are the best people in the United States, without any doubt. They have a lively curiosity and examined our troops and all our actions with evident astonishment. When they visited our camp, the girls came without their mothers and entered our tents with the greatest confidence.

I cannot refrain from reporting a very extraordinary custom of this charming province, which is known as "bundling." A stranger or a resident who frequents a house and takes a fancy to a daughter of the house may declare his love in the presence of her father and mother without their taking it amiss; if she looks with favor upon his declaration and permits him to continue his suit, he is at perfect liberty to accompany her wherever he wants without fear of reproach from her parents. Then, if he is on good terms with the lady, he can propose bundling with her. This means going to bed with her. The man may remove his coat and shoes, but nothing more, and the girl takes off nothing but her kerchief. Then they lie down together on the same bed, even in the presence of the mother—and the most strict mother. If they are alone in the room and indiscreet ardor leads the man to rashness or violent acts towards his Dulcinea, woe to him if the least cry escapes her, for then everybody in the house enters the room and beats the lover for his too great impetuosity. Regardless of appearances, it is rare that a girl takes advantage of this great freedom, which confirms the good faith of these amiable citizens.

❧ *November 1782* ❧

4 November We marched to Bolton——14 miles.

5 November To Windham, a small market town where we made a halt——14 miles.

7 November To Canterbury——10 miles.

8 November To Voluntown [Sterling Hill, Connecticut]——10 miles.

9 November To Waterman's Tavern [in Coventry, Rhode Island]——10 miles.

10 November To Providence. We remained two days in camp near the city, and on the third we left town to move into barracks in a wood.[162] A heavy snowfall made us appreciate the barracks, especially since most of our tents were worn out. At Providence one company from each regiment, commanded by M. d'Espeyron, major of the Soissonnais Regiment, em-

161. "Never have the troops suffered as much during the three campaigns as they did that day." Von Closen, p. 262. Break Neck Hill is in the town of Middlebury, Connecticut.

162. Upon reaching Providence the army first camped on the western outskirts of the town on the site previously occupied in June 1781 at the beginning of the march to the Hudson. See map, Vol. II, No. 27, where the 1782 camp is indicated by dotted lines. The "barracks in a wood" to which the army next moved, in what was then North Providence, is shown on map, No. 156.

barked on the *Fantasque*.[163] We disposed of our horses at a very low price. I sold mine, which had cost me 16 *louis*, for 25 piasters.

The Comte de Rochambeau left Providence for Baltimore to embark in the *Emeraude*, leaving the Baron de Vioménil in command of his army.[164]

December 1782

4 December To Wrentham——18 miles.

5 December Via Walpole to Dedham.

6 December Via Roxbury to Boston. This is a large and beautiful city, very populous and very commercial, and in my opinion the most agreeable in the united provinces. It has several notable buildings, including the Old [North] Church, Hancock's mansion, the Exchange, and the State House. The city is regularly laid out, and its streets are actually peninsulas. The main street is very long, and the houses very well built. Here began the disturbances that have had such dire consequences for England. It was near the State House that the massacre of 8 Bostonians took place, which seemed to give the signal for the revolt. Four miles from Boston is Bunker's Hill and the battlefield on which this famous combat took place between a very small number of citizens assembled there and the seasoned troops of Great Britain, backed up by cannon.

Boston harbor is rather treacherous, though vessels that come to anchor under the large fort find a good anchorage there.

The day we arrived the wind was too strong to launch the boats, so we spent the night in warehouses along the wharves.

7 December At eleven in the morning we embarked in the boats to go on board the *Brave*, a ship of 74 guns commanded by the Comte d'Amblimont, together with the companies of grenadiers and chasseurs, Fürstenwärther's company, and 120 men of Rühle's company; the rest of the [Deux-Ponts] regiment boarded the *Isle de France*.[165]

24 December We remained for some time in Boston. On 24 December the signal was made to get under way, but then the wind died down and we were obliged to wait until the next day, which was 25 December, a time of year when storms are very frequent. The first day was a happy one. We sailed up the coast to Saint George's Banks, where we cruised about waiting for the warships *Auguste* and *Pluton*, which were coming from Portsmouth.[166] On the third day the wind became very strong, especially on the Banks where the swell was very heavy and the sea unusually rough. We ran into frightful squalls and gales there, and during the night of the 28th our convoy was so scattered that by the next morning we were reduced to only 10 warships without frigates. We remained eight days in these latitudes in a very rough sea.

31 December The *Bourgogne* lost her foremast, and several others began to ship water. The heavy swell caused quite a large leak in our tiller-box. The carpenters could not get inside to make repairs for fear the bar would crush the helmsmen. That day we lost our main topgallantmast, and one of the men broke his hip when he fell on a yard during a false maneuver by the watch officer.

January 1783

1 January 1783 A fire broke out in the galley. Fortunately it happened during the day, when someone was there to put it out. Almost all the other ships suffered a great deal during the bad weather. Consequently M. de Vaudreuil, as one ship after another

163. Necessary repairs, as well as enemy ships cruising off Narragansett Bay, delayed the departure of the *Fantasque* (commanded by M. de Vaudoré) until 6 February 1783. She did not, therefore, join Vaudreuil's fleet for the voyage to Puerto Cabello but followed her own course (via The French Cape) back to Brest. The military hospital was also embarked on this ship. See account of "l'affaire du *Fantasque*" in Gontaut-Biron, *Le Duc de Lauzun* (Paris, 1937), p. 169, based on documents in the Archives de la Guerre, Correspondance générale, carton XLIX-a;

also Bouvet, *Service de santé*, p. 104.

164. See Clermont-Crèvecœur's journal, nn. 177 and 178.

165. See Clermont-Crèvecœur's journal, n. 176, and Berthier's journal, p. 257, for a list of vessels comprising Vaudreuil's fleet. Berthier was on the *Souverain*.

166. See Clermont-Crèvecœur's journal, p. 85. Clermont-Crèvecœur was on the frigate *Amazone*, which sailed from Portsmouth, New Hampshire, with the *Auguste* and *Pluton*, only on 29 December.

signaled that she was damaged, decided to wait no longer for the convoy to catch up, nor for the two missing warships,[167] and changed course to the southerly, which eased our minds considerably. We were very tired of the cold and the rough sea. We had been obliged to rig lifelines on deck to keep a footing. We spent most of the time hove to, and several men fell overboard.

Off New York the wind calmed down. But when we had Bermuda abeam, we struck a flat calm that proved more dangerous than the heavy weather, for since we had not a breath of wind in our sails, the heavy swell caused us to roll even more than we had off Boston. This was the aftermath of a storm some distance away in which the *Auguste*, *Pluton*, and *Amazone* had been caught and become separated.[168]

12 January We crossed the Tropic of Cancer and were baptized according to the custom of initiating all those who cross it for the first time. Several ridiculous ceremonies are performed, after which each victim gives a piece of money to the crew and receives a ducking in a tub of water.[169]

14–15 January During the night we chased and caught a small vessel, which turned out to be Danish. She was coming from The French Cape and reported that Admiral Hood was cruising off it with 16 men-of-war.

15 January We sighted the island of St. Thomas, and this same day the *Couronne* captured an English brig of 12 guns.

16 January The *Couronne* chased and caught up with the French frigate *Aigrette* coming from France with interesting dispatches for M. de Vaudreuil. That day we sighted the island of Puerto Rico. We learned that in the harbor of San Juan, which we sighted a cannon-shot away, there were 80 transports that had been escorted by the frigates *Aigrette* and *Cérès*, and a Spanish warship of 70 guns. This port has a superb fort[170] with, among other works, two batteries commanding the harbor entrance, as well as a covered way leading to further works. The city is quite large. It belongs to Spain. Towards evening we spied a cutter being hotly pursued by an English frigate, which we chased in turn.

17 January We lost the frigate during the night but sighted an English privateer of 18 guns on the 17th, which we chased in company with the *Hercule*. Although we gained measurably on her during the day, she was far to windward of us, obliging us to tack up to her. By two o'clock the *Hercule* had approached sufficiently to fire 12 guns of her 36-gun battery, but the balls did not carry far enough. The second time she tacked about we fired 7 shots at her from our battery of 36, which also fell short. Despite this, we continued the chase, holding up as high on the wind as possible. During the night we gained considerably on her, so that by two in the morning of the 18th we found ourselves to windward and almost within range; by some misunderstanding, however, the order was given to clear the decks for action, so that the ship, which had been sailing very well while everyone was asleep, suddenly lost her headway when everyone came on deck. After that the enemy gained on us steadily and ended up 5 leagues ahead.

18 January At noon, seeing that we could not catch her, we tacked ship to join the fleet off Puerto Rico. We spoke an Ostend ship coming from the coast of Guinea with 300 negroes aboard. We chased her under an English flag. When we hailed her in English, she replied in French, saying that she knew very well from the shape of our ensign that we were not English.[171] On the 18th we sighted two vessels en route to Puerto Rico. We made recognition signals to which they replied. It was the frigate *Néréide* escorting the *Isle de France*, from which we had become separated during the storm off Boston. We joined them on the sail

167. As noted by Verger hereafter (p. 172), 10 February, the "missing warships," *Auguste* and *Pluton*, were "found" only at Puerto Cabello, which they reached independently. The journal of the Comte de Vaudreuil (brother of the Marquis), commanding the *Auguste*, records their course and adventures. *Neptunia*, No. 50 (1958), pp. 32–35.

168. The storm is described by Clermont-Crèvecœur, who was on the *Amazone*. See his journal, p. 86.

169. Berthier's journal (pp. 226–227) includes the detailed description of a similar ceremony in which he participated when coming to America in 1780.

170. El Morro, construction of which was begun by the Spaniards in the sixteenth century.

171. "This Captain, a native of Bordeaux, saluted our flag with three *Vive le Roi!* to which our fleet replied with a '*Vas te faire f...!*' and he, '*A la bonne heure!!*'" Von Closen, p. 287.

to San Juan, which we sighted next morning. We came up into the wind very close to shore so as to inspect the fortifications at leisure. We cruised off Puerto Rico for five days in a beautiful sea.

22 January That evening we sailed off with several merchant ships under charter to the King. Since we were afraid of meeting the English, we skirted the coast of Puerto Rico, which is very beautiful, then rounded up into the Santo Domingo channel, where we had to sail very slowly so that the convoy could keep up.

24 January We were joined by the *Amazone*,[172] which had become separated from the *Auguste* and the *Pluton* in a storm off Bermuda.

28 January We sighted to the westward the island of Curaçao, which belongs to the Dutch.[173] We all thought this was to be our destination; however, we passed it to leeward.

29 January We sighted the mainland. That day we saw Curaçao at very close range, since we were obliged to keep tacking to make headway to windward. We kept trying to clear the channel between Curaçao and the mainland, but because of the very strong current, we lost during the night whatever distance we had gained during the day.

February 1783

6 February 1783 On the 6th, for instance, we were far to windward of the tip of the island [of Curaçao] when the current set us down 3 leagues to leeward of the harbor, so that we had to start all over again. However, since some of the ships had run out of water, the Admiral granted permission to the *Hercule*, *Neptune*, *Couronne*, and all the ships of the convoy to enter the port, where they found a Dutch warship of 64 guns, one of 50, and 6 frigates.

8 February We encountered a French lugger coming from Puerto Cabello, which gave us the news that the *Bourgogne* had been totally wrecked on a reef.[174] Today, believing he had reached Puerto Cabello, the

Admiral made signals to prepare to anchor. When the soundings showed 8 fathoms, he realized that our pilot was in error, and we resumed our course.

10 February On Monday at seven in the evening we anchored at Puerto Cabello, which is situated at 10° north latitude and 72° west longitude. We found there the *Auguste* and *Pluton*, which had arrived independently after capturing a brig from Antigua. Puerto Cabello, or Cavello, is on the mainland in the province of Caracas. It is quite small, and the houses poorly built. It carries on a large trade in cacao sent down from Caracas. Its garrison consists of about 1,200 men, half of them regulars who are very well turned out. Its fortifications are all built of brick and are quite large, as is its citadel, which is fully capable of defending the entrance to the secure and commodious harbor.[175] The beach, along which the town is built, is extremely hot because of the high mountains behind it.

The principal products of the country are tobacco and cacao. It also has gold mines and pearl fisheries. Its fruits include pineapples, bananas, figs, sapodilla plums, corozos, apricots, avocado pears, guavas, coconuts, oranges, lemons, and bergamots. Its trees include the palm, coconut, banana, sandbox tree, aloe, and cedar. A coconut contains about half a glass of milk. The meat has a nutty taste, the shell is used as a drinking cup, and the wood is excellent. The fibres are used to make rope and the leaves to make matting.

The game here consists of lions smaller than the African lions and very fierce tigers. Two of our soldiers were devoured by these animals. There are also monkeys, called *makakes*, wild boars, bears, sloths, and lizards. The most common birds are ortolans, parakeets, parrots, hummingbirds, and various others whose plumage is surprisingly brilliant. The rivers are dangerous to bathe in on account of the crocodiles.

This country groans under the weight of monopoly and priestcraft. The vested interests of the Caracas Company, whose principal depot is at La Guaira, deprive the people of all means of enriching themselves from their own industry. The priests exercise an un-

---

172. See journal of Clermont-Crèvecœur (who was on the *Amazone*) for this same date, p. 87.

173. Clermont-Crèvecœur's journal (pp. 90–91) includes a description of Curaçao. See maps, Vol. II, Nos. 167 and 168.

174. See Verger's journal, below, p. 173, and Clermont-Crèvecœur's journal, n. 186.

175. See map of Puerto Cabello, Vol. II, No. 169.

limited authority in the spiritual realm and are both feared and venerated by these poor people, who always salute them with respect, whereas the monks hardly deign to notice them. Even the magistrates cannot deal severely with a priest by reason of his calling, fearing excommunication and the odious tribunal of the Inquisition. There is one at Cartagena whose autos-da-fé reek often of the blood of poor Indians. Several have perished in its flames on some religious pretext, though avarice more often plays the major role.

A monk who visits a woman during her husband's absence customarily leaves his sandals at the door. When the husband comes home, he dare not enter his own bedroom if he sees that the monk is there, on pain of ending up in the prisons of the Inquisition where the least penalty is the loss of one's property. In short, nothing that one reads in the accounts of various travelers concerning this tribunal and the horrors it commits is exaggerated, because the pen simply cannot find words to express sufficient disgust for this odious institution. The peoples' trust in the saints borders on idolatry. All the inhabitants wear rosaries around their necks.

The men are polite but proud. They smoke tobacco all day long, preferring to eat only a little salt fish and some fruit rather than work at the cultivation of their land. The women go out of their houses very rarely and always dress in black. All the houses inhabited by whites have grilles at the windows, and one cannot address a woman in public without being indiscreet. The least mark of familiarity is regarded here as a crime.

Everyone is very much afraid of the Inquisition. I happened to mention to some Spaniards that they must long to have it abolished, but they replied that it would be the greatest misfortune were they to be granted freedom of conscience, and they stood up for the tribunal with fervor. However, one of them told me in private that he begged us not to mention this subject in public because they had to praise it and that, if they had the misfortune to let drop a few words to the contrary and it was reported to the priest, they would run a very great risk. He confessed to us privately that he detested the Inquisition because he knew all its abuses.

176. See Clermont-Crèvecœur's journal, n. 186.

We learned in Puerto Cabello of the loss of the 74-gun warship *Bourgogne*, commanded by M. de Champmartin. Almost 300 men were drowned, including 5 officers of the Bourbonnais Regiment, the chaplain of the ship, and a naval officer. During all the confusion many atrocities were committed, including frightful murders. The officers, instead of setting the example, were the first to save themselves, abandoning the soldiers to their fate. Fortunately the frigate *Néréide* arrived in time to save the rest of the crew. Several came overland to Puerto Cabello, having suffered so acutely from thirst that they ended by killing sheep in order to drink their blood. The ship was wrecked towards one in the morning. During the evening she had been sailing 30 leagues offshore, but the currents carried her off course and threw her onto a point of land where she suddenly filled with water.[176]

March 1783

A *polacca* arrived in port from the Canary Islands loaded with wines that were purchased for the squadron, but since they could not be unloaded in the harbor without paying 15,000 francs in duty, the Comte de Vaudreuil ordered the Comte d'Amblimont [commander of Verger's ship, the *Brave*] to prepare to depart for the Dutch island of Bonaire and unload the boat there. Consequently we set sail on 10 March at four o'clock. We should have arrived the next evening, but we were obliged to wait for the *polacca*. We tacked up and down during the night and the next morning at nine o'clock entered the harbor. It must be admitted that this so-called harbor-bay has only a very small spot where one can anchor. This is quite close to shore and has very poor holding-ground. One is obliged to moor his vessel ashore. Moreover, there is no other anchorage even though the harbor is very spacious, since everywhere—even 10 feet from shore—there are 50 fathoms or more of water.

We sailed along the coast very close inshore, but since the anchorage was to windward, we were obliged to tack in very near land to approach it. We did not reach it until the third tack; then, as soon as we had taken in our sails, a mooring was sent ashore for us to lie to; but just as we were about to anchor, the warp parted and we began to drift. We had to make sail and tack in again. At the second try we reached the anchorage and sent ashore a much stronger warp, which was moored to a tower on the bank. We had furled all our sails and were no more than the vessel's length from shore when a sudden squall arose and blew us off, so that we carried away the tower to which we were moored.

After this accident we had no time to make sail, for we were being blown onto the coast and the captain decided to throw over a bower anchor. It was not long before we perceived that this was not holding and that the ship was still moving. Since we were approaching the opposite bank, the danger was becoming acute. Our pilot had completely lost his head and announced that he would take charge of the vessel no longer. Consequently our captain decided to cut the cable and abandon the anchor (which cost the King 15,000 *livres*). Meanwhile, we had set our jib and mizzen topsail and, with the greatest difficulty, come up to windward; but since we had on too little sail to tack, we drifted back so near the rocks that we scraped the bottom of our gallery. The vessel had no more than 22 feet ahead and 24 astern in which to maneuver. All of a sudden, while we were in this predicament, the wind freshened and we were luckily able to tack. It was past midday and dinner was ready. Realizing the impossibility of anchoring, M. d'Amblimont resolved to abandon his mission, and we sailed under topsails to the bottom of the bay in order to round up, since we did not have enough wind to maneuver. Everyone but the captain went to dinner and were rejoicing that we had got off so lightly when, to our astonishment, a sailor rushed below to summon the second captain, and we were told that we were definitely headed for shore. We hurried on deck and saw land a pistol-shot to leeward, for the breeze had dropped and in three attempts to tack the vessel had failed to answer her helm. The third time she had lost all headway and had begun to drift back onto the shore, with no means of stopping her. Finally only 20 feet remained between our poop and the shore; however, since it would have been more dangerous to run the vessel ashore stern to, and since the captain

no longer saw any possibility of keeping her off, he maneuvered so as to run her bow ashore instead. No sooner had the vessel begun to turn than we felt several violent shocks and were greatly distressed to observe that we were no longer moving and were hard aground. The men below in irons, believing all was lost, hacked them off.

This coast is so bold that there is up to 50 fathoms of water only 12 feet from shore; but we had only 18 feet under us at the bow and 23 astern. The prow was touching the shore, and even though we had set all our sails in an effort to back, we never succeeded in budging the stern to one side or other. Believing the ship lost, the captain ordered his silver packed up. We feared at this unfortunate moment that the vessel would ground broadside, since the shock of hitting bottom had made her list, and the weight of the spars, being on the side where the water was 60 feet deep, could have caused her to capsize. Furthermore, even if we could get off the rocks, there was a point jutting far out into the crescent-shaped bay we were in on which we might easily fetch up, since we were to leeward and unable to use our sails.

We spent three-quarters of an hour awaiting our fate. We were all prepared to abandon ship, since we could easily have jumped ashore from the tip of the bowsprit. Our two boats were making all possible efforts to reach us from the opposite bank, and we had already fired two guns when an event occurred that one can call a miracle. The sky darkened and storm clouds appeared. We did not have long to wait before what, at another time, could conceivably have caused our ruin now proved to be our salvation. A violent wind and rain squall hit us bow on, filling our trimmed sails so as to back us. It gave us a mighty shake, which set us free, so that we turned broadside to the coast and tacked. We might still have fetched up on the point had not the wind then shifted to our advantage and blown us into the bay, to the great relief of all. As the vessel turned, it came so close to shore that we could easily have jumped from the deck onto the rocks. The water there was only 3 feet deep, and we could see bottom on all sides.

We rounded up in the middle of the harbor and directed the captain of the *polacca* to bring his vessel alongside under shortened sail to unload the wine. But when a sea made up and began to knock his vessel against ours, he set sail for Curaçao. We took only 50 barrels aboard, for which we gave him a bill of exchange for 14,000 *livres*. We set sail ourselves on the 14th.

Buenos Aires, or Bonaire, is an island belonging to the Dutch. There used to be several plantations there, but three years ago the English frigate *Licorne* came and destroyed all the houses and everything else on the island, then dragged her anchor and barely missed being wrecked. One can still see several houses, but since the island lacks water, it will never flourish.

15 March At midday we returned to Puerto Cabello. The *Couronne*, *Neptune*, *Isle de France*, and some transports arrived from Curaçao. We learned that M. Berthier, assistant quartermaster, fought a duel with M. de Saint-Hilaire, an officer of the Soissonnais Regiment, and was killed by a bullet.[177]

We learned via Caracas that peace had been concluded, but we had no confirmation of the fact. Finally the frigate *Andromaque*, commanded by M. Le Vasseur, arrived on the 22nd [24th] from Martinique and confirmed the rumor.[178] Needless to say, this news gave us great pleasure. The *Clairvoyant*, a cutter commanded by M. d'Aché, was sent to Jamaica under a flag of truce.

23 March The *Andromaque* left for The French Cape to announce the peace. On the next day a naval officer got into a dispute with some Spaniards, one of whom drew a stiletto (which they always carry with them) to stab the officer, when a young sublieutenant of the Soissonnais Regiment who was present drew his sword and held it against the Spaniard's chest so that he dared not budge. This allowed time for some officers and other Frenchmen to arrive. However, knowing he was bound for the café, the Spaniards lay in wait for him in the street that evening in order to

stab him, but he arrived with such a large number of comrades that they did not dare attack him.

31 March The *Couronne* was sent off to meet the frigate *Néréide*. The Comte [Christian] de Deux-Ponts, returning from La Guaira in a little Spanish boat, met up with an English frigate, which captured her and then came to reconnoiter our squadron in Puerto Cabello. After the frigate was out of sight of us, she captured a much better schooner stocked with fresh provisions, which she exchanged for the first [and sent the prisoners home in her].[179]

We learned that there were 4 English frigates in the neighborhood and that Admiral Hood was cruising between Puerto Rico and Curaçao.

❧ *April 1783* ❧

3 April We received orders to get under way. By five o'clock that evening we were under sail. Since the Admiral had ordered us to take a merchant vessel in tow, we had to wait for her. The sea was rather rough, so it took a long time to bring her up to us. Meanwhile, the current was fast setting us in towards shore. When we sounded during the night, we found that we were very close to shore. During the night the tow-line parted, and since the sea continued rough, we abandoned the merchantman.

Next day we saw the flagship [*Triomphant*] and the *Auguste* still in harbor. That evening they, too, got under way. Our course was set for the windward channel between Bonaire and the Aves Islands.

6 April We entered the channel to windward of the Aves Islands where a French squadron commanded by M. d'Estrées had had several ships wrecked on the rocks.[180]

177. The victim was Charles-Louis-Jean Berthier de Berluy, aged twenty-four, younger brother of Louis-Alexandre Berthier, who relates the full story of the duel in his journal (pp. 260–266). Aside from the brother's story (hitherto unpublished), Verger's reference to the incident is the only one known to the Editors. Verger's journal further identifies the adversary, who is not designated by name in L.-A. Berthier's account.

178. The Comte de Vaudreuil (*Neptunia*, No. 50, p. 35) dates the arrival of the *Andromaque* at Puerto Cabello as

24 March. Preliminary articles of peace between Great Britain and France and between Great Britain and Spain had been signed on 20 January 1783. Tornquist ([3], p. 123) notes that the ships' crews showed their joy at the news of peace by repeated *Vive le Roi*'s, "happy to return to their fatherland after such long and difficult journeys."

179. On this incident, see Clermont-Crèvecœur's journal, n. 199.

180. A squadron commanded by Vice Admiral Jean d'Estrées (1624–1707) was wrecked here on 11 May 1678

9 April That morning we sighted Puerto Rico and were almost becalmed.

10 April We tacked back and forth, trying to clear two uninhabited rocks called Mona and Monito.

11 April We passed Desecheo to leeward. A fairly heavy sea was running, and all the ships of our squadron were scattered. Curiously enough, we had very strong north winds in the channel between Puerto Rico and Santo Domingo, instead of the westerlies that generally prevail in these parts. This obliged us to tack to windward through the channel with great difficulty.

12 April We carried little sail in order to rally the ships of our squadron, which had become separated.

14 April We sighted La Grange [Punta de la Granja], a great land mass that ordinarily serves as a landfall because of the ease with which one can recognize it, being shaped like a grange.[181]

15 April We reached The French Cape, situated at 19° north latitude and 69° west longitude. The harbor entrance is very difficult. One has to keep very close to shore, then stand up to windward in order to negotiate the narrow passage between the rocks. Flags have been attached to the underwater rocks to mark them, but despite this warning, ships are often wrecked here. One passes beneath a fort called Picolet that is the only defensive fortification in the passage. This battery is so badly built that it looks like a house of cards. It is not large and contains two batteries of about 25 cannon, not counting mortars. There are no fortifications at the top of the mountain, and if one climbed to the summit, one could demolish the fort by throwing stones down upon it. Having been built on uneven rocks, it cost a lot of money. Its only advantage is that any vessel entering the harbor must

sail past it, running the risk of bombardment with hot shot. The harbor is good and is quite spacious, being able to accommodate 600 vessels.

On our arrival we found a Spanish squadron of 10 vessels under the command of [M. Thomasson]. These were the *San Luis*, *Velasco*, *San Sacramento*, *Dragon*, *San Nicolas*, *San Juan*, *Francisco Dansa*[?], *San Ramon*, and *San Pedro*. This squadron had left Havana on 6 February to fetch the Spanish troops who have been at The Cape for a long while.

16 April On the next day a ship flying an Imperial [Austrian] flag arrived loaded with negroes from the coast of Guinea. They all go naked aboard these ships, women as well as men. The former, who are always kept separated from the men, sleep on the quarter-deck. One was the daughter of a prince and could be distinguished by the different designs cut into her skin. At The Cape I saw these unfortunates branded in order to identify them. With a brush dipped in lampblack mixed with a corrosive acid their names are written in large letters across their chests. The acid makes the letters swell so that they can never be erased. I was present when some negroes were sold. The inhabitant who bought them tied their hands together and led them to his estate. The poor slaves believed that their last hour had come, but it is the custom to speak softly to them the first day and treat them considerately at their work.

The land on the plantations is cultivated by negroes and there is always one of them who has a big postillion's whip in his hand with which he pitilessly beats those who neglect their work. Each blow is hard enough to break the skin.

The city at The Cape is large, rather well built, and would pass for a very fine city in France.[182] The

---

when on its way to attack the Dutch at Curaçao. Ch. de La Roncière and G. Clerc-Rampal, *Histoire de la Marine française* (Paris, 1934), p. 106; J. H. Hering, *Beschryving van het Eiland Curaçao* (Amsterdam, 1779; reprint, Aruba, 1969), pp. 64–68. The memory of the disaster was also kept alive by Abbé Raynal, who mentioned it in his *Histoire philosophique et politique des établissements des Européens dans les deux Indes* (Amsterdam, 1770, and many subsequent editions), Book 12—a work many of the French officers had read.

181. See map, Vol. II, No. 171.

182. Moreau de Saint-Méry (*Description . . . de la Partie*

Française de l'Isle Saint-Domingue, ed. Maurel and Taillemitte, I, 296ff.) gives an exhaustive account of the city (now Cap Haïtien) as it was in the 1780's, describing in detail the buildings that caught Verger's eye. The "government house" (pp. 370–375, 384–387) had served that purpose since 1763, following the expulsion of the Jesuit order from France. One of the "two squares" was certainly the Place d'Armes, also known as the Place Notre-Dame (pp. 324ff.); its "beautiful fountain" (pp. 327–328) was erected in 1769. Complementing Moreau's text is his *Recueil de vues* (1791), which includes views of the city and of individual monuments (among them the fountain

streets are laid out regularly and lined with superb shops filled with sugar, coffee, etc., etc. The government house is above the city and was formerly the Jesuit monastery. There are two squares, one of which has a beautiful fountain in the center. This city is thoroughly commercial and offers every luxury one could desire. There are several superb cafés where one may play for high stakes, as well as public baths and beautiful promenades. Luxury is evident to a supreme degree, even among the blacks. Some of the mulattresses are so richly dressed that their finery must be seen to be believed. They count their victories by the number of merchants they have forced into bankruptcy.

The fortifications are in very bad condition. There are several small batteries of little consequence on the peaks; however, there is a very fine arsenal and some magnificent barracks, which can accommodate 12,000 men. The hospital,[183] half a league from town, is handsome and very well maintained. It has a very beautiful garden bordered with lemon and acacia trees. From it one has a superb view of the plain below on which are several sugar and coffee plantations. The harbor, too, offers a most curious spectacle, with its large amount of shipping giving the effect of a thick forest.

Much attention was paid to Prince William of England, who came in a corvette to see The Cape.[184] As his squadron neared the entrance to the harbor he ex-

pressed a desire to see the troops, so Assembly was beaten and the troops lined the streets. A ball was given and plays presented in his honor. He remarked to M. de Bellecombe, the governor, that he and Admiral Hood had long been expecting to see the Marquis de Vaudreuil at Jamaica, whereupon M. de Bellecombe replied very wittily that the Prince would not have seen the Marquis alone because he, as governor, would have had the honor of accompanying him.

M. Gálvez, the Spanish commander, wrote a letter to His Highness telling him that, because the Spanish troops were scattered in the countryside, he had not been able to render him honors as did the French. However, knowing His Highness's tender heart, he believed he could give him a greater pleasure by offering to pardon in his name three Natchez Indians who were British subjects and who had been condemned to death for revolting against the government of Louisiana. He, Gálvez, as governor, had the final say in their execution; therefore, if His Royal Highness wished to pardon them, he was sure that his king, who was generous, would approve.

The Prince returned to his squadron the next day.

18 April A lugger arrived from France bringing us orders from the Court to return to France. The same day the frigate *Nymphe* arrived and several Spanish transports departed, loaded with troops.

20 April[185] We saw a very amusing sight. The Span-

in the Place d'Armes, Plate 6) as well as the "Plan de la Ville du Cap François" (Plate 18), reproduced in part below, Vol. II, No. 176.

183. "Maison de la Providence." See Moreau de Saint-Méry, *Description*, I, 393–408, where even a list of civic-minded benefactors is given.

184. This was Prince William Henry (1765–1837), George III's third son, who was later to reign as William IV (1830–1837). His visit to The French Cape had taken place ten days prior to the arrival of Vaudreuil's ships, but it was still the talk of the town when Verger rehearsed it here in his journal. Prince William was at the time a very young midshipman in the Royal Navy. He had been fêted in British-held New York in the autumn of 1781 and, more recently, had sailed from New York, 26 October 1782, on Admiral Hood's flagship *Barfleur* for the West Indies. His visit to The Cape took place on 5 April 1783, two days after the cessation of hostilities. An extended account of his visit is given in a 4-page supplement to the *Affiches Américaines*, the newspaper published at The Cape (see illustration). Verger had certainly read

this and gleaned from it some of the details noted here in his journal. Although caught unawares by the sudden appearance of the Prince—who reached General de Bellecombe's gateway before a welcoming escort could be sent to meet him—the French and Spanish officials rose to the occasion and improvised a strenuous round of festivities, including a military review and gala theatrical performance followed by a sumptuous supper and dress ball. The regularly scheduled play for that evening was cancelled; in its stead the Prince witnessed *L'Anglois à Bordeaux*, which seems to have amused him. After two hours' sleep His Royal Highness rejoined his ship early on the morning of 6 April, having been granted only twenty-four hours' leave by Admiral Hood. At eleven in the morning the English fleet set sail for Jamaica. The *Affiches Américaines* for 7 May 1783 published a letter from the Prince, dated 13 April from Jamaica, thanking Don Bernardo Gálvez for his humane action in pardoning the Louisiana prisoners.

185. 20 April 1783 was Easter Sunday.

iards commemorate the death of Christ by crossing their yards and firing several guns. Then they dress up a statue to represent Judas Iscariot, holding a purse in one hand and scales in the other, and hang it from the end of the bowsprit. They then keelhaul the effigy twenty times. This is a punishment practiced by sailors and consists of throwing a man overboard, leaving him in the water for a moment, and pulling him [under the ship and] back on board. At the end of this ceremony the dummy was beaten with sticks and torn to pieces by the crew, who performed this nonsense with the greatest gravity. When the Spaniards are becalmed at sea, they cry several times "Fresco San Antonio!" and, if the wind does not freshen, put the statue of the saint overboard and tow it behind the ship.

Their ships are poor sailers and few have copper sheathing. The caliber of their guns is much inferior to ours. None of their warships carries 36-pounders.

I went to visit in the plain a very fine sugar plantation, which belongs to the Chevalier de Walsh, and saw sugar being made.[186] The mill in which the sugar is expressed from the cane is built in two storeys; on the upper storey are two heavy iron cylinders turned by horses, which walk round and round in a circle. The cylinder in the bottom storey and the one on top revolve on a third in the middle. The cane is fed into the cylinders end on and is pressed progressively while the juice runs off into a small trough leading to another building equipped with five large cauldrons, each resting on a stove. The juice runs into the first kettle, which is only moderately warm. Then a negro pours

it into a second, which is hotter, and so on until it reaches the fifth, where it begins to congeal. Then it is poured into earthenware pots shaped like crucibles with a small hole at the tip. These rest in larger earthenware pots. When the sugar is poured in, the best part congeals and the rest runs off into the pot in the form of molasses. The sugar, which is still brown, is then stored in magazines, and a layer of potter's clay, to which the brown coloring-matter adheres, is spread over the surface until, at the end of a week, the sugar is bleached white. When dry it is removed from the pots. The negroes cut into loaves the yellowish parts, and the rest is thrown into a large bin where it is broken up and crushed by the negroes and negresses.

I have watched them work, singing all the while, with a mulatto standing behind them, whip in hand, to punish the negligent. This is the hardest kind of work, at which they spend the whole day except for the two hours they are allowed for dinner. They must take advantage of this rest period to go and cultivate the plots of land allotted for their subsistence, because the planter does not concern himself at all with their food; so these unfortunate people eat a few potatoes and return immediately to work.

The coffee requires no further preparation after picking. Indigo is another important article of trade here.

There were several plays at the theatre, which were attended by M. and Mme de Gálvez. She is a charming woman who, because of her beauty and sweetness, meets with universal approbation.[187]

186. The Walsh plantation was near Limonade, ten miles or so east of The Cape. The owner was "Milord" Antoine-J.-B.-Paulin Walsh (d. 1797) of an Irish family established in Nantes. Walsh had other plantations in the southern part of the island near Les Cayes. See Moreau de Saint-Méry, op.cit., III, 1559, Index. Several members of this family served in the Régiment de Walsh, an old Irish regiment on the French establishment.

187. Bernardo de Gálvez's wife, a French Creole whom he married in New Orleans, was Félicie de Saint-Maxent, widow of Jean-Baptiste-Honoré d'Estréhan. "By all accounts they were a very happy couple; certainly the marriage enhanced Gálvez's popularity and political appeal as well as his financial standing. The Louisianians were flattered that their governor selected a daughter of the colony to be his wife. Nor was the charm and winsomeness of Doña Félicie of merely local appeal; she won just as enthusiastic approval in Mexico City and was one of the

chief factors in her husband's great popularity there as viceroy." John W. Caughey, Bernardo de Gálvez in Louisiana (Berkeley, 1934), p. 84. While she and her husband were at The Cape, Madame de Gálvez gave birth to a son, Michel, who was baptized there on 20 January 1783, the birthday of His Catholic Majesty the King of Spain. The baptismal ceremony, attended by detachments from the Spanish and French regiments, is described in the Affiches Américaines, 29 January 1783. Following the ceremony the French military and social élite were Gálvez's guests at a banquet given at "Charrier," the fine estate overlooking the harbor that had been lent to him as a temporary residence. Although Jupiter Pluvius dampened the illuminations and fireworks, this festivity, according to the Affiches Américaines reporter, "fera à jamais époque dans les fastes de la Colonie Française de Saint-Domingue." A month later, on 19 February, there was another Franco-Spanish fête organized by the Spanish officers in honor of

27 *April* The Spanish squadron and its convoy departed from The Cape, leaving behind only two ships. One, the *San Juan*, dragged her anchors and drifted down on the *Pluton* and our ship. She reanchored in the nick of time, but since she was too close to us, an officer was sent on board the Spaniard's ship to find out by what means they proposed to move away. He found that the captain was taking his siesta and that no one on board dared wake him, in spite of the perilous position of his ship.

30 *April* At eight in the morning, we got under way. That night we were becalmed and, through the negligence of the watch officer, were on the point of going aground. Since a flat calm prevented us from maneuvering and the current was carrying us into Limonade Bay, which is full of dangerous reefs, all our boats were launched to tow us. This proved effective.

⚜ May 1783 ⚜

1 *May 1783* On the next day three more vessels joined us, so that we were eight in all. We could not make sail for lack of wind, and it was not until the morning of 4 May that we got under way. Since the wind was favorable, we sailed to windward of the Turks Islands, leaving on our right Mouchoir Bank, a sandbar full of shoals. The usual passage sailed by vessels leaving The Cape passes to leeward of the Caicos Islands, which are uninhabited. The coasts in these parts are full of hidden dangers and ships are often wrecked here.[188]

4–5 *May* We had a storm during which the lightning and thunder, together with a black sky and a very rough sea, presented a curious spectacle. We fired cannon and set off rockets during the night to rally the squadron. Throughout the next day we had a very good breeze from the southeast, which pushed us along at 3 leagues an hour[189] under topsails alone.

6–7 *May* We crossed the Tropic during the night.

The wind continued from the southeast, which is rare in these parts. We had a flat calm all afternoon, and it was very hot.

10 *May* We saw a waterspout, which came quite close to us. This is a column of air from the highest clouds that descends to the water and absorbs from the sea a quantity of moisture sufficient to saturate it, whereupon the weight of the water causes it to burst and the water falls in a torrent within a small area. It is dangerous for a ship to pass at the moment when the waterspout bursts, for its weight can dismast and even sink her.

14 *May* We sighted the island of Bermuda, which we could see clearly. This island, though not producing great wealth, is extremely useful to England. Sailcloth is manufactured there, and during the war it provided a haven for many privateers. It has no harbor where large vessels can anchor.

We met some heavy weather in these latitudes, followed by calms. These waters are feared by mariners because of hidden reefs.

Several days later a man fell overboard from our ship while we were making between 5 and 6 knots. Fortunately for him he knew how to swim, for since we were sailing before the wind, it took us a long time to turn round. We threw him our life buoys, which fell beyond his reach, and also fired a gun and hoisted our red flag, the signal for "man overboard." The *Hercule*, which was close behind us, also threw him a buoy, which came close enough for him to grasp. We promptly launched a boat, which brought him back aboard. Fortunately the man never lost his head but swam clear of the *Hercule*, fearing that she might run him down.

We had another piece of good fortune when some days later we escaped being dismasted or capsized in a storm. The weather was calm during the night and we had all our sails and stunsails set when the officer of the watch was warned that a squall was making up. Not having perceived the danger, he paid no heed to

Gálvez. This included a bullfight in the best Spanish tradition, graced by the presence of Madame de Gálvez, and was followed by a supper and ball at "Charrier." The *Affiches Américaines* (12 March 1783) hinted that the bullfight was not entirely to the taste of the "âmes tendres" of the French; the reporter also noted that the grounds

at "Charrier," as the festivities proceeded, offered subjects worthy of the brush of a Teniers.
188. See map, Vol. II, No. 177, and descriptive note thereto.
189. About 10½ knots.

the warning until it was too late to do anything, and a furious gale whipped off our stunsails and royals and heeled us way over. It was amazing that we lost none of our masts.

26 May A storm ripped our main topsail and carried it away. We had very heavy weather day and night, during which we spoke an English brig. The sea was still very rough the next day when we sighted a Spanish merchantman, which cut across the squadron. Since she did not immediately display her colors, M. de Vaudreuil fired two cannon balls at her, whereupon she promptly hoisted her national ensign. For several days we had headwinds and had to tack back and forth.

28 May We had a fairly good breeze.

June 1783

11 June We passed the Azores. Several days before we reached them we saw a large topsail still attached to its yard and several heavy ships' timbers, which were doubtless the debris of the English squadron that was wrecked in this latitude. From this point on we had a southwest wind that drove us 50 leagues a day until we reached our anchorage.

16 June We sounded around four o'clock in the afternoon and found bottom at 110 fathoms. The sea was very rough and we had the wind astern, pushing us along between 8 and 9 knots. Our coastal pilot claimed that we were only 9 leagues off the island of Ushant, but our own pilot estimated the distance at 50 leagues. The weather was foggy and we could not see more than 5 miles ahead. The Admiral sent the frigate ahead to signal us in case she sighted land. We sailed all night, making 10 knots under mizzen alone. Everyone was busy on deck, looking for the land. During the night we sounded and read 70 fathoms on the line. The wind was steadily increasing, and no one was happy. We were worried because, according to our reckoning, by morning we should have been off the island; when no land appeared, we feared we might have entered the English Channel. In a very strong wind and an extremely rough sea we bowled along all

morning at 10 knots. What increased our anxiety was the fog. Our coastal pilot was at the topgallant helm when he slid down a rope crying "Breakers ahead!" In front of us there were rocks, which we could barely distinguish because breaking all around us were seas that looked just like the breakers on a reef. Luckily for us we had a fair wind and could quickly veer to port. The pilot recognized the reef as the Pont des Saints, a chain of underwater rocks a sea league in length. We promptly signaled the Admiral of the danger, just in time to avoid shipwreck. One minute later the squadron would have been done for, because just then the fog became thicker, blown in by a sudden squall from astern, which would have prevented us from spotting the reef. We were only half a league away from it and running at 10 knots (about 3⅓ leagues per hour). Thus, had we had the misfortune to sight it a moment later, the fair wind would have driven the vessel hard on it before anything could have been done to avoid it. We were right on course, and what had caused our astonishment at not sighting land was the fact that we had passed Ushant and were already in the Iroise Passage without knowing it. We continued our course with caution, and to our delight the weather cleared and we sighted Les Pierres Noires and Saint-Mathieu and found ourselves in the channel almost before we knew it.

17 June 1783 We anchored in the harbor of Brest around four that afternoon. We found the *Romulus* and *Guadeloupe* there with the detachment of the Saintonge Regiment commanded by M. de La Valette.[190] On the next day the Bourbonnais Regiment landed, on the 19th the Saintonge, and on the 20th, our [Royal Deux-Ponts] regiment. That night we slept ashore in Brest.

We saw many disarmed vessels in the harbor, including 5 three-deckers: the *Royal Louis*, *Bretagne*, *Invincible*, *Terrible*, and *Majestueux*. At Brest you see a sample of the power of the King of France in the multiple storehouses filled with all necessary provisions to equip several fleets, the large number of workmen employed in the port, the special machines to keep the harbor from silting, the yard where the masts of vessels are stepped, the superb drydocks where ves-

190. This was one of the detachments left at Baltimore the previous year, as noted by Verger, p. 161. See also Clermont-Crèvecœur's journal, n. 156.

sels are repaired, the mechanical pumps to expel water, and many other devices revealing to what heights man's industry has carried him in this field.[191]

The city is divided by the harbor into two sections. The northwestern part is called Recouvrance and contains the main fortifications. This section is very well fortified. The city of Brest is very badly laid out, and one has to climb stairs to enter certain streets. The climate is poor, and it rains quite often. This keeps the streets continually dirty. The main square is, however, quite beautiful. The theatre is most undistinguished.

The next morning we were reviewed by the Baron de Vioménil and M. de Langeron, commandant of the garrison. The port commandant is still M. Hector. The first thing that struck me on my arrival in Brest was finding myself surrounded by beggars asking for alms,

something I never saw in America, which speaks very much in its favor. The regiments on garrison duty here, in addition to the sailors, are the Béarn and the Aunis.

21 June We arrived at Landerneau, a small town with a harbor that vessels of 300 tons can enter at high tide.

22 June Via Landivisiau to Morlaix, a very amusing town with quite a pretty harbor from which many privateers sailed during the war. This place is much frequented by the Dutch. It was here that the Naval Council, presided over by M. de Guichen, sat in judgment on M. de Grasse.[192]

23 June To one league this side of Belle-Isle.

24 June To Guingamp, a rather pretty town that was designated as our refreshment billet. The Baron de Vioménil assigned the leaves, and the Minister

191. Cf. Van Blarenberghe, views of Brest, Vol. II, Nos. 1 and 2. Verger's impressions of Brest have a counterpart in Chateaubriand's *Mémoires d'outre-tombe*, Part I, Book II, Chap. 8. As a young country nobleman from Combourg, then only fourteen, Chateaubriand spent several months in Brest in 1783 when unsuccessfully seeking an appointment as a midshipman in the navy. He not only describes the busy port and naval installations he observed during his solitary walks along the Penfeld but also recalls the excitement caused by the arrival of a fleet from overseas (perhaps Vaudreuil's): "All Brest came running to the waterside. Small boats detached themselves from the fleet and arrived alongside the mole. The officers as they came ashore, with their sunburnt faces, had that foreign look of men returning from another hemisphere, and something about them that was gay, proud, and bold, like men who had retrieved the honor of the national flag."

192. After his defeat in the Battle of the Saints in April 1782 (see Clermont-Crèvecœur's journal, n. 145) Admiral de Grasse, as a prisoner of war, returned via Jamaica to London and thence to Paris in August 1782. He subsequently had printed his *Mémoire du comte de Grasse* (see "Checklist of Journals") justifying his role in the battle and raising serious charges against his subordinates. On 29 April 1783 the King ordered a council of war to collect testimony from those who had taken part in the battle. This special court of inquiry, presided over by Rear Admiral de Breugnon and including, among others, Rear Admirals de Guichen and La Motte-Picquet, sat at Lorient from January to May 1784. The results of its investigation were summarized in the printed *Jugement rendu par le Conseil de Guerre Extraordinaire de Marine, tenu à L'Orient par ordre du Roi, 1784*. Although de Grasse was not actually "tried," and thus neither condemned nor acquitted, the council nevertheless rejected

many of the charges de Grasse had circulated in his *Mémoire* and exonerated many of the officers whom he had implicitly blamed. Dissatisfied with the council's judgment, de Grasse appealed to the King for a new examination of his role in the battle. The King's reply, transmitted in a letter from the minister of marine, the Marquis de Castries (2 June 1784) concluded: "His Majesty is willing to suppose that you did all in your power to prevent the misfortunes of that day, but he cannot have the same indulgence regarding the acts that you unjustly impute to those officers of his navy who have been acquitted of the accusations. His Majesty, displeased at your conduct in this respect, forbids you to present yourself before him. It is with pain that I transmit to you his instructions, and that I add to them the advice to retire, under the present circumstances, to your country estate (*à votre province*)." De Grasse's imprudent conduct in printing and distributing his justificatory *Mémoire* prior to the official court of inquiry—that is, trying his case in public—seems to have been a greater factor in his disgrace than his actual conduct during the Battle of the Saints. The whole episode left much bitterness in naval and governmental circles. De Grasse died at the Château de Tilly on 14 January 1788. Verger's statement that the naval council sat *at Morlaix* appears at first glance to be inaccurate, but it is probable that depositions from some of the witnesses were being taken there, perhaps as early as May 1783. Tornquist ([3], p. 125) notes that after his arrival at Brest he and other Swedish officers were given permission to return home but "before our departure each one of us individually had to be heard under oath by the deputies from the General Court-Martial, concerning the battles of Count de Grasse on the 9th and 12th of April, and besides deliver signed extracts of our Journals."

wrote a letter thanking the regiment for its services and announcing that each lieutenant would receive a bonus of *75 livres*—which will not bankrupt France!

We witnessed a fête that occurs every five years, called the *Fête des Pardons*, for which close to 10,000 peasants arrived. They have different penances assigned them in order to gain indulgences; for example, they must go several times around the church on their knees, but never an even number of times. The women raise their skirts above their knees to make the penance harsher. At night they all sleep in the streets, and the priests walk about with candles to light the darker places whither the lovers go to seek solitude.

Next day there was a gathering of the *Frairie Blanche* [White Friars], a confraternity of gentlemen from the neighborhood. There were more than 100 of them. We had a very fine supper of 200 covers, which included 60 women. The ball that followed was very gay.

The suburbs of this town are very diverting. I lodged at the house of a wheelwright, but the continual noise made during the night by his wife's lovers was disgusting; besides, she had the failing of getting drunk, which obliged me to leave. I then took very comfortable lodgings at the house of an elderly spinster, where I stayed until our departure on 20 July. We regretted very much leaving Guingamp because of its good society and the welcome we received in all the houses.

❧ July 1783 ❧

20 July We arrived at Saint-Brieuc, a dirty town with very narrow streets. It has a small harbor half a league from town. I lodged with a widow who was certainly over forty but who missed no opportunity of informing me that she was only thirty. The bishop of the diocese resides in this town.

21 July We left, as before, at two in the morning and arrived very early at Lamballe, quite a pretty town. I lodged with an elderly spinster.

22 July Since most of the regimental horses were nothing but pack animals, I had to content myself with one. The First Battalion stayed in Broons, and I went on 2 leagues beyond with the Second to a little village called Caulnes. I was lodged out in the country at the house of some sort of nun, who was very pretty. She had a sister and also a brother who looked even more ridiculous than the paintings of Aesop.[193] We talked very little at the beginning because she wished to maintain decorum, but little by little she became very gay. I was given a room next to hers through which I had to pass to leave mine. Getting up early in the morning, I was so clumsy as to wake her, and she was kind enough to get up and light the candle, though I begged her not to trouble herself.

23 July We were again detached from the First Battalion, which went to Montauban, while the Second went on to Bedée. I was lodged in a very mean little inn where after a good deal of arguing I succeeded in obtaining clean sheets.

24 July To Rennes, the capital of Brittany, which has a *parlement* of nobles. The city is very beautiful. After a great fire burnt up a large part of it, it had to be rebuilt. There is a very fine bronze equestrian statue of Louis XIV and a standing figure of Louis XV here. The palace where the *parlement* assembles is most handsome. Its halls are worth a visit because of the beautiful paintings they contain. We went to visit a menagerie, which had no extraordinary animals except a mandrill or "man of the woods." We then went to a see a bull fight against dogs and also a donkey, a bear, and two wolves. There were only two dogs, and they were very good fighters.

Brittany possesses an inestimable advantage in her *parlement* and her Estates, which are composed of the leading noblemen of the country. Without remuneration they render justice and have the noble firmness to uphold at Court the rights of their compatriots, often to their own detriment. This province contributes very large sums to the King without placing a very heavy burden on its people, because each community sends its own money to the Receivers of the

193. The Greek fabulist was traditionally depicted as a hideous hunchback, following the fictitious medieval Life of Aesop which prefaced many editions of the *Fables*. See, e.g., the engraved portrait of Aesop, "the ugliest of mortals," in *Les Fables d'Esope . . . nouvelle édition . . . augmentée de la Vie d'Esope, avec figures . . . dédiée à la jeunesse* (Rouen, Lallemant, 1760). Velasquez's portrait of Aesop in the Prado reflects this same tradition.

Estates, who turn it over gratis to the Royal Treasury. They have a Farmer General and an Intendant, but fortunately neither has any power.

26 July We marched 9 leagues and arrived very tired at Vitré. The town is very old, with dark and narrow streets. The fortifications are crumbling into ruins. I lodged at the house of the organist. The town is thickly populated, and I have been told that there are half again as many girls here as boys. The former are very pretty.

27 July We arrived in a spell of very hot weather at Laval, a large town, very populous, in the province of Maine. Before entering we were searched for contraband salt, which can be smuggled in from Brittany where it is only a *sol* a pound, while here it is 13½, which constitutes a very heavy tax. Of this large sum only a third reaches the King, the rest being paid out to the tax-farmers and their employees. The customs, the costume, the speech, and especially the women's clothes are very different from those of Brittany, since the latter province is much more remote than the others, particularly the lower part. I found my hostesses at Laval very entertaining as well as very pretty. Their father was an old soldier who had fought in all the campaigns in Flanders, and I had to listen to a long account of his exploits that I cut short only by leaving him.

28 July The next day we had a very bad storm and an almost continuous rain all the way to Mayenne, where we made a halt. This city is built on the side of a steep mountain and offers nothing of interest. I lodged with an old spinster whom I found very hospitable. The next evening I was invited to take supper with the old ladies next door, who fed me very well, and we drank some excellent Spanish wines. The Duchesse de Mazarin has quite a fine mansion here.

30 July We left Mayenne at half past eleven at night and, after a long march of 9 leagues, arrived at Pré-en-Pail, a small hamlet which could provide lodg-

ings for only half the First Battalion. I was detached to a billet in the country some 3 miles beyond, in the house of a well-to-do peasant where I received every kind of service. He told me that his taxes had just been raised ten percent and again by fifteen percent. This had made it necessary for several peasants to cease cultivating their land, which could no longer yield enough to cover the expenses. How it is possible for the King to be adored as he is by his subjects in spite of the horrible vexations they endure in his name is simply beyond my understanding. They beat Assembly at half past nine that night, and the regiment formed on the road.

31 July We arrived at Alençon in the province of Normandy. This is a rather large and handsome city, where we had an excellent dinner. We paid an official call on the Intendant, who is magnificently housed. We also saw a play that was quite good, considering that it was played by provincial actors. We left at half past ten for Mortagne, where we arrived quite late. It is a small town, thickly settled, where I lodged at the house of a tanner. From here a group of our officers went to visit the monastery of La Trappe along the route.[194]

❧ August 1783 ❧

We spent a long hot day marching to Verneuil, where we made a halt. The town is very crowded and has quite a fine tower built by the English. Not far from here a battle was fought between the Huguenots and the Catholics.[195] We watched the pilgrims who were returning from Santiago de Compostela walk through the church; they marched barefoot behind a religious procession, wearing loose capes and carrying staffs in their hands. I lodged with a very kind widow.

We slept next at Dreux, a very old town that con-

194. The Abbaye de la Grande Trappe is situated some ten miles north of Mortagne near Soligny (Orne); it was here that the Abbé de Rancé, in 1662, instituted the austere discipline henceforth associated with the Trappist order. A guide book of Verger's time notes that at Mortagne "travelers who seek edification generally go from here to visit the Abbaye de la Trappe." Piganiol de la Force, *Nouveau Voyage de France, avec un itinéraire et*

des cartes, new edn. (Paris, 1780), I, 180.

195. Although numerous battles were fought during the Wars of Religion in this general region of Normandy (including the Battle of Ivry, 14 March 1590), Verger may be confusing them with an earlier battle of the Hundred Years' War, when the English defeated the French at Verneuil in 1429.

tains the ruins of an old castle. There was another bloody battle fought near here during the Civil Wars.[196] The Catholics lost it, and their anxiety for peace led them to make great concessions to appease the rebels. It was as a result of this battle that the Court began to hatch the plot that produced the Massacre of St. Bartholomew's Day.

I was very well lodged here, and we went to a very poor concert at the Hôtel de Ville.

6 August We arrived at Houdan, a small hamlet. I lodged at an inn where there were two Englishmen who did not dream that I understood English and talked freely about France. They were very much astonished and dismayed to find that I had understood their conversation. The horse I rode had been galloped too much before I rode him. They had to bleed him in all four feet, which caused me considerable anxiety.

7 August We arrived in Mantes, a completely rebuilt city on the Seine. It is quite large, has a very fine bridge and some beautiful promenades, and carries on a fairly large trade. I was lodged at the house of a youngish spinster who was so poorly dressed that on entering I mistook her for the servant and asked her to conduct me to her mistress. This put me in her black books.

8 August Next day I left with the vanguard and arrived at Pontoise, where I lodged at a notary's house. I began making an arrangement with three of my comrades to take our meals along the way. The bill at the inns always came to a *petit écu* per person. I

asked the major's permission to take four days' leave to go to Paris, which was granted. The four of us hired a carriage and arrived early in Paris, where the first thing I did was to buy a pair of pumps, silk stockings, and a nankeen waistcoat and breeches in order to make myself presentable to my relatives. Then, having lost the whole morning, I could think of nothing better to do in the afternoon than go to the opera, where *Renaud* was being presented.[197] The role of Armide was divinely played, the scenery was magnificent, and the orchestra and music excellent. This was followed by a ballet in which the principal dancer [Vestris] of the Opéra outdid himself.

9 August The next morning I went to call on M. de Losmier, who had moved from his previous lodgings to the Hôtel des Feuillans.[198] I learned from him of the death of M. de Bombelle, *maréchal de camp*.[199] At four [two?] I left in a court carriage for Versailles and drove to the house of M. Gauthier, commissary of the Naval Bureau. I went to visit the King's garden where one can see the artificial rock and caverns that have been built at great expense. The King often walks there. The prettiest spot was the Orangerie, where I saw the Dauphin and the son of the Comte d'Artois.[200] I did not go to visit the other buildings, which I had seen four years ago.

At seven o'clock that evening I left for Paris, where I arrived at ten.

10 August I dressed and went to dine in a restaurant, and from there I went to the Café Militaire, where I acquired several companions. After reserving

196. A royal and Catholic army commanded by the Maréchal de Saint-André defeated the Protestant army of Condé and Coligny at Dreux on 19 December 1562. Henri IV besieged and took possession of Dreux in 1592. There was no direct relationship between these battles and the Massacre of Saint Bartholomew's Day (24 August 1572), as Verger implies.

197. *Renaud, tragédie-lyrique en trois actes*, libretto by J.-J. Le Boeuf, music by Antonio Sacchini, had its first performance at the Académie Royale de Musique (i.e., the Paris Opéra), 25 February 1783. Mlle Le Vasseur had the role of Armide. The *premier danseur*, who appeared in the ballet concluding the opera, was the famous Vestris. See *Journal de Paris*, 8 August 1783.

198. A new apartment house that the Feuillant Fathers

had built next to their convent in the Rue Saint-Honoré. It was designed by the architect Jacques-Denis Antoine and still stands at 225–235 Rue Saint-Honoré in the vicinity of the Place Vendôme. L. V. Thiéry, *Guide des amateurs et des étrangers voyageurs à Paris* (Paris, 1787), I, 120; Michel Gallet, *Demeures parisiennes, l'Epoque de Louis XVI* (Paris, 1964), pp. 82, 171.

199. Verger was related to this family through his maternal grandmother, who was Charlotte-Renée de Bombelle.

200. The Dauphin (b. 1781), whose birth had been celebrated in America the previous year; see Clermont-Crève-cœur's journal, n. 159. The son of the Comte d'Artois (future King Charles X, 1824–1830) was the Duc d'Angoulême (b. 1775).

a place in the diligence the next day, I went off with them to the Foire Saint-Laurent,[201] a street containing several music-halls, including Audinot's and Nicolet's, and various curiosities such as the Chinese Redoubt, admission 36 *sols*. We had the pleasure of walking in a garden frequented by all the beauties of Paris. Once you have paid your entrance fee, you can amuse yourself playing various games, such as *courir la bague*, etc., etc. A café in an artificial grotto has every imaginable refreshment to offer, and above it is a ballroom where all those who wish to may dance. Overlooking the ballroom is a very large gallery for spectators. The whole façade of the building is lit in the Chinese style, that is, with brightly colored lanterns hung in a bizarre pattern. There is also a pyramid that is very well illuminated, with the most charming effect.

There were many Englishmen in the ballroom. One of them, whom I had befriended after the capitulation of York, recognized me and was delighted to find someone who spoke English. We joined some other Englishmen who had just arrived and spent a very pleasant evening together. We went during the eve-

ning to see "The Burial of Malbrouck," the most idiotic show you can imagine.[202] The same craze that seems to possess all the provinces we have visited is still raging in Paris in regard to that cursed song [*Malbrouck s'en va-t-en guerre*], which, with this nation's well-known passion for novelty, the Parisians take such pleasure in singing. We saw some very good dancing at Nicolet's and Audinot's. I should have left that evening to join my regiment, but I was obliged to wait for the departure of the Soissons diligence.

11 August The next morning I went to the Café Anglais, then on to the inn in which I was staying, where I dined with two Dutchmen. At half past five I went to the Comédie Italienne, the most popular theatre in Paris. The Queen attended with the Comtesse d'Artois. The plays being given were *Annette et Lubin* and *Blaise et Babet*, both operettas.[203] The music of the latter is divine, and the orchestra was excellent. The harmonious voice of the singer [Madame Dugazon] who sang the role of Babet won applause from the whole audience. The theatre was almost sold out half an hour before the performance and

201. The Foire Saint-Laurent, an annual summer carnival, which lasted from the end of June to Michaelmas, had grounds in the Faubourg Saint-Laurent, between the Rue du Faubourg Saint-Denis and the Rue du Faubourg Saint-Martin in the neighborhood of the present Gare de l'Est. See L. V. Thiéry, *Almanach du voyageur à Paris . . . , Ouvrage utile aux Citoyens, et indispensable pour l'Etranger, Année 1783*, pp. 199–200, which includes the description of a new attraction built two years earlier, the "Redoute Chinoise" mentioned here by Verger. Nicolas-Médard Audinot's company of juvenile actors, which had moved out to the Foire Saint-Laurent for the summer, generally performed at the "Ambigu Comique," a music hall situated along the Boulevards. J.-B. Nicolet's troupe featured acrobats and tightrope artists as well as pantomimes and skits.

202. *Le Combat et la Mort de Malbrough* was the latest of the spectacles, ingeniously combining fireworks and pantomime, put on by the Ruggieri brothers in their Vauxhall-type gardens, which were situated in the Rue Saint-Lazare on the lower slopes of Montmartre in the vicinity of the church of Notre-Dame-de-Lorette. The old song celebrating the erroneously reported death of John Churchill, Duke of Marlborough, with a tune reputedly borrowed from the Saracens by the crusading soldiers of Saint-Louis, was all the rage in 1783, having been revived

by the Dauphin's nurse, Madame Poitrine. Had they gone on to the Variétés Amusantes, Verger and his companions might have seen this same evening a play called *Churchill amoureux, ou la Jeunesse de Mal'broug*. Concurrently, pseudo-medieval battlements known as "Marlborough's towers" were springing up in fashionable "English gardens" throughout Europe. *Journal de Paris*, 10 August 1783; Lachouque-Brown, *Anatomy of Glory*, p. 211. Von Closen (p. 128), 13 September 1781, relates that, when he and Cromot Dubourg, bound for Yorktown, arrived at the small town of Upper Marlboro in Maryland, they spontaneously burst out singing *Malbrouck s'en va-t-en guerre!*

203. *Annette et Lubin*, by Madame Favart, had been in the repertory of the Théâtre Italien since 1762. *Blaise et Babet, ou la suite des Trois Fermiers*, libretto by J.-B. Boutet de Monvel and music by De Zède, was first performed in 1783, with Madame Dugazon in the role of Babet. *Journal de Paris*, 11 August 1783. The Comédie Italienne, or Théâtre Italien, one of the three theatres sponsored and subsidized by the King, traced its name back to a seventeenth-century troupe of Italian players and in turn gave its name to the Boulevard des Italiens. Its new neoclassic building designed by Heurtier was completed in 1783. The present Opéra Comique is on the same site. L. V. Thiéry, *Almanach du voyageur, Année 1783*, pp. 294–296.

I could not get a seat in the orchestra, so my English friend and I bought seats in the first balcony. He was enthusiastic about the performance.

That evening at eleven o'clock I climbed into the diligence and arrived on the 12th in Soissons. There we found the Bourbonnais Regiment. I lodged at the house of a merchant who treated me very well. We stayed an extra day in Soissons. The city has a very fine hospital.

14 August We arrived early on the 14th at Fîmes, a small town very sparsely populated. I learned from my hostess that this part of the country had been entirely devastated by hailstorms and that more than 300 unfortunate people had nothing to eat.

15 August I joined the vanguard on the march to Rheims. This is a large city with very fine buildings. The main square, which has a statue of Louis XV, is very beautiful. Our colonel came to meet us, and we paid an official call on the Archbishop, who is a member of the Talleyrand family.[204] He could not have us all to dine because he already had his chapter dining with him, so only ten of us went, including myself. We had a very good dinner, after which I visited the church of Saint-Nicaise, which is remarkable for its trembling pillar.[205] This is a supporting column of the building, extending to the roof. By swinging a certain bell in the adjacent steeple, you can see the pillar tremble very perceptibly, a phenomenon that no physicist has yet been able to explain. From there I went to visit the monks at Saint-Rémi to see the Holy Vial, which, according to tradition, was brought there by an angel.[206] We were assured that this was true by a monk who became angry when we expressed doubts.

The treasures in the cathedral are very rich. It was the feast of the Assumption and there was a great procession, which the Archbishop honored with his presence. The cathedral has sixty canons, and I was amazed by the number of monks I saw. The city has very beautiful promenades. The façade of the cathedral is generally acknowledged to be one of the most beautiful in the realm.

16 August The Second Battalion was detached to a pretty village containing a number of small houses. I was very pleased with my quarters at the house of a prosperous wine-grower who paid 200 francs in taxes and was devoted to the King. The village had just received a new parish priest, and this was the occasion for a very gay festival. His predecessor had died suddenly while playing cards.

17 August On the 17th we arrived at Châlons-sur-Marne, a very handsome city where they are building a bridge, which must cost three millions, in order to connect the two arms of the river. There is a fine administration building (*intendance*) here, also the bishop's palace. A company of the Garde du Corps is stationed here. The cathedral is very beautiful. We stayed here through the 18th.

19 August We marched to Vitry-le-François, a small town where the Normandy Cavalry is garrisoned. The town has ramparts built of earth.

20 August To Saint-Dizier, part of which was burned eight years ago and rebuilt anew. The women here are very beautiful.

21 August To Bar-le-Duc, which is divided into two parts, one of which is at the top of the mountain and the other below it. It is surrounded by vineyards and is a very pleasant town where one meets very nice people.

23 August The next day our Second Battalion was

204. Alexandre-Angélique de Talleyrand-Périgord (1736–1821). He was an uncle of the more famous Charles-Maurice de Talleyrand and of the latter's younger brother, Boson de Talleyrand, who appears in Berthier's journal (p. 266 and n. 105).

205. Saint-Nicaise, a large and magnificent thirteenth-century Gothic church, was demolished at the time of the French Revolution. The guide books of Verger's day related that Peter the Great of Russia, during his travels in Western Europe, had climbed to the top of the steeple to study the cause of the movement of the famous *pilier tremblant*. Unable to fathom the mystery and exhausted by his efforts, the prince-philosopher fell asleep in his lofty perch. Piganiol de la Force, *op.cit.*, II, 232–233.

206. The Holy Vial, or *Ampulla Remensis*, reputedly filled with inexhaustible holy oil and brought by an angel to the baptism of King Clovis in 496, was used in the coronation of the French kings until it was shattered during the Revolution. A fragment was piously preserved and moved to the cathedral, where it was used for the coronation of Charles X in 1825.

LE CASTOR

LE SARIGUE FEMELLE.

THE BEAVER AND THE OPOSSUM, AS DEPICTED IN BUFFON'S *HISTOIRE NATURELLE* (*see p. xxv*)

SUPPLÉMENT AUX AFFICHES AMÉRICAINES,

Du Mercredi 9 Avril 1783.

C'EST avec le plus grand empreſſement que nous donnons au Public la relation de ce qui s'eſt paſſé pendant le ſéjour que vient de faire au Cap Son Alteſſe Royale le Prince Guillaume-Henri, Duc de Lancaſtre, troiſieme fils du Roi d'Angleterre.

Samedi dernier 5 avril, à 8 heures du matin, l'Eſcadre Angloiſe, en ſtation ſur nos côtes, fut ſignalée par nos Vigies ; à midi, un Brigantin, ſous pavillon parlementaire, vint mouiller en rade ; & M. William-Auguſtus Merrik, Capitaine commandant le Vaiſſeau de Sa Majeſté Britannique *le Prince-William*, écrivit à M. de Belle-combe, pour le prévenir qu'il étoit chargé pour Son Excellence d'une lettre de l'Amiral Lord Hood, & que S. A. R. le Prince Guillaume-Henri, qu'il avoit l'honneur d'accompagner, n'attendoit que ſa permiſſion pour deſcendre à terre.

Auſſitôt M. le Général envoya M. de Lilancour pour compli-menter S. A. R. & prendre ſes ordres : mais l'empreſſement du jeune Prince ne lui ayant point permis d'attendre la réponſe de M. de Bellecombe, M. de Lilancour le rencontra à l'entrée du jardin du Gouvernement, entouré d'un peuple nombreux, qui faiſoit écla-ter par ſes acclamations l'allégreſſe que ſa préſence inſpiroit.

M. le Général ne s'attendant point au bonheur de voir S. A. R. auſſi promptement, ne put la joindre qu'à la grille ; & en lui ren-dant ſes devoirs, il lui témoigna ſon regret de ce que ſa marche précipitée ne lui avoit pas laiſſé le temps de ſe préparer à lui rendre les honneurs dus à S. A. R. & d'aller l'attendre au bord de la mer avec un cortege convenable.

Le Prince lui répondit très-obligeamment, qu'il s'étoit empreſſé de le voir pour lui confirmer les nouvelles de la paix ; qu'ayant fort peu de temps à reſter avec lui, il ne vouloit point en perdre ; & qu'en ſa qualité de Garde de la Marine, l'Amiral Hood ne lui avoit pas permis de s'abſenter plus de vingt-quatre heures. M. le Général demanda à S. A. R. le mot de l'Ordre, qu'elle lui donna *Louis*.

DE L'IMPRIMERIE ROYALE DU CAP.

PRINCE WILLIAM HENRY'S VISIT TO THE FRENCH CAPE IN APRIL 1783, AS DESCRIBED IN *LES AFFICHES AMERICAINES* (see p. xxv)

Tome 5. Page 410.

Tigé Dme XII. Page 178.

Pl. CCXXXI.

Dessiné par Perignon, P.tre du Roi.

II.ᵉᵐᵉ VUE DE LA VILLE ET CHATEAU DE DELEMONT,

Dans la Principauté de Porentru.

A. P. D. R.

Gravé par Née.

N.º 41

DELEMONT, VERGER'S BIRTHPLACE IN THE BISHOPRIC OF BALE (*see p. xxv*)

JEAN-BAPTISTE-ANTOINE DE VERGER AT THE AGE OF FIFTY-TWO, COMMANDER OF
THE BAVARIAN GENDARMERIE KORPS (*see p. xxvi*)

detached to a small village less than a mile from Saint-Aubin.

24 August We arrived drenched at Toul, a pretty town where the Royal Lorraine Regiment is garrisoned. We thought it very singular that they did not give our regiment a dinner, considering that we had once given them a very fine one at Sarrelouis.

25 August To Nancy, one of the most beautiful towns in France. The Place Stanislas, which contains a statue of Louis XV, and the *allée* leading to the government house opposite are magnificent, and the surrounding buildings superb. The promenades are very wide and well cared for. This square is enclosed by a gilded iron fence. All the streets are perfectly straight. The cathedral is beautiful, and so is the Place d'Alliance. A group of us dined with the Duc de Châtelet, and another in the officers' mess of the Régiment du Roi. As it was the festival of Saint-Louis, the town was illuminated that evening. The Artois Dragoons are also in garrison here. They are very well dressed and mounted.

26 August We left the next day in the rain and arrived at Lunéville, quite a pretty town, which was formerly the residence of King Stanislas of Poland. The palace, now occupied by the Gens d'Armes, is handsome, as are its gardens. The first day we dined with M. d'Autichamp, their colonel. This corps is quite strictly run and is on call at night. I took supper with my host, a lawyer. This town is very dissolute.

28 August We marched to Blâmont, a small town where we saw the ruins of an old castle that was once very large.

29 August To Sarrebourg. During our march it rained continuously. Our company was detached to a village some distance away.

30 August We arrived in Phalsbourg, a fortified town commanded by an eminence within cannon range of the fortifications. We stayed there two days, and the Régiment de Foix gave our regiment a very fine dinner. During our stay a squadron of *chevau-legers* was there. I left the second morning to ride posthaste to Saverne, where I had the pleasure of seeing my two sisters. I dined and supped with one of my old comrades and went to visit the new cardinal's palace. It seemed to me that the architecture was disappointing, and several rooms failed to live up to the grandeur of the building,[207] but the garden is magnificent.

September 1783

1 September 1783 We already notice a complete change in the costume of the peasants and in the farming methods. We arrived at Hochfelden where Prince Max de Deux-Ponts came out to meet the regiment a half a league from town.[208] He gave us a superb dinner and showed the officers every courtesy.

2 September We went to Haguenau, a pretty town where the new hussar regiment will be raised.

3 September To Soultz, a small village with saline baths.

4 September To Wissembourg, a fortified town that draws its greatest advantage from its lines of entrenchment, which can be flooded.

5 September To Landau,[209] where we arrived drenched. We found the Conflans Hussars there and the Royal Hesse-Darmstadt Regiment, who gave us an official dinner where everyone drank a lot and ended by smashing the plates and bottles.

207. The Château of Saverne, one of the residences of Cardinal Louis de Rohan, bishop of Strasbourg, was destroyed by fire in 1779. It was rebuilt by the architect Nicolas de Salins de Montfort.

208. Prince Max, future King Maximilian I Josef of Bavaria, was at this time in the French service as proprietary colonel of the Régiment d'Alsace. See Editors' Introduction to Verger's journal, n. 16.

209. Landau, the frontier garrison town some twenty miles west of the Rhine, to which the Royal Deux-Ponts Regiment returned, was under French rule in 1783. It had changed hands several times during the wars of the seventeenth century but remained in French possession throughout most of the eighteenth century. At the end of the Napoleonic wars it passed to Bavaria as part of the Bavarian Palatinate. It is now in Rhineland-Palatinate, West Germany. Landau was close to the Duchy of Deux-Ponts (Zweibrücken).

9 November 1783 I left Landau for Delémont, stopping for the night at Haguenau.

10 November To Strasbourg, where I lunched at the Hôtel du Corbeau.[210]

11 November To Colmar.

12 November To Bâle

13 November To Delémont.[211]

9 December Left Delémont for Bâle.

11 December Crossing the Rhine at Brissac, I arrived in Strasbourg, where I spent three days.

14 December To Lauterbourg.

15 December To Landau.

17–18 January 1784 During the night there was a great flood, followed by fire, in Landau.

210. The venerable Strasbourg hostelry known as the "Corbeau" closed its doors in 1854, but the building still exists, 1 Quai des Bateliers. The name survives in the "Cour . . . ," "Place . . . ," and "Pont du Corbeau." Hans Haug, *Strasbourg* (Paris, Editions "TEL," 1946), p. xx, Fig. 64.

211. Delémont (Delsberg) in the principality of the Bishopric of Bâle (now a part of the Canton of Berne, Switzerland) was Verger's birthplace and the home of his parents. See Editors' Introduction to this journal and illustration. This was the last time that Verger saw his father, Henri-Joseph-Antoine de Verger (b. 1718), who died at Delémont on 18 December 1783.

Journal

OF LOUIS-ALEXANDRE BERTHIER

LOUIS-ALEXANDRE BERTHIER AT THE AGE OF THIRTY-SEVEN
PAINTED BY LEFEVRE IN 1791 (*see p. xxvi*)

Editors' Introduction

Of our three journal writers, Louis-Alexandre Berthier sprang from the humblest origins, rose to the greatest heights of fame, and came to the most inglorious end.[1] Louis-Alexandre (1753–1815)—or plain Alexandre, as he came to be known—was the eldest of four sons born in Versailles to Jean-Baptiste Berthier and Marie-Françoise l'Huillier de la Serre. The second son, Charles-Louis (1759–1783), died in America, as related below in his brother's journal. César-Gabriel (1765–1819) and Victor-Léopold (1770–1807) both rose to the rank of general in the armies of the Republic and Empire, and their half-brother, Alexandre-Joseph (1792–1849), the child of Jean-Baptiste's late second marriage, continued the military tradition of his elders into the period of the Restoration and the July Monarchy.

The rise to prominence of this talented military family owes much to the ability, foresight, and ambition of Jean-Baptiste Berthier (1721–1804), who was born at Tonnerre in Champagne, the son of a wheelwright.[2] Encouraged by a retired officer in whose château he was employed as a servant, the young man went to Paris and enrolled in the Ecole de Mars, a cadet school for the training of officers. During the War of the Austrian Succession Jean-Baptiste was given employment as a topographical engineer and the rank of lieutenant attached to the Royal Comtois Regiment, in which capacity he joined the army of the Maréchal de Saxe soon after the victory of Fontenoy. He was present at Lawfeld (Laaffelt, near Maastricht) where the French again defeated the English, 1–2 July 1747, and drew a series of plans depicting successive phases of the battle. After the close of the war in 1748 he was entrusted with other cartographical surveys in Belgium and along the northern frontier. Soon after his return to Versailles (where he was married in 1749) he was attached to the Ministry of War. In 1751 his initiative in extinguishing a tenacious fire in the Grande Ecurie, set off by fireworks celebrating the birth of the dauphin, brought him favorable public notice. During the Seven Years' War he was entrusted with the direction of the topographical engineers and of the Dépôt des Cartes et Plans, the army's depository for

1. Although Berthier inevitably appears in the countless works dealing with the Napoleonic period, there is no wholly satisfactory biography of him. The only full-length biographies, both by army officers, are Victor Bernard Derrécagaix, *Le Maréchal Berthier, Prince de Wagram et de Neu-*

maps, located in the ministry at Versailles. Ever alert to display his talents, Jean-Baptiste Berthier was responsible for the design and construction of a new building for the Ministry of War—the so-called Hôtel de la Guerre—as well as an adjacent office building for the Navy Department and the Ministry of Foreign Affairs. Upon the occasion of the King's visit of inspection (26 June 1762) to the War Department's new home, Berthier had a sham fire prepared, extinguished in four and a half minutes, in order to demonstrate the fireproof construction of his building. The King was evidently impressed by the spectacle, for numerous marks of His Majesty's favor were showered upon

châtel, 2 vols. (Paris, Chapelot, 1904–1905), and S. J. Watson, *By Command of the Emperor, A Life of Marshal Berthier* (London, Bodley Head, 1957), which is mainly a summary of the earlier French work. Derrécagaix's biography is based for the most part on the archives of the French War Department (Archives de la Guerre), though he appears to have consulted some of Berthier's own papers then still at Grosbois. Berthier's extensive personal archives, preserved for a century or more by his descendants at the Château de Grosbois, were widely dispersed in the 1930's. His American journals and maps are now in the Princeton University Library; records concerning the administration of the Duchy of Neuchâtel were acquired by the Archives de l'Etat de Neuchâtel (Switzerland) and are there designated as the "Fonds Berthier." Other papers are recorded in a Sotheby & Co. auction catalogue (London, 1 March 1938), *Napoleon & Berthier, Catalogue of Autograph Letters, Manuscripts, Historical Documents and Maps relating to the Battles of the Napoleonic Wars, the Expeditions to Egypt and San Domingo, English, Italian, Spanish and German Affairs, the Campaign in Russia, the Mission of Berthier to Vienna, 1810, papers relating to Chambord and Versailles, etc.*; for auction purposes this extensive segment of Berthier's papers was arbitrarily divided into 90 lots, each comprising many individual items. A smaller group of papers relating to Berthier's diplomatic mission to Spain is described in a Maggs Brothers catalogue (London, 1936), *The Secret History of the Retrocession of Louisiana by Spain to France in 1800, negotiated by General Berthier on behalf of Napoleon, The Original Documents from the Archives of General Berthier.*

The Derrécagaix and Watson biographies (written without benefit of the journals and maps published in the present work) give only summary treatment to Berthier's early American campaigns. Michael Strich's well-documented work on Berthier's last years, *Marschall Alexander Berthier und sein Ende, nach archiv-*

alischen Quellen (Munich, A. Reusch, 1908), based upon Bavarian, Prussian, and Austrian archives (and superseding an earlier brochure by Friedrich Leitschuh, *Alexander Berthier, Fürst von Neufchatel und Wagram*, Bamberg, 1887), was published after Derrécagaix's work and was apparently not known to Watson. Strich's conclusions are summarized by Arthur Chuquet in "Le Suicide de Berthier," *Etudes d'Histoire*, 3rd ser. (Paris, ca. 1910), pp. 175–189. The brief articles on Berthier in the standard biographical reference works (including the recent *Dictionnaire de biographie française*) are not always reliable. Frédéric Masson, "Le Major Général Alexandre Berthier," in his *Jadis* (Paris, 1905), pp. 349–368, provides an excellent short account. Genealogical details on the Berthier family will be found in Chaix d'Est-Ange, *Dictionnaire des familles françaises anciennes ou notables à la fin du XIXᵉ siècle*, IV (Evreux, 1905); a summary of Berthier's military services is in George Six, *Dictionnaire biographique des généraux et amiraux français de la Révolution et de l'Empire* (Paris, 1934). Other sources consulted by the Editors in preparing the present account are mentioned in subsequent notes.

2. Charles Hirschauer, "Jean-Baptiste Berthier et la décoration de l'hôtel de la Guerre et des Affaires Etrangères," in *Revue de l'Histoire de Versailles et de Seine-et-Oise*, XXXII, No. 2 (April–June 1930), 137–157. "The Papers of Jean-Baptiste Berthier . . . over 750 pieces, arranged chronologically in three large portfolios" are very summarily described as Lot 90 in the Sotheby & Co. auction catalogue (1938). An album of plans of the Battle of Laaffelt, 1–2 July 1747 (War of the Austrian Succession), beautifully executed by J.-B. Berthier, is in the Bibliothèque du Ministère des Armées "Terre," Paris. A portrait of J.-B. Berthier (possibly posthumous), which formerly hung in the Château de Grosbois, is owned by the Prince de La Tour d'Auvergne. See also, below, L.-A. Berthier's journal, n. 2.

Berthier the following year. In July 1763 he was brevetted chief of the topographical engineers (*ingénieur-géographe en chef des camps et armées du Roi*), given the lifetime governorship of the Hôtels de la Guerre, des Affaires Etrangères, et de la Marine, and as a supreme reward was granted hereditary nobility by letters patent signed by Louis XV at Compiègne. The son of the wheelwright from Tonnerre, now aged forty-two, was henceforth "le Sieur Jean-Baptiste Berthier."

Jean-Baptiste Berthier's eldest son, Louis-Alexandre, the author of the journal published here, was born at Versailles on 20 November 1753 and baptized the next day in the Royal Church of Saint-Louis. He grew up, as he later said, in the Hôtel de la Guerre with the topographical engineers. As early as 1768 he was working actively with this corps under his father's tutelage;[3] by 1770, at the age of seventeen, he was a lieutenant. While pursuing his work at the Dépôt de la Guerre (during two winters, for example, he did drawings for the plates illustrating a tactical manual compiled by the Baron de Pirch), he also had a variety of temporary assignments that were designed, according to his father's plan, to complete his training by active service in the field. In 1772 he was attached to the infantry of the Légion de Flandres for the express purpose of teaching drawing to the young officers. For several months during the summer of 1775 he was present at the maneuvers of the Strasbourg garrison and prepared reports that drew praise from the inspectors. Another inspector who had seen him at work, the Baron de Vioménil (later second in command of Rochambeau's army in America), supported his request for promotion to captain (approved 2 July 1777) with the comment: "has great talents for staff work and is a good soldier (*un bon sujet*) in every respect." Berthier also served with Lambesc's Lorraine Dragoons, perfecting his skill and establishing his reputation as an accomplished horseman. In 1779 he was with the Army of Normandy, assembled there with an invasion of England in view. Then, the following year, Berthier and his brother Charles-Louis managed, through a series of adventures described below in his journal, to join Rochambeau's army in Newport, Rhode Island, where they were temporarily attached to the Soissonnais Regiment.

Berthier left for America from Brest on 26 June 1780 and returned there three years later on 17 June 1783. In his service record and petitions for advancement he counted this tour of duty, according to current practice, as "four campaigns": one for each of the years 1780, 1781, 1782, and 1783. The absence of his beloved brother Charles-Louis, who had died in Curaçao the previous February, must have cast a shadow over the reunion with his family in Versailles. His mother, too, was absent from the family circle, for she had died on 27 March this same year. Nevertheless, a few weeks later, with that resilience that seems to have characterized his whole career, twenty-nine-year-old Louis-Alexandre was off again on a three months' journey to Prussia and Austria.[4]

3. A recapitulation (*relevé*) of Berthier's military record, drawn up by an archivist in 1880, pièce 2 in Berthier's dossier in the Archives de la Guerre (reprinted in Derrécagaix, *op.cit.*, II, 613–616), dates his military service from 1766. However, the dates given in this recapitulation cannot always be reconciled with those in the original documents also in the dossier. Several of the latter indicate 1768 as the beginning of Berthier's service. The dates were perhaps manipulated a bit when he was attempting to establish seniority over other candidates for promotion.

4. Berthier's journal of his "Voyage en Prusse du 2 Août 1783 . . . ," a manuscript in 4 cahiers comprising 132 pages of text, is now in the Princeton Univer-

Leaving Strasbourg on 2 August 1783, he proceeded rapidly via Heidelberg, Frankfurt, Erfurt, and Leipzig to Berlin. He traveled in his own carriage, picking up fresh horses at each relay post (about four leagues apart, one florin for the horse). At Potsdam he had an audience with Frederick the Great and was invited to join His Majesty for the late August maneuvers near Breslau in Silesia. Returning to Berlin, he then went to Vienna, whence he journeyed via Ratisbonne, Augsburg, and Schaffhausen to Neuf-Brisach, entering the kingdom of France again on 22 October. With seemingly inexhaustible energy he lost no opportunity along the way to reconnoiter the battlefields of the Seven Years' War (Fulda, Rossbach, Torgau, Lissa, Breslau, Liegnitz, Zulicken, Kunersdorf, among others), all of which he described in detail in his journal, with his own comments and battle plans as illustrations. The Prussian maneuvers were discussed and illustrated with similar thoroughness. Berthier was much impressed by the organization of the Prussian Army. "One cannot too much admire," he noted, "the astonishing superiority of the battle march of the Prussians, whose precision I attribute to their constant pace of 76 steps to the minute." Watching Frederick galloping with juvenile ardor at the head of his hussars while shouting his orders (*Ventre à terre! des Coups de pistolet! des Coups de sabre!*), he remarked that the aged King (then seventy-two) appeared to be a youth of twenty. He was less impressed by Joseph II, the Austrian emperor, whom he subsequently saw in Vienna. The Emperor spoke of America, of de Grasse's defeat, but asked no questions about Prussia or the maneuvers that Berthier had just witnessed. "He tries to copy the King of Prussia in all respects," Berthier observed, but the difference between him and "the greatest and most respected King in the whole world" was not to Joseph's advantage.

Nothing escaped Berthier's observing eye. Arsenals, armories, army bakeries, uniforms, staff organization, recruiting practices, the care of horses, soldiers' pay, as well as public buildings, hospitals, orphanages, porcelain factories, and art galleries, are all described in his journal. In Vienna he admired the paintings of Rubens, Jordaens, Teniers, and Titian and visited the *maison de plaisance* where Marie Antoinette had lived as a child. A "Prussian melodrama" called "The Brigands," which he saw in Berlin, was analyzed in his journal with the same care he gave his battle pieces—as a horrible example of bad popular taste. The great Frederick (who had his own theatres for French drama and Italian opera) had dismissed it, Berthier added, with the remark that "The Brigands" was excellent entertainment for hangmen. The play, whose author Berthier did not identify, was young Schiller's

sity Library, Berthier Papers, No. 47. The battle plans and other illustrations referred to in the text of this journal and intended to accompany it are unfortunately no longer with the manuscript. It is listed as Lot 55 in the Sotheby & Co. auction catalogue (1938). Except for a selection of anecdotes concerning Frederick the Great translated and edited by Gilbert Chinard ("Alexandre Berthier's 'Voyage en Prusse,'" *Princeton University Library Chronicle*, v, No. 3 [April 1944], 92–103), the manuscript is unpublished.

Twenty-three years later, following the victorious occupation of Berlin by the French, Berthier was again in Potsdam where, on 26 October 1806, he visited Frederick's tomb in the company of Emperor Napoleon. See Derrécagaix, II, 171. The visit is commemorated in an engraving by Friedrich Arnold after Heinrich Dähling, in which Berthier can be distinguished (second from left); a reproduction is in the exhibition catalogue *Napoléon tel qu'en lui-même* (Archives Nationales, Paris, 1969), p. 87, No. 372.

drama of student revolt, *Die Räuber*. Nor could he then foresee that the author of this bad "Prussian melodrama" would a decade later be given the title of *citoyen français* by the Legislative Assembly of France (26 August 1792) in a gesture of universal fraternity that embraced such other "pathfinders of liberty" as Pestalozzi, Thomas Paine, Washington, Hamilton, Madison, and Kosciusko!

Upon Berthier's return from his journey—which might be described retrospectively as his first reconnaissance of localities that were to figure prominently in his later life—he resumed work at the Hôtel de la Guerre with the newly created General Staff service. This was where he wanted to be, as he had affirmed earlier when attached to the quartermaster-general's staff in America: "My assignment has given me the greatest pleasure. It is an open door to the General Staff of the army and can lead to general's rank for a hard-working officer who does not, like the gentlemen of the Court, belong to the class from which colonels are appointed."[5] Nevertheless, the doors were slow in opening, and his path was beset with disappointments. The new service provided for a limited number of assistant quartermasters-general (*aides maréchal général des logis*), with the rank of major or above, each assisted by an adjutant (*adjoint*) with the rank of captain. Although Berthier had actually fulfilled the functions of assistant quartermaster-general in America, he now found himself only an adjutant, still with the rank of captain. Other men who had served in the same capacity in America (Cromot Dubourg, for example) had, as he pointed out in memoranda to the minister, been given more favorable treatment.[6] In 1787 he finally obtained the designation of assistant quartermaster-general, but his promotion to major came only on 1 July 1788. At this time he received his first decoration, the Cross of the Order of Saint-Louis. The following year (11 July 1789) he was promoted lieutenant colonel and also had the satisfaction of being able to wear the eagle of the Society of the Cincinnati as evidence of his campaigns in America.[7] The rank of colonel came at last (with strong recommendations from Lafayette) on 1 April 1791, when Berthier was thirty-seven years old.[8] The ascent had been relatively slow, unjustly so in his own eyes. Meanwhile, he had had

*Berthier
Journal*

5. See journal, p. 237. A revealing example of the court intrigues involved in the appointment of a colonel is related by the Prince de Montbarey (minister of war, 1777–1780) who unwittingly named the Comte de Laval-Montmorency a second colonel in the Royal Dragoons in preference to a protégé of the Queen; see his *Mémoires*, 3 vols. (Paris, 1826–1827), II, 193–214.

6. Archives de la Guerre, Berthier dossier, pièces 36–39. Berthier is mentioned in the "Etat des services de Messieurs les Officiers de l'Etat-Major de l'Armée employés dans l'Amérique Septentrionale . . . grâces dont ils sont susceptibles," 1 March 1783, signed by Béville, quartermaster-general, and revised by Rochambeau, in the Library of Congress, Rochambeau Papers, vol. 6, pp. 645–650. Berthier's skill in map-making is singled out for special praise. The generals recommend that his assignment to the staff be con-

tinued but propose no raise in rank.

7. An invitation to membership in the Cincinnati authorizing Berthier to wear its badge, dated 7 August 1789, signed by the Comte d'Estaing (then president of the French branch of the Society), is cited among the items listed as Lot 67 ("Berthier. A Collection of Papers mostly of Biographical Interest") in the Sotheby & Co. auction catalogue (1938). Membership in the Society had originally been limited to officers who had seen service in America with the rank of colonel or above, but the French branch later extended it to include (as honorary founding members, *membres honoraires d'origine*) those who subsequently attained this rank or, in cases of special merit, to those of lower rank. See Contenson, *Cincinnati*, pp. 51ff.

8. Archives de la Guerre, Berthier dossier, pièces 50–52. Lafayette had addressed a memorandum to the King recommending Berthier's promotion on 4 July

several assignments in the field. In 1788 he was at the camp of Saint-Omer serving as chief of staff; in 1788–1789 he accompanied General Lambert, inspector general of the army, on a tour in Flanders and Hainaut. The events of the spring of 1789, ushering in the French Revolution, thus found Berthier on the northern frontier, whence he soon returned to his native city of Versailles, now the nerve center of a changing order.

Berthier and his two younger brothers, César and Léopold, lost no time in enlisting as fusiliers in the Versailles militia (*milice bourgeoise*), which was formed in the summer of 1789 on the pattern of the Garde Nationale Parisienne commanded by Lafayette (and inspired in part, perhaps, by the citizen militia of America).[9] When the Comte d'Estaing was elected commander of the Versailles organization in September, Berthier was named *major-général* (chief of staff) and continued in this capacity when Lafayette (doubling his Paris command with that of Versailles) succeeded d'Estaing in October. Since the nominal chiefs were nonresidents, Berthier as their second was virtually in command of the National Guard at Versailles; as a regular army officer he was also "commander for the King" in Versailles. After the enforced removal of the royal family to the Tuileries in Paris, Berthier was thus responsible for the protection of royal properties in Versailles and in command of the regular army troops garrisoned there. For nearly two years he strove to reconcile his military duties and loyalty to the royal family with his civic obligations and with popular demands. In his attempts to control civil disorder he had the support of many citizens and of the first elective mayor of Versailles, Dr. J.-F. Coste, another veteran of the American campaigns (chief physician in Rochambeau's army), who presided over the city's destinies from March 1790 to November 1791. Nevertheless, it was Berthier's misfortune to have incurred the hostility of a lesser member of the National Guard, a local politician and shopkeeper named Lecointre (later a member of the National Convention). Lecointre relentlessly pursued his attacks within the Guard itself, in the municipal and departmental assemblies, in the Jacobin Club, in the Paris press, and in a series of libelous tracts (in which Berthier's father was not spared). Berthier defended himself as best he could in the press and in pamphlets of his own.[10] His firmness and adroitness in ensuring the safe departure (sanctioned by a decree of the National Assembly) from the Château de Bellevue of the persons and baggage of "Mesdames," the King's elderly aunts, increased Berthier's unpopularity with the popular faction.

1790; this is endorsed "attendre." He renewed the request in a personal note to Duportail, 12 February 1791. Duportail, who had served in the American army as Washington's chief engineer, was minister of war from October 1790 to December 1791.

9. The Versailles episodes in Berthier's career are discussed in: Charles Hirschauer, "La Jeunesse et les débuts militaires d'Alexandre Berthier," *Revue de l'Histoire de Versailles et de Seine-et-Oise*, XXXII, No. 2 (April–June 1930), 158–174; Georges Mauguin, "Le Général Alexandre Berthier et la municipalité de Versailles," *ibid.*, XXXIX, No. 1 (Jan.–March 1937), 27–36.

The Sotheby & Co. auction catalogue (1938) lists as Lot 56 "Berthier. A Collection of Papers dealing with his command of the Garde Nationale of Versailles."
10. Several of these pamphlets are entered under Berthier's name in the Bibliothèque Nationale, *Catalogue . . . Auteurs*, including *A mes concitoyens* (June 1790) and *Compte rendu par le commandant de la Garde Nationale de Versailles de ce qui s'est passé à Bellevue, d'après l'exécution des réquisitions à lui adressées relativement au départ des effets de Mesdames, tantes du Roi, les 20, 21 février et 5 mars 1791.*

Matters came to a head in April 1791 when menacing shouts of *A bas Berthier! Berthier à la lanterne!* interrupted ceremonies marking the award of tricolor cockades to the old Flanders Regiment, then leaving Versailles as the Nineteenth Regiment of infantry. Soon thereafter Berthier withdrew from the frustrations of the forum and resumed his staff work in the army. He could certainly have subscribed to the words of his friend Dr. Coste who, when relinquishing his post as mayor of Versailles a few months later, admonished his fellow townsmen: "Remember, citizens, that, in social order, the more one is a slave of the law, the freer one is."[11] But the winds of social change were blowing in other directions.

During the autumn and winter of 1791–1792 Berthier, now a colonel, turned to more strictly professional and no doubt more congenial tasks: recruiting volunteers in the departments of Loiret and Seine-et-Oise, training new battalions quartered between the Somme and the Marne, and performing the duties of chief of staff for the Seventeenth Division concentrated around Paris. Already, however, the old army in which he had been trained was undergoing a transformation. Like others with his background (his old chief Rochambeau, for example),[12] Berthier was aware of the lack of training and discipline among the new recruits, the weakening of the command structure through the emigration of many aristocratic officers who were forming their own Army of the Princes at Trier, and the growing "interference" of politically oriented civilian authorities. At the same time threats of war lent special urgency to his tasks. On 20 April 1792 the Legislative Assembly declared war on Austria (soon to be joined by her Prussian ally). French troops were already massed along the frontier with a thrust into Belgium in view. At the request of General Rochambeau (recently made a Maréchal de France), commanding the Army of the North, Berthier joined him as chief of staff[13] and, when the old marshal resigned in discouragement, continued in this position under Luckner, with the rank of *maréchal de camp*. While the French armies were unsuccessfully attempting to move against the Austrians in Belgium, news reached them of the incidents of 20 June, when a riotous Parisian crowd entered the Tuileries and forced the King to don the liberty cap. From the headquarters at Menin on the Belgian frontier Berthier addressed an open letter to the King, deploring the attack on the royal person and pledging his loyalty in the joint struggle against domestic factions and foreign enemies.[14] His letter (dated 27 June) was published in the *Journal de Paris*, 2 July 1792, and was straightway denounced by Deputy Delmas in the Assembly.

11. Cited in John E. Lane, *J.-F. Coste* (1928), p. 15. See below, "Checklist of Journals" *s.v.* Coste.

12. Arnold Whitridge, *Rochambeau* (New York, 1965), Chap. 16, includes a good discussion of Rochambeau's difficulties.

13. Théodore de Lameth recalled in his *Notes et Souvenirs* (ed. Welvert [Paris, 1914], p. 428) that, when Rochambeau asked his brother Alexandre de Lameth to serve as chief of staff, the latter declined both because of his lack of qualifications and because he was then an object of hatred to certain members of the

Legislative Assembly. "True," said the Marshal, "my friendship for you had made me forget this, but whom then should I take?" "I think, sir, that it should be Berthier." "The one who was with us in America?" "Yes, monsieur le maréchal, the same. Perhaps I can be with him to command the troops, but as a staff officer he is far above me and many others."

14. At this same time Lafayette appeared personally before the Legislative Assembly on 28 June to express similar sentiments. Later in the summer, after the fall of the monarchy on 10 August, he crossed the fron-

Following the overthrow of the monarchy on 10 August, Berthier, suspected of *incivisme*, was relieved of his command by decree of the Provisional Executive Council on 21 August 1792 and formally suspended a month later on 20 September—which was, ironically for Berthier, the day of the French victory at Valmy. "Under the reign of despotism," he wrote, adopting the new vocabulary and signing himself Citizen Alexandre Berthier, "one supplicated the ministers, intrigued, and suffered in silence; under the reign of liberty, law, and legality, one asks for justice, one takes heart, and one is heard."[15] Citizen Berthier's protests, continuing through the autumn and winter of 1792–1793, were of no avail, in spite of strong supporting appeals from the commanders in the field, Luckner, Kellerman, and Custine. The latter, urgently demanding Berthier's assignment to the Army of the Rhine, expostulated: "I can speak of him with more knowledge than anyone else, for it was I who formed him in America. . . . I know of no one who has more skill or a better eye for reconnoitering a locality, who accomplishes this more correctly, and to whom all details are more familiar. I shall perhaps find someone who can replace Berthier, but I have not yet discovered him. . . ."[16] For the first time in his military career Berthier was *sans emploi*.

An opportunity to serve again finally came in the spring of 1793. The government of the Republic, then waging war on both the foreign and domestic fronts, was obliged to take strenuous measures to crush the revolts in La Vendée. Evidently needing all the talents it could muster, the Committee of Public Safety permitted Berthier to serve in the field as a simple volunteer, though still withholding his formal reinstatement. Once on the spot he earned the confidence of General Santerre, among others, and even of certain of the "representatives of the people on mission." Berthier drew up a plan of operations (27 May), participated in the unfortunate affair at Saumur on 9 June (where he was wounded and had two horses shot from under him), and served temporarily as chief of staff. When the Duc de Lauzun, now known as General Biron, arrived on the scene to assume the overall command of the Army of the Côtes de La Rochelle, he immediately singled out his old acquaintance. Berthier, he told the authorities, "has all the necessary qualifications for making an excellent chief of staff."[17] But even Lauzun could not act without the advice of a host of civilian commissioners and representatives; he himself was recalled to Paris in July. That same month Berthier accompanied General Dutruy to Paris to report to the Committee of Public Safety (now coming under Robes-

tier (19 August 1792) and was made a prisoner by the Austrians.

15. Berthier to the Conseil du Pouvoir Exécutif, Paris, 10 October 1792, "Year One of the French Republic." A duplicate copy of this memorandum, in Berthier's handwriting, is in his dossier, Archives de la Guerre. During this period Berthier took great pains to establish the fact that he was not an émigré. See, e.g., his letters to the municipality of Versailles, 1 September, 14 October 1792, printed in Mauguin, *op.cit.*, pp. 27–30. Berthier managed to obtain the return of his personal papers, which had been placed under seal in his apartment in the Hôtel de la Guerre when this building, like other royal properties, had been sequestered by the new Republican government.

16. Custine's letter to the minister of war is printed from the original in the Archives de la Guerre in Derrécagaix, *op.cit.*, I, 29–30.

17. Biron to Bouchotte, Niort, 21 June 1793, cited from the original in the Archives de la Guerre by Gontaut Biron, *Le Duc de Lauzun* (Paris, 1937), p. 318, n. 3. This well-documented biography gives a good account of the situation in La Vendée as it appeared to Lauzun. This was to be his last campaign.

pierre's domination) on the state of the army in La Vendée and the means needed to terminate the revolt. In spite of many testimonials from those who had seen him at work at Tours and Saumur, he again fell under suspicion, was detained in Paris, and could not obtain permission to return to his post. In another impassioned protest, which he circulated in printed form, Berthier proclaimed: "I am loyal; my heart is pure, and I have never stooped to intrigue; I have constantly followed the line of my duties and my principles of liberty, equality, and respect for the nation's sovereignty."[18]

Again Berthier was without employment. This time he prudently retired to Précy-sur-Oise, a village near Chantilly and Senlis, where one of his brothers-in-law had a country house. There he joined his two sisters, their husbands (MM. d'Avrange d'Haugeranville and Perrache de Franqueville, both former officers of the Gardes de la Porte du Roi), and his brother César. The family lived on good terms with the townspeople and was represented on the local *comité de surveillance*. Berthier himself, in deference to prevailing fashions, tactfully presented the commune with a tricolor flag crowned by a liberty cap to replace the cross on the belfry of the village church. The "certificates of civism" that the potentates of the hour had refused him evidently presented no problem at Précy-sur-Oise, where Berthier quietly spent the latter months of 1793 and the year 1794—the period of the Terror. He was more fortunate than other veterans of the American war. Lafayette was still a prisoner at Olmütz. Custine went to the guillotine on 28 August 1793, the Duc de Lauzun on 31 December. Rochambeau, imprisoned in 1794, barely escaped the same fate.

The "Thermidorean Reaction" following Robespierre's fall on 9 Thermidor (27 July 1794) and the subsequent establishment of the Directory (17 October 1795) brought the change in political climate that enabled Berthier to emerge from his retirement. He was officially reinstated in the army on 5 March 1795 as *général de brigade* and chief of staff to the Armies of the Alps and Italy commanded by Kellerman; on 13 June he was raised to the rank of *général de division*. Berthier straightway turned his energies to problems of staff reorganization, assigning responsibilities to his adjutants according to the four divisions that were henceforth to be the basis of his army organization chart: (1) troops movements, (2) general correspondence (including the "journal historique des opérations"), (3) reconnaissances, and (4) administration (supplies, camps, clothing, hospitals, etc.).[19] The winter of 1795–1796 found him in Chambéry, where on New Year's Day he had the misfortune to

18. *Alexandre Berthier, Général de Brigade, au Comité de Salut Public, Du 16 août 1793, l'an deuxième de la république une et indivisible.* 8 pp., Paris, printed by G.-F. Galetti.

19. Derrécagaix, *op.cit.*, I, 75–78. For a technical discussion of staff organization, with references to Berthier's contributions, see Raymond M.A. de Philip, *Etude sur le service d'Etat-Major pendant les guerres du Premier Empire* (Paris, 1900). Symptomatic of the change in political climate at this time was the appointment as minister of war of Aubert du Bayet, another veteran of the American war (second lieutenant, Bourbonnais Regiment) who had fallen from grace

during the Reign of Terror. Jean-Baptiste-Annibal Aubert du Bayet, born in Louisiana in 1759, was minister from November 1795 to February 1796; he was then sent as ambassador to Constantinople, where he died in December 1797. In a letter to General Clarke, 21 November 1795, Berthier refers to Du Bayet as "my former comrade-in-arms in America and my friend" (Derrécagaix, *op.cit.*, I, 54). Aubert du Bayet is the subject of Charles Gayarré's *Aubert Dubayet, or The Two Sister Republics* (Boston, 1882), a mediocre historical romance in which, according to the author, the "nudities of history" are "embellished under the glittering gossamer veil of fiction."

break a leg when his horse slipped on the ice. On 2 March 1796 the Executive Directory named Bonaparte commander in chief of the Army of Italy and at the same time named Berthier his chief of staff. The news reached Chambéry on 12 March. Setting forth a few days later, Berthier proceeded southward (stopping to inspect the arsenals at Grenoble and Valence) to Antibes, where he met Bonaparte on the 24th. The commander in chief and his chief of staff traveled together to the headquarters at Nice. Bonaparte was then twenty-six, Berthier forty-two. The partnership thus begun lasted for eighteen years.

The Italian Campaign opened on 27 March 1796. Moving swiftly through the Piedmont and into Lombardy, the French reached Milan on 15 May. "From the beginning of the campaign," Bonaparte reported to the Directory, "General Berthier, chief of staff, has spent his days in fighting at my side and his nights at his desk: it would be impossible to combine more activity, good will, courage, and knowledge. . . ."[20] The two names continued to be coupled in the reports and congratulations exchanged between Paris and Italy. Reporting on the action at Lodi, Bonaparte singled out "the intrepid Berthier who was on that day a cannoneer, cavalier, and grenadier."[21] Again, rating his generals, he placed his chief of staff at the top of the list, with the comment: "Berthier: talents, activity, courage, character, everything in his favor."[22] The following year, when according Monge and Berthier the honor of carrying to the government in Paris the Treaty of Campo Formio, Bonaparte added a message extolling his emissary as "one of the pillars of the Republic, one of the most zealous defenders of liberty: there is not a victory of the Army of Italy to which he has not contributed."[23] "The praise that you bestow on me," Berthier was moved to tell his chief, "is not above what I could have wished to do, but far beyond what I have done. It is my heartfelt wish never to be separated from such a great man, from a friend like you."[24] A young man on Berthier's staff, Baron Denniée, who was to serve with him for many years, recalled one of Bonaparte's terrible bursts of anger that he witnessed at Milan. When he was alone with Berthier, Denniée exclaimed, "Do you realize what an intolerable temper that man has?" "You are right, my dear Denniée," Berthier replied, "but remember that some day it will be a fine thing to be the second of that man."[25]

The summer of 1797 saw Berthier established in his headquarters at Milan. His orders and corre-

20. Bonaparte to the Executive Directory, Tortona, 17 Floréal an IV (6 May 1796), in *Correspondance de Napoléon Ier, publiée par ordre de l'Empereur Napoléon III*, 32 vols. (Paris, 1858–1869), I, 238, No. 338.

21. Bonaparte to the Executive Directory, Lodi, 22 Floréal an IV (11 May 1796), *ibid.*, I, 260–262, No. 382.

22. Bonaparte to the Executive Directory, Brescia, 27 Thermidor an IV (14 August 1796), *ibid.*, I, 548–549, No. 890.

23. Bonaparte to the Executive Directory, Passariano, 27 Vendémiaire an VI (18 October 1797), *ibid.*, III, 390, No. 2306.

24. Berthier to Bonaparte, Paris, 11 Brumaire an VI (1 November 1797), in *Correspondance inédite . . . de Napoléon Bonaparte . . . avec . . . les généraux français et étrangers, en Italie, en Allemagne et en Egypte*, ed. Ch.-Th. Beauvais, 7 vols. (Paris, Panckoucke, 1819–1820), IV (Venise 2), 400–402.

25. Pierre-Paul Denniée, *Itinéraire de l'Empereur Napoléon pendant la Campagne de 1812* (Paris, Paulin, 1842). When publishing his account of the Russian campaign, originally written as a letter sent to his father from Königsberg in January 1813, Baron Denniée added (pp. 193ff.) an appreciative account of Berthier, on whose personal staff he had served over a long period.

spondence for this period are written on stationery ornamented with an elaborate allegorical vignette engraved by Appiani to commemorate the Italian victories,[26] for Bonaparte had already enlisted the arts in the service of his glory and legend. Among the artists at Milan was Antoine Gros, fresh from his studies in Rome. Gros painted the well-known portrait of Bonaparte at the Bridge of Arcole, one of the earliest in the long series of Napoleonic icons.[27] Gros also did a companion piece depicting Berthier at the Bridge of Lodi. The incredibly boyish figure (he was actually forty-two) stands brandishing a sword against a background showing the bridge over the river Adda where he had distinguished himself in the affair of 10 May 1796.[28] General Desaix, who visited Milan in the summer of 1797, noted in his diary the presence of Gros and other artists, as well as a bevy of beautiful women, French and Italian, including Bonaparte's wife Joséphine and his sister Pauline, wife of General Leclerc. Desaix also jotted down impressions of the three Berthier brothers:

> Adjutant general [César] Berthier, the General's brother, short, well-built, honest.
>
> The chief of the topographical engineers [Léopold] Berthier, tall, cold, long-faced, dark complexion, taciturn, married. [Madame Berthier, Desaix noted elsewhere, was from Versailles, fairly good-looking, amiable, good-natured.]
>
> Berthier [Alexandre], short, stocky, always laughing, always bustling about; in love with Madame Visconti. . . .[29]

Giuseppina Carcano, widow of Giovanni Sopransi, was by her second marriage the wife of Francesco Visconti, soon to be sent to Paris as ambassador of the Cisalpine Republic. A precocious little

26. Specimens are reproduced in *Carnet de La Sabretache*, VIII (1900), 478–482, "A propos des vignettes d'Alexandre Berthier."

27. Finished portrait, Musée de Versailles; preliminary studies, Louvre and other collections. For full bibliography see the exhibition catalogue *Napoléon* (Grand Palais, Paris, 1969), pp. 14–15, Nos. 53–54. Gros began the portrait late in 1796 at the Casa Serbelloni, Bonaparte's residence in Milan. The artist wrote to his mother (6–7 December 1796) that the little time allotted him by the General could scarcely be called a sitting: "I must resign myself to painting only the character of his face, and from then on, as best I can, give it the form of a portrait." Apparently it was Joséphine's idea to place the flag in Bonaparte's hand. According to Jean Adhémar and Nicole Villa, editors of the exhibition catalogue *La Légende Napoléonienne, 1796–1900* (Bibliothèque Nationale, Paris, 1969), pp. 3–5, "the organization of the Napoleonic legend dates from the victory of Arcole in 1796, and first took shape during the Italian Campaign."

28. Shown at the Salon of 1798. See the exhibition catalogue *Gros, Ses Amis, Ses Elèves* (Petit Palais, Paris, 1936), pp. 51–52, No. 18. The original of this painting—frequently reproduced, though generally out of context—is now in the collection of the Prince de La Tour d'Auvergne; a copy, or replica, is at the Château de Grosbois. Another portrait of Berthier, with long locks and wearing a Directoire-style uniform, drawn by Mademoiselle Boze and engraved by Coqueret and Lagrenée, was published by Potrelle in Paris, *ca.* 1796–1797, as one in his series of full-length portraits of Republican generals (which also included Bonaparte).

29. "Notes de Voyage du Général Desaix, Suisse et Italie, 1797," ed. General V., in *Carnet de La Sabretache*, VI (1898), 577–591, 701–733, 801–819, and VII (1899), 2–13; description of the three Berthiers, VI, 707. Desaix's word picture tallies well with the group portrait painted by Louis-François Lejeune (1775–1848), the soldier-artist who served for a long period as aide to Berthier. Lejeune's painting (formerly at Grosbois, now in the collection of the Prince de La Tour d'Auvergne) shows the three brothers in uniform and on horseback against a northern Italian mountain landscape. It evokes the arrival in Italy, after the crossing of the Alps, May 1800, during the Italian Campaign of that year.

girl named Laure Permon (later Madame Junot, duchesse d'Abrantès), who first saw Berthier's inamorata in her mother's Paris salon, recalled that Madame Visconti "was really extremely beautiful":

> Indeed, I believe I have never seen a more charming head than hers. She had delicate but regular features . . . , the prettiest of noses, aquiline but a bit snub. . . . Her mobile nostrils gave Mme Visconti a smile which was of a finesse impossible to describe. . . . She had a row of regular teeth like little pearls and very black hair, always piled up in the purest classical taste. . . . Mme Visconti dressed very well. Like the elegant women of that period, she had the good sense to borrow from Greek and Roman models only what was becoming and proper—so that, truly, when she entered her box at the Opéra, with her cashmere shawl as picturesquely draped as Mme Tallien's, people found her no less beautiful. Poor Berthier was so mad about her in those days that he lost sleep and appetite. I use these strong words because I cannot say that his love ever made him lose his mind. But the fact remains that his love for her has made Mme Visconti a historic personage, for Berthier gave his arm to Napoleon, leaning on him when not supporting him—and so Mme Visconti is there, too, like a shadow, the shadow of a shade. . . .[30]

Portraits of Mme Visconti, one painted by Gros at Milan in 1797, another done by Gérard in 1810, confirm the Duchesse d'Abrantès's recollections.[31] Berthier's encounter with *his* Joséphine was in its way as decisive an event in his life as was his meeting with Bonaparte. The friendship lasted for the rest of his life, surviving his subsequent marriage and all manner of ridicule. "La Visconti" and her "Sandro" inevitably invited gossip and ribaldry. It was a subject that Bonaparte himself could never let lie (pursuing it relentlessly even in his repetitious recitals at St. Helena). Nevertheless, this liaison endured, and Stendhal, citing it in his *De l'Amour* as an example of the mellowing love of lengthening years, gave it a touch of immortality.[32]

30. *Mémoires de Madame la Duchesse d'Abrantès, Souvenirs historiques . . .* , 10 vols. with index (Paris, Garnier, *ca.* 1905), II, 59–61. The first installments of the *Souvenirs historiques* of the Duchesse d'Abrantès (1784–1838) were originally published with the help of the printer-novelist Honoré de Balzac, who numbered the author among his conquests.

Jules Bertaut's article, "Le Roman d'amour du Maréchal Berthier" (*Historia, La Revue Vivante du Passé*, XVIII, No. 104 [July 1955], 105–109) repeats the usual anecdotes but adds nothing new to the story. The same must also be said of Renée Madinier's "Le Maréchal Berthier et la belle Visconti," *Histoire pour Tous*, No. 136 (August 1971), 114–122.

31. The portrait by Gros (unlocated), painted at Milan at the time he did one of Bonaparte's wife Joséphine, is mentioned in J.-B. Delestre, *Gros et ses ouvrages* (Paris, n.d.), pp. 40–41; J. Tripier Le Franc, *Histoire de la vie et de la mort du baron Gros* (Paris, 1880), pp. 146, 154–155. The later portrait of Mme Visconti by Gérard (reproduced in Watson, *op.cit.*, and elsewhere) is now in the Louvre; cf. "Liste des Oeuvres du baron François Gérard," in Henri Gérard, ed., *Correspondance de François Gérard*, 2nd edn., 2 vols. (Paris, 1886), II, 405; and the exhibition catalogue *Gros, Ses Amis, Ses Elèves* (Petit Palais, Paris, 1936), p. 163, No. 258.

32. Stendhal, *De l'Amour*, ed. Henri Martineau (Paris, Le Divan, 1957), pp. 216 and 459, n. 576. "Votre maîtresse, devenue votre amie intime, vous donne d'autres plaisirs, les plaisirs de la vieillesse. C'est une fleur qui après avoir été rose le matin, dans la saison des fleurs, se change en un fruit délicieux le soir, quand les roses ne sont plus de saison." In his manuscript, following this passage, Stendhal added a note: "*For me.* Amours du Prince de Wagram. . . ." The note did not appear in the original edition of the book (1822)—perhaps out of deference to Mme Visconti, who was still alive—but has been restored in the Martineau edition.

Bonaparte's dynamic leadership and his growing influence in the councils of the Republic multiplied Berthier's responsibilities. At the end of the year 1797, while Bonaparte was in Paris preparing an expedition against England, he named Berthier commander in chief of the Army of Italy, in spite of the latter's protest that "I would rather be your aide-de-camp than commander in chief here."[33] In January 1798 Berthier received orders to march on Rome and set up a "sister republic" there. Although this political-military mission was not one that he himself would have chosen,[34] he dutifully played the role of "liberator" of the Roman people, entering the city on 15 February. While Pope Pius VI and his cardinals were held prisoner in the Vatican, General Berthier received the founding fathers of the new (and ephemeral) republic at the Capitol, offering them the homage of "the free French warriors": "They come, these sons of the Gauls, with the olive branch of peace, to mount guard over the altars of liberty on the very spot where your Brutuses first raised them!"[35] Leaving Roman affairs in other hands, Berthier was back in Paris in April; on 19 May 1798 he embarked with Bonaparte at Toulon on the flagship *Orient*, bound for the Pyramids. Resuming the more congenial role of chief of staff, he served throughout the Egyptian and Syrian campaigns, returning to France with Bonaparte only in October 1799.[36] Soon thereafter the coup d'état of 18 Brumaire (9 November 1799) overthrew the Directory and concentrated power in the hands of the First Consul. Under the new regime Berthier held the portfolio of minister of war until March 1800,[37] when he was again assigned the command of an army, the "Armée de la Réserve," which he led across the Alps through the Great Saint Bernard Pass down to the plain of Marengo, the scene of another famous victory (14 June 1800).[38] That autumn he was sent on a diplomatic mission to

33. Berthier to Bonaparte, Milan, 4 Nivôse an VI (24 December 1797), in Derrécagaix, *op.cit.*, I, 234–235.

34. "I have always told you that the Italian command does not suit me. I want to be done with revolutions. Four years in America, ten in France . . . is enough. I will fight as a private as long as my country has enemies to fight; but I don't want to be involved in revolutionary politics." Berthier to Bonaparte, Mantua, 12 Nivôse an VI (1 January 1798), in *Correspondance inédite . . . de Napoléon*, IV (Venise 2), 481–482.

35. A detailed account of Berthier's Roman mission, based in part on his own papers then at Grosbois, is in Albert Dufourcq, *Le Régime jacobin en Italie, Etude sur la République Romaine, 1798–1799* (Paris, 1900), pp. 88ff. The Bibliothèque Nationale *Catalogue . . . Auteurs* lists printed proclamations, in the form of broadsides in French and Italian, issued under Berthier's name as "Le Citoyen Alexandre Berthier, Général en Chef de l'Armée d'Italie." These include his *Discours prononcé au Capitole . . . le 27 Pluviôse an VI*.

36. The official account of the expedition, *Relation des Campagnes du général Bonaparte en Egypte et en Syrie* (Paris, Didot, An VIII/1799, and several other editions), was compiled by Berthier and published under his name. While he was chief of staff in Egypt, Berthier set up a topographic bureau entrusted with the systematic mapping of the country under the direction of Colonel Jacotin of the topographical engineers. This eventually resulted in the "Carte topographique de l'Egypte . . . levée pendant l'expédition de l'armée française . . . ," the engraving of which, in 47 sheets, was completed only in 1818. It was then issued as the atlas volume of the mammoth government-sponsored *Description de l'Egypte* (1809–1822). See Jacotin, "Mémoire sur la construction de la carte d'Egypte," in *Description*, "Etat Moderne," II, 2e partie, 1–118. This cartographical monument is comparable in many ways to the "Carte des Chasses" initiated by Berthier's father on which he himself had worked; see Berthier's journal, n. 2.

37. He was again named minister of war in October 1800 and held that post concurrently with his other functions until August 1807.

38. Berthier also compiled the official account of Marengo: *Relation de la Bataille de Marengo, gagnée*

Madrid, where he signed, on behalf of the First Consul, the Treaty of San Ildefonso (1 October 1800), by which Spain receded Louisiana to France in exchange for the Duchy of Parma.[39]

The multifarious activities just outlined set the pace and the pattern for the next fourteen years of Berthier's life. His personal history is inseparable from that of the Imperial epic. Berthier is there at Napoleon's side, at his court as on the battlefields—Ulm, Austerlitz, Jena, Eylau, Friedland, Wagram. One of Berthier's aides who often saw the two men together—"both so richly but so differently gifted"—has left this characteristic picture:

> It was Napoleon who inaugurated every plan, improvised the means for carrying it out, and by imbuing all with his own zeal made everything possible. It was General Berthier who, the plan of the chief once conceived, identified himself thoroughly with it, divided and subdivided the work to be done, assigning to each one the particular task by which he was to cooperate with every other member of the army, smoothing over difficulties, providing for every contingency. His anxious solicitude, which kept him ever on the alert, his undaunted cooperation, were never relaxed until success was achieved. . . .
>
> Berthier was also the most indefatigable person I knew, and when I one day congratulated Count Daru on his wonderful power of sustaining fatigue and doing without sleep, he said to me, "The Prince de Neufchâtel is even stronger than I am; I never spent more than nine days and nights without going to bed, but Berthier has been in the saddle for thirteen days and nights at a stretch. . . ."
>
> No one served the Emperor with more loyal devotion . . . , and while I was with him not a day passed without my noting some fresh proof of his devotion to his master, which was indeed a perfect religion with him. He was entirely without self-seeking, and yielded to his chief an affectionate and unfailing obedience often most touching in its patience and resignation. . . .[40]

Berthier's devotion did not go unrewarded. Honors and worldly wealth steadily accrued to him. He was made Commander of the First Cohort of the Legion of Honor (which he himself had helped

le 25 Prairial an VIII par Napoléon Bonaparte sur les Autrichiens . . . rédigée par Alexandre Berthier (Paris, An XII/1804, and several subsequent editions). The *Relation* was considerably revised by Napoleon before he approved its publication. A manuscript with his corrections has recently passed through several auctions: see Sotheby & Co. catalogue (14–15 November 1955), *Andre deCoppet Collection, Part V*, Lot 1040; sale at Palais Galliéra (Paris, 21–22 March 1966), *Bibliothèque René G.-D., Livres et Manuscrits*, Lot 140. A copy of the *Relation* was presented to Napoleon on the fifth anniversary of Marengo upon the occasion of a review held on the battlefield itself. The engraved frontispiece (Pauquet after C. Vernet) of the 1805 edition depicts the presentation ceremony in which Berthier, standing before the Emperor on horseback, is pointing with his marshal's baton to a map of the battle.

39. See Maggs Brothers catalogue (1936), *The Secret History of the Retrocession of Louisiana by Spain to France in 1800 . . . the Original Documents from the Archives of General Berthier.* The news of the retrocession was kept secret for some time before it eventually leaked out to American ears.

40. *Memoirs of Baron [Louis-François] Lejeune, aide-de-camp to Marshals Berthier, Davout and Oudinot,* tr. and ed. Mrs. Arthur Bell, 2 vols. (London, 1897), II, 140–142. Lejeune's memoirs were first published under the title *Souvenirs d'un officier de l'Empire* (Toulouse, Viguier, 1851).

organize) and was the first to receive its "Grand Cordon." With the proclamation of the Empire in 1804, Napoleon named Berthier the first of the newly created Marshals of the Empire[41] and, when creating an Imperial court, bestowed upon Berthier the title of "Grand Veneur," that is, Grand Master of the Hunt. Thanks to Napoleon's largesse, his "Grand Veneur" acquired the magnificent domain of Grosbois, some fourteen miles southeast of Paris, with its Louis XIII château and hunting preserve. On the eve of the Revolution Grosbois had been the residence of the King's brother, the Comte de Provence (the future Louis XVIII); confiscated and purchased by speculators in national properties during the Revolution, it next fell into the hands of the Director Barras, then of General Moreau, who was forced to sell it when banished to America by Napoleon.[42] Berthier's fine town house, the Hôtel de la Colonnade at the corner of the Rue des Capucines and the Boulevards, had been the residence of wealthy royal officials under the Old Regime and later, at the time of his marriage with Joséphine de Beauharnais in 1796, of Bonaparte himself.[43] As Sébastien Mercier remarked when comparing the old and the new Paris, "the birds fly away, but the nests remain."

"The conquered countries," another chronicler noted, "are always called upon to feed the generosity shown by the Emperor to his collaborators." Thus, in recognition of his role in the Campaign of 1805 renowned for the victories at Ulm and at Austerlitz, Berthier received a still greater prize. By a treaty signed in 1806 Prussia ceded the Duchy of Neuchâtel to the Emperor, who bestowed it upon Berthier with the title of "Prince Souverain de Neuchâtel et Duc de Valangin." Although his new subjects upon several occasions made preparations to welcome him, Berthier never set foot in his Swiss principality. Nevertheless, with his characteristic attention to administrative detail, the absentee sovereign devoted considerable time and thought to the welfare of his state.[44]

41. Berthier's designation as Marshal of the Empire was announced on 18 May 1804. His father, who died on the 21st at the age of eighty-three, thus lived to see his son reach the summit of the military hierarchy. In a note of condolence sent to Berthier ("Mon Cousin") Napoleon added: "But after all, at eighty-five it is time to finish; and when one has lived a good life, one can only aspire at that age to leave a good memory of oneself behind." Napoleon to Berthier, Saint-Cloud, 3 Prairial an XII (23 May 1804), in *Correspondance de Napoléon Ier*, IX, 370, No. 7770. Berthier's brother Léopold died in November 1806 at the age of thirty-six.

42. Henry Soulange-Bodin, *Le Château de Gros-Bois* (Paris, n.d. [*ca.* 1950?]); *Environs de Paris, Ile-de-France*, "Les Guides Bleus" (Paris, 1948), pp. 514–516. A portion of the "Carte des Chasses" showing Grosbois is reproduced below, Vol. II, map No. 10. Grosbois remained in the possession of Berthier's descendants until 1962, when it was acquired by the Société d'Encouragement à l'Elevage du Cheval Français. As an historic monument parts of the château can still be

visited by the public. Among the sights are the Empire-style furnishings and the "Galerie des Batailles" installed by Berthier. Hitler's Marshal Goering, who resided for a time at Grosbois during the German occupation of France in World War II, apparently left untouched the paintings (by Taunay, Carle Vernet, Vincent, Gros, et al.) of the battles in which Berthier took part and the busts of Napoleon's marshals, including Berthier's own by the ill-fated Italian sculptor Giuseppe Ceracchi. Several of the Grosbois battle paintings are reproduced in color in Jean Mistler et al., *Napoléon et l'Empire*, 2 vols. (Paris, 1968).

43. Jacques Hillairet, *Dictionnaire historique des rues de Paris* (Paris, 1963), I, 267–268. The hôtel was sold by Berthier's widow to the French government, which used it as the Ministry of Foreign Affairs from 1820 to 1853. It was demolished in 1855. A watercolor by Civeton, showing the hôtel *ca.* 1829, is reproduced in Georges Pillement, *Les Hôtels des Boulevards à Charonne* (Paris, 1953), p. 11.

44. See Jean Courvoisier, *Le Maréchal Berthier et Sa Principauté de Neuchâtel, 1806–1814* (Neuchâtel,

Napoleon's munificence was not always unconditional. "You see what I have done for you," he wrote to Berthier when sending him the official announcement of his Neuchâtel principality:

I place but one condition upon it, which is that you get married, and this is a condition that I place upon my friendship. Your passion has lasted long enough, it has become ridiculous, and I have the right to expect that the man whom I have named my companion in arms, whom posterity will always place beside me, will no longer remain abandoned to an unexampled weakness. I therefore wish you to marry; otherwise I shall no longer see you. You are fifty, but you are of a stock that lives to eighty, and these thirty years are those when the sweets of marriage are most necessary to you. . . . You know that nobody loves you more than I do, but you know, too, that the first condition of my friendship is that it be subordinated to my respect. Until now you have earned it. Continue to be worthy of it by conforming to my plans and becoming the founder of a good and great family. . . . [45]

It was to be another two years before Berthier found a wife—or, rather, before one was found for him. On 18 February 1808 Napoleon informed the King of Bavaria: "The Prince de Neuchâtel has asked my permission to marry Princess Elisabeth, Your Majesty's niece. It appears to me that they are in agreement. I wish therefore to be the first to announce this to Your Majesty, knowing your regard for the Prince de Neuchâtel who is so closely bound to me through my long-standing friendship for him."[46] Princess Elisabeth (Marie-Elisabeth-Amélie-Françoise de Bavière), daughter of Duke Ludwig Wilhelm of Bavaria, was then twenty-three years old (born 5 May 1784). In the presence of the Emperor and the Empress Joséphine, she was married to Alexandre Berthier, Prince

1959), an exhaustive study of the subject based in part on Berthier's own papers, formerly at Grosbois, now in the Archives de l'Etat de Neuchâtel. Berthier governed his principality first through General Oudinot and then chiefly through François-Victor-Jean de Lespérut (1772–1848), his councillor and plenipotentiary representative. The "Prince de Neuchâtel's Battalion," a military unit recruited in the principality for the Emperor's service, was familiarly known as "Berthier's canaries" because of the yellow coats of the uniform. Concerning these uniforms, see Paul Marmottan, "Notes sur le Bataillon de Neuchâtel (à propos du portrait d'un de ses capitaines)," *Carnet de La Sabretache*, II (1894), 175–181; Alfred Guye, *Le Bataillon de Neuchâtel, dit des "canaris"* (Neuchâtel, 1964). The Battalion was dissolved (19 May 1814) under the First Restoration, at which time the Principality of Neuchâtel was receded to Prussia. Berthier renounced his rights, in return for which he received by way of indemnity an annuity of 34,000 crowns, one-half of which sum would revert to his widow (Courvoisier, pp. 430–432). The provision made for

Berthier's wife (a niece of the King of Bavaria) was presumably a favor granted by Prussia to Bavaria, then an ally.

45. Napoleon to Berthier, Malmaison, 1 April 1806, in *Correspondance de Napoléon Ier*, XII, 253, No. 10046.
46. Napoleon to Maximilian Joseph, King of Bavaria, Paris, 18 February 1808, *ibid.*, XVI, 348, No. 13583. Berthier was already on very friendly terms with the King, as evidenced by Maximilian Joseph's letters to him: Marcel Dunan, ed., "Nouveaux Documents sur l'Allemagne napoléonienne (1806–1813)," *Revue Historique*, CLXXXVI (July–September 1939), 112–143. In one instance the King refers to Berthier as "mon bien-aimé neveu." The letters published by Dunan were formerly among Berthier's papers at Grosbois; they were purchased for the Archives du Ministère des Affaires Etrangères at the Sotheby sale in 1938 (catalogue, Lot. No 80). See also the well-documented note on Berthier in Marcel Dunan, *Napoléon et l'Allemagne, Le Système Continental et les Débuts du Royaume de Bavière, 1806–1810* (Paris, 1943), pp. 616–617, n. 68.

de Neuchâtel, in a civil ceremony performed in Paris by the mayor of the first arrondissement on 9 March 1808. Three children were to be born to them: a son, Napoléon-Louis-Alexandre, on 10 September 1810; and two daughters, Caroline-Joséphine (born 20 August 1812) and Marie-Anne-Wilhelmine-Alexandrine-Elisabeth (born 19 February 1816, after her father's death). In spite of the disparity in ages, this arranged marriage appears to have been happier than might have been expected. Even Madame Visconti made the best of it and, it is said, developed a kindly and motherly relationship with the young princess.[47]

The year following his marriage Berthier received still another title as a recognition of his preeminent role in the Battle of Wagram (6 July 1809). At the end of the campaign the Emperor announced from his Schönbrunn headquarters on 15 August (Saint-Napoléon's Day) the honors and rewards accorded to his victorious army. Berthier was granted the title of Prince de Wagram, while Masséna, at the same time, became Prince d'Essling, and Davout the Prince d'Eckmühl. These were not empty titles; each was provided with a princely appanage. "We have," Napoleon decreed, "erected as a principality, under the title of Principality of Wagram, the Château of Chambord, which we acquired from the Legion of Honor, with its adjoining park and forest, to be owned by our cousin the Prince de Neuchâtel and his descendants, according to the conditions set forth in the letters-patent. . . ."[48] The coat of arms of the Prince de Wagram bore the device "COMMILITONI VICTOR CAESAR"—The Victorious Emperor to his Comrade-in-arms.

The Prince de Neuchâtel et de Wagram, after spending the autumn of 1809 at the Schönbrunn headquarters supervising the application of the military clauses of the Treaty of Vienna, returned there again a few months later in still another capacity. This time he was Napoleon's ambassador extraordinary, sent to ask for the hand of Princess Marie-Louise. Napoleon's schemes for creating and per-

47. See, e.g., *Mémoires de Madame de Rémusat*, ed. Paul de Rémusat, 3 vols. (Paris, 1880), III, 344–346. Madame de Rémusat, who wrote her memoirs *ca.* 1819, indicates that "la belle Italienne" was then still in Paris and still on good terms with Berthier's widow. See also letter from Queen Hortense (wife of Louis Bonaparte, King of Holland) to her brother Eugène de Beauharnais (Viceroy of Italy), Plombières, 23 August 1809, in Jean Hanoteau, ed., *Les Beauharnais et l'Empereur, Lettres de l'Impératrice Joséphine et de la Reine Hortense au Prince Eugène* (Paris, 1936), pp. 234–236. Hortense writes that Augusta (Eugène's wife, daughter of the King of Bavaria) finds it difficult to accept the idea that her cousin Elisabeth (Berthier's wife) is on good terms with Mme Visconti and is even her intimate friend. Augusta herself has received Mme Visconti very coldly, much to the latter's surprise, as she is accustomed to being spoiled and flattered. Hortense concludes that her sister-in-law Augusta is, happily perhaps, still innocent of court life, as she herself once was, but that unfortunately "if you are surrounded by courtiers you soon learn to your sorrow that you must receive everybody cordially."

48. Napoleon to Prince Cambacérès, Archichancelier de l'Empire, Schönbrunn, 15 August 1809, in *Correspondance de Napoléon Ier*, XIX, 344–346, Nos. 15658, 15659. The Sotheby sale catalogue (1938) lists as Lots 68–69 "A Collection of Papers relating to the Château of Chambord and the Administration of the Estate." The Emperor increased the value of Berthier's property by his gift of a flock of 3,000 Merino sheep brought there from Spain. The Princesse de Wagram, Berthier's widow, put the Chambord estate up for sale in 1821, when it was purchased by public subscription for the Duc de Bordeaux, posthumous son of the Duc de Berry. The Duc de Bordeaux, under the name Comte de Chambord, figured in later nineteenth-century French history as the legitimist pretender to the throne.

petuating a dynasty had brought about his divorce from Joséphine; negotiations with his erstwhile enemy, Emperor Francis II of Austria, had fixed the choice of a bride. As Napoleon's emissary Berthier formally asked for the princess's hand and represented him in the marriage by proxy that took place with great pomp and ceremony in the Augustinerkirche in Vienna on 11 March 1810.[49] Describing a gala banquet in the palace of the Emperor of Austria, an officer in Berthier's suite commented: "Hitherto only those who could prove thirty-two quarterings of nobility, which involved tracing back a genealogy for seven or eight centuries, had been admitted to the Imperial table, but victory had broken through this superannuated etiquette, and here we were, twenty children of the people, raised up by the fortunes of war, now being courted and pampered by the descendants of Charlemagne and Charles V!"[50] Over roads that another very young Austrian princess had taken in 1770 and that he himself had first reconnoitered after his return from America in 1783, Berthier accompanied the nineteen-year-old Marie-Louise on her journey to France, where Napoleon awaited her at Compiègne. He could not then know that four years later Marie-Louise, with her three-year-old son, the Roi de Rome, would set out on her journey back to Vienna from his own château at Grosbois.[51]

The Russian Campaign of 1812 marked the beginning of the end for Napoleon. Berthier was by his side throughout this disastrous year, always lodged within his call, sleeping with one eye open, habitually joining the Emperor at table. Stresses and strains in the old partnership were nevertheless becoming apparent. After crossing the Niemen (22–23 June 1812), which marked the formal opening of the campaign, Berthier, like many others, was aware of the dangers inherent in the march to Moscow: the ever-extending lines of communication, the bad roads, the scarcity of supplies, the mounting desertions among the foreign conscripts. But the Emperor, obstinately pursuing his ambitious dreams of glory, would brook no advice nor accept counsel from his collaborators. Because he dared as an old friend to point out the perils, Berthier was a ready victim of the Emperor's wrath and a frequent butt for his taunts.[52] He was told, for example, that he was useless, that he should return to his hunting at Grosbois or join La Visconti in Paris. After one such painful scene at Ghiat, Berthier for several days absented himself from the Emperor's table. Upon another occasion he was surprised in an unguarded moment of depression by Méneval, the Emperor's secretary. "What is the good," Berthier burst forth, "of his having given me an income of 60,000 pounds a year, a magnificent mansion in Paris, a splendid estate, in order to inflict the tortures of Tantalus upon me? I shall die here

49. See Sotheby sale catalogue (1938), Lot 42, "The Marriage of Napoleon and Marie-Louise, Berthier's Papers concerning his Mission to Vienna as Ambassador Extraordinary to demand the hand of Marie-Louise." The lot includes eight letters (one reproduced in facsimile) written to Berthier by Napoleon while he was awaiting Marie-Louise at Compiègne.
50. *Memoirs of Baron Lejeune*, II, 19–20. Lejeune provides a graphic account of the whole mission.
51. Baron Charles-François de Méneval, *Memoirs illustrating the History of Napoleon I, from 1802 to 1815*, tr. Robert H. Sherrard, 3 vols. (New York, 1894), III, 264. Méneval's *Souvenirs* were first published in 1844–1845. He accompanied Marie-Louise on her journey back to Vienna.
52. Lejeune, *op.cit.*, II, 170; Denniée, *op.cit.*, pp. 62–63; Méneval, III, 41–45; Armand-Augustin-Louis de Caulaincourt, *Mémoires*, ed. Jean Hanoteau, 3 vols. (Paris, 1933), I, 383–385, 420.

with all this work. The lowliest private is happier than I am." Then, quickly gaining control of himself, he summoned his aides and turned briskly back to the business in hand.[53]

On 14 September Berthier, chief of staff of the Grand Army, entered the deserted city of Moscow and proceeded with the Emperor to the Kremlin. The next day, from their fortress, they witnessed the burning of the city. Leaving temporarily for quarters at Petrowskoïe, they returned again to the Kremlin, where the Emperor, clinging obstinately to the idea that peace was in his grasp, tarried for another month.[54] A report compiled by Berthier on 28 September indicated that the Grand Army of 420,000 men was already reduced to 93,000.[55] At last, on 18 October, orders to depart were given and the tragic retreat began. No one has described it more graphically than Caulaincourt. As the retreating army approached Smolensk, he wrote,

> Almost everyone was on foot. The Emperor, who followed the Guard in his carriage with the Prince de Neufchâtel, alighted two or three times a day, leaning now on Berthier's arm, now on mine, now on one of his aides-de-camp. The sides of the road were covered with corpses of the wounded, dead from hunger, cold, and misery. Never has a battlefield presented so much horror. And yet . . . in spite of our misery and of these scenes of horror, the sight of the spires of Smolensk, seen in clear weather and with the sun coming out, had revived the most downcast among us; many persons had regained their gaiety. . . .[56]

When approaching Vilna, at Benitsa, on 5 December, the Emperor made known his intention of leaving for Paris; Berthier was to remain with the army, which was placed under the command of Murat, King of Naples.

The chief of staff continued sending almost daily reports to the Emperor, concealing nothing of the disaster.[57] "I must inform Your Majesty," Berthier wrote from Kovno on 12 December, "that the army is totally disbanded, even your Guard, which now numbers scarcely 4,000 to 5,000 men. Generals, officers, have lost all they had, nearly all have some part of their body frozen; the roads are covered with corpses, and the houses filled with them. The army forms but a single column several leagues in length, which leaves at daybreak and arrives in no order in the evening. . . . Your Majesty may be assured that all that is humanly possible will be done for the honor of His arms. Twenty-five degrees of cold and the abundant snow that covers the ground are the cause of the disastrous state of the army, which no longer exists as such. . . ." Again, from Wirballen, on 16 December (5 A.M.), he reported that a calèche carrying the staff archives had gone astray ("I am in consternation about the loss of such important papers") and spoke of the "incoherent mass" and the inability of the gen-

53. Méneval, III, 43.
54. Mathieu Dumas, Berthier's comrade-in-arms since the American campaigns, remembered the two of them standing on the balcony of Berthier's apartment in the Russian Imperial Palace, indignantly watching workmen hack down the Cross of Ivan as a trophy for Napoleon. Dumas, *Souvenirs*, III, 455–456.

55. Report of Berthier to the Emperor, Moscow, 28 September 1812, in Derrécagaix, *op.cit.*, II, 437–438.
56. Caulaincourt, *op.cit.*, II, 131.
57. Berthier's reports, written to Napoleon after the latter's departure, are printed in Derrécagaix, *op.cit.*, II, 458ff.

erals to stem the "disorganizing torrent." "I know," he commented, "that I am distressing Your Majesty, but you must know all."

During this ordeal Berthier's thoughts often hastened forward to the journey's end and to the reunion with friends and family in Paris. He had not yet seen his second child and first daughter, Caroline-Joséphine, born in August 1812. In Moscow on 15 October he wrote letters (which they never received) both to his wife and to Mme Visconti.[58] Although assuring the latter that "the storms of life" had led him "to the greatest happiness, that of linking my fate to yours," he told her how eagerly he looked forward to seeing his young wife and children: "What happiness for us, what cares, what a charming occupation for you—in our [sic] children you rediscover your attachment for me." And to his wife he wrote: "Your letters bring me closer to you. At last, having waged a war worthy of us, I shall bring you an olive branch and a thousand kisses." Couriers from Paris eventually brought welcome letters from Princess Elisabeth. Seven of them, full of news of his children and household, reached him, along with eighteen batches of official mail in early December, when he was approaching Vilna.[59] "We are all in perfect health," Berthier promptly wrote in reply to his wife's anxious queries. Again, from Königsberg on 21 December, he reassured her: "I have rheumatic pains in my right arm, for the first time, but the gout has so far left me alone. I am suffering from the excessive cold weather, but I am still standing all this better than anyone else in the army." Ten days later, still in Königsberg, he admitted: "The truth of the matter is, I am very tired, but my energy and morale keep me in good health. . . . I need rest. I want to get to know my children and to make them love me, for the sweetest pleasure of life, especially as one grows older, is to be loved." Since he was writing on New Year's Eve, he sent his wife one kiss for the old year, one for the new—which, he reminded her, would be his sixtieth year. By the time Berthier reached Elbing the rheumatic gout obliged him to take to his bed and assign his duties temporarily to the Comte de Monthyon. Obviously concerned about the chief of staff's condition, Prince Eugène (who had taken over command of the army when Murat gave up) mentioned it to the Emperor, who replied from Paris: "Send the Prince de Neufchâtel home since he is in such bad shape."[60] Leaving Posen on 1 February 1813, Berthier reached Paris, tired and ill, on the 9th.

58. Léon Hennert and Emmanuel Martin, eds., *Lettres interceptées par les Russes durant la Campagne de 1812* (Paris, Publications de "La Sabretache," 1913), pp. 121–122, No. 89, and pp. 144–145, No. 106. The intercepted letters (many of them personal letters) reposed in the Russian archives until they appeared in a series of historical documents published by the Russian General Staff, *Otechestvennaia voina 1812 goda* (St. Petersburg, 1901–1914). The Hennert and Martin volume also includes two letters to Mme Visconti from Louis Sopransy (1780–1814), her son by her first marriage. Sopransy, who speaks affectionately of Berthier ("my august protector, a father, to whom I owe everything and to whom I am linked for life by the liveliest gratitude"), was wounded at the Battle of Borodino. He died in 1814 from further wounds received at the Battle of Leipzig in 1813. It is evident from Sopransy's letters to his mother that she lived on the Boulevard des Capucines and that he himself had a pied-à-terre there.

59. Berthier's letters to his wife, December 1812–January 1813, are partially printed in Derrécagaix, *op.cit.*, II, 454–455, 463–464, 469–470, presumably from originals formerly at Grosbois.

60. Napoleon to Eugène-Napoléon, Viceroy of Italy, commander in chief of the Grand Army in Posen, Paris, 29 January 1813, in *Correspondance de Napoléon Ier*, XXIV, 467–468, No. 19524.

After but a few weeks' rest Berthier was back again at his desk in mid-March, preparing for the next campaign.[61] This eventually led to Leipzig, where the French were defeated in the so-called Battle of the Nations (16–19 October 1813). The coalition of powers ranged against Napoleon now included even Bavaria, which had hitherto remained an ally.[62] By the end of the year the invasion of France had begun. Berthier accompanied the Emperor through the series of desperate, and often brilliant, actions that brought him finally to Fontainebleau on 31 March 1814. Paris had capitulated to the Allies the previous day. The month of April was to be a crucial one for Berthier, as it was for so many others and for the nation itself. To judge Berthier fairly, Caulaincourt wrote,

> One must see him as he then was, suffering, tortured by the perturbations (*les agitations*) of the Emperor, who for some time past had been worrying him, even frightening him with wild projects for which, he feared, he might be held responsible. The Emperor's excited state (*état de fièvre morale*) made Berthier a really sick man. The Emperor, in his own unhappy state of mind, made no allowances for Berthier's age, the physical suffering of a weakened man whom he had worn out and whose feelings he often wounded by his present ill-temper. Wounded in turn by Berthier's planning to leave, the Emperor no longer took into account the innumerable proofs of attachment and devotion that Berthier had given him. Such was the situation of the master and of his good and loyal servitor, or rather, as the Emperor often liked to call him, the friend, the faithful companion of so much glory and so many fine memories.[63]

Napoleon's unconditional abdication was signed on 5 April 1814 and made known on the 6th. "Gentlemen," he admonished the officers who were still with him at Fontainebleau on 11 April, "now that I am no longer to remain with you and you have another government, you must unhesitatingly adhere to it and serve it as well as you have served me. I urge you, indeed I command you, to do so. Thus those who wish to go to Paris before I leave are free to go; those who choose to remain [here until I leave] will do well to send in their allegiance."[64] Many (including Marshals Ney, Oudinot, and Jourdan) had not waited for this release. This same day, 11 April, Berthier transmitted to the new government the adherence of the Army: "The Army . . . essentially obedient, has not deliberated; it has manifested its allegiance as soon as its duty has permitted it to do so. Faithful to its oath, it will be faithful to the Prince whom the French nation is recalling to the throne of his ancestors. . . ."[65] At the same time, in a succinct note dated Fontainebleau, 11 April 1814, Berthier addressed his

---

61. Berthier's book of orders and reports to the Emperor for the year 1813 have been published separately: *Registre d'ordres du Maréchal Berthier pendant la campagne de 1813*, "publié par X . . . ," 2 vols. (Paris, Chapelot, 190-); *Rapports du Maréchal Berthier pendant la campagne de 1813*, also edited by "X," 2 vols. (Paris, Chapelot, 1909).

62. 8 October 1813, Treaty of Ried, by which Bavaria withdrew from the Confederation of the Rhine and agreed to join her armies to those of the Allied Pow-

ers. At Hanau on 30 October there was an engagement between Bavarian forces and the retreating French.

63. Caulaincourt, *op.cit.*, III, 352–353, 456.

64. *Mémoires du comte Belliard*, ed. Vinet, 3 vols. (Paris, 1842), III, 192–194; Caulaincourt, *op.cit.*, III, 344. Napoleon's attempted suicide occurred during the night of 11–12 April.

65. Derrécagaix, *op.cit.*, II, 578.

personal adherence to the President of the Senate.[66] Meanwhile, during this period of transition when civil war was barely averted, circumstances had placed him in the position of "interim commander of the Grand Army."[67] He continued to correspond with the Imperial commissioners and to issue orders until 17 April, when he informed the new minister of war, General Dupont, that he would cease to do so inasmuch as there was no longer a commander in chief of the Grand Army and his functions of chief of staff had thus become nonexistent.[68] Characteristically, his last official communication, dated 19 April, concerned the procurement of billets for the Old Guard.

Berthier finally left Fontainebleau on 17 April.[69] If there was any formal exchange of farewells between him and Napoleon, no record of it has survived. It was then expected that the erstwhile Emperor would set out the next day on his journey to Elba, the island kingdom which the Allies had allotted him. As things turned out, he actually left only on the 20th, when the famous scene of the "Farewell to the Guard" was enacted in the Cour du Cheval Blanc of the Château de Fontainebleau: "Be loyal to the new ruler whom France has chosen. Never abandon this dear country that has suffered so long. . . ." Thus, as Napoleon and his suite were traveling southward towards Elba, Berthier was already in Paris. He had previously written to his wife, his "dear Elisabeth," bidding her to leave "gloomy Chambord" and return to their mansion in Paris: "We must be prepared for great changes. . . . Things will turn out all right for us and the future of our children will be ensured."[70] As the senior marshal, the symbol and spokesman of the army's allegiance to the new regime, it was Berthier's lot to head the delegations that welcomed the Bourbons back to "the capital of their ancestors." On 21 April, on behalf of the other marshals and generals then in Paris, he greeted the Duc de Berry at the Barrière de Clichy: "In the name of the whole army I come to express to Your Highness our feelings of love, devotion, and fidelity for the King and his august family. *Vive le Roi! Vivent les Bourbons!*"[71] On 29 April Berthier was among those who met King

66. *Ibid.*, II, 579.

67. *Souvenirs du Maréchal Macdonald, duc de Tarente*, ed. Camille Rousset (Paris, 1892), pp. 268, 287–288. Macdonald, who was one of the three commissioners (with Ney and Marmont) designated by the Emperor to treat with the Allies, explains that it was agreed that "the command of the army should be given to the *Major-Général* [Berthier], as the senior, but with the stipulation that he would carry out only such orders of the Emperor as were agreed upon by the Commissioners and that he would give immediate notice thereof to the corps. He accepted the command, and made the promise."

68. Berthier to General Dupont, Fontainebleau, 17 April 1814, printed in Derrécagaix, *op.cit.*, II, 582–583, from the original in the Archives de la Guerre.

69. He had previously left Fontainebleau on 13 April but returned there again the next day. His last letter from Fontainebleau is dated the 17th. See Derrécagaix,

II, 582–583; Watson, *op.cit.*, p. 226. The frequently repeated reproach that Berthier was the first to abandon the Emperor cannot, therefore, be substantiated. In the Beauharnais Papers (Princeton University Library) there is a letter in Berthier's handwriting dated Fontainebleau, 14 April 1814, addressed to Prince Eugène: "*Mon prince*, it is my painful duty to transmit to you a copy of the treaty of 11 April signed between the Allied governments and the representatives of H. M. Emperor Napoleon. I am also transmitting a copy of the letter [concerning you] that I have received from Prince Metternich. With my highest consideration and my respect,—Prince de Neuchâtel, vice-connétable, Alexandre." The two enclosures are still with Berthier's letter.

70. Berthier to his wife, Fontainebleau, 9 April 1814, in Derrécagaix, II, 571.

71. *Ibid.*, II, 587.

Louis XVIII in Compiègne, where he again delivered the loyal address for the army. On 2 May he rode at the head of the group of officers who preceded the King's carriage into Paris.

Superficially at least, "things were turning out all right" for Berthier and his family. His properties were not sequestered, as they might have been had he chosen to follow Napoleon to Elba. Although he ceased to be Prince de Neuchâtel when the principality was receded to Prussia, he was still Prince de Wagram. On 1 June 1814, when the King's Bodyguard was reconstituted after the pattern of the Old Regime, he was named captain of the fifth company, known as the Wagram Company—thus lending to the Bourbons, as many were quick to point out, the luster of a name that evoked one of the glorious victories of the Empire. Berthier was also made a Peer of France and, in September, Commander of the Royal Order of Saint-Louis. He had received its Cross, his first decoration, in 1788, in recognition of his services in America. These new honors were soon to prove illusory, as rumors from Elba troubled the peace of the new-old regime.

Napoleon was already looking beyond the confines of his island kingdom. Viscount Ebrington, who conversed with him at his palace in Porto Ferrajo on 7–8 December 1814, noted how eager he was for news of France and of the state of opinion there. As the conversation eventually turned to the marshals, the Englishman asked him if he had not been surprised that Berthier was among the first to acclaim the arrival of the King. Napoleon replied with a smile: "I've been told that he's done some silly things like that; but he's not strong-minded. I advanced him more than he deserved because he was useful to me for paper-work. But I assure you that he's not a bad fellow. If he were to see me, he would be the first to express his regrets for what he's done, with tears in his eyes."[72] It has been said and repeated that Napoleon, when preparing his return, attempted to sound out Berthier, who turned a deaf ear to his advances. The supposition is plausible, though it cannot be surely documented.[73] Whatever illusions Napoleon may have cherished, the old partnership with Berthier had come to an end. Napoleon landed at Golfe Juan on 1 March 1815; by the 20th he was in Paris. His return only a year after his departure raised anew the specter of civil war and foreign invasion. Individuals were again torn by conflicting loyalties and faced with the old dilemmas. Whom to follow? Where did duty lie? How could the country's interests best be served? Or, if they had lived long and remembered too much, how could their own interests be served?

With threats of new disorder hanging over the capital, Berthier prudently sent his wife and chil-

72. "Deux Entretiens avec Napoléon à l'Ile d'Elbe," ed. Princesse Bibesco, in *La Revue de Paris*, LXXIV (Jan. 1967), 18–34; reference to Berthier, p. 25. Napoleon's interlocutor, Hugh, Viscount Ebrington (b. 1783), son of Hugh, Count Fortescue, was through his mother a nephew of Lord Grenville. The conversations took place on 7 and 8 December 1814. Ebrington recorded Napoleon's words in French. The *Revue de Paris* publication is based on a manuscript preserved by descendants of Ebrington; his account of the interviews was privately printed for his family in 1823.

73. See, e.g., *Mémoires du Maréchal Marmont, duc de Raguse, de 1792 à 1841*, 9 vols. (Paris, 1857), VII, 67–68. According to Marmont's recollections, Louis XVIII asked him to investigate a report that Berthier had received a letter from the Island of Elba and had concealed the fact from him. Berthier explained to Marmont that he had received a letter from General Bertrand asking for some books and that he had spoken to the King about it. His Majesty then admitted that Berthier had indeed told him of this, and the incident was closed.

dren (four-year-old Alexandre and two-year-old "Lina") to a safe retreat—not, this time, to "gloomy Chambord," but to her parents' residence in Bamberg, where she arrived on 19 March 1815. In Paris that same day, on the eve of Napoleon's arrival, Louis XVIII took flight from the ancestral nest in the Tuileries. As captain in the King's Bodyguard Berthier joined the great Holy Week exodus that took His Majesty and the royal household, his loyal followers, and stragglers, northward to Lille and then into Belgium.[74] Before crossing the frontier numerous royal servitors, including Marshal Macdonald, duc de Tarente, and Marshal Marmont, duc de Raguse, asked the King's permission to remain in France. But "poor Berthier," according to Macdonald, could not honorably ask the same permission, since he was on duty as one of the captains of the Bodyguard: "He told me in great distress that he would resign as soon as they reached Ghent, that he would then go to Bamberg to fetch the Princess and his children, with whom he would return to France. He begged me to inform his family and friends, even through the newspapers. I promised to do so and kept my word. He feared to be considered an émigré."[75] Macdonald indeed kept his word. A letter over his name appeared in the Paris paper *L'Observateur*, 31 March 1815, informing the public that "the Prince de Wagram especially requested me, the 23rd, at Lille, to declare and make known in his name, even publicly, that he would give his resignation to the King upon arriving at Ménin [in Belgium], proceeding immediately thence to Bamberg to fetch the Princess and his children."[76]

Berthier apparently remained with the King as far as Ghent, where he took his leave and hastened on to Bamberg.[77] There on 29 March he rejoined his family in the Neue Residenz, his father-in-law's palace in the Cathedral Square overlooking the city.[78] Did he perhaps recall that in October 1806, when Bavaria was still an ally of the French, he had been here with Napoleon in this same palace on the day the Emperor declared war on Prussia and marched forth toward the battlefield of Jena? Now, in 1815, the Neue Residenz was still a friendly roof, albeit in a hostile land. Soon after his arrival Berthier requested (2 April) from the Bavarian prime minister, the Comte de Montgelas, passports enabling himself and his family to return to France "in order to retire to our estates at Grosbois or Chambord."[79] He renewed the request on 5 April: "My family's fortune requires me to

74. The exodus is graphically portrayed in Louis Aragon's panoramic novel *La Semaine Sainte* (Paris, 1958), translated as *Holy Week*, with an introduction, by Haakon Chevalier (New York, 1961). Berthier frequently appears, notably in a long and perceptive digression beginning "Berthier . . . Berthier . . . Après tout, qu'est-ce qu'on sait de lui?" (Chap. XIII, pp. 424–453; English translation, pp. 382–409).

75. *Souvenirs du Maréchal Macdonald*, p. 379.

76. Macdonald's letter is cited in Arthur Chuquet, "Le Suicide de Berthier," *Etudes d'Histoire*, 3rd ser., p. 178.

77. The last months of Berthier's life are carefully documented by Michael Strich in his *Marschall Alexander Berthier und sein Ende* (Munich, 1908).

78. The Neue Residenz, still preserved as a historic monument with many of its eighteenth-century rooms and furnishings intact, also houses an art museum and the Staatliche Bibliothek. See the illustrated booklet by Erich Bachmann and Walter Tunk, *Neue Residenz Bamberg, Amtlicher Führer* (Munich, Bayerische Verwaltung der Staatlichen Schlösser, Gärten und Seen, 1968). Among the museum pieces is the desk on which Napoleon signed the declaration of war against Prussia in 1806; Bachmann and Tunk, pp. 19, 40; *Baedekers Nordbayern* (1952), p. 97.

79. Strich, *op.cit.*, p. 75, n. 2, where precise references to the Bavarian archives are given.

return immediately to our estates."[80] On the 10th both he and his wife wrote directly to Max Josef the King (her uncle): "We wish to return to France to live in retirement on our estates, where I wish to concern myself only with my family. There, faithful to my oaths, I shall form wishes for my country (*je ferai des voeux pour mon pays*). I am waiting for the passport that I have requested from your minister. . . ."[81] The reply, dated 13 April, finally came from Montgelas (who had previously consulted the powers in Vienna through the Bavarian ambassador Von Rechberg): "I greatly regret I cannot deliver to you the passports you have requested; the Allied Powers have invited me to advise you not to return to France; I beg you therefore to remain with the Duke your father-in-law until circumstances permit you to return to your country."[82]

Berthier thus found himself a virtual prisoner in Bamberg. Furthermore, he was subjected to secret surveillance by the Bavarian police, who instructed their deputy in Bamberg, one Schauer, never to lose sight of the Prince de Wagram.[83] Schauer had no difficulty in buying the cooperation of the servants in the ducal household. When the Princess attempted on 30 April to set out for France alone, accompanied only by two servants and her children, she was promptly turned back on the pretext that her passport had not been countersigned by the Allied military authorities. As the weeks went by, it was remarked that Berthier was taciturn and withdrawn, plunged in melancholy, often complaining of great weariness. Dr. Ziegler, who attended him, later said that he suffered from gastric complaints and intense gouty pains. Berthier himself confessed, when resigning his commission in Louis XVIII's Bodyguard (24 April): "The state of my health forces me to give up all military or civil duties. . . . I am sad, my dear Duc, I am suffering from the gout. Moral afflictions always aggravate this illness. I am old, very tired, and unfit for service. . . ."[84]

Soon after the middle of May Russian troops began to pass through Bamberg on their way to join the Allied offensive against Napoleon's reassembled army. General Barclay de Tolly established his headquarters in the Schloss Seehof a few miles from town. General Sacken's corps was encamped in the immediate vicinity. It was widely reported that Berthier met his recent adversary at his father-in-law's table on 31 May.[85] An ironic remark by Sacken, congratulating him on having remained

80. Strich, p. 76, n. 3.
81. Strich, p. 77, n. 5.
82. Strich, p. 77, n. 6. Montgelas concludes his letter with assurances of his continuing personal esteem: "Adieu, mon cher Prince, soyez toujours bien persuadé des anciens sentiments que je vous conserverai toujours." In view of Berthier's close relationship to the Bavarian royal family, the refusal of the passport, dictated by Bavaria's reversal of alliances, must have been a painful duty indeed. Cf. above, nn. 46, 62.
83. Strich (p. 8off.) quotes substantial excerpts from Schauer's reports, which, among other things, reveal the exaggerated and half-comic zeal of a petty official suddenly entrusted with an assignment of high import.

84. Berthier's correspondence concerning his resignation from the King's Bodyguard, "found among his papers after his death," is preserved in the Bavarian archives. It includes the letter to General Clarke, duc de Feltre (Louis XVIII's minister of war), cited here, as well as a personal letter from Louis XVIII to Berthier (Ghent, 12 May 1815) and Berthier's reply (Bamberg, 22 May 1815) submitting his definitive resignation. See Strich, pp. 85–86.
85. Mentioned, for example, in report from Legation Secretary von Weissenberg to Metternich, Würzburg, 7 June 1815; cited by Strich, pp. 96–97, from the original in the Austrian archives.

loyal to his king but expressing surprise at finding him in Bamberg, left Berthier at a loss for words and unable to regain his composure.

On 1 June the Prince de Wagram was in his wife's room; between noon and one o'clock he went into his children's sitting-room on the top floor of the Residenz, inquired about the behavior of the Prince [his son] and the Princess [his daughter] who were with their governess [Mlle] Gallien, complained to the latter that he was not well, that his tongue was still yellowish, paced the room lost in thought, bit his nails, looked out the window at the Russian troops filing past, remarked that the procession was endless, sighed "Poor France, what will become of you and I am here," left the window, asked Gallien when she would drive out with the children, since the carriage was waiting for them. Upon Gallien's reply that she could leave only after the Prince had left, the Prince retired into the bedroom and went into the closet. Gallien heard the opening of the door to the closet where the night-stool was, heard a rumbling noise in the closet, thought that the Prince might be indisposed, went into the bedroom, found the Prince no longer there and noticed only that the fallen stool, between the commode and the window, was still shaking. At the moment when Gallien heard the noise of the falling stool the unfortunate plunge from the window happened.[86]

That same day at about a quarter to two Anselm von Feuerbach, a prominent resident of Bamberg, was walking up the hill from the lower town to his house in the Cathedral Square.[87] Soldiers and bystanders filled the streets. From time to time a Cossack galloped by; one of them knocked over a child. As he approached the square Feuerbach met up with an excited crowd pouring out from the far side of the ducal residence. The name "Berthier" caught his ear. "Something terrible has happened," a woman told him, "Prince Berthier jumped out of a castle window, only a quarter of an hour ago, and he's still there!" Then, from behind the Residenz came four police carrying a litter on which lay a shattered body hastily covered with a sheet. It was borne across the square to the chapel next door to Feuerbach's house. At three o'clock he was allowed to go inside the chapel. The police on guard drew aside the stained sheet. Contemplating the gruesome spectacle, Feuerbach noted that

86. Summary of testimony of Mlle Gallien at inquest, Königlich Bamberger Appellationsgericht, 5 June 1815; printed by Strich, pp. 109–110, from original in the Bavarian archives. A contemporary engraving by J. Fleischmann depicts Berthier's death plunge; see our illustration and note thereto. Floor plans and photographs of the Neue Residenz are in Bachmann and Tunk, *op.cit.*, pp. 19, 44, 67 ("Grundriss des I. und II. Obergeschosses"), and Plate 8 (aerial view of Neue Residenz and Domplatz).

87. Paul Johann Anselm Feuerbach (1775–1833), "Tod der Herzog von Wagram, Marschall Berthier, am 1. Juni des Jahren 1815," in Gustav Radbruch,

Paul Johann Anselm Feuerbach, Ein Juristenleben (Vienna, 1934; reprinted, Göttingen, 1957), pp. 115–119; French translation by Mildred King, with prefatory note by Radbruch, in *Revue des Etudes Napoléoniennes*, XXVᵉ année, Tome XLII (June 1936), 340–343. The distinguished jurist, father of the philosopher Ludwig Feuerbach, was a resident of Bamberg at the time of Berthier's death; he had earlier adapted the Napoleonic Code for the use of the Kingdom of Bavaria but had more recently espoused the cause of the Allies against Napoleon. His account of Berthier's death was first published by Radbruch from the manuscript preserved among Feuerbach's papers.

the Prince was wearing a dark-green civilian coat. In the lapel was "the red and blue ribbon of some order."

On 5 June Berthier's coffin lay in state in the cathedral. From there a military escort, including Bavarians and Russians, accompanied it to Duke Ludwig Wilhelm's castle at Banz in the Main valley, some fifteen miles northeast of Bamberg. Many years later, in 1884, Berthier's remains, with those of his wife, were transferred to their final resting place in the royal castle at Tegernsee in the Bavarian Alps. In Bamberg a tablet recalls the spot where he fell to his death. In Paris his name is carved on the inner wall of the Arc de Triomphe with those of the other generals of the Revolution and Empire.

Immediately following Berthier's death an official inquest was begun by the Bamberger Appellationsgericht presided over by Freiherr von Seckendorf. Numerous witnesses—including Mlle Gallien, the last to see Berthier alive—were heard, and all pertinent information bearing on the case was formally recorded. The report submitted to King Maximilian Josef on 27 June presented the facts but drew no conclusion. The word "suicide" was not pronounced. Indeed, the Bavarian government, through a face-saving gesture of family solidarity, henceforth maintained that the plunge from the window was "accidental." Others who were familiar with the circumstances were less cautious. Baron von Strampfer, head of the Prussian legation in Munich, for example, in a confidential report to Hardenberg dated 13 June 1815 did not hesitate to use the words "der vorsätzliche Tod des Marschalls Berthier"—the intentional death of Marshal Berthier.[88] Meanwhile, cloak-and-dagger stories of revenge and masked men were bruited about and circulated in the newspapers of the day. These, too, like the official "accident" version, have been endlessly repeated and have even found their way into twentieth-century writings.

When Berthier died in Bamberg on 1 June 1815, Napoleon's Hundred Days were already running out. His army met its final defeat at Waterloo on 18 June, and the Emperor abdicated for the second time on the 22nd; in October he began his exile on the Island of St. Helena. Louis XVIII followed the Allied armies back into Paris and signed a second (and harsher) Treaty of Paris in November, while the Congress of Vienna was pursuing its task of reorganizing Europe.

In August the Princesse de Wagram, Berthier's widow, then thirty-one, had finally been granted a passport to return with her children to France.[89] In February 1816 a third child, Berthier's posthumous daughter, was born. The Princesse de Wagram (who lived until about 1849) eventually sold the Paris mansion on the Boulevard des Capucines as well as the Chambord estate but retained Grosbois for herself and her descendants. The children all married well: Caroline-Joséphine in 1832 became the Comtesse d'Hautpoul; Marie-Alexandrine in 1834, the Duchesse de Plaisance. Napoléon-Louis-Alexandre, second Prince de Wagram, was married in 1831 to Zénaïde Clary, a niece of the Queen of Sweden. The name and the title continued for two more generations. Berthier's great-grand-

88. Strich, *op.cit.*, p. 112, n. 60, citing original in the Prussian archives.

89. *Ibid.*, p. 93.

son Alexandre (born 20 July 1883), the fourth and last Prince de Wagram, served in World War I as a captain in the Sixty-sixth Battalion of light infantry. He was killed in action near Laon in May 1918 while leading his company against the enemy in the same region where his illustrious ancestor had fought his last campaign a century earlier.

Napoleon is supposed to have exclaimed at Waterloo, when waiting in vain for Grouchy's corps to arrive: "If Berthier were here, my orders would have been carried out, and I should have escaped this misfortune!"[90] Although the incident is probably apocryphal, Napoleon inevitably recalled his old chief of staff when he was refighting his battles during his exile at St. Helena. His references to Berthier as recorded by Las Cases and others were often unkind, sometimes spiteful, betraying the wounded vanity of a jilted lover. Berthier was "weak," "lacking character," "a veritable gosling whom I made into a sort of eagle."[91] But again, in a more kindly mood, when describing Berthier's admirable precision and promptness in transmitting his orders, Napoleon generously admitted that Berthier's special talents had been most precious to him: "No other man could have replaced him."[92]

Berthier has been diversely judged by later generations of Frenchmen. It has always been difficult for them to see the man in his own terms. Those whose thinking is colored by the Napoleonic legend naturally take their cues from the St. Helena "Memorial," their gospel. To the aristocrats, the men of the old nobility, Berthier, in spite of his early and late services to the Bourbons, remains something of a parvenu. To the Jacobin-Republicans, he is both a Bourbon and a Bonaparte. Berthier did not live to write his own memoirs. Others who had known him well tried to set the record straight: Caulaincourt, Denniée, Lejeune, among others, and Mathieu Dumas, his old companion in America, who said that Berthier's "ardent love of his country" was the *primum mobile*, the chief motivating force, of his whole life.[93] Thousands of examples of Berthier's "paper-work" have survived, but relatively few personal writings. Among the latter is the journal of his American campaigns, written when he was a young man in his twenties, before he became the shadow of Napoleon. In later life he did not often put aside the mask. His aide Lejeune recalled one such occasion. It was in 1811. Lejeune, who had just returned from an arduous mission to Spain and imprisonment in England, was with Berthier at Saint-Cloud for an interview with the Emperor:

> General Prince Berthier was good enough to drive me back to Paris, and the next day I went with him to join a hunting party at Grosbois. . . . This journey of six or seven leagues with the Prince was of deep interest to me, for I really got to know something of the General's kind heart,

90. Lejeune, *op.cit.*, II, 142. The proverbial words, repeated in many variant versions, probably date from Napoleon's reminiscent conversations at St. Helena, rather than from the actual day of the battle. See, e.g., the entry for 25 February 1817 in General Gourgaud's *Journal de Sainte-Hélène*, tr. S. Gillard (London, 1932), pp. 142–143.

91. Comte Emmanuel de Las Cases (1766–1842), *Mémorial de Sainte-Hélène*, ed. Gérard Walter, 2 vols. (Paris, Gallimard, Bibliothèque de La Pléiade, 1956), I, 452. The *Mémorial* was first published in 1823. The "gosling" epithet is picked up in Tolstoy's *War and Peace*, Part IX, Chap. 24.

92. Las Cases, I, 207.

93. Mathieu Dumas, "Notice sur le Maréchal Berthier," cited in Derrécagaix, *op.cit.*, II, 606.

which I should perhaps never otherwise have done, for he made a point of always appearing grave and severe with his young officers. He looked at me again and again with a happy, almost eager expression of affection, like a father who had regained a beloved son. He maintained, however, the dignified silence of a commander, breaking it now and then with an eager question, showing how great was his interest in what I was saying, and how much he felt for the sufferings I had endured. . . . Prince Berthier's career had really been more brilliant than that of any of the officers immediately surrounding our Caesar, but he never assumed any special distinction, for he was always simple, modest, polite, and natural in his manner. He was never known to utter a word that could wound the self-respect of his subalterns, but, on the contrary, he tried to the utmost of his power to increase the dignity of their position. . . . Few men have been more fortunate throughout their military careers than Prince Berthier. I often heard him congratulate himself on having served France in all four quarters of the globe. He made his debut in the War of Independence in America and returned home with very pleasant memories, for he became the personal friend of Rochambeau and Lafayette, under whom he served with the French contingent. He told me that, of all the decorations he had received during his successful career, he had been most flattered at getting the little eagle of the Order of the Cincinnati.[94]

94. Lejeune, *op.cit.*, II, 138–141.

Berthier's American journal, from which the following translation has been made, was preserved among his papers at Grosbois until the 1930's. The manuscript, which is now in the Princeton University Library, consists of a series of four "cahiers" made up from sheets of paper measuring approximately 31.5 x 41 cm., folded and gathered to make pages of 31.5 x 20.5 cm. The paper is of Dutch manufacture with the "Pro Patria" watermark of J. Kool. The first cahier, marked "No. 1, 1780 et 1781" and entitled "Journal de M. Berthier du 10 mai 1780 au 8 mars 1781," has 38 pages, the last being blank. Cahier "No. 2, 1781," 36 pages (last ten blank), continues the journal from 8 March to 26 August 1781. There is no journal for the interval between August 1781 and December 1782. The next cahier, marked "No. 1, 1782 et 1783," with the pencilled notation "Campagnes de mer," consists of 40 pages (last three blank) and covers the period from December 1782 through 13 March 1783. The last cahier in the series, marked "No. 2, 1783," continues the journal through 19 April 1783, when it stops abruptly. This final cahier has 34 pages, the last eighteen of which are blank. The manuscript of the journal is written throughout in Berthier's handwriting, examples of which are shown on the specimen pages reproduced hereafter. Interlinear and marginal corrections have been incorporated into the text of our translation. The topical headings in the margins, probably added at a later date and in another hand, have been omitted. No other manuscript of Berthier's journal has been found by the Editors.

Part 1

LAND CAMPAIGNS
10 MAY 1780–26 AUGUST 1781

Letter to a friend in the form of a journal
kept since my departure from France[1]

Brest, 10 May 1780

My dear Chevalier,

I obediently begin my first letter to you by recounting the initial adventures of my campaign. You will find in it only a poor account, but an accurate one.

April I was busy with a task for the Dépôt de la Guerre that I wished to complete before entering upon a campaign.[2] I had spent the whole winter at this work, which kept me on horseback from morning till night in all kinds of weather. This had the double advantage of pleasing His Majesty and hardening me for the fatigues of war. I heard talk of an expedition to America under the command of the Comte de Rochambeau. My taste for a profession of which I had seen only the reflection led me to make all possible efforts to join it, but the keen competition, plus my absence, rendered all my efforts futile.

Even my parents, through affection, believed my apparent willingness sufficient and, since I had been commissioned a captain of dragoons three years ago[3] at

1. The "friend" has not been identified. In writing up his journal as a series of letters Berthier was probably simply following a common literary convention.

2. The Dépôt de la Guerre was the branch of the Ministry of War responsible for collecting and preserving records, including maps; in this latter respect it might be described as the "Army Map Service." Berthier's father, Jean-Baptiste Berthier (1721–1804), was head of this service as well as the "Gouverneur," or resident director, of the Hôtel de la Guerre, the ministry building in Versailles that he had designed and where the Dépôt was housed. (See illustration.) The "task" in which Louis-Alexandre Berthier was engaged during the winter and spring of 1780 was, as explained below (p. 222), "the inspection" or field verification of the "Carte des Chasses du Roi." This famous map of the royal hunting preserves, covering an area within a 14-league radius of Versailles, was initiated by Berthier père in 1764. Although not strictly a military map, it nevertheless gave peacetime employment to the army's topographical engineers (*ingénieurs géographes des camps et armées du Roi*) over a long period and was one of Jean-Baptiste Berthier's claims to royal favor. Surveys were still being accumulated and perfected in 1780, but the completed version of the map, in 12 sheets engraved by Dondan, Tardieu l'aîné, and Boudet, was not issued until 1807, three years after its initiator's death. At the time of its publication, when it was retitled "Carte Topographique des Environs de Versailles, dite des

Chasses Impériales," Louis-Alexandre Berthier was Napoleon's minister of war. The engraved title-sheet unites the names of father and son, specifying that the surveys were made by the topographical engineers "commanded by the late Col. Berthier, their Chief," and the map published by order of the Emperor "during the ministry of S.A.S.M. le Maréchal Alexandre Berthier, Prince de Neuchâtel, Grand Veneur. . . ." The original manuscript "minutes" for the "Carte des Chasses" are preserved for the most part in the archives of the Service Historique de l'Armée at Vincennes. The Sotheby sale catalogue (1 March 1938), Lot 90 ("Papers of Jean-Baptiste Berthier"), mentions papers relating to "the surveying of the 'Chasses du Roy,' and the preparation of the maps, with engravers' proofs, accounts of expenses incurred by the surveyors, etc., 1768, etc." The plates for the engraved map have survived; restrikes from them are still available at the Institut Géographique National in Paris. Charles Hirschauer, "Jean-Baptist Berthier et la décoration de l'Hôtel de la Guerre et des Affaires Etrangères," "La Jeunesse et les débuts militaires d'Alexandre Berthier," *Revue de l'Histoire de Versailles et de Seine-et-Oise*, XXXII, No. 2 (April–June, 1930), 137-157, 158-174; René Pichard du Page, *La Bibliothèque de Versailles et le Musée Lambinet* (Paris, 1935). See also Vol. II, Editors' Introduction to "Maps and Views."

3. According to Berthier's service record, he was commissioned captain of dragoons 2 June 1777. He was born

the age of twenty-four, were quite content with my progress; however, I had always considered unearned rank humiliating, and must admit I blush to find serving under me an old lieutenant, instead of one of my ilk, covered with scars from gallant actions performed so long ago they are forgotten.

If I have enjoyed the King's favors, it was in hopes that they would give me more opportunity to fulfill my obligations to him, and I consider them as only a loan granted me which, when occasion arises, I shall do my utmost to repay.

I undertook to write a friend [M. d'Anselme], who is lieutenant colonel of the Soissonnais Regiment, asking him to deliver a letter to the Comte de Saint-Maîme on the latter's arrival from Gibraltar, requesting that he enlist me in his regiment as a chasseur for the American campaign. My friend replied that the Comte de Saint-Maîme had not yet arrived, that my zeal was admirable, but that by the time I received his letter the squadron would doubtless have left, since the whole army had already embarked and was waiting in harbor for a favorable breeze in order to get under way.

I was in despair at not being able to join the expedition when one of my comrades, who had served with me in the North,[4] came to see me and revived my hopes. He was aide-de-camp to M. de Choisy and was going to Brest to leave with the Second Division; I made him promise that, if the First had departed, he would inform me what regiments were left to come with the Second Division and would even arrange with one of the colonels a passage for me as a common chasseur.

While awaiting his reply I was kept extremely busy completing my inspection of the map of the royal hunting preserves ("Carte des Chasses du Roi") which occupied me up to 20 April.[5]

Several days after my arrival at Versailles I received a letter from the Comte de Saint-Maîme, written on his return from Gibraltar:

> I found the army embarked and kept in harbor by contrary winds. Instead of the position of chasseur, I can offer you a commission of captain attached to the regiment and a sublieutenancy for one of your young relatives or friends. My letter will serve as your credentials at the Ministry. Come at once, and if we have already left, you will come with the Second Division to join the regiment.[6]

I confess that no letter ever gave me more pleasure. I went to read it to my brother,[7] whose sole response was to embrace me, as he was only too happy to trade the inactive role of a captain attached to the dragoons for that of an infantry subaltern in combat. In thirty-six hours our orders were dispatched and our affairs put in order; with our trunks packed, we

---

at Versailles 20 November 1753 and was thus twenty-six when he began writing this journal. Archives de la Guerre, dossier of L.-A. Berthier, pièces 2, 17, 39.

4. Berthier had been at Valenciennes in 1777, fulfilling the functions of assistant quartermaster-general in maneuvers commanded by the Comte de Maillebois. Archives de la Guerre, Berthier dossier, pièce 39.

5. See n. 2, and map, Vol. II, No. 10.

6. Saint-Maîme's letter, of which Berthier here gives only a summary, is preserved in the Archives de la Guerre, Berthier dossier, pièce 24. It is dated 21 April 1780, "à bord du Neptune dans la rade de Brest," and is expressed in most cordial and friendly terms. By way of postscript Saint-Maîme adds: "The talk of the fleet is that we are bound for 'Kebecq.' Try to bring along a good map. . . ." Filed with the letter is Saint-Maîme's request, approved by Montbarey, minister of war, 26 April 1780, by which [Louis-Alexandre] Berthier, captain attached to the Second Regiment of *chasseurs à cheval*, is attached to the Sois-

sonnais Regiment with the same rank and with pay of 1,200 *livres*, and [Charles] Berthier de Berluis, captain attached to the Corps de Dragons, is attached to the Soissonnais Regiment with the rank of sublieutenant and pay of 600 *livres*. A marginal note states that on the same day each of them received an extra "gratification" of 600 *livres*. Montbarey's letter to Berthier, same date, informing him of his new assignment, is also in the file.

7. Charles-Louis-Jean Berthier de Berluis (1759-1783), who was to lose his life in America in circumstances described hereafter, was twenty-one years old at this time, five years younger than his brother Louis-Alexandre. There were two still younger brothers: César-Gabriel (1765-1819) and Victor-Léopold (1770-1807), neither of whom served in America. Balch (II, 53) erroneously includes César-Gabriel in his list of officers who took part in the American war, but omits mention of Charles-Louis. See Editors' Introduction to the present journal.

took leave of the ministers and set off at a gallop, our only luggage being a small portmanteau containing the bare necessities.

29 April We made good time day and night as far as Noyal, where the bad roads began and continued as far as Landerneau. These really deserve some attention from the government. It is really surprising to find the communications so badly maintained, and indeed the worst in the realm, in a province where travel is so heavy because of the location of the principal naval port of France. A project no less important is the policing of the post-houses whose masters confine themselves to taking money from travelers without bothering to procure the prescribed number of horses. The result is that the few they have are extremely poor. Added to their thievery, their dilatoriness in post-service and the incivility of their postillions expose every honest man to quarrels that are as unseemly as they are disturbing to the public peace.

Leaving on 29 April, it was only after turning twenty somersaults that we reached Brest thoroughly exhausted at six o'clock on the morning of 2 May.

2 May Going down into the town I saw with despair the squadron proceeding under sail out through the channel. I rushed to the house of M. Hector, the commandant, to show him my embarkation orders. He was out in the harbor. I jumped forthwith into a boat with my valise, promising 2 *louis* to the boatman if he found M. Hector for me in the harbor, and caught up with some vessel lagging behind the fleet.

I finally found the commandant and handed him my orders. Since nothing was left in the harbor but a lugger commanded by M. de Maulevrier,[8] he took me to it, charging that officer to put me aboard M. de Ternay's flagship and to inform him verbally of the minister's orders in regard to us. He wished us bon voyage, while commiserating with us for having so little luggage to take aboard. We promptly set sail, and after a good shaking-up, and having gone out through the Race (le Raz), we caught up with M. de Ternay at six that evening. A boat was lowered, and once we were aboard the *Duc de Bourgogne* M. de Maulevrier relayed the orders for our embarkation that M. Hector had received. The Admiral received us very coldly, saying that orders were not issued verbally, that he had too many people aboard his squadron already, and that he would send us back to France in the frigate *Bellone*. Although I delivered my official orders to the Comte de Rochambeau, calling attention to the fact that I was a replacement in the regiment, and although I offered to travel as a seaman, nothing could persuade M. de Ternay to keep us. He summoned the *Bellone* and sent us on board to return to France. I objected and, since his tone was not very courteous, turned my back on him and asked the Comte de Rochambeau for orders to sail with the Second Division, which he very kindly issued.[9]

We were the victims of the Admiral's stubbornness and of the pleasure he took in making M. de Rochambeau feel that on board ship the latter was his subordinate. The *Bellone*'s boat arrived and took us on board. The captain received us very kindly and showed us many courtesies, but our travel-weariness, the change of vessels, and our disagreeable situation

8. Maulevrier commanded the lugger, or cutter, *Guêpe* of 16 guns. Vicomte de Rochambeau, p. 196. For a list of ships comprising Ternay's fleet, see Verger's journal, n. 1. Maulevrier was Edouard-Charles-Victurnien Colbert, comte de Maulevrier (1758–1820); see "Checklist of Journals," *s.v.* Colbert.

9. Rochambeau reported the incident to Montbarey, the minister of war, as follows: "On board the Duc de Bourgogne, 3 May 1780. Sir, we have had a fine departure and are sailing with the best northeast wind, with no accidents, while crossing the Bay of Biscay in as beautiful weather as we could wish for. Messrs. Berthier came to join us yesterday in the rear-division cutter; they delivered your letters to us, and those from M. de Sartine, just after we had cleared the [Pointe du] Raz. They joined

us in linen jackets and breeches (*en veste et culotte de toile*), offering to come with us—as sailors. The Chevalier de Ternay had no place to assign them on his ship or on any other in his fleet; he put them on board the *Bellone*, which is returning this evening to bring news of us, and I am writing to the Comte de Wittgenstein to give them a passage with the Second Division. These poor boys are deserving and are in despair, but the Chevalier de Ternay really doesn't know where to stow them (*Les pauvres jeunes gens sont intéressants et au désespoir, mais le Chevalier de Ternay ne sait véritablement pas où les fourrer*) . . ." Archives de la Guerre, A[1] 3733, fol. 48. Doniol (v, 339) prints only the first sentence of this letter.

made us indifferent to all but honor. We wanted nothing more than to sleep. They made up a bed for us in the powder magazine, where the bad odor made me seasick for almost an hour. The next day I felt wonderfully well, and the frigate was busily engaged in chasing every sail it sighted until the 6th.

6 May The Admiral ordered our frigate to return to Brest and to inform the minister of the squadron's position at the time she left it. We were then about 120 leagues out in the Bay of Biscay. I had kept up my hopes until this moment, but nobody mentioned us and the frigate tacked about and soon lost sight of the squadron.

It was feared that the English, who had surely had news of the army's departure, had sent a squadron in pursuit. This fear kept us on our guard. Things were very quiet until the night of 7–8 May. I was sleeping peacefully when at midnight some sailors came to turn me out in order to fetch some powder from the magazine. The decks were cleared for action, since a very large vessel, previously hidden in a thick fog, had suddenly loomed abeam, a pistol-shot away. We were not the last on deck, for we were delighted at a chance to make up for being sent back; however, our joy was short-lived. The vessel was Dutch, so we wished her good night and bon voyage.

8 May After dinner next day, when we were 2 leagues from the Race (le Raz), we saw a frigate approaching. The nearer she came, the more convinced the officers were that she was English. She was painted in an unrecognizable fashion. There had never been any ship resembling her at Brest, so the decks were cleared for action. Recognition signals were mismade and misread. Since there seemed to be no further doubt, I requested a combat station. The captain posted me at his side, and in case of a boarding I was armed with a sword, two pistols in my belt, and a long musket.

When we came within one and a half cannon-shots of her, we fired a shot under our true colors; she replied by firing a shot under hers, which proved to be French also. We recommended the recognition signals, and there was no longer any doubt that she was a French ship. We approached cautiously within earshot and spoke her; she was the *Perle*, which had just

been repainted and had left Brest bound for Lorient. With my formidable armament I was left swearing at the eternal peace that pursued me.

9 May We anchored in the harbor of Brest that evening and went ashore on the 9th. Our astonished friends took us for ghosts, and those who find a reason for everything thought we were spies smuggled into the fleet whom M. de Ternay had unmasked and sent back to the minister. We were received by all the generals and admirals with enough interest to relieve the unpleasantness of our situation. They praised our conduct, while pitying us and blaming M. de Ternay. This adventure made us famous throughout Brest, where we were the chief topic of conversation for several days.

I rented lodgings and turned my thoughts to procuring suitable equipment for a second embarkation with the Second Division.

I have written M. de Sartine [minister of marine] describing in detail my reception by the Admiral—perhaps too frankly, but this is a family failing that I believe is incurable. Adieu, my dear Chevalier, I do not believe the proverb that says that misfortunes always come in pairs, since I have an opportunity to assure you of my warm friendship.

❧

[*Begun*] *on board the* Auguste *in the harbor of Brest and Bertheaume, 25 June 1780.*

I shall tell you nothing, my dear Chevalier, of the city and port of Brest,[10] which are well enough known, but shall confine myself to doing justice to the Bretons, whose customs are two hundred years behind ours, especially the city folk who know nothing but drunkenness and laziness, insolence and brutality. I assure you that I am not being facetious.

I received a letter from M. de Sartine in reply to mine about my reception by M. de Ternay, and it could not be more courteous. The minister promises to issue me orders permitting me to join the army at the earliest opportunity.

29 May Nothing interesting happened until today when the long-desired convoy arrived from Bordeaux to supply us with transports. Several ships were chosen

10. See Vol. II, views and map of Brest, Nos. 1–2 and 3.

and loaded with provisions for M. de Guichen's squadron in the Islands.

M. de Choisy, who had remained in Brest to leave with the Second Division, suggested to me that there was a chance of going to Martinique, but without any assurance that I would be able to join the army. Since the proposition came from him, I decided to accept, being convinced that he knew for certain that it would not be prudent to wait for the Second Division.[11] The minister had offered him, as well as my brother and me, the opportunity to join a convoy departing for Martinique and had provided him with orders to requisition the first frigate he found there to take us to the army of the Comte de Rochambeau, wherever it might be.

14 June M. de Choisy boarded the King's frigate *Cybèle*, which was escorting the convoy of 30 sail bound for M. de Guichen's fleet in the Islands. M. Hector put us aboard the *Auguste*, a vessel of 500 tons, where we are very comfortable. I installed myself here on the 14th and assure you that I shall not leave. Much luggage destined for Rochambeau's army has been put aboard the convoy.[12]

18 June The winds kept us in harbor until the 25th. On the 18th the King's frigates *Cybèle* and *Gloire* returned from a cruise, having sighted an English squadron of 25 warships off Ushant.

25 June At five in the morning in a northeasterly wind 150 sail left the harbor for Bordeaux, escorted by the frigates *Belle-Poule* and *Cybèle*. The *Andromaque* also set sail at five that afternoon for Saint-Domingue. Finally our turn came. The long-desired signal to get under way was made, and the frigate *Cybèle* and the 30 merchant ships went to anchor for the night in the harbor of Bertheaume, where we await further orders.

That morning two artillery officers and a Capuchin assigned as chaplain to the Soissonnais Regiment came aboard the *Auguste*. The latter returned to shore on some business and, by truly divine grace, rid us of his mangy presence, since he did not reappear.

26 June Today at six in the morning we set sail for Martinique, even though at the moment they are signaling that the English are off Ushant. I am putting this letter aboard a navy transport returning to Brest. Adieu, my dear Chevalier. I hope you will not receive any more news from me until I reach the New World.

❧

Saint-Pierre de la Martinique, 10 August 1780

Now you must have patience, my dear friend, for this letter will be long and perhaps very boring. You can easily remedy this by not finishing it.

Our vessel, the *Auguste*, armed with sixteen 8-pounders, was designated second in command and was to repeat the signals. The Baron de Clugny, commander of the frigate, granted us this distinction.

26 June We went out through the Race two hours after dinner without sighting a single sail.

8 July The King's ship *Actif* joined us and accompanied us until 8 July, when she set her course for Cadiz.

Until the 16th our crossing offered nothing to pique our curiosity; we had favorable winds so light that we

---

11. When it became evident that sufficient transports could not be assembled in time, Rochambeau reluctantly agreed to leave in France, for a later convoy, a part of the troops assembled near Brest. This "Second Division," commanded by the Comte de Wittgenstein, included the Neustrie and Anhalt regiments, "a third of the artillery," and "a third of the Lauzun Legion." This left approximately 5,000 men for the "First Division" that sailed with Ternay's fleet. Rochambeau to Montbarey, Brest, 27 March 1780, in Doniol, v, 331–332. This Second Division never did sail for America, though it figured prominently in the plans discussed by Rochambeau and Washington during the autumn and winter of 1780–1781. Only in early May 1781, with the arrival of dispatches from Versailles, did Rochambeau learn of the official decision not to send the Second Division. Ségur to Rochambeau, Versailles, 9 March 1781, in Doniol, v, 466–469. The regiments under the Marquis de Saint-Simon transported by de Grasse's fleet in August 1781 to join Rochambeau at Yorktown eventually brought the French forces more nearly up to the strength that Rochambeau deemed necessary for a decisive blow at the enemy.

12. See p. 232, where Berthier mentions supervising the transfer of this luggage from the transports to a ship bound for Rhode Island. Chastellux later complained: "the little room left to officers, and even to general officers, for transporting their effects, at the time of our departure from Europe, did not allow me to take with me any other books than those I needed for political and military knowledge of the continent where I was going to wage war." Chastellux (4), II, 457.

went twice a week to dine on board the frigate. The Baron de Clugny overwhelmed us with kindness and with fresh provisions, so that we were even better off than M. de Choisy, since we had the whole of the large council chamber to ourselves and were masters on board our ship. Our captain, a little Gascon, was most intelligent and most courteous and, what is more, had some excellent Bordeaux wine.

On the morning of the 16th we were at 26° 25′ latitude and 28° 43′ longitude; we were fishing and caught a *tazard*.[13] This fish was 4 feet 8 inches long, of a bluish color, its belly silver, and its jaws armed with 132 very sharp teeth that overlapped. You will see this detail in the accompanying drawings A and B.[14] We had it for dinner, despite the opinion of several writers that it drives those who eat it mad. Its flesh is white, not very firm, and has a nutty flavor. We ate it for two days without losing our minds. When cut crosswise its flesh forms six ovals—and the fibres and veins and two kinds of heart, one red, one white, appear as in the cross-section drawing C.

Several flying fish have been caught on our deck as they fell while fleeing from the dorado. They collided with the rigging when trying to fly over us. These fish begin to appear at 27° of latitude, where one encounters the trade winds (winds that blow constantly from northeast to southwest towards the equator). The largest flying fish I saw was between 8 and 10 inches long; its back was grey and blue, its belly silver and lilac, and the part under the eyes was yellow, as in drawing D.[15] Its wings, like the fins of our fish, could be spread and folded at will. These fish fly from 60 to 80 yards, rising 15 to 20 feet, which represents the time it takes for their wings to dry, as they serve no purpose when no longer wet; for this reason they plunge back into the sea before commencing another flight. They rise and fly in schools of several hundred, pursued by the dorado or bonita that feed upon them. Their flesh is quite delicate and they are very good to eat.

We reached the Tropic of Cancer where, when one crosses it for the first time, it is the custom to be baptized by Old Man Tropic. This is a means of paying the sailor his due, and the singular and picturesque form of this ceremony deserves at least one reading.

17 July On the eve of our crossing the Tropic of Cancer, Old Man Tropic sent a courier with a letter to warn the ship's captain to prepare for baptism those who had not entered his realm before.

Old Man Tropic's Letter to the Captain of the Ship
Sir,

The honor of making your acquaintance as you sail into my kingdom prompted me to find out about you, and only two weeks ago was I able to obtain news of you from the *Garonne* and the *Princesse d'Hénin*, which passed through my kingdom, giving me much satisfaction from their merrymaking as well as their good conduct. I am sending my courier to announce my visit. I shall visit you tomorrow or the next day, I cannot be sure which, because there is a King's frigate in the fleet; since you are second in command, you will receive the second visit. I expect to be pleased with you as usual, and with all these gentlemen who are especially courageous and who are going to fight for the honor of the French crown. You have on board M. ——— who has entered my kingdom as a plunderer. Do not be surprised if I take my revenge on him. To appease me he must take advantage of the opportunity awaiting him, for be assured that my soldiers will spare no one who is not willing to render me due satisfaction. Those to be baptized include the vessel, the longboat, and the pinnace, as well as Messrs. Berthier and d'Altecan whom I do not know, since they have never before entered my kingdom. They, as well as your son, must prepare to receive my baptism. Since there is nothing further to mention at the moment, I remain your friend,

Old Man Tropic of Cancer

13. Berthier's spelling of the word is used in the Diderot and d'Alembert *Encyclopédie* (1765); other spellings are *thazard*, *tassart*, or *tassard*. At the time Berthier was writing the name seems to have been applied to any one of several species of *Scombridae*, the family that includes mackerel and tuna. With the standardization of nomenclature undertaken by Lacepède and perfected by Cuvier and Valenciennes, the name was later restricted to the Frigate Mackerel, which still carries the Latin tag *Auxis thazard* (or *Auxis rochei*).

14. The drawings are unfortunately missing from the Princeton manuscript of Berthier's journal.

15. This drawing is also missing from the manuscript.

18 July We crossed the Tropic at noon, and at four o'clock that afternoon the ceremony commenced as follows:

We heard in the mizzen-top the cries of an old man, who was shivering with cold, and the rattling of many chains. A moment later a chaplain appeared with several bedaubed archers, a drummer, and Old Man Tropic almost naked, with a very long beard and a chain around his waist. His body was daubed with red and black, and he wore nothing but a sheepskin over his shoulders and a leather cap. Astride his shoulders was the son, stark naked, painted red and blue, who was tarred and rolled in chicken feathers. They pretended to be perishing with cold.

When the group reached the deck, the Old Man mounted the back of a sailor who played donkey on all fours, and the whole cohort began to march in procession round the ship. A cabin boy with his breeches down and his bare bottom turned in our direction was tied to each cannon on the quarterdeck. When the procession arrived opposite the poop, the chaplain mounted it and preached a sermon designed to make us well aware that our purses would play a principal part in the ceremony. The sermon ended, we repaired to the mainmast where there was a tub filled with water with a plank laid across it to sit on. Above it hung a basket, and at either side a man with a pail stood ready to scoop water into it from a barrel at his elbow. Old Man Tropic sat near a table at which his secretary recorded the names of those baptized. This performance was attended by the whole garrison in their finery.

They did me the honor of taking me first. As I sat on the little plank over the tub, the chaplain asked if I promised to respect all wives of absent mariners. I assured him that I had always respected the ladies in proportion as their age inspired this sentiment, accompanying my speech with a *louis*, which I dropped into the plate. They threw a little water on my hands while a pump sprayed in succession the bottoms of all the little boys tied to the cannon, and I was released. All

those under the captain's protection were treated thus. Afterward the ceremony proceeded in the orthodox manner. The moment the victim was seated on the little plank it was pulled out from under him. A hook had been placed in the belt of his breeches and attached from behind to a rope that passed through the middle of the tub. So, when the plank was pulled, the victim fell into the tub and was held there while the two men threw pailfuls of water into a basket hanging above. Meanwhile, the ritual of the cabin boys' bottoms continued.

My servant had asked me to pay for him. I agreed, but as I promised Old Man Tropic that the price would depend upon the thoroughness of the ducking, my servant can rest assured that no member of his family was ever so well baptized. At the end of the ceremony each of us threw water about on his own, and we were all thoroughly drenched.[16]

2 August The winds continued fair, the skies clear, and the weather very hot until the 2nd of August, when the horizon clouded over. Since we should have been quite near land, we shortened sail. At five that afternoon the horizon cleared and we saw the coast of Marie-Galante (A).[17] The *Cybèle* had taken in tow the transport *Saint-Charles*, which was making no progress. She released her in order to go and scout ahead of the fleet. At nightfall we arrived at the entrance to the channel between Dominica (C) and Martinique. In the channel we encountered a violent storm, which lasted all night and obliged us to sail very close to the wind and set many sails to keep from being dashed against the coasts of Dominica on the one hand and Martinique on the other.

3 August At daybreak, when the *Saint-Charles* had dropped some way behind the squadron, she was hit by a squall and sank before our eyes without our being able to save a single man. Several of our vessels lost their topmasts. Finally the storm ended and the good weather returned, and at seven in the morning, as we were off Point Macouba (B) on Martinique, we drew alongside one another in a calm. I was happy

16. A similar ceremony is described in Goussencourt's journal (pp. 36–38). Harry Miller Lydenberg's exhaustive compilation, "Crossing the Line, Tales of the Ceremony during Four Centuries," was published in the New York Public Library *Bulletin*, Vols. LIX–LXI (1955–1957), beginning with the August 1955 issue; the French text of

Berthier's account, from the Princeton manuscript, appears in LIX, No. 10 (Oct. 1955), 520–522.
17. The letters (A), (B), and (C) are evidently references to a map which is now missing from Berthier's manuscript. For relative position of the islands mentioned, see map, Vol. II, No. 163.

to find myself very near land. M. de Choisy had had the disagreeable experience of seeing all his belongings go down with the *Saint-Charles*.

At eight o'clock that morning the breeze freshened enough to take us past a rock called La Perle; then we were again becalmed. The convoy's approach had been signaled from the peaks[18] at Martinique and recognized as French, so M. de Joubert, the commandant at Saint-Pierre, dispatched a schooner to the Baron de Clugny to warn him to be on his guard, since two frigates and an English ship were cruising within sight of Saint-Pierre. At this news the Baron had the longboat lowered and sent M. de Choisy ashore with the most precious part of the frigate's cargo. Then he summoned the captains of the merchantmen and told them that, if the English arrived in superior force, he would run his frigate aground, putting as many cannon as possible ashore to erect a battery under whose shelter the vessels could flock together close inshore, or, if worst came to worst, would run them aground also.

The calm persisted all night, which I spent in the greatest anxiety. At midnight we saw 4 sail coming towards us. Through telescopes we had already determined that they included at least one warship and two frigates, but as they approached we saw that they were actually schooners. One passed near the frigate, which hailed her to come alongside. When she refused, we fired muskets at her and she obeyed. As her replies to our questions seemed somewhat hesitant, even though she claimed to be Dutch, she was ordered to follow the convoy.

4 August Watching this maneuver, I had no doubt that the schooner was an enemy spy. I was so frightened all night that the next morning I asked M. de Clugny to put me ashore. When he sent me the order

at noon, my brother and I disembarked with our belongings at Bourg du Prêcheur, relieved to know that we would not be captured at the entrance to the harbor.[19]

A light breeze sprang up, and seeing no sail, the convoy bound for Fort Royal [Fort-de-France] went to Saint-Pierre, only 4 leagues away, where it arrived without sighting the English, who had gone on to Fort Royal. You may guess with what anxiety the convoy read from the masthead the signals at Saint-Pierre revealing that the English were on one side while we were on the other.

On our arrival at Bourg du Prêcheur the officers of a detachment from the Auxerrois Regiment received us very kindly. While they searched for a pirogue to take us on to Saint-Pierre, they took us to the house of a lady who was being rocked in her hammock by a negro. All of this new country and its customs surprised me, and I shall speak of them later. At six o'clock our pirogue was ready, and we embarked with our luggage while two negroes dragged us along the shore to Saint-Pierre, 4 leagues beyond. These pirogues are dug out of tree trunks and are made of a single piece of wood. We arrived at Saint-Pierre without incident. We went at once to the house of the commandant, who gave us dinner. M. de Choisy arrived an hour later. He had come by land and had suffered greatly from the heat. He took lodgings with M. de Joubert, and we rented a room.

5 August The next day I paid calls on the senior officers of the garrison and the corps commanders and dined at the inn that I was told was the least expensive, though it cost me 16 *livres* in local currency.

An order arrived that evening from M. de Bouillé[20]

18. Berthier here and subsequently uses the word *morne*, the French term still widely used in the Antilles to describe the characteristic hills or peaks visible from the sea. The map of Martinique alone supplies numerous examples. The French borrowed the word from the Spanish *morro*, a peak, headland, or promontory—for example, El Morro in San Juan, Puerto Rico, or Morro Castle in Havana, Cuba.

19. Bourg du Prêcheur, Berthier's emergency landing-place on the western coast of Martinique, is now known simply as Prêcheur. It apparently took its name from an offshore rock called "Le Prêcheur," which was not far from "La Perle," mentioned above. See map, Vol. II, No.

165, which also shows the towns of Saint-Pierre and Fort Royal farther down the coast.

20. François-Claude-Amour, marquis de Bouillé (1739-1800). Although he never came to the continent of North America, the Marquis de Bouillé, through his key position as governor-general of the French Windward Islands (Martinique, Guadeloupe, etc.), played an important role in the War of American Independence and was later admitted to membership in the Society of the Cincinnati. He was an active leader in the amphibious warfare in the Caribbean, which in turn influenced events on the continent. Bouillé's relations with William Bingham, agent of the Continental Congress in Martinique, are discussed in

to send our convoy [from Saint-Pierre] on to Fort Royal. The frigate *Gentille*, which brought the order, was to join the *Cybèle* in escorting it. On the 6th the convoy anchored at Fort Royal after being chased as far as the forts by two English frigates and a warship, which arrived a moment too late. M. de Choisy also went to Fort Royal to get his orders from M. de Bouillé.

6 August While awaiting his return I went off to see the town [of Saint-Pierre]. I went to dine with the commandant and afterwards went to the theatre. The play was *Le Barbier de Séville* [by Beaumarchais], and I was much surprised to recognize my hostess as Señora Rosine. I had taken her to be a lady of quality and had surmised from her conversation that she seldom went to the theatre. Afterwards I took my revenge for her deception by saying all the uncomplimentary things I could think of about the actress who had played Señora Rosine, but I did not fool her as long as she had fooled me. This did not prevent our becoming very good friends. I shall tell you later about the performance.

7 August M. de Choisy returned and told us that M. de Bouillé was putting the *Gentille* at our disposal to take us to Newport in New England, where the army of the Comte de Rochambeau was stationed, passing by Saint-Domingue, where she would drop off her convoy.

8–9 August Since we could not leave Fort Royal before the 25th, I spent two more days at Saint-Pierre. This town is situated at the foot of some very high mountains on the seacoast at the head of an exposed harbor that is very dangerous during the months of August, September, and October, when vessels are driven ashore by the storms outside. The anchorage is defended by a good fort and strong batteries. The town is the most populous and the busiest in Martinique. It has two principal streets half a league long.

The houses are built of wood and are of only one storey. There are no panes in the windows, which are protected only by blinds or shutters, or else screens of cotton cloth. The rich people install either gauze or a sort of rush matting to keep out the insects, which are very bothersome. The continual heat makes fireplaces unnecessary, so in every house there is only one—in the kitchen, which is invariably a small building detached from the main house. The decoration is very simple, usually four bare walls with several mirrors, candelabra, chandeliers, and sofas, all more or less handsome. In almost every house there is a hammock in which the mistress has herself rocked by a negro. These same hammocks can be attached to either end of a pole carried on the heads of two negroes. The women sit in them, as in our sedan chairs, for going to town. All the beds have mosquito netting, a single curtain of gauze that covers the top and sides. You enter from below and thus are not incommoded by the large quantity of insects and mosquitos that come in at night and fly about the rooms.

The men go everywhere dressed in white linen waistcoats and breeches. The women here are very elegant and follow the extremes in French fashions, but we change them so often that the ships do not have time to bring over the new ones before they have changed four or five times. This is a great boon to our dressmakers, giving them a market for their unsold stock. The negresses, and especially the mulattresses, are extremely elegant. They wear long pear-shaped gold earrings, an India print handkerchief on their heads, a bodice and a very short skirt that is usually of fine embroidered muslin. It is the colonists' folly to ruin themselves for these women.

The society, which the colonists find most agreeable, did not strike me as such. You are socially acceptable and popular here only when you gamble, and the stakes are very high. The smallest game can cost you 20 to 25 *louis*. You pay visits and attend gatherings only in the evenings because of the extreme heat during the day. You are rarely invited to a meal because of the cost and scarcity of food.

This island produces but a small part of its subsistence. There are few cattle, and those few are poor. The greater part come from the Spanish mainland. Sheep are replaced here by miserable goats. The pig

---

Robert C. Alberts, *The Golden Voyage, The Life and Times of William Bingham, 1752–1804* (Boston, 1969), Chaps. 1–7. During the early years of the French Revolution Bouillé achieved further fame for his suppression of the mutiny at Nancy (August 1790) and his role in the attempted escape of the royal family ("the flight to Varennes," June 1791).

provides the best meat here, also the turtle. The only game is wild guinea-fowl and doves. The fruits that are good here are pineapples, oranges, lemons, figs, avocados, and sapodilla plums. The rest are very bad. The grapes grown here and harvested three times a year, though rare, are also poor. The flour brought from France almost always arrives fermented. After this description you may imagine that it is difficult to eat well here. The fish, which I have not mentioned, is the best thing here, but is not to be compared with ours. The Bordeaux wine and the local liqueur are really good. You are served by your negroes and negresses who, in spite of their great cleanliness, always smell of rancid oil, which is very disagreeable for a newly arrived European; but you grow accustomed to this as to everything else.

I shall return, as I promised, to the theatre. It is easy to understand why good actors, well paid and fêted in France, especially the women, would not come to a country where there is no amusement, where the men go to the play to kill an hour, and where they applaud an actor not because he has acted well but because he has finished his lines without the aid of the prompter. This might be a subject for investigation by the gentlemen of the Faculty, who could debate the effects of heat on the memory.

At the *Barbier de Séville* I witnessed both carelessness and forgetfulness on the part of the actors. Monsieur Figaro had administered such a poor sneezing-powder to La Jeunesse [his old servant] that, despite all his efforts, he was never able to sneeze. This rather amused the audience, as did the impatience of Rosine, who quarreled aloud with Bartholo. He stopped short, looked at her, and said, becoming more and more impatient: "Do I have to tell you that a sheet of paper

is missing and that my finger is black?" Then poor Bartholo, whose memory wandered, became even more disconcerted. Fortunately Figaro woke the prompter, who fixed everything, and the play ended, as in France, with a great round of applause.[21] You pay 5 *livres* and 10 *deniers* in French money for admission; the negresses and mulattresses occupy marked boxes and cannot mingle with the whites.

Only two kinds of men are recognized in our colonies, the white and the black. The position of the unsavory character who left France for misconduct is equal in this respect to that of the most respectable colonist. Our European servants are not permitted to serve us at table and are themselves served by negroes. The great disproportion of whites to blacks requires absolute respect for color.

The majority of the negroes wear only breeches, and the women skirts, leaving the rest of their bodies bare. In houses where they are servants they wear shirts, and those who work in the ports or the country often go stark naked. The breasts of the negresses are quite extraordinary; they begin to hang down on girls of twenty. Women who have borne one or two children can hang them over their shoulders, and at thirty they are nothing more than two folds of skin hanging over their bellies. They remain firm only to the age of seventeen or eighteen at the most. It happens that they are large to begin with, appearing at the age of twelve, and since they are never confined, they are continually being tossed about and gradually sag. All other parts of their bodies are very firm, even at an advanced age, owing to their habit of bathing three or four times a day. The morals of the colored people are very loose. They regard love as one of the prime necessities and natural urges. They stay mar-

21. *Le Barbier de Séville* by Beaumarchais had its first performance at the Comédie Française in Paris on 23 February 1775. The sneezing scene mentioned here by Berthier is in Act II, scene 7. Another comment on the theatre at Saint-Pierre, by a visiting American who was in Martinique seven months or so prior to Berthier's visit, is found in the "Private Journal of Capt. Joseph Hardy," printed in James L. Howard, *Seth Harding Mariner, A Naval Picture of The Revolution* (New Haven, 1930), pp. 212–277. Hardy, who was in command of marines on board the Continental frigate *Confederacy*, notes that on 23 December 1779 he went ashore after dinner and took a little exercise and then

"at 6 P.M. went in company with all our Officers to the playhouse." "The Piece that was performed," he continues, "is an English Farce called the Deserter and much esteemed by Europeans but in the French is much altered from the English Mode and ruined with a multiplicity of Singing. It was uncommonly short, beginning and concluding the Evenings entertainment without any addition." The piece Hardy heard was presumably *Le Déserteur*, libretto by Sedaine and music by Monsigny (first performed in Paris in 1769), from which Charles Dibdin had derived the "English farce," *The Deserter*.

ried so long as they are in love, and their children belong to the master of the mother who takes care of them. In general each color prefers its own—the negro a negress, the mulatto a mulattress, etc. etc.—and if they seem to offer themselves by preference to the whites, it is through vanity; but they are very anxious to forget the favors they have granted you.

Maroon negroes or negresses—that is to say, runaway slaves who have been recaptured—are punished by whipping, after which they are required to wear for three or four years, or for life, an iron collar with four large spokes, or are burdened to some extent with chains. There are few large establishments that do not contain such specimens. Every day you see mutinous or lazy slaves being driven to their work with whips. The stubborn ones are fastened naked to a post and severely flogged on their backs and buttocks. I have seen them working in the heat of the day after being subjected to this punishment, their backs crisscrossed with sores.

On a plantation near Fort Royal I witnessed the punishment of a pretty negress who was pregnant. She had been insolent to her mistress, who had her placed in a trap from which only her buttocks protruded (so her belly would be protected) and given 50 lashes. Such severity, which seems inhuman to a European, is necessary to maintain the authority of a handful of whites over an enormous number of blacks. Nevertheless, the negroes of good character are more fortunate than most of our peasants, who despite their labors often lack for bread.

The negroes or negresses who learn a trade work in town and give, according to their talents, 2 or 3 *louis* a month to their masters. With the balance they purchase small comforts. Some of them even accumulate enough to buy their freedom. I have noticed that these free negroes are the most unfortunate of all. They eat up all their earnings so that when they become old and lame they have to live on alms, whereas the slaves are sure of being cared for and fed to the end of their lives.

I should have liked, my dear Chevalier, to give you a picture of this colony in much greater detail, but I have been unable to travel to the plantations in the interior. My brother is sick, so I have had to stay with him. He has a low fever, which, though not serious, makes me yearn for a cool climate.

Adieu, my dear friend, I embrace you.

❧

Newport, Rhode Island
4 October 1780

My dear Chevalier,

I left the town of Saint-Pierre on 10 August for Fort Royal, 7 leagues beyond. The quickest and cheapest way was to go in a pirogue, which usually makes the trip in four hours. I embarked with my luggage at seven in the morning on a very cloudy day. For the first 3 leagues all was relatively calm, but suddenly a storm came up with a very high wind and fearful thunderclaps, punctuated with flashes of lightning that lit up the whole landscape. An angry sea made up and our crew, as well as we ourselves, were terrified. I begged the owner to run us ashore, but he informed me that we were off a point 500 feet high, with rocks and breaking seas extending out from it for three-fourths of a mile, on which we would be dashed to pieces without any chance of escape; thus our only hope lay in heading out to sea and taking the waves bow on, instead of abeam where they could either swamp or sink us. We lost sight of land while we were trying to extricate ourselves from this unhappy situation. My servant crossed himself furiously, and I rummaged in a bag to find some brandy, which I distributed in moderate amounts to the unfortunate negroes, who were spent from rowing. After half an hour the storm abated and the weather cleared. From time to time we caught glimpses of Fort Royal and finally arrived there at seven o'clock that evening. Our crew was exhausted. These poor negroes had been struggling against the seas for fourteen hours without a moment's respite. One must live through moments like these to realize what man can endure. Our danger was all the greater because these craft are very shallow, have no decks, and are designed to be rowed along the coast in fine weather.[22] What disturbed us

22. Captain Joseph Hardy (*op.cit.*, pp. 216–217) describes a similar journey from Fort Royal up the coast to Saint-Pierre on 28 December 1779: "Having private business at

St. Pierrs went ashore this morning with Mr. V. [Second Lieutenant Thomas Vaughan]. At 10 took passage in a Canoe from Town.—These Canoes will carry 6 or 7

most was a conversation we had on our departure with the owner of our boat, who told us that last year 15 of these pirogues had been lost in storms. I confess that I greatly feared ours was going to be the 16th.

My first concern on landing was to seek some supper, since we had had no dinner. It was with the greatest difficulty that we persuaded an innkeeper to remove the head of a suckling pig from a neighboring table and to add some salad and a bottle of wine, for which he charged us 24 *livres*. This we were obliged to pay. I was so happy to be ashore that I threw in some thanks for good measure.

11 August I set about finding a commodious lodging where my brother would be more comfortable, since he still had a fever, but despite all my efforts I had to take him to the hospital, a very handsome and well-run establishment, where he could not have been better cared for. Since I never left him, I saw nothing here, no more than at Saint-Pierre, of the interior of the country, so I shall tell you only about the town and its environs.[23]

Fort Royal and Fort Bourbon make this place more picturesque than Saint-Pierre. The city is laid out in regular blocks, with a tree-lined square along the waterfront. It is more military than commercial and is less healthy than Saint-Pierre, being built on a marsh that has been only partly drained. Fort Royal itself is built on a rocky point jutting into the sea, which commands the harbor entrance. The thickness of its parapets at the embrasure level and its large number of well-placed guns and mortars make it impregnable from the sea, since on entering against the prevailing headwind vessels are obliged to tack back and forth under the guns of the fort, exposing themselves to a galling fire to which they cannot reply.

During the last war the English took advantage of the heights above the fort to capture it from the land side, but this could not happen today because, to the east of Fort Royal, Fort Bourbon has been built on a

mountain that is dominated only by heights out of range. This mountain is very high, with a rocky summit on which Fort Bourbon is built with four bastions and a horn-work defending it on the inland side, from which it is more easily approached. It is equipped with very large cisterns and can sustain a long siege. It is my opinion that its position renders it impregnable to storming. I regard this place as the Gibraltar of the Windward Islands, because it can be defended with few men, and especially because sieges are not conducted in the colonies as they are in Europe. At the moment it is garrisoned by two battalions of the Martinique Regiment and one battalion each from the Bourbon, Champagne, and Walsh's Irish regiments, making a total of about 1,200 men.

At the moment the Windward Islands are completely stripped of naval forces, M. de Guichen having departed for Europe. We have every reason to complain of the small protection granted our commerce. We do not have a single warship cruising these waters, whereas the English put in a daily appearance before our ports. The Marquis de Bouillé has ordered the *Gentille*, which is to take us to Saint-Domingue and Newport, to take charge of a convoy of 18 sail bound for The French Cape.

I was given the task of having the luggage destined for the Comte de Rochambeau's army unloaded from the various transports and put on a single ship. This difficult operation was completed promptly.

24 August I went to sleep on board the *Gentille*. We received word that the English had left St. Lucia and were cruising before Martinique. This made our departure rather ticklish. We remained in port until the 30th to wait for a wind strong enough to carry us a good distance. We got under way at eight o'clock that evening in a stiff breeze. We reconnoitered St. Lucia to evade the English, who were cruising their regular route, and by daybreak we were 18 leagues from Martinique without having sighted a single sail.

---

hh"ds Sugar and ply with Freight or Passengers from here to St. Pierrs. They are rowed by five or six Negroes whose Lives appear to be as wretched as any part of the Human race. Some of them are chained by one leg to the Boat and others shew the stripes of cruelty on their Body's. In this manner these unhappy Mortals row in these Boats for Weeks without 10 hours intermission and

as Naked as the moment of their Birth. Not even the Galley Slave in Barbary is more miserable. . . . But to return to our passage we arrived at St. [Pierre] 3 PM. . . ."
23. See Ozanne's engraved view of Fort Royal (1780) and Du Perron's manuscript map of the Bay (1781), Vol. II, Nos. 164 and 166.

There the *Cybèle*, which had left with us, departed for Guadeloupe.

4 September We had a very good breeze and saw only one small privateer, which the frigate pursued. My brother felt better at sea and no longer had any fever. On the 4th we made a landfall at Puerto Rico, and after negotiating the Mona channel, then skirting the north coast of the Island of Santo Domingo, we sighted La Grange [Punta de la Granja] at six that evening.

6 September We tacked back and forth through the night so as to enter the harbor next morning on the fair breeze from outside.

7 September On the morning of the 7th we anchored in the harbor of The Cape [Le Cap Français, now Cap Haïtien][24], after being pursued and caught by a warship and two frigates, all French, which had not understood our recognition signals.

The harbor here has natural defenses on the east in the form of underwater rocks visible only by the spray on top. This leaves a single channel grazing the bold bluffs of the western side where Fort Picolet has been built on the rocks and equipped with strong batteries of guns and mortars. In case a vessel were caught in a gale and, in peril of shipwreck, entered the channel, the anchorage is defended by large batteries built along its edges. These, by firing hot shot, could burn up any ship foolish enough to enter. There is always a large garrison here. The Môle Saint-Nicolas and Fort Dauphin are the strongest points on the island.

On arrival at The Cape we could think of nothing but hastening our departure for New England. I put out of my mind anything that might detain me at The Cape, of which I shall give you only a very sketchy account.[25] This city, the Paris of our colonies, is extremely well built and inhabited by very wealthy people. You see many elegant carriages, which ply between the plantations of the rich and the beautiful northern plain whose every aspect reveals ease and abundance. My brother's continuing poor health, plus the shortness of our stay, prevented my accepting any

invitations here. As far as I am concerned, Newport is now the only place of interest.

The food here is much better than in the other colonies. The women, at enormous expense, are as elegant as those of Paris, but since the merchants of this city operate on the principle of cheating whenever they can, it is we who pay for the ladies' finery. The climate, plus the example set by the colored women, who satisfy every desire as if it were one of their primary duties towards nature, tend to make the morals of the white women rather free and easy. Their husbands make no small contribution to this state of affairs by their taste for high living and for ruining themselves for their mulatto mistresses.

It is the most dissolute city I have yet seen and the most dishonest. I bought something at a shop; finding the price asked by the merchant exorbitant, I told him I would trust him rather than try to bargain, since I assumed him to be too honest to cheat a stranger who knew nothing about prices in the colonies. He told me that in the tropics this principle no longer applied. It is true that The Cape is full of people who left France because of bankruptcy or misdemeanors. I was assured that things were different in the interior, where one might live a very enjoyable life.

The theatre is as good here as in our large provincial towns.

13 September I slept aboard the frigate *Gentille* on the 12th, and at daybreak on the 13th we got under way. The warship *Destin* escorted us as far as the passage[26] [through the Bahamas], which we reached in the course of the day after passing between Great Inagua and Little Inagua. Since we no longer had a convoy with us, we were making good headway when, on the morning of the 22nd, we sighted 3 sail, which we took for merchantmen. We passed them, whereupon, seeing them set their stunsails in order to catch up with us, we examined them more closely and saw clearly that they were a warship and two frigates. We therefore tacked about and set signals that confirmed that they were English. Our maneuver had

24. See map, Vol. ii, No. 171, and the view of The Cape drawn in 1780, No. 174.

25. The city of The Cape is more fully described in Clermont-Crèvecœur's journal (pp. 97–99) and in Verger's journal (pp. 176–177). See also Vol. ii, No. 176.

26. Berthier uses the term *débouquement* to describe the passage. See map, Vol. ii, No. 177, which shows Great Inagua and Little Inagua, as well as the other small islands and passages.

allowed them—especially the frigates—time to close the distance between us. We crowded on all possible sail, and still they gained. There was no longer any doubt that at the end of so unequal a combat we should be obliged to surrender and be captured. You can easily imagine how disagreeable it would be for me, after surviving so much, to arrive at my destination as a prisoner. We tried everything we could think of to make our frigate go faster. Finally, as night fell, the two frigates came within a cannon-shot and a half of one another, and we fired several shots astern. Fortunately the night was very dark, and the moment the captain could see nothing but the enemy's lanterns he changed courses until, having been hard on the wind, we ended up running before it. None of us slept that night. Our decks were cleared for action. At dawn we were overjoyed to find ourselves alone. The wind was light, and we were becalmed until the 26th, when it blew out of the northeast with such violence that we were obliged to heave to until the 28th. The sea was so high that it constantly washed over the deck.

28 September The wind calmed down, and we sighted Manisses Island [Block Island].[27] That evening we were 3 leagues from the entrance to Newport harbor when the wind drew ahead and we were obliged to tack back and forth outside until the 30th, when the frigate anchored in the harbor.[28] I went ashore immediately with my brother, who by then was entirely cured.

30 September M. de Choisy took me to the house of the Comte de Rochambeau, to whom I delivered our orders to join the Soissonnais Regiment. The General received us very kindly and gave us dinner. We were lodged near the Comte de Saint-Maîme,[29] and two days after our arrival we were as well established as if we had arrived with the army, having had the added pleasure of visiting our colonies and of arriving before any military operation had taken place.

The squadron escorting the army of the Comte de Rochambeau, which had left Brest on 2 May, had encountered at latitude 34° five English warships bound for France.[30] These had previously been mauled in action with M. de Guichen. While pursuing our transports, which they believed to be in their hands, they were much surprised to see 7 large warships appear. The combat was joined for some minutes and after much noise ended with 3 casualties in killed and wounded, whereupon the two squadrons resumed their respective courses, though the position of one of the English ships was such that she should have been captured by M. de Ternay.

The squadron continued on its course until it reached latitude 32°, where it captured a small vessel,

27. Other contemporary examples of "Manisses" as an alternate name for Block Island are: "A Map of the Most Inhabited part of New England . . . 1774," in Thomas Jefferys et al., *The American Atlas* (London, Sayer and Bennett, 1776), reproduced in W. B. Clark, ed., *Naval Documents of the American Revolution*, III (Washington, 1968), 98; and Capitaine du Chesnoy's "Carte du Théâtre de la Guerre en Amérique Septentrionale," reproduced in Doniol, III, 856–857.

28. Admiral de Ternay, in his journal for Friday, 29 September 1780, notes that, a frigate flying a "pavillon blanc" having been sighted by an officer on board the *Ardent*, he sent the schooner *Prudence* out to recognize her and raised the agreed-upon signals at Point Judith. At nine o'clock that evening a boat from the *Ardent* brought him a letter from M. de La Villebrune, commander of the frigate *Gentille*, which was anchored outside the "Goulet." "This frigate left Martinique on 30 August and Saint-Domingue on 13 September, leaving at The Cape a squadron of 9 ships commanded by M. de Monteil." Under the date of Saturday, 30 September, the journal records: "Light wind from the east and northeast, clear weather, at ten o'clock in the morning the frigate *Gentille* set sail to enter the bay, where she anchored at two in the afternoon."

29. According to the "Etat des logements," or billeting list for French officers in Newport, the Comte de Saint-Maîme, colonel of the Soissonnais Regiment, was lodged at the house of "Miss Coles" in High (now Division) Street. Miss Coles was perhaps the person of that name mentioned by the Reverend Ezra Stiles in the "Visiting Catalogue of his Congregation for 1773," in Stiles, *Literary Diary*, ed. Franklin B. Dexter, 3 vols. (New York, 1901), I, 428; the exact location of her house has not been determined. Although the army did not officially go into winter quarters until 1 November, lodgings in town for officers had presumably been assigned and occupied by them before that date. See Clermont-Crèvecœur's journal, n. 14.

30. The army's crossing with Ternay's fleet and the first two months of its sojourn in Rhode Island, summarized here by Berthier, are described in the journals of Clermont-Crèvecœur and of Verger.

which informed them of the capture of Charleston by the English. Off Cape Henry the squadron sighted a fleet that so frightened M. de Ternay that he ran feint courses all night without sending a lugger or a frigate to investigate its strength. The enemy were more curious and dispatched one of their frigates, which amused herself by firing on our flagship during the night and punching a hole in its mainsail. M. de Ternay learned that the convey was coming from Charleston with General Clinton and 5,000 men, escorted by a 50-gun warship and two frigates. M. de Ternay finally arrived in Newport on 12 July after a crossing of 72 days, congratulating himself on having accomplished his mission so well, though I am persuaded that the Court would not have objected had he captured Clinton and his 5,000 men.

On 26 [21] July the English squadron commanded by Rodney, which had left England to intercept M. de Ternay, appeared off Rhode Island but took no action, very fortunately considering that our troops had not unloaded a single cartridge or a single gun. After the departure of the English squadron, M. de Rochambeau, having given orders to build fortifications for the defense of his army, left secretly for Hartford, where he had an interview with General Washington.

Meanwhile, during August, Admiral Rodney had arrived in New York. There was talk of an expedition against the French army, which prompted M. de Vioménil to make elaborate preparations; but the English remained in a state of inaction.

The headquarters has been established in Newport, and the troops are encamped near the southern tip of the island with their left flank resting on the sea and their right on the town.[31] The Lauzun Legion, as the vanguard, is stationed far out on the Neck. The camp is protected by two rows of redoubts. The ships are moored broadside on and are defended by strong batteries. Everything is in readiness. I shall give you fuller details in my next letter; they will be more interesting than these, which are only a superficial account of first impressions during the short time I have been here.

Adieu, my friend, may my wish to see some action soon be granted. Although I have been chasing after it, up to now I have experienced nothing but peace. P.S. My brother has entirely recovered, and we have both been attached to the Soissonnais Regiment with the rank of captain.[32]

❧

Providence, 16 July 1781[33]

October 1780

My dear friend, I enclose herewith a memorandum on Newport, Rhode Island, giving details of the former English and American positions and those of the French, with a plan[34] that will serve to explain it. You will also find a roster of the French army.

The troops in America are at present inactive as far as military operations go. General [Nathanael] Greene has remained on observation in Carolina since the capture of Charleston. The principal English forces are occupying New York and King's Bridge, with outposts in the Jerseys. General Washington is with his troops at West Point and is holding King's Ferry. The English fleet, numbering 10 warships, maintains an observation post in Gardiner's Bay from which it constantly sends ships to cruise off Rhode Island. The French army is occupying Newport and the island of Rhode Island. I await with impatience

---

31. See maps, Vol. II, Nos. 5 and 6.
32. Colonel de Saint-Maîme had originally offered only a sublieutenancy to Berthier's brother; see n. 6. The signature on the large map of Rhode-Island (Vol. II, No. 7) mentions "Berthier et Berthier de Berlui, capitaines de dragons servant à la suite du régiment d'infanterie de Soissonnais." In the *Etat militaire*, issues of 1781, 1782, and 1783, "Berthier de Berlhuis" [*sic*] is continued on the roster as sublieutenant; the rank of captain was doubtless temporary and not made official.
33. The heading to this installment of Berthier's epistolary journal is somewhat confusing, since he was not actually at Providence on 16 July 1781 but at the Philipsburg

camp (see p. 251). It may indicate the date when he wrote up this portion of his journal or when he sent a copy of it to his "friend."
34. The plan referred to here is presumably a map drawn by Berthier soon after his arrival and not the more extensive and complete map of the whole island (Vol. II, No. 7) that he mentions hereafter (pp. 236, 237). It is quite probably the "Plan de la disposition des Français dans Rhode-Island," copies of which are in the Bibliothèque du Génie, MS A 224, "Atlas de la Guerre d'Amérique," fol. 66, and among the Service Hydrographique de la Marine maps deposited in the Bibliothèque Nationale, 135-9-2.

the first movement of all these troops now engaged in observing one another.

The English allowed us to spend the rest of the summer quietly in camp, while everyone observed. We were too weak to undertake an expedition. General Rochambeau took advantage of all the fine days to send the army on marches and to prepare positions at all points on the island where a landing might be attempted [by the enemy].

We have been much affected by the shocking treason of Arnold that has just been revealed by the arrest of Major André.[35] He planned to deliver West Point to the English. I shall send you the details of the outcome of this frightful affair, which is bound to be tragic.

I have spent all my spare time working on the map of Rhode Island, since all those we had seemed to me very inadequate.

Receiving no news from France and convinced that the Second Division was not coming to join him, General Rochambeau realized that he could never undertake any operation with the means at his disposal and

decided to send his son to France to point out the difficulty of carrying out the intentions of the Court with so few troops.

29 October The General sent the Vicomte de Rochambeau [his son] to France in the King's frigate *Amazone*.[36]

Preparations were made to put the army into winter quarters. Permission has been granted by the state authorities for the French army to take possession of all houses abandoned by the Tories, which the army would repair at its own expense in order to make them habitable for the troops, while the officers would be lodged in private homes.[37]

1 November After the repairs were made and the cold weather arrived, the army broke camp and occupied their quarters in the town. Only the infantry of the Lauzun Legion and 50 cavalry stayed out on the Neck and were quartered in the neighboring houses. The rest of the Legion went into quarters at Lebanon [in Connecticut], 45 miles from Providence, for two reasons: first, there are facilities there for procuring forage and building stables; and, second, it

35. News of the "shocking treason" coincided with Berthier's arrival at Newport. Arnold's treason was discovered on 25 September upon Washington's return to West Point from his conference (20–22 September) at Hartford, Connecticut, with General Rochambeau and Admiral de Ternay. Washington's return to his headquarters had been delayed by an unexpected meeting (24 September) at Fishkill with the Chevalier de La Luzerne, French minister in Philadelphia, who was on his way to Newport to confer with Rochambeau and Ternay. Word of the conspiracy (relayed by Lafayette in a letter to the minister, 26 September) caught up with La Luzerne while he was proceeding eastward to Newport, which he reached on 1 October. The original of a letter from Lafayette to Rochambeau (referring him to his letter to La Luzerne for further details), dated "Robertson's [Beverly Robinson's] House près West Point," 26 September 1780, is in the Rochambeau Papers, Paul Mellon Collection, as is the original, in Alexander Hamilton's handwriting, of Washington's letter to Rochambeau, "Head Quarters Near West Point," 26–27 September 1780. (See illustration.) Washington wrote: "On my arrival here a very disagreeable scene unfolded itself. By a lucky accident a conspiracy of the most dangerous kind, the object of which was to sacrifice this post, has been defeated. General Arnold, who has sullied his former glory, by the blackest

treason, has escaped to the enemy. This is an event which occasions me equal regret and mortification; but traitors are the growth of every country, and in a revolution of the present nature it is more to be wondered at, that the catalogue is so small, than that there have been found a few." Printed in *Writings of GW*, xx, 97, from a retained copy in the Washington Papers. Rochambeau replied from Newport, 30 September: "I have just received Your Excellency's letter of the 26th, and am very happy to learn of your return in good health to the army. I know not whether I should pity you, or congratulate you upon the discovery of Arnold's frightful plot; be this as it may, it proves to us that Providence is for us and for our cause, and of this I have had several examples since the beginning of this campaign." Library of Congress, Washington Papers; printed in Doniol, v, 379. In this same letter Rochambeau informs Washington that the frigate *Gentille* has arrived from the West Indies bringing Brigadier General de Choisy and "nine officers."

36. The *Amazone* was at this time commanded by La Pérouse. The Vicomte de Rochambeau, who returned to Newport only in early May 1781, gives a brief account of his mission in his journal (pp. 213–217). See also Clermont-Crèvecœur's journal, n. 21.

37. See Clermont-Crèvecœur's journal, n. 14.

would be in a position there from which it could march against parties of the enemy landing from the Sound.

December 1780 Concerned for the welfare of his little army as winter set in, the Comte de Rochambeau had a large hall built where all the officers could get together.[38] There were tables provided for games of chance, at which he himself set the example by playing for small stakes. This establishment provided a meeting-place where everyone gathered and prevented idleness from luring them to places of ill repute, where only too often you see young people brought to ruin. Our general gave charming balls for us there, and it is my opinion that this hall served a very useful and beneficial purpose to the whole army and did honor to M. de Rochambeau, who presided there like the head of a family.

18 December M. de Ternay died on 18 [15] December, whereupon M. Destouches took command of the fleet. Since the former was not popular, his death

created very little stir. It was the last event of the year that might have interested us.[39]

January 1781 I had finished my map of the island. The General was pleased with it and ordered me to make a copy to send to the Court.[40] On 12 January he appointed me supernumerary assistant quartermaster-general,[41] with a stipend of 100 *écus* a month. My brother was appointed aide-de-camp to the Comte de Saint-Maîme [colonel of the Soissonnais Regiment]. My assignment has given me the greatest pleasure. It is an open door to the General Staff of the army and can lead to general's rank for a hard-working officer who does not, like the gentlemen of the Court, belong to the class from which colonels are appointed. My brother is working with me, and we hope that before the campaign ends the General will bestow the blue uniform on him as well.[42] Now I am, as you can see, my friend, a man of importance and affluence, for I confess that the 1,800 *livres* that we had to live on between us was very meager; however, we devised an

38. Rochambeau had his headquarters in the house of William Vernon, still standing at the corner of Clarke and Mary Streets. Vernon made no charge for rent but received compensation for damages. Vernon's claim (dated Boston, 12 December 1782) for "damages sustained in his house at Newport, R.I., occupied by His Excellency Gen'l Rochambeau," amounting to 450 dollars, or £135, with receipt for this sum, is printed in Stone, *French Allies*, p. 227; a facsimile reproduction of the document is in the *Magazine of American History*, III, No. 7 (July 1879), 426. The "officers' club" was built in the garden to the north of the main house, as Vernon noted in a letter to his son Samuel: "I understand General Rochambeau had not your leave for building an Assembly-room in the garden. I can't think it polite of him." See Downing and Scully, *The Architectural Heritage of Newport* (Cambridge, 1952; rev. edn., New York, 1967), Plates 113–115, pp. 186–187 (rev. edn., pp. 453–454), and p. 194 (rev. edn., p. 462), where it is stated that the "French Hall," "a square rusticated building resembling the main house, stood until 1894, when it was torn down . . ."; this hall can be discerned in the *ca.* 1870 photographs, Plate 62 and unnumbered plate facing p. 194 (rev. edn., p. [464]). Gallatin ([1], p. 334) describes the hall in terms similar to Berthier's, emphasizing the attraction of the blazing fireplaces there: "Soon after we went into winter quarters the weather turned extremely cold. We were obliged to make huge fires in our rooms in spite of the cost of firewood for which we were assessed 15 francs a cord; it

had to be brought in quantity from a distance, as the English had stripped the island of its forests."
39. See Verger's journal, n. 28.
40. See map, Vol. II, Nos. 7–9, reproduced from the original preserved in the Bibliothèque du Ministère des Armées "Terre," Paris, L.I.D. 140. It bears an old stamp of the Dépôt de la Guerre and is undoubtedly the very map sent "to the Court." Rochambeau, in a postscript to his dispatch to Montbarey, minister of war, Newport, 1 February 1781, added: "I am enclosing a map of the entire island of Rhode Island, which has been surveyed with care and intelligence by Messieurs Berthier, to the elder of whom I have given a place as assistant aide on the General Staff (*sous-aide dans l'état-major de l'armée*)." Archives de la Guerre, A¹3733, p. 194; printed in Doniol, v, 407, where "MM. Berthier" is mistranscribed as "M. Berthier." The names of the two brothers appear on the map itself (lower left). Another copy of this map, unsigned, is preserved in the library of the Château de Grosbois.
41. *Aide maréchal-général des logis surnuméraire*. Berthier thus became attached to the staff of the quartermaster-general (*maréchal-général des logis*), Pierre-François de Béville. General Béville had a son Charles who, like Berthier, served as one of the assistant quartermasters-general.
42. Unlike the line officers, who except for the artillery wore white uniforms, the French staff officers wore blue.

arrangement that made us completely happy. We ate stew every day, and nothing else, and our friendship made this meal we ate together seem delicious. I have never been happier. I have not changed my way of life, since I wish to buy horses to take us on campaign. All our affairs have been successful: we have been praised, have kept well, and now have good horses and money in prospect.

3 February On 3 February we learned that the English observation squadron in Gardiner's Bay, upon hearing that we expected two frigates and several transports from Boston, had left to cruise off Rhode Island and that a violent storm had come up, driving the *Culloden* onto Montauk Point, where she sank with all hands, and totally dismasting the *Bedford* and the *America*.[43] The rest of the [English] fleet managed to reach open water, from which it returned to its anchorage, but in very poor condition. The first idea that came into my head was that we should take advantage of this moment to send our 7 warships in good condition to Gardiner's Bay to destroy a fleet that must be too badly damaged to put up more than a feeble resistance. The short distance of 15 leagues would not expose our squadron unduly. But we suffer from the misfortune of never being ready.

Arnold had left New York with a convoy and about 1,500 men to take up a position on the Elizabeth River in Virginia. The Marquis de La Fayette had left West Point to oppose him, but with a much smaller force. Again I said: Why are we not ready to sail with troops for Virginia to destroy the English ships and Arnold's troops? The English fleet had to remain idle at least a month before it could be repaired and could put to sea. Thus we found ourselves mistress of the sea, but as you shall see presently, we took small advantage of the situation.

9 February The same ideas had occurred to everyone. Everybody cried out against our inaction at this moment of good fortune. Finally, on 9 February, the 64-gun ship *Eveillé* was sent with two frigates to the Chesapeake Bay with orders to sail up the Elizabeth River and burn and destroy the English ships there, thus cutting off Arnold's supplies as well as his line of retreat. However, this operation would have required our whole squadron, and it was not ready.

During this expedition the English watched our movements closely and began with incredible energy to repair their fleet, which despite the loss of the *Culloden* was still stronger than ours. The *Eveillé*'s departure for what appeared to be simply a cruise disturbed them less than the activity aboard our vessels, to which all officers living ashore were returning.

20 February We received a letter written by General Morgan to General Greene telling of the victory he had just won against an English force at The Cowpens near the Pacolet River in Carolina. Here is a copy for you:[44]

Letter from General Morgan to General Greene, commander of the Army of the Southern Department.

Camp near Cain Creek, 19 January 1781.
Dear Sir,

The troops I have the honor to command have gained a complete victory over a detachment from the British army commanded by Lieut. Col.

43. See Verger's journal, n. 29.
44. Washington to Rochambeau, Headquarters, New Windsor, 14 February 1781: "It is with pleasure I transmit to your Excellency the Copy of a letter from Brigadier Genl. Morgan to Major Genl. Greene giving an account of a most decisive victory gained by him over Lt. Colo. Tarleton on the 17th. of January. I am in hopes that this fortunate stroke will at least retard the offensive operations of Lord Cornwallis, untill General Greene is in a better condition to oppose his progress than he was by the last accounts from the southward. . . ." *Writings of GW*, XXI, 225–226; the original recipient's copy is in the Rochambeau Papers, Paul Mellon Collection. In the same communication Washington informed Rochambeau: "I propose setting out from hence for Newport on Fri-

day next, if the North River should be passable, and if no unforeseen circumstances should intervene."
The English version of Morgan's letter given here is the text as printed in James Graham, *The Life of General Daniel Morgan . . . with portions of his correspondence compiled from authentic sources* (New York, 1856), pp. 309–311. Graham also prints (pp. 467–470) a slightly longer version, which he calls "the original account." Except for a few small omissions or inaccuracies and some garbling of proper names, the French translation that Berthier copied into his journal (probably made at headquarters and not necessarily his own) is substantially correct. The keen interest shown by the French in Morgan's victory at The Cowpens is reflected in several other journals; see, e.g., Chastellux (4), II, 398–400, 579–582, nn. 3–9.

Tarleton. The action happened on the 17th inst., about sunrise, at a place called the Cowpens, near Pacolet River.

On the 14th, having received certain information that the British army were in motion, and that their movements clearly indicated their intentions of dislodging us, I abandoned my encampment at Grindale's Ford and on the 16th, in the evening, took possession of a post about seven miles from the Cherokee Ford on Broad River.

My former position subjected me at once to the operations of Lord Cornwallis and Colonel Tarleton, and in case of a defeat, my retreat might easily have been cut off. My situation at the Cowpens enabled me to improve any advantages I might gain, and to provide better for my own security, should I be unfortunate. These reasons induced me to take this post, notwithstanding it had the appearance of a retreat.

On the evening of the 16th, the enemy occupied the ground we removed from in the morning. An hour before daylight, one of my scouts informed me that they had advanced within five miles of our camp. On this information, the necessary dispositions were made; and from the alacrity of the troops, we were soon prepared to receive them.

The light infantry, commanded by Lieut. Col. [John Eager] Howard, and the Virginia militia, under Major [Francis] Triplett, were formed on a rising ground. The third regiment of dragoons, consisting of eighty men under the command of Lieut. Col. [William] Washington, were so posted in their rear as not to be injured by the enemy's fire, and yet be able to charge the enemy, should an occasion offer.

The volunteers from North Carolina, South Carolina, and Georgia, under the command of Col. [Andrew] Pickens, were posted to guard the flanks. Major [Joseph] McDowell, [Sr.], of the North Carolina volunteers, was posted on the right flank, in front of the line one hundred and fifty yards, and Major [John] Cunningham, of the Georgia volunteers, on the left, at the same distance in front. Colonels [Thomas] Brandon and [John] Thomas, [Jr.], of the South Carolin-

ians, on the right of Major McDowell, and Col. [Joseph] Hayes and [James S.] McCall, of the same corps, on the left of Major Cunningham. Captains [Samuel] Tate and [John S.] Buchanan with the Augusta riflemen were to support the right of the line.

The enemy drew up in one line four hundred yards in front of our advanced corps. The 1st battalion of the 71st regiment was opposed to our right; the 7th regiment to our left; the legion infantry to our center, and two light companies, one hundred men each, on the flanks. In their front moved on two field pieces, and Lieut. Col. Tarleton with 280 cavalry, was posted in the rear of his line.

The disposition being thus made, small parties of riflemen were detached to skirmish with the enemy, on which their whole line advanced on with the greatest impetuosity, shouting as they advanced. Majors McDowell and Cunningham gave them a heavy fire and retreated to the regiments intended for their support.

The whole of Col. Pickens's command then kept up a fire by regiments, retreating agreeable to their orders.

When the enemy advanced to our line, they received a well directed and incessant fire; but their numbers being superior to ours, they gained our flanks, which obliged us to change our position.

We retreated in good order about fifty paces, formed, advanced on the enemy and gave them a brisk fire, which threw them into disorder. Lieut. Col. Howard, observing this, gave orders for the line to charge bayonets, which was done with such address that the enemy fled with the utmost precipitation. Lieut. Colonel Washington discovering that the cavalry were cutting down our riflemen on the left, charged them with such firmness as obliged them to retire in confusion. The enemy were entirely routed, and the pursuit continued for upwards of twenty miles.

Our loss is very inconsiderable, not having more than twelve killed and sixty wounded. The enemy's loss was ten commissioned officers killed, and upwards of one hundred rank and file, two hundred wounded; twenty nine commissioned officers and more than five hundred privates, prisoners, which fell into our hands, with two field pieces, two standards, eight hundred muskets, one traveling forge, thirty-five wagons, seventy negroes, and upwards of one hundred dragoon horses, and all their music. They destroyed most of their baggage, which was immense. Although our success was complete, we fought only eight hundred men, and were opposed by upwards of one thousand chosen British troops.

Such was the inferiority of our numbers, that our success must be attributed to the justice of our cause and the gallantry of our troops. My wishes would induce me to name every sentinel in the corps. In justice to the bravery and good conduct of the officers, I have taken the liberty to enclose you a list of their names, from a conviction that you will be pleased to introduce such characters to the world. . . .

I am, dear Sir,
Your obedient servant,
DANIEL MORGAN

You see, my dear Chevalier, that our good Americans know how to fight, even though most of them are without shoes and poorly fed. I shall leave their victory to return to ours.

24 February The *Eveillé*, under the command of M. de Tilly, left with two frigates on the 9th and returned on the 24th.[45] They arrived in the Chesapeake only to learn that Arnold had withdrawn as far up the Elizabeth River as possible with all his transports, a frigate, and a 44-gun ship, which he had moored broadside and from which he had removed the guns so as to lighten her sufficiently to clear the shoals.

M. de Tilly took on pilots and determined to go up the river to attack and burn them, but his good intentions proved futile. After several trials he could not find enough water for his ships to proceed up the river. This excellent officer zealously tried every trick he could think of until the *Surveillante* ran aground

and he had to abandon his project. After strenuous efforts he succeeded in freeing her, then anchored at the entrance to the Bay under an English ensign, ready to fall upon the first ship that attempted to reach Arnold and by taking prizes compensate for his inability to carry out his orders.

After several prizes had been lured in by his English ensign, he sighted a warship and a corvette outside. Getting under way immediately, he soon overtook them, thanks to his superior speed, and captured them without firing a shot. These were the 44-gun warship *Romulus* and an 18-gun corvette. He then set off for Newport, taking several other prizes en route. In all he captured 9 merchantmen and privateers, one of which was carrying 7,000 guineas to Arnold's troops. He was warmly welcomed at Newport for having made a very useful and profitable sortie, despite his failure to accomplish his mission.

M. de Tilly gave an example of unselfishness in the execution of his orders that deserves mention.[46] He had captured a merchantman loaded with a cargo worth 100,000 *écus*, but since his mission would have been delayed several hours had he stopped to unload her and since he did not wish to diminish his very small crew by manning her and sending her into a friendly port, he took off her crew and burned the ship and cargo.

25 February The King's frigate *Astrée*, which left Brest on 4 December, arrived in Boston after a crossing of 71 days; although it had reached the banks of Newfoundland in 13 days, northwest winds had pushed it down to the Azores, whence it was obliged to take the southern route. This frigate brought the army 5,000,000 *livres* as well as interesting dispatches from which we learned of the replacement of M. de Sartine [minister of marine] by the Marquis de Castries, and of the Prince de Montbarey [minister of war] by the Marquis de Ségur. This ship also brought news that the King had granted me the right of succession to my father's governorship of the Hôtel de la Guerre.[47] I accept your congratulations and am sure

---

45. See Clermont-Crèvecœur's journal, n. 15.

46. Had Tilly sent the captured merchantman into a friendly port, he would have been entitled to a share in the prize—hence Berthier's reference to his "unselfishness."

47. A draft of the official document granting this right of

succession, dated Versailles, 1 October 1780, is in the Archives de la Guerre, Berthier dossier, pièces 28–30. With this "Brevet de survivance de la Place de Gouverneur des Hôtels de la Guerre de la Marine et des Affaires Etrangères en faveur de l'aîné des enfans du Sieur Jean-

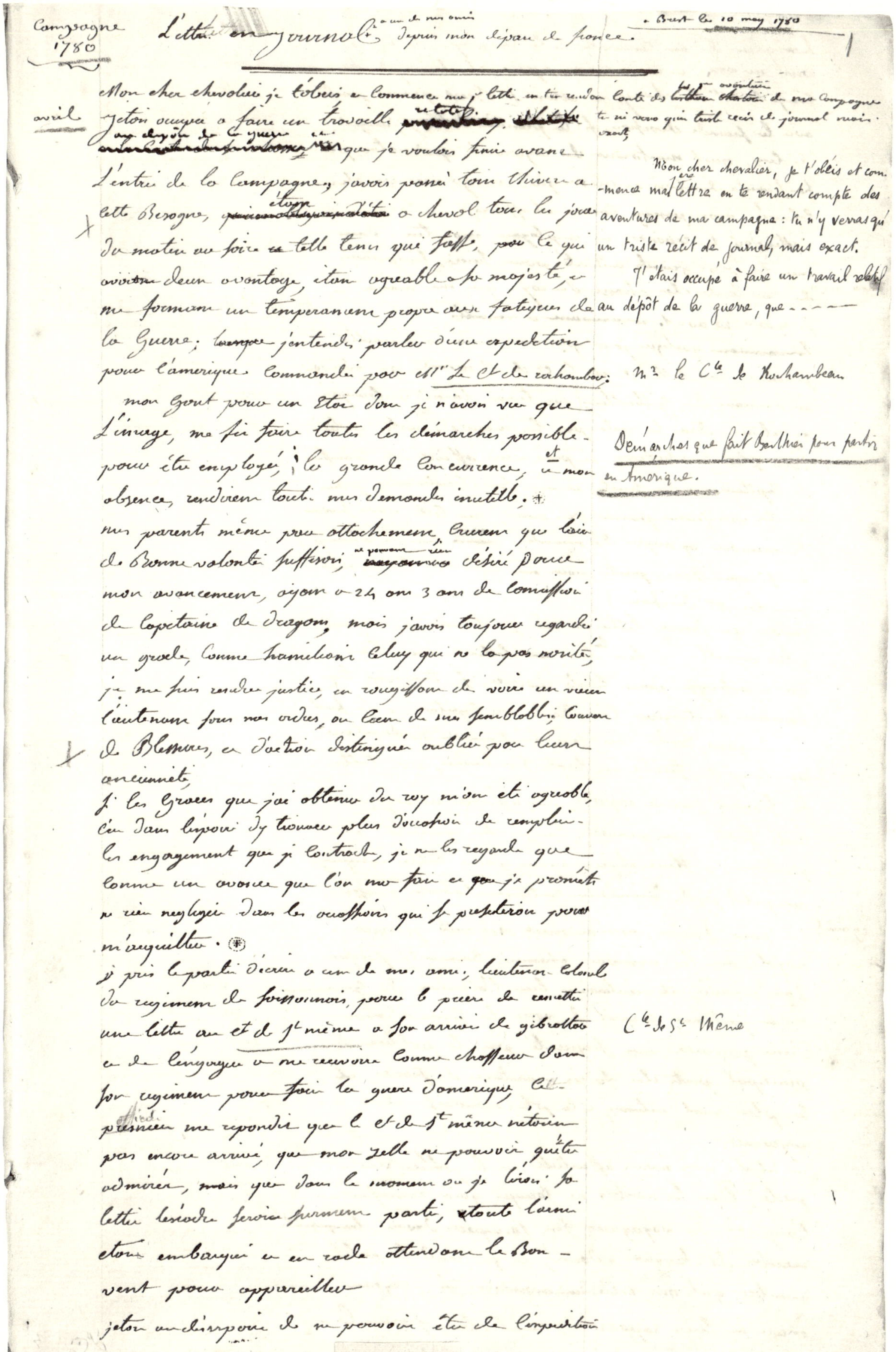

Campagne 1780

Lettre en journal à un de mes amis depuis mon départ de france. Brest le 10 may 1780

Mon cher chevalier je t'obeis et commence ma lettre en te rendant conte des aventures de ma campagne tu ni veras qu'un triste recit de journal mais exact

avril — Jetois occupé a faire un travail relatif au depot de la guerre que je voulois finir avant l'entrée de la campagne, j'avois passé tout l'hiver a cette besogne, étant a cheval tous les jours du matin au soir [illegible] pour ce qui avoit deux avantages, étant agreable a sa majesté, et me formant un temperament propre aux fatigues de la guerre; lorsque j'entendis parler d'une expedition pour l'amerique commandée par M. Le Cte de Rochambeau;

mon goût pour un état dont je n'avois vu que l'image, me fit faire toutes les démarches possible pour être employé; la grande concurrence, et mon absence, rendirent toutes mes demandes inutille.

mes parents même par attachement crurent que leur de bonne volonté suffiroit, ne pouvant rien désiré pour mon avancement, ayant a 24 ans 3 ans de commission de capitaine de dragons, mais j'avois toujour regardé un grade, comme humiliant celuy qui ne la pas merité, je me suis rendu justice, en rougissant de voir un vieux lieutenant sous mes ordres, ou ceux de mes semblables couvert de blessures, et d'action distinguée oublié pour leur ancienneté,

si les graces que j'ai obtenu du roy m'ont été agreable, c'est dans l'espoir d'y trouver plus d'occasion de remplir les engagement que j'ai contracté, je ne les regarde que comme une avance que l'on me fait et que je prometz de rien negliger dans les occasions qui se presenteront pour m'acquitter.

je pris le parti d'écrire a un de mes amis, lieutenant colonel du regiment de soissonnois, pour le prier de remettre une lettre au Cte de St Mesme a son arrivé de gibraltar et de l'engager a me recevoir comme chasseur dans son regiment pour faire la guerre d'amerique, cette premiere me repondit que le Cte de St Mesme n'étoit pas encore arrivé, que mon zelle ne pouvoit qu'être admiré, mais que dans le moment ou je lirois sa lettre l'escadre seroit surement partie, toute l'armée etoit embarquée en rade attendant le bon-vent pour appareiller

j'etois au desespoir de ne pouvoir être de l'expedition

Mon cher chevalier, je t'obéis et commence ma lettre en te rendant compte des aventures de ma campagne: tu n'y verras qu'un triste récit de journal, mais exact.

J'étais occupé à faire un travail relatif au dépôt de la guerre, que - - - -

Mr le Cte de Rochambeau

Démarches que fait Berthier pour partir en Amérique.

Cte de St Mesme

FIRST PAGE OF BERTHIER'S JOURNAL, MENTIONING HIS INITIAL EFFORTS TO JOIN ROCHAMBEAU'S EXPEDITION TO AMERICA (*see p. xxvi*)

a providence ce 16 juillet 1781

je t'envoye ci joint mon cher ami, un memoire sur —
l'occupation du new-port, et de rod-island, avec le détail
des ... position des anglois, des americains, et des françois,
avec un plan qui te servira a pour intelligence. tu —
trouvera aussi un tableau de l'armée françoise.

Les Anglois nous ont laissé passer le reste de l'été
tranquillement dans notre camp, et chacun s'observois
pour nous, étions trop foible pour rien entreprendre
Le general rochambeau a profité de tous les beaux
jours pour ... faire faire a l'armée, des marches,
et des dispositions, sur tous les points de l'isle —
susceptible de débarquemens

j'ai employé tout le reste de mon tems a travailler
a la carte de rod-island, toutes celles que nous en
avions m'ayant parus tres imparfaites.

Le General rochambeau ne recevant aucune nouvelle
de france, et assuré qu'il ne luy viendrois pas de
seconde division, et ... qu'il ne pourroit jamais
rien entreprendre avec si peu de moyens, se —
decida a envoyer son fils en france pour
representer, la difficulté de remplir les intentions
de la cour avec si peu d'armes et troupes.

le 29 il est donc parti Mr le vicomte de rochambeau
pour france sur la fregatte du roy l'amazone.

La fin de novembre ...
on se preparois a faire passer l'hiver entre les
troupes en quartier d'hivert, on obtiendra des etats
que l'armée françoise s'emparerois de toutes les
maisons abandonné par les tories, qu'on ... qu'elle
l'armée ... mettre en etat de
recevoir les troupes, ... les off. logerois chez les —
particuliers, les reparations etant ... et le
mauvais tems arrivés, le 1 novembre l'armée
leva son camp et pris ses quartiers dans les
villes, l'infanterie de la legion de l'auxun
a 50 chevaux seulement resta au neck et furent
etablis dans les maisons qui y sont. Le reste
de la legion fut pris ses quartier a lebanon
a 13 milles de providence, ce qui avoit deux
objets, la facilité des fourages, et pouvoir etre
en poste, pour prêt a marcher sur les partis
ennemis qui debarqueroint sur la ....

PAGE FROM BERTHIER'S JOURNAL MENTIONING HIS "MAP OF RHODE ISLAND" (*see p. xxvi*)

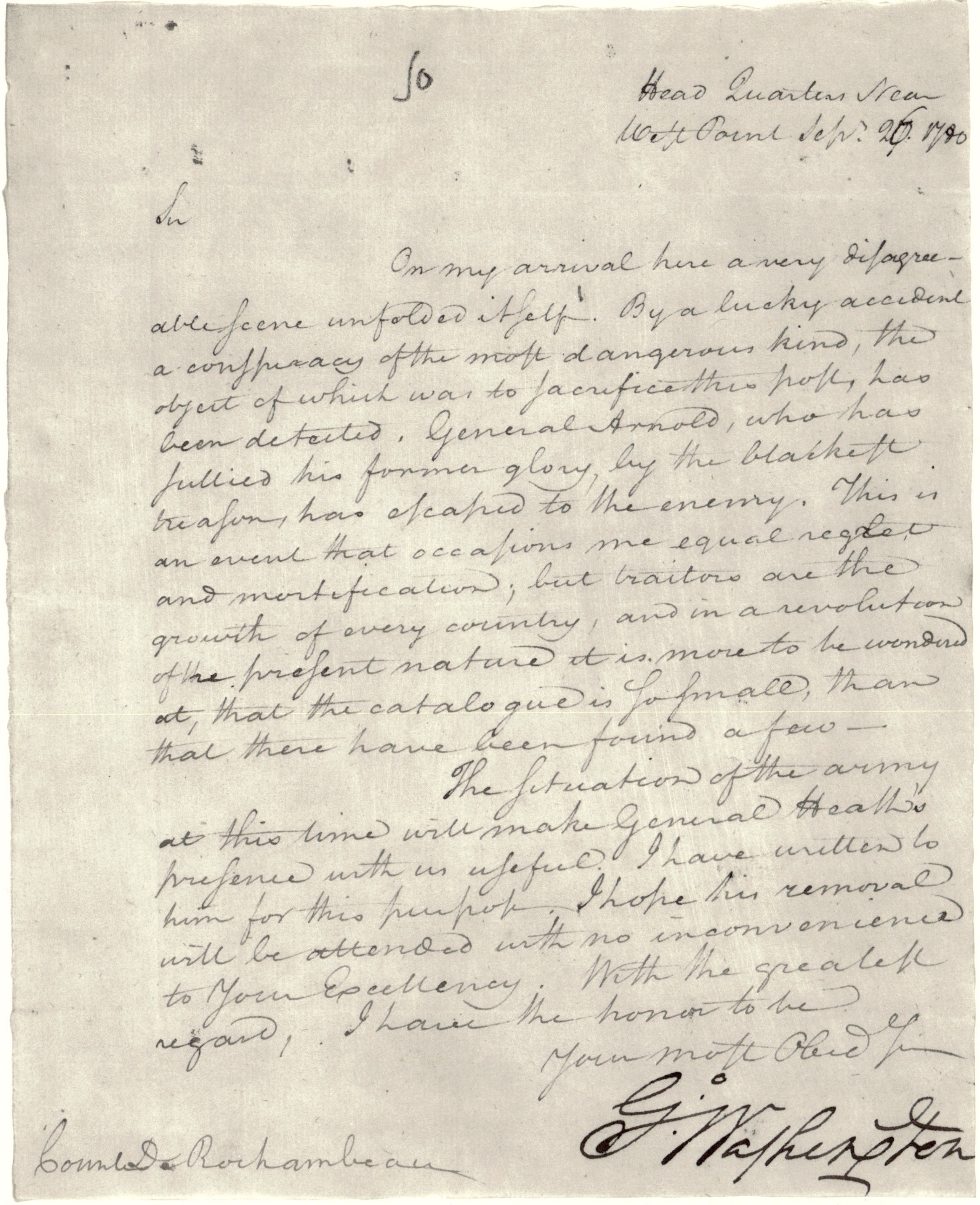

50

Head Quarters Near
West Point Sepr. 26. 1780

Sir

On my arrival here a very disagreeable scene unfolded itself. By a lucky accident a conspiracy of the most dangerous kind, the object of which was to sacrifice this post, has been detected. General Arnold, who has sullied his former glory by the blackest treason, has escaped to the enemy. This is an event that occasions me equal regret and mortification; but traitors are the growth of every country, and in a revolution of the present nature it is more to be wondered at, that the catalogue is so small, than that there have been found a few—

The situation of the army at this time will make General Heath's presence with us useful. I have written to him for this purpose. I hope his removal will be attended with no inconvenience to Your Excellency. With the greatest regard, I have the honor to be

Your most Obed. Servt

G. Washington

Count De Rochambeau

WASHINGTON'S LETTER TO ROCHAMBEAU INFORMING HIM OF BENEDICT ARNOLD'S TREASON (*see p. xxvii*)

Grace au ciel il me refte encore deux bras et une jambe pour le fervice de mon Roi.

GRENADIERS FROM THE SOISSONNAIS REGIMENT IN THE NAVAL BATTLE OF THE CHESAPEAKE,
16 MARCH 1781 (see p. xxvii)

how pleased you will be to hear this good news, which secures the fortunes of my whole family. Therefore, without further ado, I shall resume my journal.

March 1781 As a consequence of the loss of the *Culloden* in the storm and the capture of the *Romulus*, the naval forces of France and England were nearly equal. The English had but one more vessel than we; however, their ships were more powerful. Everyone was complaining of our failure to take advantage of this situation, and Arnold's raids [in Virginia] were raising quite a clamor. The Comte de Rochambeau was anxious to seize every opportunity to prove to America the interest of France and awaited only the moment when the French fleet was ready to sail in order to prove it. He persuaded M. Destouches to hasten preparations for embarking M. de Vioménil with 1,200 men and taking them to the Elizabeth River to join the Marquis de La Fayette in an expedition to capture Arnold, and he sent a courier to inform the Marquis. Meanwhile, the Admiral was ordered to moor his ships broadside in the Chesapeake in case the English should complete their repairs and come to attack him. The success of this project, which would have been assured had it been undertaken a month earlier, was compromised by the energy with which the British repaired their ships, knowing as they did that the French squadron was preparing to sail.

6 March The troops were embarked on the 6th, but the ships were held in port by contrary winds. Despite the bad weather, M. Destouches exerted himself to the utmost, but the trouble stemmed from M. de Ter-

nay, who had kept the fleet virtually idle in the harbor, unprepared for action.

Everyone was vying with everyone else to take part in this expedition.[48] With great difficulty I succeeded in obtaining permission to sail as a staff officer, and my brother accompanied the Vicomte de Noailles [second colonel of the Soissonnais] as his aide-de-camp.

General Washington, whom the French army had been expecting for several days, arrived the morning of the 6th.[49] He came by ferry and at once went on board the flagship, where he was rendered the honors of a Marshal of France. All the general officers were gathered there. He then went ashore and was greeted on the quay by the whole General Staff of the army to the booming of guns from the French batteries. All the troops were under arms, forming a great parade and lining his route on both sides of the street from the quay to his lodgings. Each general saluted him at the head of his division, while the Comte de Rochambeau with his whole staff went ahead in order to salute him at the head of the senior regiment [Bourbonnais]. Thus the General passed before the whole army. The nobility of his bearing and his countenance, which bore the stamp of all his virtues, inspired everyone with the devotion and respect due his character, increasing, if possible, the high opinion we already held of his exceptional merit.

He dined at the house of General Rochambeau. That evening he was escorted through the town, which was all illuminated. The townspeople hastened to light his path with torches and express their genuine

Baptiste Berthier qui existera lors de son décès" is the father's petition requesting it. The perquisites of the governorship included "apartments" for the incumbent. As things turned out, Berthier never succeeded his father in this post. With the advent of the Revolution the ministries were moved to Paris and the post of governor of the "hôtels" in Versailles was abolished by a law of 27 March 1791. Berthier père thus left the buildings he had designed, presided over, and occupied for some thirty years.

48. The rivalry extended even to the higher ranks. The Duc de Lauzun, for example, relates in his *Mémoires* ([2], pp. 284–285) that he himself, encouraged by Washington, had hoped and expected to be given command of the French landing forces being transported to Virginia. Upon arrival in Newport (after a winter of relative inactivity in Lebanon, Connecticut) he discovered, how-

ever, that the Marquis de Laval (colonel of the Bourbonnais Regiment) was slated for this honor. In a somewhat heated exchange with Rochambeau, Lauzun insisted that it was "my turn to march." Thereupon, according to Lauzun, Rochambeau solved the problem by entrusting the top post to General Baron de Vioménil, "who didn't want it," and demoting Laval to second place, for which the latter "has never yet pardoned him." Lauzun also maintains that by this same stroke Rochambeau was depriving Lafayette of the top command of the Virginia expedition, since, had the French forces successfully joined up with Lafayette's Americans, Vioménil would have outranked Lafayette in the allied hierarchy.

49. On Washington's visit to Newport, see Clermont-Crèvecœur's journal, n. 19.

joy. The house of a Tory who did not wish to illuminate it had all its windowpanes broken by the populace, who threw stones at it until he was forced to follow the example of the rest in order to calm their fury. General Washington went to supper with the Baron de Vioménil.

7 March That morning the Baron was on board his ship [*Duc de Bourgogne*] and I aboard the *Neptune*. As the wind was still against us, we did not get under way until five o'clock in the afternoon of 8 March with 7 warships, the 44-gun *Romulus*, the supply ship *Fantasque*, and 2 frigates.

General Washington watched us leave from the high ground on the Neck, where he had gone to inspect the fortified camp of the army.

Since M. de Rochambeau was left in an exposed position by the departure of the fleet, he had a strong battery of 36-pounders erected on the shore near the town to protect it from possible bombardment by a hostile frigate. He manned his redoubts with 600 militiamen and ordered 1,800 more held on the alert, ready to cross over to Rhode Island from the mainland at the first signal, in case the English should choose this moment for an attack.

8 March The squadron got under way at five o'clock on the afternoon of Thursday, 8 March, in a light norther that continued until Sunday.[50] At two on Monday morning, in fog and variable winds, part of the squadron was caught in irons with sails aback, and at daybreak the *Duc de Bourgogne*, the *Neptune*, the *Eveillé*, and the *Surveillante* found themselves isolated from the rest of the squadron. Our position was critical, since the English fleet could have been in the offing.

Since his ships were sailing along at a good rate, the Admiral [Destouches] seized this advantage to tack back and forth to rally his squadron, but the fog rendered his search fruitless. He thereupon decided to lay a course for the Chesapeake Bay by coming up higher on the wind, which was then blowing from the southwest.

13 March On Tuesday at seven in the morning when we were at latitude 37°, 14 leagues east-northeast of Cape Henry, the *Surveillante* signaled sails on the horizon. She was ordered to pursue and recognized the three vessels we had lost, whereupon the whole fleet was reunited.

Strong southerly winds prevented the squadron from sailing close enough to windward to fetch Cape Henry. The Admiral detached the King's frigate *Surveillante* to reconnoiter Cape Henry as soon as possible and report the position of the enemy. With the southwest winds persisting, the squadron was blown towards the north and spent two days tacking back and forth and struggling against the wind.

16 March At daybreak the wind was still blowing from the same quarter, but less strongly; the horizon was misty and the visibility poor. The squadron was running on the port tack when a frigate was sighted two cannon-shots to windward. The Admiral immediately signaled the *Eveillé* and the *Surveillante* to give chase, but shortly thereafter large ships began looming out of the fog and there was no longer any doubt that this was the English fleet, which, having been warned that the King's squadron had put to sea, had been favored by west and northwest winds and had sailed on a broad reach to the Virginia coast and arrived at approximately the same moment. Consequently the Admiral signaled the squadron to form in line of battle on the port tack. The English fleet meanwhile continued on course approximately 2 leagues to the south on the same tack. At nine o'clock the King's squadron came up into the wind and tacked about in countermarch, and half an hour later the English followed suit. At half past ten the Admiral, noting that the wind had freshened and finding that the present tack was carrying his ships too close to the reefs along the northern coast of Virginia, ordered them to resume the port tack by wearing ship in countermarch.

The enemy was taking full advantage of their greater speed and, encouraged by their superior strength, continued to come up to windward, setting all their sails and running on the starboard tack. At noon they tacked about into the wake of the King's squadron.

50. Paralleling Berthier's eyewitness account of the Destouches expedition to the Chesapeake is the official report included above in Verger's journal (pp. 126–128); see also the general note on the expedition, *ibid.*, n. 33, and Vol. II, No. 12.

Before one o'clock their vanguard had come within half a league of the tail end of the French line, which they apparently planned to attack to leeward. Up to this time the Admiral had been maneuvering so as to allow the *Eveillé* and the *Ardent* time to repair their topsail-yards, which they had broken in tacking, and had neither avoided nor sought battle. He thought only of upholding the honor of the King's arms, since he knew then that, having failed to anticipate his enemies in the Chesapeake, his expedition was no longer feasible. Taking the initiative, he bore down in countermarch upon the head of the English line, running down it to leeward on the opposite tack to give his ships a better chance to use their lower batteries in the heavy sea then running.

At one o'clock the lead ship of the French came within range of the lead ship of the English, and several moments later both sides opened fire. As the head of the English line bore away, the French vanguard followed suit in order to remain broadside to her, so that these portions of the two squadrons were fighting one another down wind. The English, who had not reckoned on the French squadron's tacking down on them, were in a sudden quandary whether to continue to windward or bear away, and two of their ships were momentarily under fire from the King's ships without any means of responding. The combat was continued before the wind by the ships bearing away in succession until the middle of the enemy line was reached. The Admiral, seeing that the maneuver of the English vanguard would permit him to reach no more of their ships while running to leeward, decided to bring his squadron back up to windward and tacked it to port in succession, thus enabling his whole fleet to file past the head of the enemy line.

This maneuver was a complete success. After receiving the broadside of the fifth French ship, their leading ship bore away and took at her poop the fire from the French vanguard and, in addition, two broadsides from the *Neptune*, which passed her within pistol range. The tail end of the English fleet had kept up to windward and found itself within combat range of the French rear guard. The leading ship of the English quit the line and sailed off before the wind, whereupon the English sent a frigate to take her in tow. The

attack of the English rear guard did little damage to the ships within range. When the 44-gun frigate *Romulus* in our line found herself quite far from her leading ship, the English three-decker *London* appeared to cut off our rear guard, but the *Romulus* delivered her a timely broadside that broke her principal topsail-yard. This obliged her to bear away and retire from the line, while keeping up a withering fire to little avail.

The *Conquérant* suffered considerable damage because while she was fighting the English vanguard her rudder had been badly damaged, preventing her from being able to follow her lead ship and thus exposing her to the fire of the whole enemy line. Her principal adversary was the *London* until the *Neptune* intervened and the *London* let go.

After the firing ceased on both sides, the French squadron found itself ahead and to leeward of the English. The Admiral gave the signal to close up the battle line on the port tack, without regard to the ships' regular positions in the line. This maneuver was executed promptly by all the ships except the *Conquérant*, which, having lost her rudder, was unable to steer. This incident prevented the Admiral from reopening the attack on the English, who were up to windward. At nightfall they headed for the Chesapeake, and we sailed to the south under shortened sail, with all our lamps lighted.

17 March On Saturday the weather was fine, and we saw no sign of the enemy. We hove to, and the captains were ordered on board the flagship to report the condition of their vessels, all of which, except the *Conquérant*, were in condition to re-engage the English. A council of war was held, and despite our slight advantage M. Destouches decided to proceed to Newport to repair his squadron.

18 March The squadron took advantage of the good weather to make repairs and resumed its voyage. Nothing of interest occurred until Sunday the 18th when at seven in the morning we saw a ship to leeward, which the *Surveillante* pursued and captured. She was coming from St. Lucia and, after stopping in the Bermuda Islands, was bound for New York. She had 4 English officers on board and a cargo of sugar, syrup, and rum. She told us of the declaration of war between Holland and England and of the capture of St. Eustatius by Admiral Rodney.[51]

21 March From the 19th to the 21st the wind blew from the northwest and north-northwest, and the squadron made little headway.

22 March On the 22nd at noon the *Eveillé*, which was leading the squadron, took a very timely sounding and found but 15 fathoms. The Admiral promptly signaled the whole squadron to tack ship, since the current had been setting us to the eastward very close to Nantucket Shoals.

23 March Off the island of No Man's Land with the coast of "Mathias Veniar" [Martha's Vineyard] and its surrounding reefs to the northeast, a furious gale sprang up from the south and southwest, which obliged the squadron to heave to, but the considerable leeway we were making so near the reefs barely 4 leagues off, placed our ships in great peril. The Admiral decided to get under way again, despite the wind, and sail as close-hauled as possible, even at the risk of being dismasted. A fog so thick that you could not see the prow of the vessel closed in, and we lighted all our lanterns and fired guns and muskets every fifteen minutes to avoid colliding with one another. When the fog lifted and the wind died down, the squadron was seen to be scattered all over the horizon. It was rallied; however, as the wind was still ahead, preventing us from laying course to clear the coasts of Martha's Vineyard, the Admiral ordered us to anchor. But then the wind hauled to the northeast and blew very hard. Several ships began to drag their anchors, so we got under way again. Most of the ships cut their cables.

25 March The squadron was again reunited, including the *Surveillante*, which had been sent to the Chesapeake and had caused us much anxiety. The wind blew fresh from the southeast, the weather was fine, and we anchored at six o'clock that evening in the harbor at Newport.

26 March The *Surveillante* had been anchored off Cape Henry when the English arrived at midnight of the 17th and anchored 3 leagues off Cape Charles. At

daybreak the frigate got under way to join the English squadron, mistaking it for ours. Since she was moving cautiously, she recognized her error. She was hotly pursued, but because of her superior speed her pursuer soon abandoned the chase. She returned a second time to examine the condition of the English fleet, which had got under way and had anchored off Cape Henry. After making his observations, the Marquis de Cillart returned to join our squadron.

The losses suffered by the French squadron on the 16th amounted to about 80 killed and 120 wounded. Among the former were Captain Cheffontaine and Ensign Kergus [both of the *Conquérant*] and 2 warrant officers.

Composition of the two fleets on 16 March

French (in order of battle)	Guns	English (in order of rank)	Guns
Le Conquérant	74	London	
Le Jason	64	(three-decker)	98
L'Ardent	64	Royal Oak	74
Le Duc de		Robust	74
Bourgogne	80	Bedford	74
Le Neptune	74	Europe	64
Le Romulus, frigate	44	America	64
L'Eveillé	64	Prudent	64
La Provence	64	Adamant	50
L'Hermione, frigate	32	——frigate	44
La Surveillante,		——frigate	32
frigate	32	——frigate	32
Le Fantasque,		Ships: total guns	562
supply ship		Frigates: total guns	108
Ships: total guns	528*		
Frigates: total guns	64		

*[Counting *Romulus* as a ship]

During our absence nothing interesting had occurred in Newport beyond the general anxiety about us. General Washington had remained with the French army for eight days, which he had spent inspecting all the defenses and drilling the regiments. At this meeting the generals must surely have settled on a plan of campaign.[52]

15 April We received word that the English fleet had anchored at Sandy Hook and that the *Robust* and

51. Great Britain declared war on the United Provinces 20 December 1780. Rodney captured St. Eustatius 3 February 1781. Cf. Clermont-Crèvecœur's journal, n. 193.

52. Cf. Clermont-Crèvecœur's journal, n. 19, concerning the plans discussed by the generals at Newport.

the *Royal Oak* had been disarmed and brought alongside the docks in New York for repairs to the damage sustained in the action of 16 March.

20 April M. de Béville, quartermaster-general of the army, returned from a trip to the Hudson River, and all signs indicated an impending movement of the army.[53] Orders were issued to transport the contents of the magazines, as well as all equipment not needed on campaign, to the magazine established in Providence.

6 May The frigate *Concorde*, which had left Brest on 27 March, arrived in Boston after a voyage of 42 days. It brought the Vicomte de Rochambeau and also M. de Barras, who came to take command of the fleet as successor to M. de Ternay.[54] The Vicomte brought news that a convoy escorted by the *Sagittaire* was en route with supplies and recruits for the army. It was scheduled to leave Brest with a large squadron commanded by M. de Grasse, who was going to the Windward Islands.

The last days of May were spent transporting to Providence everything the troops could not take with them on the march, and we received orders to prepare for a march, which could only mean that we were to join the American army on the Hudson.

The whole army had spent a delightful winter in Newport, and as each man got the word and prepared to leave, the pleasures ceased and gave way to regrets in which the whole town joined, especially the women.

Although Newport is largely inhabited by Tories, and the English had expressed such a low opinion of the French that on our arrival its residents had closed their doors to us, there was now a universal sigh of regret. Everyone's feelings had changed so much that each officer was like a member of his host's family. Even the most rabid Tories had made friends with the French. This was the result of the Comte de Rochambeau's conduct—which was courteous, wise, and calm—and the good discipline he maintained in his army.

This island, 4 leagues long and 1½ wide, is traversed by 9 superb roads and is covered with houses in which honest families live simply off their produce and practice their various religions without dissension or discussion. The race is remarkably pure. All the women here are pretty and fresh-looking, thanks to their morals, to the regularity and sobriety of their lives, and to the salubrious climate.

People here cannot believe that a man would think of seducing a girl, so the latter are allowed an extraordinary amount of freedom. Their parents often leave them alone with young men. They kiss one another quite casually. The girls seek only to please and to use their freedom in associating with men to make a good choice, on which their future happiness depends. When young people fall in love, they inform their parents and from that moment on are constantly together. They even spend half the night in conversation after their parents have gone to bed without taking the slightest advantage of this liberty, which is regarded as a sacred trust, by doing anything wrong. In

53. Washington to Rochambeau, Headquarters, New Windsor, 30 April 1781: "General de Beville will, I presume by this time, have reported to your Excellency the substance of his conference with me, and his own opinion of the different Routes from Newport to the North River. I can only, as I have done before, recommend to you to proceed in making the necessary preparations for the Field, and assure you again that you shall have the earliest notice should any movements of the Enemy make yours necessary by land. . . ." Letter in the Rochambeau Papers, Paul Mellon Collection; printed in *Writings of GW*, XXII, 12–13. The same day Washington wrote to Jeremiah Wadsworth, agent of the French army for the procurement of supplies: "General Beville having made the tour from Rhode Island to Camp, and back again on different routes, and having taken every precaution, to obtain an

accurate knowledge of the Country and roads; will be able to advise and settle with the Commanding Officer of the french army, which will be the most convenient route for the March of the Troops. . . . On many accounts, the March on the Sea Coast would certainly be the most eligible, and indeed I see no considerable obstacle in the way of it, except the Ferries." *Writings of GW*, XXII, 11–12. For a note on Wadsworth's important role in assembling supplies for the French, see Chastellux (4), I, 258–259, n. 42.

54. Concerning the arrival of the *Concorde*, see Clermont-Crèvecœur's journal, n. 21. This was not, incidentally, Barras's first visit to Rhode Island; he had come here in 1778 with d'Estaing's squadron as commander of the *Zélé*.

Connecticut it is even the custom for two lovers to lie down together on a bed for several hours during the day, or more often the evening, during which they talk of their future happiness. (This is called "bundling.") I have entered several rooms where I have found them thus engaged and where, without stirring, they continued to express their affection for one another with the utmost propriety.

Once a young lady is married, however, she becomes as discreet as she had beforehand been free in her ways and anxious to please. As a wife she belongs entirely to her husband and is subservient to his wishes, spending all her time in caring for his household, his children, and doing everything to make them happy. You have to admit, my dear friend, that things are different in France, but . . .

All the young ladies were allowed the same freedom with us. This we did not hesitate to attribute to our own charm. We were delighted to find the road ahead apparently so easy. Well, we were very foolish and were much embarrassed to find ourselves suddenly confronted with an insurmountable barrier. If some succeeded in crossing it, it was only by the vile means of false promises, a form of seduction unknown here before our arrival. But as far as the married women are concerned, there have been no such instances of seduction.

7 June We were very worried about the convoy announced by the Vicomte de Rochambeau when we learned that the vessels had just entered Boston harbor one by one after having been scattered by a storm. The *Stanislas* had been captured by an English frigate.[55]

The Comte de Rochambeau had arranged with General Washington a plan of campaign that could only be directed towards one of the two points occupied by the English: New York or the Chesapeake Bay.

He sent a frigate to inform the Comte de Grasse in the Islands of these plans, which are being kept secret.

9 June The army received orders to leave Newport. It embarked in two divisions one day apart to go and camp in Providence, 25 miles away.

10 June The camp was a mile and a half out of town on the road to Hartford. Its right flank rested on this road and its left on the Providence River.[56] M. de Choisy had remained in Newport with about 400 French soldiers and 1,000 American militia to occupy the town and guard our fleet, which was moored broadside after taking aboard all our siege artillery.[57]

Providence is a small city of the second category, well built and thickly settled. In peacetime it carries on a thriving commerce because of its situation, since frigates can come up to its docks. It is the residence of the Governor of the State of Rhode Island.

The army halted here until the 18th. Meanwhile, the recruits from the convoy arrived. We made route-marches to accustom the troops to the road and repaired all the wagons. Each company was allowed one of 1,500 pounds' capacity for all its baggage and the tents of the soldiers and officers; one wagon was assigned to the regimental staff, and each regiment was allowed a supplementary wagon, totaling 12 for each regiment.

Owing to the difficulty of procuring forage and finding enough houses for the army staff and headquarters, it was decided to march the army in four divisions and distribute the artillery between them.[58]

18 June The First Division left to camp at Waterman's Tavern, 15 miles away, under the command of the Comte de Rochambeau and was led by the Vicomte de Rochambeau as assistant quartermaster-general.

19 June The Second Division left under the command of the Baron de Vioménil and was led by the Chevalier [Charles] de Lameth, assistant Q.M.G.

55. See Clermont-Crèvecœur's journal, n. 25.
56. See map, Vol. II, No. 27.
57. Concerning the troops left at Newport under Choisy, see Clermont-Crèvecœur's journal, nn. 22 and 25. Verger was among those who remained at Newport; see his journal, pp. 130ff. The siege artillery, as distinguished from the field artillery, was eventually taken to Yorktown in the ships of Barras's squadron.
58. For further details, see Vol. II, Itineraries 1 and 2. The route is summarily indicated on the general map of camps and marches, Vol. II, No. 162, and is shown in detail in the series of road maps, Nos. 13ff., and of campsites, Nos. 26ff. The journal of Clermont-Crèvecœur (pp. 28ff.) also describes the march; he was a lieutenant in the Auxonne artillery, attached to the First Division. The dates in his and in Berthier's journal are thus staggered three days apart.

20 June The Third Division left under the command of the Comte de Vioménil and was led by M. [Victor] Collot,[59] assistant Q.M.G.

The Lauzun Legion, which had spent the winter at Lebanon, had been ordered to prepare to leave on the 20th, the day on which the First Division would arrive at Windham. This corps was to march in a separate column 9 miles to the left of the army in order to cover its left flank on the march—following the Sound by way of the Salmon River, Middletown, Wallingford, Oxford, New Stratford [Monroe], and Ridgefield, where it was to await further orders.[60]

21 June The Fourth Division left under the command of the Comte de Custine and was led by M. Berthier, assistant Q.M.G. [i.e., the writer of this journal]. It is the march of this division that I shall describe to you in my account of the army's march. It left Providence at four in the morning and marched on a very bad road to its camp at Waterman's Tavern, where it arrived at eleven. The wagon train, after many vehicles had broken down, arrived at half past six that evening, and the tail of the artillery at midnight. The camp was situated at the left of the road, facing towards the Sound.

22 June The column left its camp at Waterman's Tavern at four and arrived at Plainfield [in Connecticut], 15 miles beyond, at eleven o'clock that morning. The road was sandy and quite pretty. All the people in the neighborhood came to visit our camps. We furnished the music and they danced. Each day there was a new party.

23 June The column left Plainfield at four in the morning and arrived at Windham, 15 miles away, at ten. The camp was a mile and a half beyond the town on the banks of the little Windham [Shetucket] River. This is a town of the third category, but it is well built and the women here are very pretty.

24 June The column left Windham at four and arrived at Bolton [Center], 16 miles beyond, at eleven the same morning. This town is very small, with a few widely scattered houses.

25 June The column left Bolton at four in the morning and arrived at East Hartford, 12 miles away, at half past nine. This town has but a single street and is 2½ miles this side of Hartford. Each division halted two days here to give the artillery and train time to cross the Connecticut River. They were parked half a mile beyond Hartford on the road to Farmington.[61] This river, which is crossed by ferry, caused us no little trouble.[62] I was quite happy to get everything belonging to my division safely across on the 26th. The column halted at East Hartford the 26th and 27th.

26 June Hartford, the capital of the province of Connecticut, is situated on the west bank of the river of that name. It is one of the most important cities of the second category and is large, well built, with a fine state house and some very wealthy inhabitants. Since ships of 100 to 200 tons can come up the river to the town, it carries on a lively trade.

28 June The column left East Hartford at four in the morning, crossed the river, and arrived in Farmington, 12 miles beyond, at noon. This town of the third category contains some of the handsomest houses and

59. Georges-Henri-Victor Collot (1751–1805) returned to the United States during the period of the French Revolution. After serving as governor of Guadeloupe, where he was taken prisoner when this island capitulated to the English, he came to the United States as a prisoner-of-war on parole. In 1796 the French minister Adet sent him to make a confidential survey of the Mississippi Valley, with the recovery of Louisiana in mind. Collot's movements became a matter of great concern to both Spanish and American officials (including President John Adams). Collot was among those scheduled for deportation under the terms of the Alien and Sedition Acts of 1798. After his return to France he had printed in both French and English his *Journey in North America, containing a Survey of the Countries watered by the Mississippi, Ohio, Missouri, and other Affluing Rivers . . .* , accompanied by engraved views and maps that have remained a landmark in the cartographical history of the Mississippi Valley. Although printed in 1804, the *Journey* was not actually published until 1826 by A. Bertrand, Paris; cf. Sabin Nos. 14460–61. A well-documented discussion of the Collot episode is in Arthur B. Darling, *Our Rising Empire, 1763–1803* (New Haven, 1940), pp. 249–262, "The 'Assaults' of France—Collot's Journey."

60. The route of the Lauzun Legion is described in the "Plan for marching the army . . . ," Vol. II, Itinerary 1, and is shown on the general map of camps and marches, Vol. II, No. 162. No detailed maps of its route or campsites are known to the Editors.

61. The artillery park is shown on map, Vol. II, No. 19.

62. See "Plan for marching the army . . . ," Vol. II, Itinerary 1, marginal note on "The Hartford Ferries."

best people in America. It is in the middle of the beautiful, rich Connecticut valley.

29 June The column left Farmington at four and arrived at its camp at Barnes's Tavern [in Marion, town of Southington], 13 miles away at the end of the valley, at eight o'clock that morning. We found many Americans and some pretty women in our camp. The Comte de Charlus gave a big dinner for the prettiest ones, followed by a ball that lasted all night.

30 June The column left Barnes's Tavern and arrived at Break Neck [in Middlebury], 13 miles beyond, at noon. The road across the mountains is very hard on artillery.[63]

1 July The column left Break Neck and arrived at Newtown, 15 miles away, where it joined the Third Division, which had halted there for a day. At ten that evening an order arrived from the Comte de Rochambeau to march by brigades. Without stopping here to rest, my division joined that of the Comte de Vioménil to form a brigade commanded by the latter and led by M. Collot. Our dances ceased and our camps became more military.

2 July The Second Brigade left Newtown and marched 15 miles to Ridgebury, where it arrived at eleven o'clock. It was preceded on its march to the camp by an advance detachment of grenadiers and chasseurs. I was ordered to lead them and to choose a good position for them a mile ahead of the brigade on the road to New York, where they camped after stationing sentries at all points leading in from enemy territory. Here we received a change of itinerary.[64] The First Brigade, which was to have marched to Salem, had marched to Bedford instead, and we had received the same order, when suddenly at midnight there arrived from the General another order to proceed by a forced march to North Castle [Mount Kisco] where the whole army would be assembled.

3 July The Second Brigade left Ridgebury at three in the morning and at one that afternoon arrived at North Castle, 22 miles away, where it joined the First Brigade, which had just arrived from Bedford.

The Fourth Division, which had marched without a day's halt from East Hartford, 92 miles away, made this last 22-mile march in excessive heat with a cour-

age and gaiety quite in keeping with the ardor of the French. As we approached the enemy I was sent forward with an escort to requisition wagons at the halfway point for the sick and exhausted men. Since we were now on the edge of enemy territory, I was ordered to seize by force whatever was not yielded voluntarily. Using both methods, I obtained everything I needed.

The grenadiers and chasseurs camped on a height to the left of the New York road in front of a pond that adjoins the North Castle [Mount Kisco] meeting-house.[65] The rest of the army was encamped on high ground in back of the pond and the little North Castle River [Kisco River], with their left at the meeting-house and their right resting on a wood. The position was an excellent one, since its left was protected by marshes and closed by mountains and woodland. From here the army could either march towards the enemy in three columns or retire in two: one by way of Pines Bridge, which crosses the Croton River 4 miles to the north of the camp, and the other by way of Ridgebury and Bedford, 22 and 5 miles away respectively. Defending a position in this region is made easier by the fact that troops, especially if numerous, must march on the roads and cannot make detours without coming up against woods, mountains, and many insurmountable obstacles.

North Castle [Mount Kisco] has few houses, and they are widely separated. The headquarters was very poorly housed—just how poorly you will understand when I tell you that the assistant quartermasters-general were obliged to sleep in the open on piles of straw, which was, to boot, rather too green.

This forced march and change of itinerary resulted from intelligence received by General Washington that an English force was occupying a position this side of King's Bridge. Since part of his army was assembled, he detached General Lincoln with 1,000 men to surprise the English. Lincoln was to rendezvous with the Lauzun Legion, which had been ordered to join him by a forced march. Meanwhile, Washington took the rest of his army to White Plains and camped at Philipsburg, sending word to the French army to march as rapidly as possible to North Castle where, in

63. Cf. Clermont-Crèvecoeur's journal, p. 30.
64. On the change of itinerary, see Clermont-Crèvecoeur's

journal, nn. 31–32.
65. See map, Vol. II, No. 38.

case the English had made a sally in considerable force, it would form a second line in reserve 20 miles to the rear.

General Lincoln's expedition failed through the excess of ardor of his vanguard, who fired before they were ordered, thus alerting the English and enabling them to retire in good order after a brisk fire during which several Americans were killed.[66]

5 July During the 4th and 5th the army made a halt at North Castle [Mount Kisco]. General Washington came to visit the Comte de Rochambeau and passed down our lines. The troops were drawn up before the camp in line of battle without arms and wearing forage caps.

6 July The army began its march in a single column to join the American army at White Plains, 20 miles away. The camp was located at Philipsburg on an eminence that dominates the surrounding country.[67] (Philipsburg was burnt at the time of the evacuation of New York by the Americans during their retreat to White Plains [in 1776].) The American army composed the right wing, resting on the Saw Mill River to which you descend by a steep bluff; the American artillery park occupied the center; and the French army composed the left wing, resting on the Bronx River, whose banks are very steep. The American light infantry and dragoons were strung out from the right of the line all the way to Dobbs Ferry on the Hudson River, where a battery of four 12-pounders and two howitzers was emplaced. The heights at the left of the line were occupied by the French grenadiers and chasseurs, the Lauzun Legion, and an American unit commanded by Colonel [David] Waterbury. The field pieces were laid before the camp at each opening in the front of attack. The main guards were posted in advance on the most strategic heights, guarding all points at which the enemy could approach the camp.

This position, which is 12 miles from King's Bridge, can be approached from there by three main routes:

one along the banks of the Hudson, one leading to the center of the camp, and one to its left. It has also three main avenues of retreat over roads that cross the Croton River at New Bridge and Pines Bridge: the one from the right of the camp follows the Hudson to New Bridge [at the mouth of the Croton], the middle road leads directly to Pines Bridge, and that on the left passes through Newcastle and joins the middle road at Pines Bridge. Since all these roads were in very bad condition, we have been engaged in repairing them in both directions.

The headquarters was set up behind the camp in several widely separated houses.

Being definitely on the edge of enemy territory, the army was ordered to forage in advance of the position, as close to the enemy as possible. The assistant quartermasters-general were continually employed in reconnoitering forage so as to lead the army to it. These foraging expeditions covered an area between the camp and Long Island Sound extending from Rye, Mamaroneck, East Chester, and Chester to a point as close as possible to King's Bridge.[68] When we ran out of grass, we foraged in the barns, which were all full. We also discovered along the shores of the Sound large caches of hay and oats destined for shipment to the enemy in New York. These foraging expeditions were always supported by a detachment of 1,500 men and a troop of hussars. Although we succeeded in carrying off all the forage in their neighborhood, the English never interfered. I took advantage of these foraging expeditions and their escorts to make a survey of the country, which I shall send you with a detailed memorandum of the result.[69]

This whole country gives evidence of the horrors of war. The inhabitants we find here are in communication with the English and are pillaged by American raiding parties. All the Whigs here have abandoned their houses. Among them are some very handsome ones, deserted, half destroyed, or burned, with un-

66. On the Lincoln-Lauzun expedition, see Clermont-Crèvecœur's journal, n. 33.

67. The Philipsburg camp was on the heights between the Bronx and Sawmill rivers, within the boundaries of the present town of Greenburgh, Westchester County, New York; the area is now traversed from south to north by the Sprain Brook Parkway. See maps, Vol. II, Nos. 39–41 and 46.

68. On the foraging expeditions, see Clermont-Crèvecœur's journal, n. 52.

69. Berthier's "survey" (*reconnaissance*) must mean his large map "Position du Camp de l'Armée combinée à Philipsburg du 6 Juillet au 19 Aoust," which shows the country between the Hudson and Long Island Sound over which the foragers ranged. See map, Vol. II, No. 46.

tended orchards and gardens filled with fruits and vegetables, and driveways overgrown with grass 2 feet high. Only along the borders of the Sound is there less devastation, since there the inhabitants have changed sides whenever it has proved expedient.

I shall leave for a moment these accounts of the ravages of war to take you on a tour of a staff camp made famous by the visit that General Washington paid us there.

I have already told you that the headquarters staff were widely scattered. Since the house assigned to the Chevalier de Lameth, Dumas, and me was 3 miles from that of the quartermaster-general of the army [de Béville], we resolved, in order to be more accessible to our general's orders, to camp near his house, which was situated in a hollow at the left of the French lines.[70] We asked the intendant for 5 soldier's tents, which we pitched on a knoll in the midst of a copse where there were some 30 superb trees shading a small stream that flowed between rocks. Our sylvan abode was enclosed by a screen of foliage in which we had left openings so as to create natural vistas. These openings in our arbor were protected either by ditches or by fences.

A road 500 paces long cut through the underbrush led to our general's house. We picketed our horses on a slope to the right in a picturesque shed made of logs. Two fine trees marked the entrance to the camp enclosure. To the left as you entered was a pleasant greensward with some small trees under which two tents were pitched for our servants. The vista between them extended to a lovely meadow full of cattle. To the right the brook wound its way along the foot of a great ledge, which you ascended by a steep path. Halfway up was a den in which a big English bulldog was chained to warn us of the approach of strangers. Following along the ledge you came to a "tavern"

made of green trees, with one wall made of logs, providing an impenetrable shade that kept it always cool. There we made a couch of turf on which we could rest and read during the hottest part of the day. The trees to the left were very thick and formed a natural arch through which you entered a large salon enclosed and roofed over by several large trees, with a large turf settee at the end. Above it was a vista leading to the left wing of our camp 1,200 yards beyond. To the right you could see the entrance to my tent, erected in a small clump of trees, with a grassy bank at the door. To the left were the entrances to the tents of the Chevalier de Lameth and Dumas, erected in a natural bower of lovely trees and surrounded by a bank of verdure. Returning to the salon, opposite the settee was the entrance to a study with a table in the middle and several logs serving as seats. Since its eastern end was walled in by thick foliage, we always had shade there during lunch. To the left of this study the copse was still thick, and we cut a path that wound its way to the most beautiful trees beneath which a grassy seat invited you to enjoy a moment of solitude. At the end of this path was a private door that led only lovers know whither. The salon was furnished with work-tables in front of each tent and decorated with our arms, which hung from the trees. The walks were covered with yellow sand, and the ground under the trees and woods was carefully cleared and planted with turf and clumps of flowers.

Here, my dear friend, is where we spent six weeks of perfect happiness. Everyone was talking of our little camp, and after General Washington had dined with the quartermaster-general, he came to see it.[71]

On his arrival a military band posted a short distance off played marches and continued to play until he left. As he passed our tents he looked at the papers on our tables and saw what we were studying. On Dumas's

70. See map of "Logements du quartier général," Vol. II, No. 41, where Béville's headquarters is indicated by the figure "3." This was to the west of the Bronx River in the neighborhood of present Greenville near the junction of Central Park Avenue and Underhill Road.

71. Mathieu Dumas ([1], I, 70) recalled the sylvan abode and Washington's visit: "My friend Charles de Lameth, the two Berthier brothers who had recently arrived from France and were attached to our staff, and I set up our bivouac near the headquarters of our chief, M. de Béville,

in a very attractive spot among the crags and under magnificent tulip trees. We amused ourselves ornamenting the little area where our tents were pitched, and in a short time and at little expense we made it into a very pretty garden. General Washington when inspecting the lines wished to see us. We had been forewarned of his visit, and so, spread out on our camp tables, were a plan of the Battle of Trenton, with an account of it, a plan of West Point, and several others relating to the principal engagements of this war."

table was the evacuation of Boston and the surrender of General Burgoyne's army; on the Chevalier de Lameth's were the battles of Trenton and Princeton and the evacuation of Philadelphia; on mine were the landing of the French army in America, its position in Rhode Island, and its junction with the American army commanded by General Washington, with all the related plans.[72] Despite his modesty, he seemed pleased to find thus assembled all the successful and pleasant events of the war. He then repaired to the "tavern" to rest on the couch of turf. Beside it was a table with Madeira wine and punch, according to the American custom. He drank some with our generals and his whole suite, whereupon we all mounted our horses and escorted him back to his camp.

15 July A small squadron of 5 sail came up the North River to intercept the passage of our provision ships. It lay off Tarrytown and at nightfall began to shell the town. An outpost from the Soissonnais Regiment under the command of a sergeant, together with a detachment of Sheldon's dragoons who were stationed there to guard several barges, put up sufficient resistance to prevent the English from landing. During the night a boat loaded with bread accidentally drifted into the midst of the squadron and was captured. The squadron, whose flagship carried 16 guns, paid dearly for this incursion and was badly mauled by our 12-pounders and howitzers under the command of MM. de Neuris and de Verton.[73] When one of the vessels caught fire, 20 men jumped overboard. One swam ashore and reported that our shells had set the ship afire and that she had been pierced by more than 20 balls.

19 July General Washington and the Comte de Rochambeau made a reconnaissance in the Jerseys, from where they examined all the enemy works on New York island. They saw 4 or 5 small camps guarding those facing the North River, the largest of which was occupied by two battalions.[74]

21 July At eight in the evening a detachment of 5,000 men, including 2,500 French with six 12-pounders and four howitzers commanded by Major General the Chevalier de Chastellux, marched towards King's Bridge.[75] The detachment left camp in three columns; those on the right and center were ordered to rendezvous at Valentine Hill six miles away. The Americans forming the right-hand column marched along the banks of the Hudson, while the Bourbonnais and Deux-Ponts regiments composing the center column, which I was ordered to lead, took the road to Valentine Hill. The left-hand column, made up of the grenadiers and chasseurs of the Soissonnais and the Lauzun Legion and led by the Chevalier de Lameth, marched along the Tuckahoe Road.

This march over execrable roads, on which the column was halted every few minutes by guns that had bogged down or overturned in the pitch darkness, took all night. The Marquis de Laval, who commanded the column, had the artillery bring up the rear and did not wait for it to catch up, though I protested that, since we had no guide to leave with it, it might get lost.

22 July At one o'clock in the morning the column arrived at Valentine Hill, where General Rochambeau ordered the grenadiers and chasseurs to deploy in absolute silence, sent outposts forward, and placed the Bourbonnais and Deux-Ponts regiments in T-formation on the flanks. He sent me ahead of the American column to inform General Washington of his arrival. On my return the artillery had not yet arrived; the

72. It is evident that Berthier and the other young staff officers were drawing not only maps relating to the current campaign but also retrospective maps of earlier events in the war, especially Washington's victories. Examples of such maps have survived, including one that may have been among those exhibited to Washington on this occasion. This is a "Plan de la Surprise de Trenton, et de la marche sur Princetown, et Somerset, par le Général Washington" (presumably based upon Faden's engraved map, London, 1777, which would already have been available to the French), preserved in the Bibliothèque du Ministère des Armées "Terre," Paris, L.I.D.

166; the map is embellished with sprigs of laurel.
73. For Verton's later recollections of this incident, see Clermont-Crèvecœur's journal, n. 40.
74. On this reconnaissance, see Clermont-Crèvecœur's journal, n. 44.
75. On the reconnaissance in force of 21–23 July, see Clermont-Crèvecœur's journal, n. 45. The places mentioned in Berthier's narrative are indicated on his comprehensive map of the New York area, Vol. II, No. 46. This provides the best general picture of the events of 21–23 July, while Nos. 43–45 supply details of the actual reconnaissances made at that time.

General was obviously annoyed that it had been left behind, so I told him of the Marquis de Laval's order.

The American column passed Valentine Hill, followed by the French. The left-hand column composed of the grenadiers and chasseurs of the Soissonnais and the Legion marched towards Delancey Mills [on the Bronx River] in order to drive in all the pickets along the Sound from Morrisania to Horseneck.[76] The General ordered me to go back and find the artillery, which he believed had gone astray, and not to return until I had found it and urged it forward with all speed to join the troops. Being obliged to leave my American guide with the column, I found myself alone without knowing where I was going in a perfectly strange country full of enemy bands of Refugees [Loyalists]. Although sorely perplexed, I resigned myself to retracing my steps. I stopped at each fork in the road, but the night was so dark that I could see nothing. In order to find out whether the artillery had taken another road, I was obliged to dismount and feel the road at every crossroads to see if there were any tracks imprinted by its wheels in the dirt. Finally, after doing this for 2 miles, I felt ruts at a fork where it had taken the wrong turn. I galloped after it as fast as my horse's legs could carry me and was pleased to catch up with it. It was fortunately on a road that led back into the right one. At daybreak I reached the heights above King's Bridge where the detachment had occupied a fairly good position.

Generals Washington and Rochambeau, with their respective engineers, aides, and myself, made a reconnaissance of all the English works along the Harlem River between King's Bridge and Morrisania.[77]

When we reached Morrisania, we surprised a sort of light corps of about 20 Loyalists, including foot and horse, which had not had time to cross the river. General Washington had left his escort of light infantry a mile behind, so he sent forward the 8 dragoons who were still with him to charge them. MM. de Damas, Vauban, Closen, Lauberdière, and I joined them. We set off at a gallop, but when we arrived on the scene, they took refuge in a house from whose windows they greeted us with musket fire. As we surrounded the house firing our pistols, their fire diminished somewhat; then we called on them to surrender, threatening to give them no quarter and to burn the house if they refused.

While we kept up a very lively fire with our pistols

76. Berthier's statement, included as a marginal note in his manuscript, is difficult to decipher and interpret. The last part of the sentence appears to read: "pour replier tous les postes depuis le Sund, jusques Morisania et horseneck." Since "Horseneck" was a contemporary name for Greenwich, Connecticut, he probably is referring to the enemy pickets stationed along the shore of the Sound in the area extending from Greenwich, on the east, westward to Morrisania.

77. Washington's engineers included Duportail, chief of the American Corps of Engineers, and Bechet de Rochefontaine—both Frenchmen in the American service. Rochambeau's chief engineer was Colonel Desandroüins. In reporting on the reconnaissance Rochambeau also mentions the presence of Béville, his quartermaster-general; see "Journal de ce qui s'est passé depuis l'arrivée du Corps français au Camp de Philipsburg," in Doniol, v, 518–519. It will be noted that Berthier does not class himself among the engineers. Although he had been trained as a topographical engineer (ingénieur géographe des camps et armées du Roi), these topographical engineers were not a part of the Corps of Engineers (Corps Royal du Génie), which was a distinct branch of the army, in general somewhat jealous of its separate status and prerogatives. The results of the reconnaissance of 22 July were embodied in numerous maps, which fall into two groups:

(1) a "Plan of the Northern Part of New York Island," showing the forts on the northern end of Manhattan, with the east bank of the Harlem from Kingsbridge down to the site of the present 181st Street bridge (cf. Vol. II, No. 43); and (2) a "Plan of the Eastern part of New York Island opposite the junction of the Sound and Harlem River," showing Hell Gate, Buchanan [Ward's] and Montresor [Randall's] islands—corresponding to the present Triboro Bridge area (cf. Vol. II, No. 44). Signed examples of these maps by Desandroüins and Crublier d'Opterre of the French engineers and by Rochefontaine of the American engineers have survived. A comprehensive map of New York and vicinity, incorporating the more detailed reconnaissance, is preserved in the Archives du Génie, 14-1-3 (Places Etrangères: New York), with a staff paper entitled "Analise d'un mémoire sur l'attaque de l'Isle de New York et dépendances. . . ." This significant document, keyed to the map, discusses the various factors involved in an attack on New York, landing points, naval cooperation, etc. A somewhat similar paper entitled "General Observations on the manner to pass over [to] the island of New York" was prepared by Duportail for Washington; partially printed in E. S. Kite, Brigadier-General Louis Lebègue Duportail (Baltimore, 1933), 201–202.

and carbines, they called out that they were surrendering, but once out of the house, seeing that about 200 men had gathered across the river to support them and were firing at us with muskets as well as 4 field pieces loaded with grapeshot, they attacked us furiously. One of them approached me shouting "prisoner!" as he drew a brace of pistols from under his coat and fired on me at 5 paces, grazing my ear and crying, "Die, you dog of a Frenchman!" He was about to fire the other one when I got ahead of him by putting a ball through his chest, which killed him on the spot. We sabered, shot, or captured the rest, who had become bolder after seeing the Count de Damas's horse shot from under him. We captured 10 men and 7 horses. The rest flung themselves into the river, where some of them perished.

The generals watched this little skirmish, which lasted five minutes, at very close range.[78] We went back to join them, taking our prisoners to them, and after the reconnaissance was finished, we returned to camp. Meanwhile, the Lauzun Legion had captured about 30 men and horses. The loss of the Count de Damas's horse was the only casualty inflicted by the fairly heavy fire from the forts, batteries, and guardships of the enemy, not to mention the profuse sniping of their chasseurs, both horse and foot.

The detachment bivouacked all night and retired the next afternoon [23 July] without any opposition from the English.[79]

❦ August 1781 ❦

At the beginning of August the Comte de Rochambeau received by a frigate the Comte de Grasse's reply to his dispatch in regard to the coming campaign.[80]

Everything was now decided, and the secret was well kept. Although it was announced that we were going to attack New York, I believed that this was the least important point, for all signs indicated that we were about to move. We were ordered to repair and mark all the roads in the rear of the army and afterwards, under strong escort, all those leading to New York, probing as close to the enemy as possible. Feigning secrecy, the General ordered a commissary to build ovens in Chatham, New Jersey, which convinced the enemy that some troops would cross the Hudson River and march down the west bank to threaten Staten Island. We did not know what to think, for all signs indicated that a move was imminent. Even Clinton believed that we were threatening New York and worked continuously to prepare a warm reception for us.

Finally, on 18 August, all the French artillery and the paymaster's wagons were ordered to march back up to King's Ferry by way of Pines Bridge, forming the center column of the [allied] army.

On the 19th the whole army received the same order. The Americans formed the left-hand column, following the Hudson River to New Bridge, while the French, forming the right-hand column, were to proceed to North Castle [Mount Kisco] and Pines Bridge one day behind the artillery, which was to precede it by twenty-four hours.

The Comte de Vioménil, leaving on the 20th with the grenadiers and chasseurs, formed the rear guard.

I was assigned to lead the artillery column to King's Ferry, to have it camp as expediency required, and, since I was marching twenty-four hours ahead of the army, to take my orders on arrival from General Washington.[81]

78. For the locale of the skirmish see map, Vol. II, No. 44. Von Closen, who lost and recovered his hat amidst a rain of bullets, also gives a lively account in his journal (pp. 99–100). Many years later the incident was commemorated in a painting by the Bavarian artist Albrecht Adam; see Vol. II, No. 47, and descriptive note. Apparently the skirmish distracted the engineers from their observations, for Von Closen notes (p. 101) that on the following day (23 July), after making a reconnaissance from Throg's Neck, the engineers returned to Morrisania to complete their work there: "they stole ahead alone so as not to be disturbed in their observations." This

accounts for the double date, 22–23 July, on Desandroüins's signed version of his map of the Morrisania reconnaissance.

79. Berthier apparently did not accompany the generals to Throg's Neck, from which a further reconnaissance was made on the 23rd. See Clermont-Crèvecœur's journal, n. 51; and map, Vol. II, No. 45.

80. The crucial news from de Grasse reached the Philipsburg headquarters on 14 August. See Clermont-Crèvecœur's journal, n. 54.

81. Clermont-Crèvecœur accompanied the wagons of the artillery park in the column led by Berthier; see his jour-

THE CENTER COLUMN, composed of the artillery and the paymaster's wagons, scheduled to reach King's Ferry on the 21st.

THE RIGHT-HAND COLUMN, composed of the French army, scheduled to reach King's Ferry on the 22nd.

18 August

All the artillery, plus the paymaster's wagons, got off at eleven in the morning. I located the camp at the Abraham house, 9 miles away. The horses had suffered so much during our stay in Philipsburg that half of the artillery broke down 4 miles from camp. I rented oxen, which I sent back to retrieve it, and it arrived at four in the morning [19 August]. I collected others to draw it the next day and sent a messenger off at top speed for a remount of artillery horses that awaited us at Crompond.

19 August

At five in the morning the column set off for Pines Bridge, 10 miles beyond. I went ahead with 50 workmen, since I knew how bad the roads were. Fortunately the remounts arrived at the halfway point, but in spite of all the assistance the head of the column did not reach Pines Bridge until ten that night during a frightful storm. The bridge was down, so we had to ford the river. I had great fires built on either bank and the first wagons crossed without too much difficulty, though the night was so dark that some overturned. We had to work in the water, and the weather was so bad that, unable to persuade any of the American guides to remain in the ford to lead the vehicles around the rocks, I stayed there myself.

20 August

Finally, at two in the morning, the last wagon crossed. The camp was 200 paces beyond on the opposite bank. The poor soldiers, tired from pulling wagons the horses had refused to pull and soaking wet, had no tents and had to spend the night in bivouac, working to repair the broken gun-carriages. I ordered them to cut as much wood as they could burn.

21 August

Finally, on the next day, the column left for Peekskill. Finding this day's march too long, I halted it 2 miles short of the town. We arrived in camp very early and spent a more restful night.

19 August

The whole army set off in a single column, in reverse order, for North Castle [Mount Kisco], 20 miles away. The weather was so bad and the roads so cut up that the few wagons accompanying the troops, which carried their tents, could cover but half the distance. Consequently the army bivouacked in the mud all night in the pouring rain.

20 August

The column was obliged to halt on the 20th [at North Castle] to wait for its wagons.

21 August

After the wagons had joined the column, it set out to cross the Croton at Pines Bridge, then went on to camp at Hunt's Tavern, a distance of 8 miles in all.[82] The Comte de Vioménil, with the grenadiers and chasseurs who were serving as rear guard, followed it as far as Pines Bridge. It is very fortunate that the English sent no troops to hinder our withdrawal, which the bad roads and bad weather had thrown into such disorder. At Pines Bridge the army had converged on the same route as the center column, which it henceforth followed to King's Ferry.

nal, pp. 40–41. The route is described in the "Itinerary of the Marches of the Army from the Camp at Philipsburg . . . ," Vol. II, Itinerary 3. See also maps, Nos. 25 and 48.

82. See map of the camp at Hunt's Tavern, Vol. II, No. 61, and road map, No. 48, where the Hunt's Tavern camp is also shown but not so designated.

22 August The column [now a single column, led by the artillery and military chest] began its march to King's Ferry, 6 miles beyond.

I myself left two hours before daybreak to reconnoiter two roads, the one prescribed being the shorter. I found this road so bad that I decided to take the longer one. Consequently the artillery arrived without incident, though it had to march 3 miles farther.

I then went to General Washington for orders. He was on the river bank, presiding over the crossing of the troops and watching with great attention to see whether the English would send any armed boats or frigates to bar our passage. The General ordered me to bring up all the artillery to the ferry and begin loading it aboard and take it across immediately to the opposite bank, where I was to choose a convenient place for it to camp and to set up the forage magazine there. I carried out his orders promptly and returned to report to him that I had found a spot 2 miles from the river, near Haverstraw,[83] and had assigned the right and left wings of the camp to the artillery commander. I then returned to the ferry, where I stayed until the last gun had crossed. The energy of our soldiers, as well as of the Americans who ran the ferry boats, was such that we crossed the river, which is 2 miles wide there, in eight hours without the slightest accident. This column was composed of wagons, caissons, guns, and horses.

General Washington was impatient to get all the troops across the river. He sent me back to tell the Comte de Rochambeau to send his army up as quickly as possible. I left immediately and at nine that evening arrived at Peekskill, where M. de Rochambeau had arrived ahead of the army, which was 10 miles back at Hunt's Tavern. I reported to him General Washington's wishes and described the condition of the shorter road. He ordered me to go back at once to the army, procure 200 workmen, and return that same night in order to reach the bad road at daybreak and repair it so that the troops and wagons could use it the next

day. I reached the camp [at Hunt's Tavern] at midnight.

23 August I left with my 200 workmen at one in the morning and by a forced march got back to the bad road at five. By ten o'clock that morning, just as the army was arriving, my tremendous task was completed.

The army reached the ferry at noon and camped on the bluffs. It started to cross the river immediately and continued until midnight of the 25th, by which time it was all in camp at Haverstraw 2½ miles from the west bank.

The ferry is defended on the east bank by Fort La Fayette and on the west bank by the fort at Stony Point that the Americans took by storm in 1776 [1779].[84] Below King's Ferry the Hudson takes a more majestic course, its bed widening to 3 miles; this portion is called the Tappan Zee as far as Dobbs Ferry, where it narrows again to about 3,600 yards.

General Washington had gone ahead of the French army with 4,000 Americans to cover our left flank by marching via Paramus and Chatham. He occupied a position on the heights above Springfield [in New Jersey]. The English had no doubt that we planned to attack Staten Island and worked without respite to entrench themselves in their positions there.

The French army was to march in two brigades. The Chevalier de Lameth and I were attached to the Second Brigade.

25 August The First Brigade left Haverstraw for Suffern, 15½ miles away. I remained at the ferry to supervise the crossing of the wagons and camped there until midnight of the 25th, when the last vehicle crossed the river.

26 August At two o'clock in the morning I returned to the camp at Haverstraw. After reporting to the Baron de Vioménil that everything had crossed the river, I left at three the same morning with the camp detail to go ahead and arrange the billets. The Second Brigade left that day for Suffern, 15½ miles away.

27 August . . .[85]

83. This spot was in the present village of Stony Point (as distinguished from the fort on the Point proper), which was within the area known in 1781 as Haverstraw (then more extensive than the present township of that name). Cf. map, Vol. II, No. 63.

84. See maps, Vol. II, Nos. 48 and 62.

85. Berthier's manuscript ends at this point. The sequel—describing the march to Virginia, the Siege of Yorktown, the winter quarters in Virginia, and the 1782 northward return march to New England—has not been found, if indeed it was ever written. However, Berthier's activities during this interval of a year and a half are amply docu-

Part 2

SEA CAMPAIGNS

DECEMBER 1782–APRIL 1783

[The following letter addressed to Berthier by Quarter-master-General de Béville may appropriately find its place here as a preface to what follows. The original letter is preserved in the Archives de la Guerre, Berthier's personal dossier, pièce 42.

Providence, 28 November 1782

I have the honor to inform you, Sir, that you are included on the list, transmitted by the Comte de Rochambeau to the Baron de Vioménil, of the officers who are to embark in the Marquis de Vaudreuil's squadron, which is now at Boston.

You will continue, Sir, to be attached to the General Staff that is leaving for the Islands, as you were here. I am much pleased that this is the case, and offer you my sincere congratulations.

I enclose, Sir, the army's marching orders for leaving Providence and proceeding to Boston. As I have selected you to find quarters for the First Division, it will be necessary for you to leave on the 30th of this month, thus preceding the division by twenty-four hours. If the locality permits, you can lodge the lieutenant colonels and majors, and I beg you also to watch out for the sick officers.

I have the honor to be, very truly, Sir, your very humble and obedient servant

Béville

Since this letter was written it has been determined that the Bourbonnais Regiment will leave on December 1st, Soissonnais on the 2nd, Saintonge on the 3rd, and Royal Deux-Ponts on the 4th. Nothing is changed in respect to the march of the assistant quartermasters-general.]

Puerto Cabello, 16 February 1783

My dear Chevalier,

December 1782 As I sent you word by the frigate *Iris*, I embarked at Boston on 20 December in the *Souverain*, and my brother in the *Neptune*. On the 22nd the Marquis de Vaudreuil[86] went aboard his flagship. He sent the *Amazone* to Portsmouth with orders to the *Auguste* and *Pluton* for their departure to make a rendezvous with the fleet.[87] He proposed to cruise off Boston, a very dangerous procedure so late in the season, when severe storms are encountered. I should have preferred that he wait here in the harbor for the two vessels, since it is easier for a few ships than for a whole squadron to keep out of danger.

The Baron de Vioménil went aboard the flagship *Triomphant* on the 23rd. As he left the shore the fort, as well as the castle on Governor's Island, saluted him with 13 guns. They had done the same the day before for Admiral de Vaudreuil, whose ship had returned the salute.

24 December At noon the squadron got under way in a northwest wind.[88] The *Warwick* ran aground and was wrecked through the fault of her pilot. We carried little sail that night. On the 25th we set our course for Cape Anne off which we were to cruise until the ships from Portsmouth joined us. The winds were very light, but on the 26th they backed to south-southeast,

---

mented by the maps and itineraries preserved among his papers at Princeton and printed below in Vol. II. Itinerary 6, in particular, which describes the march of the wagon train from Annapolis to Williamsburg, is to some extent a personal journal. The next installment of Berthier's journal, strictly speaking, resumes the narrative of the campaigns with the author's departure from Boston for the West Indies in December 1782.

86. Although Berthier in his manuscript consistently calls the admiral of the fleet the *Comte* de Vaudreuil, he was actually the *Marquis* de Vaudreuil (Louis-Philippe de Rigaud, marquis de Vaudreuil [1724–1802]). The cor-

rection has been made here and subsequently, wherever the context requires it. The Marquis's brother, Louis de Rigaud, comte de Vaudreuil (1728–1810), commanded the *Auguste*, one of the ships at Portsmouth, N.H.

87. See Clermont-Crèvecœur's journal, p. 85ff. Clermont-Crèvecœur went to Portsmouth on the frigate *Amazone*.

88. In the Berthier manuscripts at Princeton (No. 41) there is a second but less complete version of this journal for the period 20 December 1782 (embarkation at Boston) through 15 February 1783 (arrival at Puerto Cabello). This is a succinct log-book, copied in formal clerical

blowing very fresh and rolling up a steep sea. Then they shifted to southeast, and a storm came up. The wind steadily increased, and at two in the morning we lost our topsails and ripped our foresail. As the storm

---

LIST OF THE FLEET[89]

In Boston

Warships	Guns	[Commanders]
Triomphant	80	[flagship, Marquis de Vaudreuil; flag captain, Montcabrier]
Brave	80 [74]	[Amblimont]
Souverain	74	[Glandevez]
Neptune	74	[Renaud d'Alein]
Hercule	74	[Puget-Bras]
Couronne	74 [80]	[Mithon de Genouilly]
Bourgogne	74	[Champmartin]
Duc de Bourgogne	74 [80]	[Charitte]
Citoyen	74	[de Thy (d'Ethy)]
Northumberland	74	[Médine]
Frigates		
Amazone	[36]	[Gaston, sent to Portsmouth]
Néréide	[40]	[Froger de l'Eguille]
Iris		bound for France [Traversay]
Transports		
Isle de France	[36]	[Elyot]
Reine de France	[14]	
Allégeance	[14]	
Fantasque	[36]	[Vaudoré, remained in Providence]
Clairvoyant, cutter	10 [14]	[d'Aché]
Warwick, corvette		[Kersabiec, remained behind]
[*Shirley*]	[14]	
[*Prudence*]	[14]	

In Portsmouth

Warships		
Auguste	80	[Comte de Vaudreuil]
Pluton	74	[Albert de Rions]

---

handwriting, noting only the weather and daily positions of the ship.

89. Berthier's list of the ships composing the Marquis de Vaudreuil's fleet has been collated with similar contemporary lists in Cromot Dubourg (2) and Von Closen, pp. 276–277, as well as with the one included in Noailles, *Marins et Soldats*, Appendix XI, p. 406. Discrepancies and

increased in violence, waves broke over the vessel. Our last hope was the mainsail. Since we were too close to shore to heave to, our sole chance of avoiding shipwreck lay in sailing as close to the wind as possible. The squadron spent that night in the greatest peril and would have been sunk with all hands had the storm lasted four hours longer. We were only 5 or 6 leagues from the reefs off the southern coast of Acadia [Maine] and east of the New Hampshire coast, which forms a gulf where rocks jut out 2 or 3 leagues from shore, leading to danger on either tack. Our last recourse would have been to put into Frenchman's Bay in enemy territory, but its navigation, of which we were ignorant, would have been dangerous in this misty weather. Fortunately at six in the morning the wind veered to northwest. Although it continued to blow as hard and the sea was appalling, we were able to sail out of danger to the open sea, and at four that afternoon we hove to. The Admiral gave the *Iris* permission to proceed to France.

27 December Our ships were scattered far and wide, and we had not been able to rally them before nightfall. By daybreak we had lost sight of the *Néréide*, the *Clairvoyant*, and all our transports. Only the warships remained, and all of them were damaged. During the day of the 28th we cruised off St. George's Bank, hoping to pick up the ships from Portsmouth.

29 December The winds blew very fresh from the northwest. The Admiral gave up his plan to wait for the *Auguste* and resumed his voyage.[90] On the 30th we were hove to. The seas were so steep that we had to extinguish the fires in the galleys and brace ourselves continually to avoid injury as the ship rolled from side to side. We kept shipping waves through the captain's cabin, which set the 'tween decks awash in water 6 inches deep. At nine o'clock on the morning of the 31st the *Bourgogne* lost her main topmast, and we reduced our speed to hers.

1 January 1783 The new year commenced with

additional information from these and other sources are given here in square brackets.

90. The course and adventures of the *Auguste*, from Portsmouth to her rendezvous with the fleet at Puerto Cabello (5 February 1783), are recorded in the journal of the Comte de Vaudreuil, *Neptunia*, No. 50 (1958), pp. 31–35.

more moderate winds. On the 2nd we were off Bermuda at ten in the evening, though not without some anxiety. All the ships passed very close to it. Although some were sailing high of his course, the Admiral, being surer of his position, did not bring his ship up. The discrepancies that exist between charts well deserve the attention of our Navy's hydrographic office (*Dépôt de la Marine*). M. de La Crenne's charts[91] vary more than a whole degree of north latitude from one of those in an English chart book by —— [blank in MS]. This atlas seemed to me carefully compiled according to the most recent observations.[92] M. du Rouret, lieutenant of the *Souverain*, had a copy. However, I forgot the small anxieties of the moment for one more imminent. I heard one of our officers tell a lieutenant in confidence that there was a fire aboard. This little joke seemed to me quite serious. I went to investigate, but fortunately several pails of water extinguished all my anxiety. The fire had started in the rope of a lantern that hung in the 'tween decks. It is always surprising, considering the prevailing negligence in this respect, that these fires do not occur more frequently. The galley stoves, the bake-ovens, the lamps in the sleeping cabins, and the smokers in the fo'c'sle should all be watched by a wise and prudent man who does nothing else.

Nothing of interest occurred until the 14th, when we sighted land at Puerto Rico. We chased and captured an English brig. Then, discovering a frigate under the land, we pursued her. She was the French frigate, *Aigrette*, coming out of San Juan, Puerto Rico. She had arrived two months before with 80 vessels loaded with provisions for The French Cape. The English fleet cruising off Samana had forced her to take refuge in San Juan. She brought us the first news of the Cadiz fleet that was to be commanded by the

Comte d'Estaing for the expedition to Jamaica. She warned the Marquis de Vaudreuil that Admiral Hood was cruising off Samana with 16 ships to waylay him.

An American brig, which had left Boston a few days after us, informed the Marquis de Vaudreuil that three hours after his departure an aide-de-camp of the Comte de Rochambeau had arrived from France in the frigate *Danaé*, commanded by M. de Capellis, with dispatches from the Court. This frigate had run aground at the entrance to the Delaware, which had not prevented her from landing all her dispatches and 2,000,000 *livres*. Several days later she had been freed and taken to Philadelphia. The dispatches had immediately been taken to Portsmouth and delivered to the Comte de Vaudreuil on the *Auguste*.

The Admiral ordered the *Aigrette* to return to Puerto Rico and send out 17 of the fastest provision-ships. He cruised up and down until the convoy, as well as the *Néréide* and the *Isle de France*, joined the squadron on 21 January. Don Solano, who had proposed the general rendezvous on the Spanish Main for the coming campaign, should have been on his way from Havana to join it. He was now due at Puerto Rico. Our admiral hoped by cruising along this coast to join up with him, for then we should be 22 warships against the 16 English. We would fall upon Hood, who did not anticipate such a junction, and fight him under very favorable circumstances; however, our castles in Spain did not materialize.

By the 21st we had had no news of the Spanish fleet, nor of the *Auguste* or the *Pluton*. After chasing two English frigates sent to watch us, our squadron lost no time continuing its journey, hugging the coast of Puerto Rico during the night so as to reach the entrance to the Mona Passage by morning. Since this is the only leeward passage to Puerto Cabello, it was

91. Jean-René-Antoine, marquis de Verdun de La Crenne (1741–1805), a French naval officer, had participated in an important hydrographic survey a decade earlier. The results of the expedition of the *Flore* were published in a work entitled *Voyage fait par ordre du roi en 1771 et 1772 en diverses parties de l'Europe, de l'Afrique, et de l'Amérique; pour vérifier l'utilité de plusieurs méthodes et instruments, servant à déterminer la latitude et la longitude, tant du vaisseau que des côtes, isles et écueils qu'on reconnoît: suivi de recherches pour rectifier les cartes hydrographiques, par Messieurs de Verdun de la Crenne*

. . . le chevalier de Borda . . . et de Pingré, 2 vols. with maps and tables (Paris, Imprimerie Royale, 1778). As a loyal son of the Dépôt de la Guerre, the army's map service, Berthier was quick to find fault with the navy's counterpart, the Dépôt de la Marine.

92. The English chart book, which Berthier does not identify, was perhaps *The English Pilot, The Fourth Book, describing The West India Navigation, from Hudson's Bay to the River Amazones . . .* (London, J. Mount and T. Page, 1773).

essential to hide our movements from the English lest they pursue us or cut us off from entering the passage. In this case we should have been obliged by our inferior numbers to take refuge in the Bay of Aguada [Aguadilla Bay] and anchor there. At daybreak we reached the entrance to the channel and started through it without sighting any sail. At eleven o'clock, upon spying a corvette, the Admiral changed course towards the southern coast of Santo Domingo. When he had lost sight of her, he resumed his southerly course, sailing as close to the wind as possible.

28 January We sighted Curaçao as we sailed to leeward. According to Don Solano's instructions, nothing was easier than sailing up the channel between Curaçao and Bonaire to Puerto Cabello, about 30 leagues to windward, skirting the coast of the mainland, which he had described as very bold, with a strong breeze blowing off the land. Consequently our inflexible admiral gave the signal to sail up to windward and to keep as close to the flagship as possible. During 30 and 31 January and 1 and 2 February the squadron succeeded in making good only about 2 leagues to windward. Some of the transports made so much leeway that they lost hope of making any progress, and since their provisions were exhausted, they headed for Porto Bello [Puerto Rico?], Jacmel, and other ports to leeward. The rest made little headway, so a frigate was left behind with them.

We were then off Curaçao. The *Neptune*, which had a damaged rudder, retired to that port, thus postponing my reunion with my brother [who was on that ship]. This disappointment was offset by the opportunity it gave us of making the acquaintance of two different places in the Dutch and Spanish colonies. The other ships confidently tacked back and forth along the coast of the mainland, but the currents were fearsome and there was no wind off the land. The squadron began to run out of water. Most of the ships had suffered damage aloft. The *Couronne* had lost her mizzen-topmast, the *Souverain* had no sails, and the *Duc de Bourgogne* had 40 inches of water in her hold, etc.

We proposed to the Admiral that he put in at Curaçao or at least take pilots aboard, but he stubbornly

directed all the ships to sail on without knowing whither. Meanwhile, his ship caught a breeze, which carried her out of sight to windward. Finally, at midnight on 6 February, while tacking back and forth along the mainland, we heard intermittent gunfire to windward and saw flares and several rockets. Our fears that one of our ships had been wrecked, which proved only too well founded, prompted all those to leeward to tack. Next morning the *Bourgogne* was missing, to our intense anxiety. The Admiral reappeared, and the *Hercule* and *Couronne* went to Curaçao. The rest of the fleet, which had opened their sealed orders, made for Puerto Cabello. We skirted the coasts of Curaçao and Bonaire, following the best course to windward and avoiding the strongest currents. Had we followed Don Solano's instructions, we should have wrecked the whole fleet. The coast of the mainland was full of deep spots and amazingly strong currents. M. Bellin's charts are full of errors, and we should do better without them.[93] There is a Dutch chart that is quite good. Finally, on 15 February, the last ship anchored at Puerto Cabello, and the transports at Curaçao.

The coast of Caracas is extraordinarily bold, containing a branch of the Cordillera Mountains, which rise to a height of about 5,000 feet. Puerto Cabello has a very good harbor sheltered from the sea by reefs.[94] The entrance faces west and is closed by a chain defended by a strong fort built on rock and a battery on the town side. Ships of 74 guns can come up fully armed to the quay, which can accommodate about 80 warships. At its mouth is a sheltered roadstead defended by a strong battery and earthwork. The town built along the waterfront is quite small and behind it is a lone mountain with three peaks (*mornes*) within cannon-range of the shore. On these peaks are three forts mounted with cannon. The batteries at the entrance to the harbor and roadstead are closed and defended by a hornwork, resting on a marsh on one side and the sea on the other, whose battery is in excellent condition. This position is most vulnerable to attack, however, by troops landing on the beach at night and storming it in force.

The town is very unhealthy because of the miasmas

93. See map of the Venezuelan coast, from Bellin's *Petit Atlas Maritime*, Vol. II, No. 168.

94. See map, Vol. II, No. 169.

rising from a large marsh to windward that extends to the base of the houses; thus it is inhabited only by those required to serve the King. The heat is oppressive and the sky often overcast. There is a regiment of regular troops stationed here, with an artillery detachment. Don de Narva, the commandant of the forces in [the province of] Caracas, has moved here for the duration of our stay.[95] We are lodged as guests of His Majesty the King of Spain—that is to say, the General Staff and the invalid officers, for the rest of the troops are quartered on board the ships. This will preserve the lives of many for our King's service.

Farewell, my dear Chevalier. They are pressing me to send this letter to Curaçao to a neutral ship that is leaving for Europe.

P. S. We learned here [at Puerto Cabello] the details of the loss of the *Bourgogne*.[96] This warship, while tacking back and forth along the coast of the mainland, which it believed clear of obstacles, suddenly grounded at one o'clock on the morning of 6 [4] February, 1½ leagues from shore. Everyone lost his head, everyone wanted to take command, and instead of all sails being backed, they were crowded on. The ship came to a stop, shipping a great deal of water, and its masts came down on deck. No one thought of bringing provisions up on deck, and everything was forgotten in the general disorder aboard. They broke the guns in trying to jettison them. At daybreak they had a raft built, which was seized by the officers with the captain [Champmartin] at their head. Seeing themselves abandoned, the men yielded to desperation. They fired pistols and committed acts which, rather than being recorded, had best be forgotten for the honor of the human race. Finally the raft got away, loaded with all the officers and as few soldiers and sailors as possible. Since the sea was very rough, the craft was very unstable and a number of men slid off. Ten officers and about 50 men were drowned.

When the news reached Puerto Cabello, a frigate [*Néréide*] was dispatched and rescued the rest of the soldiers and crew, who were suffering only from hunger and thirst, but not for so long as to endanger their lives. All the misfortunes were due to the weakness and incapacity of the captain, whose name should be lost in oblivion. How unfortunate he is to have failed on such an occasion to display the firmness and self-possession required by every man in the face of death! Farewell.

❧

Saint-Domingue, 25 April 1783

Alas, my dear Chevalier, the most miserable of men is writing you. What a painful existence for a man of feeling, to emerge from nothingness! What we call pleasures are only chimeras, whereas pain is only too real.

During the past twenty years I have known but the most rare and true happiness of comradeship. I had a brother who shared my life, with all the joys and sorrows that the hopes and experiences of this world afford. If it is possible to be happy, I was. Alas, all is changed! In losing my brother, the closest of friends, I have lost everything. How insane is man to take so much trouble to preserve his life! He does not think that an illness, an accident that he avoids, may be the source of pain a thousand times more cruel than death that offers him release. I am gathering all my strength, my dear Chevalier, to banish the thoughts that lead me too far and recount to you in detail the event that condemns me to a grief I shall carry with me to the grave.

Following our orders, my brother had embarked in the *Neptune*, and I in the *Souverain*. Our privation in being separated was balanced by the pleasure each of us took in being at his post and sharing the perils of the sea on two different ships. The *Neptune* suffered damage on the voyage to Puerto Cabello and had to put in at Curaçao. The rest of the fleet went on to Puerto Cabello, and I with it; hence we found ourselves 80 leagues apart.

95. Broglie ([2], pp. 86–87) and Ségur ([2], I, 471–472) both pay warm tribute to this Spanish official. Broglie notes that "Don Pedro di Nava," a colonel in the Spanish forces and special protégé of the minister in Madrid, had been sent by the governor-general to Puerto Cabello to provide the French fleet and army with any aid they might require: "He fulfilled his mission with a politeness, care, attentiveness, and activity that we are not generally accustomed to expect from a Spaniard." Von Closen (p. 302) also echoes this favorable opinion. It was Narva who urged several of the French officers to travel to Caracas and who facilitated their journey.

96. Concerning the wreck of the *Bourgogne*, see Clermont-Crèvecœur's journal, nn. 186–188.

On 16 February the *Hercule*, after her repairs were completed, returned to the fleet. I received the following letter from my brother. Although I was far from suspecting the truth, you can imagine that I had every reason to be anxious.

Curaçao, 11 February 1783

One must confess, my dear friend, that extraordinary things can happen in this world, and I am now confirmed in my belief that our lives depend not so much upon the pains we take as upon sheer luck. Having been involved in a duel of the most unfortunate nature, my life has become a matter of indifference to me. Ever since 4 January the only thing that has mattered to me is to preserve my honor and take personal vengeance for the wrong done me, by killing my enemy or being killed myself. Consequently I chose the most dangerous weapons—pistols. On our arrival at Curaçao on 3 February we went ashore about five o'clock that very afternoon to fight our duel. I myself measured out 6 ordinary paces, and at a signal from a grenadier subaltern who accompanied us we fired and we missed. We fired again with the same result.

Then I moved closer to my opponent, standing only 4 paces away with the utmost coolness. My resolution was too firm to have any fear of death. We missed again. We tried a fourth time, then night fell and we postponed the duel until the next morning, when we arranged to meet on the battlefield at daybreak.

I measured out 4 short paces, the signal was given, and my opponent fired without touching me; however, my pistol failed to go off. I told him: "My pistol did not go off." He replied: "So you want to shoot me? Wait until I reload." I said: "No, Monsieur, you must not reload, and I do not want to shoot a man in cold blood." I fired my shot in the air, saying that we should use a more equitable weapon. Consequently we each drew our swords and fought with those. I pricked him twice, and he broke his sword. He had to stay in his room until today, when we fought again. I received a small

cut on the thigh. I wanted to continue the duel, but I was unable to make him fight again. I met Caldaguès,[97] to whom I recounted all that had happened. He told me that he was surprised that we had fought again, that our comrades had talked about it and wanted to settle the affair, after the way we had behaved, and I in particular. Therefore I must go aboard in the morning.

You can easily see how much this letter upset me, since the duel had not yet been concluded. He did not mention the offense. I finally learned something about it from a friend. This increased my alarm, for I knew how brave and how sensitive my brother was. What a misfortune that I was 150 miles away at such a moment! I was tempted to leave without permission, but by then the duel must have been over. The Comte d'Estaing was due at any moment, and I was afraid to be absent from my post. Finally I decided to write one of my close friends, Mauduit-Duplessis.[98] The honor and courage of this good man soothed my fears. With his equanimity he could be more useful to my brother than I. I sent him the following letter by the quickest route:

Puerto Cabello, 17 February 1783

My dear Mauduit,

Friends are rare. If I consider that I have one in the army, it is you, and I am asking you to do me a very great favor.

Since I learned of my brother's unfortunate affair, I have been the most miserable and anxious of men, and particularly since I heard of it only indirectly and know no details. It is terrible at such a moment to be chained to your post 80 leagues from a brother whom you love. His delicacy and his sense of honor both reassure and alarm me. However, since in affairs of this kind one cannot oneself gauge the consensus of opinion, I beg you to take my place and play my part at this crucial moment. I vest all my rights in you. Tell him whether his conduct is approved. Restrain his youth in order to satisfy the consensus of opinion. In short, be his brother. I ask

97. Pierre-Raymond de Caldaguès (born at Aurillac, 1747) was a first lieutenant in the Soissonnais Regiment, promoted captain in May 1781.
98. Concerning Berthier's friend Mauduit-Duplessis, see

Clermont-Crèvecœur's journal, nn. 82 and 146. Mauduit-Duplessis later lost his life in the West Indies when attempting to quell a riot at Port-au-Prince in 1791. See "Checklist of Journals," *s.v.* Mauduit.

this of you, my dear Mauduit, and if I have any consolation it is in the knowledge that you are near him. Farewell, my dear friend. Send me news of that which interests me more than anything in the world.

Several vessels arrived from Curaçao. I had received no news, and my anxiety became acute. On 22 February the frigate *Néréide* arrived from that port, and I could no longer hide my misery. One of my comrades came to prepare me for the fatal blow that has banished happiness from my life forever. At his first word I saw everything clearly and steeled myself to hear the dreadful news that my poor brother, not satisfied with the settlement proposed by the officers of the Soissonnais Regiment, had continued the duel with pistols on 16 February. Taking the Comte de Chabannes[99] as his second, he stood 80 paces from his adversary, and they approached one another, determined to fire at will. My brother, overly brave, walked towards his enemy with his pistol in the air, intending to fire from 3 paces, since he had already missed him six times. When still 15 paces off he was shot in the lower abdomen. He fired a wild shot as he fell, wishing to end the duel once and for all. My imprudent brother had used poor weapons in the earlier duels and had rashly overloaded them, spoiling his aim.

He lived until 18 February. He did not suffer and did not believe himself seriously wounded until the last moment, when he died with all the courage that honor and irreproachable conduct can command.[100]

The lightning that strikes down a victim is as nothing compared to the storm within my soul. My first reaction was a desire for vengeance, but a moment later I plunged into the depths of despair, in which my friends have come to my rescue. As my grief took possession of my whole being, I forgot about vengeance. The whole army, from the General down, expressed their sympathy. They came to see me, not to console me but to share my legitimate grief, which was inconsolable.

I spent two days in a state that defies description. Finally my friends saw that it was necessary to talk to me of my misfortune, in order to make me weep. They brought me a letter from my dear friend Mauduit. He had written me two, but the first had been torn up, since they did not wish me to know the details of the quarrel. You shall see from the second, which they gave me, what a brother I had lost and in what a friend I had placed my trust.

Curaçao, 20 February 1783

How I pity you, my dear friend! You no longer have a brother. The virtuous and respected young man is no more. I saw him draw his last breath. What soul, what feeling he had! How he loved you! What strength of character was his! Alas, my friend,

---

99. This was either Jacques-Gilbert-Marie de Chabannes, assistant quartermaster-general, or his younger brother, Jean-Frédéric, aide-de-camp to Baron de Vioménil, both of whom were embarked in the *Neptune*, Charles Berthier's ship.

100. Aside from this hitherto unpublished account by his brother, the documents covering Charles Berthier's death are very meager. In the official record book of the Soissonnais Regiment, Archives de la Guerre, YB 355, registre no. 41, where it is noted that Charles Berthier de Berluis (*sic*) was attached to the regiment as a sublieutenant on 26 April 1780, there is only the bare and inaccurate entry: "mort en Cuirassao en Amérique en 1782." In L.-A. Berthier's personal dossier (there is none for Charles), pièce 41, is a statement of his account with Artois, paymaster (*quartier-maître trésorier*) of the Soissonnais Regiment, dated 1 September 1783, which mentions allowances due "your late brother" paid through 17 February 1783. The statement also mentions an advance made "to your brother at Curaçao on 8 February for the purchase of effects that he sent to you at Puerto Cabello—240 *livres*"; and "expenses of sickness, etc., according to enclosed statement [missing from the dossier], a copy of which was given you at Puerto Cabello—474 *livres*, 10 *s*." Finally, among the Berthier papers at Princeton, is a copy of the death certificate, reproduced in this volume. This is a sworn statement, dated at Uzès, 1 February 1784, by Sinety de Boisselle, then captain serving as adjutant of the Soissonnais Regiment, according to which Charles Berthier de Berluy (*sic*) "died 17 February 1783 and was buried the following day on the island of Curaçao, a Dutch colony in South America, where a part of this regiment embarked on the King's ship *Neptune* had put into port." Sinety de Boisselle further states that his certificate is in lieu of an official record of the death (*extrait mortuaire*) that could not be issued, "this officer having had himself taken ashore because of sickness and having died in a room he had rented." The Berthier-Princeton copy of Sinety de Boisselle's statement is countersigned, Versailles, 21 February 1785, by d'Avrange d'Haugeranville (Berthier's brother-in-law), lieutenant colonel of the Gardes de la Porte du Roi, who states that it is a true copy conforming to the original in the hands of Maître Roland, notary in Versailles.

I should like to console you, yet I myself need consolation. I have already reported to you his quarrel with the officer of the Soissonnais. Your brother deserved only pity, but his adversary has himself to blame. He does not deserve to live in decent society. Surely they will give you justice. The Comte de Saint-Maîme is determined to get rid of him. As for you, as a most sincere friend I beg you not to think of vengeance. Take my advice and believe me, my friend, for I am not mistaken. I have consulted the commanders, many older officers, and an infinity of reliable people, and they all agree. You cannot avenge him personally. Even public opinion decrees that you are condemned in advance if you yourself avenge him.

You know my heart, my dear Berthier. Well, I swear to you that I myself should not hesitate to take the advice I am giving you. I believe that I have always taken the honorable course. I have always followed the dictates of my heart. Well, my friend, my heart says to you today: "Stop, Berthier!" For the rest, I am determined, my friend, to save you from yourself. I shall restrain you. The strength will come from my affection for you. You cannot wrest yourself from it. I shall remind you of a family in tears, a respected father, a loving mother, brothers who depend on you, sisters whom you cherish. Well, my friend, have not they suffered enough? Do you wish to drive them to despair? I plead the cause of reason; I plead my own cause, my friend. Remember what you have often told me about your family and with what tenderness you have spoken of your good parents. I admired you and believed you a worthy son of your respected sire. Well, my friend, if you now dare take your revenge by disregarding the laws of reason and justice, you will bring your family to ruin.

Finally, my friend, I am an honest man, a man of honor with a great deal of sang-froid. Well, I assure you that I myself should do what I am advising you.

Farewell, dear Berthier. Farewell, my poor friend. I do not wish to console you, but only to weep with you. I feel your great loss and know that in losing your brother you have lost your best friend. I bid you take the advice my heart dictates, after consulting the best advisors. I embrace you because I love and pity you. Weep, my friend, weep, but be a man. Once more, farewell. I cannot see what I have written, but I know it comes from my heart. Oh Berthier, I weep with you very truly! My tears are flowing.

Your miserable and affectionate friend,
the Ch^{er}. de Mauduit

This letter from my good friend brought my grief and emotion to a crisis, and I even found some relief in the excess of my sorrow. Among those who sympathized with me, how consoling were the advice and interest of that noble soul, the Comte de Ségur! I had made the passage with this good and respected man, who took an interest in my fate solely because of my sorrow. He came often to see me, and I enjoyed his visits more than the others'.

As my tears relieved my heartache, my affection for my poor brother revived in me an unconscious desire to avenge him. This feeling conflicted with the interests of my family, who, I knew, had no fortune and whose mainstay I was. The letter from my friend Mauduit, the advice of the whole army and of the commanders and officers who came to see me, all agreed that I should be universally blamed for avenging my brother personally, and that the regiment would grant me satisfaction by dismissing the officer. While my whole soul was in perpetual conflict, vengeance seemed the most practical means of assuaging my grief. At that moment the Comte de Ségur, whose kindness had helped me so much, was about to take a trip through the province of Caracas. He persuaded me to accompany him. Since wherever I went my grief went with me, one place was as good as another, and I allowed myself to be persuaded. He took advantage of a favorable moment—when he had impressed upon me the interests of my family without private means, of which I was the main support, as well as the laws of honor and reason that forbade me to take personal vengeance—to exact from me a promise not to seek it. I took his advice and gave my word not to take personal vengeance, but with one reservation. If I met this man, whom I should always regard as the author of my family's misfortune, at any time or in any place, I could not be responsible for my actions.

So I left on 25 February at two in the morning, and I assure you that the events of the journey did not interest me in the least. In vain had I asked for a letter that I was sure my poor brother must have written me at such a grave moment. My dear Chevalier, how hard grief is to bear! You die a thousand deaths. How often must we remind ourselves that such is man's lot!

Upon our return from the trip, which lasted nearly a month, the Comte de Ségur gave me two letters from my poor brother, one written to him and the other to me. My good brother had scrupulously chosen to return all his credentials to the Comte de Ségur,[101] informing him that a most unfortunate quarrel had taken place and that, until he could avenge his honor, he was returning his commission until he reached the mainland and could, by his death or that of his adversary, clear his reputation from stain and resume the right to call himself an officer.

His letter to me will prove to you how good he was, and how unfortunate in this dreadful quarrel:

On board the *Neptune*, 12 January 1783

My dear friend, I am writing only to you and to the Comte de Ségur, believing it prudent to be prepared for any eventuality in a quarrel as serious as mine. You must shut out all weakness from your heart, be a man, and class this affair as one of those unavoidable things. You will have to know the details in order to take sides in a situation as scandalous as it is harmful to peaceful relations between men and the consideration that comrades owe one another. Here is an account of my conduct. On my arrival on board I found everything so crowded that I did not know where to stow my gear. Looking about, I found a half-empty chest where I stowed my portemanteau and my possessions. Having been aboard for a long time, M. de ——— had used this chest before I did, and next morning he told me that it was not very polite of me to have put my things in his chest and that he did not want them to stay there. This beginning seemed to me so discourteous that I almost sent him packing. However, on reflection, I told him that I had not known that the chest belonged to him but that, since there was still room in it, I hoped that in view of our crowded condition aboard the ship he would be kind enough to let me

leave them there. Finally, after many rude remarks and after he threw my things out during my absence, I asked him by what right he had appropriated this space, in which I was going to replace my belongings and not move them unless ordered to do so by M. d'Alein, the captain of the ship. This scene took place in the presence of MM. de la Gardette, de Baudre, Bazin, etc.,[102] who spoke to M. de ——— about his ridiculous behavior. He then came to tell me that if there was room in the chest I could use it to store my gear. Since I found this approach very civil, I thanked him and took advantage of his offer.

When on 4 January he said to me in the rudest tone that it was very strange, but he had been robbed, and that he had had a lock put on the chest and had given a key to no one but me, I did not expect such an outburst and asked him what he meant. He repeated the same thing in a tone that became progressively ruder. It was all I could do to keep from telling him what I thought of him. I asked him if he thought I had robbed him. With much malice, he replied: "Or your servant, at least. I had some apples and a lot of little things I can't find." I almost burst out laughing. I told him that my servant could not have stolen anything, since I had always been present when the chest was opened, and that, besides, he was well known in the regiment, and it was very curious that he should be so rude about this matter. Continuing in the same vein, he ended up by saying, *foutre*, I was an impertinent fool, with such a threatening look that I could not contain myself and retorted with "Well then, *allez vous faire foutre!*" Then, utterly beside himself, he picked up a chair to throw at my head. Fortunately I parried the blow. M. Bazin, who was in his cabin, came in and got between us to prevent me from committing a folly. So that is the provocation that I believe sufficient cause for demanding the life of one of us or the other.

You can judge how cruel it is to have to live with this person whom I cannot bear and how I long to reach land. In case anything happens to me, I beg you to report this accident to our dear family whom

101. Ségur was second colonel in the Soissonnais Regiment, commanded by Saint-Maîme.

102. All captains in the Soissonnais Regiment.

à Domingue
partie nouvelle le 25 avril 1783.

la, Mon cher Chapuis. C'en le plus malheureux des
hommes qui t'écris, quelle cruelle douleur que de
d'être faite du néant d'avoir une ame sensible
ce que Nous appellons plaisir ne sont que des
chimeres, mais les peines sont trop reelles!

Depuis 25 ans je ne connoissois que le vrai
et rare bonheur de l'amitié, un frere partageant
mon existence, les plaisirs et les peines que —
l'ambition, et les usages differens, de le monde
nous Donnent; s'il est possible d'être heureux
je l'étois, hélas! tout en change, j'ai tout perdu avec
mon frere. le plus tendre des amis.

Que l'homme en insensé de prendre tant de
soin à conserver sa vie, il ne peut pas qu'une
maladie, qu'un évenement qu'il evite, en lo pousse
de chagrins affreux, mils fois plus cruelle que la
mort. qui se presente pour les luy eviter.

je rassemble toute mes forces mon cher ...
pour quitter des reflections. qui me conduiroient trop
loin, et te rendre compte des détails. d'un —
evenement qui me condamne a une d'ouleur
qui ne finira qu'avec moy.

Le 16 fevrier ... ... j'ai reçu
la lettre de mon frere; que j'étois loin d'en
soupçonner les détails, ... tu va
juger des miens trop reelle inquietudes.

à Curaçao le 11 fevrier 1783.
il faut avoir mon cher amis qu'il y ait dans
le monde des choses extraordinaire, et je me —
conforme à croire que notre vie ne dépend pas
du soin que nous en prenons, mais seulement
du hasard. après avoir eu une affaire de la
nature la plus malheureuse, la vie m'étoit —
devenue un point indifferent ne regardant que
l'offence, l'honneur, et ma vengeance personelle
tuer mon adversaire ou certain sur la place
moi même, étoit le parti que j'avois pris et
désiré depuis le 4 janvier, en consequence
je fis choix des armes les plus meurtriere —
les pistolets, arrivé à Curaçao le 3 fevrier le
même soir vers les 5 heures nous fumes nous
nous battre, je mesurai 6 pas ordinaire moi-
même et à un signal qu'un bas off. de
grenadier qui étoit avec nous, nous fit, nous
nous tirames, et nous manquames, nous —
retirames une seconde fois de même

*Douleur de Berthier son frere vient
d'être tué.*

+ cette ... et finir le plus ... pour
son ... tous ... étois embarqué sur longtem
et moy par le pouvoir cette privation. de nous
separer, étois volonté, pour l'espace d'être à sa
place chacun à son tour et de partager les dangers
de la mer, par 2 vaisseaux, le neptune ayant tant
eu des avaris fut obligé d'enter à Curaçao,
avec le rest de la flott contenu à ...
... et jetté de ce nombre, et nous tous ...
... ... de ...

Lettre de son frere : affaire d'honneur

Duel à Curaçao

PAGE FROM BERTHIER'S JOURNAL RELATING THE DEATH OF HIS BROTHER (*see p. xxvii*)

Nous Chevalier de St. Louis, Capitaine Commandant et faisant
les fonctions de Major au régiment d'infanterie de Soissonnois, Certifions
que Monsieur Berthier de Berluy, Capitaine à la suite dudit regt.
est mort le dix sept fevrier mil sept cent quatrevingt trois. et
a été inhumé le lendemain — à L'isle de Curaçao Colonie des —
Etats unis d'Hollande — dans l'amerique meridionale, où partie
de ce régiment embarqué sur le Vaisseau du Roi le neptune
avoit relaché.

En foi de quoi nous avons fait expedier le présent —
certificat pour tenir lieu d'extrait mortuaire qui n'a pu être —
delivré; Cet officier s'étant fait debarquer du bord du Vaisseaux
le Neptune pour cause de maladie —, et étant mort dans une
chambre qu'il avoit loué.

Fait à Usez le premier fevrier mil sept cent quatre
vingt quatre. Signé Sinety. et Boishelle.

Pour copie conforme à l'original produit chez Mr. Roland notaire en
fevrier de la presente année. Certifié veritable par nous Chlr. de l'ordre Royal et
militaire de St. Louis, Lieutenant colonel d'infrie major des Gardes de la Porte du
Roi, Commandant l'hotel de ce Corps. à Versailles le 21. fevrier 1785.

Lavange d'haugeranville

DEATH CERTIFICATE OF CHARLES-LOUIS BERTHIER (see p. xxviii)

Total du produit des 10 ans, soustraction
faitte de tous frais et avances quelquonque 346650ᵗ

~~~~~~

droit à   { Deductions a faire de 5 pour % de droit
payer   { de vente pour le roy, et de 5 pour % de
           { droit pour le clergé ..... ------- --------- 34665ᵗ

L'indicoterie de 30 faneque rapportera donc en
10 ans, tous avances remboursé et droit payé ..- 311985ᵗ

et plus tous les diseurs imprevue pour pompter celle qu'il faur
faire tous les 3 ou 4 ans pour affiner l'indigot.

Machine à indigot relatif
à l'explication faitte dans mon
journal.

BERTHIER'S DRAWING OF AN INDIGO MACHINE (*see p. xxviii*)

Élévation de la façade des hôtels communs aux Départemens de la Guerre, de la Marine et des Affaires Étrangères, à Versailles.

Echelle de 15 Toises

THE HOTEL DE LA GUERRE, BERTHIER'S CHILDHOOD HOME IN VERSAILLES (*see p. xxviii*)

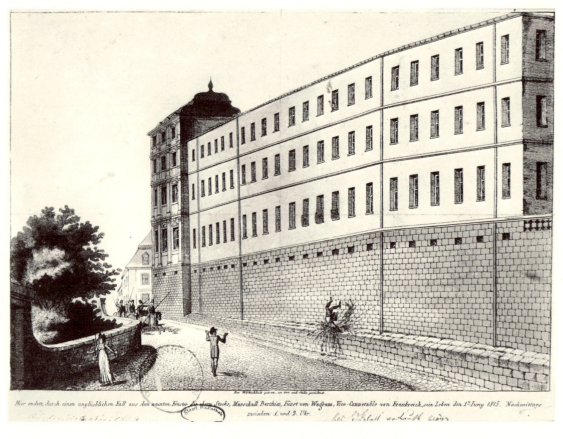

Hier endete, durch einen unglücklichen Fall aus dem neunten Fenster des obern Stocks, Marschall Berthier, Fürst von Wagram, Vice-Connetable von Frankreich, sein Leben den 1ᵗᵉⁿ Juny 1815. Nachmittage zwischen 1 und 2 Uhr.

BERTHIER'S DEATH IN BAMBERG, 1 JUNE 1815 (*see p. xxviii*)

I love so tenderly. As for you, I must tell you that I love you better than myself and that my sole regret in losing my life is not being able to prove it to you. Oh, dear friend, the violent quarrels we have had, and the pleasure we have known in seeing one another again after being separated by our army service! I beg you to forget them all and remember only our devoted friendship, and count me worthy of you.

Farewell, my dear friend, and be happy. My only regret is not having been able to contribute to that happiness, and being obliged to come to such a miserable end, though I do not consider myself beaten yet. I did not seek a duel, I had one thrust upon me. I am not afraid. In resorting to arms I place a blind confidence in fate. In case anything happens, I commit my soul to God and accept your last farewell. I embrace you.

Oh, my dear Chevalier, what a precious document! And what a fatal one! How cruel it is for my peace of mind to know all the details without being able to take revenge, but I believe I owe it to my comrades and to society to inform the commanders of M. de ———'s outrageous conduct, which is unworthy of decent society.

I had left Puerto Cabello [on 5 April] with the Comte de Ségur on a frigate [*Amazone*] for Jacmel, a seaport near his plantation on the island of Santo Domingo, to which he wished me to accompany him, when he gave me my brother's letter. As soon as I arrived at his house, I wrote the following letter to the Comte de Saint-Maîme:

At the Ségur Plantation, 14 April 1783
Monsieur le Comte,

Through the kindness of the Comte de Ségur I have received a letter from my poor brother that would have added to my sufferings had that been possible. He recounts to me the details of his duel with M. de ——— from the beginning of the dis-

pute, written at a moment when man is truthful and beyond all prejudice.

I am shocked to learn of his adversary's conduct. I have been forced to give my word not to avenge him, which is a great sacrifice for me, but I must keep it.

In the interests of society in general and of all my comrades in particular, I believe it my duty to inform you of the dangerous conduct of an ill-bred man whose brutality and studied incivility can lead men of honor, who are necessary both to their country and their families, to dire extremes.

I should regard as the greatest solace to my suffering the day when I should meet this man by chance and be afforded the cruel pleasure of avenging a brother who was my dear friend and whose conduct has ever been a model of moderation and perfect courtesy.

I am yours, etc.

P.S. I enclose with this letter a copy of the one from my brother.

Ah, my dear Chevalier, why are not all men of the world like the Comte de Ségur? What a noble soul! And how much my family and I owe him! He has saved me from myself. Ever since the tragedy he has not allowed me to leave his side. He has made me travel with him, has showered me with favors and given me moments of pleasure, if I may use the term, at a terrible time in my life. Whenever the *Neptune* joined our squadron in various ports, it was the Comte de Ségur and M. de Saint-Maîme who had M. de ——— confined to prison aboard so that I should not set eyes on him. Imagine what suffering the sight of this ship caused me, with my dear brother gone and my life still in torment! But one must be a man, and I have given proofs of it that I believed were beyond my strength.

It has been resolved that on his return to France, M. de ——— [Saint-Hilaire] will leave the regiment.[103]

103. Berthier nowhere in his manuscript journal identifies his brother's adversary. The only mention of his name found by the Editors is in Verger's journal (p. 175). Charles-Marie-Martial Bessonnies de Saint-Hilaire (born at Figeac, 30 June 1752) was a first lieutenant in the Soissonnais Regiment as of 19 March 1780, promoted second captain in 1783. There is no evidence in his dossier at the Archives de la Guerre that he was dismissed from his regiment. The *Etat militaire* for 1784 and subsequent years lists him in the Soissonnais Regiment, with the rank of second captain (first captain in 1787). The memoirs or journals of Ségur, Dumas, and Blanchard—the elder Berthier's companions on his journey to Caracas or subsequent excursion to Ségur's plantation in Saint-Domingue—

What an example! And, by the evils it avoids, how much good breeding contributes to the happiness of all! May the regiments take steps to rid themselves of those who lack it. Can they not find enough courteous and upright people to replace these scourges of the human race who should revert to the class of brutes whose manners they have adopted?

Could we but have enough self-control, my dear Chevalier, to avenge an insult without initiating another! Thus, at least, duels would never take the life of either man.

Farewell, my dear Chevalier; if grief could kill, you would lose a friend.

❧

Saint-Domingue, 26 April 1783

My dear Chevalier, in spite of my sadness I shall keep my promise to you and continue my journal.[104] I left, then, at the moment when my grief was most intense, on 25 February for Caracas with the Comte de Ségur, de Talleyrand, Marquis de Champcenetz,

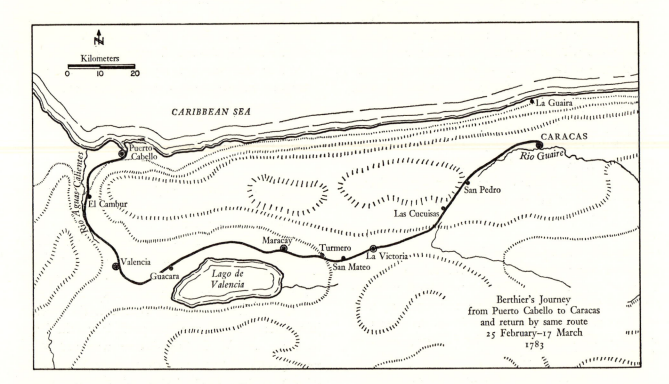

make no mention at all of the duel. There appears to have been a gentleman's agreement to consign the whole incident to oblivion. Although duelling was not officially tolerated in the French army at this time, there are at least two other examples among Rochambeau's officers. Blanchard ([1], p. 49) notes that the Vicomte de Noailles and M. de Dillon fought at Newport on 6 September 1780: "the subject of their quarrel does not deserve to be recorded." More information is available about the duel fought between Rochambeau's aides Lauberdière and Dubouchet on the eve of the army's march to the Hudson. Dubouchet, who resented the fact that he had been assigned to remain with the detachment at Newport, took offense when Lauberdière offered to buy his horses, "say-

ing that in the circumstances Dubouchet wouldn't need them." Mauduit served as second to both contestants. Lauberdière received two slight wounds, Dubouchet a more serious one. See the account based on Dubouchet's memoirs in Morris Bishop, "A French Volunteer," *American Heritage*, xvii, No. 5 (Aug. 1966), 106–107.

104. There are two versions of this portion of the journal among the Berthier manuscripts at Princeton: the original in Berthier's informal scrawly handwriting (mss, No. 3, pp. 19–35, and No. 4, pp. 1–7) and a fair copy in a formal clerical hand entitled "Voyage de Caracas" (ms, No. 5). Significant variations or revisions have been incorporated into the translation given here.

Dumas, and Dézoteux.[105] This country, so curious and extraordinary for a European, did not interest me in the least. My grief completely engrossed me.

We mounted our mules, the only means of transportation, and left at one in the morning. Two negroes served as our guides, and what luggage we had was loaded on pack animals. I shall not give you any details of the country we passed through now but will try to include them in the description of my return journey.

The only thing that struck me along the route was the crossing of the mountain range between the sea and the plain of Valencia. For nearly 17 leagues you travel on the edge of one precipice after another, confined to a trail carved out of the rock by the mountain streams. Spent with fatigue and the excessive heat, we halted in the middle of a wood beside a brook, where an Indian had been murdered the day before. While our guide was seeing to the tethering of our mules, we sat under a very fine tree at whose foot ran the brook. We ate our crust of bread there and were about to draw some water when our guide ran up in a great fright, shouting to us that we were sitting under a manchineel tree whose shade poisons not only

those whom it shelters but even the water flowing beneath its branches.[106]

There is nothing else of interest to report except the adventure of M. Dézoteux, who had hoped to reach Caracas a day ahead of us. Pushing on beyond the gorges of San Pedro, he was chased by a panther, which spent some time making up its mind whether or not to attack him. Fortunately there was a mule grazing by the roadside, which distracted the panther's attention, so it attacked the mule instead. M. Dézoteux was accompanied only by his unarmed servant. They got off with only a bad fright.

After suffering from intense heat during a five days' march through country that was nearly all wild, we arrived on the morning of 2 March in Caracas, the capital of the province of that name, 55 leagues from Puerto Cabello.

2 March Since my companions insisted that I go out in society, I shall tell you as much as I can about what I saw there.

We found apartments prepared for us, with French-speaking officers on hand to do the honors. After making our toilets, we went to the palace of the governor,[107] who received us with every mark of

105. Both Ségur and Dumas left accounts of this excursion to Caracas: Ségur (1), letters to his wife, Puerto Cabello, 9 March, 16 March 1783, and Ségur (2), I, 475–513; Dumas (1), I, 139–154. A map of the route drawn by Dumas is mentioned by Ségur ([2], I, 505–506) and by Dumas himself ([1], I, 153–154); neither this map nor any that Berthier may have drawn have been located by the Editors. For still other complementary accounts of the journey by those who were traveling at this same time, see Broglie (2), pp. 88–147, and Coriolis (2), pp. 173–189. Berthier's traveling companions Champcenetz and Dézoteux (later known as the Baron de Cormatin) were both aides-de-camp to the Baron de Vioménil. Talleyrand was Jacques Boson de Talleyrand-Périgord (1764–1830), a younger brother of the more famous Charles-Maurice de Talleyrand-Périgord (1754–1838). "Boson," as he was often called, had joined the army at Crompond, served briefly as Chastellux's aide-de-camp, and then as a grenadier attached to Ségur's regiment, the Soissonnais.
106. Cf. Dumas ([1], I, 141–142), who situates this episode at a spot near the sources of the Rio Aguas Calientes. The guide who warned them of the dangers of the manicheel tree was one of their Indian muleteers named Martini, a handsome and nimble young man of about eighteen. Girod-Chantrans, who was in the Antilles in 1782, describes at some length the manicheel ("the most poison-

ous plant in the world") in his *Voyage d'un Suisse dans différentes colonies d'Amérique pendant la dernière guerre* (Neuchâtel, 1785), pp. 100–104. In Martinique the Swiss traveler was told by two elderly colonists that, when the English had seized the island in 1758, during the Seven Years' War, their soldiers, fresh from Europe, eagerly rushed to the manicheel trees, mistaking them for apples. Disregarding all warnings, which they interpreted as mere stories concocted to preserve the apples for the owners, the invaders voraciously devoured the fruit—and not one of them escaped the fatal effects of the poison!
107. Ségur refers to the governor as "Don Manuel Gozalès" in his letters ([1], p. 201) and as "Don Fernand Gonzalez" in his *Mémoires* ([2], p. 495). Broglie ([2], pp. 102–103) calls him "don Fernando y Gonzalvo y Morenos y Torres y Gonzales," with the remark, "I found it hard to believe that such a little man [he was only 4 feet 6 inches tall] could bear the weight of such a clutter of names." The Prince de Broglie nevertheless discovered that the governor had an excellent military bearing and pleasing manners: "He heaped kindnesses upon my companions and me, spoke to us in very intelligible French, and gracefully expressed the joy he felt in receiving in his capital such a select detachment of the French nobility."

courtesy and friendship. He took us to call on several ladies. The house of Señora Aristeguieta, who has several very pretty daughters, struck me as the most agreeable in the city.[108] Our reception there will give you some idea of the informality of this society.

The Marquis de Laval, the Prince de Broglie, and others who had arrived the day before had announced our coming. They were at the house when we were introduced. As we gravely made the usual bows these lovely ladies threw handfuls of candied aniseed in our faces. This response embarrassed us and upset our composure.[109] Finally they took pity on us and on our compatriots who had preceded us and gave us some ammunition, whereupon the engagement became general; but we proved a bit awkward at this sport. This joke at our debut did not amuse me as much as it did the others. My sorrow prevented me from participating wholeheartedly in all these gaieties as well as in the parties that followed, which I attended reluctantly so as to get an idea of the life and customs of a country quite new to a European.

They sang, danced the fandango (a kind of *périgourdine*, during which they snap their fingers), and played the guitar until dinner time. The governor took us to his palace, where we had a splendid dinner, magnificently served. All the high officials of the city were there. They drank the healths of the kings of France and Spain and all others appropriate to the occasion,

so that the stag party became quite gay towards the end.

We rose from table and retired to our lodgings so as to give the Spaniards time for their siesta, a custom prevalent in this country. Every Spaniard, man or woman, sleeps for two hours after dinner. At six o'clock we returned to the palace and the governor took us for a walk in the city, and afterwards to a superb ball given for us by the treasurer of the province,[110] where everything was arranged with true Spanish grandeur. More than 50 magnificently attired ladies provided its handsomest decoration. We danced minuets, English and French dances, and fandangos. The aniseed war was much livelier than in the morning. We took supper with the governor, who used his prerogative as commander in chief to urge that we consider his house our own during our stay in Caracas.

Next morning his butler came to take our orders for breakfast, which was brought to our rooms and included everything we desired. This custom continued so long as there were any Frenchmen in the capital. At eleven o'clock we went to call on the ladies, where we passed the time precisely as the day before. Then some of us went to dine with the intendant of the province,[111] and the rest with the governor. The courtesy of the former did not in the least resemble the governor's but was somewhat strained and politic rather than spontaneous. This was later confirmed by

108. Ségur ([2], I, 496) and Broglie ([2], p. 104) both mention the "Aristeguitta" or "Aristigetta" family, naming the daughters as Belina, Panschitta, Rossa, and Theresa. Ségur adds that the famous General Miranda was related to this family. The established spelling is Aristeguieta. The genealogical ramifications of the family can be traced in Carlos Iturriza Guillen, *Algunas Familias Caraqueñas* (Caracas, 1967), I, 79–97, "Aristeguieta o Arizteguieta." Señora Aristeguieta was presumably the widow of Don Miguel Xérez de Aristeguieta y Lovera Otáñez, born in Caracas in 1704, died 25 March 1782 (a year before the French officers' visit).

109. Describing this unexpected reception, Broglie ([2], p. 110) notes that, when they had recovered from their surprise and asked for an explanation, "We were informed that since the days of remotest antiquity it was a courtly, gallant, and chivalrous custom to pelt one another with candied aniseeds (*des anis*) during the last days of the Carnival season, and that no better means had ever been found to force prudish belles to swallow the sweet compliments offered by their humble adorers. . . ." 2

March 1783 was the last Sunday before Lent. Shrove Tuesday, or Mardi Gras, thus fell on 4 March that year.

110. Broglie ([2], p. 123) refers to the treasurer as "M. Vidando"; Ségur ([1], p. 201) calls him "Don Francisco Vidando," a nephew of the minister of war, "Mousquès" (Miguel Muzquiz).

111. The intendant is identified by Broglie ([2], p. 113) as "Signor d'Avalos," and by Ségur ([2], I, 503) as "don Joseph d'Avalos." Both judge him harshly, calling him an enemy of the French, the universally detested tyrant of the colony, who monopolized imported European goods bought in the King's name, arbitrarily fixed duties and prices, and amassed a personal fortune at the expense of the colony's economic well-being. Ségur ([1], p. 202), in a letter written to his wife at the time, compares Avalos to Monsieur Turcaret, the parvenu millionaire and adventurer of Lesage's well-known comedy *Turcaret* (1709). See also De Pons, *Voyage* (cited below, n. 116), III, 46–49, where Avalos's unpopular measures taken to enforce the state tobacco monopoly are discussed.

his conduct when the army had to ask his help. After the siesta we went to walk in several parks in the city, which were not especially notable.

When we returned to the governor's palace, we found magnificent preparations there for a ball, which was attended by all the ladies in town in their most elaborate and elegant attire. Since this ball took place on the last day of Carnival [Mardi Gras], it lasted until a very late hour. Next morning you could not see the floor for the large number of partly eaten sweets that had been ground into it. They throw them into the corsages of the ladies or into their hair as they pelt one another, providing some very gay battlefields.

4 March I spent the morning walking in the city. I went to see the chief engineer, who showed me a map of the province that seemed to me to have been enlarged from engraved maps and corrected from memoranda. Although not good, it is better than the others. The engineer corps is generally neglected in the Spanish army, though the large plans of the works at Puerto Cabello and La Guaira seemed to me fairly accurate.[112]

After dinner at the governor's each of us was provided with a superb horse with saddle and housings of velvet, richly embroidered and fringed with gold. The governor took us out to a plantation about 4 miles from town, situated on an eminence overlooking the city and the fertile and well-cultivated Caracas valley.[113] The gardens of this estate were very well tended and were filled with the same flowers we have in France. Its walks were lined with orange, pomegranate, lemon, coffee, and apple trees that gave off a most delicious scent. The beds were filled with the same vegetables as ours, as well as strawberries, pineapples, and all the varied fruits of the country, giving ample testimony to its temperate climate and rich soil. The arbors were full of very large grapes that resembled our fine muscats. Such profusion, arranged with

great taste, reminded me of the fairy tales. We went to see a plantation of banana, cacao, and cotton trees, all of which, being new to us, were even more interesting. Then we returned to the drawing-room, where a very pretty young girl accompanied herself on the harpsichord. A collation was served that included all sorts of fruits, refreshments, and sweetmeats, of which they are very fond here. After this superb repast each of us was presented with a large bouquet of European flowers as artistically arranged as those of our best florists. Enchanted with all we had seen, we returned to the capital with our arms full of flowers, which we distributed among the young ladies. We spent the evening at the auditor's house, where there was a concert. The last piece was the one we liked the best, but music has made little progress in this city. Actually we found the conversation more absorbing than the music.

5 March I resumed my promenades in the city and paid several calls. After dinner there was a small dance. Despite their rigorous Lenten devotions, the ladies generously adjourned their scruples in regard to the Holy Season to entertain us Frenchmen, firmly resolved to pay for the aberration by several extra fasts. The religious fanaticism here is extraordinary; it seems to be accompanied by morals that are even more so.

On 6 March the Comte de Ségur left for the port of La Guaira whence he was to return by sea to Puerto Cabello with Captain de Thy [d'Ethy] of the navy. I stayed in Caracas, since the Prince de Broglie, who had arrived by sea, had invited me to return with him by land a few days later. This arrangement suited me, for in my situation nothing was more beneficial than travel.

We mounted our horses that afternoon to visit a sugar plantation, and at another we saw two tigers, which had been captured in the neighborhood. Everything we saw in the country surrounding this capital

112. Broglie ([2], pp. 119–120) also speaks of a visit to the chief engineer (not identified by name): "Instead of finding detailed, well-drawn plans, we saw only a bad, poorly ordered map in which the details of the back country were barely indicated. The engineer's excuse was that he had recently been transferred from another department and had found the greatest disorder here. We nevertheless saw in a very dusty corner a general plan of the province of Caracas, from which we learned that it in-

cluded five very extensive departments and that it was about 300 leagues in length and never less than 80 leagues in width. This immense country counts scarcely 600,000 or 700,000 inhabitants, including whites as well as negroes and Indians. . . ."

113. The plantation was perhaps the estate of Don Sebastián Rodríguez del Toro y Ascanio, III Marqués del Toro (1739–1787), in the present suburb of San Bernardino. Cf. Iturriza Guillen, *Algunas Familias Caraqueñas*, II, 812.

gave evidence of the fertility of the soil and the laziness of the inhabitants. On our return we met the Comte de Custine, who had just arrived and had been shown the same hospitality as ourselves. Actually the courtesies of the governor and all the residents of this capital have been extended alike to every Frenchman from the highest to the lowest ranks.

Since the round of gaieties had finally become unbearable, I spent the 7th, 8th, and 9th trying to forget my troubles by visiting the churches and monuments, drawing a view of this capital,[114] and writing down my thoughts, which in any other circumstances would have been more profound. You will appreciate my good intentions when you think of my great sorrow.

Caracas, the capital of the province of that name, is situated at [10° 30′ north] latitude and [67° 4′ west] longitude.[115] It is 6 leagues south of the port of La Guaira and 55 leagues east of Puerto Cabello, in the western part of a plain extending 4 leagues to the east. This valley is about 1½ leagues wide and lies between two exceedingly high mountain ranges. Parts of it are hilly. It is watered by a shallow river [Rio Guaire] 60 feet wide that flows from west to east, whose winding course and periodic floods make the valley quite fertile.

This plain, being open from east to west, always has a breeze blowing off the mountains where it is cooled by the damp vapors that rise from their summits; this tempers the heat of the sun, which never becomes unbearable, and makes the evenings and

mornings comfortably cool. The mountain range northwest of the city has an opening through which a cold northwest wind blows away the damp vapors that collect in the mountains when there is a lull in the prevailing easterly wind; thus the valley has perpetual spring, which makes it a delightful place to live. The rainy season extends through July, August, and September and is less disagreeable in this valley, from which the storms are diverted to the mountains.

The city lies at the foot of the northern mountains and consists of 13 parallel streets running lengthwise and 11 running crosswise, laid out in regular squares.[116] It has a population of about 20,000. The houses are of one storey, with vast, high-ceilinged rooms well adapted to the hot climate. The principal buildings are made of fieldstone, which is very scarce and hard to cut, and the rest are built of a red clay that is to be found everywhere. Two planks about 6 feet long and 3 feet high are placed parallel, separated by the desired thickness of the wall, and the space between filled with the wet clay, which dries quite quickly since the planks are carefully perforated to allow the moisture to evaporate. The planks are then placed on their sides and the next pair placed on top, and so on, so that the house is erected within a kind of mold, or form, to the required height. The roofs are constructed of very light frames made of large reeds 25 to 30 feet long and 2 inches thick, instead of laths. As at home, the outside is covered with tiles. No house has a wood floor. The doors and windows are very large and are placed opposite one another to allow

114. Berthier's view of Caracas, if it has survived, has not been found by the Editors. His mention of it is a further reminder that his training as a topographical engineer enabled him to sketch "views" as well as maps. See note to the view of Newport reproduced in Vol. II, No. 11.

115. Among the Berthier manuscripts at Princeton there is a 6-page memorandum (No. 42), in a formal hand, entitled "Notes sur la Province de Caracas nouvelle Espagne." This is an outline, not completed, for a systematic survey of the whole province. It includes some of the information noted here in the journal.

116. See map, Vol. II, No. 170, which is reproduced from an engraved plate in *Voyage à la partie orientale de la Terre-Ferme dans l'Amérique Méridionale, fait dans les années 1801, 1802, 1803 et 1804; contenant la description de la Capitainerie générale de Caracas, composée des Provinces de Venezuela, Maracaïbo, Varinas, la Guiane Espa-*

gnole, Cumana, et de l'Ile de la Marguerite. . . . avec une carte géographique et des plans de la ville capitale et des ports principaux, 3 vols. (Paris, 1806), by François Raymond Joseph de Pons (1751–1812). This work provides a systematic description of Venezuela, treating more exhaustively the subjects already touched upon by Berthier and the other French visitors of 1783. The author was a native of the French colony of Saint-Domingue and long time resident of the Antilles. De Pons's book "translated by an American Gentleman" was published in New York in 1806 (reprinted in London, 1807) under the title *A Voyage to the Eastern Part of Terra Firma, or the Spanish Main.* The translation was made by Washington Irving, in collaboration with his brother Peter Irving and George Caines, and thus ranks bibliographically as Irving's first book. The "Plan of Caracas" does not appear in the English translation.

the air to flow through. All the windows have grilles in the Spanish style and very large shutters.

As to the decoration, the walls are painted white and the rooms adorned with pictures of saints, mirrors, and a chandelier. The walls of those with pretensions to grandeur are hung partway up with tapestries surrounded by gilded moldings, or else with stuff or wallpaper framed in moldings that are either gilded or painted, depending upon the degree of magnificence.

The monuments are not noteworthy. There are three squares, two of which are quite pretty, being surrounded by arcades with balustrades under which the tradesmen sell the wares they bring to market. Each of these squares has a public fountain.

There is a bishop's palace, 4 main parishes, 2 chapels, 3 monasteries (one Fathers of Mercy, one Franciscan, and one Dominican), and 2 convents, one occupied by the Order of the Conception and the other by Carmelite nuns. These communities, which are supported by endowments, income from property, and bequests, have a total population of 600–800 religious, not counting the cathedral, which has 6 prebendary canons. The churches are adorned with gilding and very costly ornaments. They contain neither chairs nor benches. One kneels or sits on the pavement; however, the rich have a rug brought along to kneel on.

Neither the hospital, the government house, the prison, nor the warehouses have the grandeur one expects of public buildings.

This capital is the residence of the bishop, the governor, the intendant, the general treasurer, the auditor, and all the high officers of the civil, political, and military administration. The theatre is but a poor affair, the plays being acted on a stage erected in a large court where the audience sits. The best seats cost only 14 *sols*, which will give you some idea of the quality of the actors.

The garrison of this capital is composed of 3 companies of a regular Spanish regiment stationed in the province (270 men), 6 companies of militia of 80 men each (480 men), 3 negro companies (240 men), 1 volunteer dragoon company of 50 horse (50 men), and 2 engineer officers (2 men), totaling 1,042 men.

In wartime the militia drills once a week. These troops live on cornbread, for which they are allowed 2½ *sols* a pound, and meat that costs but 1 *sol*. They are paid 49 *livres* and 10 *sols* a month, of which 5 *livres* and 10 *sols* goes into the clothing fund to furnish their uniforms.

There are no defensive fortifications in the capital. The only points from which an enemy could approach are La Guaira, 6 leagues away, and Puerto Cabello, 55 leagues away, from which no artillery could be transported by road because of the numerous defiles, which constitute natural defenses. A small body of troops posted in the mountains could halt a large force that, after capturing either of these ports, was imprudent enough to venture into the interior. Therefore the interior of this province could be approached only from Lake Maracaibo and the Orinoco, which are so far from the capital that the invaders could not hope to reach it without fighting a whole campaign. I shall speak more fully on this score in my observations on the province.

Meanwhile, to return to the city, I shall divide its 20,000 inhabitants into four classes: the first white, of pure Spanish blood; the second tan, of mixed Spanish and Indian blood; the third red, of Indian blood; and the fourth negro, mulatto, etc.

The men of the first class are dressed as in Spain. The women have a uniform for church, which consists of a black skirt and bodice and a large black mantilla. They are covered with religious medals, and all carry rosaries as they come out of church, where they spend two hours every morning. The moment they return home they change into the most elegant and voluptuous negligees to receive the men. Their ball dresses consist of *polonaises* and *circassiennes* of the most exquisite taste,[117] and since they have very good figures, they wear their gowns cut very low to expose their bosoms to the maximum. Their coiffures consist

117. Berthier uses the French terms then in current use to describe characteristic elements of ladies' dress. The *Gallerie des Modes et Costumes français*, a series of engraved fashion plates published in Paris by Esnauts and Rapilly, 1778–1788, illustrates several variations of the *polonaise* and *circassienne*: e.g., "Demoiselle à la promenade du matin, en polonaise garnie de tuyaux" (Cahier J, No. 54); "Jeune demoiselle en polonaise d'indienne" (Cahier Q, No. 95); "Camisole à la polonaise avec les manches en amadices" (Cahier EE, No. 172); "Nouvelle circassienne de taffetas" (Cahier V, No. 126).

of a kind of caterpillar roll, or else a very elegant hat. Instead of a *chignon* they wear a large *catogan*, or massive "bun," reaching to their shoulders and tied with a big silk bow, which is particularly becoming, since they usually have beautiful hair. They wear very short skirts, as they have pretty legs, and most luxurious shoes. They are covered with jewelry of gold and pearls, and in general are sumptuously dressed.

The second class wear the same costume to church, though their dresses are made of less costly fabrics. Only their coiffure is distinctive, for they confine their hair in a silken net that hangs down the back of their neck and is tied above the nape with a large ribbon bow. They wear big pendant earrings of gold and pearls in the Indian style and wide gold bracelets. The men wear short jackets and wide-brimmed hats, and also capes when they go out.

The third class, both men and women, imitate the second as far as possible. Those who cannot afford black mantillas to wear to church wear white veils.

In the fourth class the women wear only a shirt and skirt, with a handkerchief on their heads. The richest ones wear long gold earrings. The men wear shirts and breeches, with caps or handkerchiefs on their heads; however, most of them wear only breeches.

These four classes unite in scrupulously observing the customs and practices ordained by religious fanaticism. Although the monks are beginning to be revered less here than in Spain, they still play a very important role compared to ours in France. They have filtered through all levels of society and are very assiduous in influencing the women. The public attributes many amorous adventures to them. Their policy of keeping the people in ignorance persists. Publishing is prohibited and literature ignored because books of every kind are banned. Moreover, one does not travel without an order from the governor, which is rarely granted to citizens and almost never to foreigners. You cannot find an inn anywhere but must beg hospitality from the inhabitants.

The climate makes the men slow and lazy and the women lively and pleasure-loving. The life of the former is spent in going to church in the morning, and at nine o'clock either to the houses of their mistresses or to their businesses. Then they dine, sleep, promenade, and go out again into society, where amorous intrigues are their principal occupation.

As for the women, they are concerned with two subjects: God and men—the first from habit and the second for pleasure. At seven in the morning they go to church, as I have already told you, dressed in black, hidden by a mantilla covered with medals, and armed with an enormous rosary. They pray to God prone on the pavement or on a rug brought by their negresses. After two or three hours of devotions they go home, where they promptly change into the most coquettish negligees to await their lovers, for they all have them. This is the universal custom, and women who rarely agree on any subject are unanimous, unalterable, and indissoluble in the matter of neglecting their husbands and obliging their lovers. The latter are received, together with all the other young people, at ten or eleven in the morning. They pass their time singing, dancing, and playing the guitar, the indispensable instrument for success in love.

The husbands are accustomed to seeing the lovers passed off as friends and calmly allow them to play the role they themselves play on another stage. When the husbands appear, they are caressed only because they are being deceived. Thus everyone stands to gain. I believe this situation to be reasonable enough, especially in a country in which marriages do not unite compatible persons so often as do the passions, which are somewhat strong here. However, this does not keep the men and women from going incessantly to confession and fasting on all the prescribed Holy Days to the point of undermining their health.

The gaiety and magnetism of our young French noblemen appealed so strongly to these ladies that they soon behaved as informally with them as if they had known one another for years. It was just as well that their lovers, knowing our stay would be very short, put no obstacles in the path of the intrigues that everyone hastened to commence. We made rendezvous with them, talked to them in the evening through the blinds of conniving friends' houses, wrote them beautiful letters, sent them bouquets; and in taking this first step each man believed he had arrived, when in fact he was about to leave. What greatly pleased all the Spanish men, who were distressed to observe that in the long run the ladies would have transferred their affections to us, was that these ladies seemed most anxious to instruct them in European manners.

I overheard a very naive remark made by a pretty woman. The Vicomte de ——— [Riccé],[118] wishing to speak to her of another woman whose name he did not mention, said in a low voice, "She is the one who has two lovers, and one of them is ———." Without giving him time to finish, she replied brightly, "Oh, that's my sister!" Even though there were fifteen of us in the room, this remark did not seem to surprise anybody.

The playful custom in society, and particularly at balls, is, as I have already said, to throw candied aniseed in the faces, hair, and corsages of the women whose gowns are cut very low. Those who receive the most are invariably the prettiest. This arouses the envy and jealousy of the others, who take this little game very seriously. Even the priests play it. I saw two monks, who were dining with me at the intendant's, carry this joke a bit too far.[119]

At these balls we saw something we had never seen before. The husbands hardly ever dance, leaving this pleasure to the younger men. They stand in the doorways and in the window-recesses wrapped in their voluminous capes, with their wide-brimmed hats pulled down over their eyes, and in this disguise spy on everything that goes on. The lovers are far more jealous than the husbands and at times resort to poniards to settle their differences; but since they have lately become more reasonable, such instances are rare.

The meal-times here are the same as ours. Chocolate is usually drunk at breakfast and often at supper in the evening. The food would be better were it prepared by a good French chef. After dinner it is the custom to serve glasses of water with little orange-flavored wafers, which they dip in the water. Everything here is very cheap except the bread, which is made of flour imported from Europe since the natives are too lazy to cultivate wheat.

Bread costs 14 *sols* a pound here. Butcher's meat costs 28 *sols* for 25 pounds and is never sold in smaller quantity. It is astonishing to see turkeys costing 16 *livres* and 10 *sols* when an ox costs but 25 *livres*. The rest costs about the same as in Europe.

The outskirts of the city and the surrounding plain are covered with plantations that are well cared for and varied as to produce, which includes sugar cane, bananas, cacao, cotton, oranges, coffee, lemons, pomegranates, and indigo. The trees are alive with every species of bird, including parrots. The fertility of the plain contrasts strikingly with the barrenness of the two mountain ranges that bound it, producing a very picturesque landscape.

On 10 March I took leave of the governor and at one the next morning left Caracas for Puerto Cabello with the Prince de Broglie and the Marquis de Champcenetz. We spent the night of the 11th at La Victoria, 15 leagues beyond. Leaving Caracas, you follow a well-cultivated valley for a league and a half, then for the next league and a half travel along the banks of the Caracas River [Rio Guaire], which you cross and recross, seeing nothing on either hand but Indian dwellings. Then you come to a house where you leave the valley, which is very narrow at that point, and take a road to the left into the mountains. You climb a steep hill for 2 leagues more and follow the crest, sometimes climbing, sometimes descending, for another league; from the crest you look down to right and left upon immense valleys extending as far as the eye can see, though most of the time the view is obscured by low clouds. You descend a league and a half to the hamlet of San Pedro, where 7 or 8 Indian dwell-

118. Gabriel-Marie, vicomte de Riccé, an aide-de-camp to the Baron de Vioménil, was one of the late arrivals who had joined the army at Crompond.

119. Describing a similar episode, Ségur ([2], I, 497–498) relates that a "reverend father inquisitor," finding the tiny aniseeds too light for ammunition, added a large almond to his volley. The bullet grazed the nose of the Marquis de Laval, who thereupon riposted with a large orange that hit the reverend father square in the face. In the midst of general consternation, with many signs of the cross by the ladies, His Reverence affected joviality (which his expression belied) and resumed the game. Ségur reflected that, had not the French army and fleet, five thousand strong, been stationed in a nearby port, the Marquis de Laval would no doubt have become acquainted with one of the dungeons that the Inquisition held in reserve for such offenders.

ings are huddled together in an exceedingly narrow gully through which flows a small stream. We breakfasted here.

Leaving this village, you climb a very steep and rocky slope for about 2 leagues. Some parts of the trail are so bad that your safety depends entirely upon the quality and skill of your mules. You follow the ridge of this mountain through a green forest with an infinite variety of trees inhabited by a prodigious number of parrots, macaws, monkeys, and stags one-third smaller than ours, of which we killed several. The tigers, which also live in this forest, do not come out of hiding unless they are famished, though you constantly hear them roar. Descending for 2 leagues, you come to Las Cucuisas, 11 leagues from Caracas, a sugar plantation on the banks of a small stream. We hung up our hammocks in an Indian cabin, and after resting from the fatigue brought on by the excessive heat in the mountains, we talked a while, dined, and resumed our journey. When traveling in this country it is customary to carry a hammock on the back of your mule. You hang it from a tree and rest there when the heat of the day becomes unbearable, and at night in the Indian cabin where you stop, if there are no beds.

For 2 leagues you follow a narrow valley through which winds a small, shallow river. The mountains on either side are densely wooded. Then you come out into an immense valley, about a league and a half wide, where a road that skirts the foot of the mountain range on your right leads into La Victoria, 2 leagues beyond. This town consists of 350 houses and about 1,500 inhabitants, and has 6 parallel streets running one way and 7 the other, forming regular squares. It contains a main square, a parish church, and a government house. South of the town is a highroad that crosses the province and leads to the frontier of the kingdom [viceroyalty] of Santa Fé.

The commandant, Don Prudhomme, received us very kindly, as did the administrator of the King's customs. The zeal displayed by the latter and by all the officials along our route, whom the intendant had ordered to make us welcome, convinced us of his despotic control over the petty tyrants of the royal government. The commandant had us lodged in the *Casa Real*, where he came to spend the evening with us. Since he spoke a little French, we were able to get to know him and to gauge his intelligence and education. We found him witty and gay as well as both learned and well read. He frets over the superstition and tyranny the Spaniards exercise over this continent. I believe he will bear watching if ever a revolution breaks out to gain independence for this colony.[120]

There are four companies of militia of 80 men each stationed here. Two are composed of white men and two of mulattos. They drill once a week.

We stayed here through 12 March and spent the afternoon walking about the town.[121] The valley is remarkably fertile, especially for wheat, which is harvested three times a year in the same field. It ears in forty days and in three months is ready to cut, with a yield of up to 30 [bushels] to the [acre]. West of the town the valley branches out to the north.

120. "He seemed curious to know in detail the history of the revolution of the English colonies and also expressed a keen desire to possess Abbé Raynal's political and philosophical history. I promised to satisfy him in both respects, and I did indeed send him from Puerto Cabello a copy of each of these two works. Thus I hope that, if a revolt of the Spanish colonies against their sovereign takes place during my lifetime, I can boast of having contributed to it." Broglie (2), p. 140. The works referred to are Abbé Raynal's *Révolution de l'Amérique* (1781) and his *Histoire philosophique et politique des établissemens et du commerce des Européens dans les deux Indes* (1770 and many subsequent editions). Ségur ([2], I, 488–489) speaks at some length of "Don Prudon's" liberal ideas and interest in the American Revolution. "In this same city," he adds, "we met a doctor who was no less dissatisfied with the government, and it was with extreme pleasure that he took us to the farthest corner of his dwelling, where he showed us, in a cleverly hollowed-out beam, the works of Jean-Jacques Rousseau and of Raynal, which he was hiding there as his most precious treasure." Dumas ([1], I, 148–149) refers to the commandant at La Victoria as "le señor Emmanuel Perdhomo."

121. According to Broglie ([2], pp. 140–143) the extra day's stay of the French travelers at La Victoria was a scheme concocted by the ladies: Señora Prudhomme, the commandant's good-natured wife, her young cousin ("la fièvreuse"), and her friend Señora Domingo ("Madame Dimanche"), an attractive thirty-five-year-old widow who was Don Prudhomme's ladylove. Señora Domingo persuaded the commandant to organize a bullfight in the French visitors' honor, while he in turn discreetly hinted to the travelers that their mules required a twenty-four-hours' rest before resuming the journey.

After our promenade we attended a bullfight opposite the commandant's house, where all the ladies in town were gathered. A young widow who looked ill interested us, and especially the Marquis de ——— [Champcenetz]. When he learned that rigorous fasting was undermining her health, his interest only increased. At the ball given for us that night by the administrator he paid her a great deal of attention and obtained permission to escort her home. Since the Marquis's principles were not identical with hers, the conversation was prolonged, requiring them to go into great detail as to what they expected of one another. Both believed themselves to be making progress with the new convert each saw in the other. Finally the pretty widow's zeal led her to offer her convert a ring made of wood from the True Cross, which he gratefully accepted and has kept. He requested, and obtained, permission to return to finish his conversation and repeat his thanks after he had made arrangements for his departure the next day. The rendezvous was granted for midnight. He met with the greatest possible success, and our pretty abstainer went into retreat for four hours that night, sacrificing all for love, while talking incessantly of the pleasure she would take in going to confession next morning. This perfectly true story, which was acted out before our eyes, will give you an idea of the morals, as well as the fanaticism, of their religion.[122]

On 13 March we left La Victoria for Maracay, 8 leagues distant. Because the heat was oppressive, we did not start until four in the afternoon. Leaving La Victoria, you cross a small stream that flows from northeast to west. There are two roads: the one on the left runs along the left-hand side of the valley; the other, which is shorter, runs halfway up the mountains, joining the first a league and a half beyond. The river, which you cross 38 times within 3 leagues, winds through a valley that is partly under cultivation. The road often leads through reeds 30 feet high, which are used to roof houses. We arrived at San Mateo, a col-

lection of 5 or 6 houses. As you leave the river the valley widens and forms a beautiful, well-cultivated plain 3 or 4 leagues across.

The roads here are lovely and are lined with hedges of orange and lemon trees filled with birds. You reach Turmero, a small town 2½ leagues from San Mateo that contains some 200 houses, a square, 2 parish churches, and a royal tobacco warehouse where each planter must bring his crop, which he sells there at 11 *livres* for 25 pounds. The same 25 pounds is then resold to consumers in the province for 66 francs. It is forbidden, on pain of being sent to the galleys or the mines, to use any other tobacco. Even the planter must buy his own tobacco from the state farm or pay the penalty. (When an inhabitant of the country wishes to grow tobacco, he must declare his intention to the government farm, one of whose employees measures the size of his field and reports it to the farm.)

There are four companies of militia of 80 men each, including two of mulattos and two of negroes. Another company of Indians armed with bows and arrows is subject to call.

After being given a collation we continued our journey. The road was not unlike the last one, but now we began to see indigo plantations. This recently established industry has met with the greatest success. As we followed the left-hand slope of the mountains nightfall overtook us, and we were treated to a curious spectacle, which is the local method of clearing the land by setting whole forests afire, lighting up the countryside for 7 or 8 leagues. Before dark, when a league and a half beyond Turmero, I came across a tree whose branches spread across a diameter of 630 feet and whose trunk was 8½ feet thick and 24 feet in circumference, though its height was normal.

We arrived in Maracay at eight that evening, and although all the administrators came to greet us, we chose to go to the house of Don Felix, the commander of the local troops, an intelligent and well-read man and a great Francophile, who in a revolution would

122. Lieutenant Coriolis of the Bourbonnais Regiment, who accompanied his colonel, the Marquis de Laval, on the journey to Caracas, also noted the prevalent taste for gallantry and the seductive manners of the Spanish women. "In short," he concluded, "they had everything needed to turn the heads of our young Frenchmen and they succeeded rather well. What a difference between these depraved morals and the simplicity, the gentleness, and honesty of the inhabitants of North America!" Coriolis (2), p. 185. Coriolis (a survivor of the wreck of the *Bourgogne*) had left North America with a heavy heart, for it meant abandoning his hope of marrying Miss Blair of Virginia; cf. Clermont-Crèvecœur's journal, n. 146.

be no less valuable than Don Prudhomme.[123] Maracay is a small town inhabited chiefly by Indians. Its appearance is most attractive. The houses are far apart, and each is surrounded by a garden containing beautiful trees. There is a square, a parish church, and a government house. The garrison consists of four companies of militia. The valley between the mountains is 3 to 4 leagues wide and is bounded on the south by Lake Valencia. It is here that the first indigo plantations were established.

We stayed here through 14 March. I went to see a species of panther the size of a large dog, the color of a lioness, and the shape of a tiger, which was a year old. She had been captured on the road to Valencia. I spent the rest of the day at an indigo plantation.[124]

These establishments are set up on plains where water is available at a sufficient altitude to water the plants and run the indigo mill. These plains are usually covered with trees, which are cut down and burned. After the land is ploughed, parallel furrows 3 inches deep are dug a foot apart, using string as a guide. In these the indigo seed is planted in September, which is still the rainy season. The first year only one harvest is gathered, and the next year three: one in June, one in September, and one in December. The roots of the plant last three or four years, after which the furrows are ploughed up and reseeded. After ten years the ground usually becomes exhausted and potatoes are planted to replenish the soil.

At maturity, indigo grows to a height of 5 or 6 feet, including the flower. After it is cut, it is carried stalk by stalk into sheds to keep the delicate plants from wilting in the sun. It is next put into vats and pressed in layers until they reach a height of 3 or 4 feet. It is then covered with water and allowed to stand for six or eight days, until it ferments to the point where it dissolves into a stringy mash. Through a very wide faucet the mash is emptied into a second vat where it is beaten by four blades fitted to a cylinder turned by a waterwheel. At the end of five hours it is completely dissolved and only a blue mud (*mat*) remains on the bottom of the vat, which is equipped with three faucets, one above the other. Through these the remaining water is gradually drained out into a trough the bottom of which is hollowed out to form a scoop to catch the small amount of indigo that runs out with the water. When all the water has run off and only the solid material is left, the spigots are closed. The *mat* is then removed with shovels and spread on frames of cloth to drain. When compact the substance is carried to extension tables that slide out from under the sheds and is exposed to the sun for several days. The tables are taken into the sheds each night and also when it rains. When the indigo is dry and very hard, it has reached perfection and is put into bags. It sells for 10 *livres* a pound. An investment of 25,000 *livres* yields in ten years, with all expenses and duty paid, 100,000 *écus* net, by the most conservative estimate. This applies to a plantation with an area of 30 *fanegas*, the equivalent of 187 by 225 French *toises*. This profit would be very handsome if all years were good, but often the crop fails because of drought or insects and not a single pound of indigo is harvested.

One of our traveling companions had contracted a fever from the heat and fatigues of the journey. I stayed behind with him in Maracay for two days, which I spent walking about, and I saw a great deal of cotton. This could become a most profitable industry. Cotton would not be difficult to produce, since it grows on every roadside and seems to go begging in this land of abundance.

I went to visit a man in Maracay who, more industrious than his compatriots, has started such an enterprise. When the boll bursts, the cotton is picked and the fiber extracted. In the fiber is a cluster of 18 to 20 seeds, which must be separated from it. This is accomplished by a machine composed of two steel cylinders an inch in diameter and a foot and half long which, placed horizontally so that they touch, are rotated in opposite directions by means of a treadle. The cotton is introduced between the cylinders, which break the cluster and expel the seeds from the fiber. Workers

123. Broglie ([2], pp. 143–144) notes that "Don Félix" was even more ardent than Don Prudhomme: "His imagination led him to envisage the revolution of the English colonies as a seductive example for the Spanish possessions in the New World."

124. Berthier also wrote up a separate description of the indigo plantation in a 4-page manuscript (Princeton, Berthier Papers, No. 43) entitled "Dépenses et produit d'une habitation d'indigot de 30 fanegues de terre pendant 10 ans." A page from this manuscript, with diagram, is reproduced as one of our illustrations.

clean it, and then it is pressed and baled. This industry is so new that the planter has difficulty disposing of his cotton, though it is as fine as that grown in the Levant.

I went from there to a cocoa plantation—the only active trade in this province. The cocoa trees grow to a height of only 20 or 25 feet and are planted in alternate rows 12 to 15 feet apart. Other trees called ————,[125] which grow very quickly to a great height, are planted between them with the sole purpose of giving shade to the cocoa trees, which otherwise would die in the hot sun. The cocoa tree puts forth a small white flower that grows out of the trunk and branches and is replaced by a large pear-shaped nut growing on a stem. This nut is the size of a pint bottle and has a rough surface. When ripe it is a deep purple. It is then harvested and the shell, which is full of seeds, is opened and the seeds extracted and dried in the sun. This is the cocoa that is sent to us in Europe. The cocoa tree bears throughout the year and the harvest is continuous. Each tree produces about 100 nuts, and the trees last from twenty to thirty years. A *fanega* (100 pounds) usually sells for around 66 *livres* and is taxed 37 *livres* and 10 *sols* in export duty when shipped out of the country.

Another industry that could, in my opinion, be very profitable is the exportation to our colonies of horses and mules. It is incredible to see this country so encumbered by its own wealth because of the shackles Spain has placed upon it and the unfortunate indolence of its inhabitants. A mule, which costs 80 *livres* here, sells for 1,500–1,800 in the French colonies, and the finest horses, which cost 8 to 10 *louis*, sell in our colonies for between 100 and 150. The oxen that we often cannot obtain sell here for 18 *livres* in the interior, where they are frequently slaughtered for their hides. You can see, my dear Chevalier, that were it in the hands of the French or British, this country would be quite different.

I left Maracay on 16 March for Valencia, 13 leagues beyond. Leaving this town, you cross a plain for a league and a half to the shores of Lake Valencia, which you at times skirt halfway up the slopes of the rather low mountains surrounding it. The lake is 15 leagues long by 6 to 7 leagues across at its widest point. There are several small islands in the middle. Its banks are dotted with small Indian villages whose inhabitants sail on the lake in dugout canoes. Since they engage in no trade, the lake is virtually useless. The sole reason, in my opinion, is the laziness and indifference of the people who dwell here, for its shores are extremely fertile and, because of the ease of water transport to the nearby towns of Valencia and Maracay, a profitable trade could be carried on.

The road that winds through the mountains affords many pleasing views of the lake. You come across many new Indian settlements in the woods. One in particular attracted my attention. This Indian family consisted of an old man and his wife, a young couple with three children, and two youths between twenty and twenty-five years old. After they had cleared the most sparsely wooded land, their first concern had been to plant a little corn and cassava and some banana trees. In the shadiest spot they had strung creeping vines from tree to tree and covered them with reeds and foliage to make a roof, under which two hammocks made of animal skins served as beds for the old people and the sick. The rest slept on mats on the ground.

Two rude earthenware pots in which they cooked the game they killed, two axes, a miserable sword blade, a bow and some arrows, and a she-goat were all their household possessions. The two youths were busy cutting wood to build a cabin while the old woman baked cassava bread and the young woman nursed her baby. The other children romped around her on all fours like two little monkeys, and as a background to this pastoral scene there was a great fire raging in the woods to clear a large area for cultivation. Although the family's clothing consisted of nothing but loin-cloths of rags or animal skins, they seemed happy and contented.

I continued my journey. As the mountains recede from the lake shore you cross about 2 leagues of low

---

125. Berthier leaves the name of the tree blank in his manuscript. Coriolis ([3], p. 175) notes that the tall trees used to shade the cacao were called "buscar," his spelling for the Spanish *bucare*, which is the Erythrina or Coral-tree, also known as Immortelle. Pons (*Voyage*, II, 188–189), in his account of cacao culture, describes two species called by the Spaniards *bucare anaoco* and *bucare peonio*.

swampland level with the lake, which you leave behind. This part is thickly wooded with green trees and shrubs and alive with monkeys, which you encounter in bands of 20 to 25, emitting piercing shrieks. Leaving the woods you come out on a fallow plain, which you cross for a league and a half to reach Cura [Villa de Cura], Colonel Taurau's plantation, 6 leagues from Maracay.[126] You then cross another league and a half of fallow land whose fine trees, however, testify to its fertility. It abounds in palms and *lataniers*[127] in whose shade grow lush pastures filled with superb cattle.

You come to the Indian village of Guacara, 3 leagues from Valencia, where the streets are laid out in regular squares and lined with Indian dwellings. Each is surrounded by a large garden planted with all the useful trees. The inhabitants live chiefly on cassava bread, smoked beef, and local fruits. Their cabins are built of wood, with walls of mud and straw, and roofed with coconut fronds. They contain three rooms, two of which are enclosed for night use, the third consisting only of a roof supported by four pillars. There they spend the hot part of the day sleeping on mats or in hammocks. At night they show a light or build a fire before their door, a custom I have observed in all the villages and hamlets, to prevent tigers from coming into the house to carry off their children or killing their cattle outside. These beasts will never come near a light. Before the cabins in the woods, where the children nearly always sleep out-of-doors, large fires are built. All travelers who stop here for the night observe this custom and consequently sleep in peace.

I continued my journey for 3 leagues on a plain similar to the last and arrived at Valencia, a city of the second category much inferior to the capital. It is situated on an eminence in a plain 3 to 4 leagues wide at the foot of the northern mountains. This plain, which runs from east to west, also extends to the north through an open valley between the mountain ranges, so that it has a healthy and temperate climate. Because of the lack of population the countryside is fallow, though fertile.

The town is laid out in regular blocks, with a large square in the center and a church. It is the residence of a commandant and several government officials. From it runs the highway leading to the frontier of the viceroyalty of Santa Fé and the headwaters of the Orinoco, passing through San Carlos, Asaure, Guanare, Barinas, and Merida, 151 leagues from Caracas. The large number of rivers you have to cross makes this journey very tedious.

On the morning of 17 March I left Valencia for Puerto Cabello, 18 leagues away. Leaving the city, you travel for 3 leagues across a plain partly planted in sugar cane. Farther on it narrows, being enclosed by several low and barren mountain ranges. You come to a miserable cabin where the muleteers stop. As you begin to cross the mountains you descend a very steep slope cut out of rock. These mountains are tremendously high and steep and are covered with very tall trees choked with vines and brambles to a height of 30 feet, making an impenetrable jungle, which contains a prodigious variety of birds. You come to a torrent, which you follow for 8 leagues across the mountain range, taking advantage of the road it has scooped out of the rocks. You are often obliged to leave this, however, when it descends abruptly into a chasm, and climb up and down the slopes of the adjacent mountains on narrow, rocky trails a foot and a half wide, which are often washed out altogether. These are so rough that only mules can take you over the obstacles. They negotiate the loose rocks by sliding from one to another or climb over them with admirable skill and incredible agility. What is even more frightening is the fact that if you fell you would roll down 700 or 800 feet into precipices so deep you cannot see the bottom. The trail between the rocky cliffs is sometimes so narrow that you must put your legs up on the neck of the mule to avoid their being crushed. As you pass under arches of rock or felled trees, you are filled with dismay to see at every turn the carcasses of mules that have died of heat or fatigue or fallen into a precipice and to hear the howling of wild beasts.

These mountains, which are inhabited by a few

126. Coriolis ([3], p. 175), who visited this plantation on 27 February on his way to Caracas, calls it "Mandono" and refers to the owner as the Marquis "del Toro."
127. In his manuscript Berthier spells the word *atanier* or

athanier, instead of *latanier*, which is the *Latania*, a species of palm characterized by its tall fan-shaped fronds. He evidently mistook the initial *l* for the definite article *l'*. See n. 130. Following a similar pattern, another eighteenth-

negroes or Indians, are dangerous to cross alone, for travelers are often murdered here. The day before I crossed them an Indian had killed a man for the half-bottle of brandy he was carrying. This is not the only danger, since when they are famished tigers and panthers often attack travelers there.

I arrived at Cambur, 8 leagues beyond. It is only an Indian cabin where the muleteers halt to drink rum. The heat was oppressive, and we hung up our hammocks and slept three hours before dinner, which, since we had no provisions with us, was served us. It consisted of smoked beef, boiled chicken, and cassava bread. We left at three o'clock. The country continued the same. On the level stretches near the mountain torrent you see Indian caravans encamped. These transport produce from the interior to Puerto Cabello on their mules. They never stop at houses but camp wherever heat or darkness overtakes them. The drivers turn their mules out to graze, stretch their hammocks between the trees, build great fires to keep off the wild beasts, and eat the food they carry with them.

Two leagues from Cambur you can smell the sulphurous vapor that rises from a hot spring 200 paces to the left of the road, on the banks of the torrent whose waters it heats for more than 200 yards downstream. You cross the mountains for 2 leagues more, leaving the torrent [Rio Aguas Calientes] on your left, and pass more and more Indian cabins until you reach the seashore. Turning left along the shore, you cross large stretches of sand, pass through an Indian village, then cross a bridge over a marsh where salt is made. Passing through a very thick wood, which is pretty and cool, you come out again upon the wet sand along the seashore and cross the Puerto Cabello [San Esteban] River at a ford to reach the harbor of Puerto Cabello.

We found that the *Couronne* had arrived from Curaçao with news of the preliminary peace negotiations, which had been brought from the Windward Islands by a Dutch vessel. This made my situation even harder to bear, for the *Neptune*, which had been repaired, had also arrived from Curaçao. The frigate *Andromaque*, which had left France and sailed to Martinique, had also arrived, bringing the preliminary peace terms to M. de Vaudreuil together with orders to cease hostilities on 3 April and leave for The Cape, where he would receive further instructions for the fleet and army. Consequently the Marquis de Vaudreuil ordered the squadron to prepare to get under way on 3 April. Meanwhile, he took advantage of his few remaining days to go to Caracas with the Baron de Vioménil.

They left on the frigate *Néréide* for La Guaira, where they learned on arrival that the Comte [Christian] de Deux-Ponts, returning to Puerto Cabello in a bilander belonging to the King of Spain, had been captured by an English frigate whose captain, after holding him and his companions two days and treating them very well, had sent them on to Puerto Cabello in a pretty vessel, much better than the King's bilander, which he presented to them complete with crew and provisions.[128] This episode determined the Admiral to send out a warship and frigate at once to act as convoy on their return journey.

On 2 April 1783 he rallied his squadron, and on the 3rd 9 warships and all the transports left the harbor. On the 4th the Admiral and his brother both got under way and joined the squadron, which had been cruising up and down all night before the harbor. On the morning of the 5th signals were made for the *Souverain* and the *Amazone* to come up into the wind, whereupon the Admiral ordered the frigate to take the

---

century writer refers to the lobelia (*la lobélie* in French) as *l'obélie*.

128. For further details about this incident, see Clermont-Crèvecœur's journal, n. 199. Berthier in his manuscript calls the ship "une bélandre," which, like the Spanish *balandra* and the English *bilander*, derives from the Dutch term for a small coaster. Coriolis ([3], pp. 187–188), who returned with the Marquis de Laval from La Guaira to Puerto Cabello in one of them (without being intercepted by the English), calls it "une lanche du Roi" and

describes it thus: "These boats are merely large sloops (*chaloupes*). They carry a crew of 20 men and are propelled by oars when the winds fail them. They belong to the King [of Spain] and are used to prevent smuggling along the coast; they are armed with two 3-pounders and some swivel guns (*pierriers*). They often board schooners three times their size." These ships were thus the equivalents of armed revenue cutters. The contraband trade, especially with the Dutch island of Curaçao, was a matter of constant concern to the Spanish authorities.

Comte de Ségur to Jacmel, a port on the south coast of Saint-Domingue only two days' journey from his plantation.

He had invited me to accompany him, so we left the *Souverain* and boarded the frigate and at eight o'clock left the fleet. Plagued by calms, we did not reach Jacmel until four o'clock on the afternoon of 12 April. The frigate landed us there and went on to join the squadron at The Cape.

The bay and harbor of Jacmel, lying between Cape Jacmel and Cape Maréchaux, are about 2 leagues long by ¾ of a league wide, narrowing as you approach the port.[129] To the right of the entrance to the harbor there is a deep spot. The town contains between 60 and 80 houses built on the high ground along the harbor. The anchorage is within cannon-range of the shore, which is defended by two batteries containing eight 4-pounders perched on a steep bluff on the left in front of the town. There are no garrison troops; however, the militia garrison this post in wartime.

We went to the commandant's house, and he sent an express messenger to Léogane to announce our arrival, since we wished to set out at once. He found us some inferior horses but was unable to procure a carriage. The oppressive heat of the day decided us to travel the 15 leagues to Léogane by moonlight, which meant riding all night; therefore we left after supper.

For the first 2 leagues you cross plantations and then enter a very thick green wood. Next, after crossing a valley between steep cliffs, you climb up and down the mountains over a well-defined trail cut out of the rock halfway up the slopes. After 7 leagues you reach more level country, covered with trees, where you see several plantations in the clearings. You reach an inlet of the sea, which you follow a while until you come out upon the plain of Léogane leading to the town 3 leagues beyond, which you cross on level roads 80 feet wide, lined with tall hedges of lemon trees or camwood trimmed breast-high, and frequently bordered with palms and *lataniers*.[130] This whole plain is covered with fine sugar plantations.

You arrive at Léogane, which is on the seacoast. It has a little harbor where small vessels can anchor. It can be rated a city of the second category. It is laid out in regular blocks with a handsome main square where the streets are wide and lined on both sides with beautiful large trees that provide a continuous shade to the houses as well as a pleasant promenade sheltered from the sun.

We did not arrive until six in the morning and were very tired. The commandant had gone to review the militia, and our messenger had retired to bed and had kept our letter without attempting to find us lodgings. Thus we were kept waiting for two hours before we could find anyone willing to take us in, since the town's only inn was full.

Finally an officiously polite citizen offered us beds. The Comte de Ségur slept while I went to make arrangements for our departure for Port-au-Prince. Our host had assured me that one could rent neither carriages nor horses but had to borrow them from the residents. I solicited aid from the wealthiest ones, not forgetting to mention the Comte de Ségur, and succeeded beautifully. Two of the richest merchants came in person to offer us their houses, to invite us to dine, and to offer us horses and carriages, all of which we accepted. After an excellent dinner we entered a fine carriage and proceeded to Port-au-Prince, 8 leagues away.

We crossed a plain, a continuation of the one by which we had come, for 3 leagues and entered a wood, where we found a post-house. After crossing the wood for 2 leagues, we came out on the plain leading to Port-au-Prince. We found traveling in a carriage far more pleasant than traveling on horseback. The carriages here go very fast, despite the heat, and cover about 4 leagues an hour. We drew up at the house of M. Vincent, the commandant, who had prepared lodgings for us in the government house; however, the Comte de Ségur preferred to stay at the inn, since he had to leave very early the next morning for his plan-

129. See map, Vol. II, No. 171, and the view of Jacmel Bay, No. 172.
130. See n. 127. Moreau de Saint-Méry, describing this same general region in his *Description de la partie française de l'Isle de Saint-Domingue*, ed. Maurel and Taille-

mitte, II, 960, mentions among the superb palm trees the *latanier*, which rises high above the others, and adds that it supplies the negroes with materials for weaving bags and baskets when resting from their labors in the fields.

tation. (There are few inns in France, incidentally, as good or as handsome as this one.)

On 14 April I was to leave at seven in the morning for the Ségur plantation, which was 8 leagues distant. Since by six the carriages had not yet arrived, we took a walk about the town, which is situated on the western side of the island on the seacoast and is laid out in regular squares.[131] The streets are very wide and the houses spaced far apart, giving the town a rather forlorn appearance. The government house is very handsome. There is a theatre here, and in peacetime this town, because of its central position in the French part of the island, is the residence of the governor of the colony as well as the intendant. The port possesses neither quay nor dry dock, so the waterfront is muddy and ill-smelling. The defensive works are of little consequence and can be ignored.

At seven o'clock we entered the carriage to drive to the Ségur plantation. We breakfasted halfway along the route with M. Blanchard, uncle of the chief commissary of the French army, who was traveling with us.[132] At eleven we crossed the boundary of the Ségur plantation.[133] As soon as the rumor of the Comte's arrival got abroad, all the negroes left their work and 300 of them ran to meet him, falling upon their knees and kissing his feet with every appearance of joy, saying that they would be happy to die now that they had seen their good master. The Comte de Ségur was astonished and his noble heart was troubled to see men

thus humble themselves before him. Almost forgetting that he was in Saint-Domingue as master of a plantation, he embraced all these miserable people as he raised them to their feet.[134]

During 15 and 16 April we toured all parts of the plantation on horseback, and on the 17th we went to see several other plantations in the valley of Cul-de-Sac.

Wishing to express his good will towards his negroes, the Comte de Ségur granted them a day's holiday from their work, regaling them with a brace of oxen, rum, and biscuit, and they spent the day dancing very gaily. When he went to see them, several of them hoisted him onto their shoulders while all the rest, uttering cries of joy, rushed forward to kiss his feet or some part of his clothing. In the end he would have been smothered in caresses had we not come to his rescue. That evening he distributed to each a shirt and breeches as a bonus. The next day the plantation resumed its normal life.

During 18 and 19 April we learned all the different aspects of growing sugar cane, of which I shall speak later.

We went to the large river whose sole function is to water the plain. This has been a great bone of contention among the planters, but fortunately the government has stopped the quarrels by assigning to each planter the quota of water he may draw from it.[135]

The valley of Cul-de-Sac is between 8 and 9 leagues

131. See the view of Port-au-Prince, Vol. II, No. 175. Moreau de Saint-Méry estimated the population of Port-au-Prince in the 1780's as approximately 9,400, whereas his estimates for The Cape were near 15,000. *Ibid.*, I, 479, and II, 1053. Since that time Port-au-Prince (present capital of the Republic of Haiti) has considerably eclipsed Le Cap Français (Cap Haïtien) in size and importance.
132. Blanchard ([1], pp. 128–129) says that on 16 April his uncle [Blanchard de Lavarie, a member of the governmental council of the colony, died 1784] gave a gala dinner of thirty covers in honor of the Comte de Ségur, who returned the courtesy at his plantation on the 19th.
133. The plantation had come into the Ségur family through the marriage of the Comte's father to a wealthy Creole, "Mademoiselle de Vernon." It was situated in the Cul-de-Sac plain at La Croix des Bouquets. "M. Seigneuret" (who was not expecting the Comte's visit) was the overseer. Ségur (2), I, 7, 517–518. Moreau de Saint-Méry (*Description*, II, 953–972) gives an extended account of "La Paroisse de La Croix des Bouquets."

134. In a letter dated "At my plantation in the Cul-de-Sac, near Port au Prince, 15 April 1783," Ségur ([1], p. 204) wrote to his wife: "I am filled with astonishment at finding myself in my house here, in the midst of a crowd of slaves who fall to their knees when speaking to me and whose life or death is in my hands. . . ." When writing his memoirs some forty years later, at a time when the plantation had long since been lost to the family as a result of the Revolution, Ségur ([2], I, 523) recalled the 1783 visit, with the added remark: "M. Berthier gave me four pretty pictures in which he had portrayed the different views and labors of my plantation, my reception by the negroes, their games and their dances; this is all that is left to me today [1824] of this rich estate." Although it is possible that Berthier's pictures still survive among Ségur's descendants, the Editors have not succeeded in tracing them.
135. See Moreau de Saint-Méry's section on "De l'arrosement procuré par la Grande-Rivière du Cul-de-Sac," in *Description*, II, 940ff. His review of irrigation projects

long, varies in width from 1 to 4 leagues, and is bordered by very high mountains. (Those on the south are very fertile and, having a cooler climate than the valley, produce many of the fruits and vegetables we grow in Europe, which they furnish to the valley and to Port-au-Prince.) Bounded on the east by a salt lake [Etang Saumâtre] and on the west by the sea and Port-au-Prince, it contains a large number of sugar plantations. The soil, which is quite parched during the dry season, has to be watered, and the river is the sole source of supply. This river [Grande Rivière] rises in the mountains to the south and flows through the middle of the valley. Its bed is 5 fathoms wide, and it is very shallow. It comes down from the mountains in waterfalls between two cliffs that are 700–800 feet high, spaced 7 or 8 fathoms apart, and that form a cave in a spot surrounded by woodland and mountains that is very picturesque. At the end of the falls a canal has been dug 20 fathoms long and 20 feet wide, ending in a crescent-shaped pool whose depth is accurately measured. This pool feeds two more canals, which carry water to the lower and upper ends of the valley for 400 fathoms, distributing it equitably among the plantations there. Each canal ends in a crescent-shaped pool that feeds water into five more canals through sluices where the water is measured by the number of inches allotted to each plantation. These are further subdivided on the same principle, so that all the inhabitants share the water in the river according to the amount of land they possess. Guards are posted to prevent planters from damming up a neighbor's canal, thereby doubling the amount of water in their own.

The old river bed is filled only during the rainy season, which is in June, July, and August. At other times it is empty, since the water has been diverted to irrigate the valley. The major part of this rich valley is uncultivated for lack of water. Without negroes and without water land on this island is worthless.[136]

and the litigation arising therefrom amply confirms Berthier's remark that water rights "were a bone of contention among the planters."

136. The Princeton manuscript of Berthier's journal ends here. The sequel describing the return voyage to France, if written, has not been found. Berthier presumably left the plantation with the Comte de Ségur on 21 April, proceeding overland "from plantation to plantation" to The Cape, whence the fleet sailed for France on 30 April–1 May. See journals of Clermont-Crèvecœur (pp. 99ff.) and of Verger (pp. 179ff.) for accounts of the passage to Brest, where Vaudreuil's fleet anchored on 17 June 1783. Berthier had thus been absent for three years; in his service record and petitions for advancement he counted this as "four campaigns": 1780, 1781, 1782 and 1783. Soon after his return Berthier was sent on a mission to Austria and Prussia (see Editors' Introduction to present journal). On 12 August 1783 he was received by Frederick the Great at Sans Souci. "The King," Berthier wrote, "asked me my regiment, my rank, and many questions about the war in America. He ended by inquiring laughingly how the French officers had managed when they found there neither perfume nor powder *à la Maréchale*. I answered that they had not only gone without these but often without bed or bread."

Checklist

OF JOURNALS, MEMOIRS, AND LETTERS

OF FRENCH OFFICERS SERVING

IN THE AMERICAN REVOLUTION

Introduction

In annotating the three journals and related documents constituting the present work the Editors have drawn heavily upon the contemporary evidence supplied by the journals of other French officers. Several such journals are well known and have long been available to historians in book form. Others have been published at various times in French or American periodicals, some of them relatively obscure. Still others have survived only in manuscript and remain unpublished. As a by-product of our efforts to locate as many such journals as possible, it seems appropriate to bring together here in convenient form the results (both positive and negative) of our investigation. This checklist is thus designed to serve both as a bibliography to the present work and, independently, as a general guide to the subject.

The term "journal" has been loosely construed and extended to include day-by-day diaries, journals (often written up from daily notes at some later date), retrospective memoirs (written long after the event, though based upon earlier documents), and coherent groups of letters written at the time. No attempt has been made to round up widely scattered single letters or to record systematically those preserved in the context of the official archives. Although the interpretation of the documents obviously requires discrimination between, for example, a daily diary and memoirs written in old age, the common denominator of the items on the list is that they all represent some sort of narrative account written by a French officer who actually participated in the American war. The accounts are limited to those by officers, for the simple reason that none written by privates (if, indeed, any such were written) have been found. The checklist includes writers from both the French army and navy, since the war was fought on both land and sea, and since their interlocking accounts often cast light on the same events. Also represented are French officers who served in the American army—the forerunners of official French participation in the war—some of whom later resumed their posts in the French forces.

The list is primarily a guide to printed materials, not a systematic survey of manuscript sources, but we have nevertheless recorded unpublished journals when they have come to our attention. We have also included a few "token references" to journals that we have not ourselves located, when their existence appears well established by the statements of others. We hope that such memoranda may be of use to future searchers. This checklist could not have been compiled without the initial help of such reference works as Sabin's *Dictionary of Books relating to America*, Frank Monaghan's *French Travelers in the United States*, and the catalogues of many libraries. It owes much besides to the information already assembled by Thomas Balch, Bernard Faÿ, Ludovic de Contenson, André Lasseray, Warrington Dawson, André Girodie, Gilbert Chinard, and other historians. Evelyn Acomb's bibliography, appended to her recent edition of Von Closen's journal, has been especially valuable. Durand Echeverria's notes to his *Mirage in the West: A History of the French Image of American Society to 1815* (Princeton, 1957) have also supplied useful indications, as have the *Bibliography of the Virginia Campaign and the Siege of Yorktown, 1781* (1941), compiled by the staff of the Historical Division, Colonial National Historical Park, and the papers of the late Harold Vreeland, now in the Library of the College of William and Mary. Although no claim to completeness is made, the Editors nevertheless believe that this list is more extensive than any of those previously published and hope that it can render services beyond its use as a bibliography to the present work.

The list is arranged by authors' names in two alphabetical sequences: first, the officers in the French armed forces; and, second, the French who served in the American forces. The spelling of the names is in general derived from documents of the time (the man's own signature where possible). However, eighteenth-century spelling is not always consistent, and later "authorities" often disagree. Spelling and form of family names have undergone modifications during the past two centuries. Furthermore, "accepted" practice in entering composite family names in alphabetical order varies between the French and the Americans, and even among the French themselves. The forms used here thus follow no single authority but represent what seem to us, from our own experience, reasonably normal forms. Titles are those held by the man at the time of his service in America.

Following the author's name is his rank, regimental affiliation, or function, *at the time of the American Revolution*. (Many of these officers were of course subsequently promoted to higher rank.)

For purposes of abbreviated citation the different bibliographical references under a single name have been numbered. In our notes to the present work a journal is cited only by name of author, and by number when there is more than one item listed under his name: for example, Gallatin (3), Rochambeau (2), or Ségur (1).

Following the bibliographical entry is the Editors' comment on the journal, indicating its content, the dates covered, etc.—that is, what one can expect to find in it. These comments are in general more complete for the less readily available or unpublished journals. A number of the items recorded are relatively insignificant or otherwise disappointing. In this respect the list may nevertheless be useful, if only as a "negative bibliography."

Finally, the checklist includes an "index" or recapitulation, in which the officers' names have been rearranged according to army, navy, regiments, or other pertinent groupings.

Ancteville, Louis-Floxel de
Cantel, chevalier d'
(1738–1785)

*Captain, Royal Corps of
Engineers; came from the
West Indies to Yorktown
with Saint-Simon's army
in 1781*

1 Warrington Dawson, ed., "The Chevalier d'Ancteville and His Journal of 'The Chesapeake Campaign,'" in *Légion d'Honneur* (American Society of the French Legion of Honor, New York), II, No. 2 (Oct. 1931), 83–96. Excerpts from d'Ancteville's journal concerning the Siege of Yorktown.

2 Stephen Bonsal, "D'Ancteville's Description of Williamsburg, and of the American Troops near Williamsburg, in 1781," in *William and Mary College Quarterly*, 2nd ser., xx, No. 4 (Oct. 1940), 502–503.

3 [Description of Williamsburg] in Jane Carson, comp., *We Were There: Descriptions of Williamsburg* (Williamsburg, 1965), p. 52.

The above brief extracts are from the more complete manuscript of d'Ancteville's journal (covering the period from 3 August to 19 October 1781) in the Archives Nationales, Marine B⁴, foll. 145–157; a transcript prepared for Warrington Dawson is in the records of Colonial National Historical Park (Yorktown, Virginia). Another manuscript copy of the journal (dated 22 October 1781) is in the Bibliothèque du Génie (Paris), bound in with maps of an "Atlas de la Guerre d'Amérique," MS A 224, pièce 66ᵇⁱˢ. There is also an incomplete copy of the d'Ancteville journal (but not identified as such) in the Archives du Génie, article 15-1-7, pièce 19; this version, covering only the period 3 August–11 October, may be a rough draft.

D'Ancteville had served as chief engineer at Môle Saint-Nicolas in the French colony of Saint-Domingue. His journal of the Chesapeake Campaign supplies details concerning the landing of Saint-Simon's troops at Jamestown (2 September 1781) and their disposition prior to the arrival of Rochambeau's army from the north. During the Siege of Yorktown d'Ancteville headed the third of the three divisions into which the engineers were grouped.

Bayac

See Losse de Bayac

Beauvoir, Charles-Louis-
Henry Hébert, comte de
(1742–1836)

Navy. Lieutenant de vaisseau

1 "Journal du vaisseau du Roi *L'Eveillé*, commandé par M. Le Gardeur de Tilly, capitaine des vaisseaux du Roy, du 21 mars 1780 sous les ordres de Monsieur le chevalier de Ternay, chef d'escadre des armées navales." Manuscript lent by Comte Henri de Beauvoir (presumably a descendant of the author) to the "Exposition rétrospective des Colonies françaises de l'Amérique du Nord" (Paris, 1929); recorded in exhibition catalogue by A.-Léo Leymarie, p. 189, No. 99. The *Eveillé*, a 64-gun warship commanded by Le Gardeur de Tilly and based with the French fleet at Newport, captured the English *Romulus* off the Chesapeake Capes in February 1781.

Berthier, Louis-Alexandre
(1753–1815)

1 Maggs Brothers, Ltd., *The American War for Independence as related in the unpublished manuscript journals and plans of Alexander Berthier, staff-officer to General Comte de Rochambeau during the American*

Captain attached to the Soissonnais Regiment; aide maréchal-général-des-logis *(assistant quartermaster-general)*

Campaign (London, 1936). Bookseller's catalogue describing a collection of Berthier's papers, until then preserved at the Château de Grosbois. The papers as described in the catalogue were acquired in 1939 by the Princeton University Library through the generosity of Harry C. Black. Cf. Gilbert Chinard, "The Berthier Manuscripts, New Records of the French Army in the American Revolution," *Princeton University Library Chronicle*, I, No. 1 (Nov. 1939), 3–8.

2 *Journal de la Campagne d'Amérique, 10 Mai 1780–26 Août 1781*, ed. Gilbert Chinard (Institut Français de Washington, 1951). Also in *Bulletin de l'Institut Français de Washington*, n.s., No. 1 (Dec. 1951), pp. 43–120. French text of the first part only of Berthier's surviving journal, not including the "Sea Campaign" in the Caribbean, 1782–1783. Excerpts concerning Rhode Island, tr. Marshall Morgan, appeared in *Rhode Island History*, xxiv, No. 3 (July 1965), 77–88.

3 "Journal of Louis-Alexandre Berthier," tr. and ed. Howard C. Rice, Jr. and Anne S.K. Brown, from the manuscript in the Princeton University Library, in the present volume.

Blanchard, Claude (1742–1803)

Chief commissary (commissaire des guerres), *Rochambeau's army*

1 *Guerre d'Amérique, 1780–1783, Journal de campagne de Claude Blanchard, commissaire des guerres principal au corps auxiliaire français sous le commandement du lieutenant général comte de Rochambeau*, ed. Maurice La Chesnais (Paris, Dumaine, 1881). Extracts from Blanchard's journal had previously appeared in an article in the *Revue Militaire Française*, 1869.

2 *The Journal of Claude Blanchard, commissary of the French auxiliary army sent to the United States during the American Revolution*, tr. William Duane (Albany, Munsell, 1876).

The manuscript of Blanchard's journal was lent by M. and J. Georget La Chesnais to the Lafayette exhibition at the Archives Nationales in 1957. It is described in the exhibition catalogue, p. 50, No. 112, as consisting of three parts: "Voyage en Italie, 1770," "Voyage en Amérique, 1780–1783," and "Voyage en Roussillon, juin 1785."

Blanchard's journal covers the entire campaign of Rochambeau's army, including the return via the Caribbean in 1783. It is one of the best, and most frequently cited, of the French officers' journals. From the author's own footnotes it is evident that he reviewed and revised his journal in the 1790's.

Bougainville, Louis-Antoine, comte de (1729–1811)

Navy. Captain, commanding the Auguste *in de Grasse's fleet at Yorktown*

1 R. de Kerallain, "Bougainville à l'Escadre du Comte d'Estaing, 1778–1779," in *Journal de la Société des Américanistes de Paris*, xix (1927), 155–206; "Bougainville à l'armée du Comte de Grasse, Guerre d'Amérique, 1781–1782," *ibid.*, xx (1928), 1–70. Kerallain's articles include substantial excerpts from Bougainville's journals.

2 *Adventures in the Wilderness: The American Journals of Louis Antoine de Bougainville, 1756–1760*, tr. and ed. Edward P. Hamilton (Norman, University of Oklahoma Press, 1964).

The manuscripts of Bougainville's journals and related documents are now in the collection of Bougainville papers in the Library of Paul Mellon, Upperville, Virginia.

Bougainville's journals provide a valuable account of the French navy's participation in the Yorktown campaign. He had earlier been in America with d'Estaing's expedition in 1778–1779 and had still earlier served under Montcalm in the Seven Years' War.

Brisout de Barneville, Nicolas-François-Denis (1746–1839)

Sublieutenant; aide-de-camp to General Baron de Vioménil

1 "Journal de Guerre de Brisout de Barneville, Mai 1780–Octobre 1781," introduction by Gilbert Chinard, in *The French-American Review*, III, No. 4 (Oct.–Dec. 1950), 217–278. Also issued separately, Institut Français de Washington, 1951. Printed from manuscript in possession of a descendant, Henri Brisout de Barneville; the manuscript is entitled "Journal depuis le 2 Mai, jour de mon départ de Brest sur le *Conquérant* jusques et compris le 12 juillet suivant, jour de mon débarquement à Newport en Amérique dans l'Isle de Rodislande. Poursuivi jusqu'à la prise de Yorktown et à l'arrivée de l'armée française à Williamsburg, octobre 1781."

The journal includes diagrams of the encounter with the English on 20 June 1780 and an extended account of the Destouches Chesapeake expedition of March 1781, in which the writer participated. As an aide to the Baron de Vioménil, Brisout de Barneville was concerned with administrative matters after the arrival in Rhode Island; his journal gives details about the purchase of supplies, horses, etc. Although he remained with the army until its return to France in 1783, no journal for the later period has been found.

Broglie, Charles-Louis-Victor, prince de (1756–1794)

Second colonel, Saintonge Regiment

1 "Narrative of the Prince de Broglie, 1782," tr. Elise Willing Balch, in the *Magazine of American History* (New York), I, Nos. 3–6 (March–June 1877), 180–186, 231–235, 306–309, 374–380. The translation was made from a transcript of the journal obtained by Thomas Balch from the Prince de Broglie's grandson; see Balch, I, 15–16. Balch's transcript is now in the Historical Society of Pennsylvania (Philadelphia), Thomas Balch Collection, bound volume. "A very lively account of the visit which he [Broglie], de Lauzun, and some others paid to the Convent at Angra [Azores], has been omitted in the translation, and also the longer part of the narrative which describes his sojourn in South America; as not being within the range of subjects entertained by this Magazine."

2 "Journal du Voyage du Prince de Broglie, Colonel en second du Régiment de Saintonge, aux Etats-Unis d'Amérique et dans l'Amérique du Sud, 1782–1783," in Société des Bibliophiles François, *Mélanges*, 2e Partie (Paris, Rahir, 1903), pp. 13–148; ed. Duc de Broglie from manuscript in family archives. An abridged version of the journal, with a brief introduction by Charles de Rémusat, was published earlier in the *Revue Française* (Paris), No. IV (July 1828), pp. 35–73, under the title "Rela-

tion du Voyage du Prince de Broglie, en 1782 [et 1783], aux Etats-Unis d'Amérique et dans l'Amérique du Sud, (Manuscrit inédit)."

Broglie went to America the year following the Siege of Yorktown on board the *Gloire*; he joined Rochambeau's army at its Crompond encampment in September 1782 and returned with it to France via the Caribbean in 1783. His account parallels that of the Comte de Ségur and the latter part of Dumas's memoirs.

Cadignan, Jean-Baptiste-Gérard Dupleix, chevalier de (1738–?)
Lieutenant colonel, Agenois Regiment

1 Extracts from Cadignan's journal, concerning Yorktown and Williamsburg, are printed in Warrington Dawson, *Les Français Morts pour l'Indépendance Américaine . . . et la Reconstruction historique de Williamsburg* (Paris, Editions de l'Oeuvre Latine, 1931), pp. 93–98; also an excerpt in Jane Carson, comp., *We Were There: Descriptions of Williamsburg* (Williamsburg, 1965), p. 48.

Dawson's extracts from the journal were transcribed from the manuscript then in the possession of one of Cadignan's descendants, M. Galin de la Garde. Contenson (*Cincinnati*, pp. 148–149) refers to it as a manuscript of 600 pages covering five years of Cadignan's service overseas.

Colonel Dupleix de Cadignan took part in the Siege of Savannah (1779), the Pensacola expedition (1781), and came to Yorktown with the regiments under command of the Marquis de Saint-Simon. The following year he was at the capture of Saint Kitts and in the Battle of the Saints.

Cambis, Charles-François, comte de [Cambis-Lézan] (1747–1825)
Navy. Lieutenant de vaisseau

1 "Extraits du Journal tenu par le Cte de Cambis à bord du Languedoc," in Doniol, III, 374–382. The manuscript of Cambis's journal is in the Archives Nationales (Paris), Marine B⁴147. It was shown in the Lafayette exhibition, 1957; cf. catalogue, p. 39, No. 68.

The Comte de Cambis served on the *Languedoc* in d'Estaing's fleet, 1778–1779. The extracts from his journal printed by Doniol cover the period 4–21 August 1778, when the fleet was off Newport, Rhode Island, at the time of the unsuccessful Franco-American attempt to dislodge the British. Bouvet (*Service de santé*, pp. 6–7) notes information about hospitals gleaned from the Cambis journal.

Capellis, Hippolyte-Louis-Antoine, comte de, and marquis du Fort (17[?]–1813)
Navy. Lieutenant de vaisseau; *aide-major d'escadre in Ternay's and Destouches's fleet (1780–1781); commander of frigate* Danaé

1 "Journal de la traversée de l'escadre expéditionnaire portant le Général Comte de Rochambeau, partie de Brest le 2 Mai et faisant route . . . pour le Cap Henri, Baie de Chesapeak." This 17-page, unsigned manuscript covering the period May–June 1780 is in the Archives de la Guerre (Vincennes), Mémoires Historiques, 248², pièce 23. On the page preceding the manuscript proper a heading added by a later hand identifies it as "Mémoire sur la campagne de 1780, par M. Duportail, officier français, commandant le génie de l'armée de Washington." This attribution is manifestly incorrect, since Duportail did not cross to America with Rochambeau's army and since he was made prisoner at the capitulation of Charleston during the period covered by the journal.

Internal evidence points to Capellis as the author of this very hard-to-decipher manuscript. The writer mentions (p. 2) that Admiral de Ternay, upon arriving in Brest, entrusted him (the writer) with the loading of the transports, "in the absence of [Ternay's] major, M. de Granchain." The Comte de Capellis, holding the rank of *lieutenant de vaisseau*, was *aide-major de l'escadre* under Granchain (*q.v.*) who was *major de l'escadre*, i.e., the chief administrative officer of Ternay's squadron. The writer also mentions (p. 3) a joint army-navy conference in Brest, at which the following were present: General Rochambeau, Admiral de Ternay, Tarlé (*intendant de l'armée*), Major General Chastellux (chief of staff), Hector (*commandant de la marine*, at Brest), "and myself." Furthermore, the writer's activities at Brest, described in the journal, are appropriate to an *aide-major de l'escadre*.

Capellis's manuscript (presumably a fragment of a more extensive journal) provides interesting details about the preparations at Brest (March 1780), the embarkation of Rochambeau's army, and the departure on 2 May. The narrative continues only through June, including the encounter with an English fleet (20 June), but unfortunately stops short of the landing at Newport, Rhode Island. Capellis mentions that Ralph Izard of South Carolina, returning from a European mission for the Continental Congress, was a passenger on the frigate *Andromaque*. Upon at least two occasions Izard came to dine on board the flagship, *Duc de Bourgogne*. Capellis records at some length the gossip he picked up from officers of the *Andromaque* about Izard's and Arthur Lee's hostility to Franklin and about Franklin's treatment of John Paul Jones. However, according to Capellis (who was himself on the flagship), when Izard came to dine with the Admiral, he was more circumspect in the expression of his opinions, knowing that they would be disapproved of and that "the French generals did not want to become involved in American quarrels" (p. 10). Capellis's remark on Ternay's "disinclination to give chase to vessels encountered along the route" (p. 6) reflects a commonly held opinion of the Admiral's timidity (justified by some, including Rochambeau, on the grounds that his chief mission was to transport the army safely to its destination). On the other hand, Capellis pays warm tribute to Rochambeau. "It is to be hoped," he writes (p. 17), "that Congress and Mr. Washington will have complete confidence in the Comte de Rochambeau, and I am convinced, ever since I have had the honor of knowing him at Brest, that it cannot be otherwise. Never have I seen a more genuine, more tactful, more honest man. These qualities, added to his military reputation, will earn for him the general esteem of the foreigners, as they have already earned for him the esteem of his own army. The Chevalier de Chastellux, his chief of staff, joins to military talent the advantage of speaking English well and a diplomatic mind. No better choice could have been made."

Charlus, Armand-Charles-
Augustin de la Croix de
Castries, comte de
(1756–1842)

*Second colonel, Saintonge
Regiment*

1 Durand Echeverria, "The Iroquois Visit Rochambeau at Newport in 1780: Excerpts from the Unpublished Journal of the Comte de Charlus," in *Rhode Island History*, XI, No. 3 (July 1952), 73–81.
2 "Dans l'Armée de La Fayette [!], Souvenirs inédits du Comte de Charlus," ed. with an introduction by the Duc de Castries, in *La Revue de Paris*, 64e année, July 1957, pp. 94–110.

The above extracts are from a manuscript journal, covering the period 3 May–29 September 1780, in the Archives Nationales, Marine B¹⁸³. Another copy of the same journal is in the Archives du Génie (Vincennes), article 15-1-7, pièce 26 (but not there identified as by Charlus). Several letters written by Charlus to his father (dated Newport, 5 August 1780, 20 April 1781, 2, 3, 5 June 1781, 12 June 1781; Philipsburg, 29 July 1781, 16 August 1781) supplement and continue the journal; these letters are in the Archives de la Guerre (Service Historique de l'Armée, Vincennes), A¹3732, pièces 59, 65, 66, 68, 72, 73, 81, 82.

The Comte de Charlus was the son of the Marquis de Castries, who became minister of the navy, replacing the Comte de Sartine, in October 1780. Charlus arrived in America with Rochambeau's army, marched with it to the Hudson and Virginia, and returned to France soon after the Siege of Yorktown on the *Amazone*. As the Minister's son and as a personal friend of Lafayette, Charlus was party to a good deal of gossip and "inside news," which he freely relayed in his letters.

Chastellux, François-Jean de
Beauvoir, chevalier (later
marquis) de (1734–1788)

Maréchal de Camp, *major
general, Rochambeau's army*

1 *Voyage de Newport à Philadephie, Albany, &c.* (Newport, Rhode Island, Imprimerie Royale de l'Escadre, 1781). Privately printed for the author in an edition of 24 copies by the printing press of the French Fleet.
2 *Voyages de M. le Marquis de Chastellux dans l'Amérique Septentrionale dans les années 1780, 1781 & 1782*, 2 vols. (Paris, Prault, 1786). First complete trade edition.
3 *Travels in North-America, in the Years 1780, 1781, and 1782. By the Marquis de Chastellux . . . Translated from the French by an English Gentleman, who resided in America at that period. With Notes by the Translator* [George Grieve], 2 vols. (London, G.G.J. and J. Robinson, 1787).
4 *Travels in North America in the Years 1780, 1781 and 1782, by the Marquis de Chastellux*, revised translation with introduction and notes by Howard C. Rice, Jr., 2 vols. (Chapel Hill, University of North Carolina Press, published for the Institute of Early American History and Culture at Williamsburg, 1963). See "Check-List of the Different Editions of Chastellux's *Travels*" (I, 43–52) for other editions not listed here.

Chastellux was with Rochambeau's army throughout the campaigns of 1780–1782; he returned to France with General Rochambeau and others on the *Emeraude* in January–February 1783, and thus did not take part in the "sea campaign" in the Caribbean. Chastellux was a man of letters, a member of the French Academy, as well as a professional military man. His account is not, strictly speaking, a general's report on military events but a narrative of journeys made between campaigns when he was free from the active duties of his command. It provides, among other things, many sidelights on the military events, and especially on the French and American personalities involved. Chastellux's journal was one of the few actually published during the years immediately following the American war.

Crèvecœur, Jean-François-Louis, comte de Clermont (1752–ca. 1824)

Lieutenant, Auxonne Regiment, Royal Corps of Artillery

1 "Rhode Island in 1780, by Lieutenant L.B.J.S. Robertnier," in Rhode Island Historical Society, *Collections*, XVI, No. 3 (July 1923), 65–78. Excerpts from the manuscript in the Rhode Island Historical Society, translated and somewhat summarily edited by Edouard R. Massey. The manuscript can now be attributed to Clermont-Crèvecœur, for reasons explained above in the present volume. A brief extract from the Massey translation appears under the name of Robertnier in Jane Carson, comp., *We Were There: Descriptions of Williamsburg* (Williamsburg, 1965), p. 62.

2 "Journal of the War in America during the Years 1780, 1781, 1782, 1783," tr. and ed. Howard C. Rice, Jr., and Anne S.K. Brown from the manuscript in the Rhode Island Historical Society, in the present volume.

Closen-Haydenburg, Hans Christoph Friedrich Ignatz Ludwig, baron von (1752–1830)

Second captain, Deux-Ponts Regiment; aide-de-camp to General Rochambeau

1 *The Revolutionary Journal of Baron Ludwig Von Closen, 1780–1783*, tr. and ed. with an introduction by Evelyn M. Acomb (Chapel Hill, University of North Carolina Press, published for the Institute of Early American History and Culture at Williamsburg, 1958). Brief extracts appeared earlier in: Clarence Winthrop Bowen, "A French Officer with Washington and Rochambeau," *Century Magazine*, LXXIII (1907), 531–538; "French Troops in Maryland," *Maryland Historical Magazine*, V (1910), 229–234; E. Acomb, "The Journal of Baron von Closen, *The William and Mary Quarterly*, 3rd ser., X (1953), 196–236. Miss Acomb's meticulously annotated edition was translated from a transcript of the manuscript made at the Library of Congress in 1904–1905; the original manuscript, which had been temporarily lent to the Library of Congress by descendants of Von Closen, was subsequently lost in a fire in Germany in 1921.

Von Closen, a German by birth, was with Rochambeau's army during its entire American campaign, 1780–1783. As a trusted aide-de-camp of the General he went on numerous special missions, thus making his account one of the most comprehensive and informative of those extant. According to Miss Acomb (p. xx): "Baron von Closen's Journal is an informal history of the French expedition, based for the most part upon firsthand sources, probably compiled many years later by a man who had kept a journal of his own participation in those events. Despite its late composition, it has a vital freshness and a very real ring of authenticity."

Colbert, Edouard-Charles-Victurnien, comte de Maulevrier (1758–1820)

Navy. Enseigne de vaisseau; lieutenant de vaisseau (*1781*)

1 Paul de Leusse, "Un Episode de la Guerre de l'Indépendance américaine," in *Bulletin de la Société Dunoise* (Châteaudun), Vol. XVII, No. 241 (1936), pp. 88–95. Offprint separately catalogued in the Library of Congress. Leusse prints Colbert de Maulevrier's long letter to Destouches, 9 March 1781, written from "Panqueteuk près York" (Pungoteague, Virginia Eastern Shore). Maulevrier, commanding the cutter *La Guêpe*, left Newport on 9 February with Le Gardeur de Tilly's expedition to the Chesapeake, became separated from the other ships, and ran aground on Machipongo Bank on 13 February. Another letter relating his adventures (not included in Leusse's article), dated "Comté de Northampton," 23 March 1781, is preserved in the Archives du Ministère des Affaires Etrangères, Etats-Unis, Correspondance politique, Supplément, Vol. 13, foll. 99–100.

2 Maps by the Comte de Maulevrier and an account of the Yorktown campaign are described in the Detroit Institute of Arts exhibition catalogue, ed. Paul L. Grigaut, *The French in America, 1520–1880* (1951), pp. 102–103, No. 260, lent by Pierre Berès, Inc. This material was subsequently acquired by the William L. Clements Library, Ann Arbor, Michigan; cf. Brun, *Guide to the Manuscript Maps in the . . . Clements Library*, Nos. 281, 359, 469, 569.

The Comte de Maulevrier, a nephew of the Comte d'Estaing, came to Rhode Island in 1780 with Ternay's squadron as commander of the cutter *La Guêpe*. After its loss in February 1781—as related in (1)—he returned to Newport and served on other ships, went again to the Chesapeake with Barras's squadron in August 1781, commanded the cutter *Le Serpent*, etc. Maulevrier later returned to the United States in 1796 as an émigré. The journal of his travels made in 1798 has been published, with introduction and notes by Gilbert Chinard, as *Voyage dans l'Intérieur des Etats-Unis et au Canada*, Institut Français de Washington, Historical Documents, VIII (Baltimore, 1935). The volume is illustrated with views of American localities from the author's sketchbook. Another of his drawings, depicting "Trenton sur la Delaware," *ca.* 1798, is in the New Jersey Historical Society; a color reproduction was published by the Society in 1962.

Coriolis, Jean-Baptiste-Elzéar, chevalier de (1754–1811)

Lieutenant, Bourbonnais Regiment

1 "Relation inédite du naufrage de la *Bourgogne*, vaisseau de 74 canons portant à bord une partie du régiment d'infanterie de Bourbonnais," with a foreword by Maurice Lachesnais, in *Revue Militaire Française*, II (1870), 262–289.

2 "Un Officier français au Venezuela (1783)," in *La Revue du Mois* (Paris), VII, No. 38 (10 Feb. 1909), 171–189. Further extracts from Coriolis's manuscript journal belonging to Maurice La Chesnais.

3 "Lettres d'un Officier de l'armée de Rochambeau: Le Chevalier de Coriolis," with an introduction by Ludovic de Contenson, in *Le Correspondant* (Paris), Tome 326 (n.s. 290), 25 March 1932, pp. 807–828. Letters written to his family from Baltimore, Providence, Boston, Puerto

Cabello, 1782–1783. Printed from originals in the possession of Jules de Coriolis.

Although Coriolis was with Rochambeau's army during the entire expedition, the above journals and letters concern only the years 1782–1783. His earlier journals were lost in the wreck of the *Bourgogne* (4 February 1783) off Punta Uvero on the coast of Venezuela. In his letters to his parents Coriolis tells of his proposed marriage to "Mlle Blaire" (daughter of John Blair) whom he had met during the winter quarters at Williamsburg. Coriolis was the brother-in-law of Claude Blanchard, commissary general.

Coste, Jean-François (1741–1819)

Chief physician, Rochambeau's army

1 *Compendium pharmaceuticum, Militaribus Gallorum Nosocomiis, in Orbe Novo Boreali adscriptum* (Newport, Rhode Island, Henry Barber, 1780). The preface is dated Newport, 25 July 1780.

2 *De Antiqua Medico-philosophia orbi novo adaptanda: Oratio habita in capitolio Gulielmopolitano in comitiis Universitatis Virginiae, die xii Junii M.DCC.LXXXII.* (Leyden, 1783). Dedicated to General Washington.

3 "The Adaptation of the Ancient Philosophy of Medicine to the New World, by Jean-François Coste," tr. and ed. Anthony Pelzer Wagener, in *Journal of the History of Medicine and Allied Sciences*, VII, No. 1 (Winter 1952), 10–67. A slightly abridged version of (2).

Although these items are not a journal, they reflect the author's activities and experiences in America during the war. The first is a pharmacopoeia compiled by Dr. Coste for the use of the medical corps accompanying Rochambeau's army. The second is a Latin oration delivered in Williamsburg when he received the honorary degree of Doctor of Physics from the College of William and Mary. Coste also received an honorary degree from the University of Pennsylvania and was elected a corresponding member of the Humane Society of Philadelphia. For a good biographical sketch, see John E. Lane, *Jean-François Coste, Chief Physician of the French Expeditionary Forces in the American Revolution* (Somerville, N.J., and New York, 1928), reprinted from *Americana*, Vol. XXII, No. 1 (Jan. 1928). Further information on Coste and on the medical corps in general will be found in Bouvet, *Service de santé*.

Costebelle, Pierre-Alexandre Pastour, chevalier de (1750–1791)

Navy. Enseigne de vaisseau *on the* Languedoc *in d'Estaing's fleet*

1 Manuscript journal in two parts entitled "Journal de la Campagne de l'Amérique Septentrionale de M^r le Comte d'Estaing, Du 21 mars 1778 au 29 juin 1779; . . . Du 30 juin 1779 au 3 septembre 1779." The manuscript was shown in the "Exposition retrospective des colonies françaises de l'Amérique du Nord" (Paris, 1929), and is recorded in the exhibition catalogue, p. 174, Nos. 53–54, as being lent from the collection of Comte Allard du Chollet, Paris. The same manuscript was also shown in the exhibition "Les Etats-Unis et la France au XVIIIe siècle" (Amis du Musée National de Blérancourt, Hôtel Jean Charpentier, Paris, 1929); cf. catalogue by André Girodie, p. 155, No. 129.

2 "Journal de la Campagne dans l'Amérique Septentrionale de la Frégate 'L'Amazone,' commandée par M. de La Pérouse, Capitaine de vaisseau;

l'escadre dont cette frégate faisait partie était commandée par M. le Chevalier de Ternay; Du 22 février 1780 au 5 décembre 1780." This manuscript journal was also lent by Comte Allard du Chollet to the two exhibitions mentioned above; cf. catalogues, pp. 175–176, No. 58, and p. 66, No. 177. A note on the title page states that "M. Pierre Alexandre de Pastour de Costebelle était embarqué sur cette Frégate." The frigate *Amazone*, commanded by La Pérouse, came to Rhode Island with Ternay's fleet; in the autumn of 1780 it took the Vicomte de Rochambeau (the General's son) on a special mission to France.

Cromot Dubourg (du Bourg), Marie-François-Joseph-Maxime, baron (1756–1836)

Aide-de-camp to Rochambeau (1781); subsequently aide-maréchal-général-des-logis auxiliaire

1 "Diary of a French Officer, 1781 (Presumed to be that of Baron Cromot du Bourg, aid to Rochambeau)," in the *Magazine of American History* (New York), in five installments: Vol. IV, Nos. 3–6 (March–June, 1880), 205–214, 293–308, 376–385, 441–452; Vol. VII, No. 4 (Oct. 1881), 283–295. The authorship of the journal is convincingly established by Balch (1, 12–15). The above translation was made from an unsigned eighteenth-century manuscript entitled "Journal depuis mon départ de France 26 Mars 1781 jusqu'au 18 Novembre de la même Année que l'Armée aux ordres de M. le Cte. de Rochambeau est entrée dans ses Quartiers d'Hiver." This manuscript was sold at the Maisonneuve sale in Paris, 15 January 1868 (described in catalogue of sale compiled by Ch. Leclerc, *Bibliotheca Americana* [Paris, 1867], No. 781); was acquired by C. Fiske Harris of Providence, Rhode Island (No. 1886 in catalogue of sale of his library by G. A. Leavitt, 1883); and subsequently came into the possession of the Historical Society of Pennsylvania in Philadelphia, where it is now located (AM 6360). The manuscript, in a near-contemporary red morocco binding (12¼ x 7⅞ inches), formerly included a series of nine maps (reproduced in the *Magazine of American History*, above) that have since been removed and placed in a separate portfolio (AM 63601), as well as a pen and watercolor view of Newport, Rhode Island, also removed and now classified with prints and drawings (Bc 68 R346). The Newport view (*ca.* March or April 1781) is reproduced in the present work, Vol. II, No. 11.

Two nineteenth-century transcripts of the manuscript exist: (1) a copy made for Thomas Balch in the 1860's, now in the Historical Society of Pennsylvania, Thomas Balch Collection, bound Vol. 3, with spine title "Rochambeau en Amérique," containing rather gaudy copies of the maps, Balch's own marginal annotations of the journal, and some of his notes and correspondence relating to it; (2) a copy in Brown University, John Hay Library, Sidney S. Rider Collection. The content of both transcripts is the same as in the HSP eighteenth-century manuscript. The Rider transcript follows exactly the pagination of the original; it does not include copies of the maps.

This portion of Cromot Dubourg's journal covers his departure from France (26 March 1781), arrival in America at Boston (6 May 1781), march from Rhode Island to the Hudson and to Virginia, the Siege of Yorktown, and establishment of winter quarters in Virginia (18 November 1781). Dubourg intercalated in his manuscript his transcripts of the "Engineers' Journal of the Siege of Yorktown" (*Magazine of American History*, IV, 449–452); of the "Journal of the Siege by M. de Ménonville [chargé du détail de la tranchée]" (*Magazine of American History*, VII, 283–288); of the "Précis de la Campagne de l'Armée Navale aux ordres du Cte. de Grasse, imprimé par ses ordres à bord de la Ville de Paris" (*Magazine of American History*, VII, 288–293); and of other staff documents.

2 "Journal des marches de la flotte française, commandée par M. de Vaudreuil, en Décembre, 1782, Janvier et Février 1783 [avec un] Résumé des événements qui se sont passés à Boston de 1764 à 1776." Manuscript in the Service Historique de l'Armée (Vincennes), Section Ancienne, Mémoires Historiques 248², pièce 30. This fragmentary unsigned manuscript includes the personal narrative of the author, covering his departure from Providence (1 December 1782), embarkation at Boston on the frigate *Néréide* (21 December), sailing (24 December), voyage to the Caribbean, and arrival at Puerto Cabello (28 January 1783); it ends abruptly with an entry dated 16 February 1783. The journal proper is interlarded with a retrospective historical account of events in Boston (pp. 6–17) and with an elaborate series of embarkation lists (pp. 19–31) recording the assignment of army officers and units to the different ships comprising Vaudreuil's fleet. The manuscript is here attributed by the Editors to Cromot Dubourg on the basis of internal evidence: the writer states (p. 17) that he went aboard the frigate *Néréide*, and the embarkation lists (p. 21) record under General Staff only the name of "Du Bourg, Aide Maréchal-Général-des-Logis" on this ship. The duties performed by the writer for Vioménil, commanding general, after the arrival in Venezuela (e.g., pp. 45 and 46) were such as would have been assigned to an assistant quartermaster-general. See also Clermont-Crève-cœur's journal, n. 197. Corroborative evidence for the attribution is supplied by the handwriting of this fragment, which is the same as that of the manuscript journal for 1781 in the Historical Society of Pennsylvania (described above).

3 "Recueil de plans de sièges et de positions fortifiées, durant la Guerre de l'Indépendance, aux Etats-Unis, 1780–1782." Manuscript atlas in the Service Historique de la Marine (Paris), Fonds du Service Hydrographique, MS 2847. Described in Charles de La Roncière, *Bibliothèques de la Marine* (Paris, 1907), p. 218; André Girodie, comp., *Les États-Unis et la France au XVIIIe siècle*, exhibition catalogue (Paris, 1929), p. 35, No. 66. This large volume in green morocco binding (approx. 26 x 40 inches), the so-called Atlas Rochambeau, comprises 9 maps, several of them folded, depicting: (1) Rhode Island; (2) Marches of the army from Rhode Island to Virginia (1781); (3) Camp at Philipsburg (July–August 1781); (4) Reconnaissance of New York (July 1781) in three parts; (5)

West Point on the Hudson; (6) Siege of Yorktown; (7) West Point, Virginia (winter quarters of artillery, 1781–1782); (8) Camp at Peeks-kill (September 1782); (9) Camp at Crompond (September–October 1782). A brief text recapitulating pertinent events accompanies each plate. Maps 3, 6, and 9 are signed "DuBourg f[eci]t" or "Dubourg f[eci]t"; the others are obviously executed by the same hand. Only Maps 1–6 have their counterpart in the HSP manuscript described above. The treatment of the two series is quite different. The HSP maps, on thin tracing paper, appear to have been copied by Dubourg from maps available to him at staff headquarters and are not the results of his personal surveys. The maps in the "Atlas Rochambeau" were worked up later, no doubt after Dubourg's return to France, as a memorial souvenir of the American campaigns. They are elaborately drawn in pen and wash on fine paper in a consciously "artistic" manner but lack the stark precision of the earlier, more utilitarian maps. Maps 3 and 9 (Philipsburg and Crompond) are embellished with charmingly romantic cartouches.

Crublier d'Opterre, Henri
(1739–1799)

Captain, Royal Corps of Engineers

1 "Journal du Siège d'York en Virginie," with two maps and related documents. This manuscript, copied in two different clerical hands, signed at the end by "D'Opterre" and dated 30 December 1781, is in the Library of Paul Mellon, Upperville, Virginia.

Crublier d'Opterre was with Rochambeau's army throughout its American campaigns. His Yorktown journal is not, strictly speaking, a personal narrative but an expanded and annotated version of the formal Engineers' record of the siege. Cf. Querenet de La Combe, Cromot Dubourg (1). Following the account of the siege the manuscript includes copies of several related documents, such as: Washington's letter to de Grasse, 25 September 1781; Washington's congratulatory "After Orders," 20 October 1781; letter from Ségur, minister of war, to Querenet de La Combe, 22 November 1781, commending the Engineers for their conduct of the siege; list of "grâces" accorded the Engineers; Cornwallis's letter to Clinton, 30 October 1781, giving his apologetic version of the siege, with Crublier d'Opterre's "observations" thereon. In addition to the two maps designed to accompany the "Journal du Siège d'York," the Crublier d'Opterre manuscripts in the Mellon Library include other manuscript maps representing other phases of Rochambeau's American campaigns: Newport, the New York reconnaissances of July 1781, Portsmouth (in Virginia), Portsmouth (in New Hampshire), West Point (in New York). Examples of these maps are reproduced in the present work, Vol. II, Nos. 5, 102, 103, 160, and 161. Also in the Mellon Collection are retrospective maps showing earlier events in the war (Trenton, Brandywine, Siege of Savannah) and engraved maps with Crublier d'Opterre's annotations. Letters of Crublier d'Opterre written from Newport, Rhode Island (13 August, 8 September 1780) are preserved with other Engineers' letters in the Archives du Génie, 15-1-7, No. 34.

Custine-Sarreck, Adam-Philippe, comte de (1740–1793)

Colonel, Saintonge Regiment

1 A journal written by Custine during the American campaign is referred to by Blanchard ([1], 64), who states under the date of 18 February 1781: "M. de Custine, who had just made a journey into the interior of America, showed me his journal and the results of his observations. This journal seemed to me most judicious and well observed. . . ." Maurice La Chesnais, editor of Blanchard's journal (1881), notes that Custine's American journal was never published and had probably disappeared. The year after Custine's death on the guillotine (28 August 1793), a work prepared by Custine's aide, Baraguey d'Hilliers, was published under the title *Mémoires posthumes du Général français comte de Custine*, 2 vols. (Hamburg and Frankfurt, 1794; reprinted 1824); however, these volumes treat only of the 1793 campaign of the Armée du Nord and contain but a passing reference to Custine's services in America.

Delavergue du Tressan, Claude-Marie-Madeleine, chevalier (b. 1755)

Sublieutenant, Saintonge Regiment

1 Group of six letters in Bibliothèque Nationale, Department of Manuscripts, Collection B. Fillon, Nouvelles acquisitions françaises, No. 21510. One of the letters is dated Newport, Rhode Island, 24 January 1781. Cf. Balch, II, 241; *Les Combattants*, p. 254; Bouvet, *Service de santé*, pp. 63–64. The writer is sometimes referred to as the Vicomte de Tressan.

Desandroüins, Jean-Nicolas (1729–1792)

Colonel, Royal Corps of Engineers

1 Abbé Charles-Nicolas Gabriel, *Le Maréchal de Camp Desandroüins, 1729–1792. Guerre du Canada, 1756–1760. Guerre de l'Indépendance américaine, 1780–1782* (Verdun, Imprimerie Renvé-Lallemant, 1887). This biography includes extensive quotations from Desandroüins's memoirs and other papers (belonging at the time of publication to a great-nephew of Desandroüins, Léon Tardif de Moidrey, of Hannoncelles in Normandy). Only pp. 341–395 concern the American Revolution.

Desandroüins, who had earlier served in America during the Seven Years' War, was the ranking engineer in Rochambeau's army. Although he was present at Yorktown, an illness prevented his active participation in the siege; his duties devolved upon his second-in-command, Lieutenant Colonel Guillaume Querenet de La Combe (1731–1788), *q.v.* As mentioned by his biographer, Desandroüins's own account of the American Revolution is less complete than might be expected, since most of his journals for this period were lost in the shipwreck of the *Bourgogne* off Venezuela in February 1783. Several letters of Desandroüins are preserved in the Archives du Génie, 15-1-7, No. 34: Newport, 10 November 1780; Providence, 17 June 1781; Williamsburg, 24 January 1782; Crompond, 20 October 1782; Providence, 28 November 1782; Puerto Cabello, 14 February 1783. The last of these letters (reproduced in the present volume) was written shortly after Desandroüins's escape from the shipwreck of the *Bourgogne*. Examples of maps signed by Desandroüins are also extant in the Archives du Génie, including one of Newport, another of the environs of Williamsburg, and maps of the New York reconnaissance of July 1781.

Destouches, Charles-René-Dominque Gochet, chevalier (1727–1794)

Navy. Capitaine de vaisseau, commanding the Neptune; *interim commander of the French squadron at Newport from Ternay's death in December 1780 until the arrival of Barras in May 1781*

Deux-Ponts, Guillaume, comte de (des) (1754–1807)

Second colonel, Royal Deux-Ponts Regiment

1 *The Destouches Papers relative to the American Revolution, comprising Letters and Documents signed by Destouches, Lafayette, Rochambeau, De Grasse, and seventeen letters signed by La Pérouse and others* (American Art Association, Inc., New York, auction catalogue for sale of 1 December 1926). The catalogue contains descriptions of 116 items, with translated excerpts. No. 108 is Admiral de Ternay's "Journal de Ma Campagne sur le vaisseau le Duc de Bourgogne, 1780." See below, *s.v.* Ternay. These papers were purchased en bloc by the Henry E. Huntington Library, San Marino, California, where they are now located.

The so-called Destouches expedition to the Chesapeake, in March 1781, is described in an official report printed at the time and entitled *Relation de la sortie de l'Escadre Française, aux ordres du Chevalier Destouches.* For a description of this publication, see below, *s.v.* Granchain, the compiler.

1 *My Campaigns in America: A Journal kept by Count William de Deux-Ponts, 1780–81,* tr. from the French manuscript, with an introduction and notes, by Samuel Abbott Green (Boston, Wiggin and Lunt, 1868). Includes the original French text as well as an annotated English translation. Green purchased the manuscript in Paris in 1867; it is now in the Massachusetts Historical Society, Boston.

Comte Guillaume was the younger brother of Christian de Deux-Ponts (1752–1817), colonel of the Royal Deux-Ponts (Zweibrücken), a proprietary foreign regiment in the French service composed largely of German-speaking troops recruited in the Rhine valley, Bavaria, Switzerland, or Alsace. Comte Guillaume's journal covers the period from March 1780 to November 1781. He returned to France soon after the Siege of Yorktown—in which he had especially distinguished himself—as one of the special messengers chosen to carry news of the surrender to the King. He left Virginia on the frigate *Andromaque* on 1 November, landing in France on the 20th and reaching Versailles on 24 November 1781. Guillaume apparently did not return to America, though his brother Christian remained with the regiment throughout the rest of the American campaigns, including the Caribbean cruise in 1783. It would appear from a reference in Von Closen's journal (p. 307) that Christian also kept a journal, though its present whereabouts (if it has survived) is not known to the Editors. Von Closen, when revising his own journal, mentions, apropos the sojourn at Puerto Cabello, that he has "in my collection" the journal of the Comte de Deux-Ponts. Miss Acomb in her edition of Von Closen assumes that the reference is to Comte Guillaume's journal (as recorded above), but we think it more likely that Von Closen then had in his possession the journal of Christian (or a transcript of it). The family connections of the two brothers Deux-Ponts, both of whom were sons by a morganatic marriage of Duke Christian IV (1722–1775) and who went by various titles (including that of Comte de Forbach), are discussed at length by Karl Theodor von Heigel in his article "Die Beteilung des Hauses Zweibrücken am nordamerikanischen Befreiungskrieg," *Sitzungsberichte der Königlich Bayerischen Akademie des Wissenschaften*, Philosophisch-philologische und historische Klasse, Jahrgang 1912, 6 Abhandlung (Munich, 1912).

Dubouchet

See French Officers in American Service.

Dumas, Mathieu, comte (1753–1837)

Aide-de-camp to Rochambeau; assistant quartermaster-general

1 *Souvenirs du Lieutenant Général Comte Mathieu Dumas, de 1770 à 1836, publiés par son fils*, 3 vols. (Paris, Gosselin, 1839). "Livre Second" (I, 24–161) concerns the American Revolution.
2 Dumas, *Memoirs of His Own Time; including the Revolution, the Empire, and the Restoration*, 2 vols. (Philadelphia, Lea & Blanchard, 1839). The chapter devoted to the American Revolution is in I, 19–80.

Dumas's service in America covered the entire campaign of Rochambeau's army, 1780–1783. For his activities as a cartographer, see Vol. II of the present work, Introduction to "Maps and Views," and map, No. 4. When Dumas wrote his memoirs in the late 1820's and early 1830's, he already had available to refresh his memory the published *Mémoires* of Rochambeau, whom he quotes freely, as well as the *Mémoires* of the Comte de Ségur and the Prince de Broglie's *Relation* (first published in the *Revue Française*, 1828). When writing of his experiences in America Dumas also consulted his own notes made at the time. His story of how these supposedly lost early papers came back to him deserves repetition here. In 1783, Dumas relates (*Souvenirs*, I, 158–159), he had expected to return from the West Indies to the United States in order to undertake a special mission for the French minister, the Chevalier de La Luzerne, but the signature of the treaty of peace changed the plan and he returned directly to France. "I had left at Dr. Bowen's house in Providence and especially entrusted to his amiable daughters a small trunk (*une cassette*) containing various papers and notes which I had collected during two campaigns. This trunk, which I believed lost, was carefully preserved by Mrs. Ward, the youngest of the daughters, who survived the rest of her family and still remembered me. After a lapse of forty years Mrs. Ward met General La Fayette in New York during his triumphal tour [1824–1825]. She was good enough to inquire after me and asked the General to bring my trunk back to me with a touching testimonial of her former friendship. The notes thus recovered have been used in preparing the summary account which I have included above in these memoirs. . . ."

Du Perron

See Revel du Perron.

Du Petit-Thouars, Aristide Aubert (1760–1798)

Navy. Garde-marine; enseigne de vaisseau

1 *Mémoires et Voyages du chevalier Aristide Aubert Du Petit-Thouars . . . ou Recueil des écrits qu'il a laissés, composant l'histoire de sa vie, jusqu'au moment où il s'est enseveli sous les débris du vaisseau le Tonnant*, published by his sister Félicité Du Petit-Thouars (Paris, 1822).
2 Amiral Bergasse du Petit Thouars, ed., *Aristide Aubert Du Petit Thouars, Héros d'Aboukir, 1760–1798, Lettres et documents inédits*, with an intro-

duction by Albert Mousset (Paris, Plon, 1937). Chaps. 1–4 include Du Petit-Thouars's account of his experiences during the American Revolution, in the form of letters to friends and relatives. This volume also incorporates material from (1).

3 See Balch, I, 10–11, for description of a manuscript of Du Petit-Thouars's "memoirs," which is now in the Historical Society of Pennsylvania (Thomas Balch Collection, bound volume). Balch purchased the manuscript from the Paris dealer Charavay on 7 December 1869. The manuscript is something of a hodgepodge, compiled by Aristide, his sister Félicité, his brother Georges-Laurent, and a brother officer, the Chevalier de Lostange. It contains material on La Clocheterie, captain of the *Hercule*, who lost his life in the Battle of the Saints.

Aristide Du Petit-Thouars was a midshipman in the French navy who participated in the Siege of Savannah (1779). Following this he came in the *Fendant* (commanded by the Marquis de Vaudreuil) to Virginia, where his ship remained off Yorktown from 20 November 1779 to 25 January 1780. The *Fendant* had brought sick and wounded northward. Du Petit-Thouars's youthful and romantic account of his stay in Virginia at this time provides a "preview" of the accounts by French officers of Rochambeau's army who were in winter quarters on the Williamsburg peninsula two years later. Du Petit-Thouars himself was not in America at the time of the Siege of Yorktown. He was, however, on the *Couronne* in de Grasse's fleet at the Battle of the Saints (April 1782) and subsequently came to Boston with Vaudreuil. When the latter's fleet sailed from Boston in December 1782, transporting Rochambeau's army to the Caribbean, Du Petit-Thouars, by then an ensign, was second in command of the frigate *Amazone*. In this capacity he took the Comte de Ségur, Blanchard, Berthier, and others from Puerto Cabello to Saint-Domingue in April 1783. At The French Cape he was given command of the brig *Tarleton* (captured from the English), which was part of a convoy taking the Touraine and Enghien regiments back to France; the *Tarleton* reached L'Orient on 29 June 1783. Du Petit-Thouars later returned to America, where he was one of the Azilum, Pennsylvania, colonists (1793–1795). As commander of the *Tonnant* he lost his life in the Battle of Aboukir (1798) during Bonaparte's Egyptian Expedition. The name was generally written "du Petit-Thouars" until the French Revolution, when it became Dupetit-Thouars, a form still retained by the French Navy when referring to its hero. For these (and further) niceties of nomenclature we are indebted to Diana Forbes-Robertson, whose biography of Du Petit-Thouars is to be published in the near future by The Viking Press.

Engineer (anonymous)

1 Bernard Faÿ, ed., "Relation sur la Guerre d'Amérique d'après une conversation avec un officier du Génie qui y étoit employé," in *Franco-American Review*, II, No. 2 (Autumn 1937), 114–120. Printed from a manuscript in the Bibliothèque Municipale de Troyes.

This "relation" is not a journal or diary but an anonymous report of a conversation with an unidentified engineer who had served in America. It provides some mildly interesting secondhand gossip about various officers in Rochambeau's army.

Engineers

1 "Engineers' Journal of the Siege of Yorktown," in the *Magazine of American History*, IV, No. 6 (June 1880), 449–452. Translated from the transcript included in Cromot Dubourg's journal. This is the official record of engineering operations during the siege, compiled by the Royal Corps of Engineers. See also *s.v.* Crublier d'Opterre, Querenet de La Combe.

Estaing, Charles-Hector, comte d' (1729–1794)

Navy. Vice admiral, commanding French fleet, Battle of Rhode Island (1778), Siege of Savannah (1779)

1 *Washington, sa correspondance avec D'Estaing*, with an introduction by Charles de La Roncière (Paris, Fondation Nationale pour la Reproduction des Manuscrits Précieux et Pièces Rares d'Archives, 1937). The correspondence extends only from July to October 1778, i.e., for the period of d'Estaing's arrival off Sandy Hook and the subsequent Rhode Island episode. D'Estaing's letters are published in their original French text (with an English translation), Washington's letters in English. One of Washington's letters (Headquarters near White Plains, 22 July 1778) is reproduced in facsimile. This publication is based solely on documents in the Archives Nationales (Marine B⁴146); the editor made no attempt to correlate them with their counterpart in the Washington Papers or with other American sources.

2 "Journal du Siège de Savannah avec des Observations de M. le comte d'Estaing," in Doniol, IV, 303–307. Doniol's heading for this document (printed from a manuscript in the Archives Nationales, Marine B⁴142, foll. 155ff.) is somewhat misleading. Actually it was d'Estaing's engineer, O'Connor, who compiled a journal of the siege, which he signed "A bord de *l'Annibal*," 22 October 1779. When transmitting O'Connor's journal to France d'Estaing added a commendatory preface and a series of marginal comments of his own, which he in turned signed "A bord du *Languedoc* [his flagship]," 22 October 1779. Doniol prints only d'Estaing's "observations," but not the journal proper. D'Estaing says that his additions concern matters that O'Connor was unacquainted with, as well as a few facts that the latter had not been in a position to observe. See below *s.v.* O'Connor.

D'Estaing's campaigns marked the first direct French military assistance to the Americans following the Franco-American alliance of February 1778. D'Estaing's fleet left Toulon in April 1778 and eventually arrived off Sandy Hook on 10 July. Deciding not to attempt an attack upon New York, d'Estaing thereupon proceeded to Rhode Island, arriving there on 29 July. The joint attempt of American land forces under General Sullivan and French naval forces to dislodge the British from Newport (the "Battle of Rhode Island") was unsuccessful. D'Estaing departed from Rhode Island waters on 21 August and retired to Boston for refitting his ships, which had been damaged in a sudden storm. The French fleet remained in New England until late November 1778, when it sailed for the West Indies. This inconclusive attempt at joint action between the Americans and their recently declared allies created considerable friction and left doubts in some American minds about the efficacy of French aid and the possibility of effective Franco-American cooperation. It should be noted, however, that several of the French officers who came to Rhode Island with d'Estaing in 1778 were to return there two years later with Rochambeau's army.

The following year, 1779, d'Estaing's fleet, with landing forces aboard, left Guadeloupe to besiege Savannah, Georgia, in cooperation with General Lincoln's Americans. Again the attempted joint action ended in failure. D'Estaing's fleet left Georgia for the West Indies late in November 1779. The Admiral's successive failures stirred considerable controversy among the French, as reflected in the anonymous publications listed hereafter.

A valuable pictorial record of d'Estaing's American campaigns has survived in a series of drawings by Pierre Ozanne, a marine artist who accompanied the fleet. See Editors' descriptive note in Vol. II, "Maps and Views," No. 164.

Anonymous officers in
d'Estaing's fleet

1 *Extrait du Journal d'un Officier de la Marine de l'Escadre de M. le comte d'Estaing* (n.p. [Paris?], 1782). There were at least three (possibly four) editions of this anonymous work: one of 126 pp., one of 158 pp., and another of 93 pp. All three have the same title and date, and all lack place of publication. The title-pages, each with a distinctive typographical ornament, are reproduced in the *Catalogue of the Wymberley Jones De Renne Georgia Library* (Wormsloe, 1931), pp. 224–225. The three editions are also in the John Carter Brown Library. A partial translation (covering only the latter pages, from September 1779 and including the Siege of Savannah) is in Charles C. Jones, Jr., ed., *The Siege of Savannah, in 1779, as described in two contemporaneous journals of French officers in the fleet of Count d'Estaing* (Albany, Munsell, 1874), pp. 55–70.

A near-contemporary manuscript copy of the above pamphlet, entitled "Relation de la campagne navale de M. le comte d'Estaing en Amérique 1778 [–1779]," is in the Princeton University Library. An "avertissement" preceding the text states: "The humiliating truths contained in this account of the comte d'Estaing's 1778 campaign in America caused it to disappear, no doubt through the efforts of interested parties, since copies could no longer be found after the first year of its printing. The author is not named, but the whole naval corps agrees in attributing it to M. de Rémusa, a naval officer employed in d'Estaing's squadron, and consequently an eyewitness of all he relates." M. de Rémusa[t?] has not been further identified. This anonymous journal, covering events of 1778 (arrival of the fleet off Sandy Hook, Battle of Rhode Island, Boston) and of 1779 (concluding with the Siege of Savannah), is, indeed, highly critical of d'Estaing's conduct of operations and generally controversial in tone. It in turn prompted an anonymous refutation—the next item recorded here.

2 *Campagne de M. le Comte d'Estaing en Amérique, ou Mémoire pour servir de réfutation au Libelle contre ce Vice-Amiral* (Bruxelles, 1782). A copy of this rare pamphlet is in the John Carter Brown Library and is described by Lawrence C. Wroth in that library's *Annual Report for 1933–1934*, pp. 2–6.

3 "The Siege of Savannah by Count d'Estaing, 1779," in Charles C. Jones, Jr., ed., *The Siege of Savannah, in 1779, as described in two contemporaneous journals of French officers in the fleet of Count d'Estaing* (Albany, Munsell, 1874), pp. 7–52. Jones's translation was made from a French manuscript, in a scribe's hand, entitled "Siège de Savannah par Mr. le comte d'Estaing, 1779." The manuscript, acquired by J. C. Brevoort of Brooklyn, New York, at the Luzarche sale in Paris (1869), later came into Jones's collection and eventually into the Wymberley Jones De Renne Georgia Library (now in the University of Georgia Library). It is described in the *Catalogue* of the De Renne Library, pp. 215–217, with facsimile reproduction of one page. This unidentified officer's detailed and circumstantial account covers the period from 19 July to 21 November 1779, beginning with d'Estaing's appearance in the roadstead of Basse Terre, Guadeloupe, and ending with his return there after the unsuccessful Siege of Savannah.

4 *Relation de l'Attaque de Savanach, Par l'Escadre de M. d'Estaing* (n.p., n.d.). A copy of this anonymous 2-page printed item is in the John Carter Brown Library; cf. Library's *Annual Report for 1933–1934*, p. 6.

5 "Journal de ma Campagne, faite sous les ordres de Mr. le Cte. d'Estaing Vice-amiral de France, commandant d'Escadre du Roy partie de Toulon le 13 avril 1778." A manuscript volume of 233 pages, covering the period from 6 April 1778 to the return of the *Languedoc* to Brest on 4 December 1779. Extracts from this manuscript (for 1 September–27 October 1779, Siege of Savannah) are published in facsimile, with an English translation, in B. F. Stevens, *Facsimiles of Manuscripts in European Archives relating to America, 1773–1783* (London, 1889–1898), Vol. XXIII, No. 2011. The manuscript was then in the possession of B. F. Stevens; it is now in the John Carter Brown Library (Codex d'Estaing 6). This journal by an unidentified naval officer is essentially a log-book of the *Languedoc*, flagship of d'Estaing's fleet. The officer remained on board his ship and did not participate in the landing operations at Savannah.

This same volume of Stevens's *Facsimiles* contains other documents (Nos. 2009, 2012–2023) concerning the participation of d'Estaing's forces in the Siege of Savannah, many of them from Stevens's personal collection, as well as the journal of the siege (No. 2010) signed by "Pechot." This is presumably a pseudonym for Tarragon; see below *s.v.* the latter's name.

6 "Journal commencé le 31 mars 1779 lors de l'arrivée du comte d'Estaing au cap françois isle St. Domingue." This anonymous manuscript journal of 150 pp., covering the period from March 1779 through May 1780, is in the John Carter Brown Library (acquired in 1960). The author begins his narrative with a list of d'Estaing's fleet upon its arrival at Le Cap Français and of the garrison troops aboard. He describes the Siege of Savannah, gives a list of the officers killed and wounded there, then describes Charleston, South Carolina, praising the inhabitants, especially the ladies, but damning the French "aventeuriers" for their bad conduct. The journal concludes with a description of the surrender of Charleston on 8 May 1780 and the Articles of Capitulation. For another journal mentioning the Siege of Charleston, see below, *s.v.* Magallon de La Morlière.

7 Journal by an unidentified naval officer on board the *Magnifique*, which was sent to the West Indies with the Comte de Grasse's division to reinforce the Comte d'Estaing's squadron. Covers the period from 14 January 1779 to 2 January 1781. This manuscript of 247 pp., bound in contemporary vellum, is in the John Carter Brown Library (acquired in 1960). The author records the departure from Brest on 14 January 1779 and the arrival at Fort Royal, Martinque, where the *Magnifique* joined d'Estaing's squadron on 20 February. The narrative includes descriptions of cruises in the West Indies, the arrival of Vaudreuil's and La Motte Picquet's squadron, and the capture of St. Vincent and Grenada on 4 July. The *Magnifique* sailed from Le Cap Français for Charleston, South Carolina, was at the Siege of Savannah, and was detached to La Motte Picquet on the return. The ship was damaged in action, was beached at Fort Royal, and, after repairs were completed by 20 March 1780, sailed out to meet Guichen. Engagements off Santo Domingo, St. Lucia, and Martinique are described. The *Magnifique* returned on 26 July to Le Cap Français, where she greeted the *Andromaque* arriving from France on the 30th. On 16 August 1780 the author's ship sailed for France with Monteil's division; during the voyage the fleet hailed (21 August) 12 American vessels ("Batiments Insurgents") coming from Le Cap Français with Guichen.

8 Although it is not a French officer's journal, we record here in an appropriate context a manuscript diary of Jonathan Lawrence, an American who helped pilot one of d'Estaing's ships from Sandy Hook to Rhode Island. Lawrence's "Memorandum of Sundry Transactions," covering the period from 15 July to 26 August 1778, is in the John Carter Brown Library (acquired in 1958). When news of the arrival of the French fleet off Sandy Hook reached Washington's headquarters, Lawrence was among those who, as he wrote, "was importuned to go on board to assist them in Endeavouring to gett into some port or in the Sound between

Long Island and the Main." He went aboard d'Estaing's flagship *Langue-doc* on 20 July; on the following day he was assigned to the *Hector* of 74 guns. His memorandum records the day-by-day progress of the ship to Rhode Island, the entrance into Newport Harbor, the attempted landing of troops, the withdrawal from Narragansett Bay and pursuit of the English, the violent storm that prevented the engagement of the two fleets, etc. Lawrence left the *Hector* on 21 August. The final pages of his memorandum contain an account of his expenses. Lawrence's diary thus provides a unique eyewitness account of the Battle of Rhode Island as observed by an American aboard a French vessel.

9 For an informed description of other manuscript material, chiefly in French archives, see Alexander A. Lawrence, *Storm over Savannah: The Story of Count d'Estaing and the Siege of the Town in 1779* (Athens, University of Georgia Press, 1951), "Bibliography, Manuscript Sources, French," pp. 183–187. Lawrence also mentions (p. 184) a manuscript in the Historical Society of Pennsylvania entitled "Journal de M. Le Comte D'Estaing, Avril 1778–Octobre 1779": "In so far as the Siege of Savannah is concerned it is more or less a digest of O'Connor's Journal. The manuscript refers to d'Estaing in the third person."

d'Ethy

See Thy.

Fersen, Axel, comte de
(1755–1810)

*Aide-de-camp to
Rochambeau; second colonel
(1782), Deux-Ponts
Regiment*

1 "Extraits des lettres autographes du Comte de Fersen à son père, pendant la guerre de France contre l'Angleterre dans l'Amérique du Nord (1780–1783)," in R. M. de Klinckowström, ed., *Le Comte de Fersen et la Cour de France, Extraits des papiers du Grand-Maréchal de Suède, Comte Jean Axel de Fersen*, 2 vols. (Paris, Firmin-Didot, 1877–1878), I, 36–73.

2 English translations of Fersen's letters, from the above Klinckowström edition, appear in the *Magazine of American History*, III (1879), 300–309, 369–376, 437–448, and again (another translation) in xv (1891), 55–70, 156–173. Also in *Diary and Correspondence of Count Axel Fersen*, tr. Katharine Prescott Wormeley (Boston, 1902), pp. 21–64.

3 *Lettres d'Axel de Fersen à son père pendant la Guerre de l'Indépendance d'Amérique*, ed. Comte F. U. Wrangel (Paris, Firmin-Didot, 1929). A more extensive selection of letters from family archives in Sweden as in (1). Whereas Klinckowström includes 25 of Fersen's American letters, this Wrangel edition has twice that number and has thus superseded the earlier publications.

Axel Fersen, a young Swede in the French service, was later famous for his role in the attempted escape of Queen Marie-Antoinette. His dutiful but lively and very personal letters to his father cover the entire campaign of Rochambeau's army, including the return via the Caribbean in 1783.

Fleury

See French Officers in American Service.

Gallatin, Gabriel-Gaspard, baron de (1758–1838)
Second lieutenant,
Deux-Ponts Regiment

1 Warrington Dawson, "Un Garde suisse de Louis XVI au service de l'Amérique," in *Le Correspondant*, Vol. 324 (n.s., 288), No. 1653 (10 Aug. 1931), pp. 321–338; No. 1655 (10 Sept. 1931), pp. 672–692. Excerpts from Gallatin's journal covering his stay at Newport and the southward march to Virginia, 1780–1781.

2 Warrington Dawson, tr. and ed., "With Rochambeau at Newport, The Narrative of Baron Gaspard de Gallatin," in *Franco-American Review*, I, No. 4 (Spring 1937), 330–340. Translation from the same journal as (1), but covering only the sojourn at Newport.

3 *Journal of the Siege of York-Town in 1781 operated by the General Staff of the French Army, as recorded in the hand of Gaspard de Gallatin*, tr. French Department of the College of William and Mary (Washington, U.S. Government Printing Office, 1931; 71st Congress, 3rd Session, Senate Document No. 322). This is not a personal narrative but Gallatin's transcription of the official General Staff account of the siege; cf. *s.v.* Menonville.

The above extracts from Gallatin's journal are all from the manuscript (in four parts) that is now in the Library of Congress. It was presented in 1932, through the good offices of Warrington Dawson, by Edmond Scherdlin, a great-grandson of the author.

Although Gallatin was with Rochambeau's army throughout the American campaigns, the surviving journal ends with the Siege of Yorktown. This Swiss officer in the French service came from the same venerable Genevan family as did his distant cousin Albert Gallatin (1761–1849), the distinguished American financier and diplomat. The similarity of names has given rise to some confusion. Albert Gallatin arrived in Boston in July 1780—as a youthful runaway from Geneva, but not as a soldier—and spent the following winter in a frontier fort near Machias, Maine. "I was for a few days left accidentally in command of some militia, volunteers, and Indians, and of a small temporary work defended by one cannon and soon abandoned. . . . As I never met the enemy, I have not the slightest claim to military service." In this statement written at the very end of his life Albert Gallatin himself refuted the legend that he had been a soldier in the Revolution.

Goussencourt [?], chevalier de

Officer with de Grasse's fleet whose identity has not been confirmed

1 "A Journal of the Cruise of the Fleet of His Most Christian Majesty, under the command of the Count de Grasse-Tilly, in 1781 and 1782. By the Chevalier de Goussencourt," tr. John Gilmary Shea, in *The Operations of the French Fleet under Count de Grasse in 1781–2, as described in Two Contemporaneous Journals* (New York, The Bradford Club, Publication No. 3, 1864), pp. 23–133. Shea's translation was made from a manuscript then in the possession of Mr. J. C. Brevoort of Brooklyn.

The journal covers the departure of de Grasse's fleet from Brest (March 1781), events in the West Indies, the Chesapeake campaign and Siege of Yorktown, and the Battle of the Saints (April 1782). The writer, who was not on one of the captured ships, subsequently returned to France, reaching Brest on 23 August 1782. The manuscript is signed "Chevalier de Goussencourt." J. G. Shea suggests in his Preface that this may be a pseudonym, since researches in records of the French navy failed to establish his identity; he could, however, have been an army officer assigned to the garrison of one of the ships. "The only indication as to his vessel is in the fact that he returned to France in the squadron composed of the *Languedoc*, 80, Baron Daross; the *Diadème*, 74, de Montéclerc; and the *Magnanime*, 74, le Begue. He bestows praise on Montéclerc for his services after the fight, and defends the conduct of Daross during it." (Preface, p. ix.) In his account of the Battle of the Saints "Goussencourt" is hostile to de Grasse. He admired the Marquis de Vaudreuil and bestows high praise on his "patriotism and ability." The journal is on the whole an interesting and fairly personal narrative. There is a good account of the arrival of the fleet in the Chesapeake and the battle of September 1781. The writer remained on board ship during the Siege of Yorktown.

Granchain, Guillaume-
Jacques-Constant de Liberge
de (1744–1805)

Navy. Capitaine de vaisseau;
major-général de l'escadre
*in Ternay's fleet that took
Rochambeau's army to
America*

1 Chevalier de Fréminville, ed., "Mémoires pour servir à l'histoire de la marine française depuis 1775 jusqu'en 1785, avec des détails inédits sur la Guerre de l'Indépendance. Correspondance de M. le comte de Granchain, capitaine de vaisseau, membre de l'Académie de marine, avec M. du Bourblanc d'Apreville," series of ten articles published in the *Revue Bretonne*, beginning in its first issue, that of 15 January 1843. The title of this periodical was expanded in 1846 to *Revue Bretonne et Maritime*. Complete files seem to be rare; there is an incomplete set of the early volumes in the Bibliothèque Municipale de Brest. (Information supplied by the Service Historique de la Marine, Paris.)

2 Abbé Adolphe de Bouclon, *Liberge de Granchain, capitaine des vaisseaux du Roi . . . Etude historique sur la marine de Louis XVI* (Paris, Arthur Bertrand, [1866]). Based on family archives, with extensive quotation from letters written by Granchain during his service in America. According to Bouclon, Granchain, or Liberge de Granchain, was also known as the "chevalier de Sémerville," and erroneously (never having had the title) as the "comte de Granchain de Sémerville." He was born at Grandchain, near Bernay (Department of Eure) in Normandy.

3 *Relation de la sortie de l'Escadre Française, aux ordres du Ch[evali]er. Destouches, & de l'affaire qui a eue lieu le 16 Mars 1781, entre cette Escadre & celle des Anglais, commandée par l'Amiral Arbuthnot* [Newport, Rhode Island, Imprimerie de l'Escadre, 1781]. This 4-page leaflet is an official account of the Destouches expedition, compiled by Granchain and printed on the fleet printing press at Newport soon after the event. Granchain's authorship is established by one of his own letters (to Bourblanc d'Apreville, Newport, 1 April 1781, in Bouclon, p. 308) in which he encloses "la relation que j'ai fait publier de ce combat et des circonstances qui l'ont amené . . ." and is confirmed by Verger who transcribed the account into his journal (p. 126). The *Relation* (which might be compared to a modern press release) was printed soon after the return of Destouches's squadron to Newport (26 March), as indi-

cated by Granchain's letter and also by a letter from Destouches to the minister of marine (Newport, 31 March 1781, in the Archives Nationales, Marine B⁴191, fol. 17) stating that he has "l'honneur de vous adresser ci-joint, Monseigneur, une relation du combat dont j'ai permis ici l'impression." Fersen in letters to his father from Newport, 3 April, 11 April (in Fersen [3], pp. 105, 107), sent copies of the printed account, as did Montesquieu in a letter of 3 April to Latapie (in Montesquieu [1], VI, 519). Blanchard ([1], p. 71) also mentions it. Berthier preserved among his papers the copy that is now in the Princeton University Library; see our illustration in this volume.

As "major" of Ternay's squadron and chief administrative officer for the navy, Granchain was also closely concerned with army affairs during the stay at Newport. He was one of the principal planners of the Destouches expedition as well as author of the *Relation* mentioned above. From Rhode Island Granchain went to Yorktown with Barras's squadron; as the latter's deputy he helped draw up the Articles of Capitulation as they affected the navy. He returned to France with Barras in the frigate *Concorde*, via Martinique, in April 1782. Granchain came back to America in 1784, commanding the *Nymphe*, on an expedition for making hydrographic surveys of the Newfoundland coast; that same year he joined Lafayette in Boston. This distinguished naval officer, of considerable scientific attainments, obviously played an important role during his association with Rochambeau's army in 1780–1781.

Grasse, François-Joseph-Paul, comte de (and marquis de Tilly) (1722–1788)

Navy. Lieutenant general (vice admiral), commander of the fleet that came from the West Indies to Yorktown

1 Institut Français de Washington, [Elizabeth S. Kite], ed., *Correspondence of General Washington and Comte de Grasse, 1781, August 17–November 4, with supplementary documents from the Washington Papers in the Manuscripts Division of the Library of Congress* (Washington, U.S. Government Printing Office, 1931; 71st Congress, 2nd Session, Senate Document No. 211). Also issued as an extra volume in the "Historical Documents" series of the Institut Français de Washington. Contains French text, with English translation, of de Grasse's letters.

2 *Précis de la Campagne de l'Armée Navale aux ordres du Comte de Grasse* [1781]. This 4-page leaflet is an official account of de Grasse's 1781 campaign, prepared under his supervision (probably by his *major de la flotte*, Vaugirauld) and printed soon after the surrender of Yorktown on the press of de Grasse's flagship *Ville de Paris* while she was still in Virginian waters. It may be considered the navy's counterpart of the army's *Journal des opérations du Corps Français sous le commandement du Comte de Rochambeau* (see below *s.v.* Rochambeau). Copies of this leaflet are to be found in various libraries, including the John Carter Brown Library (two different printings) and the Library of Congress, Rochambeau Papers, III, 336. Several officers transcribed or paraphrased this *Précis* in their journals: there is, for example, a transcript among the Berthier manuscripts (No. 27) at Princeton; Cromot

Dubourg, who copied it into his journal, specifically states that it was "imprimé . . . à bord de la Ville de Paris" (see Cromot Dubourg [1], VII, 288–293). The printing press carried by the *Ville de Paris* was not the same as the one that came to Newport, Rhode Island, on the *Neptune* with Ternay's fleet (see above *s.v.* Granchain [3]). Another example of a leaflet printed by the *Ville de Paris* press is the *Ordre Concernant les Troupes de Débarquement. A bord de la Ville de Paris*, a copy of which, countersigned by Vaugirauld and dated 22 August 1781, is in the Musée de Blérancourt.

3 *Mémoire du Comte de Grasse, Sur le Combat Naval du 12 Avril 1782, avec les Plans des positions principales des Armées respectives* [Paris? 1783?]. 28 pp. with 8 folding maps. This memoir does *not* concern the Chesapeake-Yorktown campaign of 1781 but constitutes de Grasse's apologia for his defeat in the Battle of the Saints, off Guadeloupe, in April 1782. The memoir was privately printed for the Admiral at some time after his return (via London) to France in August 1782, possibly later that year, or more probably during the year 1783. On 29 April 1783 the King ordered a court-martial to collect testimony from officers who had taken part in the battle; the special court of inquiry (Conseil de Guerre Extraordinaire de la Marine) sat at Lorient from January to May 1784 and rendered its judgment on 21 May 1784 (see below). Meanwhile, before the results of the investigation were made public, de Grasse had distributed his privately printed *Mémoire*, thereby incurring the disfavor of the government and his ultimate disgrace. For example, he sent a copy to Washington, 15 March 1784, with the remarks: "I have the honor to send you the memorials which I have submitted to the consideration of the Court Martial for their better information of my conduct. The sincere desire I have to make you judge of this affair induces me to deviate from (*passer sur*) the order I have received not to communicate these memorials in print. I request you not to show them to any body, or if you think proper to make use of them I wish you would have them transcribed." (Original letter, with the contemporary translation cited here, in the Library of Congress, Washington Papers.) Washington acknowledged receipt in a graceful but non-committal letter from Philadelphia, 15 May 1784: "I thank you for the memorials you have had the goodness to send me; it is unhappy for me however, that I am not sufficiently Master of the French language to read them without assistance; this, when fully obtained will, I have no doubt, enable my judgment to coincide with my wishes. . . ." *Writings of GW*, XXVII, 401.

4 *Jugement rendu par le Conseil de Guerre Extraordinaire de Marine, tenu à L'Orient, par ordre du Roi, 1784* (Lorient, Imprimerie de L.C.R. Baudoin, Imprimeur du Roi et de la Marine, [1784]). This brochure of 37 pages (plus cover-title) prints the findings (dated 21 May 1784) of the naval court of inquiry presided over by Rear Admiral de Breugnon. This court-martial was not the trial of a single individual but rather an exhaus-

tive investigation into the responsibilities for the French defeat in the Battle of the Saints. By exonerating many officers from the charges that had been circulated by de Grasse in his *Mémoire* and elsewhere, it did, however, implicitly censure the Admiral. The original records of the investigation fill 44 manuscript volumes in the Archives Nationales, Marine B⁴221–264. A copy of the printed *Jugement* in the Princeton University Library has bound with it a number of contemporary manuscript transcripts of letters and depositions submitted to the court by different officers involved. An abridged text of the *Jugement* is reprinted in Edouard Chevalier, *Histoire de la Marine Française pendant la Guerre de l'Indépendance américaine* (Paris, 1877), pp. 313–320. See Clermont-Crèvecœur's journal, n. 145, and Verger's journal, n. 192.

De Grasse's fleet, unidentified officer

1 *Journal d'un Officier de l'Armée Navale en Amérique en 1781 & 1782* (Amsterdam, 1783). 72 pp. Sabin 28331. Monaghan 860.
2 "Journal of an Officer in the Naval Army in America in 1781 and 1782," tr. John Gilmary Shea, in *The Operations of the French Fleet under the Count de Grasse in 1781–2, as described in Two Contemporaneous Journals* (New York, The Bradford Club, Publication No. 3, 1864), pp. 135–185.

This journal covers de Grasse's departure from Brest in March 1781, the Chesapeake Campaign and Siege of Yorktown, de Grasse's defeat in the Battle of the Saints (April 1782), his subsequent return as prisoner to England, and his arrival in France (August 1782). The author of this journal has not been identified. His account is favorable to de Grasse, and it has been suggested that the Admiral inspired it (or even that he was the author). It reflects the controversy that raged over the Battle of the Saints.

De Grasse's fleet, unidentified officer

1 Manuscript journal in William L. Clements Library, Ann Arbor, Michigan, entitled "Journal ou Campagne des Armées de Terre et de Mer." 82 pp., one map. Covers the period March 1781–May 1782.

Jennet (?), Pierre-Joseph

Naval officer (not further identified)

1 Manuscript of 300 pages in the Henry E. Huntington Library, San Marino, California, HM 578. Illustrated with watercolor drawings of ships and engagements, including panoramic view of the Battle of the Chesapeake Capes, 5 September 1781 (cf. reproduction in Richard M. Ketchum, ed., *The American Heritage Book of the Revolution* [New York, 1958], pp. 284–285). This manuscript (not examined by the Editors) is described as being the "Log Book of Pierre Joseph Jennet," who served on a series of different ships during the period 1776–1783, including the *Caméléon, Caton, Alexandre, Magicienne*, and *Zélé*.

Lannoy, César-Auguste de (1763–1853)

Navy. Enseigne de vaisseau

1 "Mémorial de M. de Lannoy (1763–1793), Notes de voyage d'un officier de marine de l'Ancien Régime," in *Carnet de La Sabretache*, whole series, XIII, 2nd ser., III (1904), 682–688, 748–765. Published from a manuscript then in the possession of the author's grandson, Captain de Marcy.

on the frigate Engageante
*in La Pérouse's expedition
to Hudson Bay (1782)*

Lannoy's "Mémorial" includes a vivid firsthand account of La Pérouse's Hudson Bay expedition in the summer of 1782. Lannoy served on the frigate *Engageante* commanded by La Jaille; La Pérouse commanded the 74-gun warship *Sceptre*, Fleuriot de Langle the frigate *Astrée*. Landing troops drawn from units stationed in the West Indies were under the command of Rostaing. After passing through the ice floes of Hudson Strait, with inadequate charts to guide them, the French destroyed the Hudson Bay Company's "factories" at Fort Prince of Wales at the mouth of the Churchill River and at Fort York. See above, Clermont-Crèvecœur's journal, n. 150. After the war Lannoy was on the *Achille* with a small squadron that visited Boston in September 1788. In order to promote good relations with their allies, Lannoy notes (p. 761), "we spent a whole month dancing, eating, and drinking the health of the Americans, which was more tiring to us than the longest of storms."

La Pérouse, Jean-François de Galaup, comte de (1741-1788)

Navy. Lieutenant de vaisseau, *commanding the* Amazone *in d'Estaing's fleet at Savannah (1779);* capitaine de vaisseau, *commanding the frigate* Astrée *at Boston (1781); expedition to Hudson Bay (1782)*

1 Series of 17 letters, February–March 1781, addressed to Destouches (commanding the French squadron at Newport), written from La Pérouse's cruising station in Nantasket Roads, Boston. English paraphrases of these apparently unpublished letters are in the sale catalogue, *The Destouches Papers* (1926), items 70–85; see above *s.v.* Destouches. The originals are now in the Henry E. Huntington Library, San Marino, California.

La Pérouse's letters give a lively running narrative of his dealings with the Massachusetts authorities (Governor Hancock et al.), a proposed expedition to Penobscot Bay, convoying of American ships along the coast, meeting vessels from France, and related matters. The following year La Pérouse led an expedition to Hudson Bay, where he destroyed the British posts there in August 1782. See above *s.v.* Lannoy. La Pérouse's role in the American Revolution has been generally overshadowed by his famous exploring expedition into the Pacific, from which he never returned. He was lost in the vicinity of the New Hebrides in 1788 (as it was finally learned during the Dumont d'Urville expedition in 1827). The voluminous literature on La Pérouse concerns chiefly this later chapter in his life. See, e.g., Gilbert Chinard, ed., *Le Voyage de Lapérouse sur les côtes de l'Alaska et de la Californie, 1786* (Baltimore, The Johns Hopkins Press for the Institut Français de Washington, 1937), and the elaborate contemporary publications sponsored by the French government, L. A. Milet-Mureau, ed., *Voyage de La Pérouse autour du Monde* (Paris, 1797), and J. J. Houton de Labillardière, *Relation du voyage à la recherche de La Pérouse . . . pendant les années 1791, 1792* (Paris, 1799). See above, *s.v.* Costebelle.

Lauberdière, Louis-François-Bertrand du Pont d'Aubevoye, comte de (1759-1837)

1 Brief extracts from Lauberdière's journal (notably his description of Williamsburg) are printed in Warrington Dawson, *Les Français Morts pour l'Indépendance Américaine . . . et la Reconstruction historique de Williamsburg* (Paris, L'Oeuvre Latine, 1931), pp. 98–100. Dawson states

*Aide-de-camp to General
Rochambeau, with the rank
of captain*

Lauzun, Armand-Louis
Gontaut, duc de (later duc
de Biron) (1747–1793)
*Colonel-proprietor-
inspector of the Legion of
Foreign Volunteers*
(Volontaires étrangers
de Lauzun)

that this unpublished manuscript journal was made available to him through the courtesy of M. Georges du Chêne.

Lauberdière, who served as an aide-de-camp to Rochambeau, was the General's cousin. He later became one of Napoleon's generals; see Six, *Dict. Biog.*, II, 70.

1 *Mémoires de M. le Duc de Lauzun* (Paris, Barrois, 1822). Numerous later editions, including the following:

2 *Mémoires du Duc de Lauzun (1747–1783)*, ed. Louis Lacour (Paris, Poulet-Malassis, 1858). Described by the editor as "publiées pour la première fois avec les passages supprimés, les noms propres; une étude sur la vie de l'auteur, des notes et une table générale." Only the last part of the memoirs, pp. 273–316 in this edition, concern Lauzun's service in America.

3 English translations of Lauzun's memoirs include one by E. Jules Méras (New York, Sturgis & Walton, 1912), another by C. K. Scott Moncrieff (London, Routledge, 1928). Excerpts from the memoirs, entitled "Narrative of the Duke of Lauzun," appear in: *Magazine of American History*, IV, No. 1 (Jan. 1880), 39–40 (the abortive attack on New York, July 1781), and VI, No. 1 (Jan. 1881), 51–53 (describing the march from Philadelphia, the Siege of Yorktown, and the return to France); *American Historical Magazine*, II, No. 4 (July 1907), 292–298 (Lauzun's return to America in 1782 and final departure in 1783).

Although doubts concerning the authenticity of Lauzun's posthumously published memoirs were circulated at the time of their first appearance in 1822, such rumors appear to have originated chiefly with ladies who had been unfavorably portrayed and have not been substantiated by later investigators. The corroborative evidence supporting Lauzun's authorship is discussed by John Austin Stevens in his article "The Duke de Lauzun in France and America," *American Historical Magazine*, II, No. 5 (Sept. 1907), 343–375.

4 R. de Gontaut Biron, *Le Duc de Lauzun* (Paris, Plon, 1937). This biography, a useful supplement to Lauzun's own memoirs, draws upon the French army archives to complete the account of the Duc's role in the American Revolution; it also quotes extensively (pp. 148–150) from a letter (in a private collection) written by Lauzun to Vioménil, Gloucester Courthouse, 27 September 1781.

"Lauzun's Legion" was created by a royal ordinance of 5 March 1780 with the official designation "Volontaires étrangers de Lauzun." It was made up largely of German, Polish, and Irish recruits. In addition to Lauzun, colonel-proprietor-inspector, the staff included the Vicomte d'Arrot, commanding colonel, and Comte Robert-Guillaume Dillon, second colonel. The Legion was comprised of 5 companies of infantry (2 of fusiliers, 1 of grenadiers, 1 of chasseurs, and 1 of cannoneers) and 2 squadrons of hussars. However, two companies of fusiliers had to be left behind when the Legion embarked for America with Rochambeau's army in 1780. (Cf. Gontaut Biron, p. 120.)

The Duc de Lauzun landed in Rhode Island in July 1780, spent the winter of 1780–1781 at Lebanon, Connecticut, and commanded the left column of the army on the march southward to Virginia, where he was stationed at Gloucester during the Siege of Yorktown. Soon after the surrender he was sent to France on the *Surveillante*, the first to bring news of Cornwallis's capitulation to the French Court. He rejoined the army in America in September 1782; after the departure of the main body of Rochambeau's army he was left in command of such detachments as remained in the United States. Lauzun accompanied these detachments back to France, sailing from Wilmington, Delaware, 11 May, and reaching Brest, 11 June 1783. The Legion, as such, was disbanded by an official order of 20 June 1783. Lauzun's account of his experiences in America lacks the precision of some of the other journals, but it is a lively and highly personal document that sheds much light on the actors in the drama.

No other journals written by officers of Lauzun's Legion are known to the Editors. A small group of papers of the Vicomte d'Arrot—chiefly letters and instructions addressed to him by Lauzun, Rochambeau, Vioménil, and others—is in the Manuscript Collections of Colonial Williamsburg, "Lafayette-Leclerc Papers."

Liberge de Granchain

See Granchain.

**Losse de Bayac,
Charles-Joseph de (b. 1742)**

*Captain, Bourbonnais
Regiment*

1 Manuscript in the University of Virginia Library, Charlottesville, Virginia, accession number 4976. Two volumes bound in vellum and boards, 181 pp. and 216 pp. Purchased in 1955 from Alexander Davidson, Jr. Vol. I, entitled "Révolution de la Nouvelle Angleterre," is a retrospective historical summary of events in America from 1763 to 1779. Vol. II is the author's personal journal of his American campaigns with Rochambeau's army, 1780–1783. It includes the arrival and sojourn in Rhode Island, the overland march to Virginia, Yorktown campaign, winter quarters in Virginia, northward march to New England, and return voyage to France via the Caribbean (1783). In March 1781 Losse de Bayac was among the land forces participating in Destouches's Chesapeake expedition; he was embarked on the *Jason*.

**Magallon de La Morlière,
Louis-Antoine, chevalier de
(b. 1757)**

*Captain, Corps of Volunteer
Grenadiers from Saint-
Domingue, at Savannah
(1779) and at Charleston
(1780)*

1 Richard K. Murdoch, ed., "A French Account of the Siege of Charleston, 1780," in the *South Carolina Historical Magazine*, LXVII, No. 3 (July 1966), 138–154. Translated from a manuscript in the Archives de la Guerre, series "Mémoires et Reconnaissances," carton 248. Brief excerpts were published earlier in Lasseray, I, 293–297. The account may have been written up from Louis-Antoine's notes by his older brother, André-Louis-Florent.

When the French troops under d'Estaing embarked for the West Indies after the unsuccessful Siege of Savannah in the autumn of 1779, some 60 sick and wounded were left behind in Charleston, South Carolina, under the command of Captain Magallon de La Morlière. The following spring, when the British besieged Charleston, this small group of Frenchmen served with General Lincoln's Americans. After the capitulation the French were exchanged for an equal number of English prisoners taken by d'Estaing at Savannah and were allowed to return to Saint-Domingue. Magallon de La Morlière arrived with his contingent at The French Cape on 23 July 1780. He subsequently returned to France and relinquished his military career.

Mauduit du Plessis

See French Officers in American Service.

Maulevrier

See Colbert de Maulevrier.

Ménonville, François-Louis Thibaut, comte de (1740–1816)

Aide-major général *on Rochambeau's staff*

1 "Journal of the Siege of York, by M. de Ménonville, Aide-Major-General," in the *Magazine of American History*, VII, No. 4 (Oct. 1881), 283–288. Translated from the transcript included in Cromot Dubourg's journal; cf. above, *s.v.* Cromot Dubourg (1).

This is not a personal diary but the official record of the siege kept by a staff officer who, as Cromot Dubourg states, was "chargé du détail de la tranchée." This is the same document as Gallatin (3), above. It was also incorporated by other officers into their personal journals—for example, by Verger (pp. 139ff). This official "Etat-Major" or General Staff journal, which gives the general orders for the conduct of the siege, has its counterpart in the so-called Engineers' journal, which deals more specifically with the engineering operations; cf. above, *s.v.* Crublier d'Opterre, Engineers, and Querenet de La Combe.

2 Balch (I, 10, and II, 180–181) mentions an unpublished manuscript journal of the Comte de Ménonville—"of great interest owing to the exactness of detail"—that was (in the 1860's) in the possession of the Comte's grandson, François-Michel-Antoine de Ménonville.

3 Three letters from Ménonville to Rochambeau, Philadelphia, 14 May, 16 May, 4 June 1781, are among the Rochambeau Papers in the Library of Paul Mellon, Upperville, Virginia. Ménonville had been sent on a mission to Congress concerning supplies for the French army. His confidential communications to the General provide an interesting report on problems of supply and the financial situation at that time.

Meyronnet de Saint-Marc Fauris, Joseph-Philippe-Auguste, chevalier de (1746–1813)

Navy. Lieutenant de vaisseau *on the* Marseillais *in* d'Estaing's fleet

1 Roberta Leighton, ed., "Meyronnet de Saint-Marc's Journal of the Operations of the French Army under d'Estaing at the Siege of Savannah, September 1779," in the *New-York Historical Society Quarterly*, XXXVI, No. 3 (July 1952), 255–287. Translated from a manuscript in the New-York Historical Society entitled "Compte rendu des opérations faites par l'armée française, commandée par Mr. d'Estaing devant Savannah (Amérique)." The NYHS manuscript is a contemporary transcript of Mey-

ronnet de Saint-Marc's account. The original of his journal is in the Bibliothèque Municipale d'Avignon, Vol. 2750, foll. 139–146, where there is also, in the same volume, foll. 2–84, a related manuscript entitled "Journal de la campagne du vaisseau le Marseillais . . . commandé par monsieur de la Poïpe de Vertrieux. . . ." The name of the author is not shown on this latter journal, but, according to A. A. Lawrence (*Storm over Savannah*, pp. 185–186), "circumstances indicate strongly that it was written by Lieutenant Meyronnet de Saint-Marc. . . . The journal is a faithful day-by-day factual account of the voyage of the *Marseillais* from the time she left Toulon in April, 1778, until December 31, 1779, when the author debarked in France. However, it is of an impersonal nature, and is to a large extent merely a log of the vessel during the American campaign."

"During the Siege of Savannah he [Meyronnet de Saint-Marc] was in charge for a time of landing boats at Thunderbolt, and the main contribution of his journal is in the detailed account of the difficulties encountered by the ships and small boats in making the landings. Being stationed at the debarkation points or aboard ship, he seems not to have witnessed the main fighting in person, but to have based his story of the siege proper and of the disastrous assault, upon word-of-mouth accounts of actual participants. . . ." Leighton, p. 256.

Miollis, Sextius-Alexandre-François (1759–1828)

Sublieutenant, Soissonnais Regiment

1 Miollis's memoirs (autograph manuscript and several transcripts in family archives in France) have not been published *in extenso*. Excerpts are included in Henri Auréas, *Un Général de Napoléon: Miollis*, with a preface by Marcel Dunan (Publications de la Faculté des Lettres de l'Université de Strasbourg, Fascicule 143, 1961). Chap. 1, "Yorktown," pp. 20–28, is based on the memoirs; see also related documents, pp. 184–185. Another recent book about Miollis—Marie-Antoinette de Miollis, *Un Compagnon de La Fayette, le Général de Miollis* (Paris, Beauchesne, 1960)—is negligible history and is mentioned here only as a caveat.

Miollis, a native of Aix-en-Provence, was permanently disfigured as a result of wounds received at Yorktown during the night of 12–13 October 1781. Auréas quotes letters written to the young man's father by J.-P. Bérage de La Boyère (second captain, Soissonnais Regiment), dated 20 October 1781 and 26 January 1782, describing the injuries. According to La Boyère, Miollis's recovery was due mainly to the care of Robillard, chief surgeon in Rochambeau's army. In his memoirs Miollis recalls with gratitude the friendship of Charles de Lameth, who was also among the wounded in the Williamsburg hospital. Throughout his life Miollis appears to have retained an optimistic view of the American Revolution and an exalted opinion of Washington. His later career took him to Italy, where he was military governor of Rome from 1808 to 1814.

Montesquieu, Charles-Louis de Secondat, baron de (1749–1824)

Aide-de-camp to Major General Chastellux

1 Raymond Céleste, "Un Petit-fils de Montesquieu en Amérique (1780–1783)," in *Revue Philomathique de Bordeaux et du Sud-Ouest*, v, No. 12 (Dec. 1902), 529–556; Raymond Céleste, "Charles-Louis de Montesquieu à l'Armée (1772 à 1782)," *ibid.*, vi, No. 11 (Nov. 1903), 504–524. Céleste's complementary articles include letters written by Montesquieu to his former tutor, François de Paule Latapie, printed from originals in the family archives at the Château de La Brède and elsewhere.

2 Octave Beuve, "Un Petit-fils de Montesquieu, Soldat de l'Indépendance Américaine," in *Revue Historique de la Révolution Française et de l'Empire*, v (Jan.–June 1914), 233–263. More letters (supplementing but not duplicating those mentioned above) written by Montesquieu to his friend the Vicomte Amand de Saint-Chamans, baron de Rébénec; the originals are in the Saint-Chamans family papers, Archives du Département de l'Aube. Some of these same letters are published from the same source (but without indication of prior publication) in Emmanuel de Lévy Mirepoix, "Quelques Lettres du Baron de Montesquieu sur la Guerre de l'Indépendance Américaine," *Franco-American Review*, ii, No. 3 (Winter 1938), 192–204.

Montesquieu, grandson of the famous political philosopher and writer, who served as aide-de-camp to Chastellux, returned to France after the Siege of Yorktown but came back to America in the autumn of 1782 and rejoined Rochambeau's army at Crompond. He returned to France with Chastellux and Rochambeau on the *Emeraude*, January–February 1783.

Naval officer, unidentified

1 Manuscript diary of French naval operations in America, 1779–1782, in Library of Congress. This manuscript, of 281 pp., is entitled "Journal histoirique De mes Voyages en ameriques melés D'un Reqüeil fidelle Des Differente Campagne que j'y ai faite Et De Different Evenement arrivée aux antilles." The author sailed from Brest on the *Robuste* in January 1779, proceeding to the West Indies, where he participated in successive Anglo-French naval engagements. He was with de Grasse's fleet at the Chesapeake in September–October 1781. The narrative continues through September 1782.

O'Connor, Antoine-François-Térance

Engineer (ingénieur du Roi); served in the Siege of Savannah

1 "Journal du Siège de Savannah, septembre et octobre 1779, avec des Observations de M. le comte d'Estaing." Several contemporary manuscript copies of O'Connor's journal are extant: one in the Archives Nationales, Marine B⁴142; another in the Archives de la Guerre, Mémoires Historiques, 248, pièce 21; and another in the Ministère de la Marine, Bibliothèque du Dépôt des Cartes et Plans. The latter is described as No. 79 in the exhibition catalogue *Exposition rétrospective des Colonies françaises de l'Amérique du Nord* (Paris, 1929), pp. 181–182. Still another contemporary transcript, illustrated with two maps, was acquired in 1951 by the John Carter Brown Library; this copy, with "observations" by d'Estaing, is described by Lawrence C. Wroth in the Library's *Annual Report for 1950–1951*, pp. 33–38.

O'Connor's journal of the siege, dated aboard the *Annibal*, 22 October 1779, was transmitted to France by the Comte d'Estaing, who gave it his official endorsement and added marginal comments of his own. See above, *s.v.* d'Estaing (2).

Ollonne, Alexandre-Paul, comte d' (1758–1822)

Sublieutenant; second aide-de-camp to General Comte de Vioménil

1 Cf. Contenson, *Cincinnati*, p. 237, where it is stated that the Comte d'Ollonne kept a journal, still unpublished, of the campaigns in America from 1 May 1780 to 30 April 1783.

Ollonne was a nephew of the Comte de Vioménil (also of the Baron) whom he accompanied to America as aide-de-camp. His elder brother, Comte Pierre-François-Gabriel d'Ollonne (1757–1831), also served in the American campaigns, as first aide-de-camp to the Comte de Vioménil.

"Pechot"

See Tarragon.

Pouzoullette, sieur de

Sous-officier, Grenadiers de la Marine Royale

1 Cf. Warrington Dawson, *Les Français Morts pour l'Indépendance Américaine . . . et la Reconstruction historique de Williamsburg* (Paris: Editions de l'Oeuvre Latine, 1931), pp. 100–101; *Français Morts aux Etats-Unis* (1936), pp. 10–11. According to Dawson, he consulted an unpublished manuscript journal by Pouzoullette, belonging to Mr. Maurice A. Hall, entitled "Journal Historique concernant les Evénements et les Expéditions faites par l'armée du Roi aux ordres de M. le comte de Grasse." Pouzoullette came to Virginia with de Grasse's fleet at the time of the Siege of Yorktown.

Querenet de La Combe, Guillaume (1731–1788)

Lieutenant colonel, Royal Corps of Engineers; acting chief engineer for the French army at the Siege of Yorktown

1 "Journal du Siège d'York en Virginie." Manuscript, dated York, 20 October 1781. Two copies of this "Journal," with related maps and letters of transmittal dated respectively York, 24 October 1781, and Williamsburg, 26 January 1782, are in the Archives du Génie, alphabetical series, "Sièges," under "Yorck." Another copy, with related maps, was presented in 1955 to the U.S. Engineer Center Museum at Fort Belvoir, Virginia, by the chief of French engineers.

This is not a personal journal but the formal Engineer Corps record of the siege. Other correspondence and maps by Querenet de La Combe are also preserved in the Archives du Génie. As mentioned above (Verger's journal, n. 98), Querenet's important role at Yorktown has been somewhat obscured for later generations by the fact that his name appeared as "Colonel Carney" in Washington's congratulatory "After Orders" of 20 October 1781. Querenet de La Combe's "Journal du Siège" was the archetype of several other surviving manuscripts, such as Huntington Library MS No. 1500. See also above, *s.v.* Crublier d'Opterre.

Revel, Joachim du Perron, comte de (1756–1814)

1 *Journal particulier d'une campagne aux Indes Occidentales (1781–1782)* (Paris, H. Charles-Lavauzelle, *ca.* 1898). Contains maps and diagrams redrawn from those in the journal. The original manuscript was acquired

Sublieutenant, Régiment d'Infanterie de Monsieur, with a detachment from this regiment assigned to the Languedoc *in de Grasse's fleet*

in 1942 by the Princeton University Library as a gift from Stuart W. Jackson in honor of Gilbert Chinard. With the manuscript of the fair copy of the journal is a second manuscript, a "brouillon" or rough draft, which carries the record through 23 August 1782, the date of the *Languedoc*'s return to Brest.

2 Gilbert Chinard, Robert G. Albion, Lloyd A. Brown, *A Map of Yorktown, by Joachim du Perron, Comte de Revel, With Notes Biographical, Nautical and Cartographical on the Journal and Maps of Duperron* (Princeton, Princeton University Library, 1942). One half of the 500 copies printed bear the imprint of the American Friends of Lafayette. Contains a reproduction in color (executed by the Meriden Gravure Co.) of one of Du Perron's maps.

The journal of Sublieutenant Du Perron (as he then called himself) covers the march of a detachment of his regiment from Besançon to Brittany and its sojourn there (May 1780–March 1781); the departure for the West Indies, 22 March 1781, on board the *Languedoc* in the fleet commanded by de Grasse; the Chesapeake expedition (Siege of Yorktown), August–November 1781; the subsequent West Indian campaign, including the capture of St. Kitts (January–February 1782); and the Battle of the Saints (April 1782). Du Perron reached France again, still on board the *Languedoc*, on 23 August 1782. Du Perron's journal is of special interest as the account of a land officer assigned to a ship's garrison, containing his descriptions of ships and navigation, and an army man's comments on the navy. At the Siege of Yorktown Du Perron was among the 800 men lent by de Grasse from the ships' garrisons and placed under command of the Marquis de Choisy on the Gloucester side of the river. His journal is one of the few firsthand records of this phase of the Yorktown operations; it includes detailed tabulations of the officers and units comprising the French forces at Gloucester, described by him as "un ramassis de détachements morcelés et sans drapeaux" (pp. 137–140). In addition to the map of the Siege of Yorktown (2), Du Perron's journal includes diagrams of the Battle of the Chesapeake Capes, a detailed map of the environs of Gloucester, and plans of the engagements in the West Indies, such as the St. Kitts expedition and the Battle of the Saints. The maps in the manuscript journal are not completely published in (1). Several of them are reproduced in the present work, Vol. II, Nos. 3, 84, 90, and 166.

Robernier (Robertnier)

Robin, abbé

Chaplain, attached to Soissonnais Regiment

See Clermont-Crèvecœur.

1 *Nouveau Voyage dans l'Amérique Septentrionale, en l'année 1781; et Campagne de l'Armée de M. le comte de Rochambeau* ("A Philadelphie et se trouve à Paris," chez Moutard, 1782). For the several subsequent editions, see Monaghan.

2 *New Travels through North-America: in a Series of Letters; Exhibiting, the History of the Victorious Campaign of the Allied Armies, under his Excellency General Washington, and the Count de Rochambeau, in the Year 1781*, tr. Philip Freneau (Philadelphia, Robert Bell, 1783).

The Abbé arrived at Boston only in early June 1781, just in time to join Rochambeau's army on its march to the Hudson and to Virginia; he presumably returned to France shortly after the capitulation at Yorktown. His somewhat superficial account is presented in the form of letters to a friend, the first dated Boston, 14 June, and the last, Yorktown, 15 November 1781. A table of the army's camps and marches is appended. With the exception of Chastellux's privately printed *Voyage*, Robin's book was the first to be published by a participant in the campaign. It thus owed its success to its current news value. Whereas most of the journals listed here were not printed at the time, this one was intended for immediate publication.

Rochambeau, Jean-Baptiste-Donatien de Vimeur, comte de (1725–1807)

Lieutenant general, commanding the French Expeditionary Forces in America

1 *Journal des opérations du Corps Français sous le commandement du Comte de Rochambeau, Lieutenant-Général des Armées du Roi, depuis le 15 d'Août.* This is Rochambeau's official report covering the operations of his army from its departure from the Philipsburg camp through the surrender of Cornwallis at Yorktown. It was sent to France by his special messengers (the Duc de Lauzun and Comte Guillaume de Deux-Ponts) with a covering dispatch to the minister of war (Ségur) dated "Au camp devant Yorktown," 20 October 1781. A summary version of the *Journal* appeared in a supplement to the *Gazette de France*, 20 November 1781; an English translation of this abridgment appeared in *The Pennsylvania Packet*, 21 February 1782, and was later reprinted in the *Magazine of American History*, VII (1881), 224–226. A complete version was published in the *Gazette de Leyde*, 30 November 1781 and supplements. It also appeared at this time as a 15-page pamphlet with the imprint (probably spurious) "A Philadelphie, De l'Imprimerie de Guillaume Hampton"; this pamphlet was reproduced in 1929 as No. 225 in the "Americana Series, photostat reproductions by the Massachusetts Historical Society." The *Journal* is reprinted from a manuscript copy in the Archives de la Guerre (A¹3734) in Doniol, V, 573–580.

There are two manuscript copies of the *Journal*, in a secretary's hand, among the Rochambeau manuscripts in the Library of Paul Mellon, Upperville, Virginia. One of these has corrections in Rochambeau's hand. This fact, as well as several statements in the first person, seem to indicate that Rochambeau himself compiled this narrative report. Similar contemporary narratives by Rochambeau covering other phases of his American campaigns are: "Journal de ce qui s'est passé depuis l'arrivée du Corps français au Camp de Phillipsburgh" (15 July–10 August 1781), manuscript copy in Mellon Library, printed in Doniol, V, 518–519, from another copy in the Archives de la Guerre, A¹3734; "Journal de la Campagne de 1782 . . . en deux parties" (1 July–1 December 1782), manuscript copy in the Archives de la Guerre, A¹3735, another copy in the Library of Congress, not in Doniol; "Journal de Notre Navigation" (Rochambeau's return on the frigate *Emeraude*, 8 January–10 February 1783), manuscript copy in the Archives de la Guerre, A¹3735, not in

Doniol. Another of Rochambeau's reports (also in the Archives de la Guerre), tr. and ed. Claude C. Sturgill under the title "Rochambeau's Mémoire de la Guerre en Amérique," is in the *Virginia Magazine of History and Biography*, LXXVIII, No. 1 (Jan. 1970), 34–64; Sturgill's claim that this is "the original afteraction report" is questionable; several names (e.g., Chastellux, La Villebrune) are misidentified by the editor.

2 *Mémoires militaires, historiques et politiques de Rochambeau, Ancien Maréchal de France, et Grand Officier de la Légion d'Honneur*, 2 vols. (Paris, Fain, 1809). The American campaigns of 1780–1783 are covered in I, 225–328. The *Mémoires* were reprinted (Paris, Pillet, 1824); a one-volume edition entitled *Mémoires du Maréchal Rochambeau sur les Guerres de la Révolution* (Paris, Ladvocat, 1824) includes only the latter part (from 1789). Rochambeau's posthumously published memoirs were written during his retirement, not long before his death in 1807. A holograph manuscript, with revisions, is in the Library of Paul Mellon, Upperville, Virginia. Although Rochambeau consulted his personal archives of the American campaigns, his memoirs give paraphrases rather than verbatim texts of such documents as the *Journal des opérations* mentioned above. It may be noted that Rochambeau's memoirs were already available in printed form when other retired officers such as Mathieu Dumas and the Comte de Ségur came to write *their* memoirs in the 1820's.

3 "An Account of the Operations of the French Army in the United States of America, during the War of their Independence; translated from the French of the Memoirs of Marshal Count de Rochambeau," in *The American Register; or Summary of History, Politics, and Literature*, ed. Robert Walsh, Jr., II (Philadelphia, 1817), 156–182. Translation of Rochambeau's *Mémoires* (Paris, 1809), I, 237–315; not to be confused with (1).

4 *Memoirs of the Marshal Comte de Rochambeau, relative to the War of Independence of the United States*, extracted and translated from the French by M.W.E. Wright (Paris; French, English, and American Library, 1838). Like (3), this includes only the portions of Rochambeau's memoirs relating to the American war.

5 "Correspondance du Comte de Rochambeau depuis le début de son commandement aux Etats-Unis jusqu'à la fin de la campagne de Virginie," in Doniol, V, 309–590. Printed, with many abridgments, from letter-book copies of Rochambeau's correspondence preserved in the Archives de la Guerre, A¹3733–3736. This publication covers the years 1780 and 1781 but regrettably does not include the correspondence for 1782 and 1783.

In addition to the materials in the Archives de la Guerre and other French government repositories (Archives de la Marine, Archives des Affaires Etrangères, etc.), further correspondence is to be found in Rochambeau's personal papers, which, as far as they relate to the American war, are now for the most part in the United States. One group is in the Library of Congress (acquired in 1883); another, acquired in the

1950's, is in the Library of Paul Mellon, Upperville, Virginia. These two segments of Rochambeau's papers, which were once together at the Château de Rochambeau, are closely interrelated. Many of the original letters received by the General when he was in America (from Washington, Lafayette, La Luzerne, de Grasse, and others) are now in the Mellon Library; letter-book copies are in the Library of Congress. Rochambeau's letters to La Luzerne (often giving more details than those he sent to the minister of war in France) are in the Archives du Ministère des Affaires Etrangères, Etats-Unis, Correspondance politique, Supplément, Vol. 15 (photocopies in the Library of Congress). This supplementary series, consisting of archives of the French Legation in the United States that were later repatriated, includes six volumes (12–17) dealing with military affairs during the American Revolution.

Rochambeau, Donatien-Marie-Joseph de Vimeur, vicomte de (1755–1813)

Second colonel, Bourbonnais Regiment

1 "The War in America, An Unpublished Journal (1780–1783)," in Jean-Edmond Weelen, *Rochambeau Father and Son: A Life of the Maréchal de Rochambeau, and The Journal of the Vicomte de Rochambeau (hitherto unpublished)*, tr. Lawrence Lee, with a preface by Gilbert Chinard (New York, Henry Holt, 1936), pp. 191–285.

The Vicomte de Rochambeau arrived in Rhode Island with the Expeditionary Forces commanded by his father in July 1780. He went back to France on a special mission, leaving on the frigate *Amazone* at the end of October 1780 and returning to America on the *Concorde* (accompanying Admiral Barras) in early May 1781. He remained with the army through the end of 1782, then returned to France with his father on the *Emeraude* at the beginning of 1783. Although the journal contains occasional interesting comments deriving from the author's special position as the General's son, it is on the whole superficial and lacking in precise details. The Vicomte's sketch of the naval engagement off Bermuda, 20 June 1780, is reproduced in (1), pp. 200–201. The Vicomte de Rochambeau was entrusted with important commands in the West Indies during the French Revolution and returned there again in 1803 with the ill-fated Leclerc expedition. He was killed in the Battle of Leipzig in 1813. His papers, like those of his father, are now dispersed in several depositories; papers relating to his later West Indian campaigns are in the University of Florida Library, others in the Yale University Library. A detailed Calendar of the Rochambeau papers in the University of Florida Library, compiled by Laura V. Monti, will be published by the University of Florida Press in 1972.

Romain, Jules de (ca. 1763–1780)

Navy. Garde-marine on the Vengeur *(1778–1779)*

1 Félix de Romain, *Souvenirs d'un officier royaliste*, 3 vols. (Paris, Egron, 1824–1829). Romain's memoirs include (1, 33–51) mention of his elder brother Jules, who served in the navy during the American war and died in Martinique at the age of seventeen. Félix de Romain publishes several of his brother's letters written to their father, including a long one dated 21 October 1779, "En rade de Savanack [*sic*]."

Young Romain served as a midshipman on the warship *Vengeur*, commanded by Du Croizet de Retz. He was at the capture of Grenada (July 1779) and later that year at the Siege of Savannah. When landing troops from one of the ship's boats Romain was obliged to spend a week ashore, during which time he "lived on biscuit, oysters, and water black as my hat" and contracted dysentery. Commenting on the siege, Romain wrote to his father: "If M. d'Estaing had not been betrayed by the Americans, who are the worst and shabbiest troops in the world, and if he had had more favorable winds when landing his troops, he would, I think, have taken the city by attacking it immediately, because the English were not at all well fortified there." In the concluding passage of his letter Jules told his father that he did not expect to see France again for another year or more—"which is a long time." "I haven't a penny left, and I would be obliged if you would try to send me some funds to Martinique, for I need breeches, shoes, and many other things and don't know how I shall manage." This was probably the last letter his father received; naval archives record Romain's death on board his ship at Martinique, 2 February 1780.

Rosel, Louis-Joseph du

Lieutenant, Saintonge Regiment

1 Dawson (*Français Morts aux Etats-Unis*, p. 11) mentions letters and manuscripts of the Rosel brothers belonging to their descendants, of which he obtained copies. Both the elder brother, Louis-Joseph, and the younger, known as the Chevalier du Rosel, were officers in the Saintonge Regiment, with Rochambeau's army.

Saint-Cyr, Marc-Antoine-Georges Bellemare, chevalier de

Captain, Saintonge Regiment

1 Dawson (*Français Morts aux Etats-Unis*, p. 11) says that the Chevalier de Saint-Cyr "left a most interesting manuscript, of which I possess a copy."

Saint-Exupéry, Georges-Alexandre-César, chevalier de (1757–1825)

Second lieutenant, La Sarre-Infanterie Regiment

1 "Journal d'un Officier du Régiment de la Sarre-Infanterie pendant la Guerre d'Amérique (1780–1782)," ed. with introduction and notes by S. Churchill, in *Carnet de La Sabretache, Revue Militaire Rétrospective*, 2nd ser., III (1904), 169–185, 240–255, 305–319, 361–383.
2 Countess Anais de Saint-Exupéry, "The War Diary of Georges Alexander César de Saint Exupéry, Lieutenant in the Regiment of Sarre-Infantry," in *Légion d'Honneur* (American Society of the French Legion of Honor, New York), II, No. 2 (Oct. 1931), 107–113. Includes excerpts from the journal pertaining to the Siege of Yorktown.

The manuscript of Saint-Exupéry's "Journal de la Guerre d'Amérique en 1780, 1781 et 1782" was lent in 1957 to the Lafayette exhibition at the Archives Nationales by the Vicomte de Saint-Exupéry; see catalogue *La Fayette, Exposition organisée par les Archives Nationales. . . .* (Paris, 1957), pp. 54–55, No. 132, where the manuscript is described and a few excerpts quoted. Also exhibited (No. 133) was another manuscript, "Routes du Vaisseau du Roi le *Triton*, en 1780, 1781 et 1782," a log-book giving detailed itineraries of de Guichen's fleet. Saint-Exupéry (an ancestor of the twentieth-century author of the same name) wrote the account of his campaigns at the suggestion of his colonel, the Duc de La Rochefoucauld d'Enville. He left Brest early in 1780 on board the *Triton* in de Guichen's fleet, as second in command of the detachment of the Sarre Regiment of infantry serving as the ship's garrison. Saint-Exupéry participated in the naval actions of 17 April 1780 off Martinique, the siege and capture of Pensacola (April–May 1781), and the expedition to the Chesapeake under de Grasse (August–November 1781). In his "journal histori-politi-philosophi-nautique," as he calls it, the young second lieutenant gives a comic account of the Pensacola affair and is extremely critical of practically everybody, including the Marquis de Bouillé, Monteil, and the Spanish admiral Don Solano. During the expedition to the Chesapeake the *Triton* blockaded the entrance to the York River; Saint-Exupéry gives a good description of the British fire-ship attack (22–23 September 1781) in which the *Triton* was first in the line of fire. He reproaches Cornwallis for not erecting abatis in the woods before Yorktown in order to delay the allied march and also blames de Grasse for not joining up with Barras's fleet and destroying the British off the Chesapeake.

Saint-Laurent, Thomas de
Navy. Garde-marine
on the Marseillais *in
d'Estaing's fleet (1778)*

1 "Journal de bord du vaisseau Le Marseillais de 74 canons au début de la Campagne de l'Amiral d'Estaing." This manuscript fragment of 28 pp., in the John Carter Brown Library, has been attributed to Thomas de Saint-Laurent, aide to M. La Poype de Vertrieux, captain of the *Marseillais*, by a comparison of the handwriting with a later portion of Saint-Laurent's journal (beginning in 1788) also in the John Carter Brown Library. This most informative fragment of the journal begins off the coast of the United States on 1 July 1778. It describes taking prizes en route to the Delaware, the wreck of the *César*, and the discussions and hesitations leading to the abandonment of an attack on New York. The narrative continues to Rhode Island, mentions Lafayette's and Sullivan's conferences with d'Estaing, reconnoitering Newport and Conanicut Island, etc. The manuscript unfortunately stops with an entry for 3 August 1778, before the Battle of Rhode Island began.

**Saint-Simon-Montbléru,
Claude-Anne de Rouvroy,
marquis de (1743–1819)**

*Major general, commanding
the army from the West
Indies transported by de
Grasse's fleet to Yorktown*

1 Ludovic de Contenson, "La Capitulation d'Yorktown et le Comte de Grasse," in *Revue d'Histoire Diplomatique*, XLII, No. 4 (Oct.–Dec. 1928), 378–399. Includes passages from Saint-Simon's journal for 5 July–9 October 1781.
2 Ludovic de Contenson, "La Prise de Saint-Christophe," in *Revue Historique des Antilles*, May 1929, pp. 17ff. Extracts from Saint-Simon's journal relating to the capture of the British island of St. Kitts, January–February 1782.

3 Ludovic de Contenson, "Deux Documents sur la Guerre d'Amérique," in *Revue d'Histoire Diplomatique*, XLIV, No. 1 (Jan.–March, 1930), 20–24. The second of the "deux documents" is a portion of Saint-Simon's journal concerning the defeat of de Grasse in the Battle of the Saints, April 1782.

The above extracts are from Saint-Simon's "Journal des campagnes de l'Amérique depuis le 5 juillet 1781 jusqu'au 12 avril 1782," a manuscript in the archives of the de Bouillé family, to whom it was given by Saint-Simon's daughter in 1828.

Saint-Simon's division at the Siege of Yorktown, comprised of troops brought from the West Indies by de Grasse's fleet, included the Agenois Regiment (1,000 men), Gâtinais [Royal-Auvergne] (1,000), Touraine (1,000), a detachment of the Metz artillery (100), and Navy volunteers (100). In addition to the Marquis de Saint-Simon, two others of this name were present at the Siege of Yorktown: the Marquis's younger brother, Claude de Rouvroy, baron de Saint-Simon (1752–1811); and their cousin, Claude-Henri de Rouvroy, comte de Saint-Simon (1760–1825), then a captain in the Touraine Regiment, who commanded the regimental gunners at the siege and later became famous as the social and economic theorist of "Saint-Simonisme." For a recapitulation of the Marquis de Saint-Simon's role at Yorktown, see Harold A. Larrabee, "A Neglected French Collaborator in the Victory of Yorktown, Claude-Anne Marquis de Saint-Simon (1740–1819)," in *Journal de la Société des Américanistes de Paris*, n.s., XXIV (1932), 245–257; and, concerning Comte Henri, the same author's "Henri de Saint-Simon at Yorktown, A French Prophet of Modern Industrialism in America," in the *Franco-American Review*, II, No. 2 (Autumn 1937), 96–109.

Schwerin, Guillaume, comte de
Sublieutenant, Deux-Ponts Regiment

1 Letters to his uncle, Comte Reingard, are in the Fürstlich Wiedische Archiv, Neuwied (Germany). Photostats in the Library of Congress. Cf. Acomb's edition of the Von Closen journal, p. 368.

Séguier de Terson, Philippe
Captain, Agenois Regiment

1 "Le Siège de Savannah (1779)," ed. Capitaine de Cazenave, in *Carnet de La Sabretache, Revue Militaire Rétrospective*, 2nd ser., 1 (1903), 240–252, 289–300. Extract from a manuscript in possession of descendants, MM. de Latour-Dejean.

Séguier de Terson embarked at The French Cape in the *Robuste* in de Grasse's division of d'Estaing's fleet on 12 August 1779, landing at Savannah on 13 September. He led the charge against the English sortie under Major Graham and participated in the final abortive assault on the English works in which Pulaski was killed and d'Estaing and General Fontanges wounded. He attributes the failure of the expedition to the lack of trained gunners and engineers in the French contingent capable of emplacing batteries and supervising fortifications, to general disorganization and laxity among the French leadership, and to the apathy of General Lincoln.

Ségur, Louis-Philippe, comte de (1753–1830)

Second colonel, Soissonnais Regiment (replacing the Vicomte de Noailles)

1 "Extraits des lettres écrites d'Amérique par le Comte de Ségur . . . à la Comtesse de Ségur . . . 1782–1783," in Société des Bibliophiles François, *Mélanges*, 2ᵉ partie (Paris, Rahir, 1903), pp. 149–200. These letters written by Ségur to his wife from America (as distinguished from his retrospective memoirs, next item) were published from originals belonging to the Comtesse d'Armaillé. See also Bessie Van Vorst, "L'Amérique au XVIIIᵉ siècle d'après un voyageur français," in *Revue des Deux Mondes*, LX (1910), 191–217.

2 *Mémoires, ou Souvenirs et Anecdotes, par M. le Comte de Ségur*, 3 vols. (Paris, Eymery, 1824–1826). Ségur's participation in the American Revolution is covered in I, 317–526. Also later editions.

3 *Memoirs and Recollections of Count Ségur . . . written by himself . . . translated from the French*, 3 vols. (London, H. Colburn, 1825–1827). Also another edition of Vol. I only published in Boston by Wells & Lilly and in New York by E. Bliss & E. White in 1825. An abridged translation by Gerard Shelley was published in London by John Hamilton and in New York by Scribner in 1928.

Ségur, son of the minister of war, was not with Rochambeau's army during the earlier phases of the American expedition and was *not* present at the Siege of Yorktown. He left France only in May 1782, on the *Gloire*, with the Prince de Broglie, Duc de Lauzun, and others. Ségur joined Rochambeau's army at its Crompond camp in September, marched with it to Boston, and returned via the West Indies with Vaudreuil's fleet in 1783. Ségur's memoirs, written during the Restoration, range backward to the Old Regime, the Revolution, and the Empire. Taken as a whole, they provide an excellent commentary on the significance of the American Revolution in the life and thought of the French aristocracy.

Soissonnais Regiment, unidentified officer

1 Manuscript in the Henry E. Huntington Library, San Marino, California, HM 621, U8 B3. Sixty-eight leaves, approx. 19 x 15.5 cm., with 4 smaller leaves tipped in. Provenance unknown. This manuscript includes an introductory narrative describing the departure of Rochambeau's army from Brest in 1780 and arrival in Rhode Island; a section entitled "Précis des Opérations et des Marches de l'Armée Combinée française et américaine pendant la Campagne de 1781"; "Journal du Siège d'York en Virginie" with related documents; and "Campagne de l'année 1782." It has no material on the 1783 campaign in the Caribbean. Of particular interest are the maps of the army's camps for the 1781 march from Rhode Island to Virginia and for the northward march in 1782. These maps, in pen and watercolor, are similar to the Berthier series reproduced in the present work (Vol. II, Nos. 26ff. and 108ff.) but smaller in size, one or more being included on a single page along with descriptive headings and text. The text provides an abbreviated itinerary of the daily marches. A number of the maps are incomplete pencil sketches only; space has been allotted for others that have not been completed.

This manuscript, which is unsigned, was evidently compiled by, or for, an officer of the Soissonnais Regiment. The first sentence of the introductory narrative states: "On 6 April [1780] the Soissonnais Regiment, which was one of those that were to form General Rochambeau's army, embarked at Brest. . . ." Furthermore, the dates of the camp plans are those of the Soissonnais Regiment, which marched as the Third Division in both 1781 and 1782. On the first page, written in a different hand, are several names, including those of "Monsieur David" and "Monsieur Debrassine[?]," residing at Roquemaure near Villeneuve d'Avignon, and the date 1786. Since no officers with such names appear in the extant rosters of the Soissonnais Regiment, they presumably refer to a person who once had the manuscript in his possession, rather than to the author or compiler. A certain de Brassine, employed in the French army's administrative services (Intendance), was still in Philadelphia in 1784, when accounts were being settled. He evidently had difficulties with his superiors, considered himself persecuted by them, and addressed several complaints to the French Legation; see Archives du Ministère des Affaires Etrangères, Etats-Unis, Correspondance politique, Supplément, Vol. 17, foll. 240–252.

Soret de Boisbrunet,
Alexandre-Claude-Louis
Mellon (1746–1818)

*Lieutenant, Angoumois
Regiment*

1 Warrington Dawson, "A New Record of the Sieges of Yorktown and Pensacola," in *Légion d'Honneur* (American Society of the French Legion of Honor, New York), IV, No. 2 (Oct. 1933), 81–85. Includes very brief extracts from Soret de Boisbrunet's journal.

Soret de Boisbrunet served with a detachment of the Angoumois Regiment on board ships of de Grasse's fleet in West Indian waters and was thus at Pensacola (May 1781) and at the Chesapeake later that year. He apparently remained on his ship during the Siege of Yorktown; the excerpts from his journal add little to the "record."

Stedingk, Curt Bogislaus
Ludvig Christoffer, baron
(and count) von
(1746–1837)

*Swedish officer in the French
service, commanding a
brigade of infantry (two
regiments) under Comte
d'Estaing*

1 *Mémoires posthumes du Feld-Maréchal Comte de Stedingk, rédigés sur des lettres, dépêches et autres pièces authentiques laissées à sa famille*, ed. General Comte de Björnstjerna, 3 vols. (Paris, Arthus-Bertrand, 1844–1847). Translated excerpts from these memoirs (including the account of Savannah mentioned below) are incorporated in the article "Count Stedingk," *Putnam's Monthly Magazine* (New York), IV (Oct.–Nov. 1854), 345–356, 492–503.

Stedingk served under d'Estaing in 1779. His letter to King Gustavus III of Sweden, written from Paris, 18 January 1780 (I, 36–44), gives an account of the Siege of Savannah in which he took part. In spite of his desires and efforts, Stedingk did not succeed in obtaining a command in Rochambeau's army; cf. his letter to King Gustavus, Versailles, 5 March 1780 (I, 49–51). Stedingk later rose to the rank of field marshal in the Swedish army.

Tarragon, Jean-Rémy,
chevalier de (1742–1804)

1 "Le Siège de Savannah. Journal de Campagne de Jean-Rémy, Chevalier de Tarragon, Capitaine commandant les Chasseurs du Régiment d'Arma-

Captain, commanding the chasseurs of the Armagnac Regiment; served as major of Dillon's division at the Siege of Savannah

gnac, employé comme Major de la Division de Dillon, 1779," ed. Lieutenant Colonel Cte. Adrien de Tarragon, in *Carnet de La Sabretache: Revue d'histoire militaire rétrospective*, xxxvii (4th ser., vii, 1934), 350–363, 404–428; also issued separately as a brochure (Moulins, 1935). Tarragon's journal, signed with the pseudonym "Pechot," also appears in B. F. Stevens, *Facsimiles of Manuscripts in European Archives relating to America, 1773–1783* (London, 1889–1898), Vol. xxiii, No. 2010, both in facsimile (from a manuscript then in Stevens's possession, now in the John Carter Brown Library) and in English translation.

Tarragon served in several actions in the West Indies where he was stationed with his regiment, but his Savannah journal (1 September–20 October 1779) is the only surviving portion of his military memoirs. Like other French participants, Tarragon attributes the failure of the campaign to the impetuosity and lack of planning of d'Estaing and his stubbornness in resisting the counsels of experienced land officers, as well as to the lack of effective cooperation of the Americans and the inadequacy of the French artillery, which, he says (p. 411), "fired grapeshot into Savannah for two hours, killing forty women and children of all colors but not a single soldier." He criticizes d'Estaing for attacking the enemy's right flank, which was unimpaired by French bombardment and the most strongly manned, against the advice of officers such as Noailles. The French attack was so confused that at its forced retreat "the disorder was so complete that not ten soldiers of any company returned to camp together" (p. 417). Tarragon's journal includes an exchange of letters between d'Estaing and Dillon.

Ternay, Charles-Louis d'Arsac, chevalier de (1723–1780)

Navy. Chef d'escadre, commanding the fleet that brought Rochambeau's army to Rhode Island

1 "Journal de Ma Campagne sur le vaisseau le *Duc de Bourgogne*, 1780." Unpublished manuscript, now among the Destouches Papers, Henry E. Huntington Library, San Marino, California. Excerpts from the journal, translated into English, appeared in the sale catalogue, *The Destouches Papers* (1926), item No. 108; see above, *s.v.* Destouches.

This journal presumably came into the hands of Destouches when he took over the command of the French squadron at Newport after Ternay's death there on 15 December 1780. It is a succinct record, little more than a mariner's log-book, extending from 23 March to 9 December 1780. The entries for 19 April–8 May and for 22 June–23 July (covering the arrival at Newport) are lacking; presumably these leaves at one time became separated from the rest of the manuscript. Of interest are marginal notes in another hand (pp. [19–20]) concerning the naval action of 20 June 1780; these contradict certain of Ternay's statements about orders given the *Neptune* (commanded by Destouches) and were probably added by the latter when the journal was in his possession.

Thy [also spelled d'Ethy], Alexandre, chevalier de (b. ca. 1735)

1 "Livre de bord du vaisseau le *Citoyen*, 29 Août–11 Septembre 1781 . . . suite du journal de monsieur le chevalier Déthy capitaine du *Citoyen*," in French Ensor Chadwick, ed., *The Graves Papers and other Docu-*

Navy. Capitaine de vaisseau, *commanding the* Citoyen *in de Grasse's fleet (1781)*

ments *relating to the Naval Operations of the Yorktown Campaign, July to October 1781*, Publications of the Naval History Society, VII (New York, 1916), 222–244. Published from a manuscript in the Archives Nationales, Marine B⁴238, foll. 108ᵛᵒ–133ᵛᵒ. Chadwick's valuable compilation (with an excellent introduction), drawn mainly from the British Admiralty archives, also includes, in addition to the extract from de Thy's journal: pp. 212–221, extracts from the "Journal de Navigation de l'Armée aux ordres de Monsieur le comte de Grasse" (the log kept aboard the flagship *Ville de Paris* by Vaugirauld, *major d'escadre*; Marine B⁴184); and p. 245, an extract from the log-book of the French warship *Pluton* for 3 September 1781 (Marine B⁴184, foll. 80ᵛᵒ–90ᵛᵒ).

The portion of de Thy's journal printed by Chadwick (presumably part of a more extensive journal) covers chiefly the Battle of the Chesapeake Capes. Although essentially a ship's log, the journal is written in the first person and includes personal comments by the commander of the *Citoyen*, a 74-gun warship in de Grasse's fleet. There is mention of the landing of Saint-Simon's troops and of the arrival of Barras's squadron from Newport. De Thy was later with Vaudreuil's squadron at Boston (1782), still commanding the *Citoyen*, which transported troops of Rochambeau's army back to France via the Caribbean in 1783.

Tornquist, Carl Gustaf (1757–1808)

Swedish officer in the service of the French navy; enseigne de vaisseau, lieutenant de vaisseau

1 *Grefve Grasses Siö-Batailler, och Krigs-Operationerne uti Vest-Indien, ifrån början af år 1781 til Krigets slut; med dertil hörande Historiske Anmärkningar: författade af En Amiralitets Officerare, under des Campagner på Kongl. Franska Flottan* (Stockholm, J. C. Holmberg, 1787). Contains maps, including one of the Battle of the Chesapeake Capes, 5 September 1781.

2 "La Bataille des Saintes racontée par un officier de marine suédois au service de la France," tr. W. Claesen, in *Revue Maritime*, March 1936, pp. 331–348. Partial translation of (1).

3 *The Naval Campaigns of Count de Grasse during the American Revolution, 1781–1783*, tr. Amandus Johnson from the Swedish with introduction, notes, and appendices, containing a "List of Swedish [Naval] Officers who took part in the struggle" (Philadelphia, Swedish Colonial Society, 1942).

Tornquist left Brest for the West Indies in March 1781 with de Grasse's fleet; was present (on the *Vaillant*) at the Battle of the Chesapeake Capes, 5 September 1781; returned with the fleet to the West Indies after Yorktown; was in the Battle of the Saints (on the *Northumberland*), April 1782; then went with Vaudreuil's fleet to Boston, and thence via the Caribbean to France, 1783. The journal includes the author's plans of the engagement off the Chesapeake Capes and of the Battle of the Saints. Tornquist ([3], p. 125) notes that upon their return to Brest at the end of June 1783 the Swedish officers were free to return to their country but that: "Before our departure each one of us individually had to be heard under oath by the deputies from the General Court-Martial, concerning the battles of Count de Grasse on the 9th and 12th of April [1782], and besides deliver signed extracts of our Journals." After his return to Sweden Tornquist submitted his diary to the *Orlogsmanna-Sälskap* (Naval Society) at Karlskrona, which sponsored its publication.

Tressan

See Delavergue du Tressan.

Vaudreuil, Louis de Rigaud, comte de (1728–1810)

Navy. Capitaine de vaisseau, *commanding the* Sceptre; chef d'escadre, *commanding the* Auguste (*after May 1782*)

1 "Notes de campagne du Comte Rigaud de Vaudreuil, 1781–1783," ed. Pierre Guiot, illustrated by Ph. Ledoux. Published in six installments in *Neptunia* (Amis du Musée de la Marine, Paris), 1957–1958: No. 45 (1st trimester, 1957), pp. 33–40; No. 46 (2nd trimester, 1957), pp. 35–42; No. 47 (3rd trimester, 1957), pp. 33–40; No. 48 (4th trimester, 1957), pp. 33–40; No. 49 (1st trimester, 1958), pp. 34–41; No. 50 (2nd trimester, 1958), pp. 29–35.

The Comte de Vaudreuil was a younger brother of the Marquis de Vaudreuil (1724–1802), also a naval officer. As related in his journal, the Comte de Vaudreuil, then commanding the *Sceptre*, left for the West Indies with de Grasse's fleet in March 1781 and accompanied it to the Chesapeake later that year. He subsequently took part in the Battle of the Saints (April 1782), after which he came to Boston (then commanding the *Auguste*) with the squadron commanded by his brother the Marquis—the squadron that was to transport Rochambeau's army back to France via the Caribbean. The *Auguste* spent the autumn of 1782 at Portsmouth, New Hampshire; she missed the rendezvous with the rest of the squadron off Cape Ann in December 1782 but later joined up with it at Puerto Cabello on 5 February 1783.

Vaugirauld (or Vaugiraud) de Rosnay, Pierre-René-Marie, comte de (1741–1819)

Navy. Capitaine de vaisseau; *"major" (flag captain) of de Grasse's fleet*

See above, *s.v.* Grasse (2) and Thy (1).

Verger, Jean-Baptiste-Antoine de (1762–1851)

Sublieutenant, Royal Deux-Ponts Regiment

1 "Journal of the Most Important Events that occurred to the French Troops under the Command of M. le Comte de Rochambeau," tr. and ed. Howard C. Rice, Jr., and Anne S.K. Brown from Verger's original manuscript in the Anne S.K. Brown Military Collection, Brown University, Providence, Rhode Island, in the present volume. The manuscript was acquired from H. P. Kraus, New York; cf. his catalogue No. 108, *The Illustrated Book*, item No. 82, pp. 61–63, Plates XLII and XLIII.

2 Mgr. Eugène Folletête, ed., "Un officier jurassien à la guerre de l'Indé-

pendance des Etats-Unis d'après le journal du lieutenant Jean-Bte.-Antoine de Verger de Delémont," in *Actes de la Société Jurassienne d'Emulation, Année 1943*, 2nd ser., XLVII (La Chaux-de-Fonds, 1944), 231–250. Selected passages from Verger's journal, preceded by a biographical sketch. These extracts were printed, not from the original manuscript, but from a nineteenth-century transcript of it.

In addition to the original manuscript, at least two transcripts of Verger's journal are extant: (1) one in the possession of Mrs. Jesse C. Johnson, Bethesda, Maryland, (2) the other in the Musée cantonal de Porrentruy, Switzerland. (1) Mrs. Johnson's copy was acquired by her father, Pierre-Joseph Frein (1869–1954, Professor of Romance Languages, University of Washington, Seattle), who purchased it in 1904 from Madame Marie Folletête, widow of Casimir Folletête (1833–1900), then residing at Saignelégier, near Porrentruy. According to Madame Folletête's extant correspondence with Professor Frein, the copy had been made by her late husband, but she did not then know who owned the original manuscript. Frein's interest in the Verger journal dated from his 1897 sojourn in the Swiss Jura region (the birthplace of his parents, who had emigrated to the United States in 1853), when he was preparing a dissertation on the local dialects for his Johns Hopkins Ph.D. The Johnson-Frein-Folletête transcript, consisting of 131 pages of text, is in a lined notebook, approx. 8¾ x 7 inches. It includes meticulous colored copies of Verger's drawings (but not his map of the Long Island engagement), which have been somewhat "improved" by the copyist (especially in facial features, anatomy of the horses, etc.). In some instances two figures appearing on separate pages in the original have been combined into a single group. (2) The transcript of the Verger journal now in the Musée de Porrentruy formerly belonged to Mgr. Eugène Folletête (died 1956, son of Casimir Folletête), who used it as the basis of his 1943 article in the *Actes de la Société Jurassienne d'Emulation* and who, like his father, was a collector of regional history. This copy, similar in content to Mrs. Johnson's copy, consists of 195 pages in a lined notebook. Both copies include, as a preface to the journal proper, Verger's curriculum vitae (through 1822), which appears to be based on notes compiled by Verger himself. This preface is not in the original manuscript.

Both transcripts appear to have been made from Verger's original manuscript journal (or possibly one from the other), which is said to have belonged at one time to Mlle Henriette Nouvion (1849–1938), who lived in Delémont. She was a niece of Ferdinand Nouvion (Verger's nephew and adopted son) and thus a grandniece of Verger. Mlle Nouvion, the last of her line in the Swiss Jura, had cousins in Bavaria. (The Editors are indebted to Mrs. Johnson and to Monsieur André Rais of Porrentruy for assistance in assembling the above information.)

Verton, Jacques-Philippe, baron de (1757–18?)

Lieutenant, Auxonne Regiment of artillery

1 Extracts from Verton's "Observations sur les 'Souvenirs et Anecdotes' de Monsieur le Comte de Ségur," written in 1826, are published as the first of "Deux Documents sur la Guerre d'Amérique," ed. Ludovic de Contenson, in *Revue d'Histoire Diplomatique*, XLIV, No. 1 (Jan.–March 1930), 20–24.

Verton's observations, in the form of a letter to the Comte de Ségur, were prompted by the publication of the latter's *Souvenirs*. Speaking of his own services in the American Revolution, Verton recalls (some forty-five years later) a conversation with Lord Cornwallis after the capitulation about the role of the French artillery in the Siege of Yorktown. He also recalls the shelling of two British frigates off Tarrytown on the Hudson in July 1781.

Viella, Louis-Henry de Labay, comte de (1764–1840)

Navy. Enseigne de vaisseau

1 A typewritten transcript of Viella's journal (made in 1936 from the manuscript original then in the possession of a descendant, A. de La Baume-Pluvinel) is in the Bibliothèque Historique de la Marine, Paris, MS No. 147.

Viella, then an ensign, served on the *Couronne* in de Grasse's fleet and later on the *Triomphant*, as *sous-aide-major* under the Marquis de Vaudreuil. He took part in the Battle of the Saints (April 1782). According to the description in J. P. Busson, *Supplément au Catalogue des Manuscrits [de la Bibliothèque Historique de la Marine]* (Paris, 1964), p. 8, Viella's journal, though compiled in 1807, is chiefly a narration of his campaigns during the American War of Independence. Cf. Contenson, *Cincinnati*, p. 278.

Villebresme, Thomas-Jacques de Goislard, chevalier de (1755–1849)

Volunteer naval officer, with La Clocheterie on the Jason

1 *Souvenirs du Chevalier de Villebresme, Mousquetaire de la Garde du Roi, 1772–1816, Guerre d'Amérique, Emigration*, ed. Vicomte Maurice de Villebresme (Paris and Nancy, Berger-Levrault, 1897). The "Souvenirs du Chevalier de Villebresme" were also published in *Carnet de La Sabretache*, IV (1896), 177–194, 256–264, 313–325, 395–400, 422–438, 543–549; but, except for the account of the Siege of Yorktown, Villebresme's memoirs of the American war were omitted in this serial publication. Excerpts from Villebresme's *Souvenirs*, translated by Henry J. Yeager, appear under the title "The French Fleet at Newport, 1780–1781," in *Rhode Island History*, XXX, No. 3 (Aug. 1971), 86–93; the "Plan de Rhode-Island" reproduced as an illustration to this article is not, as stated in the caption, a "French map of 1781," but rather a map intended to show the positions of d'Estaing's fleet in August 1778.

Villebresme's lively memoirs were written towards the end of his long life, using earlier notes. He served as a "mousquetaire de la Garde du Roi" until this unit was abolished in 1775. As a volunteer naval officer he left for America with Ternay's fleet in May 1780 on board the *Jason* commanded by M. de La Clocheterie. His account covers the transatlantic crossing, arrival and sojourn in Rhode Island, and the Destouches Chesapeake expedition of March 1781, in which he participated. In August 1781, still on the

Jason, he went from Newport to Virginia with Barras's squadron. After landing the artillery, he was permitted by the Baron de Vioménil to serve in the Siege of Yorktown with the Gâtinais Regiment, under the Baron de l'Estrade. When the British staged their raid on the French batteries, Villebresme was caught barefoot, since his valet had taken his boots off to dry, and he was wounded by stepping in his stocking feet on an abandoned bayonet. After the surrender he accompanied Vioménil to Yorktown and attended the dinner given Cornwallis by the French officers. An incurable royalist, he retrospectively chides Lafayette for "demeaning himself to copy the democratic ways of the Americans." After the siege Villebresme went to the West Indies with de Grasse's fleet, was present at the Battle of the Saints in April 1782, came to Boston with the Marquis de Vaudreuil, and returned to France via the Caribbean in 1783. Although he made the trip from Puerto Cabello to Caracas, Villebresme devotes only a few lines to it, since he had retained "such a bad memory" of this "dreadful country." Because of a similarity of names, *Villebresme* is sometimes confused with the Chevalier de *La Villebrune* (also spelled Villèsbrunne), *capitaine de vaisseau*, naval officer with Ternay's fleet in Rhode Island, commander of the captured English frigate *Romulus*, etc., who went to Virginia with Barras's squadron, convoyed troops down Chesapeake Bay from Annapolis, etc. See Contenson, *Cincinnati*, p. 211 (La Villèsbrunne), p. 278 (Villebresme).

Vioménil, Antoine Charles du Houx, baron de (1728–1792)

Lieutenant general, second in command of Rochambeau's army; assumed top command in December 1782, upon Rochambeau's departure for France

1 Apparently Vioménil left no journal of his American campaigns, and very few of his reports or letters have survived. By way of memorandum it may be noted that several of his scattered letters relating to America have been gathered into the Appendix of Roger de Montmort, *Antoine Charles du Houx, Baron de Vioménil*, tr. John Francis Gough (Baltimore, The Johns Hopkins Press for the Institut Français de Washington, 1935), pp. 41–59.

In view of Vioménil's high rank in Rochambeau's army it is regrettable that his own written record of the American expedition is so scanty. He seems to have been an "old campaigner," little given to putting his thoughts on paper. The Baron should not be confused with his younger brother, also a general on Rochambeau's staff: Charles-Joseph Hyacinthe, Comte (later Marquis) de Vioménil (1734–1827). See the next item. A third member of the family, the Baron's son Charles-Gabriel du Houx, chevalier de Vioménil (1767–1831?), served as an aide-de-camp to his father during the war in America. The Baron died on 31 October 1792 as a result of wounds received when defending the royal family at the Tuileries on 10 August.

Vioménil, Charles-Joseph-Hyacinthe, comte (later marquis) de (1734–1827)

1 "Armée de Rochambeau. Livre d'ordre contenant ceux donnés depuis le débarquement des Troupes à Newport, en Amérique Septentrionale, 1780." This manuscript volume containing 299 pages of writing, said to be in the hand of the Comte de Vioménil, is in the Archives Départemen-

Major general (maréchal de camp), *ranking third in the hierarchy of Rochambeau's army*

tales de Meurthe-et-Moselle, Nancy, E 235. It includes the Orders of the Day for Rochambeau's army, beginning with the landing at Newport, Rhode Island, in July 1780, and extending through 17 August 1781 (camp at Philipsburg, New York, before the march to Virginia).

Although this is obviously not a personal journal, it is listed here because of its great importance as the official day-by-day record of Rochambeau's army for the period covered. It has apparently been little used by previous historians; we owe our knowledge of it to Warrington Dawson's reference in his *Les Français Morts pour l'Indépendance Américaine . . . et la Reconstruction historique de Williamsburg* (Paris: Editions de l'Oeuvre Latine, 1931), pp. 91–92. A microfilm copy was obtained through the courtesy of M. Pierre Gérard, Directeur des Services d'Archives de Meurthe-et-Moselle.

The Editors have located no comparable document in the Archives de la Guerre, nor have they found (with the exception of the General Staff journal of the Siege of Yorktown) any sequel continuing the daily orders for the rest of Rochambeau's American campaigns. The presence of this volume in the departmental archives at Nancy can probably be explained by the fact that the Vioménils were a Lorraine family. The Comte de Vioménil apparently had the *Livre d'ordre* among his personal papers, which were scattered or confiscated when he was an émigré during the French Revolution.

2 "Relation de ma vie militaire." Manuscript belonging to the late Comte de Hennezel d'Ormois. Mentioned in the bibliography of Vicomte Grouvel, *Les Corps de troupe de l'Emigration française, 1789–1815*, 3 vols., (Paris, Editions de La Sabretache, 1957–1964), III, 401. Not having seen this manuscript, the Editors cannot say whether or not it contains an account of Vioménil's campaigns in America.

Von Closen

See Closen.

Yorktown, Siege of

1 For the official record of the siege compiled by the General Staff—the so-called Etat-Major journal—see above, *s.v.* Gallatin, Ménonville.
2 For the official record compiled by the Engineer Corps—the so-called Engineers' journal—see above, *s.v.* Crublier d'Opterre, Engineers, Querenet de La Combe.

Many of the officers incorporated or paraphrased one or the other of these official accounts in their own journals. Among the few strictly personal records of the siege operations are those of Clermont-Crèvecœur and Deux-Ponts.

*Major, then lieutenant
colonel, Continental Army;
brigadier general in the
North Carolina militia*

Manuscripts in European Archives relating to America, 25 vols. (London, 1889–1898), Vol. VI, No. 608. An abridged version, from the same source, is in Doniol, III, 215–222. It was also published by Ludovic de Contenson in *Revue d'Histoire Diplomatique*, XXVII (1913), 528–539.

Dubuysson served from 1777 to 1780. He was one of Lafayette's fellow passengers on the *Victoire*. He also served as aide-de-camp to Baron de Kalb and was wounded at the Battle of Camden, South Carolina, 16 August 1780.

Duponceau, Pierre-Etienne (1760–1844)

*Captain, later major,
Continental Army;
aide-de-camp and secretary
to Baron von Steuben*

1 "The Autobiography of Peter Stephen Duponceau," ed. James L. Whitehead, in the *Pennsylvania Magazine of History and Biography*, LXIII, Nos. 2–4 (April, July, Oct., 1939), 189–227, 311–343, 432–461, and LXIV, Nos. 1–2 (Jan., April, 1940), 97–120, 243–269. Four of these autobiographical letters were published earlier, *ibid.*, XL (1916), 172–186.

Duponceau's "autobiography" is contained in a series of informal letters written towards the end of his life at the instigation of Robert Walsh and of his granddaughter, Anne L. Garesché. They concern chiefly his early life in France and his first years in America, 1777–1783. Duponceau became acquainted with Baron von Steuben in Paris at the house of Beaumarchais. He accompanied the Baron to America as an English-speaking secretary and aide-de-camp, landing at Portsmouth, New Hampshire, in December 1777. They proceeded to Boston, then to York, Pennsylvania, where Duponceau was brevetted a captain in the Continental Army. He spent the winter of 1778 at Valley Forge, where he aided Baron von Steuben in the preparation of the latter's *Regulations for the Order and Discipline of the Troops of the United States* (Philadelphia, 1779). In the spring of 1781 he was in Virginia but returned north to Philadelphia because of ill health. That autumn he was employed by Livingston as a secretary in the foreign department of the United States. Duponceau henceforth made his permanent home in the United States, becoming a distinguished citizen of Philadelphia, lawyer, and scholar (notably in the field of philology); he was President of the American Philosophical Society from 1827 until his death in 1844.

2 A manuscript diary of Duponceau, covering his first months in America, 1777–1778, is in the Historical Society of Delaware, Wilmington. It includes diagrammatic plans of the encampment at Valley Forge.

Duportail, Louis Le Bègue de Presle (1743–1802)

*Brigadier general (major
general after Yorktown),
commanding the Engineer
Corps, Continental Army*

1 Elizabeth S. Kite, *Brigadier-General Louis Lebègue Duportail, Commandant of Engineers in the Continental Army, 1777–1783* (Baltimore, The Johns Hopkins Press for the Institut Français de Washington, 1933). Contains numerous somewhat haphazardly edited letters by Duportail and related documents, chiefly from the Washington Papers and the Papers of the Continental Congress. Miss Kite's compilation also includes material on other French engineers in the American service: Gouvion, Laumoy, La Radière, Béchet de La Rochefontaine, Villefranche, Cambray, L'Enfant, et al.

Duportail was an important figure in the American army and played a crucial role in the campaign of 1781. He was taken prisoner at the Siege of Charleston in May 1780 but was exchanged and resumed his command of the American engineers in March 1781. He participated in the allied staff conferences preparatory to the Siege of Yorktown, where he shared the command of the allied engineers with Querenet de La Combe, who represented the French armies of Rochambeau and Saint-Simon. Actually the other "American" engineers (Gouvion and Rochefontaine) were also French. Duportail later became minister of war in France from October 1790 to December 1791. In 1794 he emigrated to the United States, where he acquired a farm in Pennsylvania near the old Valley Forge camp. After several years as an American farmer Duportail died on his return voyage to France in 1802.

For a fragmentary manuscript journal in the Archives de la Guerre, erroneously attributed to Duportail, see above, *s.v.* Capellis.

Durousseau de Fayolle, Pierre (1746–1780)

1 "Journal d'une campagne en Amérique (1777–1779)," ed. M. le général L. Segretain, in Société des Antiquaires de l'Ouest (Poitiers), *Bulletin et Mémoires*, 2nd ser., xxv (1902), 1–48.

Durousseau de Fayolle went to America with Lafayette on the *Victoire* in 1777. His commission as lieutenant colonel in the American army was not confirmed by the Continental Congress. He returned to France in 1779 but came back to America on the *Hermione* the following year. He died shortly after his arrival in Boston.

Fleury (or Teissèdre de Fleury), François-Louis (b. 1749)

Captain, major, later lieutenant colonel, Continental Army; major, Saintonge Regiment, Rochambeau's army

1 "Journal of the Siege of Fort Mifflin," in Worthington Chauncey Ford, ed., *Defences of Philadelphia in 1777* (Brooklyn, N.Y., 1897); reprinted from the *Pennsylvania Magazine of History and Biography*, xviii–xxi (1894–1897), pp. 74–76, 80–81, 97–99, 106–108, 123–125. Ford prints only the latter installments of the journal. The manuscript in John Laurens's hand (presumably translated by him) is in the Library of Congress, Washington Papers (microfilm edition, Reels 41–42). Maps by Fleury (including several drawn during the Siege of Fort Mifflin) are listed and described by Peter J. Guthorn in his *American Maps and Map Makers of the Revolution* (Monmouth Beach, N.J., 1966), pp. 22–23.

Fleury's journal of the Siege of Fort Mifflin (Mud Island), where he served as engineer and was wounded, covers the period 15 October–14 November 1777. It is an exceptionally vivid and moving account—far more than a routine report. In recognition of his brilliant services he was promoted by Congress to the rank of lieutenant colonel (26 November 1777). Fleury later served in the Rhode Island campaign (1778) and at Stony Point (1779), for which latter service he was awarded a special medal by the Continental Congress. He returned to France on furlough in 1779 but came back to America in 1780 with Rochambeau's army as a major in the Saintonge Regiment (while retaining his higher rank of lieutenant colonel in the Continental Army, from which he was technically on leave). Fleury thus participated in the Yorktown campaign with the French. In October 1782, when it was feared that British naval forces might attempt an attack on Portsmouth, New Hampshire, Fleury was sent there with a detachment of French troops drawn from the "Island" regiments garrisoning the ships of Vaudreuil's squadron at Boston.

Kermorvan

See Barazer de Kermorvan.

Lafayette, Marie-Joseph-Paul-Roch-Yves-Gilbert de Motier, marquis de (1757–1834)

Major general, Continental Army

1 *Mémoires, correspondance et manuscrits du général La Fayette, publiés par sa famille*, ed. F. de Corcelle, with preface by G. W. La Fayette, 6 vols. (Paris, H. Fournier l'aîné, 1837–1838).
2 *Memoirs, correspondence and manuscripts of General Lafayette, published by his family*, 3 vols. (London, Saunders and Ottley, 1837).

Although Lafayette (or La Fayette, as the name was frequently written in the eighteenth century) belonged to the American army, his importance as an intermediary between the Americans and Rochambeau's French army is obvious. In addition to the posthumously published *Mémoires*, an extensive body of his correspondence for the period of the American Revolution is extant. Much of this has been printed in scattered publications. For a detailed recording of these letters, see Stuart W. Jackson, *La Fayette, A Bibliography* (New York, W. E. Rudge, 1930); Monaghan; and especially the bibliographical notes and critical discussion of sources following each chapter in Louis Gottschalk's series: (1) *Lafayette Comes to America* (Chicago, 1935; second impression with corrections, 1965); (2) *Lafayette Joins the American Army* (Chicago, 1937); (3) *Lafayette and the Close of the American Revolution* (Chicago, 1942); (4) *Lafayette between the American and the French Revolution, 1783–1789* (Chicago, 1950); (5) *Lafayette in the French Revolution, Through the October Days* (Chicago, 1969). The originals of Lafayette's letters to Rochambeau are in the Library of Paul Mellon, Upperville, Virginia. A substantial part of Lafayette's papers, formerly at the Château de Chavaniac, is now in the Library of Cornell University; another part is at the Château de La Grange. Various items in French archives and in private collections are recorded in the catalogue (compiled by André Girodie) of the "Exposition du Centenaire [de la mort] de La Fayette," held in the Musée de l'Orangerie, Paris, 1934, and in the catalogue of the exhibition, "La Fayette," commemorating the bicentenary of his birth, Hôtel de Rohan, Archives Nationales, Paris, 1957.

Landais, Pierre (1734–18? [after 1820])

Captain, Continental Navy, commanding the frigate Alliance

1 *Memorial, to justify Peter Landaï's Conduct during the Late War* (Boston, Peter Edes, 1784). *The Second Part of the Memorial to justify Peter Landaï's Conduct, during the Late War* (New York, Samuel Loudon, [1785]). Illustrated with battle charts.

Landais, a veteran French naval officer who had sailed around the world with Bougainville in 1767–1769, was commissioned captain in the Continental Navy in 1777. A mutiny aboard his ship *Alliance* resulted in a court-martial held in Boston harbor in 1781, whereby he was separated from the service. Still earlier Landais had quarreled with John Paul Jones at the time of the engagement between the *Bonhomme Richard* and *Serapis* in 1779. "The Landais book," according to Lawrence C. Wroth (John Carter Brown Library, *Annual Report for 1953-1954*, pp. 29-34), "is a bitter, unhappy story, a full-length exposition of a tragedy of personality. In addition to its specific interest in naval history, the first part is an element in the story of Franklin in France; the second part is another chapter in the story of our earliest diplomatic mission, the Deane-Franklin-Lee controversy." Landais resumed service in the French navy; his activities during the French Revolution are summarized in Six, *Dict. Biog.*, II, 51. He spent the later years of his life in the United States, where he died some time after 1820. An autograph letter written 9 December 1805 to the Massachusetts Congressman Samuel Holten, which was added by a collector to the Princeton University Library's copy of Landais's *Memorial*, indicates that he was at that date still pursuing his claim for prize money due him from the time of the American Revolution. Moré de Pontgibaud's *Mémoires* (see below) include mention of his encounters with Landais.

La Rouërie, Charles-Armand Tuffin, marquis de (1750-1793)

Colonel of Continental Partisan Legion; brigadier general, Continental Army (1783)

1 "Letters of Col. Armand (Marquis de la Rouërie), 1777-1791," in New-York Historical Society, *Collections*, XI (1878), 287-396. Consists mainly of "Colonel Armand's" letters (in his own brand of English) to General Washington.

For an informed discussion of his role, see John H. Stutesman, Jr., "Colonel Armand and Washington's Cavalry," *The New-York Historical Society Quarterly*, XLV, No. 1 (Jan. 1961), 4-42. Concerning the subsequent career of this Breton nobleman, see G. Lenôtre, *Le Marquis de La Rouërie et la Conjuration bretonne* (Paris, 1899, and later editions); Yvon Bizardel, *Les Americains à Paris pendant la Révolution* (Paris, 1972).

[De Lisle]

1 "Letters to his friends in France," in *The New-Jersey Gazette* (printed by Isaac Collins, Burlington, later Trenton, N.J.), I, No. 5 (31 Dec. 1777), No. 6 (7 Jan. 1778), No. 7 (14 Jan. 1778), No. 17 (25 March 1778). The letters are dated respectively: Fishkill, N.Y., 20 November 1777; Morristown, N.J., 9 June 1777; Reading, Penna., 28 November 1777; and Reading, 10 December 1777. The third letter only (Reading, 28 November) is reprinted in the *Pennsylvania Magazine of History and Biography*, XXXV (1911), 365-368, under the title "A Frenchman's Comments on the Discipline of the American and British Armies in 1777."

The first of these letters is prefaced by the following note to the printer of the *Gazette*, signed "H.P.": "A French Gentleman has lately favoured me with a sight of a collection of *historical* and *political Letters* to his friends in France. I have obtained his consent to translate and publish a few of them. If the following translation of one of them, which is of a modern date, should prove acceptable to your readers, I shall send you some more.

The author of them has been near two years in America, and has been introduced to the first characters on the Continent. His real name must be a secret—The name by which he has chosen to be known to the public, will be seen in the conclusion of the enclosed letter."

The letters, addressed to "My dear Count," are signed "De Lisle." The general tenure of this "French Gentleman's" letters, as well as the fluent English style (which does not sound like a translation), suggest that they may have been propaganda pieces designed to prepare public opinion for the French alliance. It may also be noted that a former artillery officer living in the French West Indies, Charles-Noël-François Roman(d) de l'Isle (born in Grenoble, 1743), came to the United States in 1776 and obtained a commission as major of artillery in the Continental Army. Cf. Lasseray, I, 86, and II, 395–398, 638.

1 Two letters from Mauduit to Mrs. Mary Willing Byrd of Westover (26 January 1782, 21 December 1782) are included in "Letters of the Byrd Family, II," *Virginia Magazine of History and Biography*, 2nd ser., XXXVIII, No. 1 (Jan. 1930), 56–59.

Mauduit du Plessis, Thomas-Antoine, chevalier de (1753–1791)

Captain of artillery, lieutenant colonel, Continental Army; later in Rochambeau's army as senior adjutant of the artillery park

The Chevalier de Mauduit (or Duplessis-Mauduit) distinguished himself at Brandywine, Germantown, Red Bank, and Monmouth. He went back to France with Lafayette in 1779 but returned to America with Rochambeau's army in 1780, remaining with it until the return to France in 1783. Although he apparently kept no journal himself, Mauduit is frequently mentioned in other officers' journals (see, e.g., Berthier's journal in this volume). Since relatively few examples of Mauduit's own writings have survived, the above letters, written in appealing English, are recorded here. They indicate, among other things, that Mauduit had been charmed by Mrs. Byrd's hospitality and that of her daughters. Mauduit's tragic death in the French colony of Saint-Domingue in 1791 is the subject of a one-act play by B. J. Marsollier des Vivetières: *La Mort du Colonel Mauduit, ou les Anarchistes au Port-au-Prince* (Paris, Cailleau, An VIII [1799]). According to the author, the play, based on a report made to the Legislative Assembly, was composed in 1792, but circumstances prevented its performance and delayed its publication. A tribute to Mauduit by Tousard, a brother officer, entitled *Aux Mânes du Colonel Mauduit*, was printed in 1791. A copy of this rare leaflet is preserved among the books of Thomas Jefferson; cf. Millicent Sowerby, comp., *Catalogue of the Library of Thomas Jefferson*, 5 vols. (Washington, 1952–1959), No. 2594. Anne-Louis de Tousard (1749–1817), who also served in the Continental Army, later returned to the United States, where he published *The American Artillerist's Companion, or Elements of Artillery*, 3 vols. (Philadelphia, 1807–1813).

[Maussion de la Bastie, Gaston-Marie-Léonard]

1 *They knew the Washingtons, Letters from a French Soldier with Lafayette and from His Family in Virginia*, tr. Princess Radziwill (Indianapolis, Bobbs-Merrill, 1926). Publishers' Note: "Historical authorities who

read these letters may differ as to their authenticity. But . . . we think they are worthy of publication if only for their literary merit." The letters had previously appeared serially in *Collier's Weekly*, 1925.

The letters are fictitious and are recorded here only as a caveat to unsuspecting readers. Princess Radziwill (Catherine Radziwill, *née* Rzewuska, 1858–1941) is also the author of the additional "Maussion" letters published in the *Century Magazine*, CXII (1926), 271–278, under the title "Washington and Lafayette, contemporary letters throw fresh light on two great men." At about this same time "Princess Razzledazzle" foisted upon the world a series of "hitherto unpublished" letters purporting to have been written by her aunt Eva Hanska to the latter's brother Count Adam Rzewuski, in which Mme Hanska discusses her love affair with the French novelist Honoré de Balzac, whom she eventually married. These letters, which had first appeared in the *Revue Hebdomadaire* (20 December 1924) and in *The Forum* (January–February 1925), under the title "New Light on Balzac's Marriage," are also appended to the Princess's French translation of Juanita Helm Floyd, *Les Femmes dans la Vie de Balzac* (Paris, Plon, 1926). Earlier in the century Princess Radziwill had forged checks under the signature of Cecil Rhodes. In his biography of Balzac, André Maurois aptly characterizes Princess Radziwill as a "mythomaniac."

Moré de Pontgibaud, Charles-Albert de (1758–1837)

Aide-de-camp to Lafayette; major, Continental Army

1 *Mémoires du comte de M . . . précédés de cinq lettres de considérations sur les Mémoires particulières* (Paris, Victor Thiercelin [printed by H. Balzac], 1827).
2 *Mémoires du Comte de Moré (1758–1837)*, published for the Société d'Histoire Contemporaine by Geoffroy de Grandmaison and the Comte de Pontgibaud (Paris, Picard, 1898).
3 *A French Volunteer of the War of Independence (the Chevalier de Pontgibaud)*, tr. and ed. Robert B. Douglas (Paris, Carrington, 1897, and several subsequent reprintings).

Moré de Pontgibaud left France in 1777 and joined the American army at Valley Forge, where he became an aide to Lafayette and received his commission as major in the Continental Army. He accompanied Lafayette back to France late in 1778, returned to America in 1780, and participated in the Siege of Yorktown with the Americans, in whose service he remained until 1783. Moré's entertaining memoirs are not always reliable in respect to dates. He came back to the United States as an émigré during the French Revolution.

Preudhomme de Borre, Philippe-Hubert, chevalier de (b. 1717)

Brigadier general, Continental Army

1 "Journal des campagnes de 1777 et 1778 au service des colonies unies de l'Amérique." This unpublished 35-page manuscript, written and signed by "Le Ch^er De Preudhomme De Borre Brigadier Des Armées du Roy," is in the Archives de la Guerre, Mémoires Historiques, 248, pièce 17. The first part of the journal is factual and precise; the latter portions are somewhat padded out with newspaper extracts and other secondary material.

Preudhomme de Borre ("General de Borre," as he was usually called in America) reached Portsmouth, New Hampshire, on 17 March 1777, proceeding via Boston to headquarters at Morristown, New Jersey, where he received his brevet as brigadier general on 7 May. He was assigned to the command of the Second Brigade in General John Sullivan's division. His brigade, of which he took command at Princeton on 21 May, included the Second, Fourth, and Seventh Maryland regiments, as well as Baron d'Arendt's "German Battalion." De Borre was in New Jersey during the early summer of 1777 and later at the Battle of Brandywine. By a Congressional resolution of 13 September he was recalled from the army pending an investigation of his conduct. He thereupon resigned his command but remained in America for another year or more. He sailed from Charleston, South Carolina on 20 January 1779 and eventually reached Brest (via the West Indies) on 5 July. This sixty-year-old officer was evidently one of those who had difficulties in adapting themselves to American conditions. His brief career in the Continental Army can also be traced in the *Writings of GW*, Vols. VIII and IX.

Unidentified officer

Came to America in 1777, expecting a commission that was not confirmed

1 "Letters of a French Officer, written at Easton, Penna., in 1777–1778," tr. Albert J. Edmunds, in the *Pennsylvania Magazine of History and Biography*, XXXV (1911), 90–102. "The . . . letters never reached their destination. They were forwarded via Boston, and the vessel carrying the mail for France was captured by a British cruiser. They were recently found, partially mutilated, among the prize papers in the records of the High Court of Admiralty, London."

The writer of these letters (dated from Easton, October 1777–January 1778) had arrived in America during the spring or summer of 1777 with others who had been led to expect employment in the Continental Army. But, in his eyes at least, Congress was guilty of "bad faith" in not honoring the agreements made by their representative in Paris, Silas Deane. Several of the disappointed aspirants had made one of their number an agent to plead their case with Congress. "You are going to ask me what I am doing at Easton. . . . The Congress is at York, behind the great and famous river Susquehanna, which forms the head of Chesapeake Bay. We have there a good many of our men and the one who is commissioned to ask for our compensation, etc. When we get news, some one will come and bring it to me here. I shall go and carry it to another man further off, and so on to Boston, which is our rallying place . . ." (letter of 23 October 1777). It appears from the last of the letters that the writer, though receiving "damages" of 2,067 *livres* from Congress, decided to put aside his uniform and engage in trade: "I am speculating and speculating well."

The letters provide an interesting case history, which can be better appreciated if read in the context of two other documents summarized by Lasseray (I, 80–109): "Etat des officiers et autres Français qui sont venus en Amérique pour y servir, tant avant le traité d'Alliance que depuis"

(Archives du Ministère des Affaires Etrangères, Mémoires et Documents, Etats-Unis, Vol. I, foll. 132–135); and "Compte-rendu à MM. les députés de l'honorable Congrès des Etats-Unis d'Amérique par M. du Coudray," the lengthy memorial submitted to the Continental Congress by Tronson du Coudray in June 1777 (*ibid.*, foll. 136ff.). Congress's long drawn-out action on the memorial, its referral and re-referral to committees, can be traced in the *Journals of the Continental Congress* for 1777, ed. Ford, Hunt, et al., Vols. VIII and IX.

Suggested identity of the author of the letters written from Easton: Louis de Récicourt de Ganot (b. 1752), a wayward second lieutenant of artillery. Cf. Lasseray, I, 81, 95, 108, and II, 388.

Villefranche, Jean-Louis-Ambroise de Genton, chevalier de (1747–1784)

Captain of engineers, major, later lieutenant colonel, Continental Army

1 No journal of Villefranche is known, but several of his maps and drawings are extant. Cf. Peter J. Guthorn, *American Maps and Map Makers of the Revolution* (Monmouth Beach, N.J., 1966), pp. 35–36; Hubertis M. Cummings, "The Villefranche Map for the Defence of the Delaware," in the *Pennsylvania Magazine of History and Biography*, LXXXIV, No. 4 (Oct. 1960), 424–434; and Cummings, "Draughts by Two of George Washington's French Engineers," in *Internal Affairs* (Monthly Bulletin, Commonwealth of Pennsylvania, Department of Internal Affairs), XXVIII, Nos. 1–2 (Jan.–Feb. 1960), 24–28. Villefranche's map of West Point (1780) and his design for the "arbor" built there for the celebration on 31 May 1782 of the birth of the Dauphin are reproduced (the latter in color) in Edward C. Boynton, *History of West Point* (New York, 1864), facing pp. 87, 161.

Recapitulation

Authors of the journals, listed alphabetically in the above Checklist, are here regrouped according to their places in the French military organization.

ARMY

ROCHAMBEAU'S ARMY

Staff:

Rochambeau
   Aides: Closen, Cromot Dubourg, Dubouchet, Dumas, Fersen, Lauberdière, Menonville, Rochambeau (vicomte de)

Vioménil (baron de)
   Aide: Brisout de Barneville
Vioménil (comte de)
   Aide: Ollonne
Chastellux
   Aide: Montesquieu
Blanchard, *chief commissary*
Coste, *chief physician*
Berthier, *assistant quartermaster-general*
Mauduit du Plessis, *adjutant, artillery park*
   (cf. French Officers in American Service)

Bourbonnais Regiment:	Coriolis, Losse de Bayac, Rochambeau (vicomte de)
Royal Deux-Ponts Regiment:	Closen, Deux-Ponts (comte Guillaume de), Fersen (1782), Gallatin, Schwerin, Verger
Soissonnais Regiment:	Berthier, Miollis, Robin (chaplain), Ségur (1782), Soissonnais Regiment (unidentified officer)
Saintonge Regiment:	Broglie (1782), Charlus, Custine, Delavergue du Tressan, Fleury (cf. French Officers in American Service), Rosel, Saint-Cyr
Lauzun Legion (Volontaires étrangers de Lauzun):	Lauzun
Auxonne Regiment, Corps royal d'artillerie:	Clermont-Crèvecœur, Verton
Engineers, Corps royal du Génie:	Crublier d'Opterre, Desandroüins, Engineers' journal, Engineer (anonymous), Querenet de La Combe

SAINT-SIMON'S ARMY
   (brought from West Indies
   to Yorktown by de Grasse's
   fleet, 1781)

Staff:	Saint-Simon

Agenois Regiment:	Cadignan
Corps royal du Génie:	Ancteville

SHIPS' GARRISONS
(with de Grasse's fleet,
Yorktown, 1781)

Angoumois Regiment:	Soret de Boisbrunet
Grenadiers de la Marine Royale:	Pouzoullette
Régiment d'Infanterie de Monsieur:	Revel du Perron
La Sarre-Infanterie Regiment:	Saint-Exupéry

NAVY

D'ESTAING'S FLEET (1778–1779, including Siege of Savannah)	D'Estaing, anonymous officers in d'Estaing's fleet, Bougainville, Cambis, Costebelle, Du Petit-Thouars, La Pérouse, Meyronnet de Saint-Marc, Romain, Saint-Laurent
Army officers under d'Estaing:	Magallon de La Morlière, Stedingk
Ships' garrisons:	*Agenois Regiment*: Cadignan, Séguier de Terson
	Armagnac Regiment: Tarragon
Engineers:	O'Connor

TERNAY'S FLEET
(transported Rochambeau's
army to Rhode Island,
1780–1781)

Ternay, Beauvoir, Capellis, Colbert de Maulevrier, Costebelle, Destouches, Granchain, Villebresme

DE GRASSE'S FLEET
(Chesapeake campaign and
West Indies, 1781–1782)

De Grasse, anonymous officer in de Grasse's fleet, Bougainville, Goussencourt, Jennet, Naval officer (unidentified), Thy, Tornquist, Vaudreuil (comte de), Viella

VAUDREUIL'S FLEET
(transported Rochambeau's
army back to France via
West Indies, 1782–1783)

Du Petit-Thouars, Thy, Tornquist, Vaudreuil (comte de), Villebresme

LA PEROUSE EXPEDITION
TO HUDSON BAY, 1782

Lannoy, La Pérouse

FRENCH OFFICERS IN AMERICAN SERVICE

Listed in separate alphabetical sequence above

Balch——Thomas Balch, *The French in America during the War of Independence of the United States, 1777–1783*, 2 vols. (Philadelphia, Porter and Coates, 1891, 1895). The second volume is a concise biographical dictionary alphabetically arranged.

Bouvet, *Service de santé*——Maurice Bouvet, *Le Service de santé français pendant la Guerre d'Indépendance des Etats-Unis (1777–1782)* (Paris, Hippocrate, 1934).

Clinton, *Narrative*——William B. Willcox, ed., *The American Rebellion, Sir Henry Clinton's Narrative of His Campaigns, 1775–1782, with an Appendix of Original Documents* (New Haven, Yale University Press, 1954).

Colles, *Survey*——Christopher Colles, *A Survey of the Roads of the United States of America*, [New York,] *1789*, ed. Walter W. Ristow (Cambridge, Harvard University Press, 1961).

Les Combattants——Ministère des Affaires Etrangères, comp., *Les Combattants Français de la Guerre Américaine, 1778–1783. Listes établies d'après les documents authentiques déposés aux Archives Nationales et aux Archives de la Guerre* (Paris, Quantin, 1903). This is the best available (though not always reliable) roster, by regiments and ships, of both officers and enlisted personnel who participated in the American campaigns. The volume was reprinted (Washington, 1905), with an index and translation of prefatory matter, as Senate Document No. 77, 58th Congress, 2nd Session.

Contenson, *Cincinnati*——Ludovic de Contenson, *La Société des Cincinnati de France et la Guerre d'Amérique, 1778–1783, ouvrage orné de 193 portraits* (Paris, Picard, 1934). This is a biographical dictionary limited to officers who were members of the Society of the Cincinnati.

Crofut, *Guide*——Florence S. M. Crofut, *Guide to the History and the Historic Sites of Connecticut*, 2 vols. (New Haven, Yale University Press, 1937).

The first volume includes (pp. 69–78) "March of the Count de Rochambeau and the French Army in Connecticut."

Dawson, *Français Morts aux Etats-Unis*——Warrington Dawson, *Les 2112 Français Morts aux Etats-Unis de 1777 à 1783 en combattant pour l'Indépendance Américaine* (Paris, 1936). Reprinted from *Journal de la Société des Américanistes*, n.s., XXVIII (1936). This is a careful compilation based both on official records and family archives and arranged by regiments or ships, but it does not include those who died during the Caribbean campaign of 1783. This was preceded by another publication by Dawson, his *Les Français Morts pour l'Indépendance Américaine de Septembre 1781 à Août 1782, et la Reconstruction historique de Williamsburg* (Paris, Editions de l'Oeuvre Latine, 1931), which includes only the list of those who died in Virginia.

Doniol——Henri Doniol, *Histoire de la participation de la France à l'etablissement des Etats-Unis d'Amérique, Correspondance diplomatique et Documents*, 5 vols. (Paris, Imprimerie Nationale, 1886–1892) and Supplement (1899).

Etat militaire——*Etat militaire de France pour l'année . . .* (Paris). The official annual army directory listing names of officers by regiments and including other information about the military establishment.

Forbes and Cadman——Allan Forbes and Paul F. Cadman, *France and New England*, 3 vols. (Boston, State Street Trust Company, 1925, 1927, 1929). The first volume includes a section on "The Marches and Camp Sites of the French Army in New England." Supplementing this is Forbes's article, "Marches and Camp Sites of the French Army Beyond New England during the Revolutionary War," in Massachusetts Historical Society, *Proceedings*, LXVII (1945), 152–167.

Freeman, *Washington*——Douglas S. Freeman, *George*

Washington, A Biography, 7 vols. (New York, Scribner, 1948–1957).

Johnston, *Yorktown Campaign*——Henry P. Johnston, *The Yorktown Campaign and the Surrender of Cornwallis, 1781* (New York, Harper, 1881; reprint, Eastern National Park and Monument Association, 1958).

Lasseray——André Lasseray, *Les Français sous les Treize Etoiles (1775–1783)*, 2 vols. (Macon, Protat, 1935). This work contains biographical sketches of the French volunteers who served in the American army (but *not* the French officers who came with the French army or navy to America, for which see Balch or Contenson).

Mahan, *Operations of the Navies*——Alfred Thayer Mahan, *The Major Operations of the Navies in the War of American Independence* (Boston, 1913). With maps and battle plans.

Monaghan——Frank Monaghan, *French Travellers in the United States, 1765–1932, A Bibliography* (New York Public Library, 1933).

Noailles, *Marins et Soldats*——Vicomte de Noailles, *Marins et Soldats français en Amérique pendant la Guerre de l'Indépendance des Etats-Unis, 1778–1783* (Paris, Didier Perrin, 1903). This is a secondary narrative history based almost exclusively on the official records in the Archives de la Guerre and the Archives de la Marine.

Papers of TJ——Julian P. Boyd et al., eds., *The Papers of Thomas Jefferson* (Princeton University Press, 1950–). 18 vols. as of 1971.

Sellers, *Portraits by CWP*——Charles Coleman Sellers, *Portraits and Miniatures by Charles Willson Peale*, which is Vol. XLII, Part 1, of *Transactions of the American Philosophical Society* (Philadelphia, 1952). A Supplement to *Portraits*, under the title *Charles Willson Peale with Patron and Populace*, was published as Vol. LIX, Part 3, of *Transactions* (Philadelphia, 1969).

Six, *Dict. Biog.*——Georges Six, *Dictionnaire Biographique des Généraux et Amiraux Français de la Révolution et de l'Empire (1792–1814)*, 2 vols. (Paris, 1934).

Stone, *French Allies*——Edwin M. Stone, *Our French Allies . . . in the Great War of the American Revolution, from 1778 to 1782* (Providence, 1884).

Washington, *Diaries*——John C. Fitzpatrick, ed., *The Diaries of George Washington, 1748–1799*, 4 vols. (New York, 1925).

Writings of GW——John C. Fitzpatrick, ed., *The Writings of George Washington*, 39 vols. (Washington, 1931–1944). This set contains only letters by Washington and not those addressed to him by others. The latter (e.g., Rochambeau's letters) are in the Library of Congress, Washington Papers, now available in a microfilm edition, with a printed *Index to the George Washington Papers* (Washington, Manuscript Division, Library of Congress, 1964; introduction by Dorothy S. Eaton).

The above list, not intended as a bibliography, does not include works cited only occasionally in a particular context. In such cases the complete reference is given in the notes. Other secondary works that have been often consulted, though infrequently mentioned in the notes, include the following.

Bonsal, Stephen. *When the French Were Here, A Narrative of the Sojourn of the French Forces in America* (Garden City, N.Y., 1945).

Chevalier, Edouard. *Histoire de la Marine Française pendant la Guerre de l'Indépendance Américaine* (Paris, 1877).

Flexner, James Thomas. *George Washington in the American Revolution, 1775–1783* (Boston, 1968).

Johnson, Amandus. *Swedish Contributions to American Freedom, 1776–1783, including a Sketch of the Background of the Revolution together with an Account of the Engagements in which Swedish Officers participated and Biographical Sketches of these Men*, 2 vols. (Philadephia, Swedish Colonial Foundation, 1953). The majority of the Swedish officers discussed by Johnson served in either the French army or navy.

Jusserand, Jules J. *With Americans of Past and Present Days* (New York, 1916). This book includes (pp. 3–133) "Rochambeau and the French in America, from unpublished documents."

Keim, DeB. Randolph. *Rochambeau, A Commemoration by the Congress of the United States of the Services of the French Auxiliary Forces in the War of Independence* (Washington, 1907). This book includes (pp. 607–645) a "List of Works relating to the French Alliance in the American Revolution," compiled by A.P.C. Griffin.

Lacour-Gayet, Georges. *La Marine Militaire de la France sous le Règne de Louis XVI* (Paris, 1905). This work includes much valuable information about naval officers, based on the French Navy Department records.

Mackesy, Piers. *The War for America. 1775–1783* (London, 1964). "The first purpose of this book is to examine the making and execution of strategy in one of England's great eighteenth-century wars, and to create a detailed model of the machine at work; the second, to judge a war Ministry in the light of circumstances rather than results. . . . This, then is not a history of the War of Independence, but a study of British strategy and leadership in a world war, the last in which the enemy were the Bourbons." (Author's Preface.)

Perkins, James Breck. *France in the American Revolution* (Boston, 1911).

Stevens, John Austin. Series of articles in the *Magazine of American History* (New York): "The French in Rhode Island," III (1879), 385–436; "The Operations of the Allied Armies before New York," IV (1880), 1–45; "The Route of the Allies from King's Ferry to the Head of Elk," V (1880), 1–20; "The Allies at Yorktown, 1781," VI (1881), 1–53; "The Return of the French, 1782–1783," VII (1881), 1–35.

Stinchcombe, William C. *The American Revolution and the French Alliance* (Syracuse, 1969). This is chiefly a survey of contemporary opinion: how American leaders in Congress, the clergy, the press, and the military "responded to" the alliance.

Weelen, Jean-Edmond. *Rochambeau* (Paris, 1934).

Whitridge, Arnold. *Rochambeau* (New York, 1965).